Political Change
in the Metropolis

Political Change in the Metropolis

Fourth Edition

John J. Harrigan

Hamline University

Scott, Foresman/Little, Brown Series in Political Science
Scott, Foresman and Company
Glenview, Illinois   Boston   London

LIBRARY OF CONGRESS
Library of Congress Cataloging-in-Publication Data

Harrigan, John J.
  Political change in the metropolis / John J. Harrigan.—4th ed.
      p.   cm.
  Bibliography: p.
  Includes indexes.
  ISBN 0-673-39848-X
  1. Metropolitan government—United States.   2. Municipal
government—United States.   3. Metropolitan areas—United States.
4. Urban policy—United States.   I. Title.
JS422.H33   1989   88-17531
352'.0094'0973—dc19   CIP

1 2 3 4 5 6 7 8 9 10 — MUR — 94 93 92 91 90 89 88

Printed in the United States of America

The author gratefully acknowledges permission to use the following material:

Page 32. *The Gallup Poll: Public Opinion 1972-1979* (Wilmington, DE: Scholarly Resources, 1978), pp. 112, 914. Copyright 1978 by American Institute of Public Opinion. *The Gallup Poll: Public Opinion 1985* (Wilmington, DE: Scholarly Resources, 1985), pg. 64. Copyright 1985 by American Institute of Public Opinion. Reprinted by permission.

Table 3-1. Alvin Chenkin, "Jewish Population in the United States," in *American Jewish Year Book* (Philadelphia: Jewish Publication Society, 1973), vol. 74, pp. 308–309. Reprinted by permission. Harold J. Abramson, *Ethnic Diversity in Catholic America* (New York: Wiley, 1973), p. 34. Reprinted by permission.

Page 83. Jack Newfield, "Mayor Daley is Alive and Well in N.Y.C.," *The Nation* (April 4, 1987): 429. Reprinted by permission.

Table 4-1. Adapted from International City Management Association, "Inside the Year Book," in *Municipal Year Book 1987* (Washington, D.C.: International City Management Association, 1987), p. xv. Used with permission.

Page 116. Karl Taeuber, *Racial Residential Segregation, 28 Cities, 1970-1980,* Center for Demography and Ecology, University of Wisconsin-Madison. Working Paper 83-12, March 1983. Reprinted by permission of the author.

Page 159. From *The Herblock Gallery* (Simon & Schuster, 1968). Reprinted by permission.

Continued on page 446

for Thomas

. . . in hope of a bright urban future

Preface

An irony of a book on political change is that change does not stop once the book has gone to press. In the four years since the previous edition of *Political Change in the Metropolis* was published, many things have happened in urban America. Most dramatically, federal-urban fiscal relations have changed sharply in recent years. Most visibly, blacks, women, and Hispanics won election as mayors of major American cities such as Chicago, Philadelphia, Phoenix, and San Antonio. Most profoundly, great economic-demographic tides of change continued eroding the vitality of some cities while carving out dynamic futures for others.

Not only do events change in urban America, but the way that scholars think about events also changes. Many topics that dominated urban scholarly thought when the first edition of this book was written more than a decade ago—the consequences of urban civil disorders, neighborhood control, red lining, metropolitan reform campaigns—are less popular today. So rapidly have events changed that some people think of these topics more as urban history than as part of contemporary politics. Other concerns, barely perceptible a decade ago, dominate urban scholarly literature today. These include such concerns as efficiency and equity in the delivery of public services, accountability in public programs, fiscal conservatism in urban management, a revival of community power theory, and above all the urban political economy. City governments across the land have become the engines of economic development, pouring countless resources into the quest for jobs and business. This quest has drawn the attention of many urban researchers seeking to find whether the benefits of this quest can match the costs and trying to sort out the biases and political implications of these efforts.

This book traces these changes in events and scholarly concerns. It also offers the reader a theoretical framework for interpreting the changes. This framework analyzes the patterns of bias inherent to the organization and operation of urban politics. Governmental structures and processes are not neutral. For example, the early twentieth century progressive reforms such as non-partisanship and at-large elections improved the political influence of upper-middle-class professionals while reducing the influence of lower- and working-class immigrants. A major question today in scholarly research and in the federal courts is whether these same biases currently hinder the political influence of blacks and Hispanics.

Part I of this book discusses the basic themes of bias, change, and the metropolitanization of America. Part II focuses on the rise, decline, and consequences of machine and ethnic politics. Part III focuses on the contemporary city. Within Part III, Chapter 5 discusses the increasingly important political roles played by blacks, Hispanics, and Asians in American cities. Chapter 6 focuses on the changing urban political economy. Chapter 7 discusses the contest for dominance in American cities, and Chapter 8 examines the difficult problem of managing city services in a time of scarce resources. Part IV shifts attention away from the central city toward the broader metropolis. Chapter 9 treats the challenge of growth to suburbia, and Chapter 10 treats the challenge of suburbia to racial segregation in housing and education. Chapter 11 covers the various strategies for reforming metropolitan government over the past three decades and analyzes the extent to which these reforms have been successful. This discussion is followed in Chapter 12 by a treatment of incremental metropolitan reforms. Finally, in Part V, Chapter 13 discusses the important role of the federal government in urban affairs. Chapter 14 offers a general summary of the major urban changes and the political biases related to them, and makes some cautious projections about the likely direction of change over the next generation in urban America.

An Instructor's Manual accompanies this book. It provides narrative chapter summaries, media suggestions, and an extensive file of classroom tested multiple-choice questions for each chapter. To aid the student in reading the book, the Instructor's Manual also contains detailed study guides for all chapters. Each study guide presents the chapter's most important terms and names that the student should be able to identify and provides a series of mastery questions that give the students a handy self test on how well they have mastered the broader questions raised in the chapter. These study guides may be duplicated and distributed to students.

For the author, few things are more gratifying than to see a book received well enough to warrant a new edition. I am very grateful to the many instructors and students who have used this book, especially those who took the trouble to send me their comments and suggestions for improving it. They will find many of their suggestions in various places throughout this edition. I continue to be grateful to the scholars who helped review manuscripts for early editions of the book, and I owe a special debt to the following persons whose reviews and critiques of this edition were indispensible: Peter Eisinger, James Lester, and David Olson. Madelon Cassavant, as always, deserves special thanks for her typing. And John Covell, as editor, provided much helpful guidance in bringing to completion what often seemed like an interminable task. To Sandy I owe a special thanks for her patience, support, and understanding throughout this project.

John J. Harrigan
Saint Paul, Minnesota

Contents

Political Change
in the Metropolis

Part I
Metropolitanization and the Development of Urban Politics: An Introduction

As background to *Political Change in the Metropolis,* it is necessary to introduce the basic concepts of *change* and *bias* as they are used in this book and to outline the major features of the metropolitanization process in the United States. This is accomplished in the following two introductory chapters.

Chapter 1 discusses the inherent bias of political organization and introduces the primary theme of this book: that changes in the organization of political power in American metropolises have had profound consequences on the groups and individuals that either benefit by or are hurt by the operations of urban governments. Three secular changes have occurred in American urban politics. First, beginning in the 1840s the European immigrants, through machine and ethnic-based politics, created a number of urban institutions that gave them influence and power in city politics. Second, beginning in the 1930s and continuing with growing momentum in the post-World War II period, the expansion of governmental services and activities led to the organization of political influence on a functional basis rather than on the ethnic and geographic bases that had predominated in the earlier era. Finally, beginning in the late 1960s with the rapid expansion of federal programs, the growing concern for coordinating and controlling these various functionally organized governmental programs, and the increasing concern for regulating future metropolitan growth, a third, contemporary secular change has been occurring in urban politics. This contemporary change we will call the emergence of the dependent city. The age of the dependent city is characterized by the stronger role of the federal government, an effort to coordinate various federal programs, and a concern for subordinating policymaking bodies to new, metropolitan-level institutions. Some of the implications of these changes are discussed in Chapter 1.

Chapter 2 defines some basic concepts of urbanization, explains why and how America urbanized, and examines the political biases that have accompanied urbanization and metropolitanization in the United States.

Chapter 1
Bias and Change in Metropolitan Politics

Urban political structures and processes are not neutral. When changes are proposed in urban political structures and processes, some groups of people benefit from the changes. Others are harmed by them.

ITEM: When civil service reforms were introduced in municipal politics before the turn of the century, ethnic political leaders objected vigorously. Civil service would destroy their access to political jobs and political influence, they charged. According to George Washington Plunkitt, Tammany Hall's most articulate spokesperson, civil service was the "Curse of the Nation."[1]

ITEM: More than half a century later, when proposals for metropolitan government were put forward in places such as Cleveland, Saint Louis, Indianapolis, and Miami, many black people objected vigorously. Metropolitan government would dilute the voting potential of blacks in central cities and diminish the access of black leaders to political decision makers, they charged.[2]*

ITEM: In the contemporary metropolis, there has been widespread resistance to attempts to equalize opportunities for housing by allowing decisions on zoning or site location of public housing to be made at levels of government higher than the local municipality or county. In metropolis after metropolis, attempts to distribute federally sponsored low-income public housing evenly throughout the metropolitan areas have run into adamant opposition.

ITEM: When attempts were made to equalize access to public education by busing public school children across school attendance boundaries for the purpose of achieving racial balance, these attempts were bitterly resisted. In Pontiac, Michigan, school buses were tipped over and burned to prevent desegregation. In South Boston, attempts to enforce federal-court-ordered busing to achieve racial desegregation led to violent opposition.

These examples of urban politics span almost a century. In spite of the great time period they bridge, they illustrate and serve to introduce several common themes of American urban politics. First, in all instances, the political participants

---

*In some other metropolises, such as Jacksonville, Florida, and Nashville, Tennessee, the proponents of metropolitan reform were able to secure black support by offering special concessions to black leaders and the black communities.

expected that a major change in governmental structure, boundaries, or decision-making processes would produce policy changes that would be biased either for or against them. Second, the more recent examples involved not only the central cities but the suburbs, the metropolitan-level structures of government, and the federal government. Contemporary politics of the central city and the entire metropolis are intertwined, not separate. Third, in all instances they key issues at stake involved changes either in the channels through which people would have political access to key decision makers, or in their direct social access to important amenities of urban life such as quality housing and education. Fourth, the latter examples indicate that the federal government is a key participant in urban and metropolitan politics. It profoundly influences public decisions on matters such as housing and education, which used to be thought of as exclusively local preroga-tives. An understanding of these themes of bias and change in urban and metro-politan politics is essential to understanding the metropolis itself, how it functions, and what its chances are of progressing beyond the contemporary stage of seemingly permanent crisis.

The Bias of Political Organization

In all the proposals for change cited earlier (civil service reforms, the introduc-tion of metropolitan government, the making of housing and zoning decisions at levels above the local government, and the use of busing to desegregate schools), the people involved in the changes that were about to occur fully expected that modification of political structures and processes would either benefit them or hurt them. The governmental structures were not expected to be politically neu-tral; they were expected to be biased in terms of the interests and policy directions they would favor or disfavor. A major objective of this book is to examine whether these people were correct in their basic assumption that there is an inherent bias in the organization of political and governmental power in metropolitan America. The chapters that follow will investigate the hypothesis that such a bias does exist.

Political bias, as that term is used here, does not necessarily imply that the polit-ical actors are purposely and consciously biased for or against given groups of peo-ple. It does imply, as political scientist Harold Lasswell has argued, that the political process itself in some measure determines *who* gets *what* political or eco-nomic benefits, *when* they get them, and *how* they get them.[3] Political bias in the metropolis, then, involves two questions. Who benefits from the ongoing political structure and process in the metropolis? And who pays the cost of those benefits? These political biases can occur either in the input into the political decision-making process or in the policy outcomes that result.[4]

In exploring the hypothesis of political bias, one must distinguish between the bias of specific actions and the patterns of bias that underlie a series of actions. In practice, *any* specific *major* action of an urban government brings disproportion-ate benefits to some people and disproportionate costs to other people. In this sense all actions are biased. There is no absolutely fair way to apportion the costs and benefits of specific governmental actions. What is fair to one person may be unfair to another. For example, construction of the central-city portions of the interstate highway systems required the demolition of tens of thousands of homes. The residents of those homes were forced to move, usually into more expensive dwellings, and thus they bore a disproportionate share of the burden of building the freeways. The main beneficiaries of the freeways were the automobile drivers who regularly rode on them, especially middle-class suburbanites who commuted into the city. However, since all actions have some bias, the bias of *individual government actions* is not nearly so important as the *patterns of bias* that may or may not occur in many metropolises. Patterns of bias are indicated when some groups are systematically excluded from the governmental decision-making process and their interests systematically neglected by governmental policy outcomes. Are some groups or categories of people systematically disadvantaged or ignored or hurt by the nature of the urban political process? And conversely, do some other people systematically benefit from the same process?

One obvious example of persistent patterns of bias in both input and output occurred in the urban renewal program of the 1950s and 1960s.[5] Semiautonomous urban renewal agencies (generically called local public agencies—LPAs) were created to carry out the objectives of the federal urban renewal program. This program enabled an LPA to use federal funds to buy property in a blighted area, clear the land of existing buildings, and sell the cleared land at a reduced price to private redevelopers who, at a profit, constructed a mix of housing and commercial enterprises on the sites.

Since the program came into effect, some of its persistent net effects in most cities have been to reduce the total amount of housing available to racial minorities, to reduce the number of independent small retail shop owners, and to rebuild central business districts and other commercial areas of central cities. The poor and the minority groups suffered a decline in housing supply. Owners of small marginal businesses were forced out of business. And middle-class payers of federal income taxes absorbed most of the costs without receiving many of the benefits. The major beneficiaries were the large construction and financial interests who profited from the redevelopment construction contracts and the larger commercial interests who saw some of their smaller competitors removed from the redevelopment neighborhood.

Not only has there been a persistent bias to the policy outputs, but there has also been a persistent bias in the inputs into the decision-making process. Until 1974, LPAs were structured and organized in ways that made it difficult for elected officials in most cities to exercise much control over them. Nor did either the middle-class taxpayers or the displaced poor have much influence on the urban renewal decisions. The most influence was exercised by bureaucrats in the federal agencies and the local LPAs and the major banking and real estate developers interested in bidding for the construction contracts. Thus there was a very obvious pattern to the bias not only of the urban renewal programs themselves but also of the governmental structures that organized power in such a way as to make the urban renewal programs so autonomous. In 1974, urban renewal was replaced by the community development program. Whether or not the community development program altered the patterns of bias in urban renewal will be examined in Chapter 13.

The Nature of Change in Metropolitan Politics

Closely related to the bias of political structures and processes are the changes that occur in the ways of organizing power in the metropolis. As political change has occurred in the United States, one of its most marked features has been its evolutionary nature.[6] Some political analysts believe that changes in the American political system historically have been evolutionary, incremental, and marginal. That is, there has never been a revolutionary overthrow of the class structure of the society or a widespread disavowal of the sanctity of private ownership of the major economic institutions. One political scientist, Kenneth Dolbeare, argues that even the Civil War and the Reconstruction, which destroyed slavery and set the stage for the far-reaching Fourteenth Amendment to the Constitution, did not provoke fundamental political change in the United States.[7] In Dolbeare's view, all political change in this country has been marginal and has left intact the basic socioeconomic structure of the nation. Most political changes have also been interdependent with socioeconomic changes.[8] As the nation's population has become increasingly metropolitan, for example, and as the nation's economy has become dominated by nationally based corporations rather than locally based proprietorships, there have been political reactions to these changes. To cope with the increasingly metropolitan population, the amount of governance in metropolitan areas increased markedly.* And to cope with the transition from a regionally based to a nationally based economy, the regulatory capacity of government, particularly of the federal government, increased markedly. Much of this change, however, in the view of political scientist Murray Edelman, has been *symbolic* rather than *substantive;* for example, the increase in regulatory capacity has been primarily a symbolic change that diverts popular attention away from making drastic, substantive changes in the distribution of power and wealth.[9] Political changes, in this view, normally focus on the symbols of power and seldom touch the substance of power.

These perceptive insights are very relevant to metropolitan politics. In relating them, however, the student should be careful not to confuse change with instability. Some political systems can undergo rapid changes in the admission of new elites, such as happens following an election, and yet remain quite stable in terms of the class structure, the tenure of governments, and the widespread acceptance of common, underlying political and cultural values of the society.[10] This seems to have been the pattern in the United States. Some other political systems become quite unstable precisely because they are not able to tolerate political changes that

---

*One feature of metropolitanization has been a continuing proliferation in the number of governments in metropolitan areas. By 1982 there were a total of 29,861 governments in the 305 officially designated metropolitan areas (SMSAs) of the United States, an average of ninety-seven governments to each metropolis.

would admit new elites into the political decision-making process.* Thus it may well be that continuous, incremental, evolutionary change leads to political stability and forestalls the need for drastic revolutionary change. It may be that change which allows emerging sectors in the society to share symbolically and vicariously in the exercise of power also enables the elites of these emerging sectors to be co-opted into the decision-making elite structure or to bring about major redistribution of wealth.

In the American metropolises, political change has also occurred in an incremental, not a revolutionary, fashion. But this is change, nonetheless. For example, the Tammany Hall political machine was not destroyed overnight. However, its tight control over New York City government, as it existed under Boss Tweed and some of his successors, was eventually destroyed. And the destruction of this control helped make a significant difference in how New York City is governed and who benefits from this governance.[11]

The evolutionary nature of metropolitan political change can be seen in the historical development of political power in American cities. Three distinct evolutionary changes can be noted. First, roughly coterminous with the age of political machines and extensive European immigration, there was an evolution of political power that was ethnically and geographically based. (This evolution is described in considerable detail in Chapter 3). Prior to 1830, political power in many American cities was controlled by very small circles of economic elites labeled variously as patrician, Brahmin, Yankee, Bourbon, or (much later) WASP (white Anglo-Saxon Protestant).† The members of these elites typically belonged to the higher-status Protestant churches in their localities. They viewed with considerable distrust both the egalitarian principles of Jacksonian democracy and the Catholic European immigrants who stood to benefit from these principles. From the 1830s until at least the end of the century, there was a steady evolution in the political influence of these European ethnic groups. Much of their political influence was founded on indigenous institutional power bases developed within the ethnic communities. The institutions that formed the base for their indigenous power remained the dominant urban political institutions up to the 1930s. The major institutions thus created were the political machines, the urban organization of the Catholic church dioceses, organized crime, certain labor unions, and certain sectors of business. In many instances, the institutions are still influential in today's metropolitan politics, although they are seldom dominant.

---

*In many Latin American countries, for example, the lack of change in admitting new elites into the political decision-making process seems to have been one of the major causes of political instability. See Karl M. Schmitt and David D. Burks, *Evolution or Chaos: Dynamics of Latin American Government Politics* (New York: Praeger, 1963), chap. 6, "Political Dynamics"; Claudio Veliz, *Obstacles to Change in Latin America* (New York: Oxford University Press, 1969); and Seymour Martin Lipset and Aldo Solari, *Elites in Latin America* (New York: Oxford University Press, 1969).

†This was true particularly in the South and in New England. It was much less true in the newer cities of the Midwest and the West. See Peter H. Rossi and Alice S. Rossi, "An Historical Perspective on the Functions of Local Politics," in *Social Change and Urban Politics,* ed. Daniel N. Gordon (Englewood Cliffs, N.J.: Prentice-Hall, 1973), pp. 49–60.

The second evolutionary change began with the progressive reform movement at the turn of the century and reached its zenith between the 1940s and the 1970s. The evolutionary change during this period was the emergence of political organization *on a functional base* as distinguished from the ethnic and geographic base of the earlier period. Within given functional areas, public bureaucracies and private interests developed. In public education, for example, the top administrators in the school systems, the teachers' unions, the superintendents' offices, and the state departments of education came to dominate public education and diminish the effective control of the boards of education—the elected public officials.[12] In public safety a similar phenomenon occurred. The police bureaucracies, the police officers' associations, and conservative citizens' groups concerned with law and order served to insulate the police from effective control by locally elected city councils and mayors.* But the most dramatic example of the emergence of functionally organized power occurred in the arena of public housing and urban renewal.[13] As noted above, the formulation of urban renewal policy soon got beyond the control of elected officials in most cities. Semiautonomous local public authorities were created in response to federal legislation, and they were largely financed by federal funds. In a sense, functional fiefdoms emerged in which the decision makers acted with considerable independence from control by elected public officials.

The functional organization of power enabled technicians and specialists to supersede elected politicians in making the most fundamental decisions about rebuilding the cities. Equally important, major decisions on metropolitan growth came to be made by specialized agencies called *special districts* rather than by general-purpose governments. Within each functional area the public bureaucracies, the special districts, and the related private interests acted in a fashion somewhat reminiscent of feudal fiefdoms in the Middle Ages when each fiefdom was

---

*The extent of police department insulation is difficult to measure, at best, and elected officials certainly affect the overall environment within which the police departments function. Nevertheless, evidence suggests that police law-enforcement practices are more the product of a bureaucratic imperative than of legislative policy made by the city council in reponse to broad community demands. Jeffrey Pressman found that the mayor and city council in Oakland were unable to alter the police department's policies regulating handgun use by police officers [see p. 515 of Pressman's "The Preconditions for Mayoral Leadership," *The American Political Science Review* 66, no. 2 (June 1972): 511–524]. John A. Gardiner studied the enforcement of traffic laws in 697 communities throughout the United States and concluded that there was "almost no evidence to suggest that the police are carrying out *publicly* established enforcement policies" [p. 171 of Gardiner's "Police Enforcement of Traffic Laws: A Comparative Analysis," in *City Politics and Public Policy,* ed. James Q. Wilson (New York: Wiley, 1968), pp. 151–172]; input from council members and influential citizens almost always occurred on an *ad hoc* basis with little implication for overall policies (p. 167). And a study by James Q. Wilson of different approaches toward juvenile delinquency by a professionalized police department and a more traditional, fraternally oriented police department found that the more bureaucratized and professionalized police force was much less sensitive to subtle community mores, was much less flexible in dealing with first offenders, and acted more in accord with the model of "an army of occupation" (p. 190 of James Q. Wilson, "The Police and the Delinquent in Two Cities," in Wilson, *City Politics and Public Policy,* pp. 173–195).

virtually autonomous and its nobility was answerable virtually only to itself. In the 1950s and the 1960s an analogous situation occurred in American metropolitan areas. Within many functional areas of public activity, the appropriate influential persons of the community were answerable virtually only to themselves. Highway, redevelopment, low-income public housing, public health, and public education fiefdoms acted independently of one another. Little thought was given to coordinating their respective actions.

The third evolutionary change began in the mid-1960s and, for lack of a better term, we will call this the period of the *dependent city.* In this stage of development, local autonomy has been sharply challenged by outside economic forces over which the local government has little control. Local autonomy has also been reduced by policy mandates from the federal and state governments, which influence not only what policies city governments can pursue but also the procedures for implementing those policies.[14] Some of the chief characteristics of the dependent-city period are an effort to coordinate the various functional fiefdoms, a concern to subordinate them to policymaking bodies at the metropolitan level, an overriding concern for public-private partnerships in the quest for economic development, and half-hearted attempts to cope with the massive social problems of poverty, crime, poor education, family breakdown, and racial separation that are increasingly the burden of the central cities.

The central city cannot by itself cope well with all its problems. It depends on state government for legal authority, on the federal government for whatever financial help it can get, on the business community for participation in economic development projects, and on surrounding suburbs for cooperation on the multitude of problems (such as pollution, transportation, education) that cross over city boundaries. Making all these interdependent relationships work for the benefit of metropolitan residents has required putting new importance in recent decades on the need for effective political leaders, especially for effective central-city mayors.

Of special importance during this contemporary period of the dependent city have been the ties between the cities and the federal government. The Johnson (1963–1969), Nixon (1969–1974), Carter (1977–1981), and Reagan (1981–1989) administrations played special roles. Under Johnson, a massive increase occurred in the federal commitment to dealing with urban problems (see pages 365–366 for details). During the Nixon administration, general revenue sharing was proposed to reverse the trend toward increasing federal dominance over domestic policies and programs. General revenue sharing, first enacted in 1972, returned about $5 billion per year to local governments to use as they saw fit, with very few strings attached, until the program was ended in 1987. Nixon also terminated some of the key urban programs started under Johnson and consolidated numerous grant programs into large *block grants* in the fields of community development, criminal justice, and employment. The net effects of Nixon's changes were to reduce the cities' share of federal spending while increasing the share of suburbs, small towns, and regional governments. Nixon's changes also tended in some ways to reinforce the political influence of state and local elected officials, while reducing the influence of some of the independent agencies such as urban renewal agencies.[15]

When Carter entered the White House in 1977, the nation's largest city, New York, was striving desperately to avoid bankruptcy, and many central cities of the Northeast and Midwest were undergoing severe financial strain. Carter responded with a National Urban Policy proposal that offered the cities little in the way of new money. Rather it called for better targeting of federal money to priority areas and tried to offer better incentives to private industry for creating economic opportunities in the nation's most distressed central cities (see Chapter 13).[16]

President Reagan promoted a New Federalism that reduced federal aid to state and local governments. He also sought to increase the authority of state governments by decreasing federal regulations and expanding the block-grant concept pioneered under Nixon. His biggest impact was a substantial reduction in federal monies to help cities cope with their problems. As we will see in Chapter 13, this has adversely affected the nation's ability to deal with one of its most vexing socioeconomic problems, the emergence of a huge urban underclass of people who lack the means to enter the economic and social mainstream of America.

To sum up, three broad evolutionary changes have been observed in the structure of political power in the metropolis. The first change was the emergence of power organized on an ethnic and a ward, or geographic, base. Second was the emergence of power organized on a functional base. Third has been the emergence of the dependent city, in which effective political power became highly fragmented among dozens of local governments and the central city lost its dominance over the metropolis. Urban politics in this contemporary period have become metropolitan in scope. From desegregation of schools to economic development, rarely is there a major public issue area that can be dealt with effectively wholly within the boundaries of the central city alone. And often the federal government becomes involved through political mandates or through financial incentives.

These evolutionary changes are of more than simple historical interest. Each of these three ways of organizing power continues to exist. The first way of organizing power did not destroy the older, closed circles of urban elites of the early nineteenth century. But it did open up new channels of political access for groups in the metropolis that did not have access under the older form. The second political change did not destroy the ethnic organization of power,[17] but it did create new channels of political access beyond the control of the ethnic-dominated political machines. Nor has the third political change destroyed the functional fiefdoms. But it has made the domestic policy and philosophy of whoever controls the White House of great importance to cities and metropolitan areas.

Political change in the metropolis, then, does not mean that one form of political organization replaces a previous form. On the contrary, it means that several forms of political organization have evolved side by side. The net result has been the emergence of a patchwork, incredibly complex structure of political organization that is continually evolving in an incremental fashion. For those who know how to navigate them, there are numerous channels of political access to decision makers. Each channel has its own set of biases. And any one channel offers access to influencing decisions only within a very limited scope of activities. Even the largest, most extensive general-purpose government in the metropolis as it now exists—the central-city government—has a very limited scope of action open to it. And in most instances, the evolution of a decision-making capacity at the metropolitan level is not very far advanced. What exists in most metropolises is a very open political situation. Anybody with the resources can do something of a limited scope (for example, construct an apartment building or delay the extension of a freeway through a residential neighborhood). But nobody has the capacity to do something of a comprehensive scope that covers several functional sectors at a metropolitan-wide level (for example, to integrate highway construction with public transit planning with sewer construction with residential construction with prior metropolitan land-use planning with equalizing social access to housing, education, and employment opportunities).

Bias, Change, and Political Power

To summarize the argument to this point, urban political structures change slowly in an incremental, evolutionary fashion. As these changes occur, they have the potential to alter the existing patterns of bias concerning the ways in which political power is organized in the metropolis.

In the presentation of this argument, the terms *politics* and *political power* deliberately have been used in a very broad sense. Politics has referred to the struggle over public decisions that determine public policies and allocate values, goods, and services; hence *politics,* as used in this book, refers not only to the election of government officials, but also to the making of public decisions and the results of public policy established by those decisions.[18]* It also refers to the broader social and economic processes that establish the constraints, needs, and capabilities that limit governmental action.

Public policies quite often result from pressure placed on government by groups and individuals having interests that will be affected by those policies. To the extent that a given group or individual has influence on what a government does or does not do, that group or individual is said to possess political power.[19] To the extent that a given group or individual lacks influence on what a government does or does not do, that group or individual is said to lack political power. Some political scientists have suggested that the concept of power is so vague and so susceptible to multiple interpretations that it ought to be avoided whenever possible.[20] However, because some individuals, groups, and public officials do have the capability to influence government actions, it seems useful to have a term to represent that idea; thus we will use the term *political power* for this purpose. Mayors, city councils, and a host of other governmental officials and agencies are politically

---

*Political power also involves what are referred to as *nondecisions.* Nondecisions are the potential issues that never get placed on the agenda for public decision making because they are beyond the pale of what is politically acceptable. The importance of nondecisions to the exercise of power is argued by Peter Bachrach and Morton S. Baratz in "The Two Faces of Power," *The American Political Science Review* 56, no. 4 (December 1962): 947–952. The significance of decisions and nondecisions in urban politics is discussed in Chapter 7 (pp. 189–190).

powerful because they have the capacity to take official action directly. Interest groups are politically powerful to the extent they can influence what the governmental actors do.

Three aspects of political power are important to understanding how metropolises function. First, metropolitan political power is generally contextual; that is, a given group usually has power only in a given context. It has power in those areas of public interest in which it chooses or is able to assert itself.* Thus, for example, real estate developers usually exert considerable influence on zoning and land-use practices, but they are seldom influential in questions of air pollution control.

A second important aspect of metropolitan political power is that it is structured:† there are patterns to the distribution of power in the metropolis, and some categories of people are more powerful than others. The participating electorate possesses power to the extent that it chooses many of the political leaders and sometimes acts as a restraint on what policymakers can accomplish. In Boston, for example, the election of neighborhood school advocates to the school committee in the mid-1960s hindered the cause of school desegregation in that city.[21] Further down the power scale from this real, if somewhat limited, power of the participating electorate is the extremely limited political power of the unorganized people and those who do not participate. In particular, the unorganized and the poor typically exert very little influence in the making of public decisions.[22] In contrast to the limited power of the participating electorate and the extremely limited power of the unorganized and the poor, some highly organized groups consistently exert considerable influence on public decisions that affect them. Certain businesspeople (especially those from the utilities, the major financial institutions, and the major local retailers) generally have a considerable voice in projects that promote their metropolitan area's economic expansion.[23] The political influence of other groups—groups such as labor unions, political parties, church organizations, or organized crime—varies from one metropolis to another. In Detroit, for

---

*This has been a sharply debated issue in community power studies. At one extreme, Robert A. Dahl, in *Who Governs?* (New Haven, Conn.: Yale University Press, 1961), argues that power is so bound up in a given context that it exists primarily in the making of key decisions on given issues. In Dahl's view, the ability to influence key decisions in one area of issues does not lead to the ability to influence key decisions in other areas. Bachrach and Baratz, in "The Two Faces of Power," seem to argue that a broad reservoir of power exists independent of specific decisions. The most common viewpoint among political scientists, however, seems to be that taken by Gordon: "Political and civic life in American communities has become sufficiently complex that no one person or group of persons is likely to want or to be able to attain power in all areas of community life" (Gordon, *Social Change and Urban Politics,* p. 61). This book, in order to avoid entanglement in the methodological argument of this point, leans to the point of view that the exercise of power and the power holders will vary from one context to another.

†The statement that power is structured is often taken to mean that a small clique at the top of a hierarchy controls politics in a given locale and that the clique is founded in the top levels of a hierarchy of business leaders. The statement does not necessarily mean this, however. It does mean that permanent relationships exist between the politically relevant institutions in the metropolis and the governmental policy outputs.

example, labor unions are a very strong political force[24], whereas unions tend to be much weaker in cities of the South and Southwest. But the important point here is that there is always a structure to the organization of political influence in metropolises. This does not necessarily mean that a small elite controls events. It does mean that political decisions do not occur randomly.

Political power is not only contextual and structured; it is also inseparable from private power. The broad sense of the term *political power,* as it is currently used by political scientists, makes drawing fine distinctions between the private and public aspects of power increasingly difficult. To take just one example, for the purely private financial reasons of trying to maximize profit and minimize losses, mortgage banks have historically been reluctant to make mortgage loans in declining areas of American cities. This practice is known as *redlining,* because the bankers supposedly draw a red line around the areas not eligible for loans.[25] Some other neighborhoods are allegedly *greenlined.* The target neighborhoods for urban redevelopment and gentrification, for example, face no shortage of mortgage bankers and real estate entrepreneurs wanting to redevelop historical buildings or put up new projects. Although mortgage lenders decide whether to redline neighborhoods for private reasons and for private profits, the decisions have far-reaching public ramifications. The urban neighborhoods that are denied mortgage loans begin to deteriorate. Governments become obliged to spend public funds on stepped-up police and fire protection, public welfare assistance, renewal, and other services to deal with the consequences of that deterioration. The greenlined neighborhoods, by contrast, thrive and see their property values go up. For these reasons, the mortgage lenders' exercise of private power is equally an exercise of public power. Furthermore, if the cities' public authorities do not or cannot use their influence to induce lenders to make loans in redlined areas, then for all practical purposes the public authorities have publicly acquiesced in and legitimized* these privately made decisions that determine which neighborhoods of the metropolis are going to deteriorate and which ones are going to prosper. It is very difficult to call decisions of such magnitude private decisions rather than public decisions, even though they might be made privately, by private businesspeople, for private motives. In this sense, the distinction between private and public has become vague. Private decisions can be public decisions in certain circumstances.

---

*Legitimacy has been defined as the "quality of being justified or willingly accepted by subordinates that converts the exercise of political power into 'rightful' authority" [Jack C. Plano and Robert E. Riggs, *Dictionary of Political Analysis* (Hinsdale, Ill.: Dryden Press, 1973), p. 45]. In this example, the acquiescence of the public authorities in the actions of the mortgage bankers enhances the likelihood of popular acceptance of the notion that bankers have a "rightful authority" to take actions that have such far-reaching consequences. According to Dolbeare, fundamental political change is first of all a process of "de-legitimizing" existing institutions and then "legitimizing" new political institutions [Dolbeare, *Political Change in the United States* (New York: McGraw-Hill, 1974), p. 8]. Thus, in this example, fundamental change would first of all involve de-legitimizing the existing right of mortgage bankers to decide which areas of a metropolis qualify for mortgage loans. The second step would be to give this right to a new institution.

This reliance on private decision makers to decide on development of extreme public importance we will call *privatism*.* According to historian Sam Bass Warner, Jr., privatism has been characteristic of American urban history.[26] But this too is changing. If one compares 1990 with 1890, one of the most marked political differences is the increased ability of governments to influence private decisions that have public ramifications. In the case of redlining, for example, government has put pressure on banks to cease the practice. One of the most important goals of the Reagan administration was to put an end to the public sector's encroachment into areas of economic life that had traditionally been private; hence the administration's support for privatization, that is, the contracting out of many public services to providers in the private sector.

Finally, privatism has its own patterns of bias. It helps make the urban system of politics more responsive to existing powerful and affluent institutions (especially banks and real estate developers) than to low-income individuals. In making the urban system of politics less responsive to low-income people, privatism inhibits the development of lower-class-based political institutions that possibly could give the poor more influence over their city governments. How does privatism do this? By fostering a set of attitudes that impel people to a self-centered individualism in which their personal ambitions for family, career advancement, and consumption of consumer goods are divorced from their concerns for the public good as expressed by ensuring decent living standards for all members of society.[27] The privatistic individual supports the political system only to the extent that the system assists his or her personal advancement. Gone is the ancient Greek belief that the purely private person is useless.

Privatism has a different effect on different social classes. On the upper middle class, privatism supports city governments that subsidize downtown redevelopment projects, but it does not support city government acts that would dramatically increase welfare or social service benefits in poor neighborhoods.[28] The effect of privatism on the poor classes is the inhibition of voter turnout and of involvement in political activities (such as protest demonstrations and collective bargaining) that would increase their collective influence on city government.

That, at least, is the theory of privatism. To date there is not much empirical research devoted to issues of privatism. But one very suggestive survey did indeed find that people who scored high on a privatism index were less inclined to engage in political or protest activity, cared less about politics, were more materialistic, and were less liberal.[29] Unless the findings of this survey are reinforced by others, we would not be justified in concluding that privatism is as pervasively biased as the argument here suggests. But these findings are indeed suggestive enough for us to take the privatism argument seriously. If the privatism argument is correct, the biases of privatism are quite apparent. Privatism helps the wealthy and the

---

*For the sake of clarification, the concept of *privatism* as defined here is distinct from the closely related concept of *privatization,* which refers to the phenomenon of governments contracting with the private sector to provide public services. Privatization became very popular during the 1980s and is discussed more fully in Chapter 8.

upper middle classes keep their privileged status in our society. And by inhibiting a class-based politics, privatism hinders the ability of the urban poor to pursue their own collective self-interest.

Summary

1. In examining the process of urban politics this book will look for *patterns of bias* to see if certain groups of people systematically benefit from the process and if other groups of people are systematically excluded from the process or are put at a disadvantage by it.

2. Urban political change has been predominantly incremental change rather than revolutionary change.

3. Three distinct periods of urban political change can be noted in America:
    a. 1830s–1930s   The period of ethnic and machine politics
    b. 1930s–1970s   The period of functional fiefdoms
    c. 1960s– ?   The period of the dependent city

4. *Politics* is used in a broad sense to refer to the struggle over public decisions that determine public policies and allocate values, goods, and services.

5. *Political power* refers to the ability to influence these public decisions. Urban political power is characterized by three features. First, it is contextual. That is, a given group usually has power only in a given context. Second, it is structured. The most powerful groups are those that are permanent and that maintain an ongoing relationship with government. Third, public power is inseparable from private power. Private institutions (such as mortgage banks) make private decisions (such as discouraging mortgage loans in redlined neighborhoods) that have consequences (such as neighborhood deterioration) to which governments must respond.

6. Finally, the tradition of privatism in urban America, it could be argued, is itself biased in favor of the upper middle classes and against the interests of the urban poor.

Chapter 2
The Emergence of
Metropolitan America

For most of its history America was shaped by rural people and small-town residents. Today, by contrast, three-quarters of all Americans live in metropolitan areas. This dramatic transformation has deeply affected the political culture and economy of the United States. Chapter 2 explores several broad questions about the process through which contemporary metropolises emerged in the United States. What is meant by the terms *urban* and *metropolitan?* What are the essential urban characteristics of the American population? Why do metropolises grow? How has the character of American urbanization changed as the cities grew into metropolises? In what ways did urbanization in the 1980s differ from earlier urban growth patterns? What are the political implications of these changes? Do these changes involve any political bias? That is, have they diminished some people's access to the political decision makers and to the social amenities of the metropolis, such as good schools and employment opportunities? If so, who are the people whose political and social access has been diminished?

Urban Characteristics of the American Population

The classic definition of *urban* has three elements: volume, density, and heterogeneity of population. The first two elements are basically demographic and the third is sociological.[1] The key criteria for distinguishing urban from nonurban places thus become: How large must a population be to be called urban? How dense must it be? And how heterogeneous must it be?

The United States Census Bureau applies these criteria by classifying as urban any incorporated or unincorporated minor civil division of 2500 or more people.* Using this definition, the 1980 census counted precisely 8765 *urban places* in the United States and found that 73 percent of the population was urban.

Although these widely accepted figures are used to indicate how urbanized the American population is, they constitute a key defect in the definition: No distinc-

---

*A minor civil division refers to the geographic territory below the county level that is the primary legal administrative subdivision according to state law. In the states where a subcounty-level minor civil division does not exist, the Census Bureau calculates a census county division for the purpose of identifying urban places. These states are found primarily in the South and the West.

What a Difference a Label Makes!

Whether federal statisticians place your hometown inside or outside an MSA can make quite a difference to you and your neighbors. Medicare payments, for example, are higher to hospitals in MSAs than they are to nonmetropolitan hospitals. MSA cities get more community development funds than do nonmetropolitan cities. And since much more data is collected for MSAs than for nonmetropolitan cities, the MSAs have a distinct advantage in the marketing and plant-location plans of the nation's corporations.

tion is made between a small Wyoming town of exactly 2500 inhabitants and New York City with its population of seven million! Both are considered urban. Neither does this definition distinguish between central cities and suburbs.

To make these distinctions, the federal government uses the terms *urbanized area* and *metropolitan statistical area.*

An *urbanized area* is the densely settled part of a metropolitan area and usually has a population density of 1000 or more people per square mile. Urbanized areas commonly exist within officially defined metropolitan areas.

The official term for metropolitan area is *metropolitan statistical area** (or MSA), and today there are 332 MSAs in the nation. An MSA is defined by the Department of Commerce Office of Federal Statistical Policy and Standards as any county containing a central city or contiguous cities of 50,000 or more people plus all adjacent counties that are metropolitan in character and economically and socially integrated with the central county. An adjacent county will meet the tests for integration with the central county if its population density exceeds 60 persons per square mile, if 35 percent of its population is urban, and if one of two work-related criteria are met: (a) at least 15 percent of its population works in the central county, or (b) at least 15 percent of those employed within the adjacent county's boundaries reside in the central county.[2] Urban areas without a central city of 50,000 are given MSA status if the urbanized area contains at least 50,000 inhabitants and the metropolitan population totals at least 100,000.

These distinctions among rural places, urban places, urbanized areas, and MSAs permit us to view a more accurate picture of the urban status of the American population. Note in Table 2-1 that while the 1980 population was 73 percent urban and 74 percent metropolitan (78 percent by 1985), only about 61 percent of the population actually resided in the urbanized portion of metropolitan areas. Within the MSAs, more people live outside the central cities than live within them. And millions of people who reside in MSAs actually live in rural, not urban, places.

These considerations point up one of the disadvantages of the MSA definition of the term metropolitan. Not only does it include many rural people within metropolitan areas, it also includes vast stretches of sparsely inhabited territory such as

---

*Prior to 1983 this term was called standard metropolitan statistical area, or SMSA. Although there are some technical differences between the two terms, for the purposes of this text they can be considered the same.

Table 2-1. Some Urban Characteristics of the U.S. Population

Population category	1970		1980		1970–1980	1985 (est.)	
	Number (in thousands)	Percentage of U.S. population	Number (in thousands)	Percentage of U.S. population	Percentage increase or decrease	Number (in millions)	Percentage of U.S. population
Total U.S. population	203,212	100	226,546	100	+11.5	238.7	100
Urban	149,325	73.5	167,051	73.7	+11.9	NA	NA
Rural	53,887	26.5	59,495	26.3	+10.4	NA	NA
Nonmetropolitan population	63,798	31.4	57,115	25.2	–10.5	53.2	22.3
Nonmetropolitan urban	26,318	13.0	21,608	9.5	–17.9	NA	
Nonmetropolitan rural	37,475	18.4	35,507	15.7	–5.3	NA	
Metropolitan population (i.e., in SMSAs)	139,419	68.6	169,431	74.8	+21.5	185.5	77.7
In urbanized areas	118,447	58.3	139,171	61.4	+17.5	NA	
In central cities	63,922	31.5	67,035	29.6	– 4.9	NA	
In suburbs in urbanized areas	54,525	26.8	72,135	31.8	+32.3	NA	
In rural areas of SMSAs	16,412	8.1	23,988	10.6	+46.2	NA	
Number of urban places	7,062	—	8,765	—	+24.1	NA	
Number of SMSAs	243	—	318	—	+30.1	281	

Source: U.S. Bureau of the Census, *Statistical Abstract of the United States: 1982–83* (Washington, D.C.: U.S. Government Printing Office, 1982), p. 15; 1987, pp. 23, 26.

that found in eastern California or Nevada. Furthermore, the relatively small central-city population criteria of 50,000 specified as the core of an MSA makes it impossible to distinguish isolated MSAs such as Billings, Montana, from chains of MSAs that together form a megalopolis. In addition, it has proven impossible to remove politics from the definitional problem. The two Long Island counties of Nassau and Suffolk were once removed from the New York SMSA for political reasons,[3] and when MSAs were defined in 1983, a number of former SMSAs such as Dallas-Fort Worth were split into two separate MSAs to please political groups from the smaller cities.[4]

Because of these disadvantages, various urbanists have attempted to develop more appropriate definitions of metropolitan. One approach has been to define as metropolitan any area with a population of at least 100,000 people that contains a central city or cities and has at least 65 percent of its economically active population engaged in nonagricultural activities.[5] This is a fairly restrictive definition that excludes many areas considered metropolitan under the MSA definition. A different approach to defining a metropolitan area has been to avoid putting precise political boundaries on what is considered metropolitan. This is done by defining an area not in terms of counties, as the MSA is defined, but in terms of commuting distance. One advocate of this approach is geographer John Friedmann, who rejects the term *metropolitan area* and introduces *urban field*. He defines an urban field as a core area of 300,000 people plus all areas within a radius equivalent to a two-hour automobile drive.[6] Friedmann prefers such a definition—which would probably classify about 90 percent of the American population as urbanized—because, he asserts, most of the American people exhibit urban social traits regardless of where they live or what occupations they have. Whatever the relative advantages of these other approaches to defining metropolitan areas, the MSA definition is the most widely accepted method of identifying American metropolises, and it is the definition according to which all federal statistical data are compiled.

In addition to urban places and MSAs, another level of urbanization, called *megalopolis* by French geographer Jean Gottman,[7] is found along the North Atlantic seacoast where the metropolitan areas are growing into one another. This phenomenon cannot be accounted for by the single MSA concept. Whereas the New York MSA has a total population of 8.5 million, its zone of influence spreads into neighboring MSAs. The same thing is true of several other urban centers.

To account for these varying degrees of metropolitanization, the Office of Federal Statistical Policy and Standards has distinguished between different levels of MSAs. It has also distinguished between the MSA and the consolidated metropolitan statistical area (CMSA), which is composed of two or more contiguous primary MSAs (PMSAs).[8] These levels are shown in Table 2-2. New York, with 17.8 million people, is the largest CMSA, followed by Los Angeles with 12.8 million, and Chicago with 8.1. The fastest-growing large CMSAs are Houston and Miami, each of which doubled its population between 1960 and 1980.

Even the concept of a consolidated metropolitan statistical area does not describe the full impact of urbanization along the northeastern seacoast, however.

Table 2-2. Levels of Metropolitan Statistical Areas: 1986

Primary Metropolitan Statistical Areas (PMSAs) and Metropolitan Statistical Areas (MSAs)		Number 332
Level A:	1,000,000 or more people	41
Level B:	250,000–999,999	115
Level C:	100,000–249,999	141
Level D:	less than 100,000	35
Primary Metropolitan Statistical Area (PMSA) An MSA of 100,000 or more people that is included in a CMSA.		51
Consolidated Metropolitan Statistical Area (CMSA) Two or more PMSAs with a combined population of over 1,000,000 that is economically and socially integrated.		23

Source: U.S. Bureau of the Census, *Statistical Abstract of the United States: 1987* (Washington, D.C.: U.S. Government Printing Office, 1986), p. 26.

The New York CMSA exists in the middle of a chain of MSAs stretching from southern New Hampshire to northern Virginia and containing more than 40 million people.[9]

The Northeast megalopolis contains distinguishing features other than a continuous metropolitan strip. Covering some 50,000 square miles with an average density of 700 people per square mile, it is one of the largest dense areas in the world. It is the world's wealthiest concentration of people, with a higher per capita income than any other population of comparable size. It also embraces one of the world's greatest concentrations of political and economic power and artistic and literary leadership. Although the Northeast megalopolis contains some of the world's greatest manufacturing establishments, few of the ores, minerals, and chemicals that its industries process into capital and consumer goods are extracted from the megalopolis itself. On the contrary, the vast majority of these natural resources are extracted from other parts of the world and fed into the megalopolis for processing or shipping.[10]

No other area of the country is comparable to the Northeast megalopolis on all these variables. However, metropolitan areas in three other regions are increasingly merging and growing together to the point that they, too, are commonly referred to as megalopolises. One of these regions is along the southern shore of the Great Lakes, particularly along Lake Michigan. Numerous MSAs branch out contiguously from key lake ports at Milwaukee-Chicago, Detroit-Toledo, Cleveland, and Buffalo-Rochester. A third megalopolis is emerging on the southern Pacific Coast from San Francisco to the Mexican border, and a fourth is developing along the Florida peninsula from Jacksonville to Miami on the Atlantic Coast and spreading out from Tampa on the Gulf Coast.

Together, the four megalopolises comprise a very small percentage of the land area of the United States, but they contain more than 40 percent of the population. The location of the four megalopolises and other large metropolitan areas can be seen clearly in the nighttime satellite photo. And Table 2-3 shows the population of the 25 largest metropolitan agglomerations.

Urban place, metropolis, and megalopolis are the three levels of urbanization that have developed thus far. A final stage of urbanization is predicted by Greek planner C. A. Doxiadis. He foresees a continued growth and urbanization of the world population well into the twenty-first century to the point where the urban areas will form part of a worldwide urban network called ecumenopolis.[11]

The Basic Determinants of Metropolitan Growth

Whether such a phenomenon as ecumenopolis will materialize is problematical at this point in history. But megalopolises exist on at least four continents, and giant metropolises exist on all continents but Antarctica. These developments have not happened by accident; they are shaped by basic economic, technological, and political forces. Only within the last hundred years have these forces converged to create the great metropolises of several million people. The great cities of antiquity and the Middle Ages were relatively small. Babylon covered an area of no more than 3.2 square miles. Athens, at the height of its glory in the fifth century B.C., contained fewer than 200,000 people. Florence in the fourteenth century was a city of no more than 90,000 people, and Venice in the fifteenth century contained about 190,000. Of all the great premodern cities, only Rome approached a population of a million.[12]

There are three reasons why giant metropolises and megalopolises began to emerge only in the late nineteenth and early twentieth centuries. First, it was not until that time that a large enough agricultural surplus was produced to enable a majority of the population to live off the agricultural production of a dwindling minority of the population. The level of urbanization is inversely proportional to the number of farmers it takes to support one nonfarmer who lives in the city. Although this may imply that city dwellers are parasites living off the agricultural surplus, in fact city dwellers perform valuable services for farmers. Urbanites transport farmers' goods, finance their investments in crops, import or manufacture consumer goods that farmers can purchase with the earnings from their crops, and administer the safety and well-being of the countryside. Without these services farmers would be reduced to living at a subsistence level. There is a vital ecological balance between the city and the surrounding farm region.*

In the contemporary era, this ecological balance has been altered by the second factor in the rise of the large metropolis—the innovations in transportation technology.[13] The contemporary metropolis requires a sophisticated transportation network in order to move food and raw materials into the area and to move the

---

*One long-standing dispute among urban theorists has been whether urbanization was dependent on increased agricultural production. For the primacy-of-agriculture argument, see Kingsley Davis, "The Origin and Growth of Urbanization in the World," *American Journal of Sociology* 60 (March 1955): 430–432. For the primacy-of-urbanization argument, see Jane Jacobs, *The Economy of Cities* (New York: Vintage Books, 1970), chap. 1.

Table 2-3. Largest Metropolitan Areas

Rank (1985)	Metropolitan Area	Population (1985)	Rank (1980)
1	New York, NY (CMSA)	17,931,100	1
2	Los Angeles, CA (CMSA)	12,738,200	2
3	Chicago, IL (CMSA)	8,085,200	3
4	San Francisco, CA (CMSA)	5,809,000	4
5	Philadelphia, PA (CMSA)	5,776,500	5
6	Detroit, MI (CMSA)	4,581,200	6
7	Boston, MA (CMSA)	4,051,400	7
8	Houston, TX (CMSA)	3,623,300	9
9	Dallas-Fort Worth, TX (CMSA)	3,511,600	8
10	Washington, DC (MSA)	3,489,500	10
11	Miami, FL (CMSA)	2,878,300	12
12	Cleveland, OH (CMSA)	2,776,400	11
13	Atlanta, GA (MSA)	2,471,700	14
14	St. Louis, MO (MSA)	2,412,400	17
15	Pittsburgh, PA (CMSA)	2,337,400	13
16	Minneapolis-St. Paul, MN (MSA)	2,262,400	15
17	Baltimore, MD (MSA)	2,252,800	16
18	Seattle, WA (CMSA)	2,247,400	18
19	San Diego, CA (MSA)	2,132,700	19
20	Tampa-St. Petersburg, FL (MSA)	1,868,700	22
21	Phoenix, AZ (MSA)	1,846,600	21
22	Denver, CO (CMSA)	1,827,100	24
23	Cincinnati, OH (CMSA)	1,679,900	20
24	Milwaukee, WI (CMSA)	1,550,300	23
25	Kansas City, MO (MSA)	1,493,900	25

Source: U.S. Bureau of the Census, *Statistical Abstract of the United States: 1986* (Washington, D.C.: United States Government Printing Office, 1985), pp. 21–23. 1985 update from *1980 Census of Population, Supplementary Report, Metropolitan Statistical Areas* (pc 80-S1-18).

area's production out to its markets. The availability of steamships, railroads, motor transport, and air transport makes it possible to supply increasingly larger populations over increasingly longer distances. These forms of transport are also much more energy-intensive than the forms of transport that supplied any previous form of urbanization. Unless new forms of transport or new sources of energy are discovered before existing supplies of petroleum are exhausted, contemporary metropolises and megalopolises will not remain viable.

In addition to the transportation network and the agricultural surplus made possible by modern technology, a third factor contributing to the growth of giant metropolises has been increasing control over death rates. Until the nineteenth century, life in towns and cities was much more hazardous than life in the rural areas. Sanitary conditions were so poor and death rates were so high that the growth of towns and cities was often very sporadic. Even as late as 1878 a two-month epidemic of yellow fever in the city of Memphis, Tennessee killed 5000 people, struck another 12,000, and caused 25,000 people to flee the city. In just two months, the city's population was reduced from about 50,000 people to fewer

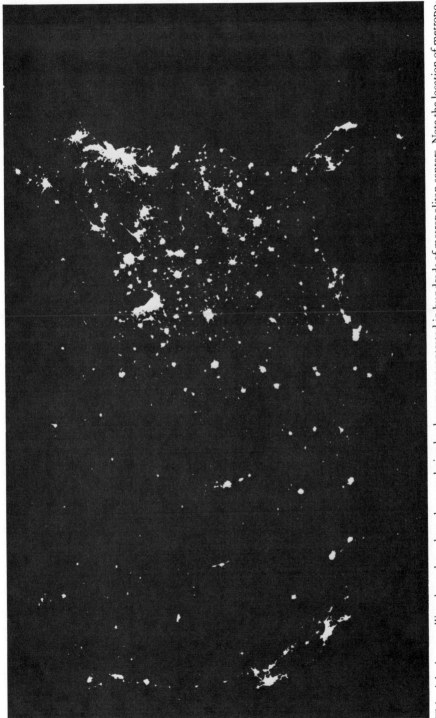

This nighttime satellite photo shows how the population has become concentrated in hundreds of metropolitan centers. Note the location of metropolises near you. Note also the Northeast megalopolis, the Florida peninsula, the Great Lakes region, and the Pacific seacoast. How many of the specific MSAs and CMSAs shown in Table 2-3 can you locate in the photo? (U.S. Air Force photo)

than 20,000.[14] Cities like Memphis could not grow into metropolises until people learned how to keep their excretion from polluting their drinking water, until they learned some elementary principles of hygiene, and until the improving practice of medicine began to eliminate the scourge of contagious diseases such as typhoid, typhus, cholera, and yellow fever. When these things occurred, the human population began to grow at an exponential rate and, in an economic sense, an excess population was created. Because of the ecological balance between the rural areas and the small rural towns, this excess population could not sustain itself in rural areas and had to migrate elsewhere. The problem became particularly acute during the nineteenth century in western Europe and England, where there was no more open land to be colonized and cultivated. Much of the excess population therefore migrated to the first great cities of the Industrial Revolution—Liverpool, Birmingham, Sheffield, and London. And much of it migrated to the Western Hemisphere, where it stimulated the urbanization of the United States.

How the United States Urbanized: Small Town to Megalopolis

The Urbanization of America: 1840–1920

The same three factors that permitted the development of large cities in general influenced the growth of cities in the United States. From 1730 to the end of the eighteenth century, the percentage of the population living in cities actually declined.[15] Large cities did not become commonplace until well into the nineteenth century. At the time of Independence the largest city, Philadelphia, contained only about 40,000 people.* The first city of 100,000 population did not emerge until almost 1820, and even as late as 1840 there were only three such cities. By 1850, that number had doubled.[16] The decade of the 1840s thus marks the beginning of intensive urbanization in the United States. The city-building phase of urbanization reached its peak by 1920, when for the first time a majority of the population lived in urban places. These eighty years of urbanization resulted from three historical forces.

Urban Migrations

The first of these forces was extensive immigration. Thirty-seven million people migrated to the United States between 1841 and 1930. Politically, they were a very important force, for they created the basic institutions of urban politics that are influential in many of the central cities even today.

As can be seen in Table 2-4, urban migrants came in different stages. The first stage was dominated by Irish and German immigration, with the Irish settling primarily in urban places in the Northeast and the German settling in both urban and rural places in both the Northeast and the Midwest.

During the second stage from the 1890s until the 1920s, immigrants came primarily from southern and eastern Europe and settled in both the Northeast and

*Other large cities in 1790 were New York, 33,131; Boston, 18,038; Charleston, 16,359; Baltimore, 13,503.

Table 2-4. Origin and Place of Settlement of Immigrants

Immigrant group	Era of most immigration[a]	Number of immigrants: 1841–1930[b]	Regions of settlement[c]	Estimated degree of settlement in urban places
Mainstream nationalities				
English	1845–1895	4,114,023	NE, ENC, South, West	Medium
Germans	1845–1885	5,747,710	NE, ENC, WNC, West	Medium
European ethnic minorities				
Irish	1845–1885	4,437,610	NE, ENC, WNC	High
Italians	1900–1914	4,648,503	NE, ENC, West	High
Catholic Poles	1900–1914		NE, ENC	High
Jews[d]	1900–1914	2,443,474	NE, ENC	Very high
American blacks	1940–1970	None	NE, ENC, South, SW	Very high
Contemporary urban migrants[e]				
Spanish-speaking	1961–1985	4,121,400	NE, ENC, Florida, SW	High
Asians	1961–1985	3,455,400	NE, SW	Very high

[a] Except for Hispanics and Asians, approximately two-thirds of all immigrants from 1841 to 1930 came during the period indicated. Hispanic and Asian immigration numbers are for the period 1961–1985.

[b] *Sources:* Bureau of the Census, *Historical Statistics of the United States from Colonial Times to 1957* (Washington, D.C.: U.S. Government Printing Office, 1957), pp. 56–59. U.S. Bureau of the Census, *Statistical Abstract of the United States: 1971* (Washington, D.C.: U.S. Government Printing Office, 1971), p. 92. Jewish immigration is taken from *Encyclopaedia Judaica Jerusalem* (New York: Macmillan, 1971), vol. 16, pp. 1519–1524.

[c] NE = Northeast; ENC = East North Central; WNC = West North Central; SW = Southwest.

[d] Jewish immigrants prior to 1880 were mostly Germans. After 1880 they were mostly Russians and Poles.

[e] Spanish-speaking and Asian immigration is probably greatly understated due to the large number of illegal immigrants. Data are taken from U.S. Bureau of the Census, *Statistical Abstract of the United States: 1987* (Washington, D.C.: U.S. Government Printing Office, 1986), p. 11.

the Midwest cities. These two waves of European immigration had a profound impact on the composition of the American population. In a 1972 survey the Census Bureau estimated that over 30 percent of the population of the United States traced its heritage to just six of these ethnic nationalities—German, Irish, Russian, Polish, Italian, and French.[17] Since the Irish, Russian, Polish, and Italian immigrants settled mainly in the metropolitan cities, they represent an even larger percentage of the metropolitan population than they do of the overall American population. The urban political institutions created by these immigrants have had a disproportionate influence on the development of metropolitan America, and we will examine those institutions in Chapter 3.

A third migration wave that profoundly altered the composition of American cities was that of American blacks coming out of the rural South into the cities. It is important to note that this migration wave differed from the two earlier waves in at least one key respect. Since the black migrants were American citizens rather than foreign immigrants, their migration into cities has been called *in-migration* rather than *immigration*. This migration wave was at its peak from about 1940 to the early 1970s.

Finally, as black urban in-migration began to taper off in the 1970s, a fourth wave of Hispanic and Asian immigrants began moving into American cities. These immigrants are dramatically altering the demographic composition and politics of several cities in the West, in Florida, in New York, and in some Midwest cities such as Chicago.[18]

Transportation Technology

The combination of innovation in the technology of transport and the frontier movement to the West created a second force toward establishing American cities.[19] The discovery of gold in California, the existence of fertile farmland from the Appalachian Mountains almost to the Pacific Coast, and the generous subsidization of the railroads to expand westward spurred a continual westward migration of the population. Along these railroad lines there began to emerge "gateway" cities, which functioned as transfer points for the exchange of goods between the railroads and the surrounding agricultural communities.[20]

In many instances the railroads created the cities. When southern Illinois towns refused to grant concessions that the Illinois Central Railroad desired in order to run its tracks through those towns, the Illinois Central ran its tracks through other locations and established its own gateway towns in competition with existing cities. A typical practice was for the railroad to acquire title to empty land, survey it, parcel it out for city lots, and then sell the lots for a profit. At Kankakee, Illinois, for example, the railroad bought the land for $18,000, sold some of the subdivided lots for $50,000, and held the remainder, valued at $100,000, for future sales. When the Illinois Central was chartered in 1851, there were only ten towns along its route. Twenty years later there were eighty-one; and the total population of all these places, excluding Chicago, increased fourteenfold, from 12,000 to 172,000.[21] The creation of these western railroad towns opened up the western farmlands and turned the United States into the world's greatest agricultural producer. The agricultural surplus that began to emerge in the nineteenth century in turn became a further stimulus to growth of American cities.

Growth within the cities was also conditioned by the technology of transportation. Sam Bass Warner, Jr. has shown how transit innovations affected the growth of Boston.[22] Until the 1850s, Boston was a pedestrian city with no transit system, and the outer boundaries of the residential areas were naturally limited to a radius of about two miles. The introduction of horse-drawn railways extended the city's boundaries to perhaps two and a half miles by 1873 and to four miles by 1887. In the 1890s, electric streetcars were introduced and the city's boundaries were extended to a radius of six miles.

The streetcar had other important effects on city development. It facilitated a form of retail strip shopping areas along the streetcar routes where retailers found it lucrative to establish their shops. Later, in the age of the automobile, these strip shopping areas would decline in most cities and the more successful retailers would move to the suburban shopping centers and malls. The streetcars also enabled the first extensive urbanization by connecting the central business district with newly urbanized places beyond the city proper. The streetcar outlined the physical growth of the eastern central cities as we know them today.

The other major technological innovations in transportation were the elevated and subway railways. New York introduced the first steam elevated trains in the 1870s, but because of their dirtiness and their occasional tendency to spew hot ashes on pedestrians walking beneath the elevated structures, they were replaced with electric elevated trains in the 1890s and subways in the early 1900s.

It is difficult to overestimate the importance of these technological changes to the prosperity of individual cities.[23] Table 2-5 indicates how dependent most cities are on prevailing modes of transportation technology and how vulnerable they are to sudden innovations. Although budding nineteenth-century river cities such as Galena, Illinois; Wheeling, West Virginia; and Louisville, Kentucky, each at one time seemed destined to grow into another Chicago, they found their growth stunted when transportation technology changed. They were bypassed because of newer, more efficient means of transporting goods and people. The newer forms of transport are highly energy-intensive, and contemporary cities that are dependent solely on them are very vulnerable to fluctuations in the availability of energy. If the petroleum problems of the 1970s were to recur and signal a permanent petroleum shortage, it is very likely that sharp declines would be suffered by cities such as Las Vegas, which is exclusively dependent on air and motor transport. The same could occur in many suburbs and satellite cities in the megalopolises. On the other hand, if sources of electrical energy are sufficient to sustain the increasingly widespread applications of electronic telecommunications technology, then settlement patterns within the megalopolises seem likely to continue dispersing and decentralizing.[24]

Emergence of a National Corporate Economy

In addition to immigration and transportation technology, the third factor that led to the growth of the metropolis in the United States was the transformation of

Table 2-5. Transportation Technology and the Growth of Cities

Mode of transport	Time period of most importance	Source of locomotion	Intensiveness			Representative city
			Capital	Labor	Energy	
Turnpike *Most important cargo: people, supplies for personal needs*	1800–1840	Animal and foot	Low	Very high	Very low	Cumberland, Md.
Canal *Most important cargo: grain from West to East*	1820–1850	Barge: first animal, then steam	Medium	High	Very low	Rome, N.Y.
River *Most important cargo: grain, agricultural products generally, people*	1840–1875	Steam, then diesel	Low	High	Very low	Galena, Ill.
Railroad *Most important cargo: agricultural products, coal, manufacturing goods, people*	1850–1920	Steam, then diesel	High	High	Medium	Vandalia, Ill.
Auto/truck/air *Most important cargo: people, manufactured products*	1920–?	Gasoline, diesel, and jet engines	Very high	Medium	Very high	Las Vegas, Nev.
Electronic communications *Most important cargo: information*	1965–?	Telecommunications, computers, fascimile	Very high	Low	High	Suburb or satellite city of a metropolis

the economy from a small-enterprise base into a national corporate economy. Until late in the nineteenth century, most business enterprises in American cities were small-scale, family-owned companies that maintained few permanent employ-ees.[25] After the Civil War, more and more business corporations set up national or regional headquarters in large cities such as New York, Chicago, and Boston. Not only did this concentration of business headquarters provide economic activity to make those regional cities grow, but the modern business offices of those corporate headquarters also created millions of new and peculiarly urban jobs in fields such as advertising, marketing, financing, accounting, typing, office management, and general office work. The creation of these occupations in turn contributed to the demand for a growing urban labor force and population. Hence the corporate business office arose and provided another stimulus to the growth of large cities.[26]

The Emergence of Contemporary Metropolitan America: 1920–1975

This urbanization process did not cease in 1920, but after that date it changed in two significant respects. First, there was a general westward drift. A marked slowdown occurred in the growth of many places that had been urbanizing prior to 1920, namely, the central cities in the Northeast and the small towns that served rural areas, particularly those east of the Mississippi River.[27] As can be seen from Table 2-6, whereas the Northeast quadrant contained 60 percent of all cities that had grown to 100,000 population before 1930, 86 percent of cities reaching that size since 1930 are in either the Southeast or the Southwest quadrant. Today six of the nation's ten largest cities are located in the Sunbelt. And perhaps nothing is more symbolic of the westward drift of population than the fact that Los Angeles in 1984 moved past Chicago and became the nation's second largest city.

The Westward Drift

Politically the westward drift is important for several reasons. With few excep-tions, such as San Francisco, the cities in these regions did not receive the millions of European immigrants that the cities of the Northeast had received, and conse-quently the style and ethnic base of their politics is different. The cities of the Southwest are also much more dependent on motor and air transport than they are on water and rail transport, and this makes them more vulnerable to potential energy shortages in the future. These cities also tend to benefit more from the new sources of wealth—Texas oil, federal defense and aerospace expenditures, and the tourist and recreation boom—than do the cities of the Northeast and the Midwest. For all of these reasons the style and character of urban politics in these new cities differ markedly from those of the older cities of the Northeast and Midwest.

Suburbanization

The second significant change in the urbanization process since 1920 has been the shifting of urban growth away from the central cities and into the suburbs. If the 1920 census was distinctive for being the first to show that more people lived in urban than in rural places, the 1970 census was distinctive for being the first to

Table 2-6. The Westward Drift of Urbanization

	Location of cities of 100,000 or more by geographic quadrant				
Year	Northeast	Southeast	Southwest	Northwest	Total number of cities
1850	5	1	0	0	6
1870	10	2	1	0	13
1900	27	3	2	2	34
1930	56	14	12	11	93
1940	50	14	12	13	89
1950	55	20	17	13	105
1960	58	27	29	15	129
1970	61	38	36	18	153
1980	53	43	50	23	169
1984	54	41	56	24	175

Northeast: Includes all cities east of or straddling the Mississippi River and north of the Ohio and Potomac rivers

Southeast: Includes all cities east of or straddling the Mississippi River and south of the Ohio and Potomac rivers

Southwest: Includes all cities west of the Mississippi River and south of the northern boundary of Oklahoma, plus all cities in the states of California and Nevada

Northwest: Includes all cities west of the Mississippi River and north of the Southwest quadrant

Not included are the cities in Alaska, Hawaii, and Puerto Rico.

Source: Compiled from U.S. Bureau of the Census, *Statistical Abstract of the United States: 1987,* pp. 31–33; *1982–83,* pp. 22–24; *1971,* pp. 21–23; *1941,* pp. 27–31; *1911,* pp. 55–56.

show that the suburban population outnumbered the central-city population.

Four factors have been responsible for the suburbanization of the United States: the automobile, the new technology in road and residential construction, the cultural dislike of big cities, and the invention of long-term, low-down-payment home mortgages.

The role of the automobile and road construction in stimulating suburbanization derived partly from the ease with which they extended the acceptable commuting distance for large numbers of people, and partly from the fact that they liberated real estate developers and retail businesspeople from having to build their residences and shops along the streetcar lines. The spread of the automobile was greatly facilitated by federal and state government highway and freeway construction. Particularly since the passage of the Federal Aid Highway Act of 1956, which earmarked the revenue from a gasoline tax for a highway trust fund to build and maintain the interstate highway system, freeway construction has stimulated the dispersion of the population throughout the suburbs. Where the roads were constructed, the population moved, and shopping facilities soon followed. The shopping centers in turn attracted more people to move into nearby areas. The first suburban shopping center appeared, fittingly, west of the Mississippi River in the country-club district of suburban Kansas City.[28]

The introduction of the automobile and the freeway systems made suburban-ization possible but not inevitable. To make suburbanization inevitable, several other things had to occur. For one thing, the mass of the population had to *want* to move to the suburbs. In the United States, historical-cultural developments worked in that direction (see the poll results on p. 32). As far back as the writings of Thomas Jefferson, one common theme of American intellectual literature has been disparagement of city life.[29] The popular media have generally idealized the small town as the epitome of American civilization.

For the metropolis to become suburbanized, people not only had to *want* to live in suburbia, they also had to *be able to afford* to live there. One device that helped satisfy this requisite was the long-term, low-down-payment mortgage loan. These loans were pioneered by the Federal Housing Administration (FHA) and Veterans' Administration (VA). Their mortgage guarantees made it possible for any qualify-ing person to purchase a home with a small down payment or no down payment at all, with monthly payments spread over a thirty-year period, and with an interest rate slightly below the prevailing conventional mortgage interest rates. Once the government-guaranteed mortgages proved that long-term, low-down-payment mortgages were financially viable, mortgage banks began to use them in conven-tional mortgage loans. Because the cheapest large plots of land existed beyond the central-city boundaries, that is where most of this new mortgage money was lent. For the first time in American history, home ownership was open to the majority of the urban population.

The government-backed mortgages were not without their critics. They were accused of being racist, because the FHA for many years agreed to restrictive cove-nants in deeds that prohibited the property from being sold to noncaucasians.[30] Even after restrictive covenants were struck down by the Supreme Court in 1948,[31] FHA instructed its officers not to approve loans that would upset the racial com-position of neighborhoods.[32] Finally in 1962 President Kennedy issued an execu-tive order prohibiting discrimination in FHA loans. Government-backed mortgages also were accused of being biased against the lower-middle-income and lower-income strata of the society, since most of the mortgages went to upper-middle-class families. And to observers concerned about the development of com-munities (as distinguished from the proliferation of housing projects), the government-backed mortgages were accused of existing primarily as a government prop to the construction industry and real estate developers.[33]

Thus the suburbanization of America after 1920 and especially after 1945 was virtually predetermined by a number of factors that met at the same point in time: the intellectual disrepute of the city, the cultural value placed on living in single-family homes in open spaces, the availability of cheap land beyond the city's boundaries, the unprecedented access to that land via new roadways, the extensive use of the automobile, and the availability of long-term, low-down-payment mortgages.

It must be noted that this analysis of the causes of suburbanization places very little weight on the cause most often cited—the flight of the white population away from the racial minorities that were moving into the central cities. Although there

Where People Want to Live

The historical disrepute of the city is reflected in popular attitudes. When survey researchers ask people where they would prefer to live if they had a choice, big cities are usually the least preferred place. The Gallup Poll found this to be true in 1973, 1976, and 1985.

1973		1976		1985	
Most preferred place	Percent	Most preferred place	Percent	Most preferred place	Percent
City	13	City of over 100,000	13	City of over 100,000	22
Suburbs	31	City of 10,000–		City of 10,000–	
Small town	32	100,000	29	99,999	29
Farm	23	Town or village of		Town of 2,500–	
No opinion	1	less than 10,000	20	9,999	23
		Rural area	38	Rural area	25
				Don't know	1
	100		100		100

Source: The Gallup Poll: Public Opinion 1972–1979 (Wilmington, DE: Scholarly Resources, 1978), pp. 112, 914. Copyright 1978 by American Institute of Public Opinion. *The Gallup Poll: Public Opinion 1985* (Wilmington, DE: Scholarly Resources, 1985), p. 64. Copyright 1985 by American Institute of Public Opinion. Reprinted by permission.

can be no doubt that much of the white population did move to the suburbs to avoid living with blacks, this fails as a sufficient explanation of suburbanization. For suburbanization occurred equally in metropolises with very small black populations (such as Seattle, Portland, Oregon, and Minneapolis) and in metropolises with very large black populations (such as Washington, Philadelphia, New York). The racial cause of suburbanization added only to the *want* factor of suburbanization. It did nothing to affect the technological factors, the availability of cheap land, and the revolution in mortgage lending practices.

Finally, it must also be noted that the rapid expansion of the urban population into suburbia does not necessarily represent an exercise of individual free choice. As indicated above, people migrated to suburbs because those were the places where acceptable housing was most likely to be found. That the acceptable housing occurred in the form of single-family homes in suburbs was not a consequence of individual choices. Rather it was a consequence of transit, housing, employment, and finance policies of the federal and state governments and the major mortgage banking institutions. How many single-family homes get constructed each year and who gets the credit to buy them is much less a consequence of individual choice than it is a consequence of government credit policies and of the policies of real estate developers and financial institutions.

The Dual Migration

The two points of racial discord and free choice are extremely important. Although suburbanization cannot be traced directly to racial prejudice or to individual choices, the fact of suburbanization has had profound consequences on race relations and the kinds of choices that are available in such social amenities as housing, jobs, and schools. Suburbanization was an integral part of the most far-reaching demographic trend of the post-World War II era: the dual migration. The first part of the dual migration was an in-migration of relatively poor, rural, and racial minority peoples into the large central cities. The second part of the dual migration was the out-migration of more affluent, middle-class whites to the suburbs.

Who Were the In-Migrants?

The third and fourth waves of urban migration shown in Table 2-4 (see p. 25) were dominated by people who did not share the European or Caucasian backgrounds of the majority of the American population. As that table shows, the in-migrants since 1940 have been predominantly blacks, Hispanics, and Asians. In a lesser number they also include American Indians and rural whites.

The third urban migration period, from about 1940 to 1970, saw a steady migration north and west of black sharecroppers who were driven off southern farms and plantations by policies of agricultural subsidies and by the mechanization of farm labor. Three migration routes developed along the principal railroad lines. From the southeastern states there was a steady migration to northeastern cities such as Washington, Newark, New York, and Philadelphia. From the more centrally located southern states of Alabama, Mississippi, and Tennessee there was a migration to midwestern cities such as St. Louis, Chicago, and Detroit. From Arkansas, Louisiana, and Texas former sharecroppers drifted westward to the large Texas cities of Dallas, Fort Worth, and Houston, and to other cities as far west as Los Angeles.[34]

Whichever route the migration took, there was some terminal city beyond which the southern blacks did not migrate in large numbers. On the East Coast it was New York. In the Midwest it was Chicago and Detroit, and on the West Coast it was Oakland. Across the river from New York City, Newark was 58 percent black by 1980, and even Hartford, Connecticut, was 34 percent black. But beyond those cities, the black proportion of central-city populations dropped off markedly. Albany was only 16 percent black in 1980, and Boston was only 22 percent black. The same thing occurred in the Midwest. Chicago was 40 percent black by 1980. Barely a hundred miles north of Chicago, however, Milwaukee was only 23 percent black, and the next central city, Minneapolis, was only 8 percent black. The same phenomenon occurred on the West Coast, where the combined populations of San Francisco and Oakland were about 24 percent black (San Francisco was 12.7 and Oakland 46.7 percent), but the population of Portland was only 8 percent black. This phenomenon is very important to understand, for it indicates that there is a very broad range of variation in racial composition from one central city to another. The black migrations were conditioned by geographical factors as much as social and political factors. Finally, it must be noted that not all urban blacks have settled in central cities. As we will see in Chapter 9, about one-fourth of all blacks now live in suburbs rather than central cities. Consequently, one must speak cautiously when generalizing about the racial problems of central cities.

The fourth, contemporary wave of urban migration has been dominted by Hispanics and Asians. There are more than 17 million people of Spanish-speaking origin in the United States, making it the fifth or sixth largest Spanish-speaking country in the world.[35] Three-fourths of these people are Puerto Ricans, Mexicans ("Chicanos"), and Cubans. About two million Puerto Ricans live in the continental United States. They have migrated principally to New York City, but large Puerto Rican settlements exist in other cities on the East Coast and as far west as Chicago. They are the most urbanized of the Spanish-speaking ethnic groups: 95 percent of Puerto Ricans live in MSAs.

Mexican-Americans, with their population of nearly nine million, constitute one of the largest ethnic groups in the United States. An overwhelming majority of Mexican-Americans live in just five states (Arizona, California, New Mexico, Colorado, Texas). But because so many Mexican-Americans are migrant farm laborers, they have formed communities as far north as Minnesota and as far east as Ohio—more than 15,000 Mexican-Americans live in Milwaukee, for example—and they are the least urbanized of the Spanish-speaking population. About 81 percent live in metropolitan areas.

About a million Cuban-Americans live in the United States, and the largest settlement is in Miami. Cuban-Americans differ from Puerto Ricans and Mexican-Americans in two respects. First, they came to the United States mainly for political rather than economic reasons, many of them being middle-class persons who escaped from Castro's Cuba in the 1960s. Second, they tend to be much more conservative in their politics than either Puerto Ricans or Mexican-Americans are. This is most apparent in matters of U.S. foreign policy; the Miami Cuban community has provided consistent support for the Reagan administration's attempt to overthrow the government of Nicaragua and has opposed Castro's Cuba whenever possible.[36]

Constituting still another category of Latin-Americans is the growing number of immigrants who come from Central America to settle in our southwestern states. Conditions of warfare and strife in Central America have prompted the gradual but steady entry of these refugees into American cities.

The second part of the contemporary urban migration wave consists of Asians. This influx stems from the change in immigration statutes in 1965 that removed the previous ceiling of 100 persons per Asian country per year. Especially after the Vietnam War, there was also a significant inflow of refugees from Indochina. These groups have an important political impact in cities such as San Francisco. But the nature of their impact is difficult to predict, because the Asian immigrants are even more diverse ethnically, linguistically, and economically than are the Hispanics. Of the 3.5 million Asian immigrants indicated in Table 2-4, the single largest number came from the Philippines (682,900), followed by Korea (603,800), China (480,100), Vietnam (419,100), and India (327,700).[37]

Finally, there also has been a migration of American Indians into the cities, although in much smaller numbers and usually localized in the urban areas fairly close to reservations. In the substantial American Indian communities found in Minneapolis and Los Angeles, these people exist in a state of poverty and disorganization that is perhaps greater than that of any other ethnic or racial group in those cities.

Dual Migration's Effects on the Cities

These migrations of relatively unaffluent people into the central cities constitute the first part of the dual migration. The second part consists of the migration of more affluent people out of the central cities. The large metropolitan areas have been compared to huge donuts with a hole in the middle. Since the suburbs become separate tax entities, the central cities do not share the increased tax revenue from more expensive homes, the increasing number of shopping centers, and the growing number of business establishments in the suburbs. Furthermore, since the suburbs normally do not belong to the same school districts as the central cities, there is less and less mingling between the poor and the upper-middle-class children in the schools. Although it is not completely true that the suburbs became affluent while the central cities became impoverished, it is true that the largest number of poor people settled in the central cities. And because suburbanization brought changes in the metropolitan political structure, the central cities found it more and more difficult to come up with the resources to handle the social problems the poor brought with them.

Dual Migration and Ethnic Succession

The dual migration of the poorer people and the racial minorities into the central cities and of more affluent, upper-middle-class people out to the suburbs has deep historic roots. As the early Irish immigrants became affluent enough to move into the better neighborhoods, their slums were inherited by Italians, Jews, and Poles. As these ethnic minorities moved out of the slums, they in turn were followed by the post-World War II urban minorities. By 1970 the black urban in-migration slowed to a trickle in most areas, while the out-migration of affluent whites has continued. The net impact during the 1970s was that central-city out-migrants outnumbered in-migrants by over 13 million people.[38] The slowdown of the in-migration of the poor has not been a great boon for cities, however. As black in-migration from the South began to taper off, that reduced the pressure on housing in lower- and working-class black neighborhoods. At the same time, open housing policies and a general rise in the incomes of middle-class, young black families enabled unprecedented numbers of blacks to migrate out of the slums into more attractive central-city neighborhoods. The net result has been a rapid deterioration in lower- and working-class black neighborhoods, which are being abandoned to what one group of commentators called "a destructive residual underclass."[39]

The Woodlawn neighborhood in Chicago illustrates this process. Located just south of the University of Chicago campus, where it serves as a residential area for university personnel, the neighborhood changed in the 1950s from a predominantly white neighborhood to a predominantly black one. During the 1960s, Woodlawn also became the locale for the most highly organized and powerful of Chicago's teenage gangs, the Blackstone Rangers. Violence precipitated by the

Rangers, together with the availability of nonsegregated housing elsewhere in the city, combined to drive out of the neighborhood most of the working-class and middle-class families who could afford to leave. At the same time, pressure on absentee landlords to bring their properties up to the standards of the city's building codes put many landlords in the untenable situation where increased rents would not offset increased maintenance and repair costs. Many landlords responded by abandoning their buildings. The abandoned buildings then became prey to vandals, looters, and arsonists. The core of Woodlawn lost 41 percent of its population during the 1960s. In the last six years of the decade, more than 400 Woodlawn buildings were demolished by the city.

This process took place not only in Woodlawn but in many other large northern cities as well. New York's South Bronx gained notoriety for its burned-out blocks. In contrast, many southern and southwestern cities continued to experience in-migration. By the mid-1980s, the abandonment process in places like Woodlawn and the South Bronx had begun to slow down, but it is too early to tell whether or not a reversal is underway.

Changes in Growth Patterns in the 1990s

As we turn from the past and look ahead to the final decade of the twentieth century, we see both continuities with and changes from the historical urbanization patterns we've just described. Among the continuities, the most significant is the population drift toward the southern and western Sunbelt regions. If anything, this trend appears to be accelerating today. The 1980 census figures showed that 89 percent of the population growth since 1970 occurred in the South and the West. The northeastern and north central regions experienced a combined net out-migration of over five million people in the 1970s, compared with a combined net in-migration of over five million in the South and West. A second continuity with the past can be seen in the continuous growth of the suburbs in metropolitan areas. There is no evidence that either of these trends will slacken in the 1990s.

Among the departures from historical urbanization trends, three significant changes began in the 1970s. First is the decentralization of the population to new urban centers in the countryside. This is seen most dramatically in the expanded numbers of SMSAs and other urban places. SMSAs increased from 243 in 1970 to 318 in 1980, and urban places increased from 7062 to 8765 in that decade. Corporations that open new executive offices or new plants show an increasing tendency to favor the smaller Sunbelt urban centers.[40] When General Motors, for example, decided to build a new automobile called the Saturn, it also decided to locate the plant in Spring Hill, Tennessee rather than in Detroit or some other traditional automobile manufacturing city of the Midwest.

How much longer this decentralization trend can continue is not known, however. A Census Bureau study in 1985 found a considerable slowdown in rural growth.[41] And the National Planning Association predicted in 1987 that 86 percent of all the jobs to be created between then and the year 2010 will occur in metropolitan areas.[42]

The second change in the 1990s is likely to be the maturation of the so-called urban renaissance that began in the late 1970s, when a number of factors combined to attract young and middle-aged professional people into certain areas of central cities. At the time, federal housing policies introduced incentives for urban neighborhood redevelopment, and energetic individuals and couples seized the opportunity to buy up deteriorated urban homes and restore them. Because this process brings upper-middle-income people back into these neighborhoods, it is sometimes called *urban gentrification.*

In view of these forces, corporations found it advantageous to increase rather than decrease employment opportunities in the cities. After virtually deserting the central cities during the 1950s and 1960s to establish their plants in more economical settings, they seemed to discover in the late 1970s that the central-city downtown areas were lucrative places to relocate their headquarters and other office facilities. Many city governments encouraged these developments by granting generous tax abatements, below-market interest rates, and other subsidies. As white-collar job opportunities expanded in downtown areas, mortgage lending institutions found themselves pressured to modify their blatant redlining practices and agree to finance homes, townhouses, apartments, and condominiums for the influx of upper-middle-income service workers who wanted to live within quick commuting distance of their new jobs.

The number of urban neighborhoods undergoing revitalization is still very small, however, and gentrification by itself is clearly not strong enough to reverse the long-term decline of central cities.[43] Nevertheless, gentrification is an important phenomenon. The gentrifiers are much more influential politically than the people they displace. And their restoration of old, previously run-down neighborhoods makes an important symbolic impact on how people think about cities. For young, single people or those who are recently divorced, for middle-aged professionals, and for the elderly, the city can be a very desirable place to live. Partially because of this, it has become commonplace to speak of a "new vitality" in the cities.[44] Although this urban vitality is most prominent in the newer cities of the South and West, old northern cities such as Chicago, Philadelphia, Baltimore, Boston, New York, and Washington, D.C. are also experiencing gentrification.

Urban Economic Transformation

Closely associated with the urban renaissance, a third influence on city growth today is the dramatic change in the economic base of cities. Earlier we cited industrialization as a motivating force behind nineteenth- and early twentieth-century urbanization. Buffalo, Pittsburgh, Cleveland, Gary, Milwaukee, and dozens of smaller Great Lake cities grew up and prospered as blue-collar factory towns. But since World War II, blue-collar jobs have been declining in the central cities and expanding in the suburbs. Today there are many more industrial manufacturing jobs in suburbs than there are in central cities.

If the city has been losing its vocation as a factory town, what economic activities have evolved to replace the factories? The answer, according to John Mollenkopf, is government jobs, third-sector institutions (for example, hospitals, universities, foundation headquarters), and advanced corporate services (such as legal, accounting, computing, advertising, and investment banking).[45] The explosion of advanced corporate services has been especially important, because cities with many such services become very attractive sites for corporation headquarters.

These economic changes have affected different cities in different ways, contributing to the vitality of some but retarding the growth of others. Mollenkopf argues that three types of cities are emerging in the 1980s. First are the old, industrial cities such as Gary, Indiana, and Youngstown, Ohio. Despite dramatic changes in the national economy that have caused the industrial manufacturing sector to decline relative to the service sector, these old cities have clung to their industrial economic bases. Gary and Youngstown are especially good examples, because their basic industry (steel manufacturing) is heavily dependent on the fortunes of the automobile industry. As that industry suffered major setbacks in the 1970s and early 1980s, Gary, Youngstown, and many other old industrial cities were economically shattered.

In an entirely different situation are the newer service and administrative centers of the Southwest. Cities such as San Diego, for example, have none of the legacy of industrial labor conflicts of the 1930s or racial unrest of the 1960s. They attracted administrative and service corporations and high-technology industries that weathered the economic storms of the 1970s better than did the old basic industries of the Midwest.

Finally, contends Mollenkopf, a third type of city has transformed its economy from old industry to banking, service sectors, and advanced corporate services. Typical cities in this category are New York, Chicago, Philadelphia, Boston, and San Francisco. Although all have suffered significant population decline, they have maintained themselves as significant locales for corporation headquarters and service-sector activities.

These economic changes pose a difficult dilemma for city leaders who want to avoid future dependence on dying industries and thus feel they must compete successfully for high-technology industries or dynamic service-sector enterprises. In this competitive quest for revitalization, can cities afford *not* to give tax concessions, community development funds, and other incentives to corporations, even though the resulting downtown revitalization may cause severe hardship for many urban poor and detour investment money away from residential neighborhoods? On the one hand, central-city mayors, newspaper editors, business corporations, and construction union officials tend to view this urban renaissance as a necessary process for stabilizing city populations,[46] making the city physically attractive, and creating job opportunities. On the other hand, many minority-group spokespersons and some scholars look at the same phenomenon and ask for whom the cities are being saved.[47] They charge that displacement and other changes central to the urban renaissance mainly benefit corporations, mortgage institutions, and real estate speculators. Few benefits, in their view, will trickle down to the poor or even to the mass of the city's working- and middle-class people. These views are supported by columnist Neal Peirce, who notes that many corporations hold out for lucrative tax subsidies in exchange for locating in a city. Peirce asks whether this is a form of industrial blackmail that forces city residents to pay for benefits to the corporation.[48] These questions about urban economic development will be explored more thoroughly in Chapter 6.

Some Political Implications of Metropolitan Growth

An underlying assumption of this chapter has been that demographic and technological forces have significant political implications. Three implications in particular stand out: (1) the nature of urban growth is shaped by political decisions; (2) urban growth inevitably leads to greater governmental activity and expenditures; and (3) urban growth obliges governments to assume the role of arbiter between conflicting groups in the urban arena.

The effect of political decisions on urban growth can be seen by reviewing some of the items previously covered in this chapter. For example, political decisions shaped the technological innovations that caused urban growth. At every stage of new technological implementation indicated in Table 2-5, governments made significant public investments. At the earliest stage, government funds financed the construction of the canals. At the railroad stage, government lands were given to the railroads, and the railroads in turn sold these lands in order to construct their railroad cities. And in the automobile / motor-transport stage, the federal government utilized the highway trust fund to provide a continual source of funding for the highways and the interstate road system. Not only have governmental decisions contributed directly to the application of new transportation technologies, but also many governmental decisions have had profound impact on determining the locations where urbanization would occur. The rapid post-World War II urbanization of southern California was due in great measure to federal expenditures in aerospace and defense industries. The decision in Nevada to legalize gambling contributed to the urbanization of Reno and Las Vegas. Finally, as indicated earlier, state and federal decisions on highway construction, home mortgage loan terms, and the subsidization of farmers to reduce acreage have contributed immensely to the dual migration that has characterized the metropolitan United States since the 1920s.

A second political implication of metropolitan growth is that increasing levels of urbanization inevitably lead to increasing levels of governmental activity and governmental expenditure. The yellow fever epidemic in Memphis cited earlier indicates how important it is for urban governments to take the initiative in such matters as sewage disposal, water supply, and public health. At the metropolitan level, suburban growth has meant greater expenditures for streets, utilities, fire and police protection, and public education. This inevitable increase in governmental activity as urbanization proceeds conflicts sharply with the political value, widely held in the United States, that governments should engage in the least possible amount of activities.

A third political implication of metropolitan growth is that governments are increasingly obliged to satisfy demands put forward by emerging groups in the growing metropolis. Often these groups ask the government to redress grievances they have against other actors in the metropolis. Other times they ask the government to help them satisfy certain needs they cannot satisfy themselves because they lack the economic resources to compete on an equal footing in the economic system. This has been true particularly in relation to the struggle of racial minority leaders and others to gain equal access to the social amenities of the metropolis—housing, jobs, and education. When they do not succeed in bargaining directly with institutions that control that access, they seek redress from the governments, and government officials are called upon to assist in the conflict.

Compared to the countryside, the urban ghetto is more conducive to militant political activity such as protesting, demonstrating, and rioting; the city brings potential leaders into direct contact with many more potential followers, and it is also more receptive to traditional forms of redressing grievances. In the city, lawsuits are brought before the courts. Lobbying is conducted before the legislatures and city councils. Candidates are run for public office. All this indicates that the more urbanized an area becomes, the more involved will its governments become in social conflicts.

These three political implications have special significance for the South and the Southwest, where urban growth rates are currently most intensive. Historically the South and Southwest have been the most conservative regions of the nation, resisting both extensive public welfare programs and political movements like organized labor that often represent the interests of dissatisfied groups. Southwestern metropolises such as Houston and Dallas have received large numbers of in-migrating Hispanics plus northern laborers driven from their native regions by economic recession and lured to the Southwest by the hope of jobs. Alfred Watkins argues that these migrants will create considerable political tensions as they seek to unionize in the Southwest and seek better welfare benefits.[49]

Political Bias in the Changes in Urban Growth

It may seem absurd to suggest that demographic movements might be biased politically, for demographic movements are neutral phenomena. Nevertheless, urban growth in contemporary America has certain patterns and consequences that favor certain groups of people above others. Three of these stand out.

First, a persistent motive force behind urban growth throughout United States history has been what Sam Bass Warner, Jr. called privatism (see p. 14). Warner wrote: "The tradition of privatism is . . . the most important element of our culture for understanding the development of cities."[50] City growth was not promoted because of a sense of community as much as it was promoted by private speculators and entrepreneurs who needed the growth to maximize their profits. Land, in particular, was seldom viewed as a public asset. On the contrary, it was a private asset on which the shrewd person not only could speculate wisely but also could build a city. The nineteenth-century masters in real estate speculation were the railroads. The twentieth-century masters were the central-city and suburban real estate developers. The provision of cultural facilities such as libraries and museums was left to philanthropists or to private subscription.[51] There was no concept of the public good for which the government could make such provisions. Even today in many cities, these facilities receive the leftovers of the municipal or county budgets.

As cities grow larger, the tradition of privatism conflicts sharply with the government's role as a provider of services and redresser of grievances. The extent to which governments at the metropolitan, state, and federal levels should try to guide the urban growth process is a hotly debated question. There are probably very few people who would any longer argue for leaving metropolitan growth totally to private initiative. But there is no general agreement on how much guidance government should provide or even which governments should provide it.[52]

A second bias of the contemporary metropolis is that it is probably more class-segregated than it was before. When the cities were so small and densely populated that all classes were concentrated within a few miles of the central business district, the residential areas of the poor, the working class, the middle class, and the wealthy were necessarily located very close to each other. The contemporary metropolises are so much larger and less densely populated that this is probably no longer true. A study of census tracts in Milwaukee and Buffalo found a very high level of class segregation in both the cities and suburbs.[53] Also, studies show that suburban neighborhoods tend to specialize in the kinds of people who live in them.[54] Although some gains have been made in black suburbanization and in reducing racial residential segregation within big cities,[55] most urban poor people and most racial minorities still live in inner-city neighborhoods.[56]

A third bias implication is that the changes over the past fifty or sixty years have made the contemporary metropolis less amenable to promoting the social mobility of the poor. The European immigrants lived within easy commuting distance from the urban growth areas where the greatest job and entrepreneurial opportunities existed. Today these opportunities have shifted to the suburban fringe. But the poor, urban in-migrant typically moves into an old residential neighborhood far removed from suburban job locations. In most metropolises, public transportation systems are not very efficient. The poor in-migrant's geographic distance from the growth area makes it much more difficult for him or her to partake in the metropolitan growth either as an employee or as a speculative entrepreneur than it was for the European immigrant who migrated into a still fast-growing city. Furthermore, the economic transformations in the past several decades have greatly reduced the number of unskilled and semiskilled jobs and have in large measure replaced small, owner-run retail stores with large retailing outlets and franchises. In summary, urban America in the days of European immigration was biased toward the entrepreneurial type who had the imagination and the capacity to profit from a growth situation. The urban America of the 1990s is much less conducive to the upward social mobility of the poor classes, particularly the poor classes within the racial minority communities.

Summary

1. In the twentieth century the American population has become overwhelmingly urban. *Urban* refers to a minor civil division of 2500 people. A *metropolitan statistical area* (MSA) consists of a central city of 50,000 people plus surrounding counties that are integrated into the central counties. A *consolidated metropolitan statistical area* (CMSA) consists of two or more MSAs bound together by rigid criteria. By 1986 there were 23 CMSAs, 332 MSAs, and more than 8700 urban places.

2. Three basic determinants of metropolitan growth have been identified: an agricultural surplus, transportation innovations, and declining death rates.

3. The urbanization of America (1840–1920) was stimulated by the immigration of millions of Europeans, the opening of the western frontier, and the creation of a national corporate economy.

4. The metropolitanization of America (1920–1975) was characterized by a shifting of the population westward and the growth of suburbs. The 1950s and 1960s were marked by dual migration. As affluent whites moved out of the cities, their place was taken by rural blacks, Hispanics, Asians, and poor whites.

5. The last two decades of the twentieth century appear to be witnessing a growing strength in small urban centers in the countryside, well removed from the metropolis. Through a gentrification process, a small but symbolically significant number of affluent whites are moving back into the central cities.

6. These urbanization patterns have definite political implications and biases. American urbanization historically has been marked by privatism. The metropolitan areas have become more class- and race-segregated as time has progressed, and the great cities have provided less of a stimulus to the upward social mobility of the poor.

Part II
Rise, Decline, and Consequences of Machine and Ethnic Politics

The tone of contemporary urban politics in the United States has been greatly influenced by late nineteenth-century machine politics and the events that caused their decline. So much has this been so that contemporary urban politics are virtually incomprehensible without some understanding of these historical forces. As the great industrial cities were born along the North Atlantic seacoast and the Great Lakes states, machine politics emerged. As governing devices, the machines were often deeply rooted in the social structures of the ethnic groups that inhabited these cities. The basic unit of political organization was a geographic unit, the ward or precinct. These developments are discussed in Chapters 3 and 4.

Because the political machines were often rooted in the social organization of certain ethnic communities, machine politics were biased toward and benefited those communities and certain businesspeople. In contrast, other groups, such as the racial minorities, benefited very little, for machine politics were effectively biased against them. However, there were very few cities with sizable racial minority populations until the twentieth century.

Machine politics were also biased to the disadvantage of certain upper-middle-class, reform-minded citizens who wanted to upgrade the level of public morals in the city. To accomplish these objectives, the reformers promoted several devices to remove city government from the control of the political machines. They were aided in their antimachine efforts by the patterns of metropolitan growth and by some actions taken by the federal government. These developments are discussed in Chapter 4.

Chapter 3
Institutionalizing Power in the Pre-World War II City

Chapter 2 indicated that the first major change in patterns of urbanization in the United States took place between 1840 and 1930, when hundreds of medium-size and large cities were created in the Northeast and Midwest by the settlement there of most of the 37 million immigrants. Politically, this process gave birth to the organization of urban political power on geographic and ethnic bases. The present chapter will show how several powerful contemporary institutions in urban politics developed out of the indigenous community structures of four European ethnic minorities: the Irish, Italians, Jews, and Poles.

The choice of these four ethnic groups is not random. Irish, Italian, Jewish, and Polish people settled almost exclusively in urban centers and, as much as any other ethnic group, shaped the institutions that dominated urban politics prior to World War II. By 1970 the descendants of these four ethnic groups numbered 30 million, about a fourth of the urbanized metropolitan population in the country, and their ethnicity continues to be important in modern urban politics.

Some of the institutions surviving from the old, pre-World War II city, such as the parish organization of the Catholic church, were integral elements of the ethnic power base. Some institutions, such as organized labor, were not integral elements of the ethnic power base, but they disproportionately tended to be led by and to serve the descendants of the European immigrants. Still other institutions, especially the urban political machines, were greatly transformed over time and fit into the power base of some ethnic groups better than others. Different ethnic groups, we will see, had different power bases. And there emerged what Ira Katznelson has called city trenches.[1] In one trench was organized labor seeking to improve working conditions; in a rival trench was the political party trying to control urban government; and in a third trench were neighborhood community organizations and government agencies trying to control the delivery of services in the neighborhoods. The leaders of the various ethnic immigrant groups competed against each other to dominate in these trenches. This competition between the rival ethnic groups and the three trenches ensured that the lower-class ethnics never banded together to form lower-class-based political movements that would protect their mutual interests against the merchant classes and the factory owners who exploited them as a labor supply and as consumers. And none of the three urban trenches or the ethnic institutions created prior to World War II have adapted very well to the needs of the contemporary black, Hispanic, and Asian minorities in the contemporary metropolis.

But we are getting ahead of our story. Let us begin this chapter by examining the size and distribution of the European ethnic settlements. We will then examine how each of the four largest groups (Irish, Italians, Jews, Poles) developed their own indigenous power base.

The Size and Distribution of Ethnic Settlements

Table 3-1 illustrates the distribution of major ethnic groups in 1970. The nine major urban ethnic groups can be divided into three general categories: (1) the mainstream nationalities that were assimilated the most thoroughly into the native white American population (especially English and Germans); (2) the European ethnic minorities that immigrated principally before World War I and still exhibit political characteristics of ethnic cohesion (especially the Irish, Italians, Slavs, and Jews); and (3) the newer racial and ethnic minorities that migrated into the cities primarily since World War II either from the American South or from abroad (especially blacks, Hispanics, and Asians). As calculated in columns 3 and 4 of Table 3-1, the mainstream nationalities comprise about a third of the contemporary urbanized metropolitan population, whereas the European ethnics comprise

Table 3-1. Estimated Ethnic and Racial Composition of the Metropolitan Population

Nationality or racial group	(1) Approximate number in United States[a]	(2) Percentage urban[b]	(3) Estimated number in SMSAs[c]	(4) Percentage of urbanized SMSA population[d]
Mainstream nationalities				**35.0**
English	29,548,000	94	25,706,960	20.9
German	25,543,000	68	17,369,240	14.1
European ethnics				**26.5**
Irish	16,408,000	91	14,931,280	12.1
Italians	8,764,000	94	8,238,160	6.7
Catholic Poles	3,829,000	87	3,331,230	2.7
Jews	6,115,000	99	6,115,000	5.0
Contemporary urban minorities				**20.9**
Blacks	22,673,000	74	16,786,000	13.6
Spanish-speaking	10,600,000	85	8,957,000	7.3

[a] U.S. Bureau of the Census, *Current Population Reports*, ser. P-20; no. 249, "Characteristics of the Population by Ethnic Origin: March 1972 and 1971" (Washington, D.C.: U.S. Government Printing Office, 1973); and *Current Population Reports*, ser. P-20; no. 264, "Persons of Spanish Origin in the United States: March, 1973" (Washington, D.C.: U.S. Government Printing Office, 1974). Alvin Chenkin, "Jewish Population in the United States," in *American Jewish Year Book* (Philadelphia: Jewish Publication Society, 1973), vol. 74, pp. 308–309. Reprinted by permission.

[b] Taken from a survey conducted among Catholic ethnics by the National Opinion Research Center. Harold J. Abramson, *Ethnic Diversity in Catholic America* (New York: Wiley, 1973), p. 34. Reprinted by permission. The Jewish population as reported in the *American Jewish Year Book* is entirely urban. Nonurban Jews were not included in its study.

[c] Estimated number = col. 1 × col. 2.

[d] Percentage = col. 3 ÷ 118,000,000 (i.e., the population of the urbanized areas).

about a fourth. The more recent in-migrants comprise about a fifth, but they are increasing faster than either of the other two groups.

The population figures in column 3 of Table 3-1 indicate the importance of the European ethnic minorities to American urban development. At the end of the nineteenth century, when some of the most important urban political institutions were being formed, the European ethnics comprised an absolute majority of the population in almost three-fourths of all cities of 100,000 or more. In the Northeast, which contained two-thirds of all such cities at the time, European immigrants and their children constituted an absolute majority in all except four cities—Baltimore, Maryland; Columbus, Ohio; Indianapolis, Indiana; and Washington, D.C. In only five big cities in the entire country did American-born whites of American-born parents comprise an absolute majority of the population. And three of these five cities were west of the Mississippi River—Los Angeles, Kansas City, and Saint Joseph, Missouri.[2]

The immediate political implications of these statistics are two. First, the black, Hispanic, and other urban minorities who today dominate many central cities found that the basic political institutions in these cities had been established long before their arrival. Most of the leadership positions in these institutions were already occupied by people not eager to relinquish them. And probably nowhere was the racial conflict over those positions sharper than in the city of Chicago, where most of the 1980s were consumed by bitter contests between leaders of the South Side and West Side black communities and the white-ethnic-dominated Northwest Side. Second, because the European ethnics historically dominated many northeastern cities, these ethnics and their institutions had a disproportionate voice in setting the tone and style that still prevail in the politics of these places. For these reasons, the political institutions developed by these European ethnic minorities are important to the study of contemporary urban politics.

The Politics of Developing Indigenous Power Bases

The Irish

The Irish were the first European ethnic group to migrate in massive numbers directly into the American city. Although some Irish were involved in urban politics as early as the 1820s, their influence remained limited until the great wave of Irish immigrants began to inundate the northeastern cities. Following the potato famine of the 1840s, Irish immigration reached a flood tide. Half a million Irish reportedly starved to death during the famine, and out of a total population of no more than 8 million, over a million people migrated to the United States in the seven years between 1847 and 1854. In the 20 years prior to 1861, more than 1.7 million Irish migrated to the United States. Although these numbers are small in comparison to present-day populations, they represented almost 10 percent of the total American population of 1840. And since the immigrants were concentrated primarily in a few dozen cities on the East Coast and in the Midwest, their localized impact was very great. As early as 1850, 26 percent of New York City's population had been born in Ireland.[3]

As their numbers increased, the Irish were increasingly considered a threat by certain segments of the dominant society that did not appreciate their strange accent, their suspect religion, their high crime rates, and their lack of preparedness for anything but the lowest forms of manual labor. A nativist movement arose to protect the integrity of American society from the supposed debilitating consequences of allowing the immigrants access to that society.[4] The Irish, like most later immigrants, found themselves in an alien and hostile environment. Periodically their churches and convents were burned and sacked by angry mobs. And an anti-Catholic book by Maria Monk, *Awful Disclosures*, was so well received in a populace apparently willing to believe the worst about the Irish and the Catholics that it went through twenty editions and sold 300,000 copies.

Politically, this nativist movement found expression in the Know Nothing party that was organized in the early 1850s. The Know Nothings hoped to restrict Irish immigration and to prevent the Irish from holding office. They enjoyed their greatest success in Massachusetts, where they won the governorship, all state offices, and huge majorities in both houses of the legislature. But they let their vigilance in weeding "popery" out of the government turn to excess. One Know Nothing legislative committee was organized to investigate convents. On a visit to inspect a particular convent, some committee members charged to the state not only their liquor bills but also the "expenses incurred in their off-duty relations with a lady 'answering to the name of Mrs. Patterson.'"[5] The revelation of these activities plus the fact that the legislature voted itself a pay increase did not endear the Know Nothings to the electorate. And when the national Know Nothing party, under the dominance of Southerners, endorsed both a proslavery platform and a proslavery candidate for the presidency in 1856, the party lost its support among the northern electorate, which was becoming increasingly abolitionist.[6] This demise of the Know Nothings as a formal political party marked the end of the last serious threat to place legislative restrictions on Irish immigration or the activities of the Catholic church.

It is difficult to compare the relative hardships that different ethnic and racial groups faced. The Irish never suffered the direct oppression of slavery or segregation that the blacks endured. They never encountered discriminatory immigration or antimiscegenation laws as the Chinese did. And they never faced the lynchings that both blacks and Italians endured.[7] But historical accounts of living conditions in Irish ghettos clearly indicate that life was brutish, oppressive, and surrounded by open hostility.

The Irish reacted to the hostilities they faced much in the way militant blacks began to react to whites during the 1960s. They took the most disparaged of their characteristics and began to stress that these were virtues rather than vices. First among these characteristics was their religion, Roman Catholicism—not only a minority religion, but a disliked and untrusted religion.

Religion as Community Development

Largely because of this distrust, Catholicism made several important contributions to the development of the social structure of the Irish community. Its first contribution was to give the Irish a symbol for psychological identification and community unification. Just as blacks a century later were to derive considerable psychological satisfaction from accentuating the very characteristics that had been most scorned by the rest of society (skin color and type of hair),* Catholicism gave the Irish their own set of distinguishing characteristics that bound them together. The liturgy, ritual, and practice of the Catholic faith distinctly marked them as different. In particular, Irish Catholics were clearly distinguished from Protestants and virtually everybody else by several practices and beliefs—confession, Sunday Mass, meatless Friday, Lenten observance, the belief that the Catholic church is the only means of salvation, ashes on the forehead when Lent began and Easter palms for decoration when it ended, religious relics carefully placed on the walls of Irish homes, and the lack of a fundamentalist puritanism about liquor and gambling.

These ritualistic observances gave the Irish the symbols of identity that were to become very useful to aspiring civic leaders in the American cities. Once a group of people begins to think of itself as different and unique, the sense of uniqueness can be exploited for purposes of political mobilization. Ethnic solidarity thus gave the professional politicians an effective way of building electoral coalitions that could cut across class lines.[8]

Whatever spiritual or religious salvation the church brought to the Irish, this symbolic identification cannot be overestimated, for it enabled Catholicism to make a second great contribution to the Irish. Very early in the period of Irish immigration, the Catholic hierarchy decided that the preservation of the Catholic faith in this Protestant land demanded the creation of parish churches and parish schools. This decision was later followed by admonitions to Catholic parents that they were bound under pain of sin to send their children to the parochial schools.[9]

These decisions had two significant results. First, by developing parishes, the Irish were bound together in *geographic* units. Catholic churchgoers not only attended church in their neighborhood; they lived there, educated their children there, and often worked there. This would prove to be an enormous advantage in electoral politics, which were also organized on the geographic units of wards and precincts.

A second result of parish development was the stimulation of considerable construction activity that channeled business opportunities to Irish contractors and job opportunities to Irish laborers. Not only were churches and schools built, but so were rectories, convents, parish halls, cathedrals, chanceries, high schools, bishops' residences, homes for retired religious persons, and seminaries. Church historian John Tracy Ellis stated that the church's energies and attentions during this period were almost entirely absorbed "by the laborious task of building churches and establishing a school system such as no other Catholic, national community had ever attempted."[10] From 1850 to 1950 the number of Catholic churches in Illinois, for example, increased fifteenfold, from 59 to 977.[11] Similar increases

---

*Malcolm X commented that blacks degraded themselves when they attempted to straighten their hair. And he stressed that they must learn not only to accept but also be proud of their natural hair and their blackness [*The Autobiography of Malcolm X* (New York: Grove Press, 1966), pp. 54–56].

THE AMERICAN RIVER GANGES.
THE PRIESTS AND THE CHILDREN.—[See Page 515.]

Source: J. Chal Vinson, *Thomas Nast: Political Cartoonist* (Athens, Ga.: University of Georgia Press, 1967), plate 48.

The anti-Catholicism that plagued the Irish In the United States during much of the nineteenth century is illustrated in this cartoon by the great political cartoonist, Thomas Nast. Note the bishops portrayed as alligators attacking the public schools, the Bible, and the defenseless women and children, while Boss Tweed leans on his elbows and smiles at the assault. Tweed was not a Catholic, but many Tammany leaders were. Tammany Hall is placed side by side with "the political Roman Catholic schools"; furthermore, its center dome is capped with a cross, whereas the two smaller domes are capped by flags of the Catholic church and the Irish. (The significance of Tammany and the political bosses will be discussed later in this chapter.)

occurred in other areas with growing Irish populations. Just before the Civil War, one Catholic weekly noted "that hardly a week passed without the laying of a cornerstone or the dedication of a new church."[12]

All of this construction activity generated a significant number of jobs and construction contracts. Quite naturally, the Irish Catholic bishops and pastors awarded these construction contracts to Irish businessmen or at least to businessmen who were willing to hire Irish laborers. The early decision to create parochial schools was a built-in guarantee that some Irish could build successful businesses in the construction trades, trucking, real estate, insurance, and related business enterprises.

The success of these early entrepreneurs was highly dependent on the very limited base of the Irish community, and their hopes for continued success made it imperative for them to reinvest a portion of their profits into religious and social institutions of the Irish community. Operating almost exclusively at the community level as small contractors, tradespeople, grocery or saloon owners, retailers, lawyers, and physicians, they depended for their continued success on adherence to what one commentator called two unwritten rules for the rising businessman or professional. "One was to live in the neighborhood. . . . The other requirement was a willingness to help the worst off in time of need. . . . No one who hoped to prosper or be well regarded in the community turned them down."[13] The very purposes behind the formation of the Knights of Columbus was in fact to institutionalize this kind of charity.

As a consequence of these unwritten rules and the ingrown nature of Irish Catholic social life, the Irish communities soon blossomed with insurance organizations, fraternal and service organizations, Catholic hospitals, high schools, Knights of Columbus centers, colleges, and even universities. An institutional framework was established to advance young men in society, to provide help for the less fortunate, and at the same time to bind the community together.

A third feature of Catholicism that contributed to Irish community development was the church's interpretation of the Third Commandment, to "keep holy the Sabbath." Whereas some orthodox Protestants interpreted this commandment as an instruction to keep stores closed on Sundays and prohibit drinking, card playing, gambling, and other pleasures, the Irish Catholics simply interpreted it to mean that they had to attend Mass each Sunday. To be sure, Catholics were supposed to abstain from any unnecessary manual labor on Sunday, but all that was really necessary to fulfill the Sunday obligation was to show up at Mass, the focal point of Catholic liturgy. And, of course, once they got to church, they were reminded that in addition to keeping the Lord's Third Commandment, canon law demanded that they contribute to the support of the church. Both of these commandments were binding under threat of eternal damnation. The net result was to turn the parish into an agency for mobilizing substantial financial and physical resources, many of which were reinvested into the development of the community, often into valuable real estate holdings.*

The key figure for guiding this development was the parish pastor. With the power to forgive sin as well as to mobilize resources, his sacral and worldly functions gave him an aura and power that kept the Roman Catholic community cohesive and unified. On occasions, the Catholic's awe of the clergy was bizarre. Archbishop Ireland of Saint Paul, for example, was reported to placate his passionate hatred of liquor by making house-to-house tours of the Irish slums and sending "whiskey bottles flying out the doorways."[14] This intrusion into the private home was a remarkable demonstration of the lengths to which the Catholic clergy could go without provoking rebellion among their Irish faithful.

Because of both the nature of its ethical rules and its extensive construction activities, the immigrant church in America came to be a significant agency for

---

*Nathan Glazer and Daniel Patrick Moynihan contend that this financial sacrifice to the church has prevented the formation of an Irish upper class in the United States. See their *Beyond the Melting Pot: The Negroes, Puerto Ricans, Jews, Italians, and Irish of New York* (Cambridge, Mass.: M.I.T. Press, 1963), p.230.

building institutions that provided social mobility for the Irish. Through the parochial school and the Sunday collection plate, the parish and the diocese efficiently mobilized both human and financial resources to build the business, educational, and religious institutions through which individual Irish could live what they considered to be productive and dignified lives.

The church not only provided jobs and business opportunities; for a long time it also constituted the focal point of institutionalized Irish social life.[15] Indeed, during the early years of immigration the only locale that seriously competed with the parish as an Irish gathering place was the saloon, which served as an informal communications network in the Irish social structure.[16] Because of the saloon's social importance, the saloon proprietors were very important personages in the Irish communities, and they often assumed positions of lay leadership in the parish organizations and societies.[17] The importance of the saloon is illustrated in the rise of the Kennedy family in Boston. Some of the early successes of Joseph P. Kennedy were traceable directly to the political and economic advantages that accrued to his father as a respected ward politician and saloon keeper.[18] During the early years, except for the saloon (and even *it* dwindled in importance as the Irish grew more affluent), the parish dominated the social organization of the Irish ghetto. Some bishops went so far as to discourage any Irish social contacts outside the confines of the church.

Politics as a Business Venture

These social institutions built through the church dovetailed neatly with urban political developments in the late nineteenth century. Already bound together symbolically, geographically, and economically by the church, the Irish developed into a cohesive voting bloc that eventually gained great influence over the Democratic party in city after city.

In the days of the long ballot, the spoils system, patronage, and other innovations of Jacksonian Democracy, control over the Democratic party and the elected city offices soon developed into the well-known phenomenon of machine politics. (Machine politics as such will be discussed later in the chapter. For now, the discussion concentrates on their implications for the Irish community.) For the Irish, the period of dominance in machine politics enabled them to secure two advantages that they have only recently given up. First, they were able to get patronage jobs in the bureaucracy. For example, the Irish in New Haven were disproportionately employed as public servants.[19] In Boston, the city government's employment practices were so heavily weighted against Italians that one Sicilian got hired only after he changed his name to Foley.[20] The pervasiveness of this patronage can be seen in the stereotype of the Irish police officer, which still contains a great deal of truth. As late as 1950 a majority of the members of New York City's police were Irish. Almost two-thirds of all the police commissioners Chicago has had since the Civil War have been Irish. And as late as 1964, forty-one of that city's seventy-two highest police department positions were staffed by Irish.[21]

A second advantage that control of the government conferred upon the Irish was that it greatly multiplied the success the church had given them in construction, real estate, and related businesses.[22] No longer was it simply churches and parish halls whose construction provided employment for Irish laborers and contracts for Irish businessmen. Now it was the physical growth of the entire city. There were contracts and jobs for schools, hospitals, precinct stations, and power lines. By controlling the city government, Irish political leaders could make sure that a disproportionate share of the jobs and business contracts went to their fellow Irish political supporters. Although few Irish city bosses got wealthy, more than one retired a millionaire.* Today, Irish ethnic political contacts no longer count for much in the way of social mobility.† But until the Great Depression of the 1930s, the relationships between city growth and business contracts provided enormously productive channels for social mobility in the Irish community. In a sense, the control over the Democratic party enabled politicians to reverse the truism of American politics that political power results from great wealth. In the case of some of the Irish, it was the political power that enabled the wealth to be acquired, rather than vice versa.‡

Although politics constituted an important channel for Irish social mobility, it should be noted that there were limits as to what could be accomplished through this channel. Steven P. Erie studied Irish ethnic politics in San Francisco and several other cities only to find that patronage work could employ but a limited number of Irish laborers, probably six percent at most. Despite the fact that as much as a third of the public workforce in big cities was Irish in 1900, over 90 percent of Irish laborers worked in the private sector. Furthermore, expansion of public jobs for Irish laborers was often limited by machine politicians who followed conservative fiscal policies. Citing these facts, Erie argues that the political channels for Irish advancement have been overstated.[23]

Although Erie correctly points out the limits of politics as a channel of social mobility, it must also be remembered that even the limited number of available patronage jobs was very important indeed to an immigrant population that was largely impoverished. For some Irish families the government connection was in fact a source of steady income that helped them get training and marketable skills for their children. By 1900, Tammany Hall controlled some 60,000 jobs in New

*Richard Croker of New York's Tammany Hall amassed a fortune of $3 million, and Hoboken's Bernard McFeeley amassed at least $1 million. However, Harold Zink's study of political bosses suggests that the millionaires were very few [*City Bosses in the United States* (Durham, N.C.: Duke University Press, 1930)]. Richard J. Daley of Chicago carefully nurtured the image that he was a man of modest means. But a report in 1974 estimated his worth to be at least $200,000—not a fortune by any means, but certainly a comfortable nest egg, considering the value of the dollar at the time [*Minneapolis Tribune*, July 12, 1974, p. 4-A].

†In his 1971 book on former Mayor Richard J. Daley, Chicago columnist Mike Royko catalogued an impressive array of contracts that enriched Democratic supporters with Irish names such as Gill, Cullerton, Horan, and Dunne [*Boss: Richard J. Daley of Chicago* (New York: Signet Books, 1971), p. 71]. It is important to stress, however, that these men belonged to the oldest generation of Irish politicians in Chicago, and few of them are around any longer.

‡This argument applies, obviously, not only to the Irish but to any politician who uses political influence as a vehicle for social mobility. See Raymond E. Wolfinger, *The Politics of Progress* (Englewood Cliffs, N.J.: Prentice-Hall, 1974), pp. 80–81.

York City. And, as Erie points out, the machines' fiscal conservatism in the nineteenth century was largely due to state controls over the cities. After 1900, many of the Irish machines broke loose from these controls in many cities and followed more expansionary fiscal policies for welfare, health, and education to meet demands that were coming from the Irish voters themselves.[24] Furthermore, the machine itself was only one of several channels for gaining political influence and social mobility. The channels created by the Irish were based on the hierarchically organized church, the Democratic party, control over the city's elective offices, and the use of that control to provide jobs and business opportunities. All of these elements were mutually reinforcing, and most importantly they provided an indigenous base of Irish political power. The Irish were symbolically bound together by a strong sense of ethnic and religious identification that in city after city gave rise to the founding of chauvinistic fraternal and social groups such as the Sons of Erin, the Society of the Friendly Sons of Saint Patrick, or the Ancient Order of Hibernians. At its most extreme, Irish nationalism led to the Molly Maguires and the Fenian movement invasion of Canada.

Irish ascendancy in the urban political process probably reached its peak at the turn of the century,* by which time the reformers' assault on machine politics and the competition of other ethnic groups threatened the Irish hegemony in the city. But by the time that occurred, the Irish were already well entrenched. Even where other semblances of ethnicity have died among them, the Irish are still disproportionately concentrated in the bureaucracies of many city governments and in the organizations of the Catholic church. For the Irish, these institutions formed the core of what sociologist Andrew Greeley calls an ethnic network of social mobility. But, as Greeley also recognizes, the ethnic network forms a trap as well, because the person who relies on that network as a channel of mobility often becomes entrapped in it and has difficulty gaining recognition outside of it.[25] If indeed the Irish have truly made it in America, the measure of their success is probably not so much their continued dominance of the ethnic networks as their ability to move out of them. The third and fourth generations of Irish have burgeoning numbers of college graduates, lawyers, businesspeople, and professionals who are making their own way in the world on their individual merits with very little reliance on the ethnic networks. In fact, as Steven Erie documents, the Irish have had more success at upward social mobility in cities that did not have machines than they have had in the machine-dominated cities. Secure possession of low-status, public-sector, blue-collar jobs may have inhibited rather than encouraged the Irish before the 1930s from moving more into higher-status careers in business or the professions.[26]

---

*Others might put the date at 1928 (when an Irish Catholic, Al Smith, was a presidential candidate) or even at 1960 (when an Irish Catholic, John F. Kennedy, won the presidency). But actually Irish control of the urban political parties began to suffer inroads from other ethnics as early as 1900. In Providence, the percentage of Irish ward committeemen in the Democratic party increased from the 1870s until it reached its peak of 73 percent in 1900. After that date it slowly but steadily declined [Elmer E. Cornwell, Jr., "Party Absorption of Ethnic Groups: The Case of Providence, Rhode Island," *Social Forces* (March 1960): 205-211].

Finally, a normative judgment is often levied against this Irish ethnic network of social mobility on two counts. First, as Daniel Patrick Moynihan and others have charged, the Irish network was extremely deficient in making intellectual contributions to American life.[27] Second, in the Irish-dominated machine's dedication to political pragmatism, it was entirely devoid of any ideological content. It was unsympathetic to becoming a class-based Labor party (as was common in Europe).[28] Historically there has been considerable merit to those charges. In some respects, however, they may be less true in the 1980s and 1990s than they were previously. Moynihan himself is evidence of Irish who are making intellectual contributions. Concerning the ideological leanings of the Irish, survey data today on racial attitudes (as shown in Table 3-2 on page 74) find most Irish to be fairly liberal. But like most other white Americans, the Irish have opposed desegregation remedies such as busing when it affected their neighborhoods and their own children.

The Italians

Italian ethnic networks of political influence and social mobility were similar to those of the Irish in some general respects. But they were very different in terms of the politically important institutions that the Italians created. Like the Irish, most Italian immigrants were unskilled laborers, and very few of them had experience as merchants or skilled tradespeople.* The greatest bulk of Italian immigrants after 1880 came from impoverished southern Italy. They settled mostly in northeastern and midwestern cities, where their initial economic function was to compete with the Irish for jobs in the general unskilled labor force.[29] Italians who migrated to California were mostly northern Italians, who were a little less destitute than—and did not get along well with—the southern Italians.[30] They also had immigrated much earlier and were much less alienated from the surrounding society.

The southern Italian immigrants tended to settle in eastern and midwestern big-city neighborhoods called "Little Italies." Normally there were several Little Italies in a big city; Chicago had seventeen.[31] Usually people from other ethnic backgrounds also lived in the Italian neighborhoods. People from the same district in Italy would settle in the same building or on the same block. Thus the buildings and sometimes the blocks were homogeneous, whereas the neighborhoods themselves were usually heterogeneous.[32]

Competition with the Irish

Although the Italians started with an occupational base and a settlement pattern similar to those of the Irish, they created an entirely different network of social mobility. No doubt much of the difference was due to the fact that the Italians

---

*One source estimates that three-fourths of the Italian immigrants were general laborers, one-seventh were skilled tradespeople, 6 percent were farmers, and about 5 percent were merchants and dealers [Rudolf Glanz, *Jews and Italians: Historic Group Relations and the New Immigration 1881–1924* (New York: Shulsinger Brothers, 1970), pp. 31–33].

arrived later, when the channels of social advancement that earlier had been open to the Irish—that is, the church and the Democratic party—were closed.

In the American Catholic church, Italians have only recently been able to penetrate the top leadership. There have been few Italian bishops. Almost 60 percent of all American bishops since 1785 have been Irish or of Irish descent,[33] and most of the rest have been German. These ethnic differences estranged many Italians both from the Irish clergy and from the institutional church, which was much more puritanical than the churches they had known in Italy.* Consequently, they demanded parishes with Italian priests and Italian-language services. The first Italian church in Chicago was built in 1881. By 1920 there were more than a dozen. The Italians were also skeptical of the parish school and preferred to send their children to the public schools.[34]† This estrangement of the Italians from the Irish-dominated church institutions was termed the *Italian problem* by some of the clergy, and the American archbishops responded by encouraging more American seminarians to study in Italy and more Italian priests to migrate to the United States.[35] Nevertheless, even today there are few Italian names among the American hierarchy. The church has not performed economic and organizational services for the Italians to the same extent that it performed them for the Irish.

Italians found the Democratic party less closed to their ambitions than the church, but it took many years for them to capitalize on its opportunities. Because the Democratic party was dominated by the Irish, politically ambitious Italians had three possible courses of action. In cities such as New Haven, where local Republicans welcomed them for the purposes of regaining control of city government, Italians tended to become Republican.[36] In cities such as Boston and Chicago, where the Republicans did not seek their support, the Italians became Democrats and fought running battles to break down Irish control over nominations and patronage in Italian neighborhoods.[37]‡ In Providence, the Italians were originally Republican, but many joined the Democrats when the Republicans failed to give them their share of the political spoils.[38] Eventually, they remained active in both parties.[39] In addition to local conditions, national political events also affected the party allegiance of Italians. Republicans gained many votes in Italian precincts during the late 1930s and early 1940s as a result of President

---

*One scholar of Italian Americans writes that "they did not feel that they could speak intimately with priests in America as they had in the old country," and consequently they tried at first to sustain their religious contacts with the village priests in Italy [Lawrence Frank Pisani, *The Italian in America: A Social Study and History* (New York: Exposition Press, 1957), p. 165]. Another scholar argues that even in Italy the peasantry was aliented from the clergy [Joseph Lopreato, *Italian Americans* (New York: Random House, 1970), pp. 88–89]. In either interpretation, early Italian immigrants had difficulty in relating to the American Catholic church.

†As the Italians grew more affluent in the post-World War II era, this changed, and Italians became strong supporters of the parochial schools [Lopreato, *Italian Americans,* pp. 89–90].

‡In Chicago, the running battle consisted of two patterns. One was a pattern of acquiescence in which the Italians let the Irish bosses dominate Italian wards as long as they got minor payoffs and jobs. The other pattern was one of overt resistance. But the Italians usually lost at this, at least until the 1920s. In one instance the cost of defeat was murder. See Humbert S. Nelli, *Italians in Chicago, 1880–1930: A Study of Ethnic Mobility* (New York: Oxford University Press, 1970), pp. 88–124.

Roosevelt's hostility to and eventual war with the Mussolini regime in Italy.[40]* But since the end of the war, the long-range trend of Italian voting has been in favor of the Democrats.[41]†

Although heavy Italian immigration began as early as the 1880s, it was not until the 1930s and 1940s that Italians began to capture many important public offices. They elected a governor in Rhode Island and a mayor in New Haven in the 1940s. Perhaps the earliest prominent Italian mayors were Angelo Rossi in San Francisco (1933–1944) and Fiorello La Guardia in New York (1933–1945). La Guardia was elected on a fusion ticket of Republicans and anti-Tammany Hall reformers. Throughout his mayoralty he greatly diminished the control of Irish-dominated Tammany Hall over the major political appointments in the city.[42] In 1949 Carmine De Sapio became the first Italian to head Tammany Hall. For the next decade he tried to balance organization Democrats and reform Democrats who were competing for control over the party.[43] Although La Guardia and De Sapio were at opposite ends of the political spectrum, they symbolize the maturation of Italian influence in New York City politics.

One reason the Italians took until the 1930s to gain political prominence involves the skill with which the deeply entrenched Irish politicians played elements of the Italian communities against each other and minimized the potential voting strength of Italians. In both New York and Chicago, the Irish political leaders gerrymandered council and legislative district lines through the Little Italies and thus divided the Italian vote into several districts.[44] In the Hull House neighborhood of Chicago, Irish ward boss Johnny Powers stayed in power until 1927, even though many years previously Irish voters had become just a small fraction of his ward. He maintained his power by giving patronage and minor political appointments to Italians who were willing to cooperate with him and intimidating those who might work against him. So secure was his position that for the last several years of his reign he did not even live in the ward. One historian writes that Italians could have ousted this absentee Irish boss many years earlier if only "the Hull House reformers and the Italian community had worked together to effect his defeat."[45]

Italians took many years to develop an indigenous power base capable of effectively challenging the Irish. When this indigenous power base finally did develop, three elements were of prime importance—the nature of the social structure of the Italian communities, Italian business, and organized crime.

Political Relevance of Italian Social Structure
One theme that pervades most of the commentary on Italian social structure is the tremendous importance of kinship and personal relations. Italians apparently

---

*Italian communities in American cities were deeply split by Mussolini's ascension to power in Italy. See John P. Diggins, *Mussolini and Fascism: The View from America* (Princeton, N.J.: Princeton University Press, 1972), chap. 6, pp. 111–143. Also see his "Italo-Americans and Anti-Fascist Opposition," *Journal of American History* 54 (December 1967): 579–598.

†Survey Research Center data for the Northeast during the 1950s found that 57 percent of Italians identified themselves as Democrats, 13 percent as Independents, and 30 percent as Republicans [cited in Wolfinger, *The Politics of Progress,* p. 39].

preferred (and still prefer) to interact with relatives and other Italians than with nonrelatives and non-Italians. As late as the 1960s, researchers found that Italians were much more prone than other European ethnics to live in ethnic neighborhoods, to visit their relatives regularly, and to visit often with others of the same ethnicity. They also were much less prone than any other European ethnics except Jews to marry outside of their ethnic group.[46] These tendencies were much stronger among the immigrant generation than they are now. A study of marriage records of an Italian church in Chicago in 1906 found that only 3 percent of the marriages were with non-Italians, and a majority of the marriages occurred between persons born in the same province in Italy.[47] Researchers also discovered other characteristics about Italian preferences, as well: Italians are less trusting than any other European ethnics except Jews and Anglo-Saxon Protestants and more authoritarian than any other ethnics except the Slavs.[48]

These data about Italian-Americans suggest an ethnic community that was bound together by a strong web of kinship and personal relationships. There was a high level of mistrust and suspicion about persons who fell outside the web (especially non-Italians), and there was a tendency toward authoritarian relationships in which roles were relatively stable, well defined, and well understood. Insiders were to be trusted insofar as they conformed to the well-defined role patterns for family members and friends. Outsiders were to be trusted only after they had established a stable personal relationship.

Several researchers have commented on the implications of these characteristics for the development of a community social structure. Historian Rudolph Vecoli suggested that in the Italian community in Chicago, trust seldom extended beyond the immediate nuclear family. "Only through the ritual kinship of *comparaggio* (godparenthood) could nonrelatives gain admittance to the family circle."[49] This emphasis on mistrust and this ethnocentricity were much stronger among immigrants from southern Italy than among newcomers from northern Italy. Edward Banfield, in researching a village in southern Italy, found the lack of trust between families to be so pervasive that the community was virtually immobilized and incapable of any cooperative action for community projects such as getting a hospital or improving schools.[50] William Foote Whyte studied an Italian slum in Boston in the 1930s and found that Italians participated in the political process principally through the device of establishing personal relationships based on mutual and reciprocal obligations. Before engaging in a campaign, younger men would often wait for cues from the dominant family members in order to avoid supporting a candidate who was disfavored by the family.[51]

This dual importance of the family in politics and of close personal relationships is most likely an outgrowth of the conditions under which Italians immigrated to and settled in the American cities. These conditions did little to make the Italians trust outsiders, and they virtually demanded that the immigrants learn cooperation in order to avoid perpetual exploitation.

The first exploiter the isolated immigrant was likely to encounter was the *padrone*. Immigrants were required to have the means to support themselves before they could enter the country. If there were no family members to meet an immigrant at the port of entry and vouch for him, labor contractors called *padro-*

nes would meet him, find him lodging, and offer him employment. For these services the padrone received a share of the immigrant's wages, and he dominated an exploitative relationship with his workers that not only included their work but often extended to other aspects of their life. The padrone system lasted from the 1880s until about 1920.[52]

About the same time, a violent form of extortion known as the Black Hand appeared. Black Handers sent notes demanding payment of money under the threat of murder or bodily harm if the money was not paid. Until strong Italian community organizations were created, there was no one to whom the isolated Italians could turn for help when threatened. The police were very ineffective against Black Handers. Black Hand activities flourished until about World War I, when they began to diminish for a variety of reasons.[53]

Not only did the immigrants face exploitation from within the Italian community; they faced open hostility from without. In the 1890s eleven Italian prisoners in New Orleans were lynched after a jury had *not* found them guilty of murdering the city's police chief. Italian residents of an Illinois town were driven out of their homes and beaten, and their houses burned, in a fit of mob hysteria. And in one of the most famous trials of the 1920s, two Boston Italians (Nicola Sacco and Bartolomeo Vanzetti) were condemned to death in a trial that included a judge who apparently was prejudiced against Italians and a jury that included no Italians and that based its decision on evidence that appeared very circumstantial.[54] Even aside from the violence, Italian immigrants commonly were cheated by non-Italian merchants or lost their savings when bankers went bankrupt.

Political Ramifications of an Ethnic Business Class

Facing these circumstances, Italians perhaps naturally turned to relatives, friends, and fellow Italians when they sought to establish business enterprises. The earliest businesses were small newspapers and retail operations that catered to the particular needs and tastes of Italian communities. Every city with a sizable Italian population soon had its Italian newspaper and was soon dotted with numerous small, autonomous family restaurants. Fruit peddlers, peanut sellers, and pushcart vendors soon plied their trade on the major commercial streets. Non-Italians increasingly dined at Italian restaurants and purchased goods from Italian merchants. These Italian businesspeople began to perform for the Italian community a capital mobilization function similar to that which the parish performed for the Irish.

Italian entrepreneurs and workers had an enormous capacity to save. At the turn of the century, when the laborer's average wage was less than $2.00 per day, the Bureau of Labor estimated that 95 percent of Italian laborers saved from $25 to $30 of their wages each month. Among Italian immigrant families in New York, 35 percent took in roomers, even though the typical tenement apartment contained only three or four rooms.[55] Many of the tenants were young men who had traveled ahead without their families. And much of the saving, of course, was by these same men, who wished to finance an eventual return to Italy or to bring their families to the New World.

Whatever the reason for this high level of saving, the net result was that the Italians aggregated capital to invest in their own community enterprises. Typically, these enterprises were restaurants, taverns, construction, trucking, the marketing of produce, roofing, and rock masonry.[56] Produce and fruit marketing in particular were lucrative for the Italians. By the turn of the century they reportedly controlled the fruit trade in Manhattan, and in Boston about a fourth of the Italian population was engaged in the fruit business.[57] Directing funerals, publishing newspapers, and developing real estate were other avenues of Italian business success.

In a community organized around strong family loyalties and personal relationships, it was perhaps inevitable that accumulated savings were deposited with Italian bankers rather than in non-Italian financial institutions. The Italian banker became an intermediary between the immigrant and the institutions of the outside world. He was a familiar figure in the Italian community, not, in the words of one historian, "an anonymous teller behind a cold steel wicket."[58]

The most successful of the Italian bankers was A. P. Giannini, who founded the Bank of America. He started his banking operations by making credit available to immigrant fishermen, fruit peddlers, small ranchers, and working people who lacked the collateral or the credit standing to get loans from the already established banks. As his banking operations stabilized and he built up trust among the immigrants, he also attracted their savings deposits. Many of these people would not put their money in a non-Italian bank.

Not only did Giannini build a huge fortune; he also kept his bank relevant to the Italian communities that he served. According to historian Andrew Rolle, Giannini "saw to it that immigrant branch managers, cashiers, lesser as well as major personnel, were Italians."[59] Giannini was not alone in his preference for Italian workers. Many of the famous California vineyards, such as Gallo and Colony, were begun by Italian families and employed primarily Italian workers.[60]

As the Italian business, professional, and middle classes developed, they maintained their preference for conducting their affairs with Italians rather than non-Italians. They developed strong ethnic networks: "The Italian doctor sees an Italian lawyer when he wants legal advice, both of them have their expensive suburban house built by an Italian contractor, and all of them vote for an Italian political leader to represent the interests of their community at city hall or the state house."[61]

Politically, the business and professional people used their new wealth to advance Italian candidates and Italian causes. Bank of America's Giannini apparently did not hesitate to use his prestige and wealth to further certain political causes.[62] And Samuel Lubell describes how the growth of Italian political influence in Providence was related directly to the increasing number of Italian lawyers who passed the bar examinations during the 1920s and 1930s. The rise of John Pastore to the governship of Rhode Island was heavily dependent on a group of newly wealthy Italians who, although Republicans, contributed heavily to Pastore's gubernatorial campaign in 1946.[63]

The Italian business leaders not only were helpful to politicians; they also helped form many Italian community organizations. Some of the organizations, such as the Sons of Italy, promoted general ethnic solidarity. Others, such as the Italian-American Labor Council or the Italian-American Chamber of Commerce, had a narrower functional base.

Italian businesspeople thus performed at least three functions in the development of the Italian community. They mobilized capital that was reinvested to produce jobs and more businesses. They contributed financially to certain Italian politicians and Italian political causes. And they helped form civic organizations that in turn promoted solidarity and cohesion among Italians.

Organized Crime: Its Myth and Reality in Italian Community Development

Few aspects of Italian-American life are more controversial than its supposed relation to organized crime. It is now widely believed that *all* organized crime in the United States is subordinated to an exclusively Italian organization called the Mafia or La Cosa Nostra. This belief stems from two general sources—official government investigations[64] and popular exposé writings.[65] According to these reports, there is a national confederation called La Cosa Nostra. It is composed of twenty-four regional groups or families located in many big cities of the Northeast, the Great Lakes states, the South, and the Southwest. Membership in these twenty-four families totals about 5000 men who are *all* Italians.[66] Their elder statesmen, who immigrated from Sicily when Mussolini cracked down on the Mafia in the 1920s,[67] form the directing group that "ratifies or rejects agreements with other non-Italian criminal organizations."[68] Through them this "Italian organization in fact controls all but an insignificant proportion of the organized crime activities in the United States,"[69] which may involve as many as 100,000 people. The net income of this organization in the mid-1960s was estimated at $6 billion to $7 billion per year.[70] The organization has infiltrated many legitimate businesses and bought off a wide range of public officials ranging from police officers to members of Congress, and it is continually growing stronger. Its ultimate aim is to control all significant legitimate business activity in the United States and to control the United States government itself.[71]

This interpretation has come under severe criticism on several counts. Former Attorney General Ramsey Clark challenged the profit estimates of $6–$7 billion as too high.[72] Other critics question whether an organization that employs so many people could exist without a corporate headquarters, but no Mafia corporate headquarters has been identified.[73] The lack of a corporate headquarters, the vagueness of the profit estimates, and the number of people involved all make the elementary problem of even defining organized crime most difficult. One critic complained that the definition offered by the Organized Crime Task Force was so vague that it was useless.[74] And this vagueness in turn prompted another critic to assert that we are "not dealing with an empirical phenomenon at all, but with an article of faith, transcending the contingent particularity of everyday experience and logically unassailable."[75]

Most criticized has been the supposed link between Italian-American organized crime and the historic Mafia in Sicily. One of the most perceptive scholars on

Italian-American organized crime, Francis Ianni, argues that until the 1920s there was little reason for Sicilian Mafia leaders to migrate to the United States. They were *all* "men of some wealth, considerable power and prestige and hard-earned status and there was no reason for them to leave the island until Mussolini . . . began arresting and killing suspected Mafiosi in the 1920s."[76] But after the 1920s, Sicilian Mafia influence appears to have been slight. Italian criminals after that time modeled their operations "not [on] the old-country oriented Mafioso . . . but [on] the more sophisticated Irish and Jewish mobsters who had mastered the secrets of business organization."[77]

Rather than being a Sicilian import, Italian-American organized crime was probably created in the United States. This would be entirely consistent with the experiences of other ethnic groups; both Irish and Jewish slums were plagued by organized criminal gangs.[78]

Italians in recent years have expressed considerable opposition to the prevailing idea of a Mafia-dominated national crime confederation, because it creates a stereotype that is difficult for many Italians to avoid. Former San Francisco Mayor Joseph Alioto won a $350,000 libel suit because of a *Look* magazine article that linked him to the Mafia.[79] Most of the evidence was highly circumstantial, and there was no evidence that Alioto had been involved in any specific crimes that may have been committed. In many other instances, Italians have successfully convinced government agencies and private organizations to stop using the words *Mafia* and *La Cosa Nostra,* which are felt to denigrate all Italians.*

Despite the criticisms of the prevailing view of organized crime as being controlled by a commission of Mafia family leaders, there is some concrete evidence that such a leadership structure indeed exists. Much of this evidence comes from wiretap evidence and testimony presented at the criminal trials of several Mafia leaders in the 1980s. Whether accurate or not, much of this evidence described a loose but highly elaborate crime structure quite similar to that portrayed by the FBI 20 years earlier.[80]

Because of the widespread belief in a close relationship between the Italian community and the Mafia, students of urban politics should thoroughly understand both the widely held beliefs and the criticisms that have been raised against them. However, neither the beliefs nor the criticisms shed much light on the importance that organized crime had in the development of *some* Italian communities. It must be stressed that in *many* cities organized crime has had no political impact on Italian community development.[81] But in *some* cities it has.

Where organized crime played a role in Italian community development, three features stand out. First, many of the criminal leaders were bound together by the "web of kinship." In a study of marriage ties among prominent crime figures, Francis Ianni found that the interactions of Italian criminals were not modeled on

*The FBI has ceased using the terms Mafia and La Cosa Nostra. Film makers were persuaded to delete any use of these words from the movie *The Godfather.* The Attorney General's office was persuaded not to allow Joseph Valachi's written manuscript to be published. Relying instead on his extensive interviews with Valachi, Peter Maas wrote *The Valachi Papers* (New York: Putnam, 1968). Maas's dispute with the Attorney General's office is described in the preface of that book.

the highly rationalized organizational structure described by the President's Commission on Law Enforcement. Rather they were based on a kinship web. In one New York-based Italo-American syndicate, *all* of the fifteen leaders had marriage or blood relationship ties. In a major midwestern city, the leaders of *all* the syndicate families were related through marriage. They also had marriage ties with criminal leaders in Buffalo, New York, and New Orleans. Ianni also examined the kinship ties of the identified participants at the famous Appalachian meeting of organized crime figures in 1957. Nearly "half were related by blood or marriage, and even more if godparenthood is included as a kin relationship."[82]

However, not all children of Italian crime figures married exclusively within the crime families. As some of them married out of crime families, the web was in some respects expanded to include the in-laws. In addition, personal friendship ties extended beyond the crime family to include people with whom crime figures had grown up or people they had dealt with in many Italian clubs or organizations. As these people began to achieve adulthood and middle-class status in the 1930s and 1940s, it was entirely consistent with the social structure of the Italian community that they would maintain ties.

> Now, the new judges, the new lawyers and prosecutors, councilmen and even police had grown up in the Little Italies along with the new leadership in organized crime. They had lived together as children and strong bonds had been established; still they kept the associations through friendship and marriage.
>
> Alliances of power, friendships and kin relationship all merged and today this presents a difficult if not impossible job of sorting out those which are corrupt or corrupting from those which merely express the strength of kinship relations among Southern Italians and their descendents.[83]

A second aspect of Italian organized crime is that it helped to finance some Italian businesses and some community organizations. Since much, if not most, of the revenue generated by the organized gangs came from non-Italians who used the services of gang-controlled numbers games, alcohol, narcotics, and prostitutes, great sums of capital were brought into Italian hands. By mid-twentieth century, much of this money was being invested in legitimate enterprises, especially hotels, nightclubs, vending machines, real estate, and even stock markets. William F. Whyte observed that the racketeers provided investment capital to some Italians in Boston to start their own business.[84] Huey Long in Louisiana invited Frank Costello to set up slot machines in New Orleans, and Costello remitted some of the profits from this enterprise back to Manhattan for investment there.[85] How extensive this legitimate investment is and how important it was for the development of Italian business is impossible to determine. But it cannot be ignored. Nor can it be assumed that such investments were always made for nefarious purposes.* What-

---

*Former Attorney General Ramsey Clark argues that many legitimate investments by crime figures are not made for the purpose of control [Ramsey Clark, *Crimes in America* (New York: Simon & Schuster, 1970), p. 73]. Others also note significant legitimate investment by organized crime figures but look on it much more suspiciously than Clark. See, for example, Richard D. Knudten, *Crime in a Complex Society* (Homewood, Ill.: Dorsey Press, 1970), p. 193.

ever their purposes, to the extent that investments were made within the Italian community, they helped provide jobs for Italian workers and they helped business-people get established.

A third way in which the Italian experience with organized crime affected Ital-ian community development was through its use of political influence. Several cities present good examples.

When New York's reform mayor Fiorello La Guardia sought to deny the Demo-cratic organization of Tammany Hall as much patronage as he could, the organiza-tion became desperate. With its traditional sources of funds (i.e., kickbacks from the patronage job holders) drying up because of La Guardia's opposition, the Tam-many organization needed a new source of money. And one source was organized crime. Daniel Bell describes how Frank Costello and Joe Adonis gradually used their newly found wealth to get Italians appointed to judgeships and elected to other offices in New York City.[86] In Boston, as William F. Whyte describes, a pro-cess of "reciprocal obligations" was established, through which a loosely knit, interlocking organization worked through both political parties by paying off the appropriate political bureaucratic leaders. The racketeers were virtually given a free hand in their business enterprises, and they were able to obtain favors for their constituents. In Chicago, a direct relationship was formed between Italian acquisi-tion of political influence and the emergence of strong crime leaders. Humbert Nelli writes, "Italians did not move up the political ladder of success in Chicago—to appointive and elective office, patronage jobs, and exemptions from the law—until the 1920s. Then, under the leadership and guidance of Johnny Torrio and Al Capone, Southerners found politics and its handmaiden, crime, to offer an increasingly important source of money as well as a means of social mobility."[87]

In Kansas City an aggressive Italian named Johnny Lazia became both a ward boss and a criminal boss. After serving a year in jail in 1917, Lazia organized a series of real estate, gambling, and bootlegging enterprises. He used his wealth to lend money to friends, to keep youngsters out of jail, to support local charities, and to help out many down-and-out Italians. Through these means Lazia built a strong following in Kansas City's North Side Italian community. In the 1928 elections, he challenged the existing Irish ward boss for political control of the Italian neighbor-hoods. Lazia conveyed the seriousness of his intentions by abducting several of his adversary's political aides. As he gained control over the North Side Democratic organization, Lazia entered an alliance with the citywide machine boss, Thomas J. Pendergast. With his political power thus consolidated, Lazia was able to influence appointments to the Kansas City Police Department, obtain gambling and liquor concessions, and get police tolerance for his organized vice operations.[88]

Whatever role organized crime might have played historically in the rise of Ital-ians to power, and however much Italians might have dominated organized crime during the 1940s and 1950s, they seem to be losing that dominance today. There is a pattern of ethnic succession in organized crime[89] just as we saw that there was a pattern of ethnic succession in control of the urban political parties and in housing patterns in city neighborhoods. Just as Italian dominance of organized crime suc-ceeded Irish and Jewish dominance of organized crime, the Italians themselves began ceding dominance to different Hispanic and Asian groups in the 1980s. As early as the 1970s black and Puerto Rican gangs successfully began to challenge Italian crime families for control over the numbers racket and narcotics distribution.[90] By the mid-1980s Colombians and Cubans had come to rival Italian crime groups as the dominant intermediaries in the importation of illegal narcotics, especially cocaine.[91]

This loss of Mafia hegemony over organized crime in the 1980s was a consequence of three setbacks the Mafia suffered in those years. Two of these setbacks were the inevitable consequences of the upward social mobility of those Italians who came from families involved in organized crime. First, as increasing numbers of the younger generations of Italians went to college they found that they had opportunities for upward social mobility in the professions and the corporate world that had been denied their parents and grandparents. So the recruitment base for future leadership was narrowing, causing the leadership ranks to become quite aged by the 1980s and leading to generational conflicts.[92] In contrast to earlier crime leaders such as Al Capone who had reached the top while still in his thirties, when the federal government succeeded in getting convictions of eight alleged top Mafia leaders in 1986, only one of them was under age 45 and their average age was 60.[93] The second setback can be attributed to ethnic succession in housing. A simple stroll through Lower Manhattan makes it obvious that Little Italy is being invaded by Chinatown. As one ethnic group vacates the slums and is replaced there by another, the first group loses its recruitment base and becomes estranged from the new customers in the slums. If there is a market for numbers, narcotics, and other illegal services in the slums today, the Italians are probably not as able to service that market as are elements of the blacks, Hispanics, and Asians who have been moving into the slum areas. The third setback to the Mafia has come at the hands of federal prosecutors who succeeded in winning several key convictions in the 1980s[94] and who began turning their attention to labor racketeering, probably the most important remaining stronghold of Mafia influence today.

Italian Power Base: Summary

What, then, is one to conclude about the emergence of ethnic-based political power among the Italians? Four conclusions seem apparent. First, by themselves the political parties and the Catholic parishes that had worked well for the Irish were of extremely limited utility to the Italians who sought political power. Second, Italian ethnic-based political power did not materialize until a distinctive social organization, built in great measure on a basis of kinship and personal loyalties, began to emerge in Italian communities. Third, Italian ethnic-based political power was dependent on large numbers of immigrants who vitally needed this kind of personalized social structure in order to survive in the very impersonalized and remote big city.

Last, the rise of Italian politicians was related directly to the rise of an Italian middle class that had developed the skills and the financial resources needed to sustain political campaigning. This middle class had a diverse economic base in business, the professions, and in some instances organized crime. As noted earlier,

John Pastore's rise was helped immeasurably by sizable financial contributions from a group of newly wealthy Republican Italians during Democrat Pastore's gubernatorial campaign in 1946. Raymond Wolfinger takes the middle-class argument one step further and argues that in New Haven it was not until the Italians developed a middle class that they were able to elect a mayor and get their share of the patronage.[95] When all three of these developments (the kinship-based social structure, the large number of immigrants, the middle class to provide leadership) matured, as they did in many cities in the 1930s and 1940s, an indigenous base of political power was created.

The Socioeconomic Base of Jewish Political Influence

The political influence of the Irish and the Italians in the United States developed through what can be called traditional channels of urban politics. The urban experience of Jews in this country has been very different and probably much more successful. The differences emerge in four major respects.

First, whereas Irish and Italian involvement in urban politics has been marked by pragmatism rather than ideology, the Jewish involvement has had a strong ideological component, marked principally by liberalism, socialism, and antimachine reformism.* There have been a few Jewish bosses, but not very many. In opinion surveys Jews consistently outscore other whites on indexes of liberalism and racial tolerance.[96]

Second, whereas the Irish and Italians have been strong Democrats, the Jews have had a much more varied partisan background. Until the 1920s Jews were mostly Republican. This stemmed in part from what Lawrence Fuchs called "enormous gratitude toward the Republic which granted them refuge," in part from dislike of the Irish-controlled Democratic machines,[97] and in part from the Republican party's abolitionist and Reconstruction origins. Jewish influence was also strongly felt in the organization of socialist movements in the early twentieth century. Much of this support was dissipated by the administration of Franklin Roosevelt, who not only supported many economic measures proposed by the socialists but also appointed many liberal Jews to high national office.[98] In return, Jewish loyalties were predominantly Democratic through the 1960s.

On the local level, since 1932 Jewish political influence has been the greatest in the Northeast, where Jews are the most heavily concentrated (see Table 3-1). Particularly in New York, Jews have fluctuated between reformism within the Democratic party and support for reform candidates put forward by the Republican and Liberal parties. Reform mayors Fiorello La Guardia and John Lindsay received some of their strongest support in Jewish precincts.[99]

Third, the economic base of the Jewish middle class differed significantly from that of the Irish and Italian communities. In comparison to the Irish and Italian male immigrants, who were mostly unskilled laborers, only 14 percent of Jewish

---

*Lawrence Fuchs comments that the early twentieth-century socialists won more votes with their denunciations of local corruption than they did with their socialist programs [*The Political Behavior of American Jews* (Glencoe, Ill.: The Free Press, 1956), p. 124].

immigrants from 1899 to 1910 were unskilled laborers; two-thirds of the immigrants were skilled laborers, many of them tailors. In addition, Jewish immigrants included a higher proportion of persons who had experience as merchants.[100] One of the most common enterprises among the early twentieth-century Jewish immigrants was to open "sweatshops." These were often begun in the entrepreneur's own apartment where he could set up sewing machines, employ many Jewish tailors to operate them, and bid for contracted work from the large garment manufacturers in New York or Boston. If successful, he could eventually move the establishment from his apartment to an actual shop; and if he were very successful, he might even become a garment manufacturer. A majority of the sweatshops were Jewish-owned, and about half of the workers were also Jewish. The working conditions in the sweatshops were deplorable, but the enterprises themselves were an agency of social mobility for the owners.[101]*

In addition to the garment trade, Jewish merchants entered small retail trades such as delicatessens, restaurants, and bakeries. Much of the capital accumulated through these Jewish enterprises was reinvested in the professional and graduate training of the immigrants' children. More than any other ethnic group, the Jews have placed a very high value on formal education and have produced a disproportionate percent of the nation's doctors, dentists, scholars, intellectuals, and creative artists. Correspondingly, Jews have been less likely to become executives of large corporations.[102]

This economic base of the Jewish community has had politically important consequences. Fewer Jews than Irish or Italians became economically dependent on political patronage jobs or on benefits to be derived from allegiance with the political machines. Even where large numbers of Jews did work for local bureaucracies, they were usually in professions such as teaching or social work that were not under the direct control of political machines. The conditions of their employment were structured by professional standards rather than political connections. Because of this, fewer Jewish leaders than Irish or Italian leaders had to support the machine for reasons of economic dependence.

The fourth difference between the Jews and the Irish and Italians lies in the social structure of their communities. The Irish and Italians had left their countries largely for economic reasons and, consequently, a substantial number of these immigrants returned to their homeland once they had saved enough money. The Jews, in contrast, emigrated largely to escape political or religious persecution. And for this reason, Jewish emigration was a one-way trip. Even if they became economically successful, Jews had nothing to return to in Europe except more persecution. For these reasons, Jews were often said to be more eager to integrate into the mainstream of American life.[103]

---

*The Jewish sweatshops in New York City were eradicated in the post-World War II period. But an ethnic succession seems to be taking place there as well as in housing, crime, and political parties. In the 1980s a new generation of sweatshops was emerging, based on the immigrant labor of Hispanics and Asians. See *The New York Times*, October 12, 1983, p.1.

One of the pervading themes of American Jewish community development has been that of reacting to anti-Semitism.[104] This was probably the most unifying element in what otherwise was a very heterogeneous people. Although all Jews nominally shared the same religion, there were strongly felt differences between those of reform, orthodox, or conservative persuasions and between the earlier German immigrants and the later Russian and Polish immigrants; and there were sharp class divisions between the upwardly mobile middle-class Jews and the poor. Even within the same economic arena—the garment industry, for example—there were sharp differences between the Jewish union leaders and the Jewish owners. In spite of all the differences, they became united because, as Jews, they were all endangered by outbreaks of anti-Semitism. Jews, regardless of wealth, faced discrimination and exclusion from the most prestigious clubs, schools, and residential areas. Even in the working-class neighborhoods of big cities, anti-Semitism erupted. Where Jewish and Irish neighborhoods abutted in northern Manhattan, Jews were sometimes beaten up by young Irish gangs.[105] Anti-Semitism led to the formation of a bond between many Jews that crossed class lines. The bonds were strengthened by the development of the Nazi regime in Germany, the horrors of World War II, and the establishment of the state of Israel. Perhaps the most obvious indicator of these bonds has been the very low rate of intermarriage between Jews and gentiles. But this is breaking down. Since 1965, almost a third of all Jewish marriages have been to non-Jews.[106]

The political consequences of these developments in the Jewish communities have been very important. As noted, the economic base of most Jews made them independent of the urban political machines. The social conditions of Jewish life and the oppression of anti-Semitism led them to support liberal causes such as civil rights and social welfare legislation that the political machines quite often opposed. Given these differences between Jews and the machines, it was probably inevitable that much of the anti-Tammany Hall reform leadership in New York's Democratic party came from the Jewish community.

In the 1960s the Jewish communities were brought into direct conflict with black communities by the various patterns of ethnic succession. As blacks moved into neighborhoods being vacated by Jews, personal contacts between Jews and blacks came in five areas: Jews were retail merchants selling their goods to blacks, landlords of black tenants, social workers among black families, educators in black schools, and allies in the struggle for civil rights. Of these contacts, only the last facilitated friendly relations between blacks and Jews, and even that contact area declined in relevance as the civil rights objectives were largely achieved and black leaders in the middle 1960s turned their attention to separatism, political influence, and other goals. The contact between blacks and Jewish retail merchants and landlords has especially occurred in the context of ethnic succession. In the late 1960s Jews owned 60 percent of all apparel stores and about 40 percent of all retail stores in central Harlem.[107] Only a miniscule percentage of these same merchants lived in Harlem, and this left them vulnerable to the criticism that they were siphoning money out of the black ghetto. Black militants demanded that Jewish and other white merchants abandon such retail establishments and leave them to be owned by blacks. In the riots of the 1960s, many nonblack stores were burned or looted.

Perhaps the bitterest black-Jewish conflicts came over public-school issues. When, for example, Brooklyn's Canarsie neighborhood (dominated by Jews and Italians) stood in the way of black neighborhood expansion, Canarsie's Jews and Italians put up bitter resistance to changing school boundaries in ways that would put their children in classrooms with black children.[108]

All of these developments have placed the Jewish leadership in a very uncomfortable position. Historically, no other white ethnic group has consistently supported black demands for civil rights and social advancement as much as the Jews have. Even today there is probably as much, if not more, support for black advancement among Jews as among any other ethnic group. Although the Jewish leadership has been divided on many specific questions, Jews were among the most ardent supporters of black demands for decentralization of urban government.

Jewish organizations have not objected very much to the demands that white and Jewish store owners be excluded from the ghetto.[109] But the demand that Jewish professionals in the public schools and the welfare departments be replaced by black professionals has caused a storm of protest. This has been so partially because the teachers and welfare workers are more articulate than the shopowners and landlords. More importantly, however, it strikes at the very core of Jewish success in America—professional competence. Although Jews were excluded because of anti-Semitism from some other areas of the economy (e.g., the diplomatic service), they have prospered in professions with fewer barriers against the exercise of individual competence. One Jewish observer wrote, "If Negroness or Jewishness has something to do with being a teacher, the Jew fears he may become an object of discrimination; equally important, he is not able to escape the condition of his Jewishness."[110] Consequently, the leaders of many Jewish organizations have opposed the concept of placing quotas on hiring. Jews have, however, strongly supported affirmative action programs that require both public and private employers to make special efforts to hire minorities and women.

The Poles

The fourth largest urban European ethnic community in the United States is that of the Poles.[111] Large-scale Polish immigration began in the 1870s and continued until World War I. The motive force behind it was primarily economic. About three-fourths of the Polish immigrants were Catholic, and the overwhelming majority entered the economy as unskilled laborers in great manufacturing cities like Buffalo, Detroit, Cleveland, Pittsburgh, Milwaukee, New York, and Chicago. Many of them found their economic base in the automobile industries, steel mills, foundries, and other heavy industries.

Much of Polish community development resulted from the activities of two large, national organizations that established local lodges in each Polish community. The first was the Polish Roman Catholic Union (PRCU), established in 1873. The PRCU was organized with a local in each Polish Roman Catholic parish. It was dominated by the Polish clergy, who sought to use the PRCU to establish a network of Polish parishes and Polish parochial schools. The Polish clergy resented the dominance of the Catholic church by the Irish, and they thought that if they could establish a strong parish and school network, the Irish-dominated church hierarchy would have to become open to the Poles as well as to the Irish.

The larger organization is the Polish National Alliance (PNA). The PNA was not restricted to Roman Catholics, and it was organized by community rather than by parish. Founded in 1880, its major goal was to achieve the liberation of Poland from its German, Austro-Hungarian, and Russian conquerors. So divided was Poland by its conquerors that many Poles acquired a consciousness of their national character only after they arrived in America and organizations like the PNA made them aware of it.[112] So successful was the PNA in attracting members through its goal of Polish liberation that PRCU was also forced to adopt liberation as a major objective. Once that objective was accomplished in 1919, both organizations turned their attention toward maintaining the Polish heritage among the immigrants and their children. The PRCU discouraged participation in non-Polish institutions. Both organizations ran a variety of activities and enterprises, which ranged from selling insurance to conducting English classes for the immigrants.

As a result of these and similar mutual-benefit organizations, a vibrant institutional life was created in Polish communities. By 1960 an estimated 830 Polish parishes and more than 500 Polish elementary schools existed in the United States. Polish convents were established, a Polish college was established in Pennsylvania, and the PRCU subsidized a seminary that trained Polish priests. Polish-language newspapers abounded. Polish businesspeople's organizations flourished. Like the Jews, the Poles made special efforts to provide higher education for their young. Both major organizations and several others maintained scholarship programs.

In summary, a strong ethnic community developed. By the 1970s, however, the strains on this community were very strong. Whereas fewer of the younger generation could speak Polish, more were beginning to marry into other nationality groups.* For many years the Polish community has resented the doctors, lawyers, dentists, and other professionals who increasingly have deserted the ethnic neighborhoods and migrated to the suburbs; frequently their professional training was received through special scholarships offered by the Polish ethnic organizations, and the doctors and lawyers often earned their income from their practices in the Polish neighborhoods. But these professionals have been accused of not supporting the Polish community organizations or being willing to live in the Polish neighborhoods. One critic noted that "the nationally minded Polish immigrants regarded their professional and intellectual class with reproach and disappointment."[113] As a consequence, the maintenance of the Polish community is left primarily to the clergy who want to maintain their Polish parishes, the businesspeople

---

*In the 1960s, National Opinion Research Center (NORC) surveys found that 50 percent of their Polish respondents were married to non-Poles. The corresponding numbers for other ethnics were Irish, 57 percent; Italians, 34 percent; Jews, 6 percent [Andrew M. Greeley, *Why Can't They Be Like Us? America's White Ethnic Groups* (New York: E. P. Dutton, 1971), pp. 87, 92].

who want to maintain their economic base, and the politicians who want to maintain their Polish constituencies.

Despite these problems, the Poles have been able to acquire significant political representation. They have a strong tendency to vote for Poles rather than non-Poles.[114] Primarily Democrats,* their greatest success has probably been in Chicago.

The major problem confronting the big-city Polish communities in the 1980s and 1990s involves maintaining the community social structure and expanding the opportunities for upward social mobility. Both of these objectives bring the Polish community leadership into conflict with the newer urban minorities who are also seeking social mobility and greater social access to employment and housing opportunities. As the most successful of the professionals abandon the old neighborhoods for the suburbs, Polish communities lose a potential liberalizing force. Local leadership is left in the hands of those who have the most to lose from contemporary social changes—the clergy and the businesspeople. Ultimately, the politicians also have much to lose because the rising influence of blacks and Hispanics ultimately means less influence in city hall for the Poles. Nowhere is this more apparent than in Chicago, where Poles are probably the single largest white ethnic constituency in the black-white battle that raged in that city for control of city government and the Democratic party after the death of former mayor Richard J. Daley in 1976.

The Relationship of Ethnic Politics to Brokerage and Machine Politics

In reality, the politics of the ethnic groups were never as isolated as they appear on being analyzed one by one. Considerable interaction existed between members of the Polish, Jewish, Italian, Irish, and other ethnic groups. The political interactions of these groups were normally handled by *brokerage* politics. In a sense, to the extent that all politics involve bargaining and the exchange of favors, all politics are brokerage politics. But here the term refers to politics characterized by material incentives in bargaining for political favors, by the jockeying for relative political advantages among the representatives of various groups in the political system, and by the tradeoff of votes or financial contributions for political favors. The political favors are always specific and material as distinguished from diffused and symbolic.[115] And brokerage politics tend to be nonideological.

Closely related to brokerage politics is the concept of *machine politics*. This term refers to a political process characterized by the presence within a political party of a political organization that endures for several years; by the rule of a "boss" who oversees the awarding of patronage jobs and the selection of party nominees; and by a reliance on patronage, awarding of government contracts, and

---

*NORC surveys of the class of 1961 college graduates found that Catholic Poles had a greater tendency to identify themselves as Democrats than any other group of college graduates except for blacks and Jews [Greeley, *Why Can't They Be Like Us?*, p. 206].

other material incentives to secure campaign workers and campaign contributions. Machines are nonideological. They usually have a political base among the underprivileged sectors of the society, and they usually portray themselves as serving as intermediary between the government and these underprivileged people. Machine politics always involve brokerage politics, but the reverse is not necessarily true: It is possible to have brokerage politics without having a machine.

Closely associated with both of these concepts is the concept of *ethnic politics*. Although machine politics do not necessarily have to be linked to ethnic politics, in the cities of the Northeast they quite often occurred together.* The political machines fit into the ethnic networks of social mobility through which some members of the ethnic communities could prosper. At the same time, the ethnic base to politics facilitated symbolic payoffs to those people who did not participate in the tangible payoff from machine politics. For these people, ethnicity played a very important symbolic role. Nominating an Italian or a Pole to high office supposedly granted recognition to that ethnic group. And either because this recognition gave them vicarious pleasure or because they hoped that their own children might rise in a similar fashion, the members of the group remained loyal to the nominating party.

The oldest and most famous combination of ethnic and machine politics occurred in the Tammany Hall machine in Manhattan.[116] The Tammany Society was founded in 1789 primarily as a sociable fraternal organization. It slowly became politicized and, particularly under the Irish, served as the mechanism for controlling the activities of the neighborhood district clubs. The district clubs were the heart of the organization. They dispensed patronage and controlled nominations within their jurisdictions. But for citywide nominations and patronage, or for settling disputes between clubs, a citywide organization was needed; and this was the role reserved for Tammany Hall. Tammany reached its greatest strength in the era that extended from the Civil War until the early 1900s under the leadership of William Marcy "Boss" Tweed, Charles F. Murphy, and Richard Croker.

Boss Tweed was surely the most colorful of the bosses. He rose from a foreman in the fire department through the positions of alderman and congressman to the position of boss of Tammany Hall. As boss he controlled the dispensing of government contracts to the point where he was able to steal millions of dollars from the New York City treasury. Tweed was finally arrested and served a jail sentence for his crimes, but few other Tammany bosses ended their careers in prison.

Despite their inefficiencies and high levels of graft, the machines, including Tammany Hall, did serve to integrate the competing demands of various ethnic groups for patronage jobs and representation in government. They also served as a link between the government and the impoverished immigrants (particularly for

---

*Raymond Wolfinger argues that machine politics and ethnic politics do not necessarily go together, and he indicates several examples of machine politics without a European ethnic base. See his *The Politics of Progress*, pp. 122–129. Elmer Cornwell argues that even where machine politics were not linked to ethnic politics, they were organized in reaction to either immigrant or black demands for inclusion in the political arena. See his "Bosses, Machines, and Ethnic Groups," *The Annals of the American Academy of Political and Social Science* 353 (May 1964), pp. 27–39.

the Irish) and provided a channel through which the larger ethnic groups (particularly Italians and Poles) were able to demand concessions from city governments and to get a share of the representation and patronage. The fact that ethnic groups could be represented as such through the machines meant that machine politics offered a way of diffusing class divisiveness in the cities: Aspiring ethnic politicians, in order to rise, had to mold a core of followers from all classes within the ethnic group.

The Tammany Hall model of deeply intertwined ethnic, brokerage, and machine politics was not, however, the only pattern that emerged. It predominated mostly in the Northeast, particularly in the North Atlantic and New England states.[117] In the South, brokerage politics had little ethnic content. In some southern states, such as Virginia and Louisiana, relatively permanent political machines developed and endured for an entire generation. In some other states, permanent machines failed to develop, and the dominant brokerage pattern was what political scientist V. O. Key called "one party factionalism." In most of the South the machines and factions had a rural rather than an urban base.[118]

In the Midwest, politics had a high ethnic content, but it evolved in two mutually incompatible patterns.[119] In Ohio, Indiana, and Illinois, politics were *jobs oriented* and similar to the politics of the Northeast. The major motivation behind political activity was to control the substantial patronage that existed in those states. Strong machines developed in Cleveland, Toledo, Indianapolis, Gary, and especially in Chicago. In Michigan, Wisconsin, and Minnesota, by contrast, politics were *issue oriented.* In Minnesota and Wisconsin, third parties developed (the Farmer-Labor party and the Progressive party, respectively) after World War I. And when they captured control of their state and local governments, they used their new-found power not so much to provide patronage jobs for their supporters as to institute broad economic and social reforms through legislation.

In the Far West, an entirely different pattern emerged. California, Oregon, and Washington all had strong progressive movements that weakened the political parties.[120] In San Francisco, machines existed in the 19th century, but in the 20th century a system of politics evolved that was characterized by an extremely high ethnic content with very little reliance on political machines.[121]

In practice, then, the concepts of ethnic, brokerage, and machine politics are distinct, not synonymous, and a variety of practical arrangements has evolved. In some places, such as New Haven, New York, and Chicago, the three types of politics are virtually indistinguishable. In other places, political machines existed even though there were no European immigrant and ethnic groups; the most prominent example was the Byrd machine in Virginia. In other places—Mississippi, for one—a form of brokerage politics existed without either permanent political machines or an ethnic base. In still other places, principally in Wisconsin, Michigan, and Minnesota, politics had a high ethnic content combined with an issue-oriented political process. And finally, in San Francisco, a type of ethnic politics developed that was characterized by neither a political machine nor an issue orientation.

The Significance of Ethnic, Brokerage, and Machine Politics Today

These patterns of ethnic, brokerage, and machine politics have more than simple historical interest. They continue to be relevant to contemporary political events. The persistence of ethnic-based politics and ethnic voting has been noted by several studies.[122] Ethnic considerations are most influential in nonpartisan elections; without the party label to provide guidance, voters look for ethnic labels. Ethnic considerations are also influential when a member of an ethnic group runs for a major office. In recent years there has been a resurgence of interest in and self-consciousness among various European ethnic groups.[123]

Assuming that this resurgence of self-consciousness among the ethnics will persist for several years, it is not clear what the political consequences will be. One possibility is a continuation of ethnic-based voting. Political scientist Raymond Wolfinger has argued that ethnic voting is most likely to occur in later generations when the ethnic group develops not only a sense of ethnic identity but also the economic and political resources to back ethnic candidates. His evidence, however, refers to just one ethnic group (Italians) in only one city (New Haven).[124] And a re-analysis of the same data by another political scientist casts doubt on the usefulness of the concept of ethnic voting, even in New Haven.[125] Furthermore, the breakup of old ethnic neighborhoods, intermarriages, and the large-scale migration of ethnics to the suburbs make a continuation of ethnic voting very difficult in the 1980s except in localities that still have cohesive ethnic neighborhoods. Nevertheless, a study of ethnic loyalties in Buffalo, New York, found that Polish Democrats has a pronounced tendency to vote for a prominent Polish Republican for mayor rather than vote for a Democractic non-Pole. This tendency, however, was weaker among the third-generation Poles than among the older generation.[126]

A continued ethnic impact on politics seems much more likely to persist on the question of social issues than on support for candidates merely because of their ethnicity. Significant attitudinal differences still tend to exist among ethnic groups about major social issues. To take just one example, Table 3-2 shows the differences between ethnic groups found in 1977 and 1985 National Opinion Research Center (NORC) surveys on two key questions of equalizing social access for blacks.

According to the NORC findings, there has been a marked decrease since the mid-1970s among all those white ethnic groups' opposition to blacks moving into white neighborhoods, but there has been much less decrease in their opposition to sending their children to schools that have a black majority. Yet many Irish in South Boston reacted violently to attempts to desegregate the high school there in the middle 1970s. And Jews in Brooklyn's Canarsie neighborhood opposed the desegregation of their neighborhood schools in the 1970s. The ethnic attitudes—probably more than the differences in voting—continue to have relevance to contemporary urban politics.

Table 3-2. Attitudes of White Ethnics Toward Social Access for Blacks: 1977 and 1985

Statement	Irish Catholics	Italian Catholics	Eastern European Catholics	Anglo-Protestants	Germanic Protestants	Scandinavian Protestants	Jews
	1977/1985	1977/1985	1977/1985	1977/1985	1977/1985	1977/1985	1977/1985
White people have a right to keep blacks out of their neighborhoods if they want to.	43%/22	46%/16	58%/34	43%/21	44%/32	43%/31	23%/20
Would object to sending their own children to a school where more than half the children are black.	39%/41	51%/32	64%/39	54%/40	46%/45	48%/47	42%/55

Source: James Allan Davis and Tom W. Smith, *General Social Surveys, 1972–1985* [machine-readable data file]. Principal Investigator, James A. Davis; Senior Study Director, Tom W. Smith. Chicago: National Opinion Research Center, producer, 1985; Storrs, CT: Roper Public Opinion Research Center, University of Connecticut, distributor.

The Bias of Ethnic and Machine Politics

Are any biases inherent to ethnic and machine politics? Three generalizations have been offered. First, some argue that both ethnic and brokerage politics have promoted a conservative bias. Except for the Jews, the immigrant generations consistently voted for conservative candidates.[127] When the Irish achieved political power, they seldom used their power to promote social programs.[128] Furthermore, the ascension to power of an ethnic group actually meant the ascension of only the *leadership* of that group; for the masses, the ascension was mostly symbolic and vicarious. The recognition accorded to a group by the appointment of one of its members to a major office was supposed to give the group enough vicarious pleasure that it would remain loyal to the appointing party. Raymond Wolfinger characterizes the ascension to power of an ethnic group as "monetary rewards for a few and symbolic gratification for the rest."[129] To the extent that this politics of recognition gave the ethnics a stake in the society by holding out the Horatio Alger promise that they too could rise to the top, Wolfinger argues that it contributed greatly to stabilizing the political system in the United States.

Because they divided the electorate along ethnic lines, ethnic politics had the additional conservative effect of muting class antagonisms. Within their ethnic group, political leaders had to appeal to all classes.

Finally, the inevitable social conflict between ethnic groups inherent to ethnic politics has facilitated incremental change in political relations.[130] Through the process of ethnic succession, newer ethnic groups were brought into the political arena. As newer groups became active, their leaders were given opportunities for personal advancement. As long as these opportunities were open to them, the ethnic population had little incentive to join revolutionary movements.

In summary, the argument for conservative bias states that ethnic politics became a stabilizing force in the urban political system. By providing a channel for ethnic leaders to gain prominence, ethnic politics obviated any recourse to revolutionary social changes but did little to improve the living conditions of the masses of the ethnic populations. A Kennedy here or a Giannini there may have entered the upper class, but the class structure itself was preserved intact.

These arguments are valid, but ethnic and brokerage politics had an equally important liberalizing bias. Within limits, ethnic and brokerage politics *did* serve as channels of social mobility for lower-class immigrants. And the machine politicians *did* represent some of the interests of their constituents. The ethnics *did* create institutional channels to represent their interests. And, certainly until 1900, it could be argued that the ethnic networks *were the only* avenues for upward mobility open to the ethnics who were contemptuously scorned by established white Americans.[131]

Nor were all the machines as devoid of social accomplishments as Tammany Hall. In Cincinnati, a Republican machine under Boss Cox muted racial and ethnic antagonisms, ameliorated conditions for the blacks, brought public improvements to the city, and ran the city government in a relatively honest and efficient fashion.[132] Furthermore, the propensity of the *antimachine, antiethnic* reform leadership to be drawn from the upper classes and the top business leadership in cities would suggest that the ethnics and their institutions *were perceived* by the upper classes as a liberalizing threat. As Melvin G. Holli has shown, when these upper-class reformers came to power in cities, their first moves were often to slash payrolls and reverse the decisions that were both opening up jobs for the lower-class ethnics and providing public services for their neighborhoods.[133]

A second bias of ethnic and brokerage politics has been against small and unorganized ethnic groups and racial minorities. The brokerage nature of the political machines was effective in ameliorating relations between groups that had their own indigenous power bases—groups such as the Irish, the Poles, and the Italians. With a few exceptions, the political machines have been notoriously unsuccessful in offering the Hispanic and racial minorities a channel to political influence.[134] There are several reasons for this. Until the 1970s these minorities were poorly organized politically and did not have an indigenous power base to confront the political machines. Even where blacks were well organized politically, as in the Dawson machine in Chicago,[135] the white political leaders very effectively minimized the patronage available to the blacks by successfully co-opting the black politicians. A major change in this situation took place when a black, Harold Washington, was elected mayor of Chicago in 1983. As we will discuss further in Chapters 4 and 5, this event precipitated a power struggle for control of the machine by Mayor Washington and a majority faction of white ethnics in the city council led by council president Edward Vrdolyak.

Until Washington's election in 1983, however, blacks did not fare very well under the Chicago machine. And as the black voting population grew larger, perhaps it was inevitable that they would come into political and social conflict with the city's white ethnics.

Because Chicago as a city has been a polyglot of ethnic and racial minorities and because of the process of ethnic succession, the social and political systems themselves inherently made racial conflict inevitable. This is most obvious in the case of the Poles and racial minorities. The pressures leading to disintegration of the Polish community in Chicago are heightened by the racial minorities' demands for social access. The oldest Polish neighborhoods along Milwaukee Avenue lie precisely in one expansion path of the Hispanic ghettos. Following a familiar historical pattern, the more the neighborhoods and schools are integrated, the greater the number of Poles who abandon the old neighborhoods. And the greater the abandonment of the old neighborhoods, the less viable become the neighborhood-based businesses, the Polish parishes, and the Polish community organizations. The national headquarters of the oldest Polish organization, the PRCU, now exists in the middle of a Hispanic ghetto in Chicago. Social access for blacks and Hispanics in Chicago is interpreted by many Polish leaders as destructive of the Polish community. As long as Polish leadership is exercised by those Poles whose vested interests are likely to be damaged by black and Hispanic expansion, social conflict between Poles and these minorities is inevitable. If this analysis is correct, the greatest threat to black advancement is not individual racism, because all but the poorest of the racists can pack up and move farther out, away from the Hispanic frontier. The greatest threat to the new minorities lies in the very structure of ethnic and machine politics in Chicago. This situation is also very threatening to the Poles, for it inherently pits the vested interests of Polish leadership against the vested interests of black and Hispanic leadership.

A third bias of ethnic and machine politics stems from their conservative and racial bias. Ethnic and machine politics are biased against systematic approaches to the great urban social issues of the 1980s and 1990s—education, race relations, housing, welfare, and crime. Because the nature of the political machines lies in the balancing of competing interests, machines of necessity approach social issues in the same manner. As Banfield and Meyerson have shown for Chicago, the machine does not deal with housing problems by setting housing goals and then carrying out a sequenced set of programs to meet those goals. Although such goals may exist on paper, the key issues on public housing, especially location, are resolved by balancing competing interests of bankers, realtors, neighborhood groups, construction unions, racial group leaders, housing experts in specialized agencies, and political leaders in the various neighborhoods of Cook County.[136] The tendency of machines to react to existing balances of power inherently makes it difficult for them to respond favorably to the needs of people without power. The machines' reliance on material incentives to attract contributions and to stay in power makes it difficult for machine politicians to place systematic policy considerations ahead of demands of the contributors and powerful groups.

Finally, machine politics was essentially a men's phenomenon. The catalogue of historic machine politicians such as Boss Tweed of New York, James Curley of Boston, or Ed Crump of Memphis was essentially a list of men. This is not surprising, however, since women were able to reach leadership positions in very few public institutions at the time. It is possible that machines were even less open to the participation of women than were other political organizations. If we judge by the receptiveness to women's suffrage, the non-machine states generally granted women the right to vote much earlier than did the machine states.

The Transition from Ethnic-Based to Function-Based Political Power

This chapter has indicated how political power developed out of ethnic social organization. Particularly crucial was the emergence of a substantial number of wealthy or upper-middle-class people whose interests or inclinations demanded that they invest their resources in the institutions of their own ethnic community. The creation of these institutions laid the foundation for ethnic political power, for the ethnic networks of social mobility, and for symbolic unity of the ethnic peoples.[137] Initially, the financial stability of the upper middle class was heavily dependent on the growth of the ethnic community institutions. As time passed, the financial base of the ethnic leaders expanded beyond a single ethnic community. The ethnic institutions still had influence, but other, more functionally oriented urban institutions developed that were not the peculiar creation of any particular ethnic group. Nevertheless, they worked as channels of social mobility for

European-American lower classes. Relevant examples of such institutions are found in organized labor and in the intellectual and artistic worlds.

Organized labor has been a very effective political voice for its members. Although unions are not principally ethnic institutions, in many ways they reinforce the influence of the more ethnically oriented institutions. The Catholic church has tended to support the economic objectives of labor, and labor has usually refrained from hostility toward the church. Numerous instances exist of close collaboration between unions and elements of organized crime. And since the 1930s labor influence in political parties has generally but not always been supportive of the Democrats.

Noticeable in the intellectual and entertainment worlds is a heavy recurrence of Jewish names. More than any other ethnic group, the Jews have used the intellectual and artistic professions as channels for advancement. So important has been their influence that it is difficult to imagine contemporary American literary or artistic life without their contributions.

Perhaps more important than questions about which ethnic groups disproportionately influence which institutions is the observation that most of these institutions have become more concerned with the *functional sector* of the society in which they operate than with either the *geographic area* in which their members reside or ethnic social advancement. The hierarchy of the Catholic church may be disproportionately staffed by Irish, but the social advancement of the Irish is no longer a prime concern of the hierarchy. The sphere of interest of the church has narrowed considerably to a much more religious focus. The sphere of interest of most institutions in contemporary society is normally focused on whatever function that institution performs. This makes it much more difficult today to create indigenous power bases in ethnic communities than it was two generations ago, when society was not so specialized.

One of the key questions now facing urban America is whether the new urban minorities of Hispanics, American Indians, blacks, Asians, and poor whites can develop institutional structures that will bring them the advancement that European immigrants found through their own urban institutions. Before we can deal with this question, we must examine the progressive reform movement and the decline of machine politics. This will be done in Chapter 4. Then Chapter 5 will return to the question of the impact of all these developments on the new urban minorities of the 1980s and 1990s.

Summary

1. In the pre-World War II city, urban political power was ultimately based on the social organization of ethnic communities. The largest of the ethnic communities were the Irish, Italians, Jews, and Poles. Each had its own particular social base for fostering political influence and upward social mobility.

2. For these urban ethnic groups, political power rested in great measure on a substantial number of middle-class people serving as clergy, lawyers, politicians,

racketeers, businesspeople, or professionals who could give their money and talent to political causes that furthered the group's cohesion.

3. Institutions such as parish churches, local businesses, and, in some instances, crime organizations were created to mobilize money and a workforce that would constitute a new investment in the community.

4. The political power that resulted from these ethnic groups was indigenous; it was not dependent on outside benevolence.

5. Although ethnic and machine politics were remarkably effective for mobilizing political power, they had biases that were inherently conservative, non-programmatic, and opposed to the effective representation of blacks, Hispanic minorities, other small urban minorities, and women.

Chapter 4
Urban Reform and the Decline of Machine Politics

The purpose of this chapter is threefold. First, it defines machine politics and examines the widespread belief that machine politics have passed away. The argument advanced here is that machine politics have not disappeared, but they have ceased to be the dominant form of political organization in most metropolises. Second, this chapter describes the forces that led to these changes in the fortunes of machine politics. Three forces have been paramount in these urban political changes: (1) the progressive reform movement of the early twentieth century, (2) the changing role of the federal government, and (3) the demographic changes discussed in Chapter 2. Finally, this chapter analyzes the bias that resulted from these changes in urban political organization.

Have Machine Politics Really Disappeared?

The years immediately before and after World War II stand as a symbolic period in urban political history. One after another, several famed central-city machines suffered significant losses. James Curley, the boss-mayor of Boston, was sent to prison,* as was Thomas Pendergast, head of the political machine in Kansas City. The Hague machine in Jersey City was defeated in 1949, as was the Crump machine in Memphis. In an attempt to defuse complaints about the corrupt practices of the incumbent Kelly-Nash machine in Chicago, the Chicago Democrats dumped boss-mayor Ed Kelly in 1947 in favor of a reform candiate, businessman Martin Kennelly. They hoped that Kennelly would draw the support of the good-government reformers. Through their astuteness, the Chicago bosses were able to maintain their power for at least another generation. But a general feeling persisted that the day of the boss was past, that urban political machines were on their way out. Novelist Edwin O'Connor portrayed the decline of the urban political

---

*Even while in prison Curley managed to get himself reelected.

boss in his novel *The Last Hurrah*, a story well worth reading by any student of urban politics.[1]*

So widespread has been this view that political machines have disappeared that it has become part of the conventional wisdom about American urban politics.[2] Yet the persistence of machine-style politics in Chicago, and the perseverance of the Tammany organization in New York City, suggest that machine politics are not entirely dead.[3] In the middle and late 1980s, indeed, New York's political organization was racked by scandals over patronage, graft, organized crime, and laundering of money in a magnitude that the city had not seen for fifty years. In Boston, Mayor Kevin White (1967–1983) kept himself in power in no small measure by using several traditional tactics of machine politics (such as patronage, dispensing of favors on a political basis, and pressuring city employees to make campaign contributions).[4]

Clearly times are changing and the machines are no longer the dominant force in most cities. But the conventional wisdom that machines are dead is at odds with the continued perseverance of machine-style politics, at least in Chicago, New York, and Boston.

One reason for the misconception that political machines are dead lies in the fact that there is no commonly accepted definition of what constitutes machine politics. What perseveres may be defined as machine politics by some observers but not by others. For example, Raymond Wolfinger asserts that machine politics have not withered away, whereas his fellow political scientist Fred I. Greenstein asserts that they are passing away. Part of the reason for their different interpretations lies in their different definitions of machine politics. Wolfinger appears to define a political machine as any organization that controls a significant number of patronage jobs and other material incentives and is more concerned with the routine operations of staffing government positions than it is with implementing ideologies or substantive policies.† Greenstein, in contrast, presents a much more restricted definition. He suggests that machine politics entail four elements in addition to patronage:

---

*O'Connor's novel is important, because its romanticization of machine politics was so popular and widely read. Most of the early twentieth-century literature presented very unfavorable treatments of machine politics. Afterward, a reaction set in and machine politics were treated much more favorably.

†Wolfinger writes of the two major Democratic party leaders of New Haven that they were "seldom present at meetings where decisions about municipal policy were made, nor did they play an active part in these matters. On strictly party topics like nominations they were, with Mayor Lee, a triumvirate. Appointments, contracts, and the like were negotiated among the three, with Lee delegating a good deal of routine patronage administration to Barbieri. But substantive city affairs were another matter; here the organization leaders were neither interested [in] nor consulted on the outlines of policy" [*The Politics of Progress* (Englewood Cliffs, N.J.: Prentice-Hall, 1974), p. 104]. Wolfinger's rationale for his definition of a political machine is explained in considerable detail in "Why Political Machines Have Not Withered Away and Other Revisionist Thoughts," *Journal of Politics* 34 (May 1972): 365–398, and in *The Politics of Progress*, pp. 101–106.

1. There is a disciplined party hierarchy led by a single executive or a unified board of directors.
2. The party exercises effective control over nomination to public office, and through this, it controls the public officials of the municipality.
3. The party leadership—which quite often is of lower-class social origins—usually does not hold public office and sometimes does not even hold formal party office. At any rate, official position is not the primary source of the leadership's strength.
4. Rather, a cadre of loyal party officials and workers, as well as a core of voters, is maintained by a mixture of material rewards and *nonideological* psychic rewards—such as personal and ethnic recognition, camaraderie, and the like.[5]

Since both of these definitions are phrased in terms of *elements* of an ideal type of political machine, the important questions become: Which elements of machine politics have passed away? Which elements have declined in use? And which have not? When observed from this perspective, the problem becomes easier to handle. Four changes can be seen to have occurred in the practice of machine politics in American cities.

First, in reference to Greenstein's criteria that machine politics demand a party hierarchy, very few such hierarchies remain operating citywide across many functional areas. The Democratic party in Chicago is one of the few remaining cases of such a hierarchy. And even in Chicago the machine hierarchy has been rent by bitter conflicts between rival factions ever since the death of the city's legendary boss, mayor Richard J. Daley, in 1976. The second-term triumph of black mayor Harold Washington in 1987 was popularly viewed as a defeat for machine politics as such. Washington had campaigned for mayor on a platform of reform, pledging that he would dance on the grave of patronage and open up the political process to those who had previously been left out. In practice, reform under Washington meant using affirmative action hiring procedures to increase the number of black and Hispanic employees in city government.[6] In this respect, Washington did not abolish the machine so much as he sought to take command of it and use it to advance the minority populations of the city. He seemed well on the road to achieving that goal when he died of a heart attack on the eve of the Thanksgiving holiday in 1987. His death opened once again the prospect of a bitter struggle between the various political factions in the city to achieve dominance over the machine. Whether Washington's successor can maintain peace between all these factions or whether the party continues to be rent by bitter rivalries has important consequences for the governance of that city. Merely stating these possibilities is evidence that machine hierarchies have not totally withered and that there is intense competition to control them.

A second change in the fortunes of machine politics concerns the role of political patronage. One of the common beliefs among political scientists has been that patronage is declining both in attractiveness to the parties and in use by them.[7] Patronage is considered unattractive because it is so difficult to administer without losing more supporters than are gained;[8] since there are always more applicants than patronage positions available, most applicants end up disappointed. In addition, civil service reforms have decreased the number of patronage jobs at the same time that the welfare system and increasing general affluence have made low-paying government jobs unappealing to many people.[9]

There can be no doubt that patronage is very difficult to administer, particularly in light of civil service, the welfare system, and a long period of increasing affluence from about 1940 to 1970. But there is evidence to indicate that patronage is still important in some regions at the state, county, and urban levels of government. It is especially important in parts of the East and in portions of the Midwest—especially Ohio, Indiana, and Illinois.[10] In short, the disappearance of patronage is not a universal phenomenon. As a result of Supreme Court decisions outlawing the dismissal of government workers for partisan reasons, however, it is not clear how much longer traditional patronage will be around.[11]

More marked than the declining use of patronage has been the proliferation of different forms of incentives—both material and symbolic. Consider the increased use of outside consultants to conduct studies or to carry out government projects,[12] the large numbers of construction jobs due to central-city redevelopment, and the number of jobs created through the awarding of cable television franchises in the 1980s. These forms of incentives differ from traditional patronage in two major respects. First, many of these public-related jobs today go to middle-class people rather than to working-class or lower-class people. Second, in most instances, the awarding of these newly created material incentives is not controlled by political party machines. In this sense, non-civil-service material incentives actually may have increased during the past twenty years. But except where strong party hierarchies exist,[13] the political parties do not usually control how the incentives are passed out. Where machine politics do exist, however, the machine leaders usually have a hand in this type of patronage. One of New York City's most experienced observers, Jack Newfield, wrote of that city:

> The machine is an infrastructure of permanent institutions. It contains law firms, landlords who make contributions, judges who channel judicial patronage to clubhouse lawyers, printing companies that get all the petitions and literature business, community newspapers that receive judicial advertising, and friendly unions. In the Bronx, it controls the community school boards and picks principals on the basis of politics, not education.[14]

A third change in the process of machine politics has occurred in their role of providing a channel of social mobility for the urban-dependent populations. Historically, the machines received electoral support from the immigrant dependent populations.[15] In turn, the machines provided certain welfare services on a sporadic basis to the poor. Furthermore, they existed as a channel for social mobility for some immigrants who were aggressive and ambitious. As these few were nominated for high office, their ethnic supporters received symbolic recognition. As immigration was curtailed in the late 1920s, the immigrant-dependent population was replaced by a new mass of urban immigrants that consisted mainly of racial minorities, Hispanic minorities, and poor whites. These new urban minorities have voted overwhelmingly Democratic. But the machines have not provided them with the same resources they provided the European immigrants. Theodore Lowi's study of the class origins of high public officials in New York City over a sixty-year period found that the Democratic party in that city *"is no longer the clear channel of social mobility."*[16] In this sense the party has declined in its ability to provide benefits for the racial minorities, the Hispanic minorities, and the poor whites, who together constitute the dependent populations of today. This does not suggest that parties are useless to the new minorities; to the extent that parties control nomination for electoral office, they can be very useful.[17] But the parties do not fit into networks of social mobility for the new urban minorities as they once did for the Irish, Italians, and Poles.

A fourth change in machine politics is that new organizations have been created to meet many of the needs that the political machines once met. Machines originally evolved in part because they filled certain needs of urban society in the late nineteenth century. In addition to meeting some of the welfare needs of the immigrant dependent populations, they filled at least two other needs. First, because of the rapid growth of cities in the late nineteenth century, city governments were faced with overwhelming demands to provide services such as streets, sewers, water supply, lights, transportation, public safety, and health inspections. But city governments were organized to perform very few of these functions. Even elementary functions such as police and fire protection were provided on a voluntary basis well into the nineteenth century. The machine offered a mechanism of getting the services provided. Second, the machines filled a need of the cities' business sector. The business sector needed appropriate responses from the city governments in the form of licenses and francises to operate streetcar lines, install natural gas, or provide electric power. By allowing themselves to be bought, machine politicians provided the appropriate responses to the business sector.[18]

Actually none of these needs has ceased to exist, but new institutions have been created to meet them. Welfare is highly institutionalized. And the most dynamic growth in public services has been occurring in the suburbs, which are usually controlled by county governments or suburban municipalities that are very independent of the central-city machines.

In summary, it is not very useful to talk in terms of the *disappearance* of the political machine, because so many cities (at least in the northeast quadrant) still retain some elements of machine politics, and in many places the party organizations are gaining new life.[19] However, the changes that have taken place in machine politics clearly indicate that *the machines have declined* in their abilities to meet many needs they traditionally were supposed to have met. For meeting these needs, the machines have been bypassed by other, usually newer, public and private institutions.

If the practice of machine politics has declined but not disappeared and the machines have been bypassed in the performance of many functions that they used to perform, then two obvious questions are (1) how did this come about? and (2) what difference does it make in terms of who benefits and who is hurt by the changes? The second question will be examined at the end of this chapter. In response to the first question, three developments have been most often cited for the decline of machine politics: the political reform movement, changes in the role of the federal government, and changes in the demography and locale of urban growth.

Reforming the Machines Out of Business

Reformers and Bosses

Tammany Hall leader George Washington Plunkitt once referred to the political reformers as "morning glories" who bloomed at election time but lacked the staying power to combat the machine on a long-term basis.[20] For many years the history of Tammany Hall bore out Plunkitt's observation. Reformers ousted Boss Tweed only to have the Tammany Society reinstated in city hall a few years later. Despite occasional defeats, the Tammany Hall machine ran New York virtually as it pleased from the 1870s until well into the twentieth century. But in the long run, Plunkitt was wrong. The reformers lost most of the battles for control of city governments, but they did succeed in restructuring the city government in ways that made it very difficult for the machines to govern.

A Conflict of Cultural Perspectives

To understand the reform movement, it is necessary to understand that its conflict with the political machines was in great measure a conflict between cultures. The machine leaders usually rose from the working and lower classes in the immigrant communities.[21] In contrast, the reformers were primarily upper-class and upper-middle-class businesspeople, lawyers, professionals, and university people. There were some sharp ideological differences within the ranks of the reformist movement; but, in contrast to the machine politicians, the reformers shared many traits. Rather than being immigrants or first-generation Americans, the reformers came from families that had lived in America for generations. They were Protestant rather than Catholic, and a great number of them had graduated from colleges and professional schools—they were not poorly educated. Rather than conducting their occupational affairs through personal and old-fashioned, informal methods as did the political machine leaders, the reformers came from occupations in which they had mastered modern, rational, and quasi-scientific methods of organization. Intellectually, they came from an antiurban heritage that placed considerable value on individual initiative, agricultural life, and a town-meeting form of democracy. Somewhat at odds with their belief in democracy was their elitist belief that government should be conducted by the best-educated and best-qualified people in the society.

Coming from such backgrounds, the reformers could never reconcile themselves to the fact that city government was dominated by the kind of people on whom the machines relied for their leadership. One group of reformers investigated the backgrounds of the delegates to the 1896 Cook County Democratic convention and revealed an intriguing cross section of Chicago's Democratic leadership.

> A Cook County convention of 1896—held, it may be well to remember, before the Illinois legislature had undertaken mandatory reform—indicates the appalling degradation that might be observed occasionally in the politics of the period. Among the 723 delegates 17 had been tried for homicide, 46 had served terms in the penitentiary for homicide or other felonies, 84 were identified by detectives as having criminal records. Considerably over a third of the delegates were saloon-keepers; two kept houses of ill fame; several kept gambling resorts. There were eleven former pugilists and fifteen former policemen.[22]*

Historian Richard Hofstadter has described the conflict between the reformers and the machine leaders in terms of two incompatible perceptions of the very *raison d'être* of politics. The immigrant politician viewed politics in personal terms. Government "was the actions of particular powers. Political relations were not governed by abstract principles; they were profoundly personal."[23] The payoffs from political involvement also were highly specific—a job for a relative, a government contract, perhaps, or advance information on a proposed government land purchase that could enable one to make a quick profit by buying it beforehand and reselling it later to the government. Even those who were not close enough to the bosses to make money from their political involvement often received special payoffs—the proverbial bucket of coal or Christmas turkey, the intercession of the ward leader with the police in certain circumstances, or even just the friendship of the precinct captains and the ward leaders.[24] In contrast to this highly personal view of politics held by the immigrant, the upper-middle-class reformers looked upon politics as "the arena for the realization of moral principles of broad applications—and even, as in the case of temperance and vice crusades—for the correction of private habits."[25] The reformers were convinced that the immigrants and machine politics were detrimental to their concepts of a democracy in which the business of the town was to be conducted directly, and in a businesslike fashion, by the best-qualified citizens.

Ethos Theory

In two very influential writings, political scientists James Q. Wilson and Edward C. Banfield attempted to apply the Hofstadter thesis to the general urban population.[26] Through a study of voting on bond referendums for hospitals and

---

*The author commented, "The policemen of Chicago at that period were not highly regarded."

THE TAMMANY TIGER LOOSE.—" What are you going to do about it?"

THE TAMMANY TIGER LOOSE—"What are you going to do about it?"

Source: J. Chal Vinson, *Thomas Nast: Political Cartoonist* (Athens, Ga.: University of Georgia Press, 1967), plate 52.

In this cartoon Thomas Nast illustrates some of the themes that irked the nineteenth-century progressive reformers. As the Tammany tiger devours the feminine figure of the Republic, the ballot box lies smashed, the law is torn to shreds, and Boss Tweed, with staff in hand, sits satisfied in the grandstand, surrounded by the Tammany spoils. In a deliberate goad to the progressive reformers, Nast reported the rhetorical question that Tweed himself so often put to his critics: "What are you going to do about it?"

public buildings, they concluded that the urban population was divided into two mutually incompatible outlooks on government activity. They called each of these outlooks an *ethos*. The first ethos was called *public regarding*. It was found mostly among blacks, Jews, and the residents of upper-class neighborhoods who voted in a "public-regarding fashion" of seeking government expenditures for the common good of the city even if it cost them more in property taxes. In contrast, a *private-regarding* ethos was discovered among the non-Jewish European ethnics who voted against such expenditures. This thesis has enjoyed widespread acceptance. The obvious implication to be drawn from it, in the words of one textbook, was that "machine-type politics thrived in a lower-class milieu, while reform-type politics flourished in a middle-class environment."[27]

Despite the popularity of the ethos theory, it has several conceptual shortcomings,* and a later attempt to identify some social groups as "private regarding" was fairly inconclusive.[28] Wilson and Banfield themselves reconducted their study in the late 1960s, using more sophisticated survey research techniques. But when they found that barely a fifth of the people they interviewed could be properly classified into the two ethos categories, they argued that the two ethos they had identified earlier were much more important historically than they are at present.[29] Another pair of scholars reexamined the same data used by Banfield and Wilson and found such a dubious relationship between private regardingness and ethnic-religious background that they rejected the validity of the concept itself.[30]

In spite of these shortcomings of the ethos theory and the inability to classify specific ethnic groups as either private or public regarding, it is very useful in practice for political leaders to portray themselves as public regarding while painting their opponents as private regarding and selfish. This in some respects is what the early twentieth-century reformers did to the political bosses. The reformers were able to create a public-regarding image of themselves and they were able to attach a singularly private-regarding image to the bosses. As we will see later, the objectives and programs of the reformers could be made to seem very public regarding. And any opposition to them could make the bosses seem venal and private regarding. If, as Wilson and Banfield's latest data suggest, very, very few people have a private-regarding attitude, the reformers obtained a certain advantage over the bosses by manipulating these two images.

Social and Structural Reformers

The above characterizations of the reformers are not meant to imply that they constituted a cohesive, monolithic bloc. They were in fact sharply divided in their outlook on the capitalistic system and its relation to government. Many reformers had complete faith in the ultimate rightness and efficacy of the system. They, after all, had benefited from it. These reformers tended to concentrate on reforms in

---

*One of the major conceptual weaknesses was the lack of definition of several key terms by Banfield and Wilson, especially terms such as *public interest, middle class,* and *Anglo-Saxon.* Nor was it clear if the difference between the public-regarding group and the private-regarding group was an ethnic difference, a class difference, or some combination of the two. There were two major deficiencies with Wilson and Banfield's methodology of testing the theory. By using referendum votes to draw inferences about individual attitudes, Wilson and Banfield committed the *ecological fallacy.* This is the attempt to draw conclusions about individual attitudes on the basis of aggregate election returns from precincts or wards. Second, the choice of bond referendums as the test of public regardingness is a very restricted test that touches the economic interests of most lower-income homeowners much more sharply than it touches the economic interests of upper-income persons. No matter how the upper-class precincts voted, they could not be labeled as private regarding, because they were not going to receive many of the direct benefits from the bond issues. At the same time, as Timothy M. Hennessy puts it [see his "Problems in Concept Formation: The Ethos Theory and the Comparative Study of Urban Politics," *Midwest Journal of Political Science* 14, no. 4 (November 1970): 537–564], the middle- and low-income renters are "precluded from behaving in a 'public regarding' manner" (pp. 544–545). Consequently, since both groups of voters are not subjected to the same testing criteria regarding the costs of the referendums, the tests are invalid. Hennessy's article as a whole is a perceptive analysis of the conceptual and methodological difficulties of the ethos theory.

Social and Structural Reformers in Power

Many social reformers sought election to public office, and a few became mayors in major cities. Some of the more prominent were Tom Johnson of Cleveland (1901–1909), Samuel "Golden Rule" Jones (1897–1903) and Brand Whitlock (1906–1913) of Toledo, and Hazen Pingree of Detroit (1890–1897). Hazen Pingree was elected mayor of Detroit just before the depression of 1893. Through his efforts at regulating the public utilities, he succeeded in getting the public lower rates on electricity, gas, and telephone service. When faced with an intransigent, privately owned transit company that refused to lower streetcar fares, he put the city in the transit business and promoted a competing streetcar line. In addition to these kinds of objectives, the social reform mayors also sought free swimming pools, park expansion, school construction, and public relief for the unemployed.

In contrast to the social reform mayors who were willing to spend public money to improve social conditions for the lower classes, most of the reform mayors were structural reformers who were most interested in honesty, efficiency, and cost cutting. Prominent examples were John Purroy Mitchell in New York, Grover Cleveland in Buffalo, and James Phelan in San Francisco. Rather than increase expenditures on services to the poor, these mayors cut payrolls, reneged on contracts to pave streets, and cut back on school expenditures. There is little argument that the structural reformers made a more honest accounting of their tax revenues than did the political bosses, but there is also little argument that costs of their honest accounting were paid mostly by the poor and by the residents of poor neighborhoods.

Source: Melvin G. Holli, *Reform in Detroit: Hazen S. Pingree and Urban Politics* (New York: Oxford University Press, 1969), pp. 393–403.

---

governmental structure that would make city government more efficient and less costly to the corporate and business taxpayers. For this reason they can be called *structural reformers.* Many other reformers were critical of the capitalistic system. They were appalled by the degrading living conditions of the urban lower classes, the social irresponsibility of many industrial corporations, and the obvious graft that seemed to characterize the relations between the business leaders and the big-city political machines. They tended to concentrate more on social reforms than on structural reforms.[31] They can be called *social reformers.*

The ideological differences between these two kinds of reformers were reflected in their practical activities. One avenue of social reform was the muckraking and reform journalism exemplified by the work of observers such as Lincoln Steffens[32] and Jacob Riis. A second channel of social reform activity was social work, particularly the settlement-house movement. A prominent social worker was Jane Addams, who founded the Hull House settlement house in Chicago to facilitate the assimilation of the immigrants and to influence government activities in a progressive direction.[33] The third tactic of social reform activity was to take over the government and use it to implement progressive policies. A good illustration of this is the activity of Detroit's mayor Hazen Pingree, described in the accompanying box. Historian Samuel P. Hays carefully examined several reform movements and concluded that the major initiators of the structural reforms came primarily from the cities' top business leadership and upper-class elite. According to Hays, the movement to reform governmental structures "constituted an attempt by upper class, advanced professional, and large business groups to take formal political power from the previously dominant lower and middle class elements so that they might advance their own conception of desirable public policy."[34] Among the many reform movements that Hays examined, he found none in which small businesspeople, white-collar workers, or artisans were represented.

The Goal of Reform

The reformers focused on destroying the control that they felt the machine bosses had over city government and the voters. They noted examples of corrupt machine control over the voters, of which there were plenty. In one Chicago ward in the election of 1896, for example:

> The bars were open all night and the brothels were jammed. By ten o'clock the next morning, though, the saloons were shut down, not in concession to the reformers, but because many of the bartenders and owners were needed to staff the First Ward field organization. The Bath, Hinky Dink and their aides ran busily from polling place to polling place, silver bulging in their pockets into which they dug frequently and deeply.[35]

The charge that elections were bought with sex, booze, and silver dollars was, understandably, a powerful tool in the arsenal of the Progressive reformers. But there is no way to know for sure how much boss control depended on manipulating the vote this way. John Allswang writes, "in boss-run cities as well as those receiving more favorable appellation, most people most of the time voted free from duress and without illusions."[36] Political machines relied not only on lower-class ethnic voters but on business connections and support from the city's middle class as well.

Nevertheless, it was the corruption, the election fraud, and the social backgrounds of the machine politicians that were most vulnerable to attack. So the reformers centered their attack on breaking the links between the bosses and (1) an untutored immigrant electorate and (2) businesspeople who were willing to partake in the "honest graft" that the machines offered them. If these links could be broken, then higher-quality persons, not dominated by the machine, could be elected to city office. City administrations could then be conducted according to accepted practices of efficiency and administrative honesty with the likely additional benefit of operating at considerably less expense. These beliefs in the inherent goodness of efficiency and honesty underlay the programs of the structural reformers.

The Programs of Structural Reform

The devices for accomplishing these strategic aims were quite simple, although it took several years for them to evolve. The heart of the problem was the party bosses. Since the bosses were very difficult to eliminate, the key to the solution lay in making them ineffective. And this was largely accomplished through two broad movements: (1) breaking the control of the party bosses over the electoral process and (2) administering the city government according to the designs that would make it efficient and honest. This demanded a restructuring of city government.

Breaking the Bosses' Control over the Electoral Machinery

Under the existing rules of the game in the process of competing electorally with the bosses, the reformers often turned out to be, as Plunkitt charged, morning glories. If the reformers were to be effective in the long run, they would have to change the rules of the game. The devices for doing this were relatively simple. If the party bosses controlled the nomination process through control of the party nominating conventions, then conventions had to be replaced with *direct primaries* in which the people would nominate their own candidates without the interference of corrupt political middlemen. If another source of the bosses' strength lay in the geographic or ward organizations through which they could channel limited welfare benefits to the needy in exchange for their votes, the logical solution was to eliminate wards and hold *at-large elections*, with every candidate for a particular city office running against every other candidate. If the long ballot meant that fifty or a hundred offices had to be voted on at local elections—numbers so large that voters relied heavily on machine endorsements to distinguish friendly from unfriendly candidates—then the logical solution was to eliminate this reliance by having a *short ballot* in which people would have to learn about the candidates for only a limited number of offices. If the machine's strength depended on its ability to control party nominations, the machine might be permanently crippled by holding *nonpartisan elections* in which partisan nominations were banned. And if the machines controlled the margin of votes in close elections by their dishonest election practices such as repeating, voting in the names of persons who had died or moved away, buying votes, substituting premarked ballots for unmarked ballots, or simply having the election officials add up the tallies incorrectly, then the final *coup de grace* might be given to the machine simply by making such practices illegal and clamping down on election-law violations.

The standard mechanisms for breaking the control of the party bosses, then, were the direct primary, at-large elections, the short ballot, nonpartisan elections, fair campaign laws, plus the separation of local elections from national elections. In addition to these standard mechanisms for weakening the party bosses, other devices were used in many places. *Proportional representation* guaranteed a minimal representation of minority factions on city councils and thus weakened party control. But proportional representation never became a permanently popular device in the United States as it has in some European countries. Referendum, recall, and initiative devices were instituted in some cities. By *initiative*, a group of citizens could draft a bill by petition and submit it directly to the voters for approval. Through the *referendum*, legislation passed by councils or legislatures could be overturned by the voters at the ballot box. Through the *recall*, voters could directly remove from office officials who displeased them.

The machines' power was further broken down by more stringent fair-campaign laws. The most notorious voting frauds were virtually eliminated. Repeating was a common fraud that could be greatly effective when handled with a certain amount of delicacy. A party worker would get up early in the morning, go to different polling places, and vote in other citizens' names before those people showed up. So common was repeating that even William Foote Whyte engaged in the practice while conducting his research as a participant observer in Boston for his classic book, *Street Corner Society*.[37] Unless it was handled carefully, however, repeating could embarrass the machine. George Washington Plunkitt himself told the story of the repeater who entered a polling place and requested a ballot under the name of Doane. "You ain't Bishop Doane," challenged the poll judge. "The hell I ain't," responded the repeater, betraying himself.[38] In addition to repeating, some other fraudulent electioneering devices were premarking the ballots, buying votes, accompanying the voters into the voting booth so they could be pressured into voting as the precinct workers wanted them to, and voting in the name of citizens who had died or moved out of the precinct. This last device was used so indiscriminately that the results were sometimes ludicrous. In 1844, for example, a New York City election had a voter turnout of 55,000 people—even though there were only 41,000 qualified voters in the city.[39] Because of these kinds of abuses, stricter controls were enacted on voter registration and on campaign practices.

To complete the assault on boss-controlled politics, many states permitted *open primaries* in which voters did not have to prove their party affiliation in order to vote in a party's primary election. Through *cross filing*, California even went to the extreme of permitting candidates to run in the primary elections of both parties.

It was easier to get the reforms instituted in places like California, where the progressive movements had been able to gain temporary control over the state government. Thus states with strong progressive movements—states like Minnesota, Oregon, Wisconsin, and California—became the leaders in the reform movements to put the political machines out of business. Where reforms were put into effect, political machines often found themselves severely contained. Studies of the effect of cross filing and open primary elections in California concluded that these devices did indeed weaken the control of the party bosses.[40]

It is important to stress that the reform movements did not eliminate graft between politicians and special interests; graft is still rampant at all levels of American politics. What the reformers did accomplish, in most cities and metropolises, was to remove the old party machine from its highly influential brokerage position right in the middle of the exchanges between the politicians and special interests. The effects of this can clearly be seen when the politics of reformed cities are contrasted with those of unreformed cities. Wherever the reform movements went into effect, the *modus operandi* of party politics became completely different.

James Q. Wilson and Edward Banfield contrast a highly reformed city, Los Angeles, with a city in which few of these reforms took hold, Chicago. In Los Angeles, one finds nonpartisan primaries, the absence of party endorsements, a high ideological or issue content in the election campaigns, and the almost complete absence of machine politics. Races are wide-open contests that anyone can enter, and the quality of media advertisement is normally the key to victory. In Chicago, elections are based on wards. Although elections for city offices are nominally nonpartisan, each party in fact promotes its slate of candidates. In the dominant Democratic party, the key step in the nomination process occurs in the preprimary convocation of the Cook County Democratic Central Committee in one of the downtown hotels, where the party leaders choose the Democratic slate for the primary.[41] Especially during the reign of Mayor Richard J. Daley, this hand-picked slate seldom was upset in primary elections.

Restructuring City Government

At the same time that reformers sought to break the control of the bosses over the election process, they also sought to have the city itself administered competently on a politically neutral basis.[42] Specifically, they wanted to eliminate patronage as a basis for employing city government workers, and they wanted to eliminate partisan favoritism from the delivery of public services. They rejected the notion that garbage collection, or any other public service, could be performed any better by Democrats than by Republicans. If it were only garbage collectors who held patronage jobs, the reformers might not have worried much, for very few reformers wanted to become garbage collectors anyway. But they did want good schools for their children, and they resented any partisan interference in school administration or in the awarding of contracts to construct new schools. They were concerned about the connections between police departments and vice in the cities. They wanted parks and open spaces. They wanted honest systems of bidding for government contracts, and they wanted efficiency in general in city administration. In fact, they had a decided tendency to conceive of city government as a problem in administration that could be solved through improved organizational techniques rather than as a problem in politics that involved the balancing of competing interests. They assumed that administrative solutions could prevail in political situations. In the logic of the reformers, it thus defied rationality that garbage collection should be considered a political problem rather than an administrative problem. Theoretically, what mattered was that garbage be picked up and eliminated in the fastest, cheapest, and least inconvenient way possible.

These general features of the reformers' mentality and the faith in the superiority of administration over politics have become such generally accepted conventional wisdoms about the way city government ought to be administered that it is often difficult to image why anybody could have opposed them. But from the point of view of the machine politicians, patronage and political favoritism in the administration of public services were essential. Without patronage there would be very little reason for the party followers to do the party's campaign work. George Washington Plunkitt reserved his most bitter scorn for attempts to eliminate patronage. Civil service was "the curse of the nation," wrote Plunkitt. "Parties can't hold together if their workers don't get the offices when they win."[43] Nor, if patronage were eliminated, could the party bosses have enough control over the bureaucrats to ensure that the services got delivered where the bosses wanted them delivered—namely, in the neighborhoods of the party followers.[44] Political favoritism in the delivery of services was thus essential to provide rewards for the neighborhoods that supported the machines. Political favoritism was also essential as a means of raising campaign funds. For Mayor Bernard McFeely in Hoboken, New Jersey, to have removed politics from garbage collection would have been political idiocy. Garbage collection was a means of granting the city garbage collection monopoly to a trash firm he himself had organized just shortly after his election in 1925. It was also a means of getting kickbacks to finance his party's coffers. That McFeely was not averse to feathering his own nest is demonstrated by the fact that although his salary never exceeded $5000, he accumulated a fortune of $3 million by the time he was finally ousted from office in 1947.[45]

For McFeely and Plunkitt and the machines they represented, patronage and political favoritism were essential. In vain the political bosses argued that the reformers were themselves politically biased and that in their efforts to get control over the government they would only rob lower-class people of the jobs and welfare benefits that the machines gave them in exchange for their votes. Plunkitt, for example, argued that the civil service was a device to deny jobs to the Irish who were not as likely to have been educated and capable of answering the questions on the examinations.[46] Mayor Daley of Chicago once explained his devotion to the Democratic machine by stating simply, "The party permits ordinary people to get ahead. . . . Without the party, only the rich would be elected to office."[47] These were very private-regarding arguments, however, and in comparison to the public-regarding posture that could be adopted by the reformers, the political bosses made themselves look very venal and petty.

The programs of the reformers were articulated and promoted by several national and regional organizations. To work for the elimination of party-controlled patronage at all levels of government, a National Civil Service Reform League was established in 1877. A Municipal Voters' League was organize in Chicago in 1896 and a Bureau of Municipal Research was organized in New York in 1906. Similar organizations were established in dozens of other large cities across the country. These organizations drew their membership and financial support from reform-minded local business leaders.[48] A major development was the formation of the National Municipal League in 1894. The League drafted a model city charter in 1900 and disseminated books, pamphlets, and other reformist literature to local groups that were seeking ways to reform their own city governments. A major organ for expressing the league's reformist views was its journal, *National Civic Review*, which is still published.[49]

Strong and Weak Mayor Forms of Government   A key target for the reformers was the weak mayor form of city government, which was thought to be more susceptible to machine dominance than was a strong mayor form. Most machine-dominated cities had weak mayors.

The weak mayor form of government derived from the traditional American distrust of executive authority. Powers over the bureaucracy and budget were typically divided into several offices, many of which were elective and most of which had considerable patronage to dispense. This division of budgetmaking and policymaking powers into many hands made it extremely difficult for citizens to know which officers were responsible for what policies.[50] It also inhibited any coordinated policy control over city government services. But as long as there was no strongly felt need in cities for governments to perform many services, the weak mayor form of government functioned well.

As the city populations grew large, however, city governments came under considerable pressure to install water lines and sewers, grant franchises for power companies and transit lines, initiate public health inspections, and perform a variety of new services. In cities with political machines, the large number of elective offices fell under machine control, since the machine dominated the nomination and election machinery. But machine dominance did not necessarily lead to improved public policy, for the machines were normally much more interested in controlling the patronage and government contracts at the offices' disposal than they were in coordinating the policies of the offices.

The weak mayor form of government thus came under attack from several points of view. It hindered public accountability. It fostered the dominance of city government by machines. And it proved incapable of coordinating all public policies in the city. One proposed solution to these defects was to create a strong mayor who would not be subordinated to a political boss and who would be able to coordinate all the policies of city government departments.

The differences between the strong and weak mayor forms of government are illustrated in Figure 4-1. Under the strong mayor form, the mayor actually assumes authority over the administration of the city government, leaving to the council the responsibility for legislative functions. Since department heads are appointed by the mayor, they become more accountable to him or her. Through the mayor they are (theoretically, at least) accountable to the voters. The strong mayor form does not eliminate politics from city administration, but it does in theory limit the government fragmentation that was felt to be conducive to machine dominance.

The Council-Manager Plan of Government   The city manager plan of government was an attempt to obtain unified control over the city administration and at the same time to isolate city administration even further from political influence. All policy was to be established by the city council. Day-to-day operations were turned over to the city manager, who took care of the administrative details and stayed out of political questions.[51]

The city manager plan of government quickly became the most popular form of city government in the United States. As noted in Table 4-1, it was adopted by a majority of all cities in the 25,000–250,000 population range. The incidence of city manager government drops off sharply in cities of fewer than 25,000 because the cost of hiring a manager becomes prohibitive for very small communities. It begins dropping off in cities above 250,000 because the sheer size of such cities increases the number of conflicting interest groups concerned about city administration. City managers function best in cities where there is a broad consensus on local politics. As cities became larger, a broad consensus is difficult to achieve, because the number of interest groups tends to be considerable. Large cities also

Figure 4-1. Strong and Weak Mayor Forms of Government

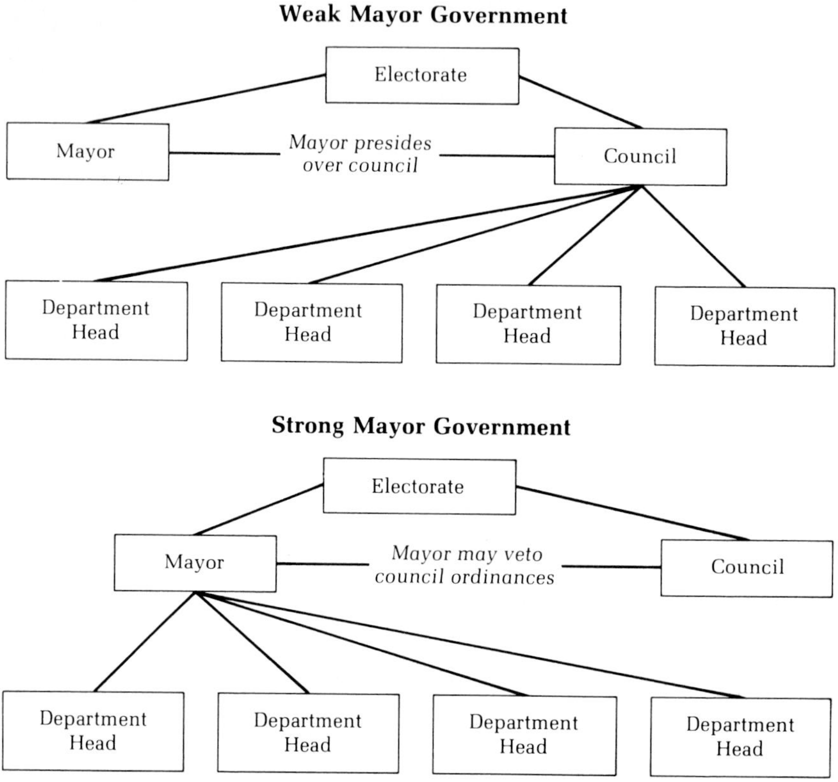

Weak Mayor Government

```
                    ┌──────────────┐
                    │  Electorate  │
                    └──────────────┘
    ┌─────────┐    Mayor presides    ┌──────────┐
    │  Mayor  │──── over council ────│ Council  │
    └─────────┘                      └──────────┘

┌────────────┐ ┌────────────┐ ┌────────────┐ ┌────────────┐
│ Department │ │ Department │ │ Department │ │ Department │
│    Head    │ │    Head    │ │    Head    │ │    Head    │
└────────────┘ └────────────┘ └────────────┘ └────────────┘
```

Strong Mayor Government

```
                    ┌──────────────┐
                    │  Electorate  │
                    └──────────────┘
    ┌─────────┐    Mayor may veto    ┌──────────┐
    │  Mayor  │── council ordinances ─│ Council  │
    └─────────┘                      └──────────┘

┌────────────┐ ┌────────────┐ ┌────────────┐ ┌────────────┐
│ Department │ │ Department │ │ Department │ │ Department │
│    Head    │ │    Head    │ │    Head    │ │    Head    │
└────────────┘ └────────────┘ └────────────┘ └────────────┘
```

tend to have more heterogeneous populations, which put conflicting demands on city government, especially if the council is elected from districts rather than at-large.[52] The largest cities with council-manager systems are Dallas and San Diego, and as their populations approach the million range both cities have seen the city manager system subjected to pressure. Some civic leaders in Dallas suggested a move to a strong mayor system,[53] and, as we will see in Chapter 7, the San Diego mayor's office was substantially strengthened in the 1970s (pp. 205–206). By contrast, in mid-sized cities and in cities where the ethnic and political composition of the population is relatively homogeneous, such as in many suburban cities, the city manager form of government is very popular.[54]

Political scientists have asked whether or not the city manager form of government has lived up to the claims of its supporters that it would remove politics from city government. If politics are defined as active participation in party affairs, one would have to answer, "Yes, city managers are nonpolitical" in this limited sense. They are highly professionalized and even have their own International City Management Association, which advises them to scrupulously avoid getting entangled in partisan affairs.

Table 4-1. Frequency of Local Government Forms

Population size	All cities	Form of government (number and percentage)			
		Mayor-council	Council-manager	Commission	Town meeting[a]
Over 1,000,000	6	6 (100%)	—	—	—
500,000 to 1,000,000	18	13 (72%)	5 (28%)	—	—
250,000 to 499,999	35	16 (46%)	17 (49%)	2 (5%)	—
25,000 to 249,999	1,069	382 (36%)	616 (58%)	45 (4)	26 (2%)
10,000 to 24,999	1,587	735 (46%)	673 (43%)	54 (4)	125 (8)
2,500 to 9,999	3,949	2,532 (64%)	1,045 (26%)	72 (2)	300 (8)
Total, all cities over 2500	6,664	3,684 (55%)	2,356 (35%)	173 (3)	451 (7)

[a] *Includes representative town meeting.*
Source: Adapted from International City Management Association, "Inside the Year Book," in *The Municipal Year Book 1988* (Washington, D.C.: International City Management Association, 1988), p. xiv. Used with permission.

If, however, the term "political activity" is more broadly defined as involvement in the process of making public policy, the city manager is very politicized. One study of city managers in Florida concluded that they exercise political leadership in three ways.[55] First, although the council is theoretically supposed to initiate policy and leave it up to the manager to carry it out, in fact the city manager is more often than not the one who initiates policy proposals to the council. Second, the council members and the citizens perceive the city manager as a political leader. The manager is well known among the leaders of the civic organizations, chambers of commerce, and service organizations in the city, and it is the manager as much as the city council to which these civic leaders look when they want a policy initiated or stopped. Third, successful city managers usually find it necessary to align themselves with the dominant factions on the city councils they serve. A study of city managers in California found that some were so aligned with factions of their councils that they even urged candidates to run for city council and participated discreetly in the resulting campaigns.[56]

Because they are appointed by the council, the managers serve only as long as a majority on each council supports them. If they either line up with a faction that is in control only temporarily or try to be too innovative as administrators, they often risk sudden dismissal. But dismissal or short tenure in office is not necessarily harmful to the manager's career. As a professional administrator, the manager is expected to lead the council in the direction of adopting innovative techniques of city governance. Aggressive leadership may bring about short tenure but may also lead to a series of short-term assignments to the more sought-after and prestigious manager cities.[57]

Because the manager career is highly professionalized, it serves as a mechanism for introducing cosmopolitan professionals into positions of local leadership. This has tended to break down the resistance of parochially oriented local governments to planning and to standardized administrative procedures. In the large cities, which (as shown in Table 4-1) tend not to have council-manager governments, many mayors have tried to avail themselves of the administrative expertise of the manager by hiring chief administrative officers (CAOs) or deputy administrators.

The Commission Form of Government   Another reform-style city government is the commission form. It was first developed in 1901 in Galveston, Texas, after a tidal wave inundated the city and killed 6000 people. Because the disaster was too great to permit the politics-as-usual conduct of government, a commission of three leading businessmen was established to run the city during the crisis. Their administration proved so popular that, after the crisis was over, Galveston adopted the commission form of government permanently.

The number of cities adopting commission government spread rapidly in the early twentieth century to about 500.[58] But commission government has not endured. As Table 4-1 shows, fewer than 200 cities use commission government today, and this figure includes only two cities with populations over 250,000 (Tulsa, Oklahoma, and Portland, Oregon).

A commission form of government uses the council members as administrators as well as legislators. As shown in Figure 4-2, each council member (commissioner) is elected directly by the voters, usually in an at-large election. In addition to being a legislator, the commissioner is also the head of a particular department of government. The commission format has proven ineffective either for running the government efficiently or for managing political conflict. Since the council members are also department heads, budget sessions frequently turn into logrolling sessions in which no overall capacity exists to budget for the city government as a whole. Coalitions form, as is normal on city councils, but council members who are left out of the coalitions find their departments left with smaller appropriations.

The Federal Government and the Decline of Machine-Style Politics

The federal government has stimulated the decline of machine politics in three ways. The first two stem from the federal reaction to the Great Depression of the 1930s, and the third stems from Supreme Court decisions.

The Great Depression was such a mammoth economic catastrophe that federal action to curb its effects was widely demanded. By the winter of 1932–1933, 25 percent of the national workforce was unemployed. Traditional forms of charity proved inadequate to cope with the immediate needs of the families of these workers. The urban political machines found themselves unable to cope with the problem, either. The magnitude of this economic depression had sharply reduced the revenues of municipal governments, and there were no surplus payroll funds that the machines could use to maintain their former high levels of patronage.* The

---

*This affected some machines more than others. In Chicago, the declining public revenues had very little detrimental effect on the machine's viability [Harold F. Gosnell, *Machine Politics: Chicago Model*, 2nd ed. (Chicago: University of Chicago Press, 1967), pp. 2–8].

Figure 4-2. Manager and Commission Forms of Government

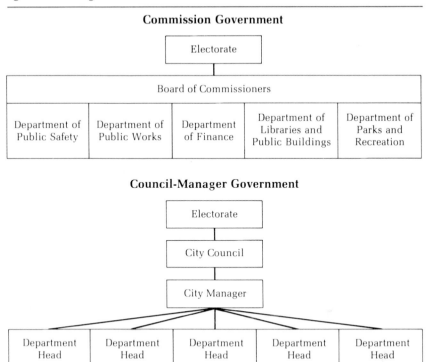

Commission Government

Electorate

Board of Commissioners

Department of Public Safety	Department of Public Works	Department of Finance	Department of Libraries and Public Buildings	Department of Parks and Recreation

Council-Manager Government

Electorate

City Council

City Manager

Department Head	Department Head	Department Head	Department Head	Department Head

machines no longer had the resources to donate food, clothing, or coal buckets on anything other than a piecemeal basis. When the federal government finally began to act in an extensive way to cope with the Depression, two aspects of its actions had a detrimental effect on the political machines.

First, the New Deal administration of President Franklin D. Roosevelt instituted a form of individual public assistance that bypassed the political machines. For workers who were dismissed from their jobs, unemployment compensation was initiated. For workers who were injured on the job, worker's compensation was begun. For mothers who were widowed or who had been deserted by their husbands, Aid For Dependent Children programs were established. As a supplement to pension plans, the Social Security Act was passed. Other welfare programs were established for the blind, the aged, and the disabled.

Two key features of all these programs made the recipients independent of the political machines. First, the recipients had a *legal right* to their assistance. They did not in effect have to buy the assistance by voting for the machine's candidates or by doing precinct work during the campaigns. Second, the assistance came *directly* to the recipients, usually through the mail in the form of a check. There was nothing that the ward leaders could do to increase the value of the checks being sent to supporters of the party or to decrease the value of the checks being sent to supporters of the opposition.* One net effect of the Great Depression and the New Deal, then, was to diminish the welfare functions the political machines had previously performed. This deprived the party bosses of some of the material incentives they had implemented to maintain party discipline.

A second general effect of the New Deal came from the rapidly expanding role of the federal government in urban areas. To support bankrupt cities, the federal government began making grants and loans directly to cities in order to finance public improvements such as water supply systems, sewage systems, hospitals, and other public works. Increasingly, however, federal programs were carried out not by city governments but by agencies especially created to handle particular services. The Federal Housing Act of 1937, for example, enabled federal housing projects to be administered not through city governments but through quasi-public corporations called *housing authorities*.

Political scientist Morton Grodzins has identified several separate channels through which federal aid was directed to urban areas. In addition to the aid channeled directly to city governments, some aid went directly to individuals (e.g., Old Age and Survivor's Insurance). Some aid was channeled through the states (e.g., highway programs). And a considerable amount of federal aid was channeled through specially created local governments called *special districts*, which were relatively independent of state or city governments. Much aid for conservation programs was of this type.[59] Because a substantial portion of federal aid was channeled into urban areas through special districts and quasi-public corporations, the federal government compounded the historic tendency in American government to fragment governmental authority.[60]

The impact of these proliferating government programs was to create new systems of material incentives that were increasingly beyond the control of the old-style machine. As the most dynamic functions of urban government came under the control of new agencies, the expansion of the machines was severely limited. Among the central cities of the West, machines are very seldom found. The functions traditionally associated with them are now performed by other agencies and there is no need for new machines to be created.

A third way in which the federal government affected machines was through federal court decisions. The most important of these were rulings that sharply restricted the ability of the party in power to fire workers for patronage reasons.[61] Less directly related to machines is the courts' tendency over the past fifty years to uphold federal laws that preempt local authority. For example, in 1982 the Supreme Court denied cities the power to grant monopolies in the awarding of such public franchises as cable television contracts.[62] By sharply restricting local authority, the Court has restricted the powers of political machines.

---

*The ward leaders were not left completely without influence, however. They could still give advice to welfare recipients on their welfare rights and benefits. And they could still try to intercede on behalf of the recipient with the welfare agencies [William F. Whyte, *Street Corner Society* (Chicago: University of Chicago Press: 1970), pp. 196–197].

Impact of Metropolitan Growth on the Political Machines

In addition to the political reform movements and the proliferation of federal programs, the decline of machine politics was also hastened by the basic demographic and technological forces described earlier in Chapter 2. The dual migration, the westward drift of the population, the decline in dominance of the Northeast, the encirclement of the central city by suburbs, and the shift of urban growth from the central city to the suburbs all made it impossible for the political machines to expand their influence.

The dual-migration movements were detrimental to machine politics because the political machines never succeeded in absorbing the new urban minorities as they had the European immigrants. In fact, the new minorities were often perceived as threats to the perquisites of persons who had worked their way up in the party. Even where the minorities were brought into the machine's operations, as in the case of the black community under William Dawson's leadership in Chicago, the machine was powerless to promote the social reforms so desperately needed in the black wards.[63] Instead, it promoted highly visible construction activity in freeways, rapid transit, airports, convention halls, a university campus, and downtown office buildings that would give the city a progressive image, please the business sector, provide jobs for white construction workers, and open up enormous sources of graft to fill the party's coffers. Very few of the benefits of this activity went to improve the collective status of the black or Hispanic minority populations in Chicago.

The westward drift of the population and the rise of urban centers in the West are also relevant to the decline of machine politics. In the Southwest, the most dynamic area of urban growth today, the elements that had facilitated machine politics were much less strong than they had been in the Northeast and the Midwest. The machines' reinforcing social institutions, in particular, were much weaker. Labor unions were not traditionally strong in the Southwest. Although ethnic communities developed in the West,[64] they seldom dominated local politics. Furthermore, many western cities developed their basic political form after the antimachine reform movements had begun to take effect. The major exception to this is San Francisco. There the ethnic base of politics has remained very strong, but the political machine has disappeared.[65]* Particularly important in the Southwest and especially in California was the fact that newspapers and television became much more effective campaigning tools than the political parties. For all of these reasons, the general westward drift of urbanization out of the northeast quadrant meant that the old machine politics would not be able to expand along with the vanguard of urbanization. It would become a sectional phenomenon limited for the most part to the central cities of the older metropolitan areas.

Even within the Northeast, the demographic and technological forces were detrimental to the survival of the machine as an adequate governing force. Metropoli-

*It is likely that ethnic-based political activity will increase in other southwestern cities as Hispanic and Asian political participation increases.

tanization had brought a monumental increase in scale in the urbanization process,[66] turning the northeastern seacoast into a megalopolis of 40 million people. Most of the population increase occurred in the suburbs, which were not controlled by the central-city machines. Even within the central cities there was an increasing tendency to bypass the parties as much as possible when it came to accomplishing concrete objectives such as urban renewal.

The Impact and Bias of the Machines' Decline

The above-mentioned developments themselves did not necessarily destroy the old political machines. Machines in Jersey City and Chicago, for example, continued to thrive despite the existence of a formally nonpartisan ballot. And the McFeely machine in Hoboken was able to thrive under the commission form of government. Furthermore, where ethnically based politics were deeply ingrained, the passage of antimachine reforms did not necessarily change voting behavior. With party labels removed, the ethnic identification of candidates assumed even greater importance.[67]

If individual political reforms did not necessarily destroy the old machines or the ethnic basis to politics, then what difference did they make? Did the reform movement make any difference at all in urban politics? There has been considerable empirical research on various aspects of these questions, and the conclusions on the reform movement tend to fall into five general lines of thought. (1) Reform movements have prospered more in certain kinds of cities than in others. (2) Individual reforms have a class bias and a partisan bias. (3) In cities where all the reforms occurred, their sum total has weakened the machines. (4) The reforms have led to an increased rather than a diminished fragmentation in city government. (5) The reforms have resulted in a lessened accountability of political leaders to the electorate.

Reform-Style Governments: Their Success in Certain Kinds of Cities

If one distinguishes between a reform-style government and a nonreform-style government, some clear differences can be discovered between the kinds of cities that have reform-style government and those that do not. A city government may be considered reform style to the extent that it has adopted the major structural innovations of the political reform movement—nonpartisanship, at-large elections, and council-manager form of government. Such governments are least likely to be found in cities with heavy concentrations of European ethnics. John H. Kessel found that the fewer foreign-born residents a city had, the more likely it was to have a city-manager form of government.[68] Other demographic relationships were found. The faster the growth rate of a city, the more likely it was to have a city-manager form of government. The more highly educated its population, the more likely it was to have reform-style government. When cities were ranked in terms of their major economic functions, there was an increasing reliance on the city-manager form as cities' economic bases became less dependent on the manufacturing, transportation, and economic bases associated with the old, historic, industrial city. The fewer Catholics a city had, the more likely it was to have reform-style government. And, finally, another study found that reform-style governments were more prevalent in the West than they were in the East.[69] From this, one can conclude that nonreform-style city government is most likely to be found in central cities, in the East, in cities with high percentages of ethnic concentrations, in slowly growing cities, and in older, industrial cities. Conversely, reform-style city government is most likely to be found in suburban cities, in the West, in cities with low percentages of ethnic concentrations, in fast-growing cities, and in newer, nonindustrially-based cities.[70]

The Class Bias of Political Reforms

Class Bias of Nonpartisan Elections

There is considerable empirical evidence that nonpartisan and at-large elections are biased to the extent that they reduce the city council representation of lower-income people and racial minorities.[71] A study in Des Moines concluded that nonpartisanship in that city reduced voter turnout among lower-income people and thus gave "upper-income groups relatively greater power in the local community."[72] Albert Karnig and B. Oliver Walter's study of city elections compared turnout in three different time periods (1935–1937, 1962, and 1975) and found that turnout in nonpartisan cities ranged from 5.4 to 11.7 percent lower than in partisan cities.[73] Some other, less obviously class-oriented consequences have been identified with nonpartisanship. Nonpartisanship gives advantages to incumbents in local elections,[74] reduces voting turnout among Democrats more than among Republicans, and usually (but not always) favors Republican candidates over Democratic candidates in local elections.[75]

Other reform devices can also reduce voter turnout. Karnig and Walter's above-mentioned study of city elections found that turnout was 8.6 to 11.9 percent lower in council-manager cities than in cities without that reform.[76] There is also some evidence that separation of local elections from national elections is biased against people of lower social status. A study in Toledo, Ohio, found that voter turnout was lower for the local election than for the national election and that it was primarily the people of lower socioeconomic status who did not turn out. The net result was to give the middle and upper classes a greater electoral voice in city affairs than they would have had if local elections were held at the same time as national elections.[77]

The Class Bias of At-Large Elections

If the majority of evidence indicates that nonpartisan elections are biased against lower-income persons, the evidence is even stronger that at-large elections have that same class bias. Timothy Bledsoe and Susan Welch, who surveyed 975 city council members from all cities of 50,000 or more in 1982, found that those from at-large cities had significantly higher incomes and educational attainments than did those in district cities.[78] And Carol Cassell's study of all cities over 2500 in population found that at-large cities had council members from markedly higher-prestige occupations than did the district cities.[79]

In short, the extremely popular reformist device of at-large elections has had a definite class bias against the representation of lower-status residents of cities and their neighborhoods. Would switching back to district elections reverse this bias? Not necessarily, say Peggy Heilig and Robert Mundt, who examined 11 cities that did just that between 1961 and 1977. Although representation from low-income neighborhoods increased when the cities adopted district elections, there was no corresponding decrease in the social status of city council members. The representation of business people declined, but they were not replaced by low-income blue-collar workers. Rather they were replaced by professionals such as lawyers, teachers, or doctors.[80] In other words, people from low-income neighborhoods tended to vote for candidates having a higher social status than themselves.

Another interesting question about the biases of at-large elections is whether it makes any difference in the electability of female candidates for local office. Most research on this question has concluded that at-large elections have little impact on the success of women in local elections; and women might even do slightly better in at-large elections.[81] A study of San Jose, California, however, where women attained a 7–4 majority on the city council in 1980, concluded that the women could not have won their majority if the city had not switched from at-large to district elections that year. The five women first elected in 1980 all said that they would not have run for the office if they had had to run citywide, which would have made the election much more costly and time-consuming. The new women council members had been very active at the neighborhood level and this gave them a bigger advantage in district elections than it would have in citywide elections.[82]

A final important question about the biases of at-large elections is their impact on the electability of blacks and Hispanics to local office. This question has been the subject of many important Supreme Court cases and considerable empirical research, to be examined in detail in Chapter 5. At this point it is necessary to say only that, with very few exceptions, most of this research concludes that black representation is reduced by at-large elections.

Class Bias in Policies Adopted by Reformed Governments

Up to this point we have seen that reformed governments have a class bias on the *input side* of the political system, in that reformed governments underrepresent the lower classes in city government. The studies do not, however, address themselves to the question of whether the *policy outcomes* of reformed governments are equally biased against the lower classes. An early attempt to answer that question was the analysis of 200 cities of 50,000 or more population by Robert L. Lineberry and Edmund P. Fowler.[83] They found that reformed cities spend less and tax less than do nonreformed cities. The reformed cities are also less responsive to sharp racial, ethnic, and socioeconomic divisions in the electorate. These are important findings, for they confirm some of the expectations of both the early reformers and the political bosses. Recall that many political reforms had been supported by businesspeople who hoped that the reformed governments would hold down both expenditures and taxes. In contrast, the bosses had opposed the reforms because they would diminish the political voice of the lower classes (i.e., patronage).

Lineberry and Fowler do not assert that political reformism is the only variable affecting policy outcomes in cities. Rather they conclude that policy outcomes are a consequence of three interrelated sets of variables: socioeconomic cleavages (e.g., ethnic or racial differences), political variables (party registration, levels of voter turnout, etc.), and political institutions (form of government, type of elections, and types of constituencies).

These conclusions of Lineberry and Fowler are partially supported by Terry N. Clark's study of fifty-one cities of between 50,000 and 750,000 population.[84] Clark found that general government expenditures on noncontroversial issues were likely to be higher in cities with decentralized decision-making structures and nonreform-style government. On controversial issues, such as the initial stages of urban renewal, the more centralized and reformed governments had the higher expenditures. The stronger correlation with high government expenditures, however, was not a political variable. Rather it was the size of the city's Catholic population. The higher the percentage of Catholics, the higher the level of expenditures.[85]

More recent research, however, has begun to question those conclusions. David R. Morgan and John P. Pelissero traced taxing and spending patterns in twenty-three cities over an eleven-year period. Twelve cities experienced a change in government structure within this period, while eleven cities kept the same structure throughout. The authors concluded that the changes in government structure had "almost no impact on changes in taxing and spending levels."[86] Nor do most people's satisfaction with or sense of access to local government appear to be greatly affected by whether they live in a reformed or nonreformed city. A survey of 1007 residents in 50 southern cities found the overwhelming majority of blacks and low-income whites to be satisfied with their local government, regardless of whether they lived in district or at-large cities. However, those living in district cities were slightly more likely to have had contacts with their council members.[87]

Another way of looking at the output side of government is the orientation of city council members. Some have a policy orientation of focusing their efforts on overall city policies. Others have a service orientation of helping to improve the delivery of city services to residents. Bledsoe and Welch's survey of 975 city council members from all cities of 50,000 or more in 1982 found that council members from district cities were much more inclined to a service orientation than were those from at-large cities.[88] Council members from district cities are also much more likely than those from at-large cities to play the ombudsman role of handling constituent complaints about city government and city services.[89]

Summary of Class Biases of Reformed Politics

In summary, reform-style politics tends to reduce voter turnout. It underrepresents lower-income neighborhoods in city councils. It tends to result in city councils that are less service-oriented than are councils in nonreformed cities. The most extensive analyses done to date find that reformed cities are also more conservative fiscally (in taxing and spending) than are nonreformed cities. But some recent studies on smaller groups of cities suggest that structure may not really affect taxing or spending policies.

Machine Politics Weakened by Reforms

Although there is no evidence to indicate that the enactment of any one specific reform drove any particular machine out of business, it is clear that when all or most of the reforms were put into effect at once, the political machines found it very difficult to operate. Even when machine politicians did get elected in reformed cities, they found it very difficult to govern. As more city jobs came under civil service protection, fewer workers felt compelled to make campaign contributions or to become precinct workers. Improved auditing procedures and a muckraking press made the "honest graft" of George Washington Plunkitt much more difficult to manipulate. Changes in government policies toward organized labor also increased the problems of the machines. The federal protection given to labor unions after the passage of the Wagner Act in 1935 created a new force that had to be taken into account in the calculus of urban political leaders. The emergence of militant public employees' unions in the 1960s, and the increase in the number of teachers, police officers, garbage collectors, and other civil servants who were willing to paralyze the city's operations through strikes if need be in order to make their demands heard, made the old-style, face-to-face, intimate-exchange politics extremely difficult to keep up. By midcentury, New York had 50,000 organized school employees plus 26,000 police officers and 13,000 firefighters who were unionized.[90] The size and magnitude of city bureaucracies, freed by civil service from dependence on the machines for jobs and organized by the public employees' unions to seek their own group interests, hampered the old-style personal politics.

Fragmentation Increased by Reform

Reform-style government tended to increase rather than decrease the fragmentation of urban political power. From the 1930s to the mid-1970s, urban services expanded unrelentingly. Welfare services were greatly expanded. Increasing numbers of public hospitals were built. More and more urban areas began purchasing private transit systems and operating them publicly. Public employment offices were established. Airports had to be built to handle the rapid growth of airlines and then rebuilt to accommodate the jetliners. With the passage of the United States Housing Act in 1949, cities were able to tear down dilapidated buildings in blighted neighborhoods and could try to replace them with housing and redevelopment projects.

One extremely important fact is that very few of these newly created services were turned over to the traditional city governments. Expanded welfare and hospital services became the province of the county governments. When privately owned transit systems were sold to the public, the general pattern was to create a metropolitan district to operate them. Usually airports were also operated by metropolitan districts. Public employment offices were usually run by the states or the federal government. Housing authorities that administered the urban renewal programs often were appointed by the city councils, but they operated under very rigid federal guidelines, and in few cities did they serve as an arm of the city government. Central-business-district redevelopment plans were usually initiated by businesspeople who had a stake in the survival of the downtown business district. Funds for redevelopment usually came from federal urban renewal programs or from private investors, and the major actions required of city councils were often limited to making the appropriate zoning changes and setting up bond referendums when they were needed.

One of the most popular agencies for performing new governmental functions has been the special district. A special district is an autonomous government created to perform a specific service. The number of special districts in metropolitan areas has increased regularly since the 1930s. Because special districts are autonomous and relatively free from control by central-city governments, their proliferation has necessarily increased the fragmentation of governing authority in urban areas.[91]

Public Accountability Decreased by Reform

A last consequence of the political reform movements was to reduce the accountability of the public officials to the electorate. Again, as in the fragmentation of local government authority, this was a result that the reformers had not counted on: The reformers had not intended to reduce government accountability, but a decrease in accountability did result from the reform measures.

Charles Adrian has asserted that nonpartisan elections prevent the groups that control the government from being held collectively accountable to the voters.[92] And Robert Wood has argued that nonpartisanship is based on some very faulty assumptions about the ability of individuals to determine who in government is responsible for what policies: "Inescapably, there is a belief that the individual can and should arrive at his political convictions untutored and unled; an expectation that in the formal process of election and decision making a consensus will emerge through the process of right reason and by higher call to the common good."[93]

Furthermore, as authority shifted increasingly from the hands of the elected officials into the hands of the large public bureaucracies, it became exceedingly difficult for the elected officials to control the bureaucrats. The doctrine that policymaking should be separated from policy implementation further served to insulate the bureaucracies from accountability to elected officials. When bureaucrats did not want to suffer the interference of elected officials on some controversial action, they could insist that the action dealt with policy implementation rather than policymaking and consequently was not subject to scrutiny by the elected officials. As the public bureaucracies became more and more insulated, they began to develop into functional fiefdoms. The implications of this will be discussed in Chapter 7.

As these changes took place in city politics, they significantly affected the fortunes of blacks, Hispanics, American Indians, Asians, and other minorities who were growing to sizable numbers in many American cities. This will be examined in the next chapter.

Summary

1. Although political machines have declined in recent years, we still see elements of machine politics, especially in the creation of new forms of material incentives to replace old-style patronage.

2. A prime motive of the early twentieth-century progressive reformers was to drive the political bosses and the political machines out of business. The reform movements were started by upper-class and professional persons who reacted negatively to the dominance of city politics by the lower-class immigrants and their political machines.

3. The programs of the political reformers to end the dominance of the machines were many: direct primaries, nonpartisan elections, at-large elections, separation of local elections from national elections, and others. In addition to reforming the electoral structure, the reformers also sought to alter the forms of city government itself. They particularly opposed the weak mayor system of government and particularly favored the council-manager form and the commission form.

4. In addition to the progressive reform movement, the federal government also contributed to the decline of the political machines. The expansion of federal welfare and assistance programs made poor people less dependent on the political machines for governmental assistance. Federal programs also led to an expansion of governmental services in urban areas. But the new services were often turned over to special districts and specialized agencies that were not under the direct control of the old-style machines.

5. Metropolitan growth has also contributed to the decline of machines. Machine politics have not fared well in the suburbs or in the South and West, where the most dramatic urban growth has occurred since the 1940s.

6. Several biases were attributed to the progressive reform movements. First, the political reforms were most likely to take place in suburban cities, in the West, in cities with low percentages of ethnic populations, in fast-growing cities, and in newer, nonindustrially-based cities. The political reforms generally worked to the disadvantage of the lower-income groups and the racial minorities while

increasing the access of the upper- and middle-income groups. The reforms helped weaken the political machines, helped fragment government, and helped decrease the accountability of urban governments to the residents of urban areas.

Part III
Politics in the Contemporary City

Although the contemporary city has inherited much of its political structure and style from the older American city discussed in Part II, today's city also differs in many important respects from the historical American city. In contrast to the European immigrants who predominated in the older city, today's most visible urban minorities are blacks, Hispanics, American Indians, other racial and cultural minorities, and poor whites. The most important question facing the American city in the last two decades of the twentieth century is whether the city today is still a place of opportunity for the upward mobility of its poorest residents and its most recent in-migrants. Chapter 5 examines this question by focusing on the changing impact that the racial and Hispanic minorities are having on city politics. Chapter 6 analyzes the fiscal and economic environment that affects how much upward mobility central cities can offer.

Chapter 7 focuses on the contest for dominance in central cities. Theories of community power and the fragmentation of power into functionally organized fiefdoms are examined. Centralized political leadership, if it is to exist, often becomes the task of the central–city mayor. To meet their responsibilities, mayors need both the objective resources for authority plus a leadership style that is appropriate for their time and place.

One major problem facing mayors and other urban executives in the 1990s is ensuring the delivery of a wide variety of public services in an environment of scarce resources. Chapter 8 reviews the rising demands in the 1990s for improving productivity in urban services delivery, the governmental structures for delivering public services, and some managerial techniques that urban administrators use to improve productivity. Finally, the chapter examines the patterns of bias in public service delivery.

Chapter 5
The City as
a Place of Opportunity:
The Politics of Racial
and Social Change

In earlier chapters it was argued that American cities played a historic role as a place of economic opportunity for poor migrants. From the mid-nineteenth to the mid-twentieth century, European immigrants and their offspring used the city as a starting place for jobs, business opportunities, education, political influence, and upward social mobility. Many European ethnics, of course, did not rise up the social ladder. Many returned to Europe. Many died in squalor at an early age. Some turned to anarchism in rebellion against a system they saw as hopeless. And in most cases, it took three or four generations to achieve middle-class status. Nevertheless, most of today's grandchildren and great-grandchildren of yesterday's Irish, Polish, Russian, Italian, and other European immigrants enjoy a better position on the social ladder than their ancestors did.[1]

As Chapter 2 described, few of today's urban poor are recently arrived migrants from Europe. Rather they are predominantly blacks who have migrated from the rural South since World War II, Hispanics from Mexico, Central America, and the Caribbean, American Indians from the western reservations, poor whites from economically deteriorating rural regions such as Appalachia, and Asian refugees from strife-ridden places such as Vietnam, Cambodia, and Laos. In the final decade of the twentieth century, is the American city still a place of opportunity for its poorest residents and its most recent in-migrants?

This chapter addresses that question by focusing on the largest of these urban groups—the blacks and Hispanics. How have their current political positions evolved out of historical circumstances? What institutions have they developed for exercising leadership in their urban communities? What themes underlie their politics in the 1980s? Are their political situations today analogous to those of the European ethnics discussed in Chapter 3? And what prospects for upward mobility are offered them through the political arena in the 1980s and 1990s?

Blacks and Urban Politics

The most dramatic social change in American cities in the last 40 years has been the great in-migration of blacks and Hispanics. As Figure 5-1 shows, fewer than half of all blacks lived in urban places in 1940; today more than four out of five blacks live in urban places.

Figure 5-1. Urban Percentage of the Black Population: 1910–1980

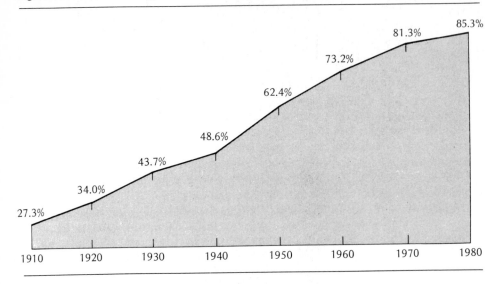

As this massive migration from rural areas to cities occurred, it tended to focus on large industrial cities which, during the 1940s and 1950s, seemed to offer the greatest job opportunities for an unskilled labor force coming off farms. Table 5-1 shows that in 1980 almost one-third of all black Americans lived in only fourteen cities, those containing 200,000 or more blacks. Eight of these cities were located in the Northeast or Midwest, five in the states of the old Civil War Confederacy, and one in California. The white population has already become a minority in six of these cities and seems well on its way to becoming a minority in most if not all of the others.

Not only are most urban blacks concentrated in a relatively small number of large cities, but historically those cities themselves have been highly segregated. Although recent studies have shown a slight decrease in residential segregation,[2] the levels of segregation are still quite high. Karl Taeuber calculated a segregation index (see the box on p. 116) for 28 cities with black populations of over 100,000. Although the average level of segregation for the 28 cities decreased during the 1970s, the index reading still stood at 81 in 1980. A similar trend appears to exist for metropolitan areas as well as for central cities. One study found an eight percent decrease in metropolitan segregation between 1960 and 1970.[3]

The most marked recent change from historical patterns has been a growth in black suburbanization. The number of blacks living in suburbs increased by nearly 50 percent in the 1970s.[4] By 1980 about one-fourth of all blacks lived in suburbs, and they accounted for 6.1 percent of the suburban population. This black suburbanization did not signal a big decrease in segregation, however. Most of black suburbanization took place in suburbs adjacent to black neighborhoods in big central cities,[5] and most blacks continue to live in segregated central-city neighborhoods.

Table 5-1. Cities with Large Black Populations

City	Size of black population (200,000 or more blacks)	Percentage of city's population	Black mayors
**New York	1,784,337	25.2	
*Chicago	1,197,000	39.8	Harold Washington (1983–1987)
			Eugene Sawyer (1987–)
*Detroit	758,939	63.1	Coleman Young (1974-)
Philadelphia	638,878	37.8	W. Wilson Goode (1983–)
**Los Angeles	505,210	17.0	Thomas Bradley (1973–)
*Washington, D.C.	448,906	70.3	Walter Washington (1967–1979)
			Marion Barry (1979–)
**Houston	440,346	27.6	
*Baltimore	431,151	54.8	Kurt Smoke (1987–)
*New Orleans	308,149	55.3	Ernest Morial (1978–1986)
			Sydney Bartholemy (1986–)
**Memphis	307,702	47.6	
*Atlanta	283,050	66.6	Maynard Jackson (1975–1982)
			Andrew Young (1982–)
Dallas	265,594	29.4	
Cleveland	251,347	43.8	Carl Stokes (1967–1971)
**St. Louis	206,386	45.6	

*Black and Hispanic populations are a majority of the city's population.
**Black and Hispanic populations exceed 45 percent of the city's population.
Source: U.S. Bureau of the Census, Statistical Abstract of the United States: 1987 (Washington, D.C.: U.S. Government Printing Office, 1986), pp. 31–33.

These patterns could clearly be seen in Florida, where an analysis of black metropolitan residential locations in 1970 and 1980 revealed several interesting facts. First, the number of blacks living in blocks that were 80 percent black dropped substantially between 1970 and 1980. Second, despite a decline in this measure of segregation, very few blacks had moved into white neighborhoods far removed from black neighborhoods. Instead, black residents gradually moved into white neighborhoods adjacent to the black areas. Third, the only cities to witness substantial movement of blacks into neighborhoods far removed from the black areas were university cities such as Gainesville and Tallahassee. Finally, when middle-class blacks sought to move out of black neighborhoods rather than moving to older established white neighborhoods, they tended to move to the expanding edge of the urbanized area where population growth was occurring and newer homes were being built.[6] In short, housing segregation appears to have ameliorated somewhat in the 1970s, but not greatly.

The continuing segregation of most blacks has many negative consequences. Concentrating hundreds of thousands of poor people into small sections of the city only compounds the severe social problems of trying to hold families together and provide an environment conducive to the educational development of children. It has also kept blacks physically removed from the most dynamic areas of the

Most and Least Segregated Big Cities

Most segregated				Least segregated			
City	Segreation index 1980	1970	Change	City	Segretation index 1980	1970	Change
Chicago, IL	92	93	−1	Nashville, TN	80	90	−10
Cleveland, OH	91	90	+1	Milwaukee, WI	80	88	−8
St. Louis, MO	90	90	0	Boston, MA	80	84	−4
Philadelphia, PA	88	84	+4	Richmond, VA	79	91	−12
Atlanta, GA	86	92	−6	Washington, DC	79	79	0
Baltimore, MD	86	89	−3	Cincinnati, OH	79	84	−5
Birmingham, AL	85	92	−7	New Orleans, LA	76	84	−8
Memphis, TN	85	92	−7	Newark, NJ	76	76	0
Dallas, TX	83	96	−13	Columbus, OH	75	86	−11
Indianapolis, IN	83	90	−7	New York, NY	75	77	−2
Pittsburgh, PA	83	86	−3	Detroit, MI	73	82	−9
Jacksonville, FL	82	94	−12	Gary, IN	68	84	−16
Houston, TX	81	93	−12	Oakland, CA	59	70	−21
Los Angeles, CA	81	90	−9				
				Average for all 28 cities	81	87	−6

The index ranges from 0–100. If every block in a city were either 100 percent black or 100 percent nonblack, that city would have an index score of 100, indicating that it was completely segregated. A completely desegregated city would be one in which the black-non-black population of every block was found in the same percentage proportion as the black-nonblack population of the entire city; its index score would be 0.

Source: Karl Taeuber, *Racial Residential Segregation, 28 Cities, 1970–1980*, Center for Demography and Ecology, University of Wisconsin-Madison. Working Paper 83-12, March 1983. Reprinted by permission of the author.

metropolis—the suburbs—where job opportunities are growing the fastest. The segregation of urban blacks into central-city neighborhoods, however, eventually came to be a source of political strength, for it facilitated political activities that had been more difficult when blacks were spread throughout the rural South. With the instruction of the federal government's Community Action Program, the spontaneous outburst of hundreds of civil disturbances, and the demand for black power in the 1960s, the effect was to mobilize black political forces in ways that had not been possible earlier.[7] Especially critical were the Civil Rights Act of 1964 and the Voting Rights Act of 1965. To understand urban black politics in the 1980s, it is necessary to understand these laws and the events that led to them.

The Civil Rights Movement

The major impetus for black political organization during the first half of the twentieth century was civil rights. Although the Civil War and the Thirteenth Amendment ended slavery, most blacks were trapped for the next 100 years in a degrading and violent segregation system. In southern states, segregation statutes prohibited blacks from marrying whites, eating in the same restaurants as whites, sitting in the same sections on buses, trains, or in theaters, using the same restrooms, drinking from the same fountains, going to the same schools, and even being buried in the same cemeteries. Voting was restricted to only a handful of blacks, and during the early part of the twentieth century, black officeholders virtually disappeared. For blacks who rebelled or tried to assert some civil rights there was always the threat of economic sanction such as being fired from a job. And there was often the threat of lynching and mob violence.

Although segregation was most pronounced in the South, it was not limited to that region. Kansas and Delaware, for example, had segregated schools. In many nonsouthern cities the schools were segregated in practice, since blacks were concentrated in their own neighborhoods, even though there may have been no segregation ordinances. And many, if not most, nonsouthern communities permitted restaurants, hotels, and other public accommodations to practice blatant racial discrimination.

Accompanying this political, psychological, and social oppression was extensive discrimination in the workplace. This job discrimination eased during the two world wars, when labor was in short supply and blacks were deliberately enticed from the rural South to take factory jobs in cities. Also, during the labor strife of the 1930s, some employers hired blacks as strike breakers even though the blacks seldom realized that these job offers were simply to break the unions and would be withdrawn as soon as the strikes were over.

In the face of this oppression and manipulation, early black leadership split into two factions. The first, under the leadership of Booker T. Washington, stressed black economic improvement and downplayed political activity or civil rights agitation. Washington's philosophy was best articulated in a speech at the Atlanta Exposition in 1895 when he called on blacks to improve themselves individually and integrate individually into the larger society rather than agitate for political and civil rights.[8]

In opposition to Booker T. Washington, W. E. B. Du Bois and others started the Niagara Movement in 1905 to press for political and civil rights. Although the Niagara Movement quickly died, its ideals were soon picked up in 1909 by a new organization, the National Association for the Advancement of Colored People (NAACP). The NAACP eventually became the largest and one of the most successful of the black civil rights organizations. Particularly effective was the NAACP/Legal Defense Fund, which financed and fought court battles to get segregation statutes overturned.[9] Its most significant victory was the Supreme Court's ruling in *Brown v. Board of Education*[10] (1954), which struck down state laws that required public school segregation. Other early black civil rights organizations were the National Urban League (1910) and the Congress of Racial Equality (CORE), founded in 1942.

Although the NAACP originally began as a radical organization, it had become much more moderate by the 1960s. Indeed, its commitment to judicial strategies was very time-consuming, and many blacks sought to speed up the move toward civil rights. A turning point in this process can be traced to an afternoon in 1955 when a black woman, Rosa Parks, refused to give up a seat in a white section of a bus in Montgomery, Alabama, and was jailed as a result. The Montgomery black community, led by Baptist minister Martin Luther King, Jr., staged a very effective bus boycott and at the same time sued in the federal courts to get the bus segregation policy overturned. By winning that suit, the Montgomery leaders showed dramatically that legal tactics could successfully combine with direct action tactics such as boycotts. The next few years saw the creation of two new organizations devoted to direct action tactics—the Southern Christian Leadership Conference (SCLC) under King's direction, and the Student Non-Violent Coordinating Committee (SNCC). These organizations systematically organized civil disobedience tactics. Typically they would get a group of people to violate segregation statutes (for example, by having blacks and whites sit down together to eat at a segregated lunch counter) and get themselves arrested. They appealed their convictions in the federal courts, but the appeals route was a slow, tortuous process, which often required going as high as the United States Supreme Court. And there was never any certainty that one's conviction would be overturned.

Even if the conviction were overturned, the process often took years; one might have completed an entire jail sentence for having violated the segregation ordinance by the time the final ruling came down. Equally as important as the legal battle was the media attention given these direct confrontations and protests. National television exposed the brutality of segregation and helped mold public support for civil rights. These efforts came to a climax in the Civil Rights Act of 1964, which outlawed discrimination in public accommodations such as motels, restaurants, or theaters. The key provisions of this act are outlined in the accompanying box.

Key Provisions of the 1964 Civil Rights Act

Public Accommodations
Prohibited discrimination in public accommodations.

Desegregation of Government Facilities
Authorized the Justice Department to initiate suits to desegregate facilities owned or managed by state or local governments.

School Desegregation
Authorized the Justice Department to initiate suits to desegregate public schools and colleges.
Authorized the Office of Education to give technical and financial aid to school districts in the process of desegregation.

Civil Rights Commission
Strengthened the Commission's role to investigate civil rights complaints.

Federally Funded Programs
Prohibited racial discrimination in programs that receive federal funds.

Equal Employment Opportunity
Prohibited private-sector employers from discrimination in employment on the basis of race, religion, sex, or national origin.

Voting Rights
Strengthened the role of the federal courts and the Attorney General in dealing with violations of voting rights.

Black Power and Racial Violence

Despite the historic achievements of the civil rights movement, by the mid-1960s black leadership was facing a crisis. After the passage of the Civil Rights Act of 1964 and the Voting Rights Act of 1965, white support for the black movement seemed to wither, and the most prominent civil rights leader, Martin Luther King, Jr., was assassinated in 1968. Furthermore, although the passage of civil rights laws gave middle-class blacks access to public accommodations such as restaurants and motels, it provided no immediate improvement in the depressed economic conditions of the overwhelming majority of blacks. New leaders began to question whether blacks could ever hope to enter the mainstream of American society. Some argued that the black community was an internal colony within American society. The dominant institutions operating within the urban ghettos (banks, schools, stores, apartment buildings) were run by white outsiders who took the money generated by these institutions out of the ghetto.[11] A study of Chicago found that black-owned and black-run institutions were dependent on and inferior to the dominant white institutions.[12] If the black ghetto was indeed a colony within American society, this cast doubt on whether blacks could ever hope to integrate individually into the mainstream of American society. Perhaps their only route was to rebel against the colonizing society and declare their independence. This train of thought led some black leaders during the 1960s to turn to black nationalism as a solution to black problems. The intellectual debate was reminiscent of W. E. B. Du Bois's arguments 60 years earlier against the individual integration philosophy of Booker T. Washington.

Perhaps the most dynamic new leader until his assassination in 1965 was Malcolm X, a successful recruiter and spokesperson for the Nation of Islam (Black Muslims). Where the civil rights leaders had worked primarily with a middle-class black clientele, Malcolm X appealed directly to poor blacks. His rejection of American patriotism in favor of black nationalism brought him into direct conflict with the mainstream of American liberalism, which had been a long-time source of support for civil rights movements.[13]

Other developments in the 1960s also led toward a politics of confrontation. Stokely Carmichael made a speech in 1966 calling for "black power."[14] A Black Panther party organized in Oakland, California, in 1966 and began preparing itself for violent confrontation with the police. In Chicago, a police squad assaulted the city's Black Panther headquarters and killed several Black Panther leaders.

The most startling change in black politics during the mid-1960s, however, resulted from the urban riots. In city after city during those years, each spring and summer saw black people looting stores in their neighborhoods, burning buildings, and engaging in confrontations with the police. Between 1964 and 1968 at least 220 people were killed, over 8300 injured, and more than 52,000 arrested.[15] In the single month following the assassination of Martin Luther King, Jr., in 1968, riots broke out in 172 cities and 27,000 people were arrested.[16]

There has never been a consensus on why the riots of the 1960s occurred or on what their consequences were. After the very destructive Watts riot in Los Angeles in 1965, the governor of California appointed the McCone Commission to investigate it, and the McCone Commission blamed the Watts riot on a few troublemakers in the black community.[17] As riots broke out in other cities, however, and literally hundreds of thousands of black people participated in them, it became apparent that much more was involved than simply the instigation of a few troublemakers. One alternative explanation was that the rioting was a black reaction to the oppression of racism in American society.[18] Another viewpoint was that the riots constituted an act of political rebellion, an attempt to break out of the colonial bonds that held blacks in subjugation to the white community.[19]

Joe R. Feagin and Harlan Hahn surveyed the research on urban rioting during the 1960s and pointed to two recurring background factors. First, cities with large black populations were more likely to have riots than cities with small black populations, and their riots tended to be more serious. Second, Feagin and Hahn traced a growing acceptance of collective violence by blacks during the 1960s as a legitimate means to achieve their goals in a political system whose conventional political channels were unresponsive.[20]

In addition to underlying background factors, a precipitating set of events is needed to trigger a riot. The most common triggering event during the ghetto riots of the 1960s was some action on the part of the police—shooting a black teenager, treating someone roughly, or engaging in some other perceived brutalities. The National Advisory Commission on Civil Disorders studied several riot cities in 1967 and found that more than 60 percent of the major and serious riots were precipitated by police actions.[21] Rumors about the incident would spread rapidly, a crowd would gather to discuss it, and violence would begin. Further police action would fail to contain the violence and National Guard reinforcements would be called in to maintain the peace. These circumstances created an adversary situation. The police and the National Guard acted much like an occupying army. Community leaders would try unsuccessfully to gain control of the scene. Moderate leaders often came out on the streets urging people to get back to their homes. Militant leaders often mingled on the streets but made no effort to discourage people from looting stores or engaging in other riot activities.

If there was no consensus on the causes of the riots, neither was it clear whether the riots benefited the black community. One study found that the Watts riot brought an immediate influx of federal poverty funds into Los Angeles.[22] However, businesses were leaving. (In Watts, for example, it was not until 1985, 20 years after the riot, that the neighborhood got another full-service supermarket.[23]) City governments reacted politically by pouring money into police services that could maintain order rather than by pouring new money into social services to meet the grievances of black residents. This was attributed by one scholar to a negative white backlash against the black community.[24]

Since the 1960s there had been very few serious incidents of ghetto mob violence until the outbreak of a major riot in Miami, Florida, in May 1980. The circumstances surrounding the Miami riot were strikingly similar to those surrounding the riots of the 1960s. Background factors of high black unemployment and smoldering resentments prevailed. While these grievances went unattended, Miami blacks apparently resented the special help being given to over 100,000 Cuban refugees pouring into the city in the spring of 1980. Many blacks looked on these refugees as competitors for scarce jobs. The spark that ignited the riot involved the local police. Six months earlier a black insurance salesman had been brutally beaten to death while in the custody of a team of white police officers. Despite trial testimony of eyewitnesses about the beating, an all-white jury acquitted the four white officers charged with the killing. The riot erupted the day that the jury's decision was announced. When the riot ended three days later, 18 persons were dead and another 400 were injured. In December, 1982, another Miami black neighborhood rioted following the fatal police shooting of a black youth in a videogame arcade.[25]

Black Power and the Politics of Advancement

Although there is little agreement on the causes of the riots or on their ultimate consequences, it is clear that they were a major dividing line in black urban history. If black politics before the decade of urban rioting were characterized by a unified struggle for civil rights and an end to segregation, black politics since 1970 have broadened their focus to many other concerns. The great civil rights organizations NAACP and the NAACP/Legal Defense Fund were beset by internal strife,[26] while CORE and the Southern Christian Leadership Conference (SCLC) lost much of their earlier dynamism. The torch of black leadership went in many directions after 1970 as blacks gained representation in most sectors of the mainstream of American life and the American economy. In terms of urban politics, in contrast with the fundamental struggles of the civil rights movement, urban black political leaders now focus on the more commonplace tasks of getting representation on city councils, getting black mayors elected, increasing job and economic opportunities, trying to reverse the deterioration of the city, and trying to target the city's resources more directly at the social problems of its minority populations.

The events of the 1960s had set the stage for significant electoral success in the 1970s. Removing the legal restrictions on black voting (such as poll taxes, white primaries, literacy tests, and other forms of discrimination), and especially the federal government's enforcement of the 1965 Voting Rights Act (see accompanying box), led to a massive increase in the black electorate, which in turn led to a dramatic increase in the number of elected black officials. Whereas only 1469 elected black officials could be identified in 1970, the number had increased to over 6000 by 1985.[27] There are today nearly 200 elected black mayors, although 70 percent of these are in small communities of less than 5000 people. Nevertheless, as Table 5-1 shows, by the mid-1980s black mayors headed numerous major cities.

Implementing the Voting Rights Act

All of the provisions of the Voting Rights Act were controversial, but the most enduring controversy surrounded the Section 5 prior-approval (or pre-clearance) requirement, which prohibited nine states and portions of thirteen other states from making any changes in election laws or municipal boundaries without prior

Key Provisions of the 1965 Voting Rights Act

Voting Examiners

Authorized the Justice Department to appoint voting examiners who could register people to vote in counties or municipalities that (1) had used a literacy test in determining voter registration for the 1964 presidential election or (2) had a voter turnout of less than 50 percent of the voting-age population in the 1964 presidential election.

Literacy Tests

Authorized the Justice Department to suspend literacy tests if it was found that they had the effect of discriminating.

Prior-Approval Requirement

In political subdivisions in which federal voting examiners had been appointed, no change in voting laws, voter qualification laws, or municipal boundaries could be approved without prior approval of either the Justice Department or a three-judge federal court in Washington, D.C.

Enforcement Machinery

Provided authority to the Attorney General and the Civil Service Commission to enforce the act. Provided fines and imprisonment for convictions of violating the act.

---

federal approval. This provision was due to expire after five years, but it was renewed several times after repeated attempts to water it down. In 1982 it was renewed for a 25-year period to expire in 2007. It now covers language minorities as well as racial minorities.

What makes the Section 5 prior-approval requirement so important, from the black perspective, is that it prevents the deliberate alteration of election laws, boundaries, and systems of representation to negate the impact of black voters. In the 1950s the City of Tuskegee, Alabama, for example, had changed the shape of its boundaries from a square to a 28-sided polygon for the specific purpose of keeping enough blacks outside the city boundaries to ensure white control of the city council. Although the Supreme Court struck that act down as blatantly unconstitutional,[28] many blacks feared that less blatant manipulations would be put into force without the prior-approval requirement.

The techniques most likely to dilute black voting influence were probably annexation and at-large elections. Annexation is felt to reduce black influence when a city annexes suburban white residents and thereby decreases the black portion of the city's electorate. At-large elections, it is charged, enable the white majority to minimize if not prevent black representation on the city council. As an example, one midwestern city had a ward system of elections in which the black ward repeatedly elected a very militant council member who was disliked by the rest of the council. To get around this member, the city changed to an election system in which each ward nominated two members for its city council seat, and they competed against each other in a citywide at-large election. Under this system the black ward nominated the militant black council member as its first choice and a more moderate black as the second choice. But in the citywide runoff at-large, the moderate was elected and the first-choice, more militant black was unseated.[29]

Whether this was an atypical result of electoral changes or whether at-large elections do in fact systematically discriminate against racial minorities has been subjected to considerable research. One study of 16 New Jersey cities found that black representation was not seriously hampered by nonpartisan elections, at-large elections, or reform-style government.[30] This conclusion was supported by some broader studies that attempted to assess the impact of at-large elections throughout broader regions.[31] Particularly in cities with minority populations that are too small or too scattered to dominate a single ward, the at-large system might well be more conducive to getting minorities elected. And one study found that the switch from at-large to ward elections did not significantly improve black representation.[32] Most systematic studies, however, have come to the opposite conclusion. Albert Karnig's study of black representation and reformism on a national scale, for example, found that the district system of representation definitely made it easier for blacks to get a fair number of council members than did at-large representation.[33] A number of other studies that focused on cities of different sizes have tended to support Karnig's conclusions. For example, a study of Texas cities that switched from at-large to ward systems found that minorities increased their representation after the switch.[34] And a highly sophisticated statistical examination (called multiple regression) of the impact of several variables, such as form of representation, socioeconomic development, and percent of the population minority, discovered that these other variables affected black representation much less than did the factor of at-large versus ward representation. The ward system consistently gave the blacks more representation than the at-large system.[35]

With the preponderance of research showing that annexation and at-large elections dilute black voting strength, it is not surprising that numerous prior-approval-requirement cases have been brought to the federal courts. On annexation cases, the Supreme Court has not consistently struck down annexation as violating the Voting Rights Act. The Court allowed Richmond, Virginia, to annex a large suburban area, thereby reducing blacks from a majority to 42 percent of the city's electorate. The mitigating factors here were that the annexation could be justified on economic grounds of increasing the city's tax base and the fact that the expanded city adopted a nine-ward city council that assured blacks a majority in four wards.[36] (Blacks in 1977 won control of the fifth ward as well, giving them a majority in the council.) Although the Supreme Court approved Richmond's suburban annexation, the Department of Justice in 1979 disallowed an annexation in Houston, Texas, which would have diluted the black and Hispanic percentage of the city population by only a few percentage points.[37] In this case, however, it is not clear what constituted the best interests of those minorities. On the one hand, annexation would have slightly diluted their share of the city population; but on the other hand, the motive of the proposed annexation was not racial deprivation but increasing the city's tax base, and that clearly would have benefited the minorities.

In dealing with at-large versus ward elections, the Supreme Court has shown a tendency to follow three patterns. First, it tends to reject attempts to move from ward to at-large elections. Second, however, it has tended not to strike down existing at-large systems even if they do have a discriminatory effect unless there has been a past history of deliberately using the system to deprive minorities of their right to vote. That was the precedent established in a case involving Mobile, Alabama, which has had a three-member, at-large commission since 1911. By the 1970s blacks accounted for 40 percent of Mobile's voters, but they had never elected a city council member. They charged that the at-large system denied them representation and asked the Court to force Mobile to adopt a ward election system. The Supreme Court refused to do so, however,[38] on the grounds that the system had not been established with the intent of diluting black votes. The third tendency has emerged in instances when at-large cities sought to make some other change that brought them under federal court jurisdiction; the federal courts have tended to force such cities to modify their at-large elections to guarantee representation for minorities. Thus when Port Arthur, Texas, sought to annex a suburban white community, the Supreme Court forced it to adopt a plurality vote rule that would give blacks (35 percent of the population) a fair chance to win two city council seats.[39] The largest cities forced to modify their at-large systems were Houston and Dallas. In these instances, the Department of Justice pressured the two cities into setting up in their at-large systems some wards that would guarantee representation for blacks and Hispanics.[40] And the nation's three largest cities (New York, Los Angeles, and Chicago), even though they already had ward systems, were forced to redraw the ward boundaries in order to give better representation to Hispanics.

With the assistance of the Voting Rights Act, blacks have been able to turn their numbers and their political resources into tangible victories at the polls. But is this political success making any substantial strides toward improving the living standards of black people? It was argued in Chapter 3 that control over city politics was one channel used by some European ethnic groups to provide economic advancement for their members. Does this opportunity still exist for more recent urban minorities in the 1990s? As blacks gain elective office and political influence in city governments, can they translate that influence into economic opportunities for their constituents?

Black Power and Machine-Style Politics

These tremendous electoral successes of blacks after the Voting Rights Act naturally raise the question of whether a revitalized Democratic party organization operating in a mode somewhat akin to the old machine-style politics might not be resurrected to promote black advancement. If black mayors, so the argument goes, could use their public office to create a mechanism for controlling nominations, influencing hiring practices, and helping to channel contracts to black businesses, they could also help improve the overall living conditions of black people in their cities.

Blacks, of course, are no strangers to political power or to machine-style politics. In New York City, black congressman Adam Clayton Powell vocally championed black causes from his position of congressional influence. In Memphis, the Crump machine made use of black voters at a time when blacks were generally disenfranchised in the rest of the South.[41] But in most cities, the white-dominated political machines minimized the political influence of blacks.[42]

Perhaps nowhere was this seen more clearly than in the influence of the black machine put together by William Dawson of Chicago from the 1930s to the 1960s. Dawson was Republican alderman on the city council during the mid-1930s but switched allegiance to the Democratic party in 1939. In return for delivering thousands of black votes for the machine candidates, Dawson was given control over substantial patronage and other material benefits that he could dispense in the black community. His ability to deliver the black wards was a substantial factor in the legendary Richard J. Daley's first mayoral victories. But because Dawson and his black machine were subordinate to the citywide machine, he did not use his power to attack the underlying social problems such as housing, employment, health, and education that blacks faced in that city.[43] In the years between Dawson's death in 1970 and the election of Chicago's black mayor Harold Washington in 1983, the Chicago machine became even less responsive to the concerns of Chicago blacks. Led by Mayor Daley (1955–1976), the machine attempted to dump black Congressman Ralph Metcalf after Metcalf criticized the city's police department. That attempt was rejected by black voters, however. After Daley died, the machine refused to replace him with the city council president pro tem, a black man, despite the feeling of many city blacks that as holder of that office he should have gotten the nod. In subsequent years, the machine rejected the bids of blacks to be appointed to police superintendent and superintendent of schools. Many blacks felt snubbed by these developments[44] as black voting support for the machine declined in the 1970s. Black voting power was finally crystallized by black leader Harold Washington, who won the mayor's post in 1983 and was reelected in 1987,[45] becoming the dominant force in the city's politics when his faction gained a majority on the city council in 1987. Only a few months after gaining this important dominance, however, Washington died of a heart attack.

The big question for the 1990s is whether Harold Washington's successors can keep the dominance he achieved over the machine and turn it into an instrument for advancing the economic conditions of Chicago's black population. Steven P. Erie argues that machine politics is likely to hinder black advancement rather than advance it. He points out that even in the case of the most successful example of ethnic-controlled machine politics (the Irish), the benefits of machine politics were vastly overstated and he suggests that more Irish would have achieved middle-class status much earlier if they had not relied on machine politics. Because of the extensive welfare system today and affirmative action programs in the public sector, blacks already get more benefits from the public sector than the Irish ever did.[46] From this point of view, reliance on the machine is more likely to hold blacks back and keep them in low-status welfare positions and public-sector jobs than it is to promote significant numbers of them to the middle class.

In one sense, however, this is a bogus argument, because there probably is little likelihood that other cities will turn to the machine-style politics as practiced in Chicago, and even in Chicago the machine is not likely to recapture the patronage levels, control over nominations, and political influence that it held during Mayor Daley's heyday. What is likely is that black mayors will use their influence over hiring practices, disbursement of city government contracts, affirmative action programs, political appointments, and political nominations to promote the interests of their constituents. This style probably will not be called "machine politics," but it will nevertheless contain some of the elements of machine-style politics that we examined in Chapter 4.

Furthermore, there already is evidence that black mayors who have operated in this mode have indeed brought some benefits to the black community. Peter Eisinger examined six large cities with black mayors and concluded that those mayors enjoyed considerable success at expanding public-sector opportunities for blacks during the 1970s.[47] Perhaps the most successful tactic for expanding public-sector opportunities was the aggressive pursuit of affirmative action policies. In five of the six cities, a black was named to head the city personnel office, and this resulted in substantial increases in black employees on the city payroll. In Atlanta and Detroit, this increase in black employees occurred despite the fact that overall city employment was declining. Affirmative action was also used to award city contracts to minority businesses. Atlanta mayor Maynard Jackson encouraged joint ventures that would enable small black firms to bid jointly with larger companies. Detroit mayor Coleman Young started a policy of preferential bidding in which city firms were preferred over firms from outside the city that were less likely to hire blacks. Newark mayor Kenneth Gibson set aside 25 percent of all federal public works funds for minority contractors. The net impact of these strategies, according to Eisinger's research, was substantial improvement in black city employment and black firms doing business with the city. In Detroit, for example, the black share of city administrators nearly doubled from about 12.1 percent in 1973 to 23.5 percent in 1977, and the black share of professional employment increased from 22.8 to 41.1 percent. The percentage of blacks on Detroit's police force increased sixfold from 5 percent in 1967 to 30 percent in 1978.

Eisinger's findings on the policy impact of black mayors were buttressed by Albert Karnig's and Susan Welch's statistical analysis of policy impacts of black mayors in all cities of 50,000 or more population. Welch and Karnig found that cities with black mayors had significantly higher expenditures for welfare services and significantly lower expenditures for parks, libraries, and fire protection. Additionally, black-mayor cities raised more money generally than did nonblack-mayor cities and they gained these additional revenues in part by importing a greater share of federal aid.[48] These data should not be interpreted to mean that the mere presence of a black mayor will substantially reduce the economic misery that prevails in most black communities, but it does suggest that black mayors in cities with large black populations may have a better opportunity than white mayors to alleviate that misery somewhat at the margins.

Black Power and Black Mayors

Although we have argued here that some of the elements of machine-style politics (hiring influence, awarding of contracts, influence over nominations, political appointments) can be very useful for black mayors in their quest to improve economic conditions among their black constituents, most mayors do not have a political machine at their disposal. For this reason we need to examine black power and black mayors a little more generally. Let us examine first the limits that black mayors face.

Limits on Black Mayors

Is it possible for black mayors to govern when they are elected in racially polarized elections, when they get so few votes from whites, and when they may not command a majority of the city council? Even if they can govern, can they give special attention to the social problems of their black constituencies?

The answer to these questions may well depend on (1) black mayors being extremely adept at balancing their need to respond to black constituents with their need to gain support among white political leaders and (2) the willingness of white political leaders to cooperate with them. In the case of Cleveland's Carl Stokes, neither condition seems to have been present. Stokes was elected mayor of Cleveland in 1967 and reelected in 1969, the first black person elected to head any major American city. Although he sought to be mayor of all the people of Cleveland, Edmond Keller states that "his primary commitment was to the black community."[49] In his first term, he added 5200 public housing units, which more than doubled the former existing number. This put him at odds with the white-dominated city council, and when he envisioned a series of low-income housing projects spread throughout the city, he was strongly opposed not only by the city council but by a majority of whites and many middle-class blacks as well.[50] In his second term, Stokes sought to improve the city's tax base by raising the city income tax and ending the city's sharing taxes with suburbs. This would have enabled property taxes to be lowered while still raising an additional $26 million for the city. The council opposed this plan and submitted its own tax proposal to the voters. Faced with these two competing proposals, the voters polarized, with black precincts favoring Stokes's plan and white precincts opposing both plans. When both plans were rejected by the voters, the city was forced to lay off some city workers and reduce some public services. Edmond Keller writes that this episode left Stokes's image severely tarnished. He was branded as incompetent and would have had a difficult time restoring the white community's confidence in him even if he had tried.[51] To Stokes's credit, he created a strong political organization in Cleveland's black community that dominated several diverse local elections and gave the black community an influential voice in the city's government. But after Stokes declined to run for reelection in 1971, the black organization splintered.[52]

It is not certain whether Stokes's problem was peculiar to Cleveland or whether it is a general problem faced by all black mayors. They are faced with high expectations from the black community that might not be attainable.[53] In some cities the resources might not exist, and it might be impossible to overcome political opposition. Like their white counterparts, black mayors often find that city government and the mayor in particular have very weak authority to cope with the social problems of black constituents.[54] Additionally, because black migrations of the 1940s through the 1960s moved disproportionately into the industrial cities of the Northeast and Midwest, cities that end up with black mayors are likely to be cities in economic decline. Even under the best of cirumstances, controlling the city government is only one of many factors in society that affect the economic status of blacks. Control over city government will not eliminate racial prejudice. Furthermore, the overwhelming majority of economic opportunities are in the private and not the public sector, and control over city government will have only limited influence on the employment patterns of private companies.

For all these reasons, there are many limits on the ability of black mayors to use their new power to promote the economic advancement of their black constituents.

A Dual Strategy for Black Mayors

Despite these constraints, the situation for black mayors also has many possibilities for success. Peter Eisinger has suggested that black mayors can successfully follow a dual strategy for improving the economic status of their black constituents.[55] The first part of the dual strategy is to stimulate economic development that will increase job opportunities for blacks in the private sector. The second part of the dual strategy is to expand black opportunities in the public sector.

The private-sector strategy of promoting economic growth in the city so that jobs will be created for black workers means getting big corporations to invest in substantial redevelopment—usually downtown. This approach has been followed with substantial results in Detroit, Los Angeles, Newark, and Atlanta, as well as in many cities not run by black mayors. However necessary this strategy might be to produce jobs in the private sector, it has many political consequences for the black mayors who follow it. It forecloses alliances of the mayor with lower-income whites, working-class whites, or middle-class whites.[56] If the mayor aligns lower-income black constituents with poor whites, that might produce a class-based politics that would alienate business interests and discourage them from investing in the city. Indeed, V.O. Key argued many years ago that the imposition of the segregation system in the South in the 1880s was partly a reaction to Populist attempts to unite black and white lower-class voters against the dominating upper-class elites.[57] The strategy of downtown development also minimizes alliance with working- and middle-class whites, since they will be competing directly with the blacks for the jobs to be created. And it does not seem to leave any meaningful role for middle-class whites to play in city politics. The strategy also puts black mayors constantly under fire in the black community for "selling out" to the white power structure. Thus, Eisinger maintains, the black entrepreneurial mayors spend considerable time reassuring their black constituents that they have not sold out.[58]

If they want to expand private-sector economic opportunities, however, the black mayors may have little choice but to ally with the downtown business community. Downtown redevelopment generates many construction jobs during the development phase and also attracts many white-collar service jobs as the new facilities go into operation. Whether this economic development strategy will actually do much to promote black economic advancement, however, is open to question. We will examine this question in Chapter 6.

The second strategy for black mayors is to expand opportunities for blacks in the public sector through aggressive use of affirmative action policies, by channeling city government contracts to black businesses and businesses that hire black workers, and by installing a substantial number of black political appointees who can function as gatekeepers to bring more blacks into city government employment. As Peter Eisinger's research suggests (see above, p. 126), these tactics can have considerable success in expanding employment opportunities for black residents of cities.

To make a broader test of whether black mayors could significantly improve public employment of their black constituents, Eisinger later examined the factors governing black municipal employment in 43 cities whose populations were 10 percent or more black.[59] He found that black employment was only slightly affected by social and demographic variables such as the city's size, whether the city was growing or declining, whether the black population was well educated or not, and whether public employment was expanding or not. The key variables were the size of the black population and whether the city had a black mayor. The larger a black population is, the more it constitutes a potential voting bloc able to compete successfully for city jobs. Black mayors have a greater impact on appointments of blacks to professional and administrative positions than on the general city government workforce. Because these appointed administrators become "gatekeepers" with the power to hire in their departments, they are able to use their position to ease the entry of blacks into the city bureaucracy. Strong mayors like Detroit's, of course, are able to use the strategy more successfully than weak mayors, since they have more administrative appointments to make. This strategy also is more likely to bear fruit in economically healthy cities whose governments are not under fiscal pressure to cut back on their public services.[60]

In support of Eisinger's contention that control over city government can help secure black economic advancement is a study of ten northern California cities. This study used the term "incorporation" to reflect the extent to which blacks and Hispanics exercised influence in those cities. Controlling the mayor and city council, of course, is the maximum incorporation. The findings of this study were stark. The more that the black community was incorporated into a city's politics, the more it was able to do for black residents. The greater the incorporation, the more responsive the city became to black protest demands, the more effectively black neighborhoods were able to block unwanted changes, the greater the representation of blacks on advisory commissions, the greater the social services in black neighborhoods (although those were sharply limited by available funds), and the greater the share of city government contracting awarded to minority businesses.[61]

To summarize all the preceding considerations, can black political power be used to make the city a place of opportunity for blacks? The answer to that question seems to depend in great measure on the peculiar circumstances of the city, the quality of the black leadership, and the ability of whites to cooperate. Carl Stokes's experience in Cleveland illustrates the constraints on black mayors. But the experience of black mayors such as Coleman Young in Detroit and Maynard Jackson in Atlanta suggests that many of these constraints can be overcome. The mayors overcame the constraints by pursuing dual strategies of encouraging private-sector economic development and promoting public-sector opportunities for blacks. If the short-term measure of mayoral success is the ability to get reelected, these mayors were very successful, since they and most black mayors succeeded at reelection at least once. The long-term measure of success is whether the economic development strategies will transform the economic misery that pervades most of the urban underclass of blacks and other low-income residents of central cities.

Black Power and the Black Urban Underclass

Unfortunately, the dramatic improvement in black political power over the last three decades has not been matched by similar improvements in living standards of the black lower class. Despite the increased number of jobs for black workers and the opening up of professional-level positions for middle-class blacks, living conditions for substantial numbers of blacks have in some respects deteriorated. In 1965 Daniel P. Moynihan drew a disturbing picture of the toll that decades of segregation and racial oppression had taken on the average black family up to that time. (This was the famous *Moynihan Report*.[62]) Moynihan charged that the family deterioration was evident in the high levels of broken marriages, births outside of marriage, dependency on welfare, and the number of families headed by women. At the time it was issued, the report was bitterly criticized as racist.[63] But in the years that have passed since then, the situation has only deteriorated further. In 1965, one-fourth of all black births occurred outside of marriage; by 1980 this figure had risen to 50 percent. The percentage of black families headed by a woman rose from 25 to 41 percent. Acts of violence in black neighborhoods increased, and welfare dependency got worse.[64] And where blacks are concentrated in big-city public housing projects, life sometimes comes close to fitting Thomas Hobbes' description of life in a state of nature as nasty, brutish, and short. One of the largest public housing projects is Chicago's Cabrini Green. In the first 9 weeks of 1981, the residents of Cabrini Green witnessed 10 murders, 35 gunshot wounds, and random sniping.[65]

In short, what has grown around us since the mid-1960s has been a double dual society. The first dual society is the one warned about in the Kerner Commission Report on the urban riots of the 1960s—a separate and unequal society of affluent, suburbanized whites separated by dozens of social and economic barriers from the impoverished black underclass of the central cities.[66] A second dual society has grown within the black community itself. The black working class and middle class has gained measurably in economic and political stature from civil rights legislation and from their own initiatives. But few of these benefits have trickled down to the huge, impoverished black underclass that has settled into the bleakest neighborhoods of American cities and threatens to become a permanent fixture on our social landscape.

The situation of this improverished underclass would no doubt be worse if the black community had not achieved political influence, because in that case there would be even fewer jobs and fewer opportunities. And because of the nature of the separate and unequal society that has emerged in urban America, leaders of the black community are necessarily very limited in what they can do for their underclass constituents. But in the last analysis, the achievements of the current generation of black leaders will probably be measured by how much they are able to do to reduce the size of the black underclass and alleviate the poor living conditions of poverty-striken blacks by increasing the number of available jobs while reducing crime rates, school dropout rates, and family deterioration rates.

Fourth-Wave Immigrants and Urban Politics

As discussed in Chapter 2, Hispanics and Asians constitute a fourth historical wave of migrants into American cities. There are today about 18.8 million Hispanics and over 4 million Asians in the United States, and over eighty percent of all legal immigrants today come from Latin America, Asia, or the western Pacific area. Are these fourth-wave urban immigrants in danger of being added to the urban underclass? Are they likely to follow the paths of ethnic succession and upward social mobility traced by the European ethnics? Or are they following a pattern different from the European ethnics or the blacks?

Hispanics and Urban Politics

The 18.8 million Hispanics in the United States account for about seven percent of the total American population. As Table 5-2 shows, the three largest Hispanic groups in America are Puerto Ricans, Cubans, and Mexican-Americans. Although Hispanics are found throughout the United States, they are concentrated most heavily in the Southwest, New York, Florida, and Illinois. The Southwest has relatively few Cubans or Puerto Ricans. It is heavily Mexican-American, although it also has sizable concentrations of people from Central and South America as well. Florida's Hispanic population is dominated by Cubans and to a lesser extent by people from Central and South America. Illinois is unique in that it is the only state where large numbers of both Mexican-Americans and Puerto Ricans reside (mostly in Chicago). If all these different groups are counted as one, Hispanics are the fastest-growing ethnic group in America. At present growth rates, they could easily outnumber blacks and become the nation's largest minority within twenty years.[67]

In one respect it makes sense to consider all these diverse peoples together as Hispanics, since they all speak the same mother tongue, Spanish. But in other key respects the groups are very different. Racially, for instance, Mexican-Americans tend to be of Spanish-Indian backgrounds, while most Cubans and Puerto Ricans are of caucasian or black African descent or some mixture thereof. In Puerto Rico's Spanish history, color differences had a meaning much different from that in the United States, and this has provoked powerful emotional reactions in some Puerto Ricans who have been required to make this adjustment.[68] Reasons for entering the mainland United States also differ for each group. Most Mexican-American immigrants seek economic opportunity, while most Cubans are political refugees from the Castro regime. Puerto Ricans are United States citizens free to travel back and

Table 5-2. Hispanic Peoples in the United States

A. Distribution by nationality group: 1987

Country of origin	Number	Percent
Mexico	11,762,000	62.6
Puerto Rico	2,284,000	12.2
Cuba	1,017,000	5.4
Central and South America	2,139,000	11.4
Other Hispanic origin	1,588,000	8.5
	18,790,000	100.0%

B. Distribution by geographic region in the United States: 1980

State or region	Number	Percentage of that region's population
New York state	1,659,000	9.5
Five southwestern states	8,788,000	19.6
(California)	(4,544,000)	(19.2)
(Texas)	(2,986,000)	(20.9)
(Arizona, New Mexico, Colorado)	(1,258,000)	(18.2)
Florida	858,000	8.8
Illinois	636,000	5.6
Remainder of the United States	2,668,000	1.9
	14,609,000	

C. Rate or urbanization: 1980

Nationality group	Percentage living in: SMSAs	Central cities
Mexican-Americans	79.3	43.4
Puerto Ricans	94.5	74.7
Cubans	96.7	39.5
All Hispanic peoples	83.5	48.2
Non-Hispanic peoples	65.9	25.3

Source: U.S. Bureau of the Census, *Current Population Reports,* "The Hispanic Population in the United States: March 1986 and 1987, Advance Report," Series P-20, no. 416 (Washington, D.C.: U.S. Bureau of the Census, August, 1987), p. 5. *1980 Census of Population*, Vol. I, Chapter B (PC80-1-B).

forth between Puerto Rico and the mainland. For this reason, the Puerto Rican community is free of the illegal-alien problems that plague other Hispanic communities. Finally, there are also important political differences among these groups. Cubans, as we will see, tend as a group to be much more politically conservative than Puerto Ricans or Mexican-Americans.

Because the space limitations of this text make it impossible to do justice to all the nuances and divisions of Hispanic America, we will focus here on the largest Hispanic-American group, the Mexican-Americans, and take a short look at the Cubans, because their experience is so distinctive.

The Political Legacy of Mexican-American History

As a result of the Mexican-American War of 1846, about 75,000 Mexicans living in the newly annexed territories that are now California, Arizona, and New Mexico suddenly became Americans.[69] Although the Mexicans numerically dominated this territory before 1846, they were soon outnumbered by "Anglos" attracted to the West by the California gold rush, the completion of the transcontinental railroad, the Army's pacification of the West, and the hope of economic prosperity. In Texas, Americans had begun settling while that area was still under Mexican domination. When they achieved sufficient numbers, they proclaimed Texas's independence of Mexico and in 1845 were annexed to the United States. The history of Mexican-Americans has left a threefold legacy for the 1990s: deprivation, oppression, and cultural nationalism.

That the Mexican-Americans as well as most Spanish-speaking Americans are economically deprived is well documented. As shown in Table 5-3, Mexican-Americans and other Hispanics lag far behind the non-Spanish population on all the major socioeconomic indicators. They are only about half as likely to have finished high school, about one-fourth as likely to have completed college, and almost half more likely to be employed as service workers or farm laborers. The Mexican-American's median family income is barely three-fourths that of non-

Table 5-3. Economic Status of Hispanic Americans

Characteristic	Mexican-American	Puerto Rican	Cuban	Hispanic total	Non-Hispanic speaking total
Education (1987)					
Percentage who completed 4 years of high school (among those 25 years old or older)	44.8	53.8	61.6	50.9	77.3
Percentage who completed 4 years of college (among those 25 years or older)	10.8	12.1	12.4	12.0	12.7
Income (1986)					
Median family income	$19,326	$14,584	$26,770	$19,995	$30,231
Occupation (1986 for employed males)					
Percentage professional and managerial (nonfarm)	8.8	12.4	19.0	10.8	26.5
Percentage craft, operatives, and laborers (nonfarm)	28.7	33.8	23.8	28.0	19.9
Percentage service worker	12.9	14.9	9.1	14.3	9.5
Age (1987)					
Median age (in years)	23.5	24.3	35.8	25.1	32.6

Source: U.S. Bureau of the Census, *Current Population Reports*, "The Hispanic Population in the United States: March 1986 and 1987, Advance Report," Series P-20, no. 416 (Washington, D.C.: Bureau of the Census, August, 1987), pp. 6–7.

Spanish families, and Puerto Ricans' median family income is less than half that of non-Spanish families. The low average income of Mexican-Americans results in part from their high concentrations in poor-paying, dead-end jobs in the garment industry, fast-food restaurants, and other service occupations.[70] As we observed in Chapter 3, one of the key resources in any ethnic group's rise to power is the existence of a substantial middle class that can provide leadership and begin moving into positions of political and economic importance. The very low percentage of college-educated Mexican-Americans slows their entrance into the mainstream of middle-class American politics.

The lag in resources caused by economic deprivation is compounded by a history of oppression. Current Mexican-American writers describe a long history of maltreatment by various government agencies. Particularly resented have been the Border Patrol and the immigration authorities whose job has been to stem illegal immigration through projects such as "Operation Wetback" in the 1950s. Under Operation Wetback:

> United States-born children were known to have been expelled with their parents. Many American-born adults were stopped and asked for proof of citizenship in cities far removed from the border—and some, reacting with anger as well as amazed incredulity, came into conflict with the officers. Because of its large scale and allegations of rough treatment, Operation Wetback became one of the most traumatic recent experiences of the Mexican-Americans in their contacts with government authority. No Mexican-American community in the Southwest remained untouched.[71]

During the Great Depression of the 1930s, welfare officials in Los Angeles and Detroit attempted to reduce welfare costs by repatriating Mexican-Americans to Mexico, even though many of those repatriated were United States citizens who objected to being deported.[72] One of the most bitterly detested governmental units was the Texas Rangers. Formed in 1835 to protect the frontier, the Texas Rangers, according to one historian, subsequently engaged in a "reign of terror against the Mexicans."[73] Nor have Mexican-American grievances against government agencies all been far in the past. In the 1960s, Mexican-American sheep grazers came into violent conflict with the National Forest Service, which attempted to drive them off the forest for conservation purposes.[74] And in 1978, Mexican-American groups in Houston, Texas, charged that city's police officers with police brutality in their relations with the Mexican-American community.[75]

Given this history of conflict, it is not surprising that Mexican-Americans have historically had low voter turnout rates and a low sense of political competence.[76] These traits in turn have held down Mexican-American political representation. Garcia and de la Garza estimated in 1973 that Mexican-American representation in state legislatures was barely half of what their numbers would be under a one-person, one-vote principle in Arizona, a fourth of what it should have been in California and Colorado, and less than a third of what it should have been in Texas. Only in New Mexico did the Mexican-Americans' share of the legislators come close to their share of the population.[77]

The impact of low participation on representation can be seen in Houston. A survey in 1980 of registered voters in that city found that even among registered voters, Mexican-Americans expressed much less interest in politics than did blacks or Anglos. Registration rates were so low that in a Houston city council district specifically drawn to represent the Hispanic population, Mexican-Americans comprised 63 percent of the population but only 42 percent of the registered voters.[78]

Mexican-American leaders are, of course, keenly aware that improved participation is critical to their electoral success, and since the 1970s the Southwest Voter Registration Education Project has worked strenuously to increase the number of Hispanic voters. These efforts plus enforcement of the pre-clearance requirements of the Voting Rights Act have markedly increased Hispanic participation in the Southwest. In Texas, which has been one of the major focal points of the Voter Registration Education Project, the number of Hispanic voters has more than doubled since 1976 and the number of Hispanic elected officeholders increased by 60 percent.[79]

Another legacy of Mexican-American history has been a growing sense of cultural nationalism. This is symbolized by the use of the term *Chicano*. Although the origins of the term are not clear, it is clear that *Chicano* implies a sense of pride in the unique Mexican-American culture. The term also is "associated with all Mexican-American militant and separatist groups."[80] The political effect of this growing sense of cultural nationalism has been a heightened militancy that Garcia and de la Garza call *Chicanismo*, a call for greater attentiveness to Mexican-American needs in several problem areas that are partially urban in nature: bilingual and bicultural education, community control of schools, fairer treatment by law enforcement agencies, better employment opportunities, an end to housing discrimination, and better health care.[81] It is not clear, however, that all or most Mexican-Americans identify as Chicanos. When asked in a 1976 survey which term they used to identify themselves, 50 percent said "Mexican-American," 20 percent said "Mexican," and only 4 percent said "Chicano."[82]

In sum, the political legacy of Mexican-American history for the 1980s is the heightened awareness among Mexican-Americans of their past and present discrimination, and a sense of cultural nationalism. Although Mexican-Americans have been marginally involved in electoral politics historically, this legacy combined with their growing numbers to make them a growing political force in the 1980s, especially in the cities of the South and Southwest.

Mexican-American Political Organization

Although the Mexican-American legacy of deprivation, oppression, and cultural nationalism has been analogous to that of black Americans in some respects, their political organization differs in one central respect. There is as yet no nationwide Mexican-American organization that enjoys the national stature of the NAACP or the Urban League. However, a number of important national organizations exist, including a Mexican-American Legal Defense and Education Fund, and the Congressional Hispanic Caucus. The most important political impacts, though, have probably been made by local and regional organizations. Garcia and de la Garza divide Mexican-American organizations into three categories. First are the early accommodationist organizations that stressed patriotism to the United States.[83] Some of these, such as the *Orden Hijos de Americas* (Order of the Sons of America), were similar to the fraternal and mutual-benefit societies of other immigrant groups. Most important was the League of United Latin American Citizens (LULAC). Viewing themselves primarily as an educational and civic group, LULAC leaders did not engage in any political activities or even attempt to increase Mexican-American voter turnout.

A second category of groups began emerging after World War II. They were much more politically oriented than the earlier accommodationist groups. Californians in 1947 founded the Community Service Organization, which used Saul Alinsky-type tactics* to get concessions from local governments. World War II veterans in Texas founded the G.I. Forum about 1947 and sought to improve voter registration and turnout among Mexican-Americans. The most politically oriented of the post-World War II groups were the Mexican-American Political Association (MAPA) in California and the Political Association of Spanish Speaking Organizations (PASSO) in Texas. Both groups tried to improve Mexican-American voter turnout, endorsed and campaigned for candidates, and engaged in a variety of community organization tactics. Probably the most renowned of the Mexican-American groups has been Cesar Chavez's United Farm Workers (UFW). Affiliated with the AFL-CIO, the United Farm Workers successfully organized grape pickers and field workers in California, battled with the Teamsters, gained for Mexican-Americans the support of prominent Anglo liberals like the late Senator Robert Kennedy, and organized a moderately successful nationwide boycott of wines, grapes, and lettuce that had not been picked by the United Farm Workers. Despite these early successes, the UFW is not adapting well to the more conservative environment that has prevailed since 1980, and today finds itself with a declining membership and severe financial burdens.[84]

Garcia and de la Garza's third category of Mexican-American groups is the radical category. Just as black politics began getting more militant during the 1960s, so did Mexican-American politics, and the net result was a proliferation of newer, more militant groups such as the Brown Berets, the Federal Alliance of Free City-States, the Crusade for Justice, and various student organizations. Some of these accepted the use of violence if that was necessary to attain Mexican-American goals. In contrast to the middle-class orientation of most of the earlier-mentioned groups, many of the newer groups, according to Garcia and de la Garza, were "composed mainly of lower-class or working-class members with a leadership corps of middle-class individuals."[85] The best known of the radical groups is the *La Raza Unida* party, founded in Texas but currently active throughout the Southwest.

Although numerous Mexican-American groups exist, they do not command the concern or awareness among their constituency that civil rights groups did

---

*Saul Alinsky was a prominent neighborhood organizer. His methods are described in his books *Reveille for Radicals* (New York: Vintage Books, 1969) and *Rules for Radicals* (New York: Random House, 1971).

among blacks during the civil rights movement. A 1980 survey of Houston Hispanics found that the only group whose name could be recalled by a majority of the
people interviewed was LULAC. No other group was identified by more than 10
percent, and the highly active and visible *La Raza Unida* was identified by only 5
percent. Only 9 percent of those interviewed were members of any Mexican-
American political group.[86] As the Hispanic population grows in size, however, it
can be anticipated that Hispanic political groups will gain visibility and prominence.

Mexican-American Mayors

As the Mexican-American population has grown and participation rates have
gone up, its political influence in urban politics has increased accordingly. What
form this influence will take is not fully determined yet. It seems unlikely that very
many cities will see a Mexican-American political dominance on the model of
black dominance of places such as Detroit or even Chicago. Mexican-Americans
dominate very few large cities numerically to the extent that blacks do. Only two
U.S. cities of 100,000 or more, San Antonio and El Paso, claim a Mexican-
American majority. Blacks, on the other hand, constitute a majority in nine such
cities.[87] Table 5-4 shows that there were only twelve cities with 100,000 or more
Hispanics in 1980, but there were twenty-six SMSAs with 100,000 or more Hispanics. This indicates that the Hispanic population in general, and the Mexican-

Table 5-4. Cities with Large Hispanic Populations: 1980

City	Size of Hispanic population	Percentage of city's population	Hispanic mayors
**New York	1,406,024	19.9	
**Los Angeles	816,076	27.5	
*Chicago	422,063	14.0	
*San Antonio	421,954	53.7	Henry Cisneros; Mexican-American (1981-)
**Houston	281,331	17.6	
*El Paso	265,819	62.5	
*Miami	194,037	55.9	Maurice Ferre; Puerto Rican (1971–1985) Xavier Suarez; Cuban (1985–)
San Diego	130,613	14.9	
Phoenix	116,736	14.8	
Albuquerque	112,084	33.8	
Dallas	111,083	12.3	
*Corpus Christi	108,175	46.6	
Denver	92,400	18.8	Federico Pena; Mexican-American (1983–)

*Black and Hispanic populations are a majority of the city's population.
**Black and Hispanic populations exceed 45 percent of the city's population.
Source: United States Bureau of the Census, *Statistical Abstract of the United States: 1987* (Wash-
ington, D.C.: U.S. Government Printing Office, 1986), pp. 31–34.

American population in particular, are much more dispersed throughout the metropolis than are the black metropolitan populations. While this greater dispersion of Mexican-Americans makes them less subject to segregation than blacks, it also disperses their potential voting power and makes it more difficult for them to elect city council members.

Mexican-Americans have also seen their voting power further diluted by the fact that they are most populous in the region of the country where central cities have historically expanded by annexing surrounding suburban settlements. As central cities annexed white suburbs, the voting power of Mexican-Americans was diluted.

Because of these trends, it was difficult for a Mexican-American to be elected mayor. But all of this changed after the Voting Rights Act was amended in 1975 to cover discrimination against language minorities as well as racial minorities. The most stunning Mexican-American victory came in San Antonio.

From the mid-1950s to the mid-1970s San Antonio had been dominated by a Good Government League composed of major business interests. Ninety-five percent of all city council members during this period were also members of the Good Government League.[88] But the Good Government League dominance splintered in 1975, when the so-called Independent Team of younger businesses pledged to concentrate city development resources on the growing north side of the city. The city's Hispanic population was poorly represented in either of those governing coalitions. In 1974 the Mexican-Americans lost on a proposal to create several district seats for the city council and end the at-large system of elections.

In April 1976 the United States Department of Justice objected to San Antonio's plan to annex sixty-five square miles that was 75 percent Anglo on the grounds that such annexation would dilute the Mexican-American voting strength from 52 percent to a minority. Under such Justice Department fire, San Antonio ultimately was allowed to effect the annexation, but only on the condition that there be instituted a ten-district city council that created five districts for the Mexican-American community, one for the black community, and four for the non-Hispanic, nonblack community.[89] (An at-large mayor would have the eleventh vote.)

Under this plan, the Mexican-Americans took control of the San Antonio city council in 1977, and in 1981 elected Henry Cisneros the first Mexican-American mayor of a major city. Under Mexican-American control the city government restricted suburban construction activities over an aquifer supplying the city's water and pursued affirmative action policies designed to bring more minorities into city government. But Cisneros maintained his support in the Mexican-American neighborhoods while working with business leaders to promote economic growth.[90] With the demise of the business-dominated Good Government League in the mid-1970s, San Antonio's politics had become much more democratic. Several political factions emerged, but none of them could dominate the city.[91] Mayor Cisneros, with his economic growth policies, was able to work effectively among these conflicting factions. After four successive two-year terms,

Cisneros himself had come to dominate the city's political landscape and to gain much national publicity for his city. By 1987 he was looked on as the Democrats' best hope to recapture the Texas governorship in 1988, but he withdrew from that contest to devote more time to an ailing son who had been born with severe birth defects.

Cuban Urban Politics

Cuban political influence is most markedly felt in Miami, a city in which Hispanics are a majority, and Cubans are the dominant Hispanic group. Most Miami Cubans are caucasians who came into the country as refugees when Fidel Castro took over Cuba in 1959. Being middle-class business people and professionals, it did not take them long to enter the middle-class mainstream of American life and, as Table 5-3 shows, they are in a much better economic position than are blacks, Mexican-Americans, or Puerto Ricans.

Politically Cubans are much more Republican and conservative than the other Hispanic groups, motivated by a fierce anticommunism. Most Cubans felt a deep disappointment with the Democrats when President Kennedy failed to overthrow the Castro regime. They have provided many of the Spanish-speaking operatives for numerous CIA missions against communism in the western hemisphere, and when President Reagan began supporting the Contra war against the Sandinista regime in Nicaragua, large numbers of Cubans gave him and the Republicans their allegiance.[92]

Using their economic power and their political savvy, some Cubans have played a leading role in providing community support for the Contra effort to overthrow the Sandinistas in Nicaragua,[93] a few have become intimately involved in illegal drug trafficking,[94] and many have dramatically transformed Miami politics. The city is ethnically divided between Cubans, who are a slight majority of the city's population; blacks, who account for another 25 percent; and a small non-Hispanic white population. Politically, the gaps between these three ethnic groupings are huge. Cuban mayor Xavier Suarez won election in 1985 by maximizing his Hispanic vote, while his opponent sought to put together a coalition of Hispanics, blacks, and non-Hispanic whites. By 1987, Suarez solidified his political support and won majorities in all three of those ethnic groupings while winning a reelection runoff.[95]

Black-Cuban relations in Miami have been exacerbated by the influx of 100,000 new, impoverished, mostly black Cuban refugees (called Mariel Cubans or Marielitos) who arrived in 1980 and an influx of impoverished immigrants from other Latin American nations. These newer immigrants have greatly displaced black Americans from low-income service jobs in hotels, hospitals, and restaurants and by doing so have created a great deal of resentment in the black American community. The Marielitos enjoy little of the middle-class achievements of the early white Cuban immigrants. And their plight received national attention in 1987 when Cubans in two federal prisons rioted when they thought they were going to be deported to Cuba.

Asians and Urban Politics

The second largest group of fourth-wave urban immigrants are from Asia and the western Pacific area. But being from the Orient is about all they have in common, as they represent different nationalities, different languages, different religions, and differing socioeconomic levels. The largest of these migrant groups are from the Philippines, Korea, China, Vietnam, Japan, and India. For the most part, however (the main exceptions being Southeast Asian Vietnamese, Cambodians, and Hmongs), Asian immigrants have much better educational levels and enjoy more prestigious occupations than do blacks or Mexican-Americans. Although they are not yet earning incomes comparable to those of whites with similar education, they seem to face, according to one study, "very few barriers to socioeconomic achievement . . . [and their] . . . story seems to be quite rosy."[96] In addition to enjoying better socioeconomic positions than most of the fourth-wave urban immigrants, Asian-Americans are also much less segregated than blacks and probably less so than Hispanics.[97]

Despite this more favorable picture for Asians, they do indeed face some distinct discrimination problems in America. The United States Civil Rights Commission in 1987 warned of a high level of racially motivated violence against Asians. Quite frequent were firebombings or attacks on Korean retail stores.[98] Asians have also complained that elite universities have put quotas on the admission of Asian students, not because the Asians do poorly in college but because they outperform most other students.

Issues of Concern to Fourth-Wave Immigrants

The three main issues of concern to fourth-wave immigrants are probably immigration, bilingualism, and jobs.

Immigration

Immigration is an issue because of the millions of people who seek better economic opportunities in the United States. Immigration today is shaped principally by the Immigation Act of 1965 that repealed previous restrictions on Asians, effectively reduced the proportion of European immigrants, and turned Asia and Latin America into the two main sources for immigration since then.[99] In 1985 there were 570,000 legal immigrants coming to the United States, with 46.4 percent from Asia (or the Pacific) and 36.7 percent from Latin America.[100]

But it is not the legal immigrants who are the center of controversy so much as it is the illegal immigrants who are mostly impoverished rural laborers from Mexico. Whether illegal Mexican aliens take jobs away from Americans, whether they should enjoy free public services such as education and welfare, and whether they pay more in taxes than they receive in free public services are hotly debated questions in both the Hispanic and non-Hispanic communities.[101] And there is no more unanimity among Mexican-Americans on these issues than there is among non-Hispanics. A 1980 survey of 200 Hispanic registered voters in Houston, for example, found 56 percent approved of tuition-free schools for undocumented aliens, and 44 percent disapproved.[102]

Social scientists who investigate these questions are no more unanimous in their conclusions than are ordinary citizens. But some definite statements can be made. There is overwhelming sentiment for doing something to curb illegal immigration into the United States. A *Newsweek* poll in 1984 found that 61 percent of Americans would approve of penalizing companies that hire illegal aliens and 55 percent favored a policy of arresting and deporting illegal aliens who are already here.[103]

Formulating a policy to cope with this demand is complicated by the fact that nobody knows how many illegal aliens migrate each year into the United States and how many are permanent residents in the country. The Immigration and Naturalization Service (INS) estimated that there were 12 million illegal aliens residing in the United States in the mid-1970s, but that figure was rejected as inflated for purposes of getting a bigger department budget from Congress. The Census Bureau in 1980 estimated between 3 and 6 million, but Census Bureau technicians later reduced the estimates to a range of 1.5 million to 3 million.[104] But these figures would seem to be too low simply because of the fact that INS apprehended and returned 1.8 million persons attempting to enter or remain in the United States illegally in 1986 alone.[105] Even discounting for repeated arrests of the same persons and realizing that most of the illegal entrants stay only for part of the year, there could still easily be 300,000 to 500,000 illegal immigrants each year.[106]

After several years of debate, Congress in 1986 passed the Immigration Reform and Control Act (usually called the Simpson-Rodino Act). This law sought to come to grips with illegal immigration by:

1. requiring employers to verify the U.S. citizenship or legal status of all employees and imposing still penalities on employees who violate the law.
2. granting an amnesty to all aliens who have resided permanently within the United States since before January 1, 1982 and allowing them to apply for citizenship.
3. granting temporary status to alien agricultural workers who worked at least 90 days in the United States between May 1985 and May 1986 and allowing them to apply for citizenship.

This intent of this legislation was, of course, to reduce the incentives for impoverished Mexicans to migrate over the border in search of low-paying jobs in the United States. Whether that goal will be achieved will probably depend on how diligently the law is enforced. Although it is too early to tell, the first year of the law's operation saw a 34 percent dropoff in illegal immigration.[107] This brought cries of alarm from West Coast agricultural interests that they could not find enough farm laborers to harvest their crops, suggesting that political pressures may build to relax the law's enforcement.

Bilingualism

A second issue of concern to fourth-wave immigrants is bilingualism. Should immigrants be obliged to learn English in order to get jobs and go to school? Or should schools be obliged to offer instruction in the native tongues of recent immigrants as a means of helping them keep up with their studies until their command of English is sufficient for them to enter regular classes? And should employees be obliged to hire workers who cannot understand written or spoken instructions in English? When some Corpus Christi oil refineries posted a rule that only English could be spoken on the job, it stirred up a hornet's nest of protest from Hispanic groups such as LULAC.[108]

The usual argument for bilingualism is that it should be used especially in schools to prevent dropouts and improve the academic performance of immigrant children. Although there is some evidence that bilingual instruciton does indeed accomplish these goals, opponents point out the absurdity of a city such as Los Angeles having to provide instruction in the native tongues of Mexican, Japanese, Indian, Philippine, Korean, Vietnamese, Cambodian, and other immigrant children who inhabit that city.[109] Opponents also fear that catering to the language problems of non-English speakers could lead to Spanish being recognized as a second official language and to a cultural separatism problem such as that of Quebec, Canada. In 1986 California voters passed an initiative proposition that declared English the official language of the state.

Jobs

The third issue of crucial importance to fourth-wave urban immigrants is whether they can find jobs to maintain themselves, whether in doing so they take jobs away from native-born low-income Americans,[110] or whether the jobs they take are so menial and arduous that native-born Americans are unwilling to do them.[111] Social science research on these questions has not yet provided definitive answers, but four generalizations seem apparent.[112]

First, there seems to be some evidence that immigration has added jobs to the overall American economy, especially in California, by providing a pool of low-wage laborers that may make some American manufacturers more competitive with low-wage foreign manufacturers. Second, this process does indeed drive down wages for existing workers, especially in manufacturing and agricultural areas. Third, some researchers fear that reliance on low-wage immigrant laborers may inhibit American manufacturers from modernizing their production processes with high technology and may in the long run retard the competitiveness of American industry. Finally, in the long run, because of demographic trends some researchers fear that a labor shortage will emerge in the United States and that large-scale immigration will have to be stimulated to fill this shortage.

The Search for a Rainbow Coalition

If low-income Mexican-Americans, Puerto Ricans, American Indians, native whites, and Asians could form an electoral coalition capable of swinging election results, that act alone would vastly increase their political influence. The most prominent spokesman for this movement is, of course, Jesse Jackson, who in his

1984 and 1988 presidential campaigns coined the term "rainbow coalition." Just as the rainbow's natural beauty lies in the spectrum of colors it presents, the political rainbow coalition would embrace a spectrum of people of different colors: whites, browns, reds, yellows, and blacks.

Scholars, as we have seen, have devoted considerable energy to the question of why a cross-nationality electoral coalition did not emerge among lower-class European immigrants in the late 19th and early 20th centuries. As we have seen, ethnic divisions, religious divisions, the tradition of privatism, the hope of upward social mobility, workplace-oriented unions (as distinct from class-oriented unions), non-ideological machine politics, and repression of ideological movements by the law, the police, and various national guards all conspired in the past to prevent the emergence of institutions that would enable the lower classes to advance their political and economic self-interests. Has anything changed from the past that might permit the emergence of something akin to Jesse Jackson's electoral coalition in the 1990s and the 21st century?

Let us analyze this question first from the viewpoint of the central-city black leader seeking to put together a multiethnic electoral coalition capable of winning office. The most logical allies would seem to be lower-class whites, since they face many of the same economic problems faced by lower-class blacks (poor housing, poor schools, need for social services, and need for more jobs.)* The tendency of lower-class blacks and lower-class whites to form a united constituency has not been analyzed very thoroughly, but one study of voting patterns in the South between 1960 and 1977 suggests that such alliances are very difficult to forge. In partisan elections, lower-income whites had a fairly strong tendency to support the same candidates as those supported by blacks—as long as the candidates were white. But this support dissipated when the candidate was black or when elections were non-partisan.[113]

A more successful voting alliance for blacks has been with white liberals. In Berkeley, California, for example, a sizable black middle class coalesced with liberal academic whites to get black representation on the city council.[114] The most successful citywide black candidates have held the loyalty of a small minority of

---

*Three possibilities seem to exist for black-white voting alliances. The first, as discussed above, is that blacks could align with lower-income whites and support the same candidates. This has been argued by Chandler Davidson in *Biracial Politics: Conflict and Coalition in the Metropolitan South* (Baton Rouge: Louisiana State University Press, 1972), pp. 215–219. The second possibility is that blacks could align with upper-income whites, who tend to have the least prejudicial attitudes and would be least threatened by black advancement. James Q. Wilson argues that "the natural ally of the Southern Negro, for the foreseeable future, is the cosmopolitan white bourgeoisie"; see his "The Negro in Politics," in *The Negro American*, Talcott Parsons and Kenneth Clark, eds. (Boston: Houghton Mifflin, 1966), p. 427. A third possibility is that urban society is so complex and has so many issues cutting across racial and economic lines that voting patterns are not likely to be consistent. See Robert A. Dahl, *Democracy in the United States: Promise and Performance*, 2nd ed. (Chicago: Rand McNally, 1976), pp. 359–362. These three possibilities are summarized and tested in five southern cities by Richard Murray and Arnold Vedlitz, "Racial Voting Patterns in the South: An Analysis of Major Elections from 1960 to 1977 in Five Cities," *The Annals of the American Academy of Political and Social Science* 439 (September 1978): 29–39.

whites while getting an extraordinary turnout of blacks. In the 1977 election of Ernest N. Morial as New Orleans' first black mayor, for example, Morial received only 19 percent of the white vote but 95 percent of the black vote, and three-quarters of the city's eligible black voters turned out.[115] In Richard Arrington's election as the first black mayor of Birmingham, Alabama in 1979, Arrington also won only 10 to 15 percent of the white vote but was aided by a large black voter turnout.[116] The same pattern held true for more recent black mayors elected for the first time. Philadelphia's W. Wilson Goode won about 20 percent of that city's white votes but an estimated 97 percent of the black vote in 1983.[117] Chicago's Harold Washington won few white votes but an estimated 97 percent of the black vote in 1983.[118] Both men were aided by extraordinary turnouts of black voters, over 95 percent in Philadelphia and 82 percent in Chicago. Of all the big-city black mayors, only Los Angeles' Thomas Bradley won a majority of white votes in his initial election to the office in 1973.

A third possible voting alliance for blacks is with Hispanics. An important example of a black-Hispanic coalition emerged in Chicago where Mayor Harold Washington won an estimated 57 percent of the Hispanic vote in 1987[119] and relied on Hispanic support to gain control of the city council.[120] But in most cities, blacks and Hispanics do not seem to coalesce very easily. Houston mayor Kathy Whitmire was supported by a majority of blacks in her 1983 election but opposed by a majority of Mexican-Americans. New York mayor Edward Koch has enjoyed warm support from Puerto Rican leaders but coolness from black leaders. A number of California cities have both black and Hispanic populations, and in a few of these cities, such as Sacramento, black-Hispanic coalitions did emerge. But the preeminent analysis of minority-group politics in northern California describes black-Hispanic alliances as difficult to achieve.[121] Across the continent, in Miami, black-Cuban relations are openly hostile.[122]

If black leaders face innumerable problems in building a rainbow coalition, can the same be said of Hispanic leaders? On the face of it, urban Hispanics could logically ally themselves with several other disadvantaged groups in the city—principally American Indians, blacks, and lower-class whites. Garcia and de la Garza think that racial and cultural differences preclude a successful coalition with lower-class whites.[123] They do point out, however, that some successful alliances have been made between American Indians and blacks. As we discussed earlier, however, several pitfalls hinder black-Hispanic alliances, despite the fact that both groups suffer from similar economic and discriminatory handicaps. Ironically, the most successful political alliances have been with upper- and upper-middle-class whites, who provided considerable financing and support for the United Farm Workers' struggle with the Teamsters and various agricultural landowners in California.

Like the blacks, historic Hispanic allegiance has been to the Democratic Party but to a much smaller degree. By a traditional survey research measure of party identification, about 58 percent of Hispanics in a 1986 New York Times poll identified themselves as Democrats.[124] Another measure of Hispanic partisanship would be their participation in primary elections. In Texas in 1986, Hispanic voters accounted for nearly 24 percent of the voters in the Democratic Party primary but only about 2 percent in the Republican primary,[125] suggesting that Democratic-oriented Hispanics outnumber Republicans by a ratio of 12 to 1. Some critics think that this Democratic inclination has been a blind allegiance that is not always in the best interest of Hispanics.[126] These critics would play Democrats and Republicans against each other by giving Hispanic support to the party that offered the most benefits or by supporting a Hispanic-based third party, such as *La Raza Unida*.

Finally, there are important partisan and ideological differences that would have to be bridged to create a successful rainbow coalition in the 1990s. These are illustrated in Table 5-5. This table suggests several things. First, in terms of party allegiances, there are great similarities between blacks and Hispanics. But American Indians, lower-class whites, and Asians do not seem likely to join such a coalition, since they have the highest percentages of Republicans of any ethnic group outside the northern and western Europeans.

In terms of ideology, blacks stand alone as the most liberal of the ethnic groups. Asians are the most polarized of the ethnic groups, having the largest percentage who are conservative and the second largest who are liberal. American Indians and lower-class whites appear closer to the European ethnics than they do to the blacks and Hispanics.

On specific policy issues there are also some important differences. On support for increased military spending, the blacks, Asians, and Hispanics line up as the most opposed, while the American Indians and lower-class whites are even more supportive than the European ethnics. Using support for a law prohibiting the sale of pornography as a surrogate for social policy conservatism, Hispanics, American Indians, and lower-class whites line up with the European ethnics on the conservative side, while Asians and blacks line up on the liberal side of the issue. Using support for increased welfare spending as a surrogate for economic policy liberalism, Asians and lower-class whites desert the rainbow coalition of blacks, Hispanics, and American Indians and in fact are even more conservative than the European ethnics. Finally, in terms of their subjective social class identification, Asians are more like the Europeans than they are like the other elements of the rainbow coalition.

If partisanship, ideological beliefs, and issue positions make a difference in terms of who joins a political coalition (and they usually do make a big difference), there appear to be important roadblocks in the way of a rainbow coalition. Asians appear to desert the coalition on subjective political ideology and welfare expenditures. Blacks desert it on opposition to capital punishment. American Indians appear to desert it on military spending. And Hispanics appear to desert it on support for right to choice on abortion. Few of these issues, of course, are overtly urban in character and astute political leadership might be able to overcome the differences. But simply in terms of political beliefs and attachments, the obstacles are important.

Table 5-5. Ethnic Divisions

Variable	N & W European	S & E European	All lower- or working-class whites	Asian	Latin American	Blacks	American Indians
PARTY IDENTIFICATION							
% Democratic	34.8	47.0	49.8	32.8	61.3	70.0	47.9
% Independent	34.7	37.0	37.4	48.8	32.6	23.2	35.2
% Republican	30.5	16.1	20.8	18.4	6.1	6.0	17.0
SUBJECTIVE POLITICAL IDEOLOGY							
% Identifying as liberal	24.7	30.5	25.0	35.0	33.3	39.6	27.0
% Identifying as moderate	38.8	42.2	44.6	32.0	42.7	37.2	45.1
% Identifying as conservative	36.5	27.3	20.4	33.0	23.9	23.2	27.9
NATIONAL DEFENSE IDEOLOGY							
% Saying we are spending too little on arms	27.0	23.4	28.4	18.7	19.8	20.2	32.2
ECONOMIC POLICY IDEOLOGY							
% Saying we are spending too much on welfare	58.2	56.8	55.3	54.7	38.3	22.4	48.5
SOCIAL POLICY IDEOLOGY							
% Opposing freedom of choice on abortion	54.1	49.4	59.8	46.3	79.8	62.9	65.3
% Supporting law prohibiting distribution of pornography	46.3	42.4	45.4	27.5	42.5	34.9	44.4
SUBJECTIVE SOCIAL CLASS							
% Identifying as lower or working class	46.8	46.8	100	44.9	71.6	69.8	65.0

Source: James Allan Davis and Tom W. Smith, *General Social Surveys, 1972–1985* [machine-readable data file]. Principal Investigator, James A. Davis; Senior Study Director, Tom W. Smith. NORC ed. Chicago: National Opinion Research Center, producer, 1985; Storrs, CT: Roper Public Opinion Research Center, University of Connecticut, distributor.

This table uses the sum of all the data from 1972 through 1985. This is done to avoid the problem of insufficient subsample size for the smaller ethnic groups that would be inherent if the survey results for only a single year were used. Single-year surveys of the GSS have a sample size of about 1500, while summing all of the surveys yields a total sample size of 18,586. Using the multi-year sample also has the advantage of giving a more balanced overall picture of political beliefs over the entire fourteen-year period than would be possible if only one year's survey were selected.

Bias in Contemporary City Politics

In the competition of contemporary city politics, the newer urban minorities (especially blacks and Hispanics) do indeed possess strengths in the 1990s to a much greater degree than they did in earlier decades. Their greatest asset is their large share of the urban population. That, combined with the politically important development of a sense of cultural uniqueness (black and Hispanic pride) facilitates a race- and ethnic-based voting pattern that has brought increasing numbers of blacks and Hispanics to positions of political influence in urban America. Furthermore, a number of outside political forces benefited black and Hispanic causes. Until the Reagan administration, the federal government's espousal of affirmative action, for example, worked hand in hand with minority demands for better job opportunities.

Despite these strengths, the non-middle-class portions of minority communities still face definite biases in the urban political system. Three kinds of biases have been identified in this chapter. First, there are several internal aspects of the minority communities that work to the disadvantage of the lower- and working-class portions of those communities. These people lack extensive personal resources such as money, self-esteem, confidence, and leisure time that are so important in politics.[127] Further, they have high transiency levels that hinder long-term political allegiances. Welfare families are often relocated around the city, breaking up political communication networks. Competent and upwardly mobile minorities get coopted into managerial positions with established institutions, thus draining off the lower class's ability to maintain internal leadership.

If the first bias stems from the internal social structure of the minority communities, a second bias stems from the political and governmental reforms discussed in Chapter 4, especially at-large elections, nonpartisan elections, civil service hiring procedures, and racially motivated boundary changes. Although none of these procedures has eliminated minority influence in local politics, the general conclusion of the empirical research on this question is that it dilutes minority influence. The structure of city government does not facilitate upward mobility for blacks and Hispanics nearly as much as it did a century ago for European immigrants.

It is possible that a third bias stems from the economic and fiscal situation of the cities in the 1980s and 1990s. Does the city offer the same economic opportunities to unskilled laborers that it did a century ago? Career-ladder positions now inevitably require some schooling or training. There are fewer unskilled labor jobs in industrial factories than there were a generation ago. The most dynamic growth areas of the metropolitan economies are on the suburban fringes. The inner-city minorities no longer live where job opportunities are rapidly expanding. This was not true a century ago, when inner-city job opportunities were expanding rapidly and were within easy commuting distance of the poorest neighborhoods. Finally, does the fiscal condition of many cities in the 1980s and 1990s enable them to expand their workforces and function as an employer for lower-income populations as the political machines did a century ago? These questions about the economic and fiscal abilities of the city to perform its historic role as an arena of social mobility are so important that we will devote all of the next chapter to these topics.

Summary

1. As a result of black and Hispanic migration into the cities, the white population is becoming a numerical minority in some cities. The new urban minorities bring to urban politics a tone infused with militant rhetoric. It has not fit very well into the mold of machine politics, and the old political machines have not met the needs of these new minorities very well.

2. Black urban politics have shifted away from emphasis on the struggle for civil rights that characterized black politics before and during the 1960s. By the 1980s, black urban politics centered around getting representation in city government, increasing job and economic opportunities, trying to reverse the deterioration of the city, and trying to target the city's resources more directly at the social problems of minority populations. Black mayors have had some success with a dual strategy of encouraging business investment to increase jobs in the private sector and using affirmative action strategies to increase job opportunities for blacks in the public sector.

3. Hispanic politics have become increasingly militant over the years. Like black politics, Hispanic politics face questions of the most appropriate electoral strategies and political coalitions to follow in order to maximize Hispanic influence. San Antonio serves as an example of Mexican-Americans seeking political control through conventional means and using that control to promote economic development. Key issues for Mexican-Americans center around bilingualism, immigration, and jobs. Cubans dominate Miami, are much more economically successful than other Hispanics, and are much more conservative.

4. Asians constitute the largest block of legal immigrants today. They are more successful economically and are less segregated than blacks or Hispanics.

5. Despite the appeal of a rainbow coalition among lower-income racial minorities, several obstacles stand in the way of such a coalition materializing.

6. Three patterns of bias affect today's urban politics. First, several internal aspects of black and Hispanic politics reduce their potential political influence. Second, the reform-style politics discussed in Chapter 4 inhibit the political influence of blacks and Hispanics. Third, there are limits to the socioeconomic advancement that can be achieved through political power.

Chapter 6
The City as a Place of Opportunity: The Changing Urban Political Economy

As earlier chapters have documented, nineteenth- and early-twentieth-century European immigrants found the American city a useful place for gaining political influence and economic advancement. In today's American cities those ethnic groups have been succeeded to a great extent by blacks, Hispanics, and other minorities. Chapter 5 described how blacks and Hispanics have begun to use their growing numbers to gain city council seats, mayoral office, and other positions of political influence. On the face of it, this suggests that the process of ethnic succession is working for today's urban minorities just as it worked for the European ethnics a century ago. At least the process of ethnic succession seems to be working in the urban political sphere.

Whether or not the process of ethnic succession is also working in the economic sphere poses a very important question. In the waning years of this century, is the American city still a place of opportunity for its poorest residents, its minorities, and its most recent in-migrants?

This chapter addresses that question by focusing on four major changes that are taking place in the political economy of American cities. First, which changes in the national economy are important for American cities? Second, how are these national changes affecting the economic outlook for cities as we move to the end of the twentieth century? Third, what is the changing fiscal outlook for cities? Fourth, what economic development strategies can cities follow to improve their economic and fiscal position? After examining these four questions, we shall explore whether today's economic and fiscal changes contain any biases either for or against Hispanics, blacks, and other urban ethnic minorities.

The Changing Economic Climate for Urban America

To appreciate how the prospects for black and Hispanic upward mobility differ from those of the European ethnics a century ago, we must first examine four broad trends taking place in the American economy. First is the transformation from an industrial to a post-industrial economy; second, the intensification of foreign competition; third, the changing class structure of American society; and fourth, a more slowly growing economy.

From Industrial to Post-Industrial Economy

Economists distinguish among three sectors of the economy. The primary sector refers to extractive activities such as oil production, mining, timber production, or farming. The secondary, or industrial, sector refers to manufacturing activities. The tertiary sector refers to a broad range of service activities from retail trade to banking to hospital management. As Table 6-1 later shows, the growth of manufacturing jobs in the secondary or industrial sector in recent years has lagged far behind the growth of the labor force in general. In contrast to the manufacturing sector, which produces fewer jobs and less income (relative to the whole economy) than it did in the past, the service sector of the economy has been growing. The relative decline of industrial manufacturing and the relative growth of the service sector have led some social scientists to note that America has been shifting from an industrial to a post-industrial economy.[1]

Within the manufacturing sector of the economy, dramatic changes are also occurring that have devastating impacts on many central cities. The most dynamically growing parts of the manufacturing sector have been high-technology manufacturing of products such as computers, lasers, and sophisticated medical equipment. These are among what economist Lester Thurow calls the "sunrise industries",[2] those whose day in the sun is just beginning. In contrast to them are the "sunset industries" such as radio and television manufacturing and old, heavy-industry manufacturing of steel and automobiles. These have been badly damaged by foreign competition and have lost badly in their share of the market.

In a dynamic economy, jobs are always disappearing and new jobs are always being created to replace them, so on the face of it there should not be much alarm as sunrise industries replace sunset industries. But two important questions about the current process of job loss and job creation are relevant to urban America.

First, are the new jobs in the sunrise industries and the service sector as plentiful and as lucrative as the disappearing jobs in the sunset industries? Many observers say they are. About 5.1 million jobs were lost in the five-year period from 1979 through 1983, according to the Bureau of Labor Statistics (BLS),[3] but a Congressional study found that this was more than compensated for by the 8 million new jobs created during a comparable period of 1979 through 1984.[4] Furthermore, business publications tend to argue that these jobs are better than the old factory jobs being lost and that they will eventually provide a better standard of living for more people.[5]

To many critics, however, these assertions are not convincing. An increasing body of research is pointing consistently at the conclusion that the newly created service jobs pay less and provide fewer hours than the manufacturing jobs that are disappearing. The Bureau of Labor Statistics (BLS) estimated that in 1983 the average nonsupervisory manufacturing worker earned $478.98 per week, while the corresponding nonretail service worker earned $238.71 per week and the retail service worker earned only $171.05 per week.[6] The BLS study of the jobs lost/jobs created relationship also discovered that of the 5.1 million jobs lost from 1979 through 1983, 80 percent were in the manufacturing sector. What happened to those workers who lost their jobs? By 1984, 40 percent were still unemployed or had dropped out of the labor force altogether. Of the 60 percent who did succeed in finding new jobs, 41 percent were working at lower pay than they had received at the jobs they had lost.[7] In short, the jobs that were disappearing paid much better than the jobs that were being created, on the average.[8] Nor do prospects appear much brighter for the immediate future. The BLS projected that the five occupations that would produce the greatest job growth from 1982 to 1995 were building custodians, cashiers, secretaries, general clerks, and sales clerks. Obviously, none of these are high-wage jobs.[9]

The second question about the dynamics of the jobs lost/jobs created relationship is: Are the new jobs being created in the places where the old jobs are being lost? And the answer is "not for the most part." With a few significant exceptions, most industrial job losses are occurring in the belt of northern industrial cities stretching from the Hudson River on the east to the Mississippi on the west. Most new jobs are being created in suburbs rather than in central cities and disproportionately in the southern and southwestern regions. The main exception is New England, especially the Boston area, which has enjoyed a remarkable economic resurgence since about 1980. The other exception can be found in the "oil patch" areas of Texas, Louisiana, and Oklahoma, where the economic boom collapsed in the 1980s. Because of the glut in the world's oil supply, these areas have been pushed into hard times. Aside from these and a few other exceptions, however, the long-term economic growth trends have worked to the disadvantage of the central-city poor, especially those in the Northeast and the Midwest whose industrial belt has been eroding. At some point in the future, the Northeast and Midwest economies will stabilize. But for the moment, they are not very dynamic job creators for the urban poor.

Intensification of Foreign Competition

Although the United States has never been totally independent of the world economy, our economic interdependence with the rest of the world today dwarfs any interdependency of the past. Table 6-1 shows that exports have nearly doubled their share of the gross national product (GNP) since 1965 and that imports have more than doubled their share. These shares are likely to grow further in the future.

On the positive side, this interdependence enriches the quality of American life by making a greater variety of imported goods and services available. Moreover, aggressive expansion of American exports opens up larger world markets to American companies, thus creating more jobs and income. In theory, the increased need to compete in both the import and export markets leads to better products at the most reasonable prices.

On the negative side, many corporations and communities are poorly prepared to compete in international markets. Foreign nations have become increasingly competitive in their ability to manufacture and market high-quality consumer products such as automobiles and television sets. Much American manufacturing

Table 6-1. Changes in the American Economy

Selected aspects	Year	Percentage
International interdependence		
1. Percentage of new automobiles sold that were manufactured domestically	1965	94%
	1983	74
	2015	?
2. Exports as a percent of GNP	1965	5.9
	1983	10.2
	2015	?
3. Imports as a percent of GNP	1965	4.6
	1983	10.4
	2015	?
Postindustrialization		
Growth of labor force employed in manufacturing compared with growth of the total civilian labor force, 1975–1983, in percentages		
in manufacturing		2.5
in total economy		17.5
in services		28.4

Source: U.S. Bureau of the Census, *Statistical Abstract of the United States, 1981* (Washington, D.C.: United States Government Printing Office, 1981), pp. 624, 421, 390, 733; *Statistical Abstract: 1985*, pp. 404, 432, 595, 703, 770.

is done in outmoded plants using old-fashioned production methods, compared with highly automated plants in, for example, Japan, with their extensive use of robots and other innovations. Labor costs are usually cheaper in Japan (although comparative labor costs vary from year to year depending on the relative value of the dollar and the yen). And labor costs are cheaper yet for our major third-world competitors, such as Korea, Brazil, Mexico, Taiwan, Hong Kong, and Singapore, where multinational corporations have set up manufacturing plants. Apple Computer Corporation, for example, now does most of its manufacturing in production plants set up in third-world countries. Further complicating the problem for American communities, much of the foreign competition comes from countries with authoritarian governments that curb free labor unions, hold down wage costs for multinational corporations, and do not force their local plants to adhere to environmental and safety standards that are prevalent in the United States. Additionally, the host governments often subsidize the export of their products to the United States (what American-based manufacturers call dumping). Despite huge transportation distances and costs involved, these and other factors combined to give many imported products in the 1970s and 1980s a distinct price advantage over comparable American products.

To counter their foreign competition, American businesses have expressed their hope of narrowing the wage gap between U.S. factory workers (who averaged $13.09 per hour in 1987) and the much, much lower wages of factory workers in

Brazil, Korea, Hong Kong, Mexico, Taiwan, and Singapore.[10] Although publicly stating that this wage gap must be narrowed by bringing up the wages of the third-world countries, in fact most businesses attack the problem by taking tough stands on collective bargaining with their American employees while at the same time supporting authoritarian regimes that hold down labor costs for many of our third-world competitors.

The Dwindling Middle Class

As the American economy adapts to these technological and foreign challenges, that adaptation has profound consequences for the social and political structures of metropolitan America. Economist Lester Thurow flatly charges that the American middle class is shrinking.[11] As shown in Table 6-2, the percent of middle-income families has decreased since 1970, while the number of lower- and upper-income families has increased. If this trend persists, it could signal a shift in America toward a more bimodal society in which a comparatively smaller middle class is less able than in the past to reduce tensions between the fairly wealthy and the fairly poor.

Slower Economic Growth

A fourth important aspect of the national economy is that growth rates today are lower than they were in the 1970s. And 1970s growth rates were lower than those of the 1960s. The gross national product (GNP) grew at a real annual rate (that is, adjusted for inflation) of 4.4 percent in the 1960s but only 3.5 percent in the 1970s and only 2.7 percent in the first half of the 1980s.[12] Between 1961 and 1969 there were no recessions, and inflation rates were low compared with the 1970s. Four recessions occurred since 1970 (1969–1970, 1974–1975, 1980, and 1981–1982), and the recovery periods in the 1970s suffered from extraordinarily high rates of inflation.

Table 6-2. The Receding Middle Class

Family income category	Percentage of families in category in:			
	1970	1975	1980	1985
Lower income	32.6%	33.8%	34.3%	34.0%
(Under $20,000 contant 1985 dollars)				
Middle income	54.4%	52.3%	50.6%	47.7%
($20,000 to $49,999 contant 1985 dollars)				
Upper income	13.0%	13.9%	15.1%	18.3%
($50,000 or more constant 1985 dollars)				

Source: United States Census Bureau, "Money Income of Householders, Families, and Persons in the United States: 1985," Current Population Reports. Series P-60, Number 156. (Washington, D.C.: Census Bureau, August 1987), p. 8.

On the face of it, the overall economy of the 1980s should have been better than previous decades, since it was marked by a dramatic decline in inflation rates and had more than six consecutive years (1983–1988) of sustained growth. But, as Figure 6-1 shows convincingly, the prosperity of the 1980s did not extend itself very well to the less affluent part of the population. Both poverty rates and unemployment rates were uncomfortably higher than in the 1970s.

The Changing National Economy and the City as a Place of Opportunity

How have these four trends affected the ability of cities to perform their historic roles as places of opportunity for the poor? The answer to that question depends in great measure on how dynamic the central-city economy will be in creating new jobs and economic opportunities. Many central cities have been badly hurt by the decline in the manufacturing sector and by foreign competition. Nowhere do these changing economic conditions provoke more problems than in the typical large- or medium-size central city, especially the old industrial cities of the Midwest.

The Bipolar City

As total economic growth slowed down, the central-city economies and the opportunities that central cities offer their poorest residents also slowed down. During the nineteenth- and twentieth-century period of urban European ethnic advancement, central cities grew faster than the rest of the economy, which was a major reason for European ethnic upward social mobility. Likewise, the less dynamic urban economy of recent years is a major reason for the very limited upward mobility of today's urban minorities.

Especially damaging to many older cities has been the decline of the industrial-production sector of the economy. Unskilled racial and Spanish-speaking minorities migrated by the millions into old industrial cities like Buffalo, Cleveland, Detroit, Gary, and Pittsburgh only to find that the industrial job market was starting to decline. Job growth was taking place disproportionately in the suburbs, but the minorities were housed in the central cities, and the industrial cities could not expand their economic opportunities fast enough to absorb the influx of unskilled laborers who came looking for jobs in the urban factories.

Over the past two generations, the politics of central cities in the Northeast changed from that of growth and dynamism to that of consolidation and holding the line. The housing supply deteriorated and even declined in some cities. Many cities lost large numbers of jobs. The precise number lost is difficult to calculate because regular employment data are usually published on a county basis rather

Figure 6-1. Growth, Poverty, and Unemployment over Three Decades

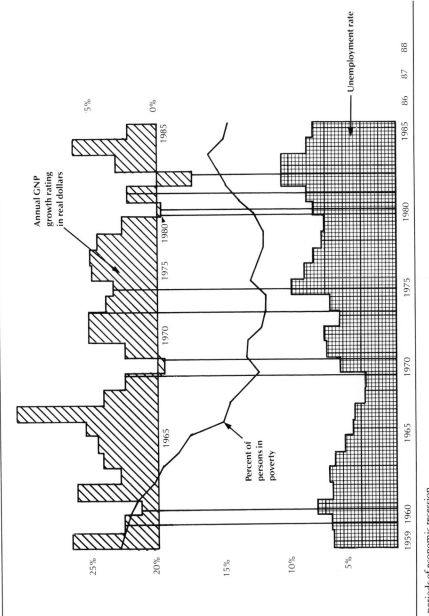

Shaded areas are periods of economic recession.
Source: *Statistical Abstract of the United States: 1987* (Washington, D.C.: U.S. Bureau of the Census, 1986), pp. 371–375, 416–417, 442, 531.

155

than on a city basis. But in places where city data are available, the results tend to be very discouraging. New York City lost 195,000 jobs between 1973 and 1981. Baltimore lost 65,000 jobs in the same period and St. Louis lost 84,000. Philadelphia County lost 105,000 jobs.[13] Very few were the cities in which the growth in good jobs for unskilled laborers kept pace with the in-migration of unskilled laborers.

The consequences of these developments are shown in Table 6-3. On the average, central-city residents have substantially lower incomes than suburbanites, and they are more than twice as likely to be living below the poverty line. The central cities have high concentrations of racial minorities, elderly people, and one-parent families headed by females. As Table 6-3 shows, these categories of people tend to have extremely low incomes and extremely high poverty levels.

What is emerging, according to George Sternlieb and James Hughes, is the bipolar city.[14] At one pole is a large, low-income population. Such a city may have a racial minority percentage sufficient to elect a black or Hispanic mayor. But as the city no longer offers enough manufacturing jobs that pay well, these new urban residents are forced to settle for lower-income jobs or to rely on government social services and welfare. In Boston, one of the most economically prosperous cities of the 1980s, one out of every five households had incomes below the poverty line in 1980.[15]

At the other pole of the bipolar city is a small elite of upper-income professionals who work in the sleek downtown office buildings and live in the gentrified high-income neighborhoods. Squeezed out between these two poles and fast disappearing, argue Sternlieb and Hughes, are the "middle groups who find both

Table 6-3. Socioeconomic Background of Central-City Residents: 1986

	Median family income	Percentage of individuals below the poverty line
By location		
Metropolitan suburbs	$38,445	8.4%
Central cities	26,679	18.0
Outside metropolitan areas	23,229	18.1
All whites	30,809	11.0
People with high concentrations in central cities		
Blacks	17,604	28.0
Hispanics	19,995	24.7
Persons over age 65	13,845	12.4
Female-headed households	13,647	34.6
Black female-headed households	9,300	50.1
Hispanic female-headed households	9,423	51.2

Source: Bureau of the Census, *Current Population Reports* P-60, no. 147, "Money Income and Poverty Status of Families and Persons in the United States: 1986" (Washington, D.C.: Bureau of the Census, July 1987), pp. 3, 22, 23, 89.

the lifestyles and economic opportunities of suburbia (and increasingly exurbia) affordable and much more fulfilling.''[16]

In this pessimistic scenario, the central cities are losing middle-class people, losing jobs, and losing their dynamism as places of economic opportunity for their millions of low-income residents. This scenario for cities was articulated succinctly by Norton Long, who said that the central city had become a "reservation for the poor, the deviant, the unwanted, and for those who make a business or career of managing them for the rest of society."[17] George Sternlieb compared the city to a sandbox for the poor, a place where society's problem people were given enough public programs to keep them busy while the real business of society got carried on in the suburbs.[18] Much of this pessimistic scenario is depicted in the Herblock cartoon on p. 159. The impoverished central city increasingly seems to be surrounded by affluent and dynamic suburbs.

The Patterns of Central-City Impoverishment

Central-city impoverishment is not universal, however. Table 6-4 shows that older central cities are much more likely than newer ones to be poorer than their suburbs. All the regions that reached SMSA size before 1880 are poorer than their surrounding suburbs, but in only a minority of the metropolises that reached SMSA size since 1940 are the central cities poorer than the suburbs.

The size of a metropolis also affects the discrepancy in affluence between central cities and suburbs. The largest metropolitan areas had the most severe discrepancies between central-city poverty and suburban affluence. In the smallest metropolitan areas, the central-city residents were at least as affluent as the suburban residents. This is shown in Table 6-5.

Not only are newer and smaller central cities more affluent than older and larger cities in comparison with their suburbs, but cities in the western and southern

Table 6-4. City/Suburban Differences by Age of SMSA: 1970

Period established	Number established in decade	Number of SMSAs in which the suburbs are more affluent than the central cities in:		
		Median family income	Percentage of adult population who are high school graduates	Percentage of population below poverty level
1800–1860	16	16 (100%)	16 (100%)	16 (100%)
1870–1880	17	17 (100%)	17 (100%)	17 (100%)
1890–1900	37	32 (87%)	34 (92%)	34 (92%)
1910–1920	55	42 (76%)	40 (73%)	46 (84%)
1930–1940	31	19 (61%)	21 (68%)	25 (81%)
1950–1960	62	30 (48%)	29 (47%)	36 (58%)
1970	24	11 (46%)	10 (42%)	14 (58%)

Source: U.S. Department of Commerce, Bureau of the Census, *1970 Census of Population: General Social and Economic Characteristics* (Washington, D.C.: U.S. Government Printing Office, 1972), tables 83, 89, 90 for each state.

Table 6-5. City/Suburban Differences by Size of SMSA: 1970

| | | Number of SMSAs in which the suburbs are more affluent than the central cities in: | | |
Size	Number	Median family income	Percentage of adult population who are high school graduates	Percentage of population below poverty level
Greater than 500,000	65	57 (88%)	56 (86%)	62 (95%)
100,000 to 499,999	152	101 (66%)	99 (65%)	115 (76%)
50,000 to 99,999	25	9 (36%)	12 (48%)	11 (44%)

Source: U.S. Department of Commerce, Bureau of the Census, *1970 Census of Population: General Social and Economic Characteristics* (Washington, D.C.: U.S. Government Printing Office, 1972), tables 83, 89, 90 for each state.

parts of the country are better off as well. This is undoubtedly related to the fact that most metropolises in the Southwest are newer than the metropolises of the East.

In great measure, central cities of the Northeast and Midwest have been hit by an economic disinvestment problem with two facets. First, population growth, growth in jobs, and growth in economic opportunities have been switching from the central cities to the suburbs. Second, there has also been a regional disinvestment from the Northeast and Midwest to the South and Southwest Sunbelt.

The disinvestment from northeastern and midwestern central cities in part is a result of the changing fortunes of the manufacturing sector of the national economy. Sunbelt cities such as Houston, Dallas, and Phoenix are much less likely to depend on an industrial economic base than are midwestern or northeastern cities. Dallas and Houston especially provide examples of Sunbelt cities that have become service and financial centers. The federal government's siting of the NASA (National Aeronautics and Space Administration) space center in Houston has helped make that region attractive for aserospace, computer, and high technology corporations. Light industries have also flooded into the region. By the end of the 1970s, Houston had a highly diversified local economy, but it was also an economy whose major sectors (processing oil production and other services) were dynamic parts of the national economy, at least until the oil crash of the mid-1980s.

Of course, as the Sunbelt cities become inundated with impoverished migrants, their growing economies could also be overloaded by job seekers. Alfred Watkins argues that in the past, in-migrants to southwestern cities tended to be "white, middle-class, well-educated professionals."[19] But today more and more in-migrants tend to be relatively poor Hispanics or factory workers displaced by the loss of manufacturing jobs in the North. The net impact of these migrants on Sunbelt cities is not clear. As we saw in Chapter 5, some research suggests that the impoverished Mexican immigrants actually helped the economy of California by providing a pool of cheap labor that kept manufacturers from going abroad.[20]

"Help!"

Source: From *The Herblock Gallery* (New York: Simon & Schuster, 1968). Reprinted by permission.

The plight of the older central cities is illustrated in this 1966 cartoon by Herblock of the *Washington Post*. Herblock has drawn several cartoons that show the central city overwhelmed by its problems. This one is particularly distinctive for its portrayal of the isolation of the central city and its forlorn cry for help that obviously cannot be heard above the tall buildings.

This type of labor, however, will not prevent the bipolar city from emerging. Sunbelt states are less likely than states of the Northeast or the Midwest to have public policies that encourage redistributing the new economic prosperity to the lower classes. With the exception of a few states like California, Sunbelt states have less progressive tax systems. Their unemployment compensation, workers' compensation, and general welfare benefit levels are much less generous. They are more likely than northeastern or midwestern cities to have state laws that prohibit union shops and discourage union recruitment drives. Because of these factors, Sunbelt cities might not offer any more advantages for lower-class upward social mobility than are offered by the declining cities of the Northeast.

Cause for Optimism?

Although the economic prospects for central cities are portrayed rather grimly here, it would not be fair to leave the topic of central-city economies without noting that some observers have a much more optimistic viewpoint.[21] The urban optimists view commercial redevelopment as perhaps the cornerstone to their more hopeful view of the city. During the 1970s and 1980s corporations began to look more favorably on expanding their facilities in central cities than they had during the 1950s or 1960s. Many cities have offered attractive incentives (described on pp. 175–176) to encourage corporations to undertake central-city development. Some of this development deliberately took place in minority neighborhoods where the corporate facilities could symbolize the company's concern for minority employment problems. But the most visible sign of corporate investment in central cities has been in the construction of office buildings in the central business districts. This approach was pioneered in the 1950s with the urban renewal programs in places such as Newark and New Haven. The pacesetters in the 1970s and 1980s were architecturally stunning developments such as Atlanta's Peachtree Center or Detroit's Renaissance Center. Miami, Buffalo, Washington, and Atlanta used federally available mass transit funds to start subway systems running through their downtowns. Chicago's Watertower Place, two marble-facade skyscrapers, literally transplanted the most luxurious retail shopping facilities from the downtown Loop to a new location a mile north, while the Loop has become mostly a jumble of massive office buildings. Boston rebuilt the historic Quincy Market into a chic downtown shopping area. And San Francisco's Fisherman's Wharf has been turned into a huge sprawling collection of tourist-oriented businesses. Similar consumer-oriented projects were also erected in Baltimore, San Antonio, and other big cities. The scholarly urbanists may criticize that such projects do little to revitalize urban neighborhoods or cope with deep-rooted social problems, but there is strong optimism on the part of chambers of commerce, labor union leaders, mayors, and central-city planning staffs that such redevelopments are the leading edge of urban revitalization.

In addition to corporate- and government-sponsored commercial redevelopment, many cities are also experiencing *gentrification*. This is the process whereby upper-middle-income and young people buy houses in older neighborhoods of cities, rehabilitate the houses, and in general drive up property values. This seems to be a widespread development from Beacon Hill in Boston to Nob Hill in San Francisco. Although this process has been confined to only a small number of people so far, the process is significant because it brings more spending money into previously impoverished neighborhoods, improves the tax base of cities, and upgrades the physical appearance of the neighborhoods. It also leads to the founding of new restaurants, specialty shops, and other commercial activity that can feed off the higher incomes of these gentrifiers and make their neighborhoods more lively. The negative side of gentrification is that it displaces the previous, poorer residents of the gentrified neighborhoods and forces them to seek generally more expensive housing elsewhere in the city.[22]

The Changing Fiscal Outlook and the City as a Place of Opportunity

Closely related to the urban economy is the urban fiscal situation. In contrast to the term city economy, which refers to the level of business activity and growth, the term *fiscal* refers to revenues and expenditures of the city government. We are going to analyze changing patterns of city finances over the past two decades. And in doing so we are going to note not only that there is relatively less money available for urban problems today than there was two decades ago, but also that there have also been important shifts in the sources of city revenue and the purposes for which it is being spent.

All of these changes (in the amounts of revenue, the sources of revenue, and the purposes of expenditures) can be traced in no small measure to the economic fortunes of central cities. As these fortunes sagged in the 1960s and 1970s, the fiscal capacity of urban governments to raise revenue fell behind the demands placed on them to provide more services. Low-income people cannot pay as much in property taxes as upper-income people. Tax assessments for old, run-down houses and deteriorating retail stores in older sections of cities are not as high as those of large, new suburban houses and air-conditioned shopping centers.

National economic forces since 1970 have also placed severe fiscal hardships on city governments. The inflationary environment of the 1970s put most cities in a fiscal squeeze. This was because inflation drove the cost of performing the same government activities higher than cities were able to raise their revenues.[23] Compounding the squeeze of inflation on cities, the four recessions since 1970 drove up city unemployment rates, which in turn limited city revenues and put pressure on city and county unemployment compensation budgets as well as welfare budgets. The economic recovery years since 1982 have helped city economies generally, but the recovery failed to bring back the growth rates of the 1960s.

In addition to the pressure of the national economy, two specific pressures on urban governments until the 1980s were rising energy costs and employee costs. Like all users of energy, urban governments were hit hard as gasoline prices quadrupled in the 1970s and the cost of fuel oil and natural gas also rose sharply.

Employee costs have always been a high share of city budgets; one study estimates that 60 to 80 percent of the typical city's budget goes for personnel costs.[24] As these employees unionized and sought salary increases that would keep them ahead of inflation during the 1970s, they put considerable pressure on government at all levels. Unlike corporations, urban governments have not been able to pass all these costs on to the consumer.

How Cities Get and Spend Their Revenue

There are some major reasons why city revenues have found it hard to keep pace with expenditures. One is that a declining or slowly growing city economy finds it hard to produce increasing amounts of tax revenue. Cities with growing economies suffered much less from the fiscal squeeze of the 1970s and 1980s than did declining cities.[25] Another reason for the fiscal squeeze is that cities have legal limits on their borrowing power, property tax levies, and on the other kinds of taxes or charges they can levy.

Figure 6-2 shows the main sources of city revenues—utilities and liquor revenues, current charges and fees, property taxes, other taxes, and intergovernmental aid. Utility and liquor revenues come from public electric, gas, or water supply systems and liquor stores, which many cities run. Current charges and fees are derived from such services as parking garages, public swimming pools, licensing fees, and sewer charges. Nonproperty taxes include income taxes, sales taxes, restaurant taxes, motel taxes, and entertainment taxes. Although each of these specific revenue sources is small, collectively they are important because they add up to more than one-fourth of city government revenues. The single largest tax revenue is the real estate tax, accounting for nearly one-fourth of locally derived revenue. A person's property tax is based on two factors—the assessed value of the property and the tax rate that local government levies on it. Thus property tax revenue can be increased either by raising the assessed value of people's homes or by raising the tax rate. However, cities are usually limited by law as to how much they can raise either the assessed values or the tax rates. This means that a city's best tactic for increasing property tax revenue is to increase the tax base of the city either by getting more industry to come in or by getting more expensive homes to be built. This is one of the reasons why downtown redevelopment is so attractive to big-city mayors. By replacing old, cheap buildings with modern skyscrapers, the city government can significantly improve its revenue base.

Until 1980 the fastest-growing city revenue source was intergovernmental aid, and even today it accounts for one-fourth of city revenues. Many cities have become heavily dependent on intergovernmental aid. Federal grants to Buffalo, Cleveland, and Detroit in the late 1970s, for example, amounted to nearly 70 percent of the locally generated revenue in those cities.[26] The hard-pressed cities of the Frostbelt are much more dependent on federal aid than are the growing cities of the Sunbelt. A 1983 study, for example, found that Detroit and St. Louis relied on federal funds to finance over one-fourth of their spending on such basic services as public works, sanitation, and police and fire protection. Houston and Los Angeles,

Figure 6-2. Sources of City Government Revenue: 1985–1986

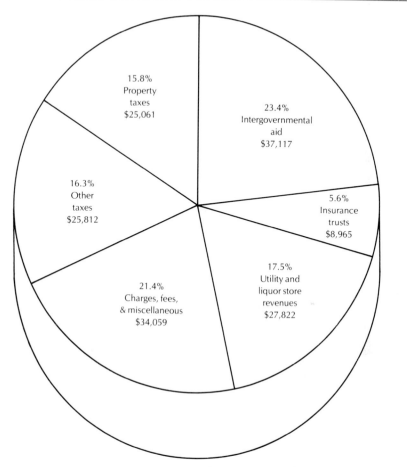

15.8%
Property
taxes
$25,061

23.4%
Intergovernmental
aid
$37,117

16.3%
Other
taxes
$25,812

5.6%
Insurance
trusts
$8,965

21.4%
Charges, fees,
& miscellaneous
$34,059

17.5%
Utility and
liquor store
revenues
$27,822

Amounts are expressed in millions. Total: $158,836

Source: United States Bureau of the Census, *Government Finances in 1985–86*, GF-86, No. 5 (Washington, D.C.: U.S. Government Printing Office, November 1987), p. 7.

in contrast, relied on federal funds for less than five percent of spending on those same services.[27] When federal aid was cut sharply by the Reagan Administration in the 1980s, dependent cities like Detroit and St. Louis wre forced to make much sharper reductions in public services than were the growing cities of the South and West. In 1987 cities throughout the country were fiscally hit when the Reagan administration finally eliminated general revenue sharing, which had been sending $4.6 billion annually to local governments to spend virtually as they wanted.

In addition to declining federal aid, many cities were also hit by property tax reduction movements. The most dramatic of these took place in California and

Massachusetts. California voters in 1978 passed an initiative called Proposition 13 that reduced property taxes by 60 percent. Massachusetts voters in 1980 passed an initiative called Proposition 2¹/₂ that limited the property tax in that state to 2¹/₂ percent of assessed real estate value. Thus California and Massachusetts municipalities could not raise their property tax rates to make up for the lost federal aid. Both states were obliged to increase state aid to local governments to help replace lost federal aid and property tax revenues.

In contrast to the situation in California and Massachusetts, property taxes as revenue sources became more, rather than less, important in some other states. Minnesota, in the Frostbelt, cut state aid to local governments sharply in the 1980s, resulting in greater reliance on the property tax for funding basic services. Texas, in the Sunbelt, saw its oil revenues decline, reducing its ability to provide state aid to its cities.

As a consequence of the property tax revolt of the late 1970s and the Reagan revolution of the 1980s, a subtle shift has occurred in the sources of city revenues. Reliance on integovernmental aid has dropped from 27.4 to 23.4 percent of city revenue sources between 1981 and 1986, and reliance on property taxes has declined from 16.9 to 15.8 percent. To make up for these reductions, there has been an increase in charges and fees from 19.7 percent to 21.4 percent and an increase in other taxes from 15.2 percent to 16.4 percent.[28]

One final source of revenue not shown in Figure 6-2 is borrowing. Cities, like other governments, engage in two types of borrowing—long-term and short-term. Short-term borrowing is used to cover expenses while waiting for tax or other revenues to arrive. Many cities receive their property tax revenue at only two payment dates during the year. Federal and state aid arrives more frequently, but seldom on a monthly basis. While they wait for these revenues to come in, cities must pay their employees, pay for supplies, and meet other obligations. If they do not have enough cash on hand to pay these costs, they borrow the money for the short term by issuing *revenue anticipation notes* or *tax anticipation notes*.

Cities use long-term borrowing to finance large capital expenditures such as buildings, heavy equipment, or land acquisition. There are two types of long-term borrowing—general obligation bonds and revenue bonds. *General obligation bonds* are backed by the taxing power of the city and a portion of them are paid off each year from city tax revenues. States usually limit the amount of general obligation bonds that can be outstanding, and most general obligation bonds have to be approved by voters before they can be issued. *Revenue bonds* are used to finance construction of a facility such as a toll bridge, a convention center, or an industrial redevelopment project. They are not backed by the taxing power of the city, but are paid off instead from the revenues generated by the facility.

For what purposes do cities spend their money? This question is hard to answer definitively, because expenditure patterns vary widely across the country. Figure 6-3, providing data for all cities, shows that about three-fourths of city budget monies are spent for physical maintenance or traditional services such as police and fire protection, parks, streets, libraries, and for utilities such as water and sewer systems, gas, and electric power. Beyond those traditional basics, virtually all central

Figure 6-3. City Expenditures: 1985–1986

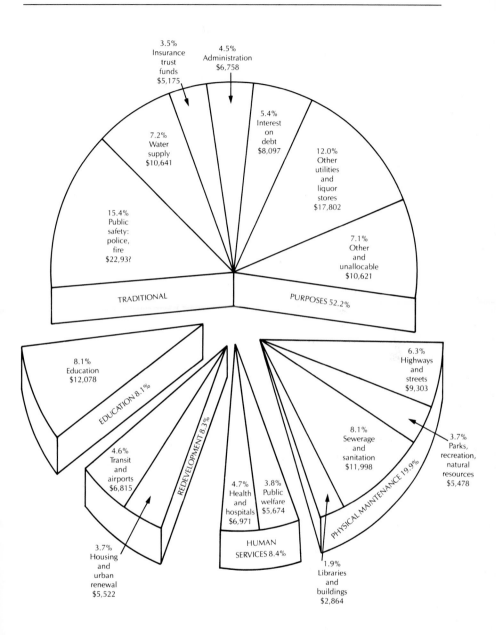

3.5%
Insurance
trust
funds
$5,175

4.5%
Administration
$6,758

5.4%
Interest
on
debt
$8,097

7.2%
Water
supply
$10,641

12.0%
Other
utilities
and
liquor
stores
$17,802

15.4%
Public
safety:
police,
fire
$22,93?

7.1%
Other
and
unallocable
$10,621

TRADITIONAL   PURPOSES 52.2%

8.1%
Education
$12,078

EDUCATION 8.1%

6.3%
Highways
and
streets
$9,303

REDEVELOPMENT 8.3%

4.6%
Transit
and
airports
$6,815

8.1%
Sewerage
and
sanitation
$11,998

3.7%
Parks,
recreation,
natural
resources
$5,478

PHYSICAL MAINTENANCE 19.9%

4.7%
Health
and
hospitals
$6,971

3.8%
Public
welfare
$5,674

HUMAN
SERVICES 8.4%

3.7%
Housing
and
urban
renewal
$5,522

1.9%
Libraries
and
buildings
$2,864

Amounts in millions. Total: $148,732

Source: U.S. Bureau of the Census, *Government Finances in 1985–86,* GF-86, No. 5 (Washington, D.C.: U.S. Government Printing Office, November 1987), p. 13.

cities engage in some redevelopment activities. Few cities engage in the level of education and human services indicated in Figure 6-3, however; those figures are heavily weighted by cities in the Northeast. In the rest of the country, education tends to be provided by independent school districts whose funding is independent of city finances. Outside of the Northeast, welfare and social services are provided by countries more commonly than by cities.

If we compare the data in Figure 6-3 with similar data from only a few years earlier, we note some subtle but important changes in expenditure patterns. There is a small but important decrease in the percent of city funds spend for education, human services, street maintenance, parks, and recreation. There is an increase in the percent of city funds spent for sewerage, public utilities, water supply, and redevelopment. This shift in expenditure patterns is not accidental. As Paul Peterson has pointed out, it is harder for cities to raise money for redistribution purposes (such as social welfare) than it is to raise money for purposes linked to redevelopment that can be viewed as contributing to growth in jobs and business activity.[29]

Urban Fiscal Stress

Squeezed by increasing demands for expenditure and decreasing sources of revenue, many cities have suffered severe fiscal stress in recent years. Wayne County, Michigan, the nation's third largest county, lacked resources to meet its payroll in October, 1979, as did the Chicago school system in November of that year. Cleveland was forced into default on its bond payments in 1979, and the San Jose school district was so short of resources that it declared bankruptcy in 1983.[30] Most cities fared better than these urban governments, but few cities escaped the fiscal problems of the late 1970s and early 1980s. A survey by the Joint Economic Committee of Congress found that 47 percent of medium-sized cities (pop. 50,000–99,999) ran operating deficits in 1982.[31] Perhaps the most famous cases of urban fiscal stress were those of New York City, Chicago, and Cleveland.

Three Cases of Fiscal Stress

Like many northeastern cities, New York underwent a dramatic in-migration of low-income people since mid-century—especially Puerto Ricans and rural blacks. As these people migrated to the city, they needed help from the city's welfare, health, education, and housing agencies. During the 1960s, militant community organizations put increasing pressure on city agencies to meet these needs better. In responding to these demands, New York City saw its budgets soar during the 1960s. The number of city workers grew rapidly. Salaries increased much faster than salaries of workers in private enterprise. Even more important, fringe benefits such as pensions increased liberally. Many city employees were able to retire in their early forties with pension benefits equal to half their last year's salary.

The city's tax revenues did not rise fast enough to cover all these expenditures. To make up this deficit between revenue and expenditure, the city got into the practice of borrowing short-term money by issuing municipal notes in order to make interest payments on its long-term obligations. By 1975 the city was running a deficit of $800 million and the debt repayments totaled $1.6 billion per year. The city was unable to make these payments in 1975 without borrowing more short-term money. However, the fact that the city was in danger of defaulting on its bond payments made its credit rating drop, and investors were unwilling to buy new city bonds or short-term notes.

The threat that the nation's largest city might default had more severe consequences than would have resulted from the same threat by a smaller city or by any individual person no matter how wealthy. This forced the state of New York and the federal government to act.

The state of New York responded by creating two new institutions—the Municipal Assistance Corporation (MAC) and the Emergency Financial Control Board (EFCB). MAC was authorized to issue $3 billion in long-term bonds and use those funds to buy up the city's short-term obligations. The city would make regular payments to MAC to pay off the bonds, and the city would thus be saved from immediate default. The MAC bonds themselves did not become marketable, however, until prospective bond purchasers were assured that the city's financial management was being put back in order. In order to straighten out city finances, the Emergency Financial Control Board was given power to oversee the city budget. Since three members of the seven-person board were top executives of major New York corporations and two members represented the state, New York City effectively gave outside forces ultimate control over its budget. The EFCB used its powers to ensure that city costs were cut, welfare benefits reduced, charges raised at the City University of New York, reductions made in the city workforce, and severe cutbacks made in public services. Even this left the city with substantial deficits, however, and city leaders turned to the federal government for more aid. The federal government was very reluctant to provide aid until more economies were forced on the city. Finally, in 1978, the federal government extended a number of long-term loan guarantees that got New York City back on a timetable for meeting its financial obligations. To demonstrate the commitment of public employees to the financial rescue plan, New York City and state pension funds agreed to buy a large share of the MAC securities. This package "ingeniously linked the destiny of the city, the state and their employees," wrote two observers.[32] EFCB members could hope that these links would force labor to moderate its demands on the city. If city employee unions in the future bargain for benefits that drive the city to the edge of default, those employees will be the ultimate losers, because so much of their pension funds are tied up in the city's debt.

With the federal guarantees, the employee pension fund involvement, and the stringent financial controls installed as part of the rescue plan, New York's fiscal affairs were soon put back in order. By 1983 the Municipal Assistance Corporation had built up a surplus large enough to pay off the guaranteed loans and get the city out from under the thumb of the EFCB.

While these events were taking place in New York, Chicago, the nation's second largest city, seemed to be quite solvent. Commentators began calling it the "city that works" in comparison to New York, which apparently was judged not to work. By the end of the decade, however, Chicago found itself in a fiscal bind very reminiscent of New York City's. When Jane Byrne became mayor in 1979, she found that the city had for several years been making up budget deficits by borrowing money from several escrow funds set aside to finance equipment purchases and other recurring expenses. However, the city did not repay the money to the escrow funds. And by 1979 this had created a cumulative deficit of $100 million that the city had to repay.[33]

Just as that fiscal problem was coming to light, it was discovered that the Chicago School Board had been engaging in dubious financial practices over the years and by 1979 had accumulated a deficit of about half a billion dollars. The district had failed to pay the Internal Revenue Service $16 million it had withheld in payroll taxes, and $44 million had simply disappeared and could not be found by a team of auditors appointed to untangle the board's complicated finances. School teachers did not receive paychecks for three consecutive paydays in December 1979 and January 1980. Three thousand teachers were laid off, and a strike closed the schools temporarily in January 1980.

Cleveland's fiscal situation was even more disastrous than New York's or Chicago's, since Cleveland actually did default on some debt payments and at one point sold off city property to get funds to meet other bond payments.

At issue in Cleveland were the fate of the city-owned power company, Muny Light, and the city's flamboyant mayor, Dennis Kucinich. Muny Light was in direct competition with a private power company, Cleveland Electric Illuminating Company (CEI), which for years had been trying to purchase Muny Light from the city. Until 1970 Muny Light had been profitable and had contributed a substantial subsidy to the city government's budget each year. But Muny Light began losing money in the 1970s in no small measure because CEI was able to block Muny's bid to purchase extra power from outside suppliers in order to prevent power outages. As Muny began losing money and required a subsidy from the city budget rather than contributing to the budget, pressure built up from the Cleveland business community to sell the company to CEI.

It was opposition to this proposed sale that brought Dennis Kucinich to prominence and enabled him to win election as mayor in 1977. But when Kucinich blocked the sale of Muny Light to CEI, Cleveland banks threatened to retaliate by not rolling over several short-term notes that were coming due. In the summer and fall of 1978 two bond rating agencies lowered the city's credit rating, and this strengthened the position of the banks and CEI in forcing the mayor to sell Muny Light. When Kucinich still refused to sell, the debate between the mayor's office and the business community grew increasingly acrimonious. The chairman of the Cleveland Trust Company referred to Kucinich as the "little canker downtown"[34] and Kucinich in turn called the bankers "blood-sucking vampires."[35]

As the impasse dragged on, the city defaulted on $14 million in notes that came due in December 1978. The mayor and city council finally worked out a compromise in which the voters were asked in a special election whether the city should sell Muny Light and whether they would approve a 50 percent increase in the city income tax to pay city debts that were due. The voters in February 1979 approved the tax increase and rejected the sale of Muny Light by 2 to 1 margins. Kucinich was then able to use the income tax receipts to pay off the notes and other debt, but the controversy severely damaged his reputation and he was defeated in his 1979 bid for reelection. The new mayor, George Voinovich, worked closely with the city's business community to cut city government expenses, improve fiscal management practices, and negotiate an agreement with the banks whereby short-term city debt was exchanged for long-term bonds.[36]

Why Fiscal Crisis?

In all three of these fiscal crises, there was plenty of blame to go around. Some observers blamed the crises on bankers, charging that they lent too much money too easily before the crises began and then deliberately turned off the money spigot when they saw a chance to gain influence over city expenditures. Others blamed the crises on fiscal mismanagement, and still others blamed the demographic changes that had turned the cities into havens for the poor and the unwanted. New York mayor Abraham Beame blamed his city's crisis on the city's big heart; New York's generosity toward the poor exceeded its revenue base, he theorized.

We can sort these various explanations into two general schools of thought—the external, socioeconomic explanation and the internal, political vulnerability explanation. The external explanation attributes the fiscal crises to external demographic and socioeconomic forces beyond the cities' control.[37] The influx of racial minorities and poor people into the cities, the loss of jobs and middle-class residents to suburbia, the slowdown in national economic growth, and the decline of the industrial sector have all combined to place a fiscal squeeze on the cities. At the same time that they have been losing their tax base, the central cities have been flooded with poor people who place a high demand on urban services.

The second school of thought attributes the urban fiscal crises to internal city political vulnerabilities. City bureaucracies, according to this viewpoint, tend to be bloated and inefficient.[38] They exert pressure for hiring more employees and expanding their budgets. They are supported in this task by the public employees' unions, which not only have the power to cripple a city through strike but also constitute a substantial voting bloc in mayoral and city council elections. A New York City Sanitary Workers' head once commented, "We have a natural advantage no [private-sector] union has. We can elect our employers."[39] Compounding these pressures for driving up city expenditures is the fact that many mayors have become politically vulnerable to such pressures. They have become vulnerable because of the deliberate weakening of the political parties, as we discussed in Chapter 4. Wherever mayors lack a strong partisan electoral base, according to the internal vulnerability school of thought, they are forced to make electoral alliances with the bureaucratic leaders, public employees' unions, and private-sector citizens' groups that also want to expand public services. In New York City, for example, the most dramatic expansion of the city's fiscal commitments took place under Mayors Robert Wagner (1954–1965) and John Lindsay (1965–1973), who followed precisely that electoral strategy. Once in office, they found it difficult, if not impossible, to turn down the demands of the very groups that had helped elect them.[40] Ken Auletta expressed this viewpoint when he wrote that "New York was, paradoxically, the victim of too much—and too little—democracy; a plethora of special interest groups combined with short-sighted politicians and a self-centered electorate."[41]

Which of these theories is closer to the truth? Perhaps there is a bit of truth in each. A Congressional Budget Office study viewed the external socioeconomic forces as long-term factors contributing to fiscal crisis and viewed the internal political forces as short-term factors.[42] Pietro S. Nivola sought to see if cities suffering from fiscal stress correlated more closely with cities suffering economic hardship or cities susceptible to some of the political vulnerabilities we have cited. He found no significant relationship between economic hardship and fiscal stress. But he did find some empirical support for the political vulnerability thesis, in that fiscal stress was significantly higher in cities supporting a high percentage of unionized workers, high average employee salaries, and high employee retirement costs.[43]

The most sophisticated study of the causes of fiscal stress was probably that done by Terry N. Clark and Lorna C. Ferguson, who conducted a multivariate statistical analysis of 62 cities between 1960 and 1977. They concluded that fiscal stress has more to do with political leadership than with economic conditions. They also systematically deny that urban fiscal stress is caused by regional imbalances, declining population, job loss, recession, or inflation.[44] Many northern cities suffered economic hardships at least as serious as those of New York or Cleveland without the city government defaulting on debt payments.

But part of Clark and Ferguson's conclusion can be traced to the distinct way in which they use the term fiscal strain, an imbalance between city government expenditures and the taxpaying potential of the local city economy.[45] In their terms, if a major resource such as population "declines, and spending does too, the city will not suffer fiscal strain."[46] Such reductions might not be stressful statistically, but they will be very stressful politically for city council members who have to face the painful practical task of cutting services, reducing library hours, eliminating some recreational facilities, firing employees, and raising fees for parking meters, recreational programs, and other services.

To see how cities adapt to fiscal strain in practice, it is useful to examine an actual case study of a community in the throes of fiscal stress. Irene S. Rubin conducted such a study of an anonymous midwestern city that she called Southside.[47] Although a small central city of 75,000 people, Southside experienced most of the economic and demographic changes typical of midwestern cities. Its black population grew, and its middle-class white population increasingly moved out to the suburbs. The city recaptured many of those out-migrants by annexing them back into the city, but this had the effect of increasing service costs out to the new areas. Those economic and demographic changes had a long-term effect of worsening the city's fiscal position, but in themselves they did not precipitate the fiscal crisis. Neither did she find that unionization caused the crisis. The unions became militant only after the crisis had started and the city manager sought to deal with it by refusing to negotiate with the unions.

Rubin suggested that two developments precipitated the crisis. The first was a drive after the 1968 riots to expand the size of the police force and to professionalize it. Ironically, increasing the number of officers did not lead to increased patrolling in riot-torn neighborhoods. Rather, patrols increased in the downtown business district. The second precipitating event was the city's desire to issue bonds to finance a downtown redevelopment project. Moody's bond rating agency lowered the city's credit rating, and this action brought to light the fact that the city manager and city council had for a number of years been concealing a growing budget deficit.

Once precipitated, the crisis was prolonged by city attempts to hide the size of the deficits and by a political conflict that ensued when the city manager sought to weaken the public employees' unions. In the last analysis, however, Rubin found that Southside's fiscal problems were self-correcting. The decline in property tax valuations had led the city to adopt redevelopment policies and this led in turn to the reduction in the city's credit rating. Once the budget deficits became highly visible, the city was obliged to take corrective action by reducing expenditures and raising taxes.[48]

Coping with Urban Fiscal Problems

If Rubin's analysis of Southside is applicable elsewhere, it suggests that urban fiscal stress is the product of both external socioeconomic variables *and* internal political variables. In the cases of New York, Cleveland, and Chicago, political ineptitude and fiscal mismanagement worsened a situation that would have been very bad even with excellent financial management. All three cities had been faced with escalating demands for public services as well as demands from public employee unions for better pay and fringe benefits. Large amounts of intergovernmental aid had the effect on most cities of stimulating higher levels of expenditures.[49] Compounding these pressures that drove expenditures up was the fact that all three cities also faced pressures that kept local revenues from rising as fast as expenditures. All three cities faced a long-term economic decline relative to their surrounding suburbs and the Sunbelt region. And all three city governments faced the severe fiscal squeeze resulting from the 1970s' economic environment of severe recessions sandwiched between runaway inflation.

Although most cities do not face the danger of bankruptcy as did New York, Chicago, and Cleveland, often they do face the same kinds of fiscal pressures described earlier. Like Southside, many cities have a limited flexibility to react to those pressures. They can (1) cut services, (2) try to share their tax burden with other governments, (3) increase productivity so that they get more services for the same amount of expenditure, and (4) try to attract new investment into the city to improve the tax base.

Cutting services was adopted in New York, Chicago, and Cleveland. Although these cuts often put a burden on the least affluent people, they were a political necessity in those cities to overcome the huge deficits that had built up. In New York, cutting services was politically necessary to get the federal and state aid that eventually kept the city from going bankrupt. Service cuts, in fact, have become common in cities since the mid-1970s.

The second strategy, sharing the tax burden, usually means importing as much federal aid as possible. Urban governments relied heavily on federal CETA funds to provide jobs and meet their payrolls. When CETA was abolished in 1981, these governments were forced to lay off many workers. Cities became heavily dependent on revenue sharing (which was abolished in 1987), community development block grants, and other forms of federal aid (see Chapter 13). Urban areas also continue to rely on state aid to cover substantial education costs and welfare costs. One of the most imaginative revenue-sharing schemes was the Minnesota Fiscal Disparities Act of 1971. Under its provisions, the tax from all commercial real estate built in the Twin Cities metropolitan area after 1972 has been split, with 60 percent going to the local community where the real estate was built and 40 percent going into a metropolitan pool to be shared by all the municipalities in the area. This especially benefits the central cities. They do not get as much new real estate as the growing suburbs, but their large populations give them the largest portion of funds going into the metropolitan pool. By 1988 this pool had reached nearly $2 billion in property values.

A third way for cities to cope with the fiscal squeeze is to increase productivity. This approach began receiving considerable attention in the late 1970s as mayors and other political leaders began searching for ways to maintain service levels while budgets and workforces were being cut back. The productivity movement will be discussed more thoroughly in Chapter 8.

The fourth strategy is to attract new business investment into the city. This investment will add jobs to the local economy and will also increase the real estate tax base to support city services.

Of course, all cities will not react to fiscal stress in the same way. Clark and Ferguson discovered from their study of 62 cities that a particular city's reaction to fiscal stress is greatly influenced by the type of political culture the city has.[50] Cities with a traditional New Deal Democratic culture, for example, are likely to resist the privatization of city services, while Republican cities are apt to encourage privatization. In the culture that Clark and Ferguson label New Fiscal Populism (San Diego under Mayor Pete Wilson, for example), cities are apt to adopt improved productivity as a means of coping with fiscal stress. But perhaps the most widely emulated strategy today is to promote and encourage economic development.

Urban Economic Development Strategies

Urban economic development seeks to increase the economic activity in an urban area and improve the area's fiscal base. To accomplish those goals, cities have been very active over the past ten years encouraging firms to move in or to expand their operations. The strategies used in economic development rely on close interaction between city governments and their states.

The Business Climate Debate

Perhaps the most visible issue in development politics is the business climate. Cleveland mayor Dennis Kucinich was put on the defensive, as we saw above, by the charge that he was creating a poor business climate in the city. And political leaders in most states are also vulnerable to the same charge if they press too hard on issues such as taxes or environmental protection that are resisted by the local business community. No political leader wants to be blamed if a major employer closes a large facility and blames it on the business climate.

What qualities it takes to create a positive business climate is not absolutely clear, and it may vary from one type of business to another. The Chicago-based industrial consulting firm of Alexander Grant and Company publishes an annual rating of the business climates for manufacturing firms. Those ratings focus on factors such as labor costs that are important to industrial manufacturing firms. Not surprisingly, states with strong unions and generous workers' compensation programs score poorly.[51] By contrast, *Inc. Magazine* recently rated state climates for small business.[52] Labor cost is less important to small businesses than is state action to facilitate venture capital that can assist small firms as they get underway. Not surprisingly, this study came up with rankings far different from those of the Grant study. Minnesota, for example, in 1983 was rated fifth in climate favoring small businesses but thirty-second in climate for industrial manufacturing.

What issues are most involved in creating a favorable business climate? Taxes, labor costs, and the level of government expenditure on public services are the most politically controversial issues. Many business organizations in the high-tax and high-spending states of the Northeast and Midwest claim that the low-tax and low-spending states of the South and Southwest are more attractive to industry. According to this viewpoint, when firms decide to relocate or to expand they often go South or West in order to avoid the "punitive" tax structures of the Northeast and Midwest.

Attempts to trace empirically and systematically the causes and effects of corporate relocations do not tend to support the tax-structure theory. Although corporations continuously monitor their branch operations (deciding to open some new plants, expand some existing ones, and shut down others), they do not commonly relocate whole facilities from one state or region to another. One of the most widely respected studies of the impact of corporate in- and out-migrations on jobs was David Birch's study of over two million firms in the early and middle 1970s. He found that such migrations had a practically negligible impact on the number of jobs a state gains or loses.[53]

To the extent that firms do relocate facilities, to what extent do those relocations result from companies leaving a state to avoid high tax structures? Roy Bahl surveyed numerous studies of the impact of taxes on decisions to relocate from one state to another and concluded, "The consensus of a great deal of such research would seem to be that taxes are not a major factor in interregional location,"[54] although taxes do affect relocation within a metropolis. State taxes are a relatively small percentage of a firm's income and most firms can save relatively little on taxes by moving from one state to the next.

The limited impact of taxes on locational decisions was also discovered by Roger W. Schmenner's study of location decisions by 410 of the Fortune 500 companies. Schmenner found that "tax and financial incentives have little influence on almost all plant location decisions." At best they are "tie breakers" when competing sites are otherwise equally desirable.[55]

More important than taxes is the cost of labor. States with low average wages, weak unions, so-called right-to-work laws that inhibit union strength, and low unemployment and workers' compensation benefits may have a significant advantage in attracting industry over states that are on the high side on all of those criteria. Offsetting this factor, however, is the fact that many firms also want a labor force that is relatively well educated and has a reputation for reliable, hard work. For this reason a state that reduces taxes by cutting back on the public schools and higher education that produce quality workforces may in the long run worsen its business climate rather than improve it.

Finally, many locational criteria are not very directly under a state's control. Other things being equal, a moderate weather climate would be more attractive than an extreme climate. Access to low-cost energy was a major plus for Texas in attracting industry during the energy-conscious 1970s, for example. A region with a variety of first-class cultural, sports, and entertainment amenities would be more attractive than a state without such amenities. And perhaps most important, a region close to a firm's markets would be more attractive than a region far from those markets.

To sum up, a state's business climate is composed of many variables that give each state its own peculiar combination of strengths and weaknesses. But seldom discussed is the question of how much difference the business climate actually makes in promoting a state's economy. If business climate were the single most important factor in economic development, states like South Dakota and Mississippi would be among the highest in economic development, while states like New York and California would be underdeveloped. In fact, the reverse is true. An overall comparison of the relationship between the Grant Thornton business-climate rankings of 1985 and the number of jobs gained or lost in each state in the same year found no relationship between the two variables. Of the 24 states that gained the most jobs that year, 13 were in the fifty percent of states with the worst business climates.[56] Nor do the good business-climate states score especially well in projected job growth in the future. The National Planning Association projects that nearly half the total growth in jobs between 1986 and the year 2000 will occur in just 30 metropolitan areas. Only 12 of these metropolises are located in the good business-climate states, while 17 are in the poor business-climate states.[57]

None of this data indicates that business climate is irrelevant to corporations when they make location decisions. Rather, it reflects the fact that corporations do not have unlimited discretion to move where they want. They are constrained by proximity to markets and suppliers, availability of a competent workforce, and other factors.

Incentives for Economic Development

In addition to facilitating a favorable business climate, states and communities also have a broad range of incentives to attract new industries and to retain established ones. Most states use public relations through advertising in business magazines. Most have established central agencies to coordinate business promotion efforts. And most states and communities provide a range of tactics to promote business. Some of the most prominent of these tactics are urban enterprise zones, a range of financial incentives, and venture-capital efforts.

Urban Enterprise Zones

By the mid-1980s twenty-seven states had set up urban enterprise zones.[58] These are zones in blighted neighborhoods in which taxes are reduced and government regulations relaxed for any firm that will set up shop and employ local residents. In Connecticut, for example, up to six enterprise zones were authorized for any city neighborhood that had at least 25 percent of its 1981 population below the poverty line, on welfare programs, or unemployed. A firm that locates a facility in one of these zones and hires more than 30 percent of the facility's employees from the zone will have the facility's corporate income tax cut in half for ten years, will receive a $1,000 state grant for every zone job created, and will have its local property tax reduced by 80 percent for five years.[59]

Financial Incentives

Local governments are often very aggressive in promoting economic development, and over the years they have developed a variety of financial incentives to attract new business.[60] First among these incentives is probably the *tax abatement*. This is the tactic of forgiving a firm's property taxes for a number of years if it expands in the particular city. Although the preponderance of evidence suggests that tax abatements do not have very much effect on the investment decisions of corporations,[61] tax abatements are widely used. Cities can also provide seed money for firms to locate. For example, suppose a firm wishes to expand in a city but is hampered by the lack of developable land. Using its powers of eminent domain, the city can force the owners of a desirable piece of land to sell and move out. Purchasing and clearing such land is extremely expensive, but cities have many sources of financial aid for this purpose. From the federal government, cities are likely to use Community Development Block Grant (CDBG) funds and Urban Development Action Grant (UDAG) funds for this purpose. They can also raise money through their power to issue bonds. The two most popular types have been Industrial Development Revenue Bonds (IDRB) and Tax Increment Financing (TIF).

The IDRB allows the city to act as an intermediary to help a company raise development money at a cost lower than if it had to go directly to the market and sell its own bonds. Because the interest earned by municipal bonds is exempt from federal income taxes (and usually state income taxes in the state issued), they carry lower interest rates than corporate bonds. A city will entice a corporation to expand by issuing IDRBs. The bonds will be paid off by the revenues from the company's development project. This will reduce the interest costs for most corporations without putting any cost on the city. The entire cost is paid by the federal government in the form of lower income tax revenues. Until 1987 IDRBs were the single most popular method of funding urban economic development. But in 1986 Congress put a cap on the amount of IDRBs that each state would be allowed.

Under tax increment financing (TIF), the city will declare a tax increment financing district in the neighborhood it wants to develop. The city will issue bonds to clear the land and entice a developer to come in and build some commercial structure on the site. Because the new structure will be more valuable than the older uses of the land, it will generate more property taxes. This increment, or increase in property taxes generated, will be used to pay off the tax increment financing bonds that were issued. Thus the new development will not bring new property taxes into the city's general revenues until after the TIF bonds are paid off. But the development itself will probably create many new jobs for city residents and ultimately improve the city's fiscal picture.

Venture Capital

At least 20 states today have *venture capital* programs to invest start-up capital in new companies that have excellent prospects for growth. The Sky Computer Company of Lowell, Massachusetts, for example, badly needed capital in 1982 to market plug-in computer boards for scientific and engineering applications. The Massachusetts Technology Development Corporation (MTDC) then invested public funds in the company to help it get off the ground. Within three years the company's workforce expanded from 15 to 85 and the annual sales shot up to $10 million. By using its governmentally supplied venture capital for projects like this, MTDC has been able to increase the number of jobs in the state. Between 1979, when it was created, and 1984 the MTDC invested about $5.7 million in venture capital in 27 companies, which has resulted in over 1,000 jobs and $2 million in state income tax collections each year.[62] In addition to public venture-capital corporations like MTDC, three states (New York, New Jersey, and Michigan) allow public employee pension funds to invest in venture-capital projects.[63] Although venture capital is extremely risky, the Massachusetts example shows that under the proper circumstances it can produce benefits that far exceed the costs.

Assessing Urban Development Strategies

Cities are under so much economic and fiscal pressure that they have little choice but to do whatever seems likely to improve the local economy. Several questions should be asked, however, before a city enters into a public-private venture of the sort described here.

First, do the development projects result in a *net* increase in jobs? Development projects always generate new jobs. But they usually also destroy jobs that existed on the site prior to the project. Before a city undertakes a public-private development project, it should ask whether the project will create more jobs than it destroys. It should also ask whether the people who lose jobs will find new ones in the city.

Second, do the projects bring a *net* fiscal benefit to the area? Wellston, Ohio, for example, suddenly got 980 new jobs when Geno's, Inc., decided to consolidate its $200 million-per-year pizzamaking facilities in that city. To help Geno's locate in Wellston, the local county and the state of Ohio lent the firm over $5 million at a $1^7/_8$ percent interest rate. But once the new facility began operations, its waste products clogged the city sewerage system with a mass of cheese, meat, and other ingredients the consistency of toothpaste and the color of tomato soup. When the EPA threatened to close down the plant as an environmental danger, Ohio had to give the firm $500,000 to find a way to clean up the wastes.[64] In the long run, Geno's may be a net fiscal contributor to Wellston, the county, and the state. But in the short run, the location inducements appear to have been fairly costly.

Third, does a public-private redevelopment project actually generate new economic activity, or does it just relocate activity that would have occurred anyway? Much of the redevelopment of the 1970s and 1980s has focused on central-city downtowns. It is a fair guess that if the city governments had not acted, most of the investments would have been made anyway. They probably would have been made not downtown but in the suburbs of the same metropolitan areas. Larger suburbs have learned that they, too, must compete for new development, so now they also are engaged in the game of offering a variety of tax or bond inducements to promote development. Many older regions probably had good reasons to redevelop their old, run-down central business districts. But from today's metropolitan-wide perspective, one has to ask whether it any longer makes sense to have cities competing with one another offering tax incentives for development projects that in all likelihood would occur someplace in the same metropolitan area if no government offered any inducement. As we will see in Chapter 9, no American metropolis has a governmental institution capable of planning and acting from such an area-wide perspective.

Fourth, what recourse will a city have if, after granting lucrative incentives to a firm, the firm eventually moves out? Yonkers, New York, in 1972 put up over $2 million of a $13 million public financing package to help Otis Elevator build a modern factory and thereby keep its manufacturing facilities in that city. In the 1980s, Otis's parent company, United Technologies, began phasing out the factory and announced that it would have to be closed because it was technologically obsolete. Mayor Angelo Martinelli charged that the firm had breached a contract and sued in court to get back the city's investment.[65] Can a company legally accept millions of dollars in public assistance and then turn its back on the city that aided it?*

A related issue arose in Detroit, where in 1980 the city razed 1100 homes in a neighborhood called Poletown. Having spent nearly $200 million to do this,

*The answer to this question is not yet resolved. Yonkers lost its suit against Otis Elevator but has appealed it. Other cities and states have also sued various companies, following the Yonkers example, but no definitive court decision has yet been made.

Detroit offered the site to General Motors for $8 million and offered the company a $5.4 million annual property-tax break to build an assembly plant on the site. General Motors built the plant, but at about that time the bottom fell out of the automobile market, and the employment levels at the plant have yet to match the promises that were made.[66] Given the vast number of public incentives bestowed on companies by cities in recent years, issues such as this are likely to recur. Unless a major court decision rules against such actions by companies, the cities are in a poor bargaining position. The tougher a city is when negotiating with a company, the less likely the company is to construct the facility the city wants so badly.

Fifth, what will be the unanticipated consequences of a redevelopment project? Although no one can predict the future, analysts ought to try and forecast what unintended byproducts might result from the project. Often community leaders are so eager to begin a project that will generate a lot of economic activity that they accept the developer's projections at face value while downplaying the objections of critics. Nowhere was this clearer than in the case of Atlantic City, where casino gambling was adopted partly in the hope that it would revitalize the city. But George Sternlieb's account of the casinos' impact on Atlantic city shows precious little revitalization occurring.[67] Atlantic City appears to have lost the gamble. The housing supply has gotten tighter. The number of local services such as supermarkets have declined. Crime has risen. The pervasive role of organized crime in the city appears to have grown. The community development fund that was supposed to be set aside for renewal in the city never matched expectations. And few of the 40,000 jobs created by the casinos went to Atlantic City residents. Eighty percent of casino employees live in Atlantic City suburbs and surrounding communities. A 1985 survey found that 63 percent of the employees would not even think of moving into Atlantic City because of the crime, poor schools, and increased housing costs.[68]

Finally, whatever states and communities do, the prestigious business organization Committee for Economic Development (CED) urges them to do it within a broad economic strategy. Rather than skipping from construction project to construction project, the CED recommends that states adopt a strategy to "define priority actions, to give cohesion to government actions, and to avoid actions which may be harmful to the economy."[69] CED recommends that each state start with a diagnosis of its own economic conditions, its potentialities, and how it is affected by changing national economic conditions. The state must then develop a vision that focuses not on "the conventional emphasis on recruiting firms *to* the state, but [on] creating an environment that facilitates change and is conducive to development and entrepreneurship *within* the state."[70] Finally, states should take actions that are compatible with the diagnosis and the strategy.

Combating Business Closures

Although not an economic development strategy strictly speaking, combating the closure of business facilities is a tactic that communities sometimes use. Governments cannot prevent plants from closing, and most economists probably would argue that they should not do so. From a national economic perspective, it makes little sense to force a corporation to keep in existence an inefficient plant that can be replaced by a new, more automated, more efficient one. Protecting such inefficiencies, so the argument goes, will in the long run only make American manufacturers less competitive in the world economy. Instead, economists argue, we should encourage disinvestment from failing sunset industries so that those resources can be reinvested in more viable sunrise economic activities.[71]

On the other hand, many business closings in the 1980s have had very little to do with plant efficiencies. They resulted from corporate buyout plans by so-called corporate raiders who use borrowed money to purchase a corporation that is undervalued in the stock market. The raider then reduces total corporate employment and sells off the pieces of the corporation individually until he has made enough money to pay back his debt and leave himself a profit. The result is a decimation of a corporation, hardship on the employees and communities involved, and usually no evident redirection of the investment into productive sunrise industries. Indiana and some other states have passed laws that would make it more difficult for raiders to buy out local plants for these purposes.

Plant-Closing Legislation

Although states cannot prevent plant closings, they can pass legislation that softens the blow to local communities.[72] Four states have passed such legislation (Connecticut, Maine, Massachusetts, and Wisconsin), and in 1988 Congress passed a federal law that requires 60 days' notification of plant closings to give workers more planning time to make necessary arrangements. The most extensive law is in Massachusetts. It encourages companies to give 90 days' notice. The legislation also provides for an extra three months of health insurance, unemployment compensation, and job retraining.[73] At a minimum, each state would seem to want to require the closing companies to provide severance pay and funds for retraining and job counseling. Many companies do provide severance benefits, but the results are not always as good as the promises. U.S. Steel Corporation established a job counseling program for laid-off workers when it closed its Clairton mills outside Pittsburgh. Despite counseling and motivational sessions, few workers were able to find full-time jobs in the area. Heavily dependent on the now closed mills, the local economy simply was not strong enough to absorb all the laid-off workers.[74]

Buy the Plant and Run It

A far more daring strategy is for the local community to purchase the failing facility and operate it. Twenty-five states have passed Employee Stock Ownership Plan (ESOP) laws that provide financial aid and other assistance to help employees purchase plants that are threatening to close. But few communities have been able to do this successfully. Formidable obstacles lie in the way.

The obstacles involved in purchasing a plant were demonstrated in Youngstown, Ohio in 1977. Religious leaders sought to purchase a factory of the Youngstown Sheet and Tube Company, which announced it would close its Youngstown plant, putting 5,000 people out of work. One month after the announcement, a group of religious leaders led by Catholic Bishop James Malone formed an Ecumenical Coalition to find a way for the community and workers to buy the doomed plant. Barely had these plans been formed than opposition developed. The parent company of the steel plant (Lykes Corporation) opposed the sale for fear of creating a plant that would compete with its remaining steel mills in other parts of the country. Local leaders of the United Steel Workers (USW) did not support the plan because of their ambivalence about being put into a managerial role if the workers were to become part-owners of the mill. Putting a viable plan together took several months. During those months, the markets served by the now-closed Youngstown plant had turned to other suppliers, and it was doubtful that the Youngstown mill could recapture this lost market share. Finally, banks refused to lend the coalition the $500 million needed to purchase the plant unless the federal government would guarantee the loan. But the government refused to make loan guarantees. In the face of those obstacles, the Ecumenical Coalition was unable to complete its purchase of the plant.[75]

Change and Bias in the Urban Political Economy

The major change in the urban political economy in the last two decades has been the solidification of the central-city mayor's role as a promoter of public-private partnerships seeking to increase economic activity in urban areas and to improve the city's fiscal base. Cities use a variety of strategies, from offering tax abatements to supplying seed money to working out complicated lease-back arrangements. What biases, if any, permeate this urban political economy?

First, despite the infusion of new money into urban redevelopment projects, the economic benefits for the poor and the minorities have been disappointing. As indicated earlier in this chapter, numerous central cities have experienced devastating losses in numbers of jobs over the past two decades. Even in the Sunbelt, where cities are still growing, population increases may have outpaced job increases, and most of the growth occurs on the expanding edge of the city, not in the low-income residential neighborhoods. Whatever the reason, the percent of most cities' residents living in poverty, unemployed, or on welfare is as bad or worse today as it was two decades ago.

Second, part of the reason for the lack of improvement in the cities' poverty statistics must be attributed to the biases inherent in the urban redevelopment process itself. One of the most commonly used redevelopment tools, the industrial development revenue bond (IDRB), for example, does not appear to be used to stimulate economically depressed regions, despite the fact that this rationale, offered in legislation establishing it, usually names that as a prime objective. To examine how extensively IDRBs were aimed at depressed locations, Thomas A. Pascarella and Richard D. Raymond sought to see if high-unemployment areas in Ohio used IDRBs more than low-unemployment areas, but they found no relationships. They then looked at the types of jobs created by IDRBs in Cleveland and

Akron, and did find that they created twice as many jobs in occupations with a workforce surplus than they did in occupations with a workforce shortage.[76] IDRBs are now used in forty-seven states, and they became so popular that by the mid-1980s they comprised 70 percent of all municipal bond issues, whereas in 1970 they comprised only 33 percent.[77] The most frequent use of IDRBs has been for the installation of pollution-control equipment, for the construction of hospitals, and for the construction of publicly subsidized housing. They also are often used to finance fast-food franchises, discount-store locations, and similar commercial facilities that have little developmental power. In short, the IDRB as often used does little to generate permanent, well-paying jobs in poverty-stricken neighborhoods. In part because of these disappointments, Congress in 1986 put limits on the amount of IDRBs that a city could issue each year.

There are limits to what the city can raise money for, Paul Peterson has argued.[78] In Peterson's view, a city that tries to raise too much money for redistributive services for needy residents will drive out its middle-income residents to the less redistributive-oriented suburbs. Cities should focus on raising money for economic development, according to Peterson, and leave redistributive policies to the federal government.

Whether Peterson's vision is true or not is impossible to prove. But most cities engaged in the redevelopment game today act as though they think his vision is true. That is, the most-praised and successful redevelopment in the 1970s and early 1980s has focused on economic activities in the mainstream of the nation's economy—primarily providing support and office space for service industries and retail commerce. Much has also gone into retaining or attracting manufacturing facilities. This has not reversed the decline of heavy industry in the Frostbelt, but it may have been helpful to industrialization efforts in the South and Southwest over the past decades. Urban redevelopment activities seem to be reinforcing the bipolar city discussed early in this chapter. Much public money has been spent supporting downtown projects and gentrification projects, but no one has yet found the formula that would provide enough economic opportunities to make a permanent dent in the percentage of urban poverty. Small, owner-run retail establishments, which in the past assured the city of a substantial middle-class population, have been squeezed out.

A further bias in the urban political economy relates to the mechanisms for passing the costs of urban redevelopment on to the federal treasury. This may be a good or bad development, depending on one's viewpoint. But the trend is clear that much of the stimulus for urban redevelopment has come from the federal treasury in the form of direct appropriations of CDBG and UDAG subsidies. More important have become the growing popularity of indirect subsidies such as the IDRB and lease-back and tax-increment financing. These subsidies are not in the form of direct appropriations but in the form of tax reductions (tax expenditures, to use the federal budget jargon).

People have a very difficult time evaluating much of the urban redevelopment and gentrification activities of the past decade. Remembeering the seedy and run-down appearance of many big-city downtowns two decades ago, comparing them to the elaborate redevelopments in many of these same cities today, and noting the increased number of people, jobs, and activities, it is hard to say that the cities should not have initiated these projects. At the same time, however, many central-city residential neighborhoods have had trouble holding their own as their former middle-class occupants moved out to the suburbs, and today they are increasingly occupied with people subsisting on marginal incomes. Many cities are moving toward a bipolar status, as Sternleib and Hughes expressed it, and the urban redevelopment activities have not slowed that trend. They may even have hastened it.

Summary

1. Economically, the typical large American central city is in danger of becoming a bipolar city. At one pole is a large lower-income population, and at the other is a small elite of professionals working in sleek office buildings and often living in chic gentrified neighborhoods. Squeezed out are the middle-income families who did so much in the past to provide social stability to city neighborhoods. The bipolar city is much further advanced in the Northeast and Midwest than in the South and Southwest.

2. Fiscally, cities have found themselves squeezed between increasing demands for urban services and a tax base that has not grown as fast as the demands for city expenditures. Until the late 1970s, cities filled these revenue gaps by getting increasing amounts of federal aid. Federal aid has declined since the late 1970s, however, pushing cities back to their own revenue sources and state aid. Many cities have gone through difficult periods of fiscal stress. To avoid or overcome fiscal stress, cities raise taxes, try to share the tax burden with other governments, cut expenditures, and promote economic development.

3. Cities seek to cope with their fiscal and economic plight by promoting public-private redevelopment projects. These projects aim to increase the city's level of economic activity and improve the tax base.

4. Three main biases were found in the contemporary urban political economy. First, the higher rates of poverty and unemployment compared to twenty years ago suggest that the city has not been a very dynamic place of economic opportunity for its lowest-income residents and for many of its racial-minority residents. Second, the urban redevelopment process, however necessary it may be for other reasons, offers slim hopes of advancing the economic prospects for the urban minorities and the poor. Finally, much of the cost of urban redevelopment has been passed on to the federal treasury.

Chapter 7
The Contest for Dominance in Central Cities: Community Power, Functional Fiefdoms, and Executive Leaders

Who really runs American cities?

And for whose benefit?

These questions jump out when reflecting on our discussion in the previous chapter on economic development. A great many American cities over the past three decades have spent a great deal of public money (your money, if you are a federal or state taxpayer) and built up a huge amount of public debt (your debt) that will have to be paid off by future taxes (your taxes) in order to rebuild their downtowns and stimulate business investment. Whether or not these public actions attain their goals, they will have an impact on your own quality of life in future years if you live within metropolitan America (as three-fourths of Americans do). For these reasons, it seems fair to ask: Who really influences what governments do in American cities? And for whose benefit do they exercise that influence?

These questions are as troubling to urban scholars today as they have been for the last fifty years. Some people respond that cities are run by elite power structures. Others say that cities are run through the interactions of various interest groups and power centers. These two responses have been termed the *elitist* and *pluralist* models of community power, respectively. The elitist and pluralist models constitute the starting point for exploring the contest for dominance in American central cities. To understand this contest we must examine these two models as well as some other important related changes taking place in urban politics—the emergence of what we will call functional fiefdoms, the challenge to strong mayoral leadership, and demands for community control and citizen participation in local governance.

Accordingly, this chapter will ask the following questions. First, are the central cities dominated by a stratified power structure? Second, what is meant by the emergence of functionally based governmental power, and why is the strong mayor proposed as an antidote for it? Third, what is the nature of the charge that contemporary urban government is unresponsive to the citizenry, and why is community control proposed as an antidote for this alleged unresponsiveness? Last, does the organization of public power in the contemporary metropolis lead to consistent patterns of bias?

Are Central Cities Dominated by Stratified Power Structures?

Who runs American cities? Are they controlled by a unified, upper-status elite that usually operates behind the scenes and is capable of subordinating the formal governmental apparatus of the city to its own interests? In other words, is community power in city governance *elitist?* Or is control over the city divided among several competing groups and power centers? Is it *pluralist?* For over three decades the elitists and the pluralists have debated basic methods of research, basic assumptions about the exercise of power, and basic conclusions about its dispersion.

The Elitist Model of Community Power

Although several sociological and anthropological community studies had commented on local politics,[1] the first community study that devoted itself exclusively to the exercise of power was Floyd Hunter's *Community Power Structure.*[2] His book is worth examining in some detail, because it establishes one major strand of basic research methodology and substantive conclusions that have influenced community studies since its publication in 1953. Hunter, a sociologist, set for himself the task of answering the question, "Who runs Regional City?" (For *Regional City*, read *Atlanta, Georgia.*) To identify the leadership of Regional City, Hunter compiled lists of prominent civic leaders, government leaders, business leaders, and status leaders. He then selected a panel of six knowledgeable people to examine the lists and identify the most influential individuals and the most influential organizations on each list. From these selections, Hunter identified forty individuals at the apex of the power structure in Regional City. Most of these forty served on the boards of directors of the same corporations and belonged to the same social clubs. Beneath the top leadership was a cadre of what Hunter called "understructure personnel" who carried out the will and the instructions of the top power structure.

Not only did Hunter identify a top power structure in Regional City; he also contended that this power structure initiated most of the major developments that occurred in Regional City and that it successfully vetoed projects it disliked. Enterprising newspaper or journal writers lost their jobs when they disagreed with the power structure. Social welfare professionals were carefully constrained not to raise issues such as public housing that might violate the interests of the power structure. On certain key issues, such as limiting the supply of public housing, Hunter pictured the governor, the United States senators, the key state legislators, the party leaders, and other officials with very few exceptions as subordinated to the top power structure. Power, in Hunter's view, was cumulative. That is, power in one area of activity gave a person power in other areas as well (see the accompanying box).

As an example of how things were done in Regional City, Hunter describes how a top business leader named Charles Homer used a dinner meeting at an exclusive club to launch a project to establish an international trade council:

> When we meet at the Club at dinner with the other crowds, Mr. Homer makes a brief talk; again, he does not need to talk long. He ends his talk by saying he believes in his proposition enough that he is willing to put his own money into it for the first year. . . . The Growers Bank crowd, not to be outdone, offers a like amount plus a guarantee that they will go along with the project for three years. Others throw in . . . I'd say within thirty or forty minutes, we have pledges of the money we need. In three hours the whole thing is settled, including the time for eating.
>
> We went into that meeting with a board of directors picked. The constitution was all written, and the man who was to head the council as executive was named . . . a third-stringer, a fellow who will take advice.
>
> The public doesn't know anything about the project until it reaches the stage I've been talking about. After the matter is financially sound, then we go to the newspapers and say there is a proposal for consideration. Of course, it is not news to a lot of people by then, but the Chamber committees and other civic organizations are brought in on the idea. They all think it's a good idea. They help to get the Council located and established. That's about all there is to it.

Source: From Floyd Hunter, *Community Power Structure* (Chapel Hill, N.C.: The University of North Carolina Press, 1953), pp. 173–174.

Critiques of Hunter

In summary, Hunter described Atlanta as dominated by a very small and conservative business elite that acted for its own rather than the public benefit. Public officials were subordinated to this power structure, and power was cumulative. Because of this dominance of the city by a nongovernmental elite, Hunter's thesis is referred to as an elitist or stratification theory of community power. When the book appeared, it provoked a furor in the academic community, particularly among political scientists, for, in a sense, Hunter's downgrading of governmental structures as totally subservient to the economic structures made the traditional political scientists' concern over forms of city government seem irrelevant. If true power was to be found outside the governmental structure, what difference did it make if the city government was organized under a strong mayor, a city manager, or a commission? Consequently, the appearance of Hunter's book precipitated a new rush of inquiry into the study of local government.[3]*

*The study of urban politics might be roughly divided into four stages. Prior to the appearance of Hunter's book in 1953, the dominant themes of the study of urban politics were highly normative, nonempirical, and devoted more to public administration than to political processes. Typical studies dealt with the relative administrative advantages of the city manager form of government vis-à-vis commissioner forms and weak-mayor forms. From 1953 to the middle 1960s, urban political studies were dominated by questions of community power. A third stage emerged in the early 1960s and continues today. This stage has been characterized by highly sophisticated empirical studies of the determinants of public policy in urban areas. A fourth stage emerged in the 1980s as urban scholars were forced to explain intellectually how the economic dynamism of extensive urban redevelopment and the public economy fit into community power theory.

Political scientists generally disagreed with Hunter's conclusion, but since no political scientist had conducted empirical studies that could refute Hunter's thesis, their strongest criticisms attacked his research methods and his assumptions about power.[4] By asking knowledgeable observers to identify the most influential leaders, said Hunter's critics, he had not really measured the exercise of power. He had merely measured the reputation for power.[5] Hence Hunter's approach to measuring community power was called the *reputational method*. To measure power validly, argued some of Hunter's critics, one would have to use a decision-making approach; that is, analyze the actual decisions through which power is exercised.

The Pluralist Model of Community Power

The first major empirical work that used a *decision-making* approach to measure power rather than Hunter's reputational approach was the study of New Haven by Robert Dahl in *Who Governs?*[6] Dahl deliberately set out to test the hypothesis that New Haven is governed by the kind of economic and social elite that Hunter had discovered in Atlanta. He isolated thirty-four important decisions in the three functional areas of urban renewal, education, and the selection of party nominees for mayor over a period of time that extended from 1941 to 1959. He established rigid criteria for defining the economic and social notables of New Haven. Contrary to Hunter's findings, Dahl discovered that in New Haven there was *no significant overlap* between the economic and social elites, that these elites had almost no influence on the decisions he studied, and that power in New Haven was *noncumulative* (that is, power in one functional area did not lead to power in other functional areas).

In the three issue areas that concerned him, Dahl conducted extended interviews with forty-six top decision makers. He found very few instances in which an individual person was involved in more than one major decision, let alone more than one issue area. The major exception to this was the mayor of New Haven, Richard C. Lee. Lee was a supreme political tactician at bargaining with the leaders of all the major functional fiefdoms in New Haven plus some others in federal and state agencies that had programs in New Haven. Through his bargaining skill, he was able to initiate and carry out the kinds of programs he envisioned for the growth and prosperity of the city. Dahl perceived Mayor Lee as occupying the critical position in what Dahl referred to as an "executive centered coalition" of a plurality of interest groups in New Haven. Because this view sees power as noncumulative and dispersed among several power centers, Dahl's theories about community power are called *pluralist* theories.

Early Refinements of the Two Models of Community Power

Following the publication of the initial studies by Hunter and Dahl, increasingly sophisticated research methods were used to examine every conceivable subtlety of these two models. Comparative studies were conducted of community power in more than one city,[7] and in some studies, reputational methods of analysis were combined with decision-making methods.[8] A survey of almost three dozen community power studies found that sociologists had an overwhelming tendency to use the reputational method, whereas political scientists were much more likely to use the decision-making method of analysis. Political scientists were also much less likely to come to stratificationist conclusions than were sociologists.[9]

Some of the early communities were restudied. Hunter revisited Atlanta a quarter-century later and found that little of basic importance had changed: "fundamental power relationships have not altered."[10] New Haven was also revisited by the stratification theorist William G. Domhoff, who reanalyzed some of Dahl's data and came to the conclusion that New Haven fundamentally really was run by an economic elite.[11]

In great measure the pluralists and the stratificationists were talking past one another, starting from different assumptions and leaving this "important area of study . . . in disarray," as Clarence N. Stone expressed it.[12] If Stone is correct that this large and growing body of research is really in disarray, what conclusions can we draw about the contest for dominance in cities? Four aspects are relevant here—the role of business, the importance of nondecisions, the great variety of power relationships that exist, and a renaissance in urban political theory in the 1980s.

The Role of Business

Subsequent research has tended to dispel the picture of top businesspeople operating as a cohesive clique and dominating city public affairs, the picture that Hunter presented of the businesspeople in Atlanta. However, it is conceivable that Hunter's observations of Atlanta were accurate for that time period, and that businesspeople did indeed dominate the city's politics during the early 1950s.* Hunter's findings of business dominance is consistent with the overwhelming majority of early anthropological and sociological community studies, which asserted the same kind of business dominance over their cities that Hunter found in Atlanta. Particularly dominant were the owners of key businesses in one-industry towns. The classic example was the dominance of Muncie, Indiana, by the Ball family, referred to as Middletown and the X family, respectively, by Robert and Helen Lynd in their monumental works *Middletown* and *Middletown in Transition*.[13] In one famous passage, the Lynds quote a Middletown man's comments on the pervasive influence of the X family over all aspects of life in Middletown.

> If I'm out of work I go to the X plant; if I need money I go to the X bank, and if they don't like me I don't get it; my children go to the X college; when I get sick I go to the X hospital; I buy a building lot or house in an X subdivision; my wife goes downtown to buy clothes at the X department store; if my dog stays away he is put in the X pound; I buy X milk; I drink X beer, vote for X political

---

*Edward C. Banfield argues that businesspeople may have dominated Atlanta in the early 1950s, but by the middle 1960s they were only one of two important blocs in the city. See his *Big City Politics* (New York: Random House, 1965), pp. 18–36. Also see M. Kent Jennings. *Community Influentials: The Elites of Atlanta* (New York: The Free Press, 1964).

parties, and get help from X charities; my boy goes to the X Y.M.C.A. and my girl to their Y.W.C.A.; I listen to the word of God in X-subsidized churches; if I'm a Mason I go to the X Masonic Temple; I read the news from the X morning newspaper; and, if I am rich enough, I travel via the X airport.[14]

Despite the protestations of the pluralists that stratificationists such as Hunter and the Lynds were exaggerating the business dominance of local politics,* many other cities in addition to Muncie and Atlanta seem to have had a particular business elite that dominated local affairs. United States Steel Corporation planned and built Gary, Indiana, and exercised considerable influence over its government. The Mellon family had disproportionate influence in Pittsburgh. One-company mining towns often stayed under the control of their patrons for decades. And even today the Anaconda Corporation exerts extensive power over Butte, Montana.

In more normal situations, however, where central cities are not dominated by one locally owned industry, pluralists have argued that the patterns of business involvement in city politics are much more complicated than elitists have recognized. Most sectors of the economy are now dominated by national corporations rather than local companies. Some corporations are not very concerned about local issues. In towns dominated by national corporations, business leadership is often bifurcated between a local elite of retailers who are very much interested in local affairs and the managers of the national corporations whose careers and interests impel them to pay more attention to the internal affairs of their corporation than to local politics.[15] Unless the corporation has a significant business reason to be interested in the local affairs of a community, the corporation executives often limit their involvement in local affairs to activities designed to do little more than maintain a positive corporate image. However, in cities where local affairs *do* affect the economic interests of national corporations, their managers are much more likely to become involved locally.[16]

Not only is the business sector divided between the owners of local businesses and the managers of national corporations; it is also divided into several functional categories. Few businesspeople exhibit much interest in civic affairs that lie beyond their functional sphere. Thus urban renewal agencies routinely seek out the advice and collaboration of real estate brokers and the financial community, whereas other kinds of businesspeople—such as retail merchants, automobile dealers, or shopping center owners—are often quite uninterested. Utilities seek to promote a city's population, income, and employment, whereas railroads often display little interest in city politics.[17] Because of this divergence of interests, the business community is not nearly as cohesive in its approach to local politics as Hunter's portrayal suggests. It is highly competitive. And the resources with which businesspeople can influence public affairs depend on the functional area involved, the issue, the interests of the businesspeople, and the homogeneity with which they can act.

---

*Polsby in particular argues that the stratificationist conclusions of the elitists not only were inaccurate but also were inconsistent with much of the data that the authors recorded. See his *Community Power and Political Theory* (New Haven, Conn.: Yale University Press, 1963), pp. 14–68.

Another study of businesspeople in local city politics discovered that they do indeed play a very significant role, although an anticipatory role rather than the manipulative role described by Hunter.[18] Political leaders anticipated the needs and desires of businesses before taking any actions that might affect them. Businesspeople seldom initiated or vetoed public policies; however, their acquiescence in certain projects was often crucial for the project's success due to the considerable prestige that they enjoyed. When business fails to support a public project, this fact is noted by the people in the community who respect the key figures of the business sector and take cues from them. If the projects require any private investment, the cooperation of business is deemed especially essential, for they are the ones who will have to raise the private funds.

The Importance of Nondecisions

If subsequent research on the role of businesspeople in city politics tended to dispel the stratificationist notion that they manipulate public affairs as one cohesive, well-organized bloc, it also found flaws in the decision-making approach to analyzing community power. Political scientists Peter Bachrach and Morton S. Baratz charged that the concentration on actual decisions ignores "the fact that power may be, and often is, exercised by confining the scope of decision-making to relatively 'safe' issues."

> Of course power is exercised when A participates in the making of decisions that affect B. But power is also exercised when A devotes his energies to creating or reinforcing social and political values and institutional practices that limit the scope of the political process to public consideration of only those issues which are comparatively innocuous to A. To the extent that A succeeds in doing this, B is prevented, for all practical purposes, from bringing to the fore any issues that might in their resolution be seriously detrimental to A's set of preferences.[19]

Such an exercise of power is referred to as coming to "nondecisions." Nondecisions are much more difficult to identify and measure than are actual decisions. The key area where nondecisions predominate is in preserving the dominant values, myths, and established political procedures of a community. Only certain kinds of questions are put on the agendas of the decision-making agencies. Other kinds of questions are never put on those agendas and hence never reach the point where decisions about them can be made.

Furthermore, some people have fewer resources for waging political battles than do others. The people with few resources usually lose these battles, and they quite often are the poorest people in the city. Many issues stay in the realm of nondecisions because these people lack either the resources or the will to fight for them. In the words of Clarence Stone, "Because people have no taste for waging costly battles they are sure to lose, much goes uncontested."[20]

Although researchers have expressed doubts about the usefulness of the concept of nondecisions, pertinent examples have been cited in the literature on local politics.[21] In his study of New Haven, for example, Robert Dahl paid very little attention to the black community because it did not figure in the major decisions he analyzed. Even the urban renewal decisions, which deeply touched the lives of large numbers of New Haven blacks, were made without much input from the local black community. When a riot broke out in New Haven in 1967, some people began to ask why decisions had not been made on questions the blacks themselves apparently considered important.[22] The answer seems to be that the blacks did not constitute a strong enough interest group to have their demands placed on the decision-making agenda. The needs and demands of people who do not have the backing of strong interest groups and powerful civic leaders are likely to remain in the realm of nondecisions.

The Variety of Power Relationships

Finally, pluralists pointed out that power is structured differently in different communities, and the structures change over time. Atlanta of the late 1980s is vastly different not only from the New Haven that Dahl studied but even from the Atlanta that Hunter studied in the early 1950s. For one thing, it is a black majority today compared to only a black minority at the time of Hunter's analysis. Atlanta has had black mayors for the past decade, an accomplishment that would have been impossible if the city's power structure were still the same as the one described by Hunter. Not only do power structures change over time, but a city located in the middle of a large megalopolis will be subjected to outside political influences that will have less impact on a comparable city surrounded by a rural setting.[23]

Highly stratified power structures are most likely to be found where city leaders share a consensus on the role of government and where power is not shared extensively with the mass of the people. On the other hand, much more democratic power structures can be found in cities where the leadership is competitive about rather than unified on the role of government, and where power is broadly distributed among the residents. Highly stratified power structures are most likely to be found in isolated communities dominated by a single industry, in small homogeneous communities, and in the South. Pluralist power structures are most likely to be found in metropolitan areas, communities with a heterogeneous population, and communities with a diversity of economic foundations and social cleavages.

Renaissance of Urban Theory in the 1980s

By the end of the 1970s, the status of community power theory could reasonably be summarized by the abovementioned three propositions (that the role of business is complex, that nondecisions are as important as decisions, and that different kinds of communities have different kinds of power structures). But several things had happened to cities from the 1960s through the 1980s that could not be explained very well by early pluralist or elitist theories. Especially prominent were the eruption of riots during the 1960s, the staggering economic decline of many cities throughout the period, widespread fiscal stress in the late 1970s, and more than anything the impressive downtown and economic redevelopment schemes that blossomed across the land. If the stratificationists were correct that a small group of business elites controlled the cities for their own benefit, why would they have collaborated with the economic disinvestment that has been so disastrous for so many cities? And why did so many of the economic redevelopment schemes appear to originate not in company boardrooms but in city halls? If the pluralists were correct in their optimistic view that a plurality of interest groups governed the city through competition and coalitions, then how do we explain the fact that the huge central-city underclass (as noted in Chapter 5) was almost always left out of the governing coalition? And how do we explain the fact that the economic redevelopment schemes have had so little payoff at the neighborhood level, where the rank-and-file members of the supposedly powerful interest groups lived?

These questions are very difficult to answer within the framework of early elitist or pluralist theories. But just as nature cannot tolerate a vacuum, the human mind cannot tolerate unexplainable facts. So it is not surprising that urban political theory enjoyed a renaissance in the 1980s as scholars sought new explanations for today's urban reality. At great risk of oversimplifying a large number of complex ideas, five theoretical approaches stand out today: (1) neo-Marxist and structuralist approaches, (2) growth machine theory, (3) the unitary interest theory of Paul Peterson, (4) the systemic power and regime paradigm theories of Clarence Stone, and (5) what for want of a better term we might call the pluralist counterattack.

Neo-Marxist and Structuralist Theories

Perhaps the most philosophical contribution to new urban political theory has been that of the neo-Marxists. It is important to stress here that to call these theorists neo-Marxists does not mean that they are active communists. They are Marxists in the sense that they believe that a class struggle for control over capital and the means of production is the underlying force that explains the key events in urban politics, especially the decline of cities and the economic redevelopment boom of recent years.

Cities are in decline today not because of a conspiracy of economic elites (as seems to underly much of the analysis of the early stratificationists)[24] but because the evolution of American capitalism has made the traditional American city obsolete. Richard Child Hill writes: "The city is forged upon the hearth of a given mode of production. . . . A particular city cannot be divorced from the encompassing political economy with which it is embedded and through which it manifests its particular function and form."[25]

From this viewpoint, the old industrial city of the Midwest was formed a century ago because labor-intensive industrial manufacturing required large numbers of workers to be assembled in concentrated areas. It was the job of city government to provide the infrastructure (streets, sewers, water supply, land preparation) that would enable this concentration of laborers to take place. It was also the job of the city to provide sufficient police protection and political services to keep the laborers from organizing collectively against the factory owners. For today's capital-intensive factory, however, large concentrations of workers are no longer needed. The Dodge plant at Poletown in Detroit employed many more workers at the height of its operations in the 1950s than have ever been or are likely to be employed by the Cadillac plant built on the same site in the 1980s.

Not only is today's factory capital-intensive rather than labor-intensive, but also capital is mobile; corporations can move the production facilities out of troublesome locations into more receptive locations. Cities, by contrast, are stationary; you cannot move Detroit to the Sunbelt. Detroit, in fact, has been suffering from flight of capital out of the city for years as corporations closed down plants in the city and built new ones in the suburbs, in the Sunbelt, or overseas. Between 1960 and 1976, Detroit lost 200,000 jobs, about 30 percent of all the jobs that had existed only 16 years earlier in 1960.[26]

When General Motors in the late 1970s decided to invest $40 billion in building new automobile production plants, there were probably 100 places around the globe in addition to Detroit where GM could profitably make the investments in new plants. The juxtaposition of the stationary city with highly mobile investment capital puts Detroit and every other city at a disadvantage in dealing with GM. Nowhere was this seen more clearly than in Detroit's bid to get the site for GM's new Cadillac plant in 1980 and 1981. GM adopted an uncompromising take-it-or-leave-it attitude on the site specifications for the new plant. To produce the site, the city had to destroy a neighborhood (Poletown), suffer severe attacks on its public image as a result of that destruction, and spend over $200 million to turn the site over to GM. There is no realistic projection under which increased city revenues and tax base could repay that $200 million within the next two decades.[27]

From a neo-Marxist perspective, the politics of urban redevelopment and the conflict between corporation and neighborhood is a contemporary replay of the class conflict in today's city. The corporation seeks to maximize profit and looks to the city government to prepare the infrastructure for the corporation's involvement. As in Poletown, this task often puts the city in the middle between the corporation and the city's own neighborhood residents. In this sense, the class struggle appears to be taking place today between capital and neighborhood as a substitute for the historical struggle between owner and worker.

These concepts of the neo-Marxists have come under severe criticism. With some exceptions,[28] much of this theory is highly deductive in nature with little foundation in systematic empirical research[29] and little relation to the lives of ordinary people on city streets.[30] And some important case studies of redevelopment politics explicitly reject neo-Marxist explanations. An analysis of economic development politics in the New York region, for example, argues that huge development institutions such as the Port Authority of New York and New Jersey have policy agendas of their own that are quite independent of business leaders in the region.[31]

Growth Machine Theory

Despite these criticisms, the great contribution of the neo-Marxists to the community power debate was to take attention away from elites as behind-the-scenes conspirators in the city and to refocus attention on the larger politico-economic forces that influence city politics. From one school of thought, the most important of these forces is what sociologist Harvey Molotch called "a growth machine."[32] Molotch argues that local elites with substantial local land holdings dominate community policymaking and that these leaders' common interest lies in promoting growth. Growth will make their land more valuable. To secure their investment, these local land-based elites dominate local government and seek to co-opt local political leaders by bringing them into the pro-growth machine.

Growth machine theory differs from neo-Marxist theory in at least two key respects. First, the goal of the growth machine is not to *maximize profit* from selling goods and services in a national market as is the goal of the corporation. Rather, the goal of the growth machine is to *maximize rental returns* through renting space to the businesses and people who will use the facilities built by the growth machine.[33] In this sense, from the viewpoint of the growth machine advocates in Detroit, the possibility that the city might never recover the $200 million it invested in the Poletown site was less bothersome than the prospects of nothing being built on the site. Second, due to its interest in land use rather than maximizing profit, the growth machine is not composed of the national upper class or even the leaders of the national corporations. Instead, the elites of the growth machine are local real estate owners, bankers, developers, construction unions, and central-city newspapers whose circulations and advertising revenues will expand with growth in the metropolis.

In dealing with the growth machine, city government plays two conflicting roles. First, it must support the growth machine's promotion of economic growth and redevelopment on the grounds that growth will bring in jobs for city residents and will make land in the region more valuable. Second, since it represents people in local neighborhoods, city government often finds itself playing an intermediary role in the conflicts that arise when neighborhood residents oppose particular redevelopment projects.

Cities as a Unitary Interest

In contrast to the neo-Marxist and growth machine interpretations of urban decline and redevelopment is Paul Peterson's concept of "unitary interest," spelled out in his highly influential 1981 book *City Limits*.[34] At great risk of over-simplifying a complex set of ideas, the heart of Peterson's theory focuses on the role that city governments can effectively play in the local political economy. Like the neo-Marxists and the growth machine theorists, Peterson also placed great emphasis on the role of investment capital in determining the fate of cities. Cities are in competition with each other to capture as much investment capital as they can. A city also has export industries (automobiles in Detroit; computer hardware and software in the Silicon Valley area; health services in Cleveland) that provide a lot of jobs and bring money into the city. The business leaders of the city, political leaders, and ordinary residents have a *unitary interest* in protecting those export industries and helping attract new investment capital that will help them expand in the future. Thus it is not a "growth machine" that impels the mayor to pursue downtown redevelopment. It is simply a mutual recognition of the best interests of all the city's residents.

Peterson's theory leads him to an extremely important normative conclusion as we saw in Chapter 6. If city leaders have a unitary interest in promoting the city's export industries, then city government should limit its expenditures for redistributive social or welfare services to the minimum; it should maximize expenditures that facilitate the unitary interest. Redistributive and welfare costs should be shifted to the national government.

This argument provides a powerful justification for the economic redevelopment activities of most cities. But, like the other theories, it too has been criticized.[35] The key interests of business leaders diverge sharply from those of political leaders. Although political leaders may care most about maximizing the city's export industries, the self-interest of most corporate leaders necessarily lies in maximizing the profits of their particular corporations, and in most instances this goal is divorced from the well-being of the cities in which the corporation resides. Finally, neighborhood residents might or might not benefit from downtown redevelopment. In fact, one could make a powerful argument that strengthening neighborhoods is a more important unitary interest of a city than is downtown redevelopment. If crime rates are low, the middle class is not moving out, city services are good, and schools are excellent, then a city will be a very attractive location for many kinds of businesses. This is precisely the situation in many suburban cities. But simply redeveloping the central-city downtown or putting in an automobile production plant will not necessarily pull in the middle class, improve the schools, reduce the crime rates, or make the neighborhoods better places in which to live.

Systemic Power

Despite these criticisms, Peterson's unitary interest thesis of the limited city has become the dominant model of American urban theory in the 1980s.[36] The most likely alternative model is that of systemic power, articulated by Clarence Stone.[37] Like Peterson, Stone sees three power clusters in cities: (1) the business elite, (2) the elected city government leaders and their top appointees, and (3) the city residents and the variety of neighborhood groups, labor union locals, political party organizations, and other political groups to which the residents belong. The mayor (as the most visible elected political leader) is elected to office by the residents. But once in office, the mayor and other top political leaders can gain very few additional rewards from the city voters or their representative groups. Instead it is the business elite and to a lesser extent other institutional elites who control access to most of the things that most reasonable mayors are likely to want (a thriving city economy, a successful administration, prestige, respect, and possibly post-mayoral employment at a high salary). Ordinary city residents can give a mayor none of these things.

Because they control access to these goals that most reasonable mayors seek, business and institutional elites exercise *systemic power* over the city government. Their exercise of power will seldom be overt, but the mayor will psychically identify with the top institutional elite rather than with the masses. The mayor will anticipate the reactions of the elite to mayoral initiatives before the initiatives are taken. And it makes little difference if the mayor is black, white, male, female, Democrat, or Republican. Mayors and high public officials generally "find themselves rewarded for cooperating with upper-strata interests and unrewarded or even penalized for cooperating with lower-strata interests."[38]

No better example of Stone's analysis could be made than that of Dennis Kucinich who, as we saw in Chapter 6, aligned himself with Cleveland residents opposing the efforts of Cleveland banks to pressure the city into selling Muny Light to the Cleveland Electric and Illuminating Company in 1978 and 1979. As a result of Kucinich's opposition, the banks refused to roll over the city's debt, the city defaulted on loan payments, Kucinich was discredited, and he lost his reelection bid in 1979. His successor, George Voinovich, was much more cooperative with the business community, has presided over considerable downtown redevelopment, enjoys considerable respect as mayor, and (ten years later) still holds the office.

What is at work in most cities, according to Stone's analysis, is a regime of systemic power. There is no unitary interest binding the masses, the mayor, and the business elite. Rather, successful elected officials subtly and almost invisibly align themselves psychically with the upper-strata interests of the area and keep themselves in power by convincing a majority of the average voters that all of this will benefit them in the long run.

The Pluralist Counterattack

Although neo-Marxist, growth machine, unitary interest, and systemic power theories provide powerful (if not always consistent) explanations for economic decline and redevelopment in American cities, they are not convincing arguments to most pluralists.

A prime example of the pluralist counterattack is the analysis of Poletown by Bryan D. Jones and Lynn W. Bachelor.[39] Earlier we cited Poletown as an example of economic elites dominating a city. But Jones and Bachelor persuasively argue the opposite. First, they find no unitary interest between Detroit's or any city's business elite and the top political leaders. General Motors faced considerable competition from foreign automobile manufacturers, and GM's chief aim was to locate its new Cadillac production plant in a location that would contribute to the goal of successful competition. This put GM's primary interest at odds with Mayor Coleman Young, whose primary interest was not GM's profits but increasing the level of economic activity within the city of Detroit. In this sense, the mayor's job is akin to "making water run uphill; attracting capital where it would not normally flow . . . [getting] . . . businessmen to do things that they would not do on their own."[40]

Although this situation clearly put GM in a privileged bargaining position in dealing with Mayor Young, Young was by no means powerless. Indeed, the only reason GM even considered the Poletown site in the first place was because Young had vocally badgered GM chairman Thomas Murphy about previous location decisions that had excluded Detroit.

In summary, Jones and Bachelor view the destruction of Poletown not as an example of either big capital trampling on the rights of a minority or a mayor systematically deferring to upper-strata interests rather than to lower-class needs. Instead they view Poletown as an example of a democratically elected mayor, supported by the overwhelming majority of the city's residents, engaging in extremely effective political leadership to bring the city a very important economic resource it would not otherwise have had.

Finally, the pluralist counterattack also disagrees with the deterministic outlook that prevails among neo-Marxist, growth machine, and systemic power theories. Unitary theory perceives a common consensus among the residents, the business elite, and the political leaders that city government's primary concern is to protect the city's export industries. Neo-Marxism, growth machine, and systemic power theories perceive the same goal, attained by upper-strata interests co-opting the politicians who in turn convince the lower-strata voters that they share in the interests of the upper strata. But in either view "local policymaking on economic development issues becomes deterministic, barring occasional mistakes on the part of decision makers."[41] Mayors simply act out roles that are predetermined by the economic structure, much as a baseball player's role allows him to stand at the plate until he gets three strikes. Wade Boggs of the Red Sox does the batter's job better than most (just as Coleman Young does the mayor's job better than most), but when Boggs (Young) is gone, the game still goes on as before. He is replaced by another batter (mayor) who plays out the same role without questioning the rules or even the point of the game.

Pluralists argue that this is too deterministic a view of city politics. In fact, considerable evidence shows that there is a great deal of latitude in which different political leaders may act in very different ways for many different purposes. As we saw in the preceding chapter, the fiscal policies that a city follows are greatly influenced by the quality of public-employee unions and their leadership.[42] And how cities adapt to fiscal retrenchment depends greatly on the ideological values of their mayors.[43] For all of these reasons, pluralists reject the all-encompassing nature of neo-Marxist, unitary interest, and systemic power theories as an explanation for urban decline and redevelopment.

In sum, a rich variety of research has emerged in recent years seeking to explain the role of city government in the local political economy. Neo-Marxists focus on contemporary twists to the historical class struggle. Growth machine theorists and systemic power theorists focus on a local, land-based elite and its relations with the local political system. Peterson's unitary interest theory focuses on the proper role for city government to play in handling urban problems and on the very real limits confronting those governments. And pluralists generally tend to reaffirm city government's independence in these conflicts, asserting that it is not simply a passive actor playing out a predetermined role.

The Emergence of Functional Fiefdoms

Although this book cannot resolve the differences between the various models of community power, it can at least present two important conclusions that tend to be consistently supported by the research findings. First, whichever approach one uses to examine community power, the number of important decision makers discovered is relatively small.* Second, the political influence of the important political participants derives form their positions of institutional leadership. The important participants are business leaders, labor leaders, party leaders, government leaders, or leaders of some other institutions that have interests at stake in the governmental process of their cities.

One of the most striking institutional changes that has occurred in the governmental process over the past two generations has been the growing importance of functionally organized political power. The traditional general-purpose governmental structures (the city council and the mayor) have been bypassed to a considerable degree. Especially created governmental agencies have been given substantial authority to operate specific, key governmental functions. Each agency acquires governmental authority in its determined functional sector. It develops a professional bureaucracy that soon identifies its own set of vested interests. It is nominally run by a board of appointed officials who are often eager to demonstrate their independence from politics and to set new milestones in the functional area. In addition, outside of the government structure there are labor unions, church spokespersons, downtown business interests, racial organizations, highway lobbyists, construction contractors, teachers' organizations, professional organizations, and a host of other special-interest groups that establish ties with the agencies that operate the functions of most concern to them.

Political scientist Theodore Lowi coined the term *functional feudalities* to describe these ties between the professional bureaucracies and their related interest groups.[44] The feudal analogy is very appropriate. Just as the elite nobility in the Middle Ages enjoyed relative autonomy in the conduct of affairs within their fiefdoms, so for the past 50 years the elite bureaucratic officials have traditionally enjoyed considerable autonomy from effective outside interference by citizens and political parties (but not from members of Congress) in the conduct of their specialized operations. Just as the feudal nobility was not elected to its position of dominance but was maintained in it through a complex system of secular and ecclesiastical laws, the bureaucratic elite of the contemporary United States city is not elected to office but enjoys tenure through an equally complex system of laws and administrative rules. In Lowi's terms, the various functional feudalities constitute a "bureaucratic city-state."[45] The major inapplicability of the feudal analogy is that the fiefdoms of the Middle Ages were geographic in scope, whereas the fiefdoms of the contempoary bureaucracies are primarily functional in scope.

At the core of the functional fiefdoms are the administrative bureaucracies—what Lowi calls the new political machines. These new machines arose to perform service functions the old political party machines were supposed to have performed. They also arose to perform new service functions (urban renewal, for example) that require more formalized administrative procedures than the old machines could provide.

---

*In his review of *Who Governs?*, Floyd Hunter noted that despite Dahl's rejection of the elitist model, the actual number of participants in the large number of decision studies in New Haven never added up to more than 0.5 percent of the city's population. See his review of *Who Governs?* in *Administrative Science Quarterly* 6 (1961–1962): 517–518.

In several respects the new machines, the functional fiefdoms, exhibit many of the characteristics of the old party machines. They pursue rational organizational goals, and each bureaucracy develops its own set of loyalties that must be protected by all members. In some instances, an ethnic base has been found in the new bureaucratic machines. This is most pronounced in New York City, where the Irish are disproportionately employed in the police and fire departments, the Italians in the sanitation department, the Jews in the public school system and the welfare department, and the blacks and Puerto Ricans in public hospital and health care services.[46] The public employees' unions associated with the new bureaucratic machines are influential in negotiating employment contracts with the city governments. The main differences between the old party machines and the new bureaucratic machines are that the bureaucracies are functional in scope rather than geographic; they are more numerous and diverse than the old party machines; they rely for their legitimacy on the authority of law rather than on popular acquiescence; and in the conduct of their affairs they are probably less prone to graft than were the old-time party machines.[47]

Lowi's concepts of functional feudalities and the new bureaucratic machines are drawn primarily from his study of patronage in New York City, but the fragmentation of political influence and the emergence of functional fiefdoms can be found in other cities as well. A similar fragmentation was found in Cleveland.[48] In Oakland, California, the critical agencies dealing with housing (Redevelopment Agency and Housing Authority), port development (Board of Port Commissioners), and poverty (Economic Development Council, Inc.) all operated independently of one another and of city hall.[49]

A good example of a functional fiefdom in operation is the construction of urban freeways as part of the Interstate Highway System. This construction has largely occurred beyond the control of elected local officials. A federal highway trust fund was established in 1956 to earmark the revenue from federal gasoline taxes for the construction and maintenance of the Interstate Highway System. In addition, many states established their own highway trust funds. Both state and federal trust funds operated through state highway departments that, because of the automatic availability of the earmarked trust fund revenues, were able to become very independent of the policy preferences of mayors, governors, and state legislatures. Urban freeway planning was conducted by specialized technicians who showed very little regard for communities that might be broken up or displaced. Although freeways, bus service, and rapid rail service are all interrelated components of urban transit systems, the highway planners were soon reinforced by highway construction lobbies. Together they were able to establish highway construction as the highest transit priority at the federal, state, and local levels. Given the rapid growth of automobile usage in the United States, this was not unreasonable. But the consequences for public transit were disastrous. In Los Angeles a subsidiary of General Motors and Standard Oil of California purchased the city's transit system and was accused of tearing up its rail service.[50] And in city after city, public transit ridership peaked in the late 1940s and declined throughout the 1950s and 1960s. It was not until the 1970s that the ridership on public transit began to increase[51] and cities began to fight successfully to gain some control over the location of their freeways.[52]

The Fiefdoms' Effects on City Government

Two major consequences have resulted from the proliferation of functional fiefdoms in American cities. First, this proliferation has inhibited, but not necessarily prevented, the exercise of unified political leadership in tackling urban problems. Second (as will be seen later in the chapter), functional fiefdoms have compounded the problem of making urban government responsive to the citizenry.

The first consequence is apparent in two respects. First, political authority is so fragmented among competing agencies that the establishment of a clear-cut policy often becomes almost impossible. There often is no consensus among bureaucratic chiefs and public employees' unions on how programs should be run or even whether they should be run. This has particularly been the case in New York City, where, as political scientist David Rogers charges, "the centers of power . . . if indeed there are any, are in its municipal employees' unions and associations . . . [which] . . . veto innovative social development programs almost as a reflex reaction."[53] In this kind of situation, it takes an extremely adept mayor to exercise unified leadership. The second reason that the functional fiefdoms inhibit unified leadership follows upon the development of close ties between city bureaucratic chiefs and their federal counterparts, who have the same professional backgrounds and operate in the same program areas.[54] In setting up new programs, bureaucrats in federal agencies tended to bypass the general-purpose local governments. Instead, they put new programs into the hands of their colleagues in specialized lower-level agencies. In Oakland, California, for example, only about 1 percent of all federal spending in that city was administered through city hall.[55] For better or for worse, this insulates the programs from centralized policy direction by city hall.

The overall impact on city governance of this proliferation of functional fiefdoms has been to create a highly complex mechanism of city government that operates efficiently enough but is not very susceptible to unified policy guidance by the city council or the mayor. In the words of one pessimistic observer, the city has become "an intractable jigsaw puzzle" that is ungovernable.[56]

The result of functional fiefdoms in most cities is a juxtaposition of impressive power to act in urban redevelopment on the one hand with an inability to move dynamically on a myriad of social problems that afflict cities on the other. Detroit's functional fiefdom in redevelopment can work with GM to build a factory in Poletown and can work with Ford to build the impressive Renaissance Center. But the city government has been markedly unsuccessful in coping with high crime rates, high school dropout rates, deteriorating city services, and a fleeing white middle class.

This anomaly of powerful functional fiefdoms and weak ability to attack urban social problems exists in part because city governments have traditionally been weak. Although it is the most visible of urban governing institutions and the one institution that people hold responsible for solving urban ills, its authority to cope with those ills is sharply circumscribed not only by the existence of other powerful, competing institutions but also by law and by constitutions. A long-standing principle of municipal law holds that municipal governments can exercise only those powers specifically granted them by state legislatures or those powers indispensable for carrying out the responsibilities that the legislatures have assigned them. This principle is called *Dillon's rule*, after Judge John F. Dillon, who formulated it. Dillon stated that, "Any fair, reasonable, substantial doubt concerning the existence of power is resolved by the courts against the [city government], and the power is denied."[57]

Consistent with Dillon's rule has been the historical tendency to minimize the number of functions a city government performs. Nearly all city governments are responsible for the traditional functions of police and fire protection, street maintenance, park maintenance, and the operation of water and sewer, zoning, building permit, and building inspection services. Only a small minority of cities, however, are responsible for other urban services such as welfare, courts, hospitals, or schools. The newer a city is, the fewer services it is likely to provide.[58] Furthermore, as new services (for example, airports, highway construction, or public welfare) have been created in the twentieth century, the tendency has been to insulate these services from mayors and city councils. The federal courts have tended to support federal programs that preempted local authority.[59] (Perhaps the most notable departure from this principle came in the Housing and Community Development Act of 1974, which made it possible for mayors and councils to reassert their authority over federal urban renewal programs. For more about this, see pp. 370–371.

For the past several decades, there has been a movement away from applying Dillon's rule and toward increasing the power of city governments. This so-called *home-rule* movement seeks to give each city a home-rule charter that would authorize the city to redraw its own charter and reorganize the structure of its government without the express permission of the state legislature. Consistent with the home-rule movement, a number of states have begun giving their cities broader constitutional authority to act without getting prior permission from state legislatures.[60] Although these developments are not cure-alls for urban governing problems, they can be used to strengthen weak city governments.

Antidotes for Functional Fiefdoms: Strong Parties and Strong Mayors

Today, one of the major concerns of urban governance has come to be that of overcoming the fragmentation of governmental authority into functional fiefdoms. Two courses of action have been proposed: (1) reviving the political party as a potent force in city politics and (2) strengthening the big-city mayors.

Reviving the Political Party

One of the most prominent advocates of reviving the political party as a potent force in city politics is political scientist Theodore Lowi. His prescription is aimed primarily at New York, but presumably he means for it to apply elsewhere as well.

> The City has little to fear and very much to gain from restoration of the machine. If parties do not reclaim primacy in policy-making and implementation, the chief executive will continue to be faced with the *ad hoc* adjustment of claims. Particularism will continue to spread, and the "ordeal of the executive" will remain unresolved. Executive discretion—and therefore elective responsibility—will continue in its secondary role to a kind of functional representation.[61]

Many proponents of revitalizing the political party's role in city politics point to the model of Chicago. Despite some highly publicized deficiencies of its system of government, Chicago's system enabled an extreme amount of formal fragmentation of government to be overcome through the informal centralizing tendencies of the political machine.* Because of the machine's influence, Chicago received a disproportionate share of antipoverty program funds and received them more quickly than most cities, such as New York and Los Angeles.[62] Organized labor did not dominate the city's politics as happens in some other cities.[63] Interest groups generally were forced to work through the party,[64] and the mediating influence of the machine lessened the ability of potential demagogues to take office by inflaming the electorate.[65] While New York City was undergoing its bankruptcy crisis in 1975–1976, Chicago boasted proudly that it was a "city that works."

From the perspective of the 1990s, however, the benefits of the Chicago machine certainly appear to have been oversold. Chicago shares all of the problems of big industrial cities of the Northeast and Midwest, and some of them may well stem from Mayor Richard Daley's concentration on downtown redevelopment to the detriment of neighborhood renewal as well as Daley's covering up some fundamental fiscal problems that did not surface until after his death in 1976.

As the Chicago machine declines in stature, there is less and less inclination to look to the political party as the model way to strengthen city government. Despite some evidence of revival in local party organizations,[66] strong voter identification with the parties has declined considerably. And in the conduct of elections, city-wide campaigns rely less on party organization than they do on television, comput-

---

*The major deficiencies of the Chicago system are that it is unresponsive to the demands of poorly organized groups and the minority communities and that it is conducive to extensive graft. On the question of unresponsiveness, see Edward C. Banfield and James Q. Wilson, *City Politics* (New York: Random House, 1965), pp. 124–125. For charges of graft and a generally polemic indictment of the Daley machine, see Mike Royko, *Boss: Richard J. Daley of Chicago* (New York: E. P. Dutton, 1971). For a discussion of the centralizing influence of the machine, see Banfield and Wilson, *City Politics,* pp. 101–111.

ers, and direct-mail techniques.[67] However desirable it may be, party revitalization is not a very likely mechanism for strengthening urban governance in the 1990s.

Strengthening Central-City Mayors

A more viable model for urban leadership is the strong mayor. In the view of strong mayor advocates, the fragmentation of government authority is not so much a cause of mayoral weakness as it is an opportunity for skillful mayors to pyramid their power by bargaining with the various power centers, particularly with the technical specialists in the bureaucracies and with the downtown business leaders.[68]

If mayors are to become dynamic leaders, at least two things must happen. First, they must be given the legal and political resources to do their jobs. Jeffrey Pressman has identified seven factors that he calls the preconditions for strong mayoral leadership.

1. sufficient financial resources with which a mayor can launch innovative social programs
2. city jurisdiction in the vital program areas of education, housing, redevelopment, and job training
3. mayoral jurisdiction within the city government in those policy areas
4. a salary sufficiently high that the mayor can work full-time at the office
5. sufficient staff support for the mayor for tasks such as policy planning, speech writing, intergovernmental relations, and political work
6. ready vehicles for publicity, such as friendly newspapers and television stations
7. politically oriented groups, including a political party the mayor can mobilize to help achieve particular goals[69]

Unless mayors have these objective resources, claims Pressman, they are probably doomed either to frustration or to serving in a very minimal capacity.

In addition to these objective resources, an effective mayor must also have a subjective vision of what needs to be done in the city and how it can be done. A mayor who has no vision of how the mayoralty can be used to improve the lives of the city's residents will not become a great mayor regardless of his or her objective resources. On the other hand, a very dynamic personality with a sharp understanding of what can be accomplished may be able to have a lasting impact on the city even if he or she lacks some fo the resources identified by Pressman.

In trying to gain some understanding of the subjective vision of the mayor and mayoral leadership, John P. Kotter and Paul R. Lawrence studied mayors in twenty different cities during the 1960s and isolated several variables that contributed to mayoral success.[70] Of critical importance were: setting a decision-making agenda; controlling their time; expanding their political alliances to attract new supporters; building a large staff to whom they could delegate appropriate responsibilities; and gaining political control over city government. If we juxtapose the objective preconditions with the subjective-vision dimension, we derive four types of leadership: the ceremonial mayor, the caretaker mayor, the crusader mayor, and the program entrepreneur. These are shown in Figure 7-1.

Figure 7-1. Styles of Mayoral Leadership

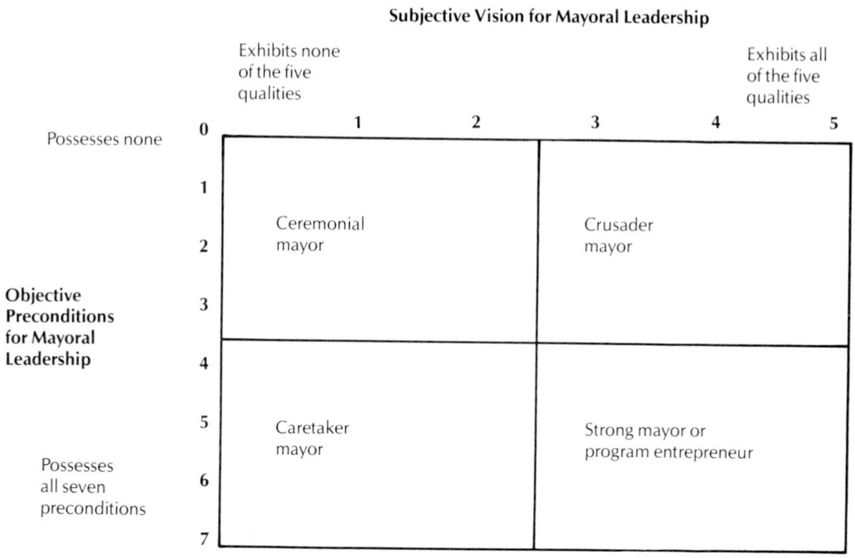

By juxtaposing the objective preconditions with the subjective vision for mayoral leadership, we can identify four major styles of mayoral leadership.
Source: This table was composed by juxtaposing criteria developed in Jeffrey L. Pressman, "The Preconditions for Mayoral Leadership," *American Political Science Review,* 66, no. 2 (June 1972): 511–74; John P. Kosser and Paul R. Lawrence, *Mayors in Action: Five Approaches in Urban Government* (New York: Wiley, 1974), Chap. 7; and Douglas Yates, *The Ungovernable City* (Cambridge, Mass.: M.I.T. Press, 1977), p. 165.

The Ceremonial Mayor

Ceremonial mayors make little effort to set a decision-making agenda for dealing with city problems. They have no broad goals to be accomplished. Rather, they simply deal with problems individually. They have modest staffs and do not try to build new political alliances to cope with city problems. Rather, they rely on past friendships and personal appeals. In coping with mayoral tasks, ceremonial mayors attempt to tackle each task personally rather than delegating authority to others to do them. As an example of a ceremonial mayor, Kotter and Lawrence point to Walton H. Bachrach of Cincinnati (1963–1967). They write of Bachrach:

> Walt was a very personable guy and just about everybody loved him. He'd walk down a crowded street and say hello to nearly everyone—by their first name.
> As mayor he spent nearly all of his time in ceremonial activities. He gave speeches at banquets, he welcomed conventions, he cut ribbons at all types of openings, he gave out keys to the city, and so on. He really looked the part and he played it with grace and dignity.[71]

The Caretaker Mayor

Like the ceremonial mayors, caretaker mayors also do not set an agenda of goals to be accomplished. They too simply deal with problems individually. They make more of an effort than do ceremonial mayors to build political alliances, to surround themselves with loyal staffs, and they are more able to delegate authority to others, especially to the established bureaucracies.

The prototype of a caretaker mayor was Ralph Locher of Cleveland (1962–1967). Locher dealt with city problems with a nonsystematic approach. He let his own daily agenda be dictated by other people who placed demands on him and by regular office routines such as opening the mail and dictating letters. There is no evidence that Locher attempted to establish goals for some of Cleveland's broader social problems. He was simply a caretaker for the city. Locher himself said:

> You know, I suppose it could be said that Burke [a previous mayor] and I were custodial mayors. We tried to keep the city clean and swept and policed. Some say that wasn't enough. Let me just say this about that complaint. You can't nurture flowers and good thoughts and ideals when you're living in a rat-infested squalor and your city services aren't being done.[72]

The Program Entrepreneur

Program entrepreneurs are the most ambitious of all the mayoral types. Their agenda is much more detailed. They not only have broad goals but even have a list of objectives or priority areas to be covered. Only a small portion of their daily work schedule is spent reacting to events. The rest is spent on activities tied into long-range and yearly objectives. Program entrepreneurs skillfully build political alliances and surround themselves with a substantial staff.

The prime example of a program entrepreneur is Richard C. Lee of New Haven, Connecticut. Lee built up a solid alliance around the major interest groups in the city—the city bureaucracy, federal renewal agencies, the city council, the business community, organized labor, the Democratic party, and Yale University.

Much of the basis for Lee's success was his strong political support in New Haven's Democratic party. With this strong political backing, he was assured of renomination and reelection, thus giving him a long tenure as mayor. The long-term mayor has advantages in dealing with the bureaucracy that the short-term mayor does not have.[73] It is easier for bureaucratic officials to oppose or ignore the wishes of short-term mayors, because they might not be around very long. One of Lee's first goals upon becoming mayor was to establish control over the city departments and bureaucracies.[74] He was able to maintain control over New Haven's urban renewal projects, a feat not performed by mayors in other cities such as Newark or New York.[75] At the center of what Robert Dahl called an executive-centered coalition, Lee was able to line up business leaders, university leaders, union leaders, and other civic leaders behind his redevelopment goals.[76]

The Crusader-Mayor

In addition to the above three mayoral styles, Douglas Yates has also identified a crusader-mayor.[77] The crusader style emerges when the mayor's office is occupied by a very active, imaginative, and ambitious personality who has a very weak political power base. Yates points to former New York City mayor John Lindsay as a crusader. Lacking the political strength to control the city bureaucracies and dominate the government, Lindsay adopted a crusading, symbolic style of leadership. During the riots of the 1960s, he went into the streets in the riot-torn sections and urged people to return to their homes. He traveled often to Washington to testify before congressional committees and to serve as a spokesperson for the nation's urban problems. He engaged in political battles with New York State governor Nelson Rockefeller. Despite the battles, the conflicts, and the publicity, however, it is hard to identify Lindsay with very many significant accomplishments.

The Minority Mayor

Although not a distinct style of leadership, the minority mayor is a very visible and increasingly common phenomenon. Minority mayors include blacks such as the late Harold Washington (Chicago), Wilson Goode (Philadelphia), Thomas Bradley (Los Angeles), Coleman Young (Detroit), and Andrew Young (Atlanta); Hispanics such as Henry Cisneros (San Antonio) and Federico Pena (Denver); and women such as Kathy Whitmore (Houston) and Annette Strauss (Dallas).

Minority mayors may confront problems and opportunities that white mayors do not face. Writing particularly about black mayors, political scientist Peter Eisinger argues that they are faced with a problem of divided loyalties.[78] In their initial election campaigns, they usually win a small minority of the white vote,[79] which means that they rely on overwhelming support from black communities. But to initiate the economic development activities they seek, black mayors have to make alliances with upper- and upper-middle-class whites who have the economic power to put economic development programs into action. The more that minority mayors cater to their minority constituencies, the more problems they create with their economic development coalitions, and vice versa.

If minority mayors have special problems, they also have special opportunities to increase employment and business prospects for the minority populations. Eisinger's studies of black mayors show that they are indeed able to increase the number of blacks employed by city government at all levels.[80] A similar study among female mayors found that they are able to increase the number of women holding city jobs.[81]

Can Mayors Be Strengthened?

At the beginning of the 1980s, it did not seem likely that there would be enough resources for many mayors to serve successfully as program entrepreneurs as did Richard Lee during the 1950s and 1960s. Federal community development funds did not grow as fast as inflation, and many local governments encountered strong voter resistance to big spending projects. This led many mayors to become very concerned with efficient management of the city's scarce resources.[82] Despite these fiscal problems, many mayors found imaginative ways to raise funds for economic development projects.

Additionally, considerable progress has been made toward the seven objective preconditions outlined earlier for strong mayors. One study found that mayoral staffs in Boston and Philadelphia had more than doubled between 1960 and the early 1970s.[83] By the mid-1970s, the New York City mayor had a staff of over 1,000 people and a budget of more than $20 million.[84] And a study of mayoral influence in ninety-three cities found that mayors with a strong political base of support tended to enjoy considerable success in getting their program proposals adopted.[85]

Finally, even where the mayor's formal powers are slim, it has been possible for dynamic individuals to exercise strong leadership. This could be seen in San Diego where a city-manager format presided smoothly over a growth period of the city during the 1950s and 1960s. By 1970 San Diego had grown to nearly 700,000 people. Severe opposition arose to the ethos of unrestricted growth, and the city manager proved unable to negotiate effectively between the city's pro-growth and no-growth political factions. This led to the emergence of Mayor Pete Wilson in the 1970s, who gradually strengthened the mayor's office, weakened the city manager, built a strong electoral coalition, and successfully balanced the city's competing pro-growth and no-growth factions.[86]

To sum up, there was a general awareness by the 1980s that a need existed to strenghten central-city mayors if urban problems were to be addressed successfully. Some steps were made in this direction in many cities during the 1970s—especially in curbing the functional fiefdom of urban renewal. Indeed, by the 1980s the mayor's office had become a much more prestigious place than it had in the past, often attracting dynamic candidates who were able to use the city as a stepping-stone to higher office. For example, San Diego's Pete Wilson and Indianapolis's Richard Lugar moved up to the United States Senate. Today's mayor is likely to move on to higher office as is a governor or United States representative.[87] An interesting phenomenon in recent years has been the number of women elected mayor of major cities.

Antidote for Charges of Nonresponsiveness: Decentralization

Charges of Nonresponsiveness

In addition to coping with the demands and interests of powerful functional fiefdoms, city governments must also cope with the demands and needs of unorganized citizens, of smaller and less powerful groups, and of newly emerging power centers. When the urban political process is viewed from the perspective of these factors, it is often portrayed as something beyond the influence or even the understanding of ordinary citizens. Michael Parenti studied three unsuccessful attempts of the Newark Community Union Project (NCUP) to obtain major gains for the residents of a poor, black neighborhood in Newark during the mid-1960s.[88] NCUP was organized by local black militants and white members of Students for a Democratic Society. Over a three-year period, NCUP attempted to get the city government to enforce the city's building codes and to install a traffic light at a particularly dangerous intersection. When these attempts failed, NCUP tried to elect new black candidates to the city council and the state legislature. But this attempt failed, too. Throughout these efforts, the tactics employed by NCUP ranged from traditional voter registration and electioneering to protest activity and agitation that involved rent strikes, sit-ins, and blocking traffic at the intersection where the traffic light was desired. Although NCUP held together and persisted in its efforts for three years, none of its three major projects was successful.

Drawing on his observations of these unsuccessful experiences, Parenti describes the urban political process as seen from below. First, "there exists the world of the rulers and the world of the ruled." Second, one of the crucial elements of power is the capacity to set the agenda of the struggle, to determine that certain questions will not come up for consideration by government agencies. These are the so-called nondecisions. "Much of the behavior of Newark's officials can be seen as a kind of 'politics of prevention' . . . designed to limit the area of issue conflict." Third, Parenti rejects the pluralist concept of "latent power," which in this case would imply that the ghetto dwellers possess a latent or "potential power that would prevail should they choose to use it."[89] On the contrary, the resources of the poor are seen as infinitesimal in comparison to the resources of the interest groups. In contrast to Robert Dahl, who states that power is noncumulative, Parenti maintains that the *lack* of power is cumulative. Ghetto dwellers exist in a state of *cumulative inequalities* in which their unequal status in education, income, jobs, and discrimination all accumulate to reduce their potential collective political efficacy. Because of their cumulative inequalities, they are unable to translate their needs into effective demands. Since politicians respond to *demands* more readily than they respond to citizens' needs, the cumulative inequalities of the poor increase their difficulty in getting the government to meet their needs. Furthermore, politicians who do respond to ghetto dwellers' demands on certain kinds of issues such as building code enforcement "might incur the wrath of high political leaders or powerful economic interests." For this reason, "party regulars have little inclination to entertain the kinds of issues" pushed by organizations such as NCUP, and "they also try to discredit and defeat those reformers who seek confrontations on such issues."[90]

Not all studies of attempts to mobilize the poor have been as totally pessimistic as Parenti's study, but a remarkable consensus exists on the extreme difficulties of organizing the poor to articulate their demands in ways that will oblige government agencies to respond positively. One of the most common political tactics of the poor has been protest activity. But a study of rent strikes and protest activity in New York found that protest as a tactic has severe limitations, particularly over the medium and long range.[91] Protest groups are inherently unstable and difficult to keep together. In order to get the attention of the mass media, protest leaders tend to overstate their strength and their accomplishments, only to lose credibility with reporters when they are unable to produce on the statements and claims they make. In order for protests to be successful, the leaders have to capture the sympathy and often the financial support of third parties, particularly white liberals. This usually involves moderating their position or making compromises that lose them support from other members of the protesting groups. In the Harlem rent stikes of 1963 and 1964, government officials and slum landlords were able to use delaying tactics and wait for the indignation aroused by reportage of slum housing conditions to wane. When public interest declined, the rent strike coalition collapsed.[92]

The limitations of protest as a political tactic probably exist in other cities as well. The only comparative research on protest activity studied protests in 43 cities over a six-month period in 1968. During that period, 120 protest actions were taken, but in only 18 cases were concessions made by the particular government to meet the demands of the protesters.[93] This pattern of the poor and their demands being mostly ignored is also supported by numerous case studies in the 1960s in Toledo, Ohio,[94] Chicago,[95] Oakland,[96] and Brooklyn.[97] The brunt of scholarly research by 1970, then, clearly supported the "powerlessness of the poor" viewpoint.

Although these studies stress the powerlessness of the poor and the racial minorities, their powerlessness is not total and the power relations are not static. They do change. Changes have been most obvious in the arena of electoral politics. As noted earlier in Chapter 5, the number of black elected officials increased dramatically from 1469 in 1970 to 6300 in 1986, and most of the cities with large black populations now have black mayors (see p. 115, Table 5-1). Even where blacks did not elect their own mayors, they have seen an increase in their collective political influence. In Providence, Rhode Island, for example, blacks took control of the Community Action program away from its dominance by the mayor and the city's political machine.[98] And a study of protest activity in California showed that protest combined with organizational activity indeed helped the racial minorities to be drawn into the governing coalitions of cities.[99]

What conclusions can we draw about this research into the powerlessness of the poor and the racial minorities? Three conclusions are warranted. First, blacks, by engaging in community organization, direct political action strategies, and electoral competition, have been able to get middle-class black leaders drawn into the governing coalitions in most cities where blacks constitute a substantial portion of the city population. Second, despite being able to use this new-found power to make modest increases in black public-sector employment, there is no systematic evidence that black mayors have yet been able to make substantial improvements in the living conditions of the huge black urban underclass.

Third, despite the black success, there still is no systematic evidence that unorganized people, regardless of race, get any more positive reaction from city governments today than they did thirty years ago. Commentaries on certain white ethnic groups, poor white communities, and many big-city residents interviewed sporadically indicate that they also feel powerless to influence city politics.[100] This white powerlessness may not be limited to the poor; there may well be a sense of middle-class powerlessness as well. In Chapter 9 we will argue that this sense of powerlessness within the city is one of the reasons for the white exodus to the suburbs. And for whites who cannot afford to move to the suburbs, there is often a frustrating sense of loss of control over their neighborhoods. In the Canarsie section of Brooklyn, these frustrations often exploded in acts of violence against blacks whom the whites saw as invading Canarsie.[101]

Decentralization as an Antidote for Nonresponsiveness

Given the widespread perception that city governments and their functional fiefdoms are not very responsive to unorganized city residents and their neighborhoods, it is not surprising that the past twenty years have seen a succession of decentralization proposals to give citizens more influence in the programs operated by the functional fiefdoms. To date, urban decentralization has evolved through three stages: (1) the Community Action and Model Cities programs of the 1960s, (2) the community control movement of the late 1960s and early 1970s, and (3) a continuing emphasis on citizen participation and neighborhood revitalization in the late 1970s and 1980s. All three of these concepts held considerable potential for reducing the power of existing functional fiefdoms over urban governments.

Community Action and Model Cities Programs

The Community Action programs (CAPs) were created by the Economic Opportunity Act of 1964, and the Model Cities program was created two years later. Although important differences existed between the programs, they had three similar objectives: (1) to provide and improve public services for the poor, (2) to mobilize both public and private resources to cope with the problems of poverty, and (3) to engage the maximum feasible participation of the poor in carrying out the programs.

Participation of the poor was most advanced in the Community Action programs. Community action agencies (CAAs) were created to implement the Community Action programs. The CAAs were originally made independent of the city government, and neighborhood representatives dominated their boards of directors. But as time went on and as the federal funding agency (the Office of Economic Opportunity) was terminated, CAAs became highly dependent on local city halls for their survival. Although many cities have continued to fund their own CAAs, the CAAs now function more as an arm of city hall rather than as independent political organizations for the poor. Whatever merits they may have today in terms of delivering public services to the urban poor, they are clearly no longer a major force for decentralizing political influence to bring it to the neighborhood level.

Community Control

A second prescription in the 1960s and 1970s for making urban governments more responsive to the citizenry was that of sharing control over governmental services between centralized bureaucracies and community residents who receive the services. A wide variety of control-sharing schemes was advanced under a bewildering array of labels as diverse as community control, consumer representation, decentralization, little (neighborhood) city halls, neighborhood advisory councils, and neighborhood corporations. Each of them is based on different assumptions about the nature of urban government and each would have different results in dealing with the problem of bureaucratic unresponsiveness. In all community control plans, an important distinction must be made. Does the control sharing plan simply decentralize the *delivery* of services? Or does it decentralize *political control* as well?[102]

There have been many instances of practical attempts to achieve decentralization of political control and/or delivery of services. Three of these have evoked the most interest among observers: (1) decentralization of education, (2) decentralization of city hall and public services, and (3) neighborhood advisory committees or councils.

Decentralization of Public Education   In central cities with large numbers of poor children or racial minorities, the public school systems have been resoundingly criticized as being unresponsive to children's needs.[103] Because of residential segregation, big-city schools have traditionally been racially segregated in fact, even though there may have been no laws demanding their segregation. Schools for the racial minorities were also commonly the oldest, shabbiest, and most poorly supplied with facilities. Teachers with enough seniority to have a choice tried to avoid teaching in the minority neighborhoods.

Black leaders attacked these problems for many years by seeking more school integration, but in few cities were they successful. Consequently, when the concept of decentralizing control over schools was advanced in the mid-1960s, it quickly won acceptance from those blacks who despaired of ever getting truly integrated schools and at the same time deplored the inferior quality of the black schools. Local control of schools was also consistent with the then-growing philosophy of black separatism. Two of the most noteworthy experiments in decentralized control of schools occurred in New York City and Detroit.

In three of the most impoverished neighborhoods in New York City, the Board of Education established locally controlled demonstration districts to experiment with locally controlled schools. A local governing board was created in each district, and the members were chosen by popular election by residents of the district.[104]

In the Ocean Hill-Brownsville district, an explosive controversy soon developed between the local governing board, the school bureaucracy, and the teachers' federation. When the governing board attempted to transfer some teachers out of the district and replace them with others, it ran into the solid opposition of the United Federation of Teachers (UFT). Since some of the teachers to be transferred out were Jewish, the local blacks were accused of anti-Semitism, even though it should be noted that most of the retained teachers were also Jewish. A long, drawn-out struggle ensued in which the schools were closed by a teachers' strike and the police had to be brought in to protect the peace. There was little popular support for the demonstration district's side of the strike outside the black community, and even among blacks barely a majority supported it.* The strike proved so unpopular and

*Louis Harris conducted a survey of New Yorkers in April and May 1969. On a question of whether the teachers' federation was more right or the demonstration district governing board was more right, the percentage favoring the teachers versus the percentage favoring the governing board was 63 to 8 among Jews, 48 to 9 among Catholics, 35 to 20 among white Protestants, 21 to 12 among Puerto Ricans, and 14 to 50 among blacks [Louis Harris and Bert E. Swanson, *Black-Jewish Relations in New York City* (New York: Praeger, 1970), p. 132].

divisive that the demonstration district experiment was brought to an end by the New York legislature in 1970. In its stead, thirty-two local school boards were created whose authority was sharply limited.[105]

In Detroit, the attempt to decentralize public schools also developed into an explosive controversy.[106] In 1969 the Michigan legislature passed a bill that created new local school boards that would be subordinate to the citywide board. The citywide board was dominated by liberals who were determined that decentralizaton would not be allowed to impede their plans for school integration. Consequently, they drafted a plan for local school boards in which about 9000 pupils would be bused across local boundary lines in order to accomplish integration.

The public reaction was swift. Behind the leadership of a conservative board member who opposed the integration, protests and demonstrations erupted. Under local pressure, the state legislature quickly revoked its 1969 law and passed a new law that outlawed such busing of students and mandated the decentralized school boards to be organized on the basis of neighborhood schools. That obviously meant that the schools would not be integrated. In addition, the new law gave each of the eight local school boards one representative on the previously at-large, citywide Board of Education. A recall petition was filed in June 1970 and, in a special recall election, all of the liberal members of the citywide Board of Education were removed from office and replaced with conservatives. The former conservative member who had led the anti-integration demonstrations was elected board president. Local neighborhood boards were given extensive sway to establish policies as they saw fit. In a black district, a principal was removed. In another district, the local board was permitted to refuse to administer a statewide achievement test to students. And a district in a white region was allowed not to implement voluntary desegregation guidelines that had been established.

The decentralized schools in Detroit seemed to come much closer to the neighborhood government model of decentralization than did those in New York. Their net impact, however, was to impede integration in Detroit, inflame latent racial tensions, and cut back educational programs. They also failed to increase the representation of the poor or the minorities in school policymaking. As in New York, Detroit's local school board members came largely from middle-class professional, technical, and managerial positions.[107]

Perhaps in reaction to the experience of New York and Detroit, school decentralization efforts elsewhere have shied away from granting political control to subdistrict units. Instead, the tendency has been to expand the use of community advisory councils that give parents input into decision-making on some curriculum matters and certain federal programs.

Little City Halls   A second approach to decentralization has been to establish little (neighborhood) city halls throughout the city. A little city hall is simply a mayoral branch office that seeks to expeidite the provision of city services in neighborhoods and to improve ties with neighborhood residents. Little city halls were strongly recommended by the National Advisory Commission on Civil Disorders[108] as one means of lessening citizen alienation from the government. In terms of the three models of decentralization, little city halls contain elements of the status quo, the representational, and the bureaucratic models. They do not contain elements of the neighborhood government model, because they are basically a branch of the mayor's office.

Some form of decentralized delivery of services has been found in at least seventy-five cities, and in at least twenty-five of them are significant enough to be called little city halls.[109]

In New York City, mayor John Lindsay established an Office of Neighborhood Government to interact with district offices in that city. In some districts a district cabinet was established to bring representatives of all city departments together to improve the delivery of their services in those neighborhoods, and a district manager was given authority to coordinate these operations. Although New York's Office of Neighborhood Government and the district manager plan fall much more into the bureaucratic model of decentralization than into the neighborhood government model, some observers judge them to be very successful at making the city more responsive to neighborhood needs.[110]

Neighborhood Advisory Councils   Similar to the little city halls are neighborhood advisory councils (NACs), established in St. Paul, Minnesota, Washington, D.C., New York City, and many other cities. The NAC plan typically divides a city into small geographic districts (17 in St. Paul, 36 in Washington, and 59 in New York City), provides funds for a neighborhood office and a full-time district manager, and allows for an elected or appointed representative board. Typically, councils are responsible for advising the central-city government on land-use decisions, budgeting, and the delivery of services in the neighborhood. Where the NACs are elected, as in Washington, voting turnout rarely exceeds 20 percent of the registered voters,[111] and where they are appointed, as in New York City, there are inevitable complaints that the appointed board members do not reflect neighborhood viewpoints.[112]

Although NACs have little formal authority, they can, if they are astute, parlay their advisory role into political results. The New York City NACs have given neighborhoods an influential role in planning many big development projects. Department heads have also been able to capitalize on NAC complaints to get larger budgets to improve services in the neighborhoods.[113]

Decentralization in the 1990s

By the late 1980s much of the thrust for community control had dissipated. The most advanced form of community control was that of Milton Kotler, who advocated dividing cities into neighborhood governments that would have legal authority to handle all neighborhood-level governmental issues.[114] But Kotler's model was not adopted anywhere.

More enduring were the moderate forms of control sharing. The New York City demonstration school districts, for example, disappeared very quickly when they attempted to exercise real power. The less powerful local school boards created after the Ocean Hill-Brownsville crisis, on the other hand, continue to function. One study of neighborhood programs in four midwestern states also found that neighborhood program participants expressed greater satisfaction with the program if it provided only for moderate levels of participation rather than high levels and if the program was of a moderate scope rather than a comprehensive scope.[115] Neighborhood advisory councils seemed to fit much better into the less militant mood of the 1980s.

There is today some concern about how to revitalize neighborhoods without turning them into subcity governments. The American Institute of Architects called for a national growth policy based on preserving the quality of life in neighborhoods.[116] Mortgage lending institutions came under attack for the practice of redlining—that is, making it difficult for certain neighborhoods to get home mortgage loans. Federal legislation attempted to curb redlining. Federal community development funds and public housing funds under the 1974 Housing and Community Development Act made it easier to preserve buildings and to restore old neighborhoods of historic interest. This gave an added stimulus to the gentrification process of upper-middle-income people moving back into inner-city neighborhoods. The Carter administration established an office for coordinating federal programs on a neighborhood basis. During the Reagan administration, however, this office was disbanded.

Decentralization—A Critique

Despite the eclipse of the community control movement in the 1980s, it would be a mistake to write it off entirely as a historic aberration of the 1960s. Some of its more moderate tenets (such as client representation and neighborhood advisory councils) are accepted practices in many cities today. Although these practices have not revolutionized the life styles of urban dwellers, the practices often have modified the plans of big-city institutions to make them more accommodating to local residents. We will see in Chapter 9, for example, how local groups in Boston and other cities halted the construction of freeways through their neighborhoods. And New York City's Office of Neighborhood Government seems to have had some success in making that city's bureaucracies more attentive to service-delivery problems at the district level.[117]

Control sharing has the potential to reduce citizen alienation from government. Giving citizens a voice in the management of their neighborhoods gives them an alternative to moving out to the suburbs when they become dissatisfied with the delivery of local public services.[118] Poorly organized or ineffectual control sharing, of course, can easily lead to bitter conflict that reduces confidence in government. But evidence does exist that meaningful and effective participation can also increase satisfaction and trust in local government.[119]

Finally, there is also reason to belief that vibrant neighborhood politics make the city more governable. Matthew Crenson studied neighborhood politics in Baltimore and concluded that they made several contributions to the effective government of that city. If neighborhood groups and a system of informal politics can be created, they can often deal with the hundreds of daily problems (such as vandalism, people who fail to maintain their property, trash removal from private property, even snow removal from alleys) that arise in a big city. This shields the central-city leaders from having their energies torn in many different directions at once and allows them to focus their energies on the big problems of the city. By delegating "authority to a host of small-time operators . . . [the downtown leaders] . . . will have more opportunities to behave like big-time operators themselves."[120]

In conclusion, the concept of control sharing was one of the most creative concepts to come out of the turbulent decade of the 1960s. Although much more moderate and much less extensive, the concepts of citizen participation and neighborhood revitalization continue to have meaning in the 1990s. The citizen participation movements have led to political mechanisms and expectations that make it easier for citizens groups in the 1990s to demand meaningful input into governmental decisions.

Bias in Contemporary Urban Government

Several themes about contemporary urban government have dominated the foregoing discussions. First, although no consensus exists on whether the elitist or pluralist theories of community power are more accurate, it does appear that individual citizens are generally much less influential than institutions. Second, the institutional dominance of cities can be described by the concept of functional fiefdoms. A functional fiefdom consists of an urban agency operating in some general arena of public affairs, consisting of its bureaucracy, its professional staff, its public employees' union, its board or commission of directors; its counterpart agencies in the state and federal government; and the private businesses, labor organizations, and interest groups that serve as a clientele for the agency. Third, the functional fiefdoms pose enormous problems for the exercise of decisive political leadership in large cities. Fourth, the existing structure and organization of power in urban areas, be it pluralist or stratified, is biased against people who are unorganized. This bias is felt more heavily by the poor and the racial minorities. Finally, two entirely different remedies have been prescribed by social scientists and others as antidotes for the deficiencies of functional fiefdoms. For the weakness of inhibited political leadership, the antidotes most often prescribed have been a simultaneous strengthening of the political parties and the big-city mayor. For the anti-poor bias of the functional fiefdoms, the prescription has been some form of shared control with, or citizen control over, urban government.

The two antidotes appear to be contradictory; it is not clear how a geographic decentralization of government can be consistent with strong mayoral leadership. But if Matthew Crenson's analysis of neighborhood politics in Baltimore is correct, the two antidotes may not necessarily be contradictory. Effective politics at the neighborhood level help to shield the mayor from dealing with petty squabbles, and enable him or her to concentrate on the overriding citywide issues.

The controversy over community control has exposed the biases of the status quo. The advocates of community control demand it not simply because they think that the bureaucracies are doing a bad job of helping the poor and the racial minorities. If that were the case, the problem could be remedied through the application of modern techniques of public administration and program analysis. Rather, in the writings of the advocates of community control, the functional fiefdoms are *inherently* biased against the interests of the disorganized, the poor, and the racial minorities. This is a direct result of the peculiar form of representative democracy that has developed in the United States. Legislatures and bureaucracies are most responsive to constituent and client groups and to citizens who participate in the political process. For a variety of reasons, the poor and the disorganized do not participate very well in these groups, in electoral activity, in campaigning activity, or in lobbying activity. The major institutional reasons for their lack of participation is that there is no institutional mechanism that can mobilize them into action.[121] The closest thing to such a mechanism has been the affiliation of organized labor, by means of the New Deal coalition, with the Democratic party. The labor unions can mobilize their members to vote and can pressure the government for legislation that will benefit their members. But no institution in American society has mobilized the poor and the disorganized in the same fashion.

In this view, then, the key failure of the bureaucratic state is that no institutional mechanism exists for representing the interests of the disorganized and the poor. And, in this respect, community control is championed as the new institutional creation for accomplishing this representation directly in the administrative bureaucracy.

In fact, however, there is good reason to doubt that the poor would gain very much from community control. All the evidence we have reviewed to this point indicates that upper-status people participate in neighborhood politics more than lower-status people do. And Matthew Crenson argues that the upper-status neighborhoods are also believed to have more influence in city politics than lower-status neighborhoods have. "Decentralization achieved through community organizations would probably accentuate existing political inequalities between rich neighborhoods and poor neighborhoods."[122] The most effective thing that city governments could do for poor neighborhoods, asserts Crenson, is to encourage more middle-class people to move into those neighborhoods so that all of the city's neighborhoods would be more socially integrated. It is the middle-income people in generally poor neighborhoods who are most likely to engage in the informal politics that Crenson views as so favorable for city governability.

Bureaucratic decentralization has been accomplished without decentralizing control over policy. Steps have been taken to place token client representatives on the boards of public agencies without cutting into the autonomy of the bureaucracies involved. The proliferation of federal programs for compensatory education, health planning, community development, and so on has led to an equal proliferation of federally mandated and funded citizens' advisory councils. And, despite the experiments with Model Cities and Community Action programs, no true neighborhood governments have been established. Instead, the emphasis has shifted from community control to neighborhood revitalization. Finally, whatever its revolutionary potential, the concept of neighborhood government via the Milton Kotler model clearly is not the wave of the future for American cities.

Summary

1. Two competing theories of community power are the elitist, or stratificationist, theory and the pluralist theory. These theories were traced to early research conducted in Atlanta, Georgia, and New Haven, Connecticut. More recent community power research has modified the early elitist interpretations of the business community's role in community power, has attributed greater importance to the concept of nondecisions, has shown that a variety of community power relationships exist, and has found that community power relationships can change over time. In the 1980s and 1990s the community power debate has been revived by neo-Marxist growth machine, unitary interest, and systemic power theories and a pluralistic counterattack.

2. A distinguishing feature of power in urban America has been the emergence of functional fiefdoms. These are power relationships within specific functional sectors (urban renewal, for example) that involve bureaucratic officials at more than one level of government and private interests that work with those officials.

3. The emergence of functional fiefdoms has tended to inhibit unified political leadership in tackling urban problems and has compounded the problem of making urban government responsive to the citizenry.

4. Strong political parties and strong mayors have been proposed as antidotes for the fragmentation of power that occurs with functional fiefdoms.

5. Getting strong mayors requires giving mayors the objective legal and political resources needed to do their jobs and getting mayors who have a subjective vision of what needs to be done in the city and how to do it.

6. To cope with the problems of making city government more responsive to citizens, experiments have been conducted with Community Action programs, Model Cities programs, and various schemes for community control and political decentralization.

7. Several biases were found in the contemporary patterns of urban government. Citizens are not as influential in urban politics as are institutions, particularly institutions tied into a functional fiefdom. This bias against citizens is especially pronounced against unorganized citizens. These biases have been exposed in the struggle over community control.

Chapter 8
Managing City Services
in a Time of Scarce Resources

Because of the forces discussed in the previous two chapters, urban governments today are being pressed to become more efficient and productive. As shown in Chapter 6, many if not most central cities are beset with serious economic and fiscal restraints in financing their public services. And as shown in Chapter 7, even if the cities had sufficient financial resources, they are buffeted by political forces that severely hamper their ability to deal effectively with the urban problems they face. The current reaction to these limitations on city governments that seems to draw the most favorable response from urban observers is the demand that urban governments become more productive and efficient. Although there is little agreement on what is meant by managerial efficiency or increased productivity, there is no doubt that these concepts have become central demands on city governments. If the 1960s were characterized by riots, confrontation politics, and the demand for political influence by new constituent groups such as blacks, Hispanics, senior citizens, and women, urban politics since 1980 have been characterized by different concerns. These are the delivery of public services, fiscal pressures on central-city governments, and especially concern over the effective management of urban governments.

In this chapter we shall first review the reasons for this rising concern with improving urban management. Second, we shall examine the governmental structures for delivering urban services. Third, we shall outline some recent managerial innovations with which public administrators hope to increase the productivity of their organizations. Then we shall examine a complex of personnel problems involving hiring, affirmative action, and collective bargaining. And finally we shall inquire about the equality of public-service delivery and ask what patterns of bias, if any, characterize them.

A Rising Concern with Improving Urban Management

One reason for the growing concern with urban management is traced to the atmosphere of financial retrenchment that pervaded the late 1970s and much of the 1980s.[1] This was symbolized by the passage of Proposition 13 in California in 1978, which effectively lowered property taxes in that state by nearly 60 percent and encouraged tax reform movements in other states. By 1978 nineteen states in addition to California had put some statutory limits on government spending.[2]

Not only has there been political pressure to reduce government's share of the national economy, but the economy itself slowed down from an average annual real* GNP growth rate of 3.9 percent in the 1960s to 2.9 percent in the 1970s to 2 percent in the first half of the 1980s.[3] Because of these political and economic forces, city governments will continue to face fiscal pressures. To provide the same level of services with less money will require increased productivity. To maintain the same level of productivity with no real increase in expenditures will necessarily mean a reduction in public services. The threat to urban services is real. Potholes in streets will go unfilled. Neighborhood libraries will cut their hours, perhaps closing on Saturdays and some evenings. Parks will not be well maintained. Zoo animals will not be cared for properly. Public swimming pools will raise their fees. Less efficient bus lines will be cut, and the patrons of these lines will be sent back to their automobiles, even though it is in the national interest for them to keep using the buses. Class sizes in the schools will increase. Police patrols will come around less frequently and will respond to complaints more slowly. Former HEW secretary Joseph Califano expressed the problem facing urban governments:

> Today the liberals and progressives of our society must match their compassion and generosity with competence and efficiency. Unless we accept and meet the challenges of austerity with good management, we will surrender to an undiscriminating Proposition 13 mentality that will do violence to the concepts of social justice on which the programs of the New Deal and the Great Society are so soundly based.[4]

A second reason for the interest in improving urban productivity can be traced to a deeply held belief that city bureaucracies were not very efficient in comparison to private bureaucracies of corporations.[5] In the early 1970s it was found, for example, that it cost New York City garbage collectors $39.71 to collect a ton of garbage, but private companies in adjacent suburbs could collect the same amount of garbage for only $17.28[6] In Chicago, the city spent $1.23 to read a single water meter, but a private firm in Indianapolis was able to do the same job for 27.5 cents.[7] And a comparison of city-run fire departments with the private companies that provide the fire protection services for Scottsdale, Arizona found that the private companies were more economical.[8]

The reader is cautioned not to accept all of this at face value as evidence of the inferiority of the public sector. Some European nations enjoy very high standards of living and have a much larger public sector than we do in the United States. And the reasons for inefficient garbage collection and meter reading in New York and Chicago might have as much to do with the peculiar characteristics of those cities as they do with whether the services are administered publicly or privately. In other places the public sector might be more efficient. The residents of Runaway Point, Georgia, an unincorporated suburb of Savannah, asked that the city annex their

---

*Adjusted to compensate for inflation.

area in 1984. They sought annexation in part because the garbage collection by private contractors in the suburb cost each home $12 a month compared to only $2.50 by the city garbage collectors.[9]

Having expressed these reservations, however, even the most pro-city-government adherent would be forced to admit that cities might benefit from greater productivity. And by the late 1970s demands for greater urban productivity were widespread. The prestigious Committee for Economic Development published a booklet in 1976 calling for *Improving Productivity in State and Local Government*.[10]

Before proceeding to examine how urban governments deal with these demands for greater economy and productivity, it is important to remember that there is more at stake than simply reducing the cost of urban services. The effective delivery of urban services makes a significant difference in the quality of our lives. If the potholes in our streets are not filled, our lives are less comfortable. If the police do not respond to our calls, our lives are less secure. It is reported that when residents of the South Bronx need emergency help fast, they often pull the fire alarm rather than call the police.[11] They know that the fire department always responds quickly, but they do not know how fast—or even if—the police will arrive. This, of course, is a very expensive way of getting help. And for the urban manager in the 1980s it illustrates some of the main problems. How do you ensure that the most appropriate agencies deliver the right services most effectively to the target people on time? And how do you meet the demands of cost-conscious groups that all these services be delivered at the lowest possible cost per unit of service?

The Structure for Delivering Urban Services

Who Does What

There are 80,000 local governments in the United States. Because there are so many different ways to provide public services, from North to South and East to West, it is impossible to make a generalization that applies in every region of the nation. To get an overall picture of who does what, it is necessary to sort out the services by the types of government responsible for them. Table 8-1 uses data from the U.S. Census Bureau to do this.

Table 8-1 shows that five different types of local government (counties, municipalities, townships, special districts, and independent school districts) spend the vast majority of money being allocated to local services. The biggest share of money ($153 billion) goes for public education, which in most regions is administered by an independent school district. In most central cities the school district has the same geographic boundaries as the city government, but the school district is independent, having its own elected school board and its own separate administration. There are several major exceptions to this characteristic, however. In much of the South, the county rather than the central city forms the boundaries of the urban

Table 8-1. Who Does What in Local Government

| General category of local service | Expenditures for all services in the category by type of local government: 1985–86 (in billions) | | | | | |
	County	Municipality	Township	Special district	School district	Total
Human and social services (welfare, hospitals public health, corrections)	$26.6 (57.2%)	$12.6 (27.2%)	$0.4 (0.8%)	$6.8 (14.8%)	0 (0%)	$46.6 (100%)
Physical maintenance (highways and streets, sewerage, water supply, parks, recreation, libraries, natural resources)	$15.1 (27.8%)	$29.6 (54.4%)	$3.9 (7.1%)	$5.8 (10.7%)	0 (0%)	$54.4 (100%)
Other traditional city government services (police protection, fire protection, sanitation)	$32.4 (22.7%)	$82.0 (57.3%)	$5.5 (3.8%)	$20.6 (14.4%)	$2.6 (1.8%)	$143.1 (100%)
Redevelopment activities (transit, housing and community development, airports)	$2.3 (10.9%)	$12.3 (56.6%)	$0.1 (0.8%)	$12.6 (31.7%)	0 (0%)	$27.3 (100%)
Education	$11.9 (7.8%)	$12.1 (7.9%)	$3.1 (2.0%)	$0.0 (0%)	$125.4 (82.3%)	$152.5 (100%)

United States Bureau of the Census, *Government Finances in 1985–86*, GF-86 No. 5 (Washington, D.C.: United States Government Printing Office, November 1987), p. 13.

school districts. And in Hawaii, all local school systems are subordinate to the statewide school district.

Table 8-1 also shows an interesting division of responsibility between city and county governments. Except for parts of New England (where counties are insignificant), counties bear the heaviest responsibilities for human services (such as welfare, hospitals, public health, and corrections). The heavy county expenditures for physical maintenance and police services shown in Table 8-1 take place primarily in the suburbs and rural areas, not in the central cities. Within the central cities, the municipal governments dominate the traditional services and the physical maintenance services. Special districts play a significant role in physical maintenance services, and about three-fourths of their physical maintenance expenditures shown in Table 8-1 were for sewerage and water supply. Special districts and municipalities share responsibility for redevelopment activities such as public housing, urban renewal, and transportation.

Although the patterns identified nationally differ from one part of the nation to another, the Bureau of the Census data do permit some generalizations to be made about who does what in urban America. Dividing public services into the five categories shown in Table 8-1, the provision of local public services in central cities is handled as follows:

1. Public education is normally provided by independent school districts, which, outside of the South, are coterminous with the central-city boundaries.
2. Noneducational human and social services are provided principally by county governments, but in New England and some other areas, central-city governments play a major role.
3. Physical maintenance services are provided mostly by central-city governments, but many regions have established special districts to provide sewerage and water supply services.
4. Other traditional government services such as police and fire protection, street maintenance, and recreation are handled almost exclusively by city governments.
5. Redevelopment activities are divided mostly between central-city governments and special districts, with counties accounting for most of the balance.

How Urban Governments Are Organized

Urban services are delivered by counties, cities, special districts, and school districts, and these governments are organized in similar fashion. The counties, as will be discussed more fully in Chapter 11, are governed by an elected board of commissioners (sometimes called board of supervisors), which functions as the legislative body. Often, a variety of administrative officers (sheriff, registrar of deeds, auditor, assessor, coroner) are also elected, and there is seldom an overall chief administrative officer (CAO) accountable to the legislative body.

Cities, as discussed in Chapter 4, are headed by elected councils that serve as legislative bodies, and have either a mayor or city manager as the CAO. Special districts are governments that normally provide a single service (although some provide multiple services). As will be discussed in Chapter 9, they often have an appointive rather than elective legislative board, and their CAO is an appointed executive director. School districts are the most prevalent kind of special district, and they are usually governed by an elected school board, which appoints a superintendent of schools as the chief administrative officer.

How these governments are organized for urban service delivery is illustrated in Figure 8-1. Although no specific governmental organization chart would be as simplified as Figure 8-1, most government organization charts distinguish between a policymaking level and an implementation level as shown in the figure.

Policymaking

Policymaking at the local level is formalized through a policymaking board such as the city council, the county board of commissioners, the school board, or the special district's board of directors. The policymaking board is greatly affected

Figure 8-1. Bureaucratic Hierarchy for Delivering Urban Services

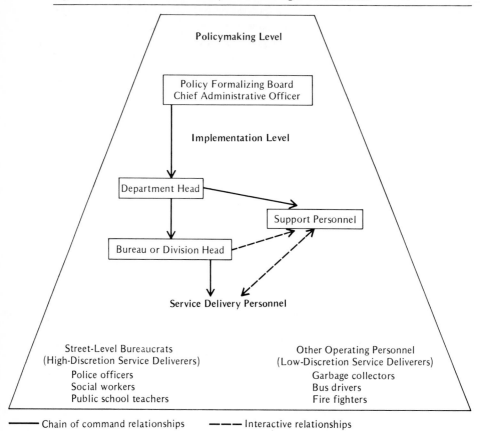

Policymaking Level

Policy Formalizing Board
Chief Administrative Officer

Implementation Level

Department Head

Support Personnel

Bureau or Division Head

Service Delivery Personnel

Street-Level Bureaucrats (High-Discretion Service Deliverers)	Other Operating Personnel (Low-Discretion Service Deliverers)
Police officers	Garbage collectors
Social workers	Bus drivers
Public school teachers	Fire fighters

——— Chain of command relationships   — — — Interactive relationships

by state and federal law. On numerous issues its policymaking function is limited to determining how a particular federal or state policy can be tailored to local circumstances. For example, federal law and (usually) state law prohibits racial discrimination in governmental hiring practices, but these laws are often very broad, and a local government has considerable flexibility in adopting its own equal opportunity and affirmative action policies.

The chief administrative officer is a critical factor in policymaking. In the city, the CAO would be the mayor or the city manager (depending on the type of city government). Most rural counties do not have a CAO, but urban counties have increasingly hired county administrators and county managers. In school districts the local superintendent of schools is the CAO, and in special districts it is the executive director.

The chief administrative officer is critical in policy formulation for several reasons. If the position is strong, as in the case of a city manager, the manager controls the flow of communications between council members and the city department heads. The manager consults with the presiding officer of the city council to prepare the agendas for council meetings. By preparing the agenda the manager effectively decides what matters come to the council for policy decisions. This is especially the case in making budget policy. In Oakland, California, for example, it was found by Meltsner and Wildavsky that the manager is the key actor in budget making. "He guides the city council in its considerations. He feels it is his budget. And he uses it to make his influence felt throughout city government."[12] An astute manager will prepare the budget for the council's approval and will effectively narrow the council's decision-making choices to that of either increasing or decreasing amounts suggested by the manager and department heads. Rarely does the council initiate new budget policy proposals. Normally it functions as an oversight entity that reacts to the proposals made by the manager.[13]

Policy Implementation

Once made, policy must be implemented, and this is accomplished at the administrative and service delivery levels. Below the mayor or city manager are several department heads. From a policy perspective, one of their main tasks is to establish routines or decision rules[14] that will permit public services to be delivered in a predictable manner and in a way that is consistent with the government's policies. For example, the director of a county welfare department must ensure that the county's procedures for dispensing AFDC (Aid for Families with Dependent Children) are consistent with ever-changing federal, state, and county regulations. The director also must ensure that the services get delivered predictably. Each application for AFDC must be judged by the same criteria and processed the same way. This necessarily requires applicants to fill out numerous forms, undergo a financial investigation, and persevere through a waiting period while the application is being processed. These delays are sometimes criticized as needless "red tape," but such routines are necessary if the delivery of services is going to reflect public policy and if the services are going to be delivered consistently, predictably, and fairly.

Within each department it is ultimately the department head's responsibility to enforce the routines and decision rules. Beneath the department head are several bureau or division heads (although the precise terminology may differ from place to place.) Some divisions are responsible for what public administrators call *line* services, whereas others are responsible for *staff* (or support) services.[15] Although the distinction between line and staff personnel can often become quite fuzzy,[16] it is useful to refer to those workers who actually deliver the services (the police officer, the bus driver, the garbage collector) as line personnel and to refer to those workers who provide supportive services (run computers, process checks, administer personnel departments) as staff personnel.

Because staff personnel play such a critical role but do not actually deliver services, and because they are on the same horizontal level in the hierarchy as the line personnel or line divisions, the "chain of command" notion of a hierarchy illustrated in Figure 8-1 is diluted considerably in practice. For example, according to the chain of command, the department head and the division head in a welfare department might give orders to a child protection worker to intervene in a family where a child was reportedly abused by its parents. To accomplish this intervention, however, the protection worker is likely to need cooperation from the police, the county attorney, the courts, and the staff person in charge of placing children temporarily in shelter homes or foster homes. Even though all of these people may work for the same county government, there is no line of command requiring them to obey any of the instructions the child protection worker may have received from his or her supervisor. Given this ambiguity in the protection worker's authority, the most effective workers are likely to be ones who have developed the skills of supplementing their authority with negotiations and persuasion.

As shown in Figure 8-1, the line personnel who actually deliver urban services may be of two types. On the one hand are the operating personnel whose job routines are highly fixed and who exercise little discretion in how they deliver their services. Bus drivers and garbage collectors, for example, must follow the same routes every cycle and must adhere to a fixed time schedule.

The other type of line personnel are what Michael Lipsky calls street-level bureaucrats.[17] They exercise considerable discretion as they perform their jobs. Typical street-level bureaucrats are teachers, police officers, and some social workers. Teachers exercise much discretion in the way they conduct classes, relate to children, encourage learning, build up children's self-esteem, or discourage bad learning. The police officer's job is especially characterized by a high degree of discretion and ambiguity.[18] A team of officers might get called to investigate a family disturbance, for example, and find a drunken husband who has just beaten his wife who in turn has picked up a butcher knife to defend herself. Once the officers get her to put down the knife they must swiftly choose from among a number of possible courses of action. They could arrest both parties, arrest one but not the other, or threaten to make an arrest if they are called back. They could quiet down the couple and then leave the scene, or they could spend some time with the two spouses and urge them to get marital or chemical-dependency counseling. Thus the officers have considerable discretion, and what is an effective course of action in one situation might be counterproductive in another. This puts a premium on good judgment.

So, too, with the social worker. Consider, for example, the child protection worker discussed above. There are so many instances of parents breaking their children's bones, sexually molesting them, abandoning them, or most often neglecting to feed or house them adequately that every major metropolitan welfare department in the nation has several social workers whose sole job is to protect children from abuse and neglect. When confronted with a specific case of abuse, the protection worker must make many decisions about it. Has the abuse experience left the child functioning poorly in school or even not attending school? If so, what can be done to ameliorate the situation? Could the child benefit from counseling? Should the worker seek a court order to remove the child from the home temporarily until the family situation improves? And in cases where the situation does not improve, should the worker seek a court order to remove the child permanently and place him or her for adoption? Was the abuse a criminal offense, such as incest or assault? If so, should the worker recommend that the county attorney prosecute the offending parent? Or would these particular parents be capable of responding to less extreme measures such as mandatory counseling? Workers in such cases have a wide range of optional courses of action. If they choose the right ones, they may set a family back on the road to recovery. But if they choose the wrong ones, a child might end up being badly injured or killed in future abuse. And whatever they choose, they are simply dealing with the tip of an iceberg of personal relations and family problems that may have taken years to emerge and are not likely to be cured in the short time a given social worker is handling the case. Like the police officer, the case worker's judgment and discretion are critical to effective action.

In all of the above service delivery situations, it is impossible for even the most intelligent administrator to create enough routines and decision rules to cover every situation the street-level bureaucrat will encounter. Yet the judgment and discretion exercised by the street-level bureaucrats must also fit within the system of routines and decision rules that promote predictability and consistency in policy implementation and service delivery.

If the system of decision rules is not effective and street-level bureaucrats use their discretion arbitrarily or unwisely, the consequences can be severe. In Chapter 5 it was noted that the fatal beating of a black insurance salesman by a team of white police officers was instrumental in sparking the 1980 Miami riot that left 16 people dead and over 400 injured. Because of other abuses of their authority (such as using coercion to get confessions out of criminal suspects), police have seen their discretion somewhat limited by federal court restrictions on what kinds of evidence can be admitted in trials.[19] They have also become more vulnerable to citizen groups that demand influence on the behavior of police officers.

A similar phenomenon has occurred with some other street-level bureaucrats. Jonathan Kozol's *Death at an Early Age* charged that public school teachers in Boston's black ghetto tended to be middle-class whites whose indifference to the special needs of their pupils stunted the intellectual and emotional growth of the children.[20] As similar charges were made of other big-city schools, one response was the formation of citizen groups in city after city to influence the formulation and implementation of school policies. When welfare departments discouraged eligible people from applying for benefits, poor people's interest groups began to bring complaints against the departments.

As these examples suggest, there have been a considerable number of complaints that too many street-level bureaucrats just do not care very much about the clients they serve, that they are so hemmed in by bureaucratic decision rules that they cannot respond very well to the needs of their clients, or that they treat low-income clients and racial minorities worse than upper-income people and whites.[21] This critical picture is probably much too pessimistic. A national survey in the 1970s found that 79 percent of all the people interviewed felt that they had been treated fairly by government agencies with which they had dealt.[22] This feeling was given support by John Clayton Thomas's case study of citizen contacts with public bureaucracies in Cincinnati. Thomas found some evidence that homeowners felt they had been treated better than renters did, and whites felt they had been treated better than blacks did. But overall, Thomas concluded that public servants in Cincinnati strived to perform their duties competently and without bias. He attributed part of the disaffection of blacks to the fact that they presented bureaucracies with more complicated problems than did the whites.[23]

The Citizen's Role in Urban Service Delivery

These developments of the 1960s and 1970s have greatly complicated the jobs of street-level bureaucrats and underscore the need for intelligent and sensitive people to fill these jobs. These developments also signal a change in the citizen's role in urban service delivery. Twenty years ago the citizen who dealt with a public bureaucracy was primarily a *client* who received help from bureaucrats in what were called the helping professions (social work, education, counseling, health care). Today citizens perform other roles as well. The three most important, perhaps, are service on *advisory committees*, working with *interest groups*, and placing demands on urban bureaucracies by *contacting* them to complain about service levels.

Bureaucrats tend to resist creating advisory committees with substantive authority. Police departments, for example, resist police review boards with authority to make investigations and prescribe disciplinary action in cases of police brutality. But many public services typically have citizen advisory committees that make policy recommendations and serve as a channel for investigating citizen complaints. Outside of the bureaucracy, interest groups act as a source of policy recommendations and as advocates for clients with complaints about their treatment by the bureaucracies. Finally, citizen-initiated contacts with public officials are a major source of feedback to officials on how effectively public services are meeting citizen problems.[24]

The Intergovernmental Connection in Service Delivery

One factor that complicates public service delivery problems in today's city is the fact that no government has exclusive authority over any major problem. Despite the specialization in services suggested by Table 8-1, authority is generally shared among many governments at the federal, state, and local levels. Morton Grodzins once used the sanitarian to show how all levels of government are involved in the implementation of many specific local policies.[25] Today the child protection worker is probably the best example of this intergovernmental connection.

Usually employed by and paid by the local county welfare department, the child protection worker is financed partly from county funds, partly from state funds, and partly from federal welfare grants. Although a county employee, the child protection worker functions as an agent of many different governments, acting as a federal officer when getting a client to apply for federally funded food stamps or AFDC and as a state officer when investigating a complaint about a violation of state laws prohibiting abuse of children. When bringing a client to a mental health center in a county hospital, the worker functions as a county officer; but because the center is funded by a federal program, the worker also functions as a federal officer. Investigating a complaint that a city family lets an infant crawl unhealthfully on a floor strewn with the feces of several family pets means acting as a city officer, investigating the ordinance on health and the ordinance on the number of pets permitted in a home. Following up on court orders to ensure that abusing parents continue with court-ordered family counseling means serving as an officer of the court. Visiting a man in jail for having sexually abused his daughter and investigating whether he is taking part in the counseling program there means serving in part as a state corrections officer. The child protection worker may also act as a negotiator with several other local governments and private agencies, such as negotiating with local school districts to get clients into special programs, or with neighboring counties to purchase services for clients that the worker's own county does not provide, or with private agencies, foster homes, halfway houses, or church groups to get their resources applied to clients.

In short, this county-hired street-level bureaucrat acts partly as an agent of the federal government, party as an agent of the state, and partly as an agent of the county. In getting decisions implemented successfully, this worker cannot rely on any automatic hierarchical chain of command but must constantly consult and negotiate with a wide variety of people both in and out of the government.

Child protection services may perhaps be an extremely complicated example of public service delivery. Certainly driving a bus would not require all the intricate decisions needed to rectify a child abuse case and prevent future abuse. But the extreme complexity of this example serves well to illustrate how interconnected many urban services are and how their successful implementation requires the cooperation of officials of many different governments.

To raise productivity, cost effectiveness, and efficiency among street-level bureaucrats like the social worker raises many interesting questions. The first of these are: Can it be done? If so, how?

Better Productivity Through Better Management

The Cry for Cost Effectiveness

To ask if urban governments can be made more productive is generally understood to mean this: Can urban governments be made more cost effective? Can more units of service be provided at a lower per-unit cost?

For some urban services the criterion of cost effectiveness raises few objections. For example, can more water meters be read per dollar? Can more snow be removed per dollar? Can more garbage be picked up per labor-hour of work? The Chicago Democratic party might object to applying cost-effectiveness criteria to its patronage workers who read water meters. And New York City's sanitation workers' union might object to cost-effective criteria requiring each garbage collector to pick up more trash each week. But in today's environment, they would be voices in the wilderness. Few citizens would value the political machine's patronage or the municipal unions' overstaffing demands higher than the efficient performance of meter reading or garbage collection.

For some public services, however, cost effectiveness clashes with values that are more widespread than are patronage and overstaffing. In these conflicts of values, public officials must make a tradeoff. In public education, for example, per-pupil costs could be lowered dramatically simply by doubling class sizes and giving each teacher twice as many students. However, doubling class sizes would probably reduce the amount of material that pupils learn and lead to complaints from parents, teachers' unions, parent-teacher organizations, and student organizations. School board officials who want not only to reduce per-pupil costs but also to maximize learning and minimize complaints have to find tradeoff points between these values. How high can you raise class sizes before learning suffers and constituent groups start complaining?

In reality the clash of cost effectiveness with other values would rarely be this simple. In the case of the child protection problem discussed earlier, the clash of cost effectiveness with other values would be much more complicated. A new county board of commissioners might respond to tax-revolt pressures or declining federal funds by dramatically increasing the caseload of social workers, by reducing the amount of time a social worker can keep a case open, and by reducing the amount of money available to place children in foster homes. These steps would undoubtedly be cost effective and would probably reduce the welfare budget perceptibly. But these steps would also clash with other values. Some cases might be so severe that they should not be closed within the prescribed time. If the protection worker's caseload were increased too much, he or she might pay so little attention to each case that the amount of abuse or neglect might actually increase rather than decrease. As the new funding limits on foster homes require that problem children be taken out of foster homes and returned to their previous environments, their problems might reemerge and bring them into trouble with the law. And it is conceivable that the cost-effective measures used to reduce the county welfare budget might lead to increased costs in the county's corrections budget.

One problem facing cost-conscious administrators, then, is to identify what other values cost effectiveness might clash with and to calculate acceptable tradeoffs to resolve the conflict. When put in terms of tradeoffs, administrators and policymakers find that many governmental services could be done more cheaply without imposing unacceptable costs on other values. Having the city employ large numbers of inefficient patronage workers might well be an important political value to Chicagoans, as long as services do not break down. But when that patronage-dominated system failed to clear the streets after a series of blizzards dropped seven feet of snow in 1978–1979, Chicagoans rebelled and voted the incumbent mayor out of office. In a rough way, the Chicagoans placed the value of snow-removal effectiveness above the value of patronage.

Public administration specialists have introduced several innovations in recent decades to make public management more effective and efficient. Among the most important of these are (1) budget innovations, (2) management by objectives, and (3) program evaluation.

The budget is perhaps the most potent weapon that mayors, city managers, and county executives have to control their administrators. Their ability to wield this weapon, however, depends on the extent to which they have moved from traditional budgeting practices to newer approaches such as program budgeting and zero-based budgeting.

Traditional Budgeting

Traditional budget making is an incremental process.[26] An increment is simply a small step, and an incremental process is one that moves in one direction in small steps. Budgeting is an incremental process because most agencies get a budget increase each year that is slightly larger than the previous year's level. Only under extraordinary circumstances, such as the creation of a new agency or the introduction of a new program, does a department get a substantial increase that greatly exceeds the overall budget's rate of increase. Incrementalism produces stability in the budgeting system. Since each agency knows it will get a slight increase each year, it also knows that it will not get cut back sharply or cut out entirely.

Why do budgets change in incremental steps rather than in response to changing policy priorities? One reason is the reluctance of city councils to do a comprehensive review of the whole budget document each year.[27] In San Antonio, Texas, the city council in a recent year made budget changes of less than $100,000 out of a total budget request of $68 million. One San Antonio budget official commented that generally "the council doesn't interfere" with the budget.[28] A comprehensive review each year would "continually reopen past accommodations between the parties interested in each item of an agency's program. This would make each item always controversial, would preclude administrators or clients from counting on the continuation of current programs."[29] Nor would public employees be able to count on keeping their jobs permanently. To terminate whole sectors of city employees and public services each year as priorities changed would make city government chaotic.

In addition to incrementalism, traditional budgeting is also characterized by the line item. Line-item budgeting refers to the way budget authorizations are listed. For example, a school district budget would typically authorize line-item expenditures for items such as the superintendent's office, the business office, travel, and teachers' salaries. If reading levels cause a significant problem in the district, however, the line-item budget fails to tell school board members and superintendents how much money the district is spending for reading programs and how those expenditures compare to other instructional programs such as English grammar, science, mathematics, or social studies.[30]

Program Budgeting

In the early 1960s Secretary of Defense Robert McNamara introduced a new concept, planning program budgeting (PPB), to the U.S. Defense Department. The concept quickly spread to other departments and then to the states[31] before it was abandoned in the early 1970s. Although abandoned, it was an important experiment because it spun off innnovations such as program budgeting, cost-benefit analysis, the definition of program objectives, and zero-based budgeting, which assumed increasing importance.

PPB was an extremely complicated budgeting device that attempted to eliminate the separation between program planning and budget planning that was inherent in the line-item budget. Instead of organizing the budget by traditional line items, PPB organized a budget by programs. In addition, PPB also demanded that each program's objectives be defined. Rather than simply asking for more funds to continue activities that had been carried on in previous years, agencies were obliged by PPB to define each activity's objectives and to indicate how the budget amounts related to the objectives, alternative ways to accomplish the objectives, and whether the objectives were being accomplished. This involved a *cost-benefit* analysis of programs. In the school district budgeting program cited above, a program budget would show how much money was budgeted for each instructional program (reading, for example) and how this money was divided up among certified teachers, noncertified staff, and other expenses. In a full-blown PPB exercise, the costs of alternative ways of achieving the goals of the reading program would also be indicated. School board members and the superintendent would be able at a glance to compare expenditures for reading not only with each of the other instructional programs but also with alternative ways of reaching the reading goals. And the most cost-effective way of reaching the goals could be chosen.

Tying all the elements of PPB together turned out to be such an enormously complicated task that the federal government eventually abandoned it. A few states managed to establish some effective variations of program budgeting; Hawaii, Pennsylvania, Wisconsin, and Alaska were among these. However, in most states the elaborate PPB process never got off the ground.[32] At the local level, PPB was tried with very limited success in Ann Arbor, Michigan.[33]

Zero-Base Budgeting

As PPB began to wither, budget reformers turned their attention to zero-base budgeting (ZBB). Under ZBB, each agency is forced to justify its own budget from a base of zero dollars as though it were just starting to operate for the first time. In practice, ZBB rarely asks a department to justify its activities from a base of zero. Rather, the process follows several steps.[34]

1. All the city's services and functions are divided into alternative ways of performing them. For example, trash collection might be handled by the city or contracted out to private haulers.
2. Performance levels or levels of effort are determined. These might range from 50 percent of the current level to 125 percent of the current level. For trash

collection this might vary from twice-a-week pickups to twice-a-month pickups.
3. A budget figure is calculated for each service level.
4. Each department ranks its service levels in order of priority.
5. The chief administrative officer (CAO) compares the rankings of each department, combines them into a citywide ranking that reflects the CAO's priorities, establishes a priority cutoff line at the level of expenditures the CAO wants, and deletes the budget requests for lower-priority service levels that fall below the cutoff line.

Early experiments with ZBB occurred at the state level in New Mexico[35] and New Jersey.[36] Jimmy Carter also introduced ZBB while governor of Georgia and awakened much interest in the concept when he suggested that it should also be applied to the federal government. At the local level, ZBB was successfully introduced in Garland, Texas, in 1974.[37] And perhaps the most interesting use of it to date was the experience in Wilmington, Delaware, in 1976.

Thomas C. Maloney was elected mayor of Wilmington in 1973 and began looking for ways to improve that city's budgetary process.[38] He complained that the traditional budget did not give him enough information on how money was spent on services or who benefited from them. City departments took their previous year's level of expenditures as a given and sought automatic increases. Budget requests exceeded the city's revenue, but the existing budget process provided Maloney with no means for making tradeoffs among the various services. To make matters worse, he could see no hope that revenues would grow or that the city council would pass a tax increase. Compounding his problems, wage settlements were locked in due to existing union contracts and about half of the city's expenditures were fixed either by law or by previous agreements.

In 1975 Maloney decided to introduce ZBB. City departments wre divided into budget units that corresponded to services actually delivered. For example, the public works department was divided into eleven units, the police division into six, and the fire division into three. After this, alternative service levels were identified for each budget unit and the costs were calculated for each service level. For example, the sanitation budget unit calculated how much it would cost to fund trash collection at each of three different service levels ranging from weekly garbage pickup at the curb to twice-a-week pickup from the rear or side yard. These data were then consolidated at the department level and sent on to the mayor. In all, 196 separate service levels were identified.

To achieve a balanced budget the mayor had to cut the budget requests by $1.2 million (out of a total budget of $20 million). His staff engaged in long budget hearings with each department before the city council's finance committee.

Of the 196 service levels, 34 provided such basic services as police patrol or garbage pickup that it was decided to fund these at the previous year's levels. This left 162 service levels, which the mayor divided into high, medium, and low priorities. A cutoff point was established at the point where the city's budget would balance, and all of the high- and medium-priority service levels were above the cutoff point. About half the low-priority service levels fell below the cutoff point, and these were not recommended for funding. The budget report was presented to the city council, which adopted it with minor changes. Not only did Mayor Maloney balance his budget, but also the ZBB process helped him make rational choices among cost-effectiveness criteria and competing values.

Management by Objectives

Under management by objectives (MBO), each department head stipulates his or her objectives for the upcoming year.[39] These objectives include both personal and agency goals. A personal objective might be, for example, to make more public speeches during the coming year. A superintendent of schools, for example, might set an objective to reduce the number of school dropouts. Once the superintendent's objectives are defined, the assistant superintendents propose their objectives, which will be consistent with those of the agency head. The building principals then define their objectives for the year in relation to those of the assistant superintendents. Theoretically, all the employees of a given department work to attain a common set of objectives for the departments as a whole. Throughout the year, supervisors evaluate their subordinates' progress toward the objectives. In systems that provide merit pay, MBO can be tied to pay increases for employees; employees who exceed their objectives get special raises. In this way, MBO and merit pay can be tied together in a comprehensive system of incentives.

In practice, of course, MBO rarely works this neatly. Public employee unions generally resist MBO if it involves the concept of merit pay. Nevertheless, the concept of MBO has become popular with high-level administrators who feel that it has greatly increased their capacity to control the services they administer.

MBO began in the private sector in the 1920s but became popular in the public sector in the 1970s. At the federal level, MBO was viewed as a means to improve the performance of the government's large departments and bureaucracies.[40] At the local level, Charlotte, North Carolina, implemented an MBO plan in the early 1970s with some success.[41] To be successful locally, MBO requires consistent support of the CAO and the various department heads. MBO must also be viewed as a long-term process. It takes several years for the process to be accepted in the organization and for employees to become comfortable with the extensive paperwork involved.

Program Evaluation

A third management tool for improving productivity is program evaluation. Without evaluation, government officials cannot know what programs are successful, what administrative practices work, or even which groups of employees are most competent. To practice program evaluation, urban managers must be able to measure the outcomes and costs of their programs. Without some measured evaluation, urban managers would have to rely on less rigorous techniques (such as guesswork or just following previous years' precedents) to make choices about which programs to expand or reduce.[42]

There are three types of program evaluation. First is the *social science* or *behavioral* approach. A social science evaluation might, for example, conduct surveys of residents in a redevelopment neighborhood to determine the impact of the program on their lives. Experimentation has also been used. Different neighborhoods might be identified as control and experimental sites to test rent subsidy or social service programs. The social science approach has definite uses, but it also has limits. Administrators can affect the conclusions of the evaluation, and programs administered in separate cities may differ so much that they cannot be compared as part of controlled experiments.[43]

A second approach is based on *cost-effective* models that assume that costs and benefits for specific programs can be measured. When forced to choose between alternatives, administrators can choose the approach that has the lowest cost-benefit ratio, that is, the approach that produces the most benefits for the least cost. Although attractive in theory, the cost-benefit approach has been difficult to implement. Many programs have multiple goals that are difficult to rank and that may evolve over time. Administrators tend to state goals in vague, general terms to give themselves as much flexibility as possible. All this makes evaluation of goals difficult, and also makes it difficult to measure whether the goals are attained.[44]

A third type of evaluation is *eclectic*.[45] Eclectic means selecting unsystematically from various approaches. For example, when asking for a large budget increase in a given program, administrators might make an eclectic evaluation of the program by listing a series of rationales and data to show that the program is effective. Such data will be unsystematically gathered and perhaps be totally unrelated to the prestated objectives of the program. But if presented well, the administrator may be able to use this kind of evaluation effectively.

In sum, program evaluation can be a powerful management tool. Because of the vast number of programs operating in urban America, a pressing need exists for independent evaluations to test the effectiveness of these programs.[46]

Privatization of Public Services

A fourth, and perhaps the most controversial, management tool for improving productivity is simply to contract public services out to private companies. Scottsdale, Arizona, contracts out its fire protection to private companies, for example,[47] and Butte, Montana, has its municipal hospital run by a private firm. Hundreds of other cities have followed these examples in recent years and have entered into contracts with private firms to provide a wide variety of services, the most common ones being trash collection, streetlight operation, vehicle towing, hospital management, solid waste disposal, street repair, and traffic signal maintenance. Twenty-five percent of all cities contract out these services.[48] The big competitive advantages that private firms have over public bureaucracies are flexibility and cheaper workforces. The private employees are often non-union, which means that they work for substantially lower wages and are less likely to refuse working flexible shifts and odd hours.

The key to understanding the theory behind privatization is making a distinction between the arrangements for (or *provision* of) public services and the actual delivery of (or *production* of) those services. Some public services (public education, for example) are provided for by state law but are actually produced by local governments. Some other public services (garbage collection, for example) are provided for by local governments but are often produced by private collection companies that are actually given a franchise to handle garbage collection in a specific area.

Types of Privatization

Given this distinction between provision of and production of public services, E.S. Savas has noted ten different possible combinations of public-private services.[49] The most noteworthy of these are illustrated below in Figure 8-2.

The Private Economy   The marketplace dominates this sector. It includes goods and services purchased privately (such as consumer goods) and voluntary services (such as charity). In this sector, governments are limited to a regulatory role but do not produce services directly or seek to arrange for their production.

Figure 8-2. Types of Service Arrangements

The Provision of Public Services

		Privately Provided	Publicly Provided
The Production of Public Services	Privately Produced	**The Private Economy** Consumer goods Voluntary services Self-service	**The Public-Private Economy** Contracting Grants Franchising Vouchers
	Publicly Produced	**The Government Vendor Economy** Government-vended services	**The Public Economy** Government-produced and -provided services

Source: Adapted and altered from E.S. Savas, *Privatization: The Key to Better Government* (Chatham, N.J.: Chatham House Publishers, Inc., 1987), pp. 58–92. Reprinted by permission.

Note: Savas diagrams his types somewhat differently than they are diagrammed here, and unlike this diagram he includes vouchers under the category of privately provided-privately produced services.

The Public-Private Economy   In this sector, governments find a variety of ways of arranging for public services to be provided, but the actual production and delivery of those services is left to private organizations or individuals. Under *grants,* a local government provides funds to an organization (such as a mental health clinic) to deliver the services that are needed. Under *contracting*, a government employs a private organization to provide some service for it. Services commonly contracted out include data processing, golf course management, and school-bus driving. Under *franchising*, city government awards a private firm a monopoly to offer a particular service in a particular area. Commonly franchised services include telephone, water supply, electric power supply, and cable television. Finally, *vouchers* are certificates that have a cash value for a certain commodity and are given to individuals by the government to enable individuals to purchase those commodities or services. Food stamps are essentially vouchers that enable people to purchase groceries. Hotly debated during the 1980s was the issue of whether vouchers should be issued for public education and for public housing assistance.

The Government Vendor Economy   Government vending occurs when a private organization contracts with a government agency to produce a service for it. For example, a private rock concert being held in a private arena might contract with the local police department to provide police protection services during the concert. In this example, the police department vends out its services to the private organization.

The Public Sector   In this sector, the services are both provided by and produced by government. For example, all states provide for the public education of all children through high school, and the most common way of producing those educational services is through local school districts.

Assessing Privatization

During the 1980s, with considerable support from the Reagan administration, privatization became a very popular cause, and there was especially a dramatic expansion in the contracting out of public services. The advantages of privatization are quite marked. It usually offers much greater flexibility in service delivery than a government agency can offer. And, depending on the particular service and the circumstances, as noted above, private firms can often deliver the same services more cheaply.

Privatization of services is not problem-free, however. In some instances, public provision of services is cheaper than contracting out.[50] There is tremendous potential for contracting out to become a form of patronage associated with bid rigging, political favoritism, and financial kickbacks through campaign contributions. The savings by going private may disappear if the contractor makes a "low-ball" bid the first year and then recovers the losses by boosting prices once the contract has been won. If contractors default or fail to perform adequately, the city may be left holding the bag. St. Paul, Minnesota, contracted out the operation of a facility with a machine to turn diseased elm trees into wood chips that could be marketed as cheap fuel. The private contractor never learned how to run the machine and failed to market the chips successfully. The city was saved from a financial loss on the operation only when the chips accidentally caught fire and were destroyed.[51]

Contracting out is controversial because it touches on a central values issue in urban politics: Is cost effectiveness the highest value in public life? (See pp. 227–228.) Or is there also room for other values such as maintaining stability in a public workforce and ensuring that the providers of public services get paid more than minimum wage? Cost-conscious citizens do not necessarily want to force public service workers into poverty-level wages, but they perceive the public bureaucracies as essentially wasteful. Unions, on the other hand, tend to perceive contracting out as a threat to the livelihood of their members.

Better Productivity Through Better Personnel

In many respects, productivity is related to the quality of the workers who are delivering the services and providing staff support. Are the most competent people being hired and promoted? Are they being paid adequately? Are they relatively satisfied with their work environment? Are they highly motivated to be productive? Do grievance procedures work smoothly? Are workers cooperative with management and eager to implement overall policies? Or are they uncooperative and do they put roadblocks in the way of implementing policy? We shall investigate these questions by examining the merit system of employment and the problems that arise in personnel management.

The Merit System of Employment

The merit system, or the civil service system, is a recruitment method by which employees are hired and promoted on the basis of their training and competence to perform specific jobs. Once employees are given civil service status, they are protected from arbitrary removal.

One gets civil service status by passing a test. A job description is drawn up for each civil service position, which is called a classified position. The position is classified at a specific level and assigned a pay range. Promotion to higher positions is achieved by competition, with promotions ideally going to the candidates whose experience, qualifications, training, and test scores best fit the responsibilities of the jobs.

The first state civil service system was established in New York in 1883. Since then it has spread to all states[52] and to most large cities. Most of these civil service systems have been established since 1939 in response to federal laws and court decisions that prohibit patronage employment in federally funded programs.[53]

Merit systems are administered in one of two ways—either by a civil service commission or by a personnel office directly under the CAO. Most cities use the second approach. A department with a job opening files the job opening with the personnel office, which advertises it, tests applicants, and then sends the three or four best-qualified applicants to the department for a job interview. The supervisory people in that department thus do the actual hiring, not the personnel office. The personnel office functions as a screening device. If it screens out minorities or people over forty-five or women or handicapped people or Polish Catholics or Jews, it will be very hard for the city to hire those people.

Problems in Personnel Management

Bias

Civil service systems have been increasingly accused of bias in hiring and promoting. Racial minorities complain that civil service procedures are biased against them. Feminists complain that the procedures systematically exclude women from the highest civil service positions. Both charges are confirmed by employment data. Up to and during the 1960s, the federal government attempted to cope with this bias by promoting equal employment opportunities. Federal grants and loans for programs administered by local governments could be denied unless the recipient government hired its employees without regard to race, sex, religion, or country of origin. This equal employment opportunity principle was written into the 1970 Equal Employment Opportunity Act. However, equal opportunity did not substantiallly increase the number of women and minorities in top policymaking positions.

Because of the failures of equal opportunity principles to overcome traditional biases in hiring practices, minorities and women began promoting the concept of affirmative action. Under affirmative action guidelines, each government receiving federal funds must develop a plan for increasing the number of women and minorities in top positions.

Police and fire departments are among the city agencies most often criticized for bias in their hiring practices. Frank Thompson has described the roadblocks that the Oakland, California, fire department put in the way of an affirmative-action-minded personnel officer who tried to increase the number of minority firefighters. The fire chief opposed changes in the educational requirements and the qualifying examinations that would make it easier for minorities to be hired, and he found other ways to obstruct the objective of affirmative action.[54] In Minneapolis, Minnesota, minority applicants for the fire department found that the federal courts were a more powerful ally than the city personnel office. That city's fire department had not hired a single black during the 1950s and 1960s, even though twenty-four blacks had taken the examination and six had passed it. A federal court ordered the fire department to give preference to minorities in the next twenty positions to be filled.[55] Peter Eisinger has shown that black mayors have enjoyed considerable success in increasing the number of black city employees.[56]

In addition to facing discrimination in hiring, minority and female workers also are most likely to be laid off if the public workforce must be cut. This is mainly because of civil service laws and collective bargaining contracts that require job seniority to be followed in laying people off. In the early 1980s Boston was forced by a severe fiscal crisis to lay off large numbers of firefighters and police officers. In a deliberate attempt to implement an affirmative action policy, the city laid off whites with higher seniority rather than several minorities, who retained their jobs. The laid-off white workers sued that their rights under civil service and collective bargaining were being violated. Before the suit reached the Supreme Court, Massachusetts passed a law rehiring the laid-off workers and requiring seniority to be followed in any future layoffs. By the time the suit reached the Supreme Court, three complicated issues had emerged. First, the public employees' union (supported by the Reagan administration) wanted the affirmative action order by a district federal court struck down, because the union considered it an unconstitutional and illegal instance of reverse discrimination. Second, the white employees wanted back pay for the time that they were illegally (in their view) laid off. However, this issue was not formally included in their original appeal to the Supreme Court. Third, the National Association for the Advancement of Colored People (NAACP) wanted the Supreme Court to uphold the validity of the original layoffs, thereby strengthening the affirmative action position in potential similar cases around the country. These issues gave the Supreme Court an opportunity to resolve some of the ambiguity about affirmative action and the seniority clauses of collective bargaining contracts. However, the Court made a very minimal response by dismissing the case on the grounds that the issues were moot. Since the laid-off workers were all back at work, they no longer had a bona fide controversy.[57] While this decision upheld the affirmative action principle in this particular case (since the minorities were allowed to keep their jobs), it did not establish a decisive principle for courts to follow in future affirmative action cases.

Comparable Worth

Closely related to the issue of bias in the public sector is an issue of particular concern to women, *comparable worth*. This is the demand that jobs of equal skill requirements receive comparable pay. This demand is different from the more familiar demand of equal pay for equal worth. The equal pay for equal work principle would guarantee that a female licensed practical nurse (LPN) would earn the same salary as a male LPN with the same seniority and experience. But it would not guarantee that LPNs (a field dominated by women) earn as much income as persons in male-dominated fields with comparable or lower skill requirements. For example, state-employed LPNs in Minnesota (95 percent of them women) in 1979 earned $1,382 per month, wheas state-employed general repair workers (99 percent of them men) earned $1,564 monthly. A state study evaluating the jobs on the basis of knowledge, skill, problem solving, accountability, and working conditions gave the LPN job 183 job-evaluation points and the general-repair-worker job only 134 points.[58] Despite having jobs that were more demanding, the female LPNs received about 12 percent less pay than the male general repair workers.

There are two general ways to reduce this inequity. Opponents of the comparable worth concept point out that the pay differences for different jobs reflect the differing economic values of the jobs as determined by the marketplace. Accordingly, they argue, women who wish to earn more money should seek jobs that pay more. Proponents of comparable worth argue that the value of all jobs in a state or local government should be assessed on objective, gender-free criteria, and the pay scales for those jobs should be set accordingly.

This issue came to national prominence in 1983 when a federal district court ruled that the State of Washington had discriminated against many female employees by paying them much less than it paid male employees in jobs with similar or lower value. This ruling called on the State of Washington to readjust its pay schedule to reflect the content of each job. As a result, the state was ordered to pay about half a billion dollars in back pay to 15,100 female workers for the previous four years. In many other states, chapters of the American Federation of State, County, and Municipal Employees (AFSCME) took a cue from the Washington case and began pressing for comparable-worth studies in their states. To date, comparable-worth legislation has been defeated in a number of states (Florida, Missouri, Nebraska, and Pennsylvania) and is being implemented in at least five states (Iowa, Minnesota, New Mexico, Wisconsin, and Washington).[59] The California legislature passed a comparable-worth law in 1986, but it was vetoed by Governor George Deukmejian. The largest city to implement comparable worth is Los Angeles, which included comparable-worth provisions in its public-employee collective bargaining contracts.[60]

Merit

Although civil service is ideally based on the merit theory, which holds that the most qualified applicants and the most competent employees get hired and promoted, in practice the system seldom rewards superior performance and instead makes it virtually impossible to fire incompetent workers. A New York City management advisory board complained that the combination of that city's civil service rules and more than 100 separate union contracts had made it virtually impossible to fire anybody for poor job performance.[61]

Collective Bargaining

Collective bargaining by public employees made very little progress until the 1960s.[62] During that decade, strikes of teachers, police officers, and other public employees led to state laws that permit employees to bargain collectively and in some states to strike under certain circumstances. By 1975 most states permitted some form of collective bargaining for public employees.[63] Only seven states (Alaska, Hawaii, Minnesota, Montana, Oregon, Pennsylvania, and Utah) permit public employees to strike.[64] But making the practice of striking illegal has not stopped it. In 1975 there were 466 work stoppages in local government.[65] And in 1980, antistrike legislation did not halt Chicago work stoppages in the public schools, the fire department, and public transit.[66]

The foremost public employee union is the American Federation of State, County, and Municipal Employees (AFSCME), which by 1983 had 959,000 dues-paying members.[67] About 40 percent of all state and local employees are unionized today,[68] with the greatest unionization occuring among firefighters, sanitation workers, and teachers.

Although collective bargaining has helped raise public employee pay, it also aggravates the civil service problem of providing merit incentives. The bargaining unit typically negotiates a master contract that stipulates conditions of employment, grievance procedures, salary schedules, and seniority provisions. If low tax revenues force public agencies to lay off personnel, the seniority clause of the contract causes the layoffs to be made on the basis of seniority, with no regard for job competence or for affirmative action.

Equality and Bias in Urban Service Delivery

Having surveyed the demand for greater productivity in urban services and the institutional structure that delivers them, are there any patterns of bias in the distribution of services in the city? Are services delivered equally? Or do some people benefit more than others from them? To answer these questions we need to (1) determine what equality of service distribution means, (2) seek out any potential patterns of bias in urban service delivery, and (3) ask what consequences follow from the cutbacks in urban services that have generally followed the deteriorating fiscal conditions of many cities since the mid-1970s.

The Problem of Defining Equal Services

Equality in public services does not mean the same thing to everybody. As Robert L. Lineberry notes in his study of service distribution in San Antonio,[69] equality itself has been treated differently by philosophers,[70] social scientists,[71] and constitutional law. In constitutional law the key question is whether the equal protection clause of the United States Constitution means that all public services have to be distributed equally to everybody. Court rulings on this question are not consistent. In cases of gross inequities, such as Shaw, Mississippi, where 97 percent of the homes lacking sanitary sewers housed black people, the courts struck down the inequities as violating the Constitution.[72] A federal court also ordered that Washington, D.C. distribute its educational financial resources equally among all the city's schools.[73] But the Supreme Court refused to intervene in fiscal disparities between school districts,[74] and Lineberry argues that with this decision the Supreme Court closed the lid on Pandora's box, removing any expectation that the Supreme Court will oblige all units of government to deliver their services equally to everybody.[75]

Even if the Supreme Court were to order equal distribution of public services, one's definition of equal distribution may well depend on whether one is philosophically a liberal, a conservative, or a radical.[76] The conservative's response to the question of distribution of public benefits is the *equality of opportunity*. This is akin to James Coleman's concept of *input equality*.[77] If each child is given the same educational resources, each child has equal opportunity to take advantage of these resources.

Liberals attack equality of opportunity (or input equality) as perpetuating inequalities that existed before the child even got to school. To use a sports analogy, a person 5 feet tall has equal opportunity to try out for a basketball team that averages over 6 feet in height. Just as the overwhelming majority of 5-foot-tall people will not be able to take advantage of this equal opportunity to make the team, the overwhelming majority of children from lower-income families will not be able to take advantage of equal educational resources to achieve academically at the same rate as children from middle- and upper-income families. Input equality does not in fact lead to *output equality*. Liberals favor the concept of output equality and argue for *compensatory* services that would overcome lower-income people's social handicaps and lead to output equality. The only federal program aimed at compensatory goals occurred in public education. Title I of the 1965 Elementary and Secondary Education Act (ESEA) allocated about a billion dollars per year to local school districts for compensatory education for children from low-income homes.[78]

The radical approach to inequality is *leveling* or *redistribution*. Income is continuously redistributed until everyone has an equal amount. Although some redistribution of income from rich to poor was accepted for years in the concept of the progressive income tax, Americans usually rebel at the socialist idea of a complete leveling of income and social status. Lee Rainwater wrote that "the idea of essentially equal distribution of resources does not seem attractive to most people."[79]

Patterns of Bias in Urban Services Delivery

If there is conventional wisdom about urban services, that wisdom is probably that low-income neighborhoods and racial minority neighborhoods get poorer public services than do upper-income neighborhoods and neighborhoods that house the city's political and social elites.[80] The charge is often made, for example, that police patrol less frequently in poor neighborhoods; libraries are less accessible; and city parks, pools, and recreation facilities are more poorly maintained. Streets are in poorer repair, and in the wintertime the snowplows come to the poor neighborhoods last.

Since the early 1970s, scholars have spent considerable energy trying to measure whether this conventional wisdom is accurate. Unfortunately, except for a study showing racial discrimination in the pattern of urban library services,[81] these studies tend to be case studies about specific cities, making it impossible to draw any confident generalizations. Nor are all the findings consistent. In Prattville, Alabama, and San Francisco, California, for example, racial minority neighborhoods got less park and recreation space than did white neighborhoods.[82] Other studies, however, failed to find this bias consistently in other cities. Philadelphia was found to make capital expenditures for recreation equally in all neighborhoods.[83] In Detroit, park services favored the lower-income neighborhoods.[84] And a study of public services in Oakland found that the biases in service delivery all depended on the service. Some public service "mechanisms were biased toward the rich. Other mechanisms favored the poor." But none favored the middle-income neighborhoods.[85]

One of the more comprehensive case studies to date is Robert L. Lineberry's analysis of service delivery in San Antonio, Texas.[86] He set out to measure inequalities in the (1) distribution of the property tax burden, (2) access to parks and recreation, (3) availability of police patrols, (4) distance from fire stations, and (5) access to library resources. After a detailed collection of data on each of these measures, Lineberry concluded:

1. Racial minority neighborhoods and low-income neighborhoods neither suffered a higher tax burden nor were they discriminated against in each of the above municipal services. In fact, black neighborhoods had the lowest tax rates. Police patrolling was allocated evenly among neighborhoods. And access to parks, recreation facilities, and libraries showed what appeared to be *unpatterned inequalities*. The neighborhoods did not all have equal access, but it was impossible to find a high correlation between services and socioeconomic status or race.

2. Neighborhoods that housed the political elites of the city neither got lower property taxes nor did they get better services than other neighborhoods. Indeed, the neighborhoods with the most political elites had the highest property tax rate.

3. The most significant variable for understanding the distribution of services was that of *decision rules* made within the bureaucracy. For example, in distributing library books among the city's branch libraries, the library board did not try to implement a compensatory principle by putting more library books in the neighborhoods with the lowest levels of education. Nor were books distributed equally among all the libraries. Rather they were distributed according to a decision rule that the most books should go to the branch libraries that had the highest circulations. A decision rule existed, for all practical purposes, that library resources would be distributed according to the demands of the marketplace rather than demands of equality.

Lineberry's theory of unpatterned inequalities and distribution of public services by bureaucratic decision rules has been both supported and criticized by subsequent researchers. Supporting the importance of decision rules was a study of department heads (of fire, police, and public works departments) in a majority of all the cities of over 5000 population. This study concluded that although political officials (mayors and council members) sometimes try to influence how services are delivered, the departmental decisions about service delivery are "based primarily on neutral criteria."[87] This finding that public bureaucracies strive to avoid partisan or electoral influences in delivering their services was also supported by Mladenka's studies of service delivery in Chicago. If any city in the country would be expected to deliver public services on partisan criteria, the machine city of Chicago would be the one most likely to do so. Nevertheless, Mladenka found that the machine did not effectively use service delivery to reward the party supporters.[88] Also supportive of the idea that public services are distributed on the basis of bureaucratic decision rules rather than racial, political, or class biases was a study of bureaucratic responses to citizen-initiated contacts in Dallas [89] and Cincinnati.[90]

Critical of the unpatterned inequalities/decision rules theory was a study of delivery of seven specific public services in 62 different neighborhoods in New York City.[91] This study reached three major conclusions about equality of service delivery. First, like Lineberry, it found no evidence that lower-class neighborhoods were systematically discriminated against in the provision of public services. Second, contrary to Lineberry's notion of unpatterned inequalities, it did find important patterns to the inequality of service delivery. The upper-income neighborhoods got significantly better police, fire, and sanitation services than the other neighborhoods. Some people look on these as property-tax-related services because in great measure they protect property. For this reason the authors of the study argued that tax-related services follow a *contributory pattern*. The better neighborhoods, which paid the highest property taxes, got the most return for their taxes paid. In contrast, the lower-income neighborhoods received significantly more in human resources, health, and public school services than did the other neighborhoods. This, the authors argued, suggests a *compensatory pattern*. Their third conclusion was that the discovery of these patterns also suggests that the decision rule theory of service delivery needs to be modified. Although decision rules may exist in the bureaucracies, the finding of patterned inequalities implies that these decision rules are not made independently of the surrounding political and economic environment. Rather, the decision rules of a bureaucracy are in part a response to the social, political, and economic forces that impinge on the bureaucracy.

Consequences of Urban Service Cutbacks

A common trend in the late 1970s and 1980s was cutbacks in urban services in the face of fiscal difficulties. This was especially acute in the financially pressed Frostbelt cities such as New York City, Detroit, Cleveland, and Chicago. Chicago, for example, laid off 3000 teachers in November 1979 in order to avoid a financial collapse of the school district. Following its fiscal crisis in 1975–1976, New York City made wholesale cutbacks in police protection, fire protection, trash collection, and other services. Nor were these cutbacks limited to the Frostbelt. As a consequence of Proposition 13 in California, many cities laid off workers, raised fees for city services, and cut out some services altogether.

If urban services have been suffering cutbacks and are not likely to resume expanding again in the 1990s, who benefits from this?

If people become dissatisfied with central-city services, Albert O. Hirschman argues that they have two basic options—voice or exit.[92] *Voice* is the option of protesting and fighting to redress one's grievances. And there is considerable evidence to show that people in poor neighborhoods need to exercise their voice option by organizing themselves in order to get city policies directed at their grievances.[93] *Exit* is the option of looking elsewhere to get the services. And there are two ways to do this. The first is to substitute private services for deteriorating public services. Send your children to private schools; join the YMCA or some private club and use its recreation facilities rather than the poorly maintained public ones; band together with your neighbors and hire private security services to patrol your streets. Obviously, only people with very high incomes can afford to do all these things.

The second way to exercise the exit option is simply to move out to a suburb with superior services. Although you do not have to be quite as rich to do this as you do to purchase all your services privately, it is also clear that the option of moving to an affluent, well-serviced suburb is not open to many lower-middle- and lower-income people. In short, by driving upper- and upper-middle-income central-city residents to exercise their exit options, declining public services have an inherent bias against low-income people. To explore this question more deeply, Chapters 9 and 10 take a closer look at the exit option and the rise of suburbia.

Summary

1. The late 1970s and the 1980s have seen a growing demand for increasing productivity in the delivery of local government services. This demand can be traced to a slowdown in the growth of the public sector, inefficiencies in the organization of many urban governments, and disillusionment with many urban programs.

2. Although there are wide variations in urban service-delivery patterns across the nation, Bureau of the Census publications do indicate some tendencies toward specialization. Public education services tend to get performed by independent school districts. County governments tend to specialize in human and social services, and outside the central cities they also perform extensive police patrol and road maintenance services. Central-city governments dominate the traditional city services such as public safety and physical maintenance of streets and sewers. Central cities combined with special districts dominate redevelopment activities.

3. Urban governments are theoretically organized in a hierarchical manner that distinguishes between policymakers and policy implementers. Two factors, however, dilute this hierarchy in practice—the rising importance of support staff and the high level of discretion demanded of street-level bureaucrats (for example, teachers, police officers, and social workers).

4. The example of the child protection worker illustrates many of the complexities of urban service delivery. This street-level bureaucrat exercises considerable discretion and personal judgment about the implementation of bureaucratic decision rules and policies. This job also illustrates the intricate nature of the intergovernmental service delivery system. And it illustrates how the value of cost effectiveness can clash with other equally important values.

5. The cry for better productivity in public services is normally understood to be a cry for cost effectiveness. Although cost effectiveness may outweigh other values in some services (e.g., reading water meters), it clashes with other important values when applied indiscriminately to all public services.

6. Among the management tools for improving productivity in public services, much attention has been given in recent years to program budgeting, zero-base budgeting, management by objectives, and program evaluation.

7. The personnel practices critical to improving productivity have led to many problems. Although civil service was introduced as a merit system that would lead to more productive workers, this has seldom been the result. Merit systems have not overcome historic biases against minorities and women in hiring people for policy-level and higher managerial positions. Collective bargaining contracts put seniority above merit when it comes to salary increases and laying off employees. There is little evidence that the so-called merit system actually rewards merit.

8. Examining the question of bias in urban service delivery leads to three major generalizations. First, there is no agreement on what would constitute a fair and equal distribution of urban services. The conservative definition of equal delivery of services is equal opportunity. The liberal definition is output equality or compensatory services. The radical definition is redistribution until everyone is at the same level on all criteria. Second, although analyses of urban service-delivery patterns produce very inconsistent findings, there seems to be little evidence that urban services for poor neighborhoods or racial minority neighborhoods are consistently poorer than they are for the rest of the city. Third, declining quality of public services will stimulate upper-middle- and upper-income people to exercise their exit options and either purchase their services privately or leave the city for suburbia. To the extent that this happens, it constitutes a bias against lower-middle- and lower-income people, who cannot afford these options.

Part IV
Suburbia and the Multicentered Metropolis

With the transformation of the city into a metropolis, new political structures were needed to deal with the physical and social problems associated with suburban growth. Suburbs wanted to maintain political autonomy and independence, yet few suburbs were large enough or had enough resources to provide their own water, sewage disposal, roads, schools, and other physical systems needed for growth. Chapter 9 describes the metropolitan response to this problem, concentrating on the two policy sectors of transportation and land use management.

In addition to the challenge it posed for the management of physical growth, suburbanization also posed a challenge of social exclusion, especially in the sectors of housing and education. Whereas racial and cultural minorities predominate in central-city neighborhoods and central-city schools, they are present only in small numbers in the suburbs. Has this paucity of minorities in suburbia resulted from free choices people make about where they want to live and go to school? Or has it resulted from deliberate policies of exclusion designed to keep the minorities and the poor out of suburban neighborhoods and suburban schools? These questions are examined in Chapter 10.

As an approach to coping with the problems of growth and exclusion, some metropolitan reformers have argued that the entire multicentered system of governance ought to be scrapped and replaced by a single metropolitan government. Other observers have argued that a system of governance could be achieved without creating a metropolitan government. Chapter 11 examines these arguments, the attempts to create metropolitan government, the patterns of bias associated with metropolitan reform, and the reasons for success and failure of metropolitan reform.

In the absence of broad-scale success at creating metropolitan government, the years since the mid-1960s have seen an emphasis on incremental change, metropolitan planning, and the creation of metropolitan policymaking agencies such as councils of government. These developments and their biases are discussed in Chapter 12.

Chapter 9
Suburbia and the Challenge of Growth

Today more people live in suburbia than in rural areas, nonmetropolitan cities, metropolitan central cities, or any other identifiable type of place. Suburbs have become the locale for the largest growth of jobs and businesses. Politically they have gained a larger share of representation in Congress and the state legislatures. By 1980 the suburbs had become central to American politics. However, despite a number of recent studies about suburbia and politics,[1] our thinking about suburbs is in many ways still dominated by several myths that started in the 1950s and deserve reexamination today. These myths portrayed suburbia as a large dormitory housing a homogeneous collection of white, upper-middle-class, conservative Republicans who universally ignore the country's social needs while they quietly pursue the acquisition of private wealth.[2] Although this is probably the dominant view of suburbia, it is an extremely misleading picture.

Chapters 9 and 10 examine these myths and the realities about contemporary suburban politics. This chapter focuses on the politics that surround the growth and physical maintenance of the suburbs. Chapter 10 then analyzes the suburban politics of access and exclusion. On the one hand are those who demand that their suburbs have a right to be socioeconomically exclusive. On the other hand are those who demand that the suburbs be opened up and made accessible to all people.

The Heterogeneity of Suburbia

The suburbs of American cities are as heterogeneous as the neighborhoods of the cities they surround. Just as there are different types of city neighborhoods, there are also different types of suburbs. They can be differentiated in several ways—by functional specialization, by the kinds of people they house, and also by their spatial arrangements.

Functional Specialization

One way in which suburbs differ is in the basic functions they perform. Some suburbs, called *residential* or *dormitory suburbs*, primarily perform the function of housing people; they provide little industrial or commercial activity. Others, called *employing suburbs*, function primarily as the location for industries and employment centers. Sociologist Leo Schnore examined 300 suburbs in the twenty-five largest metropolitan areas and discovered a third type as well, a *mixed suburb* that provided both residential and employment functions. Schnore's analysis clearly demonstrated that only a small minority of these suburbs (about one-third) were the stereotyped dormitory suburbs. The other two-thirds were almost evenly divided between mixed suburbs and employment suburbs.[3]

Other studies have shown some suburbs to be even further specialized by the functions they perform. Some suburbs exist primarily as territorial enclaves to give large property tax advantages to industries or utilities plants. Others exist primarily as locations for racetracks. Racetracks require considerable space, and since they do not make congenial neighbors in residential areas, they usually are built in suburban regions that are thinly populated.[4] And still other suburbs exist primarily as enclaves for honky-tonk bars, nightclubs, gambling, prostitution, and narcotics traffic.[5] Examples can be found within easy commuting distance of many major cities.[6]

Class Specialization

Just as the myth of suburbia as a dormitory does not withstand close analysis, neither does the myth about upper-middle-class homogeneity in suburbia. A 1978 survey of New York area suburbanites found that 28 percent considered themselves working class and 16 percent reported relatively low incomes.[7] They hardly fit the upper-middle-class stereotype. Particularly among the smaller and newer metropolises, suburbanites are not more affluent than central-city residents. In many areas they are less affluent. (See pp. 157–158.)

The Exclusive Suburb

Although suburbia as a whole is very heterogeneous, individual suburbs are often homogeneous and house people with very similar incomes and social backgrounds. Some suburbs are exclusive enclaves for the wealthy, others are predominantly upper middle class, and still others are working class. Residents of a distant and wealthy suburb might refer to themselves as exurbanites and live in stately homes on large lots far removed from the center city. The government of an upper-class suburb is usually very nonprofessional and small, and most of the employees do not even live in the suburb.[8]

The Middle-Class Suburb

The middle-class suburb, in contrast, is much more likely to have a professional city manager and to have local residents engaged in controversies over local policies. The issues that arouse citizen concern will most likely be schools, zoning regulations, public improvements such as sewers or street paving, and public services such as recreation or garbage collection.[9] It is this middle-class suburb that has served as the focal point for so much sociological research and popular literature on the supposedly homogeneous, conformist suburbia.

The Working-Class Suburb

The working-class suburb has become an increasingly common phenomenon. A survey of AFL-CIO membership found that about half of the members live in the suburbs rather than in the central cities; among the younger union members, as many as three-fourths live in suburbia.[10]* According to one study, moving to the suburbs did not change basic working-class behavior patterns. Auto workers retained such un-middle-class behavior as carrying lunch buckets, shunning church attendance, and continuing to vote Democratic.[11] The working-class suburb differs in several respects from the middle-class suburb:

> The working-class suburb is quite likely to be unincorporated. It is cheaper that way, and the residents must look for ways to save money so as to preserve their status as homeowners in time of economic difficulties—and in order to spend money on luxuries in imitation of the middle class. If the county or township administers the area, part of the cost of governmental protection and services may, through the property tax, be transferred to residents in wealthier areas, and costly services are less likely to be demanded of a more distant government than one's own municipal organization. If the area is incorporated as a separate municipality, less participation in government is likely than is the case in the middle-class suburb.[12]

The Black Suburb

Other social classifications of suburbs exist as well. An increasing phenomenon is the predominantly black suburb. Three distinct types of black suburbs have been identified. First are the old black neighborhoods that often predated the post-World War II black migration to central cities. These suburbs typically contain very inexpensive homes and often lack access to public water and sewer facilities. Second are the densely populated black settlements that have arisen near major employment centers, particularly in the North. Finally, since the 1960s new suburban residential areas have been developed predominantly and sometimes exclusively for blacks. Most of the recent black suburbanization has occurred in this third type of suburb, and their residents are more affluent than most other blacks. These are often "spillover" suburbs, where the central-city black population has expanded into adjacent suburbs.

The 1980 census showed that the previous decade had seen the greatest growth in black suburbanization in history, with the number of suburban blacks increasing by forty-four percent from 4.0 million to 5.8 million. Twenty-three percent of the black population lived in suburbs by 1980.[13] The degree of black suburbanization varies greatly from region to region. While more than a third of all blacks in the West live in suburbs, less than nine percent of southern blacks live in suburbs,

---

*There may be important regional variations in working-class behavior patterns, however. One study of a very small sample of blue-collar families in the Minneapolis–Saint Paul SMSA found that the suburban blue-collar men were more status-conscious than the central-city blue-collar men, were more concerned with upward mobility, and were both less liberal and less inclined to the Democratic party. See Irving Tallman and Ramonn Morgner, "Life Style Differences Among Urban and Suburban Blue-Collar Families," *Social Forces* 48 (May 1970): 324–348.

and about twelve to fifteen percent of blacks live in suburbs in the northeastern and north central regions.[14]

Has this increased suburbanization of blacks in the past decade brought them greater affluence and integration? In terms of affluence, suburban blacks historically were poorer than central-city blacks. This pattern has now been reversed. The average black suburban family is now slightly more affluent than the average black central-city family.[15] In terms of integration, black suburbanization has been less successful. Increasing numbers of blacks now live in integrated suburban neighborhoods, but most suburban blacks still live in census tracts that are a black majority.[16] Growth patterns of the late 1960s and early 1970s suggested to some observers that the suburbs would become more integrated.[17] But census data does not yet show that a significant breakup of suburban segregation has occurred.[18] A study of 1980 census data for metropolitan Saint Louis found that suburban blacks in that area lived in only slightly less segregated neighborhoods than did central-city blacks.[19]

The Elderly Suburb

A final type of suburb that may be emerging is the elderly suburb. Many people who settled the early post-World War II suburbs are today becoming senior citizens, leading to a phenomenon that has been called "the graying of suburbia."[20] The most famous of the 1950s suburbs was Levittown,[21] a New Jersey subdivision with relatively inexpensive homes inhabited by growing families. Today a similar Levittown in nearby Long Island has grown much older and the shortage of growing families contributes to a local school district population that is declining at a rate of over 100 students per year.[22] As suburbs like these Levittowns age, they are likely to lead to increased welfare costs for services to the elderly. As the commercial strips of these older suburbs get supplanted by the centralized shopping malls, the older suburbs begin to take on some of the declining economic characteristics of the older central cities[23] and some of their fiscal characteristics as well.[24] For example, their real estate tax base by the 1980s was no longer growing as fast as demands on them to provide local services.

Specialized Spatial Patterns

In addition to differences in function and in kinds of residents, one of the most important variations between suburbs is their difference in spatial arrangement. Some scholars see the metropolis as developing in a series of *concentric rings* radiating from the downtown central business district. Immediately adjacent to the central business district are the warehouse zones and the heavy industry zones, followed by the poorest residential neighborhoods, the working-class neighborhoods, the middle-class neighborhoods, and finally, on the fringes of the metropolis, the residential areas of the upper middle class and the wealthy.[25] Other scholars see the metropolis as developing in a pattern of *sectors*. Certain subareas of the city or the metropolis become specialized for serving as centers of certain activities and especially for serving as the residential neighborhoods of given classes.[26] The sectors do not exist in the form of concentric rings. Rather they emerge along

the major transportation arteries. A third theory views the metropolis as developing a pattern of *multiple* and *interrelating nuclei.*[27]

These three theories are not mutually exclusive as they apply to suburbia. Elements of the concentric-ring theory have general relevance because many central
cities are surrounded by several tiers or rings of suburbs. Immediately adjacent to
the central city lie the inner-ring suburbs, often incorporated during the interwar
years. These suburbs tend to have relatively high densities. Their residential character is indicated by apartment buildings lining the freeways that radiate from the
central cities and by small houses in older neighborhoods of single-family homes.
They are more likely than not to be working-class suburbs, but scattered throughout the inner ring are pockets of upper- and lower-income neighborhoods.[28] A
second ring of suburbs exists, beyond the inner ring, in which the great post-
World War II housing boom created the sprawling subdivisions of fairly standardized, small houses. As the original residents of these suburbs have become more
affluent and have moved farther out, their place has been taken by lower-income
persons. In many of the older tract developments, signs of neighborhood deterioration are already appearing, causing some observers to predict that these will
become the slums of the future.[29] Beyond these second-tier suburbs exists a third
ring inhabited primarily by professional and business people with substantial
incomes who are able to afford living in large homes on large lots, and who trade off
the inconvenience of long commuting distances for their more comfortable sur-
roundings.

Although the concentric-ring theory of metropolitan development seems to
explain well the growth of several tiers of suburbs surrounding the central city,
other elements of suburban growth seem more readily explained by the sector and
the multiple-nuclei theories. In none of the rings of suburbs are the populations
really homogeneous. Some of the wealthiest suburbs can be found in the inner
ring and some of the poorest in the outer rings. Also, in most metropolitan areas,
the central business district shares an ever-decreasing portion of the commercial
life, the social life, and the cultural life of the region. Particularly in areas such as
Los Angeles, the multiple-nuclei theory of metropolitan growth seems to be much
more appropriate than the concentric-ring theory.

Finally, the very fact that none of these metropolitan growth theories can adequately explain the diversity of the suburbs is additional reason for rejecting the
homogeneous model of suburbia. The serious student of urban affairs can no
longer look at the suburbs in such simplistic terms. The suburbs simply must be
seen as diverse and heterogeneous places.

The Politics of Suburbia

Partisanship in Suburbia

If the myth of a homogeneous, affluent, upper-middle-class, white suburbia
does not withstand empirical analysis, neither does the myth that all of suburbia is
Republican. This myth arose because the suburbs on balance have tended to vote
Republican. In particular, during the 1950s some suburbs voted heavily Republi-

can for Dwight Eisenhower for President. Shortly after Eisenhower's victory in 1952, Senator Robert A. Taft predicted that the Republicans would continue to dominate suburbia and, through suburbia, the White House.

Two hypotheses were offered to explain these early Republican successes in the suburbs. The first was the theory of *conversion*, which stated that central-city Democrats who move out to the Republican-dominated suburbs convert to Republicanism in order to minimize partisan cross-pressures. Furthermore, becoming property owners for the first time, these ex-city dwellers then become more conscious of the property tax effect of government expenditures.[30] In other words, they are influenced by their new status and new neighbors to vote Republican and conservative.

In contrast to the conversion theory was the *transplantation* theory, which had two versions.[31] The first version stated that it was primarily Republicans who moved out of the central city to the suburbs. Suburbanites were not converted Democrats; they were simply transplanted Republicans. The second version said that it was upwardly mobile Democrats who were moving to suburbia from the central city. Being upwardly mobile, they were ripe for a transformation from a Democratic to a Republican allegiance. However, the transformation occurred before rather than after the migration, so they, too, were transplanted Republicans rather than converted Democrats.

The problem with both the conversion and the transplantation theories is that they are based on the assumption that the suburbs are overwhelmingly Republican. This was true in the presidential elections of 1952 and 1956, when the Republican candidate, Eisenhower, won 58.5 and 62.5 percent of the suburban vote. But in 1960 and 1964, Republican percentages dropped to 50.2 percent and 36.2 percent, respectively, as the Democrats won the White House. This suggests that the Republicans did not dominate the suburban vote nearly as much as was earlier believed[32] and that strong Democratic candidates have a realistic shot at winning the suburban vote. These conclusions were confirmed by an analysis of congressional and presidential voting from 1952 to 1964 in fifty-one suburban congressional districts; suburban voting patterns were found to follow national trends.[33] The classic election study *The American Voter* also rejected the conversion theory. "The absence of a really unique change in political allegiance among ex-urbanites . . . further indicates that movement out of the metropolitan centers cannot stand as the factor responsible for changes in partisan loyalties that cut across non-movers as well."[34]

Data from more recent years, however, seem to confirm the Republican advantage in suburbia. Table 9-1 shows that Republicans have dominated the suburban vote in three of the five presidential elections since 1964 (1972, 1980, and 1984), but they have never gained a majority of the central-city vote. Among white suburbanites, the Republican advantage is even stronger, as Table 9-1 shows. Whether because of transplantation, conversion, or simply desertion from traditional loyalties, suburban whites have consistently voted overwhelmingly Republican in presidential races since 1964.

In terms of partisan identification, however, Republican dominance of subur-

Table 9-1. Presidential Vote among Suburbanites and Central-City Residents

	All races				Whites only			
	Centr. city	Inc. suburbs	Uninc. suburbs	All voters	Centr. city	Inc. suburbs	Uninc. suburbs	All voters
Percentage voting for the Republican presidential candidate in:								
1984	45.0%	68.3%	63.4%	60.8%	57.1%	71.5%	66.4%	66.1%
1980	35.5	56.1	49.3	47.8	47.0	58.6	52.1	52.7
1976	35.3	47.9	51.7	44.6	41.6	50.2	53.6	44.8
1972	42.4	66.2	66.7	59.5	52.7	68.0	68.8	73.5
1968	33.5	52.3	53.8	47.4	44.4	53.1	54.9	50.4

Note: The figures for 1968 and 1980 are necessarily reduced by the fact that third-party candidates in those years drew approximately 12 and 7 percent of the vote respectively.
Source: Davis, James Allan and Smith, Tom W.: General Social Surveys, 1972–1985 [machine-readable data file]. Principal Investigator, James A. Davis; Senior Study Director, Tom W. Smith. NORC ed. Chicago: National Opinion Research Center, producer, 1985; Storrs, CT: Roper Public Opinion Research Center, University of Connecticut, distributor.

bia looks shakier, even among white suburbanites. Republicans prevail in the incorporated suburbs, but in the unincorporated suburban fringes, Democrats still outnumber Republicans by a 4-to-3 margin. These data tend to support a much earlier study done by Benjamin Walter and Frederick M. Wirt, who followed voting patterns in 407 different suburbs in the 1950s and 1960s. They found, as shown in Table 9-2, that *a slim majority of the suburbs leaned Democratic* rather than Republican.[35]

Table 9-2 also shows a very strong relationship between a suburb's affluence and its tendency to vote Republican. The Republican suburbs exhibit a much wider range of affluence than do the Democratic suburbs. And there is also considerable overlap in the categories, with some Democratic suburbs being more affluent than some Republican suburbs. But the overall pattern is quite clear. The most Democratic suburbs are clustered at the lower end of the affluence index. And the most affluent suburbs tend to be Republican.

These data from the 1960s are supported by more recent surveys of the National Opinion Research Center (NORC). A 1985 NORC survey showed that suburbanites at all income levels were much more inclined to call themselves Republicans than were central-city residents. But the richest suburbanites were much more likely (46 percent) to call themselves Republican than were either lower-income (31.4%) or middle-income (34.7%) suburbanites. This is shown in Table 9-3, which also shows two other important relationships. First, at all income levels, residents of unincorporated suburban areas are much less likely to be Republican than are the residents of incorporated suburbs; and second, in no income grouping are a majority of suburbanites Republican. These data suggest that the Democratic suburbanites are most likely to be found in three areas of the suburbs: the black suburbs, the low-income incorporated suburbs, and the unincorporated fringe areas of the metropolis.

Table 9-2. Party Competition and Socioeconomic Status in Suburbia

Majority party in presidential elections of 1956, 1960, 1964[a]	Number of suburbs (and percentage)	Score on affluence index[b]	
		Mean	Range of scores
Democratic	70 (17.2)	−0.8	−1.5 to −0.1
Leaning Democratic	141 (34.6)	−0.4	−1.0 to +0.3
Leaning Republican	160 (39.3)	+0.3	−0.5 to +1.2
Republican	36 (8.9)	+1.3	+0.3 to +2.3
Total	407 (100.0)	0.0	−1.5 to +1.3

[a] Although there were eight possible combinations of patterns to the vote, the only combinations that actually occurred are the ones shown in this table.

[b] This index is composed of affluence factor scores that Walter and Wirt computed from a factor analysis of eleven separate education, income, and occupation variables in the 407 suburbs. The scores range from the least affluent suburb (−1.5) to the most affluent suburb (+2.3). The mean score of all suburbs is 0.0, and the scores are in a normal distribution around that mean. Each score represents its standard deviation from the mean. Thus, the affluence index for the 70 Democratic suburbs, for example, indicates that the mean of the 70 Democratic suburbs is a 0.8 standard deviation below the mean for all 407 suburbs and that the affluence scores for the 70 Democratic suburbs range from a 1.5 standard deviation below the mean for all 407 suburbs to a 0.1 standard deviation below the mean for all 407 suburbs.

Source: Adapted from Benjamin Walter and Frederick M. Wirt, "The Political Consequences of Suburban Variety," *Social Science Quarterly* 52, no. 3 (December 1971): 750–753. Copyright © 1971 by The University of Texas Press. Reprinted by permission of the publisher, The University of Texas Press.

Are Suburbs Conservative?

Perhaps a more relevant question than political partisanship is whether the supposed conservatism of suburbanites impels their policymakers to act more conservatively. Because there are few rigorous empirical analyses of this question, it is difficult to answer with finality. But one fairly consistent finding is that central-city residents have public service preferences that differ from those of suburbanites. A study of suburbanites and city dwellers in the Dayton, Ohio, metropolitan area found that the suburbanites tended to be more dissatisfied with their available public services than were the central-city residents.[36] And a survey of Columbus, Ohio, area residents found some differences between the problems that concerned central-city residents and those that concerned suburbanites. Central-city residents were much more concerned with the environment and slum housing, whereas suburbanites were more concerned with schools and transportation.[37]

A study of five metropolitan areas in Wisconsin found that although suburbanites preferred spending more money on public education than did city dwellers, they were not as willing to spend as much on other municipal services. The suburbanites preferred to scrimp on municipal services such as central water supply or sewerage. Through the use of wells and septic tanks, these services could be shifted to private expenditures, and sometimes the central cities could be induced to provide the services for the entire urbanized area.[38]

Table 9-3. Partisanship of Suburbanites and Central-City Residents: Controlling for Income, 1985

	Poorest quartile in family income			Middle half in family income			Richest quartile in family income		
	Centr. city	Inc. suburb	Uninc. suburb	Centr. city	Inc. suburb	Uninc. suburb	Centr. city	Inc. suburb	Uninc. suburb
Party identification									
Dem.	54.4%	34.3%	58%	48.2%	32.2%	44.4%	42.9%	22.1%	26%
Ind.	25.2	34.3	22	34.2	33.1	27.8	26.8	31.9	36
Rep.	20.4	31.4	20	17.6	34.7	27.8	30.3	46.0	38

Source: Davis, James Allan and Smith, Tom W.: *General Social Surveys, 1972–1985* [machine-readable data file]. Principal Investigator, James A. Davis; Senior Study Director, Tom W. Smith. NORC ed. Chicago: National Opinion Research Center, producer, 1985; Storrs, CT: Roper Public Opinion Research Center, University of Connecticut, distributor.

In addition to these differences between central-city residents and suburbanites on service preferences, are there also ideological differences between them? The earliest research on this question tended to be negative. Perhaps the most important early study, based on Survey Research Center national samples, found "that there is little or no difference between some urban-suburban attitude and activity patterns and that the nationwide urban-suburban division is the *least* rather than the most influential of the forces used to explain" urban and suburban differences.[39]

This may have been true in the 1960s, but the central city–suburban ideological differences have become starker in the 1980s, and it is getting more difficult to explain away those differences as caused by something else. The differences may well be caused by something else, probably income and educational variables, but the differences exist nonetheless. Data in Table 9-4 show several differences between white suburbanites and white central-city residents. First, central-city residents are about twice as likely to call themselves liberal as are suburbanites from incorporated suburbs (20.0%) or those from unincorporated suburban areas (19.1%). Conversely, the suburbanites are much more likely to call themselves moderates or middle-of-the-roaders than are central-city residents. Second, whites from incorporated suburbs are decidedly more conservative than central-city whites on only four of the nine statements in Table 9-4 (statements E, G, H, I) that tap some aspect of the desire to isolate oneself from urban social problems. They are marginally more conservative on two of the statements (A, C), and they give less conservative responses on 3 statements (B, D, F). Third, whites from the unincorporated suburban fringes are decidedly more conservative than central-city residents on five of the statements (A, E, G, H, I), marginally more conservative on two statements (C, D), and give less conservative answers on two statements (B, F).

In summary, white suburbanites are indeed more conservative than white central-city residents on the average. But it is not a simple matter to predict how

Table 9-4. Ideological Differences Between Suburban and Central-City Whites: 1985

	Centr. city	Inc. suburb	Uninc. suburb	National average
Percentage calling self:				
Liberal	37.8%	20.0%	19.1%	23.9%
Moderate	28.9	40.9	37.7	38.1
Conservative	33.3	39.1	43.3	38.0
Percentage giving a conservative rather than liberal response to each of the following statements:				
A. We are spending too much money on the problems of big cities.	13.7	17.5	23.8	19.7
B. We are spending too much money on improving conditions for blacks.	25.6	18.6	24.1	24.4
C. We are spending too much money on welfare.	41.3	44.8	44.9	49.8
D. There should be laws against marriages between blacks and whites.	24.7	22.6	32.1	28.4
E. Blacks shouldn't push themselves where they are not wanted.	47.2	69.0	64.8	61.4
F. White people have a right to keep black people out of their neighborhoods if they want to, and blacks should respect that right.	23.9	20.6	22.6	26.2
G. Would object to sending one's child to a school where more than half of the children were black.	42.2	48.0	49.4	47.5
H. Oppose the busing of black and white schoolchildren.	75.2	80.5	82.1	80.9
I. On the average, blacks have worse jobs, income, and housing than white people because blacks just don't have the motivation or will power to pull themselves up out of poverty.	51.6	60.8	68.4	60.8

Source: Davis, James Allan and Smith, Tom W.: *General Social Surveys, 1972–1985* [machine-readable data file]. Principal Investigator, James A. Davis; Senior Study Director, Tom W. Smith. NORC ed. Chicago: National Opinion Research Center, producer, 1985; Storrs, CT: Roper Public Opinion Research Center, University of Connecticut, distributor.

these ideological differences will impinge on actual policy decisions. For example, an analysis of the voting records of central-city and suburban Congressional members during the Johnson administration (1963–1969) failed to find significant differences. Where differences were discovered, they were traceable primarily to partisan differences.[40]

The sharpest differences in policy preferences are found not between the suburbanites as a whole and central-city dwellers as a whole, but between persons of different socioeconomic status. In a study of Philadelphia suburbs, four political scientists asked both residents and public officials about their policy preferences about keeping the tax rate down, acquiring business and industry, and keeping undesirable people out of the suburb. They discovered sharp differences in policy preference between suburbs of a lower social rank, those of a middle social rank, and those of the upper social rank. Even within suburbs of the same social rank, there were sharp differences from one suburb to another.

The only issue in the Philadelphia study that failed to provoke a direct breakdown along social class lines was that of keeping undesirables out.[41] On this question overwhelming agreement existed, and the middle-class suburbs were the most adamant. The racial overtones to the question are obvious. Race is the one question on which white suburbanites demonstrate an implacable, united front in their attitudes. But the data in Table 9-4 show that there are plenty of exceptions, even on issues related to race. On only about half of the statements in that table are the suburban whites markedly different from the central-city whites.

Is There Anything Distinctive About Suburban Politics?

In sum, suburban political attitudes and behavior are much more complex than the suburban stereotype. Saying this, however, is not to say that there is nothing distinctive about suburban politics. Three distinctive features give suburban politics a tone that is different from politics in central cities or nonmetropolitan areas.

The Politics of Autonomy

First, suburbs are politically distinctive because of their quest for political autonomy, for a government that is small enough and close enough to home that the average citizen can have a personal impact on it. Robert Wood argues that suburbia is essentially an attempt to recreate Jeffersonian democracy on the fringes of the cities.[42] The outward growth of population and business *could have occurred* without the establishment of a ring of municipal governments surrounding the central city, and central cities *could have* continued to grow by annexing the newly settled areas. The fact that this did not occur reflects the strength of the political motivation to keep the new settlements separate from the old central cities.[43] This motivation was supported by scholars who argued that city governments function best if the cities are kept at a population range of 40,000 to 50,000,[44] a size that fits nicely into suburbia. Many people hoped that a proliferation of small, politically autonomous towns would enable their residents to have the best of two worlds— the intimacy of small-town government and the advantages of metropolitan facilities. Accordingly, one of the key themes that has pervaded many specific issues of suburban politics has been that of defending local autonomy from encroachment by big-city or metropolitan government.

This motivation behind suburbanization is similar in some respects to the motivation behind the demand for community control in central cities.[45] But community control and the proliferation of suburban governments are very different in other respects. Even the most ardent advocates of neighborhood government within cities favor retention of an overall citywide government. The staunchest advocates of suburban government, however, have opposed an overall, metropolitan-wide government. Politically, then, suburbia is distinct in that there is no overall suburban or metropolitan government; there are many governments. Governmentally and politically, the metropolis has become multicentered.

The Politics of Growth

A second distinctive feature of suburban politics has been the politics of regulating metropolitan sprawl. Typically, someone would buy a farm within easy commuting distance of a city or a major employment center, subdivide the farm into suburban-sized home lots, and contract with construction firms to put in a subdivision complete with houses and streets.[46] If the subdivision were far enough removed, the homes would get their water from wells and dispose of their waste through septic tanks. Eventually the high-density use of septic tanks would pollute the well water, and local governments would be called on to provide a community water supply as well as a sanitary sewer system. This growth would also demand other services. Storm sewers were often needed to prevent basements from flooding. In the North, snow had to be removed from the streets in winter. Police and fire protection had to be increased. Schools had to be built. Park space had to be bought and developed. Hospitals had to be provided.

The goals of autonomy and growth seemed to conflict. The goal of autonomy called for small-town suburban governments. But providing the infrastructure for growth (highways, sewers, water supplies, hospitals, schools) was too expensive for small-town governments to do on their own. If the system of autonomous small-town suburban governments was going to be maintained, some mechanisms had to be created to provide those expensive essential services. The creation of these mechanisms and the politics of managing growth was the second distinctive feature of suburban politics.

The Politics of Access

A third distinctive feature of suburbia is the politics of access. Especially in the larger and older metropolises, the suburbs do not house a proportionate share of racial minorities, low-income people, welfare recipients, or subsidized housing tenants. On the contrary, these people are disproportionately housed in the central cities of these metropolises. Michael N. Danielson has argued that a series of legal mechanisms were used to keep low-income people out of the exclusive suburbs and penned up in the city or the poorer suburbs.[47] These exclusionary politics have occurred largely in public education, zoning, and in home construction and sales. These arguments will be examined closely in Chapter 10.

Maintaining the Multicentered Metropolis: Practical Strategies

As discussed above, one of the most serious suburban problems was that of finding the physical and financial resources needed to supply urban services such as streets, sidewalks, sewers, water, lighting, schools, and police and fire protection. The traditional ways of financing these improvements through locally imposed property taxes obviously became more and more impossible as the services themselves, especially schools, became exceedingly expensive. The attempts to reimplant small-town democracy on the fringes of the metropolis caused most suburban cities to end up, financially speaking, with the worst of both worlds. On the one hand, they were too small to possess the broad tax resources of the central city or to practice its economies of scale. And on the other hand, they were too numerous and too competitive for any one of them to become *the* commercial center for a broad geographic region, as was characteristic of rural small towns. In the rural small town, a natural ecology limited the population growth to the number of families and business enterprises needed to serve the surrounding rural area. The suburban cities' services quickly became overburdened. The most obvious way to compensate for these disadvantages was for each city to (1) attract commerce or industry in order to broaden its tax base, and (2) restrict its housing supply to relatively expensive homes that would add to the property tax base.

Although this course of action was a reasonable one for individual suburbs to follow, for metropolitan areas as entities it was a formula for disastrous competition for commercial and high-value residential real estate that would increase the local property tax base. Since there was seldom enough industry to go around, there were more losers than winners in the competition.[48] In the quest to provide a reasonable level of services without forsaking the political autonomy of the small town, some alterntive had to be found that would at the same time enable the suburbs to use economies of scale in providing services, keep the costs of local government reasonable, and enable suburbs to retain their small-town image.[49] Three imaginative answers to these problems were contracting for services, special districts, and metropolitan districts.

Contracting for Services: The Lakewood Plan

When a suburban community was too small to practice economies of scale in supplying services, the most ingenious device created was to separate the production of services from the provision of services.[50] The production could be left to the municipalities, counties, or special districts large enough to take advantage of economies of scale. The smaller communities could then handle the provision of services by purchasing them from the larger unit. This practice is sometimes referred to as the Lakewood Plan, because the Los Angeles suburb of Lakewood was the first in the nation to exist completely on the basis of purchasing almost all its basic services from another unit of government. In just the four years from 1950 to 1954, Lakewood grew from sparsely settled farmland to a suburban municipality of 50,000 people. Because Lakewood is the most renowned example of providing its public services by buying them from other governments, its plan is well worth examining for its advantages and its disadvantages.

Prior to 1954, Los Angeles County was allowed to provide its services only in unincorporated areas. The services provided in these unincorporated areas were paid for not only by taxes derived from those areas but also by taxes derived from municipalities that did not receive any of the county's services. Residents of these incorporated municipalities complained that they were being charged for services that went only to the unincorporated areas. And in the unincorporated areas, the residents were beginning to desire more control over their own territory. However, if they incorporated in order to get that control, they not only would lose the services that the county was providing but also would be subject to the extra tax burden that was levied on the residents of municipalities.[51] The impasse was resolved in 1954 by the compromise known as the Lakewood Plan. The plan allowed suburban municipalities incorporated after 1954 to purchase a package of services from the county. The plan also authorized local sales taxes as an incentive for incorporation. Under the provisions of the Lakewood Plan, Los Angeles County signed more than 1600 agreements with all seventy-seven municipalities for more than fifty-eight types of services that the county supplied. Some of the major services and the number of cities that purchased each one are shown in Table 9-5.

From one perspective, the Lakewood Plan and the device of contracting for services was an overwhelming success. It guaranteed local suburban municipalities both their autonomy and the ability to utilize economies of scale in providing municipal services to their residents. Not only did the Lakewood Plan guarantee the existence of suburbs, it even gave them several alternative producers from whom they could purchase the services. They could, in many instances, produce a needed service themselves; they could purchase it from another municipality; they could enter a joint powers agreement with another municipality to provide the service jointly; and, in some instances, they could purchase the service from a private firm. In summary, the Lakewood Plan made the suburban government like a shopper entering a supermarket and purchasing the most appropriate products at the lowest price. If the county wanted too high a price for a given service, the purchaser could look elsewhere for a cheaper price.

Table 9-5. Services Provided to Cities by the Los Angeles County Government: 1972

| | Cities contracting for service | |
Standard form agreement	Number	Percentage of all cities in the county
Maintenance of city prisoners in county jail	76	99
City health ordinance enforcement	74	96
Subdivision final map checking	70	91
Emergency ambulance program	67	87
General services agreement	65	84
Animal control services	38	49
Hospitalization of city prisoners	37	49
Industrial waste	31	40
Building inspection	30	39
Law enforcement services	29	38
Street construction and maintenance	28	36
Parcel map checking	14	18
Tree planting and maintenance	5	7

Source: Advisory Commission on Intergovernmental Relations, *Report A-44. Substate Regionalism and the Federal System: The Challenge of Local Governmental Reorganization* (Washington, D.C.: U.S. Government Printing Office, 1974), vol. III, p. 71.

If the Lakewood Plan solved the immediate dilemma of providing large-scale urban services without sacrificing local autonomy, it was not without its critics. Because of its position as the major producer of services, the county dominated any bargaining with local municipalities over the quality of services and the costs at which they will be provided. The Lakewood Plan also led to a proliferation of municipal government incorporations in the county, because the passage of the plan in 1954 gave tax incentives to suburban residents to incorporate rather than become annexed to the City of Los Angeles or even remain unincorporated. Whereas only two cities incorporated in the county between 1930 and 1940, thirty-two cities incorporated in the next 20 years. Some of these new cities were special-interest cities created to secure particular tax advantages. The City of Industry was a tax shelter for factories and warehouses. Another suburb, Dairy Valley, was a farming enclave. In Rolling Hills, all the streets were owned by a private company. And Hidden Hills is literally walled in. When its gates are closed, outsiders cannot enter.[52] One study found that the Lakewood Plan was biased in favor of business and upper-status interests seeking a tax break. A majority of business-sponsored incorporation attempts were passed, but only one of 21 resident-sponsored attempts passed.[53]

The Lakewood Plan did not cause the incorporation of these municipalities, but by enabling them to purchase services they were incapable of producing for themselves, it gave them a tax incentive to incorporate. Since it guaranteed the county government's position as the preeminent producer of public services in the region, county officials or bureaucrats had no incentive to seek a broader, metropolitan-wide government.[54]

Whatever might be the merits of these criticisms, the practice of contracting for governmental services is very popular. A survey of eighty-six metropolitan counties found that 65 percent of them reported some form of integovernmental cooperation in providing public services.[55] These forms of cooperation range from interlocal agreements to transfer of functions to a higher level of government to consolidation of functions. It also has become very popular to purchase services from private companies, as indicated in Chapter 8.

Special Districts

A second common device for providing public services in the suburbs is the *special district*. The use of special districts has increased steadily over the past few decades. Until the 1940s there were only about 9000 special districts in the entire country. Today there are that many just in the MSAs, and there are over 29,000 nationwide. Table 9-6 tabulates changes in the number of local governments in MSAs between 1977 and 1982. While the number of school districts declined, the number of municipalities and special districts continued to increase, with special districts accounting for more than 95 percent of all the increases in local governments during that period.

Most of these special districts have been created in the suburbs to provide services that might be needed in an unincorporated area or that might be needed for a

Table 9-6. Incidence of Special District Governments in MSAs: 1977 and 1982

Kind of local government	Number in MSAs		Change from 1977 to 1982
	1977	1982	
School districts	5,751	5,692	− 59
Towns and townships	4,752	4,756	+ 4
Counties	670	670	0
Municipalities	6,923	7,018	+ 95
Special districts	10,640	11,725	+ 1,085
	28,736	29,861	

Source: U.S. Bureau of the Census, *Census of Governments: 1982, Vol. I, Governmental Organization* (Washington, D.C.: U.S. Government Printing Office, 1983), p. 43.
The number of MSAs refers to the 305 MSAs existing in 1982.

large area that encompasses more than one suburban municipality. In suburban Houston, for example, the provision of water supply has been accomplished almost universally by the creation of Water Control and Improvement Districts, the number of which grew from 221 in 1971 to 392 in 1979.[56]

The major reason for the popularity of special districts undoubtedly lies in the fact that they can raise money for needed services at the same time that they maintain a low political and fiscal visibility. Municipalities and counties are quite often restricted by state laws from assuming responsibility for the needed services or from raising their debt to the level that would be needed to provide the services. In these instances the problem can be solved by creating special districts with their own taxing powers and their own debt level. Because the taxes generated by these districts are normally collected by the county, many voters are confused about the origin and distribution of the property taxes they pay. This confusion gives special districts low fiscal visibility and helps shield them from criticism when citizens' groups protest against rising taxes. Table 9-7 shows that special districts providing natural resources, fire protection, and community development services account for about a third of all special districts.

Despite the evident popularity of special districts, their proliferation has caused some serious problems both for the governance of the metropolis and for making the government responsive to the electorate and to the citizens' needs. A study of more than 500 special districts in the San Francisco Bay area[57] found that few citizens knew that the special districts existed, let alone what they did. Once created, districts are hard to dissolve because of vested interests that grow up around them and incumbent officeholders who are understandably reluctant to lose their positions. A study of special districts in the Houston area discovered serious lack of accountability. Many water control districts (WCDs) were established by suburban land developers to use public money to finance the construction of suburban subdivisions. The water control districts were typically created before any residents

Table 9-7. Special District Governments by Functional Class: 1982

Functional class	Total of special districts in SMSAs performing the function indicated
Single-function districts	25,991
Natural resources	6,232
Fire protection	4,560
Housing and community development	3,296
Water supply	2,637
Sewerage	1,631
Cemeteries	1,577
School buildings	960
Parks and recreation	924
Other single-function districts	4,174
Multifunction districts	2,597
	28,588

Source: U.S. Bureau of the Census, Census of Governments: 1982, Vol. I, Governmental Organization (Washington, D.C.: U.S. Government Printing Office, 1983), p. xii.

lived in the subdivisions and they issued bonds that then had to be paid off by taxes on the properties of the residents when they moved in. In this way, the builders enhanced their own profits by passing on a substantial portion of development costs to the taxpayers. In one instance, developers were the only ones who voted in the election to create the water control district. Once created, developers dominated the governing board during the crucial early years when the WCDs' bonds were issued. And even after local residents were elected to the governing boards of the WCDs, they necessarily viewed the WCDs' chief constituency not as the residents who elected them but the bond owners who often were closely affiliated with the original developers.[58] Because of these affiliations, the original WCD bond issuers had no incentive to keep interest rates down. After all, the interest rates would be paid by somebody else, while they themselves would benefit from high rates. The use of water control districts to finance suburban land development costs is not limited only to Texas but has also been common in California, Colorado, Tennessee, Kentucky, and Kansas.[59]

Metropolitan Districts

The *metropolitan district* is a special district that produces a specific service on either a countywide or a multicounty level. The number of metropolitan districts, like the number of special districts, has increased in the larger MSAs. The services performed by the metropolitan district are those that transcend most municipal boundaries and can be performed most efficiently on a regional or county level. Typically such services include transit, sewerage, water supply, parks, and sometimes airports.

A Special District in Action: The Port Authority of New York and New Jersey

The most famous and most successful metropolitan district is undoubtedly the Port Authority of New York and New Jersey. It was established in 1921 by an interstate compact between New York and New Jersey to develop commercial and transportation facilities in the region. It is directed by a twelve-member governing board of commissioners appointed by the governors of New York and New Jersey. Once appointed, the commissioners become virtually immune from removal.

The commissioners are selected from upper-level executives of the major corporations in the two states. With few exceptions, the Port Authority has had a succession of extremely capable executive directors who have employed equally competent staff personnel and have provided some of the most consistently successful leadership of any government in the nation.

The Port Authority was given no taxing powers; once created, however, it quickly developed lucrative profit-making enterprises. By 1931 it was operating four toll bridges and the Holland Tunnel. The next year it opened a freight terminal. In 1944 it opened a grain terminal, and in 1948 it took over its first airport. During the 1950s it acquired the rest of New York's major airports. During the 1960s it entered the real estate business and constructed the 110-story twin towers of the World Trade Center. By the mid-1980s, the Port Authority's various enterprises brought in about $1.2 billion in annual revenue.[60] Port Authority facilities included six interstate bridges and tunnels, two bus terminals, six airports, ten truck terminals, the World Trade Center, facilities for international shipping and other commercial activities, and one railroad system. It was the last of these facilities that symbolized one of the Authority's most severe headaches.

Despite the Port Authority's enormous success, critics have long complained that it was neglecting commuter rail service, one of its original responsibilities. Rather than relieving New York's traffic problems, it was charged, the Port Authority's bridges and tunnels were making New York's traffic congestion worse by bringing in more automobiles. The Authority was increasingly pressured to invest some of its ever-increasing revenues into commuter rail transit. After a long, drawn-out battle in which the Port Authority eventually was attacked on the issue by the governors of both states, the Metropolitan Rapid Transit Commission, the New Jersey legislature, the mayor of New York City, many local leaders in New Jersey, a committee of the United States Congress, and a variety of groups and citizens concerned about the transit problem in New York, a compromise was finally arranged in 1962. The Port Authority agreed to purchase one small commuter railroad. In return the Authority was given permission to build the World Trade Center, and the two state legislatures passed a bond covenant forbidding the Authority from taking on any other rail activities if the deficit from existing rail operations exceeded 10 percent of the Authority's general reserve fund. These two concessions seemed to guarantee that the Authority's finances in the foreseeable future would be so tied up in constructing the World Trade Center and subsidizing the deficits on the PATH (Port Authority Trans-Hudson) Railroad that there was no danger of it being forced to subsidize any other mass transit operations.[61]

Despite the bond covenant of 1962, political forces in New York and New Jersey continued to pressure the Authority to take on more mass transit responsibilities. In a complicated set of agreements in 1973 and 1974, the Authority agreed to use more of its revenues to support rail transit in the region and to construct rail lines linking Manhattan with Newark and Kennedy airports. The New York and New Jersey legislatures in 1974 repealed the 1962 bond covenant, and the Port Authority increased its bridge and tunnel tolls to pay for the $240 million it was going to spend on these projects in New York and New Jersey. However, these agreements fell apart in 1977 when the United States Supreme Court ruled that the legislatures' repeal of the 1962 bond covenant had violated the obligation of contract clause of the United States Constitution.[62]

As these events unfolded, the Port Authority was also rocked by internal conflicts among its various divisions and the only scandal in its 60-year history. Auditors found that Authority executives had used shady methods of letting out bids for contracts, had accepted financial favors from politicians and corporations, and had illegally padded their expense accounts.[63] As the scandal came to light, one senior officer committed suicide and others were disciplined.

In the wake of the internal conflicts and the scandals, a wide personnel shakeup took place. An agreement was worked out between the governors of New York and New Jersey to bring in a new executive director and chairperson who were committed to increasing the Port Authority's role in mass transit. A legal compromise was reached that enabled the Port Authority, without violating its 1962 bond covenant, to provide more aid for mass transit. This aid was spent for commuter bus equipment, roadways, and other transit costs.[64]

Controlling Metropolitan Districts

Although the profitability of the Port Authority and the extensiveness of its operations make it unique among metropolitan districts, its very uniqueness illustrates the major advantages and disadvantages of metropolitan districts. The major advantage is that a given service can often be performed on a metropolitan scale very effectively, efficiently, and economically. Operating expenses will often be covered by fees collected from the service, and capital expenses for constructing new facilities will normally be covered by an issue of public bonds paid off from the operating revenue plus a small property tax. Federal grants are often available to the district under many federal grant-in-aid programs. Because of the federal grants, the bonding authority, and the fees collected from operating the public services, the metropolitan districts enjoy considerable financial independence from city councils. And this financial independence can make metropolitan districts very popular with economy-minded public officials.

Metropolitan districts such as the Port Authority of New York and New Jersey, the Southern California Metropolitan Water District, and Chicago's Metropolitan Sanitary District sell vitally needed services—and, as shown by the example of the Port Authority of New York and New Jersey, can often sell them at a profit. For these kinds of services, the metropolitan district approach works very well. But many vital metropolitan services such as mass transit or air pollution control must operate at a deficit rather than a profit and, as the case of the Port Authority of New York and New Jersey demonstrates, getting profitable metropolitan districts to take on needed but unprofitable services is often difficult. Even the enormously successful Port Authority lost over $100 million in 1986 on its bus terminal and its Trans-Hudson Railroad. However, these losses were effectively subsidized by the Authority's profit-making enterprises.[65]

A related problem posed by metropolitan districts is that of coordinating the different functions each of them performs separately. The transit problem of a metropolis can only get worse if the plans of the highway planners are not coordinated with those of public transit planners. Similarly, if metropolitan sprawl is to be contained, there must exist a high level of coordination between plans for sewer construction, water line construction, highway construction, construction of public transit lines, shopping center construction, solid waste disposal, and open space preservation, to name a few major metropolitan concerns often handled by isolated metropolitan districts. It does little good if water lines run in one direction, sewerage lines in another, highways in a third, and transit lines in another, and no provisions are made for the preservation of open space.

In order to subordinate metropolitan districts to elected political officials and to coordinate the activities of different metropolitan districts, three tactics have been attempted: the constituent unit method of representation, the multipurpose district, and the use of a review and planning authority.

The *constituent unit* method of representation seeks to subordinate the metropolitan districts to the major elected government bodies by having the most important government bodies represented directly on the boards of the metropolitan districts. A metropolitan transit commission, for example, might be composed of council members or mayors from the central city and the principal suburbs. The rationale for such representation is that these government representatives will oblige the metropolitan district to be responsive to their constituents. All too often this does not work in practice. In many instances, the commission is torn by political conflicts between commissioners who represent the interests of their own cities. Even where the constituent unit method of representation does succeed in subordinating a metropolitan district to the local elected officials, *different* officials will be on *different* metropolitan districts and consequently cannot coordinate the activities of various districts. Nevertheless, because it enables some control by elected officials, the constituent unit method of representation has been quite popular.[66]

A second approach to coordinating the activities of metropolitan districts has been to consolidate several isolated single-purpose metropolitan districts into one *multipurpose district* that would exercise overall policy control over each function and ensure that the various services were coordinated. A recent example of this has been in Seattle, Washington, where sewage disposal and transit are combined under a metropolitan district called the Municipality of Metropolitan Seattle, and Portland, Oregon, where until 1979 the Metro Service District coordinated the policies of all the metropolitan districts in that metropolis.

A third approach to coordinating the activities of metropolitan districts was adopted in Minneapolis–Saint Paul. The Metropolitan Council is given very broad review powers over metropolitan districts in that region. The Metropolitan Council appoints the members, oversees the budgets, and sets the general policy plans for the three metropolitan commissions responsible for transit, sewers, and regional park development. For the two other metropolitan commissions, responsible for airports and sports facilities, the Metropolitan Council has less authority, but it nevertheless has power to disapprove their capital expenditure budgets. The net result of this in the early 1970s was that the Metropolitan Council forced the airports commission to abandon its plans to build a second commercial airport and also forced the transit commission to abandon its plans for a rapid rail system. Although some critics argue that these decisions will turn out to be major mistakes, the Metropolitan Council claims that these decisions saved the region's taxpayers more than a billion dollars. Whichever side of the argument is correct, the Minnesota approach to controlling metropolitan districts does appear to have demostrated some considerable success.[67]

As a governing device, metropolitan districts serve partly to maintain the multicentered metropolis and partly to create new forms of governance. In the respect that they provide a mechanism to deal with specific functional problems on an areawide basis, they represent a break with the parochialism of suburban municipal politics. But they protect the multicentered metropolis in several respects. Because of their unifunctional orientation, controlling and coordinating the policies of several districts is difficult. Like contracting for services, and like special districts, metropolitan districts do not restrain the proliferation of governments in the metropolis. Finally, because of the way in which their boards are constituted, metropolitan districts are not normally held accountable to the electorate. There is no known instance of the voters rising up and throwing out of office the members of any metropolitan board.

Transportation and the Politics of Metropolitan Growth

The Federal Initiative

As discussed in Chapter 2, transportation technology and policies have played a significant role in urban growth patterns. Few if any transportation policies have affected these patterns more than the federal government's decision in the 1950s to build metropolitan freeways and the Interstate Highway System. Although the federal government has aided highway construction since 1916, it was not until the highway legislation of 1944 and 1956 that metropolitan freeway systems became commonplace. The Federal Aid Highway Act of 1944 approved a 41,000-mile interstate highway system to connect the major urban centers. The Federal Aid Highway Act of 1956 provided the means of financing this interstate highway construction. It established the federal highway trust fund, which was derived from a four-cents-per-gallon (today, nine cents) federal tax on gasoline. The Bureau of Public Roads (now called the Federal Highway Administration) was given authority to determine the routes for new interstate highways. Ninety percent of the construction was financed from the highway trust fund, and the other 10 percent was financed by individual states whose highway departments assumed responsibility for the actual construction and maintenance of the new highways.

The interstate program has had four major consequences on the metropolitan centers. First, by tearing up enormous tracts of residential housing in the cities, the urban freeways displaced countless numbers of people and destroyed many viable urban neighborhood communities.[68] Second, because the local residents whose neighborhoods were torn up found themselves powerless to stop the freeways, the freeways contributed to an increased public alienation with city government during the 1960s and 1970s. Third, by effectively subsidizing the construction of roads for automobiles, the federal government neglected the needs of public transit, and public transit facilities throughout the nation deteriorated progressively after World War II.

The fourth major consequence of federal highway programs was their contribution to the out-migration of population, shopping facilities, and jobs to the suburbs. The major freeway interchanges became growth centers for a wide variety of businesses and housing developments. Downtown department stores and major retailers such as Ward's, Penney's, and Sears expanded into the suburban shopping malls. The malls supplemented these department stores with a variety of specialty shops. Unlike the strip shopping in the cities, the suburban shopping centers provided large parking areas. Soon these shopping centers, located at the major freeway interchanges, attracted other service-oriented businesses, medical buildings, lawyers' offices, motels, theaters, restaurants, and other amenities. Downtown businesspeople had originally supported the construction of freeways as a means of speeding traffic through the city and bringing shoppers downtown swiftly. Instead, the freeways sent city shoppers out to the suburbs and the placement of the freeways enabled long-distance travelers to bypass the city entirely.

Conflict over Transportation Policies

By the 1970s several explosive reactions to freeway construction began to occur. In the central cities, antifreeway groups began to oppose additional freeway construction. Although these groups were ineffectual at first, by the late 1960s they began scoring some significant victories. In Boston, a coalition of citizens' groups protested so successfully against the construction of a freeway through their neighborhoods that the governor of Massachusetts ordered an end to all freeway construction in that city.[69] Congress in 1966 reacted to lobbying from conservationist groups and forbade the construction of freeways through public park systems unless there were no alternative routes. And in 1971 the Supreme Court upheld a suit filed by conservationists against a proposed freeway through a park in Memphis, Tennessee.[70]

It was not until 1974 that Congress provided significant federal subsidies for mass transit. Those subsidies were increased in 1980, 1982, and 1987. The net result has been that since 1970, the federal government has spent $28.8 billion in grants for mass transit.[71] As a consequence of this aid, most metropolises have expanded their bus and rail service. This in turn led more people to use mass transit. Whereas ridership on public transit systems had declined steadily from 1945 to 1970, ridership increased during the 1970s until it began falling off again in the 1980s.[72] The transit systems themselves began to spread beyond the cities into the suburbs. The Bay Area Rapid Transit District in California built a subway linking San Francisco and Oakland to some suburbs, and Washington's METRO rapid rail linked the District of Columbia with suburbs in Maryland and Virginia. By the mid-1980s, 10 cities (New York, Chicago, Philadelphia, Boston, Cleveland, San Francisco, Atlanta, Miami, Baltimore, and Washington) had rapid rail systems and a dozen had started light-rail-vehicle (LRV) systems.

Today, many of these metropolitan transit systems are greatly overextended. The increase in public ridership during the 1970s had come largely from federal and other subsidies that had been used to keep fares from inflating, to purchase new buses, to expand new bus routes into the suburbs, and to subsidize operating deficits. But rising fuel costs and wage demands in the inflationary economy of the late 1970s made it impossible for many transit systems to balance their budgets even with heavy federal and state subsidies. Facing increased political resistance from tax-revolt-conscious legislators and other political actors, the public transit systems once again had to begin cutting back operations and raising fares in the late 1970s and early 1980s.

Public transit advocates today face a very difficult dilemma. On the one hand, unless public transit continues to expand, dependence on the automobile will increase, suburban sprawl will continue, vulnerability to petroleum shortages will continue, and people without automobiles (principally the poor, the elderly, and the handicapped) will be denied access to the economically dynamic areas of the metropolis (the suburbs). On the other hand, evidence from the 1970s suggests that public transit subsidies are sometimes not very well spent, the metropolitan transit commissions do not exercise very effective cost control, and they could easily absorb billions of dollars yearly in subsidies without making an appreciable dent in suburban sprawl. Compounding this dilemma over subsidizing public transit is the continued deterioration of the existing freeway system, bridges, other roads, and the associated transportation infrastructure.

Commenting on these developments, one team of transportation writers referred to a "current malaise of urban transportation policy."[73] While the urban road network is virtually complete, except for unfinished links of the interstate system, capital-intensive public transit planning has promised more results than it has produced. This is especially evident in the analyses of San Francisco's BART system. One prominent urban planning scholar, Peter Hall, included BART among a list of six great planning disasters, mainly because BART has failed to attract the number of riders predicted, it is experiencing large cost overruns, it runs at a large deficit, and it has made no dent in the California choice of automobiles over public transit. Hall asserts boldly, "Had the citizenry of the Bay area the ability to foresee the true future, there seems little doubt that they would have rejected the whole BART proposal out of hand."[74]

If BART was a planning disaster, as Peter Hall asserts, it has not dissuaded other cities from going ahead with their own systems. In most of those places, the rapid rail systems also are falling short of their projections and are costing more than anticipated. One of the most interesting schemes is Detroit's People Mover, an elevated monorail that shuttles people around the central business district. It is too early to know whether the People Mover will reach its projected ridership, but there is no doubt about the cost. Construction costs totaled over $200 million,[75] which works out to about $1,088 per inch of the 2.9-mile monorail.

In fairness to Detroit, San Francisco, and other cities that have built capital-intensive rail systems, it may well be that it takes more than a decade for the benefits of the system to begin outweighing the costs. The subway systems of New York City and Chicago were initiated late in the 19th century, and it is quite conceivable that an early assessment of them would have been just as negative as Peter Hall's assessment of BART. Yet today they are invaluable assets for New York and Chicago. It is quite conceivable in the long run that BART and the other BART-like systems built in the 1970s and 1980s may also be viewed as positive assets twenty or thirty years from now. Since BART's original $1.6 billion construction bonds have much lower interest rates than prevail today and are being paid off by dollars cheapened by inflation, the BART taxpayer in the 1980s and 1990s may well be purchasing an extremely valuable asset at a cost that could not be duplicated today.

Land Management and the Politics of Metropolitan Growth

As highways and automobiles extended commuting distances farther and farther from the old central city, suburbs began to sprawl along these commuting lines. Environmentalists, urban planners, and other critics began to lament this. Sprawl was denounced as unsightly, a waste of precious farmland, a waste of energy, expensive, and a major factor in the nation's dependence on imported oil.[76] Put purely in terms of cost to tax-conscious citizens, urban planners pointed out that it would cost much less money to provide pavements, sewers, water, and other urban amenities in a metropolis with planned and orderly growth than it does in existing metropolises sprawling over the countryside.

Particularly lamented in this view by metropolitan planners was the fact that no authority existed at the metropolitan level to regulate land use. Traditionally, land use was either unregulated or regulated by the lowest-level government. Typically, a land developer gets a permit from the local government responsible for the land. The project must conform to any plans, zoning ordinances, building codes, or subdivision regulations that already exist there. Especially on the metropolitan fringes (where the process of sprawl takes place), these regulating governments tend to be smaller suburban municipalities and townships, which often lack a comprehensive planning process or a professional staff to examine requests for building permits. Additionally, these communities often seek growth in order to get a larger tax base. As a result, development permits are often granted quickly, uncritically, and in complete disregard for the impact of that particular community's growth on neighboring communities or on the region as a whole.

This decentralized system of regulating land use may have worked well in the rural nineteenth century, but it has produced undesirable consequences in the urban twentieth century. Letting owners manage their land as they saw fit led to racial segregation, shoddily constructed housing, oil spills along the coastlines, dumping of untreated industrial wastes into waterways, and inadequate septic tanks in densely populated housing developments. More and more open space was lost to suburban sprawl. More and more people built homes on the nation's seacoasts and other shorelands. As these phenomena received increasing publicity in the last third of the twentieth century, pressure mounted for more effective land use management.

Among the various approaches to land use management, four stand out.[77] First are the limited-growth zoning plans adopted by a variety of cities. Second are the statewide land use controls in Hawaii, Vermont, and Maine. Third are attempts— like the coastal zone protection plan in California—to protect designated areas. Fourth are efforts to channel future metropolitan growth into predesignated areas, typified by the development framework of the Minneapolis–Saint Paul region.

Model 1: Limited-Growth Zoning

In the limited-growth zoning model a single municipality designs a zoning plan that will put definite limits on the amount of growth it will allow. This model was pioneered in Ramapo, New Jersey, a New York City suburb of about 60,000 people, which in 1968 adopted a zoning plan that would limit future building permits to about 300 to 350 per year. Ramapo adopted a capital improvement program that staged the addition of future capital improvements such as sewers, roads, and fire stations over an 18-year period from 1968 to 1986. It then adopted a building permit process that measured each developer's proposal on a 23-point scale depending on how close the project was to existing service facilities. Permit applications that failed to get at least 15 points were rejected. When challenged as an illegal taking of property, the Ramapo plan was upheld by the state courts,[78] and the city went ahead with its program.

Across the continent another limited-growth plan was adopted in Petaluma, California, a growth center in the San Francisco Bay area. Petaluma limited its future growth to about 500 units annually. Petaluma differed from Ramapo in that its point system also included aesthetic features such as landscaping and it also provided for low-income housing. Like Ramapo, it was also challenged in the courts. Originally a federal district court rejected the plan as an unwarranted restriction on people's right to travel. But this was overruled by a federal circuit court of appeals, and the Petaluma plan was allowed to go into effect.[79]

With these two successful examples to serve as models, the idea of limited-growth zoning became very popular during the 1970s. Boulder, Colorado, a fast-growing satellite city of about 90,000 people 30 miles from Denver, adopted a plan that would limit its growth to about 2 percent annually.[80] Even major central cities became attracted to the concept, as shown by the examples of San Diego and San Jose,[81] California, which adopted measures in 1977 and 1978 to limit their fast-growing populations.

Whatever utility limited-growth zoning might have for local towns that do not want any newcomers, it provides no solution for the broader metropolitan growth problem. It might even make the sprawl problem worse. If one or many suburbs refuse to accept more growth, the growth pressure is increased on the other communities in the metropolis. And if all suburbs restricted their growth, then poor and moderate-income people would never be able to move out to the suburbs. For this reason, some critics charge that limited-growth zoning is basically nothing more than a dressed-up version of exclusionary zoning designed to keep poor people and minorities out of certain suburbs.[82] (See Chapter 10.)

Model 2: Statewide Land Management

An approach to land use regulation that avoids the parochialism of limited-growth zoning is simply to let the state regulate land use. This has been tried successfully in Hawaii, Vermont, and Maine. The most elaborate plan exists in Hawaii, where the Hawaii Land Use Law of 1961 created a state Land Use Commission. The commission divided the state into four zones—urban, rural, agricultural, and conservation. Within each zone, land can be used only for purposes specified by the law. Thus, for example, extensive urban development is prohibited in the agricultural zone. A developer with a proposal that is not consistent with the specified uses of a zone can apply to the state Land Use Commission either for a boundary change or for a special use permit. In the urban areas, local zoning bodies continue to issue building permits.

Vermont's Land Use and Development Act of 1970 established an environmental board and eight district commissions to cope with rapid residential and commercial development that began in the 1960s,[83] as the state became a popular place for second homes, recreational developments, and people eager to escape the crowded Northeast megalopolis. The environmental board is responsible for the state land use plan, whereas the district commissions make the actual decisions on permit applications. The overwhelming majority of permit applications have been approved. Rather than deny permits, the commissions used their authority to impose conditions that would make them consistent with the state plan.

Although statewide land use regulation copes with the metropolitan problem much more effectively than does the limited-growth zoning model, it is not likely that this model will spread to the other forty-seven states. Conditions in Hawaii and Vermont are very unusual. Both states are small. Hawaii's plan was passed early in its statehood, and in Vermont, few local governments had historically imposed land use regulations. This meant that there was much less local opposition to a statewide plan than would be likely in most other states.

Model 3: Protecting Designated Areas

A third approach to land use regulation has been simply to establish a dual permit system to protect areas that are designated as environmentally endangered. The most far-reaching example of this is the California coastal zone plan, which protects that state's 1000 miles of coastline. When the California legislature failed to pass coastal zone protective legislation after the disastrous Santa Barbara oil spill in 1969, environmentalists used California's initiative process to put a coastal zone bill directly on the ballot in the 1972 general election. This initiative passed by a 10 percent margin. [84]

Pursuant to this act and a subsequent law passed by the legislature in 1976, a statewide coastal zone commission is responsible for a statewide plan, and six regional commissions are responsible for applying the plan in their region. Developments within 3000 feet of the coastline or up to 3 miles out to sea require a permit from the appropriate regional commission in addition to a traditional permit from the appropriate local government. Thus a double permit system exists. If the local government issues a permit that violates either the regional or the state coastal zone plan, the regional commission can for all practical purposes veto the local permit. Developers must now placate the regional commissions as well as the local governments.

Although the coastal zone plan has not stopped coastal development (about 90 percent of permit applications are approved), the regional commissions have negotiated changes with the developers in order to make the projects more environmentally sound and consistent with commission policies. [85] Thus coastal development is no longer uncontrolled and unregulated.

Model 4: Metropolitan Policymaking with Local Implementation

A fourth approach to managing land use has been to establish a metropolitan-level policy and oblige local governments to implement that policy as they go about their normal process of issuing building permits. This model is currently being experimented with by the Minneapolis–Saint Paul Metropolitan Council. [86] Rather than establishing a dual permit system, the Minnesota Legislature gave the Twin Cities Metropolitan Council policymaking authority over the land use plans of local governments. Under this authority, the Metropolitan Council established a Development Framework Plan that divides the entire metropolitan region into four planning areas: (1) the central cities and a few adjacent suburbs, which were designated as a fully developed area; (2) the second-tier suburbs, which still had substantial areas of vacant land and were designated the area of planned urbanization; (3) the rural area, which was to be preserved from urbanization and preserved mostly for agricultural use; and (4) thirteen satellite cities in the rural area, which were designated freestanding growth centers. The Metropolitan Council planned to channel the majority of future growth into the area of planned urbanization and the freestanding growth centers. This would preserve the rural area for agricultural use and would contain the sprawl of the urbanizing region.

To implement this plan, the Council has drawn a metropolitan urban services area (MUSA) line around the area of planned urbanization and has stated its intention not to allow sewer lines to extend beyond the MUSA line (except in the free-standing growth centers). Since the Council, as pointed out above (pp. 268–269), controls the budget of the sewer commission, it has the authority to carry out this intention. Without access to sewers and with a stiffening of septic tank regulations, the rural areas beyond the MUSA line can absorb only limited growth. Furthermore, Minnesota law requires local governments to submit comprehensive land use plans to the Metropolitan Council to make certain that they are consistent with the development framework plan. As a deterrent to local governments deviating from the development framework and other metropolitan policies, the Council has a number of legal powers to insist that local governments adhere to its policies.

Although the Minnesota model is the newest approach to regional land use management, it has not been in existence long enough to know whether it will be successful. And just as the success of the statewide land use plan may not be transferable from Hawaii, Vermont, and Maine to other states, the same might well be true of the Minnesota model.

In some places of the country it may already be too late to change metropolitan sprawl patterns. Many metropolitan areas of the Northeast appear to have reached the limits of their growth,[87] due to a slowdown of population growth, the population shift to the Sunbelt, and lifestyle changes that are making the central cities more attractive to childless couples and single adults. The continuing emergence of new metropolitan areas, however, and the rapid growth of Sunbelt and western metropolitan areas is evidence that land management policies are still very much needed. The four land management models examined here may serve as examples to be followed in some of these growing metropolises during the late 1980s and 1990s.

Assessment

In summary, policymakers have not yet found an overall cure for the problems of suburban sprawl. Four interesting experiments have been tried over the past decade, but none seems likely to be adopted throughout the country. The limited-growth zoning model is perhaps the most popular of these four models, but it is essentially a parochial approach that does nothing to alleviate the metropolitan-wide problem of sprawl. The statewide land use regulation model probably is not feasible in states with a long history of local control over land use. The dual permit model used to protect California's coastal zone seems to have considerable potential, but to date the model has been used only to protect environmentally endangered areas, and nobody has tried to apply it to traditional problems of suburban sprawl. The Minnesota model of metropolitan policy implemented by local governments is very imaginative and might well become very successful in that region. However, it is a direct product of the peculiar form of metropolitan governance created in the Twin Cities and probably is not transferable to regions with different forms (see Chapter 11).

Finally, the efficacy of all these growth control models was thrown into question by a Supreme Court ruling in 1987 that requires local government to compensate landowners for "undue burdens" that growth control ordinances may put on their land.[88] The First English Evangelical Lutheran Church of Glendale, California had been forced to close a campground for handicapped children, because the camp lay in a flood control area where Los Angeles County had banned construction. The county had passed the ordinance after a flood through that area had destroyed several buildings and killed several people. But the church argued that this ordinance deprived the church of "all uses" of 21 acres it owned in the area and sought compensation for the economic losses it incurred. When the Supreme Court agreed with the church's claim of compensation, the Court made it possible that local governments everywhere will face a vast number of lawsuits over growth control measures they have enacted.[89]

The Consequences of Unrestricted Suburban Growth

As the population spread out to the suburbs, as shopping and service facilities decentralized from the central city out to the shopping malls on the freeway interchanges, and as municipalities, special districts, and intergovernmental contracting plans became popular ways of providing public services, the metropolis was no longer centered on the old central business district. In many respects the metropolis by the 1980s had become multicentered. And these multicentered metropolises were characterized by several distinct consequences and biases.

Uncontrolled Sprawl

If there is any one distinguishing physical feature of the North American metropolis, it is the sprawl of the suburbs over the countryside. As discussed above, this sprawl is accentuated by the fact that control over zoning decisions is left in the hands of individual suburban municipalities. A study of zoning disputes in New York concluded that although individual zoning decisions "do not appear to have great significance by themselves, the total metropolitan development pattern is the result of a patchwork of local decisions, overlaid by transportation networks imposed by the state and Federal governments."[90]

The multicentered metropolis prevents a coherent approach to controlling metropolitan growth, to channeling the growth into areas designed for it, and to preserving other areas for permanent recreational green spaces or drainage, or even for vital groundwater recharge purposes. Despite the suburbs' lower population densities, they often have less park space or recreational space per capita than do the central cities. Typically, suburban growth has occurred before sewer and water lines were constructed, and this growth in many areas has thus posed a threat to the safety of the water supply. Furthermore, the outer suburbs are characterized by very low density, and the population concentrations are often separated by great distances. When low-density suburbs finally are forced to install public sewers and water supplies, the cost is much higher than it would have been if the growth had been planned in conjunction with the need for utilities. In the face of all this, suburban land use policies, particularly zoning laws, have been very unsuccessful in regulating where and under what conditions developers can build. Despite the ineffectiveness of suburban zoning controls, suburbanites tend to oppose vociferously any attempts to transfer zoning power to a higher level of government, such as the county.[91]

Ironically, the more that suburban sprawl continues, the more suburbanites are afflicted by the problems they sought to avoid by moving to the suburbs in the first place. Automotive gridlock is one of the most frustrating of these. Washington, D.C.'s suburban Tyson Corners is gridlocked daily in the morning and evening rush hours by traffic jams that would rival those of the central city itself.[92] Similar suburban gridlocks occur in many other metropolitan areas.[93] As suburbs sprawl, another consequence is to take more agricultural land out of production. One study estimates that at the current rate of loss, the next 50 years will see losses of cropland equal to the size of Missouri. Much of this loss is due to suburban sprawl.[94]

Loss of Accountability for Public Decisions

Although the suburbs were supposed to bring the government closer to the citizen, evidence indicates that on many vital questions the opposite has occurred.[95] Retention of the multicentered metropolis has necessitated a proliferation of single-purpose governments to provide the services the suburban municipalities cannot provide individually. Since the municipalities, the metropolitan authorities, and state and federal agencies all exercise some portion of responsibility in any given suburban municipality, it is virtually impossible for the ordinary citizen to know which government is responsible for what.

Proliferation of Governments

Perhaps the most visible consequence of the multicentered metropolis has been the proliferation of governments, principally of municipalities and special districts. Beginning early in the twentieth century and extending to the 1960s, state legislation made it relatively easy for metropolitan fringe communities to incorporate. And there has been a steady escalation in the number of special districts. As these districts proliferate, the problem of getting collective action to achieve an overall public good becomes increasingly difficult. In suburban Houston, for example, each of the over 400 water control districts (WCDs) sees its task as providing sufficient water for its particular sub-area of the region, and no individual WCD has any incentive to restrict its water production. But for the metropolitan area as a whole, the total impact of all 400 WCDs taking as much water as they want from the underground aquifers (water supply) is a substantial reduction of the aquifer's water volume. This in turn causes land to sink (subsidence). In some parts of the Houston region, land is sinking at the rate of two inches per year.[96] Given the proclivity for hurricanes and storm waves in the coastal Texas area, the sinking land (if allowed to continue unabated) creates the potential for a flooding disaster causing unprecedented damage to property and loss of human life.[97] In some parts of Florida, subsidence caused by the exploitation of a relatively shallow aquifer is dramatically shown by the sudden appearance of sinkholes, sometimes resulting in the destruction of property such as houses and automobiles.

The Biases of Unrestricted Suburban Growth

It can be seen from the above discussion that some people receive benefits because of the decentralized political structure of the multicentered metropolis. Certain other people are disfavored.

The multicentered metropolis is biased to favor those who profit from uncontrolled sprawl—particularly land speculators, real estate developers, and large retailing enterprises. Local municipalities, which make zoning decisions in most metropolises, seldom turn down proposed real estate developments that will increase the local community's tax base, such as shopping centers or expensive single-family homes. Nor do they consider how the development fits into areawide growth patterns. And once the overall permission for a shopping center is granted, specific decisions as to the kinds of shops and their owners or managers may be left to the shopping center management, without input from the local municipality or residents.

Although it is clear that the multicentered metropolis favors large-scale developers by granting them considerable autonomy in their operations, it is not as clear who is directly hurt by this process. Nor is it clear that the direct profits of development would be more widely shared if zoning decisions were made at the metropolitan rather than the municipal level.

A second bias may exist in the multicentered metropolis: a bias against the public good. To the extent that the "public good" consists of the objectives of minimizing pollution, protecting open space, equalizing the availability of public services, and equalizing access to housing, shopping, employment, and educational facilities, contemporary suburbia is probably biased against the public good. But it is doubtful that universal agreement exists that these objectives constitute the public interest. Furthermore, many steps have been taken toward many of these objectives in the past decade.

Third, the multicentered metropolis is biased against effective citizen input. With such a wide variety of government agencies operating within any given geographical region, concerned citizens may find it extremely difficult to express grievances effectively because they do not know which agency has responsibility for their particular grievance. In theory, suburbanites are very close to their city council and their school board, and they are much more likely to know one of these officials personally than are central-city residents. But they also are likely to discover that some of the most important governmental activities that concern them—streetlight location, sewerage, transit service, welfare problems, and in some suburbs even water supply, fire protection, and police protection—are not handled by these local officials.

Finally, it must be asked whether the concentration of poor people and racial minorities in the central cities constitutes another bias of the multicentered metropolis. This question will be examined in Chapter 10.

Summary

1. On examination, the myths about suburbia as a homogeneous collection of white, upper-middle-income, conservative Republicans is not borne out by the facts. Although many individual suburbs may house a limited range of people, there are indeed many different kinds of suburbs. They differ by their functional specialization, by the kinds of people they house, and by their spatial arrangements.

2. In partisan politics, neither the transplantation theory nor the conversion theory has proven to be accurate, because the suburbs are not overwhelmingly Republican. Although suburbanites on balance tend to vote Republican slightly more often than they vote Democratic, there are more Democratic or Democratic-leaning suburbs than there are Republican suburbs or suburbs that lean Republican. Also, the tendency of a suburb to vote Republican is directly related to the suburb's affluence.

3. Although it is misleading to characterize suburbs as more ideologically conservative than central cities, three distinct political features of suburbs do exist. They seek political autonomy from the central city. They are much more affected by the politics of metropolitan sprawl. And they face bitter conflicts over the questions of practicing exclusion or facilitating social access.

4. There have been three recurring strategies for preserving small-town suburban governments while at the same time providing the physical services needed for growth—contracting for government services, special districts, and metropolitan districts. The most successful example of a metropolitan district is probably the Port Authority of New York and New Jersey. It illustrates the difficulties in getting special districts or metropolitan districts to be responsive to the elected officials of general-purpose governments and in getting them to adapt their policies to the changing needs of the times.

5. The federal highway trust fund and the Interstate Highway System have contributed to the metropolitan freeways that did so much to encourage suburban sprawl. In the 1970s, central-city residents began to fight successfully against a number of freeway projects in their neighborhoods. The 1970s also saw a renaissance in public transit. Petroleum shortages endangered the continued

growth of American metropolises. Federal and state subsidies to mass public transit increased during the 1970s. But the cost effectiveness of these subsidies was in doubt by the start of the 1980s.

6. During the 1970s, there were significant movements in the direction of regulating land use at a level of government higher than the local municipality or township. Four imaginative models that will have some relevance for the fast-growing Sunbelt metropolises in the 1990s are (a) local limited-growth zoning, (b) statewide land management, (c) protection of designated environmentally endangered areas, and (d) metropolitan land use policymaking combined with obligatory local government implementation.

7. Uncontrolled metropolitan growth since World War II has had some distinct consequences. It has led to suburban sprawl, loss of accountability for many public decisions, and the proliferation of local governments.

8. Uncontrolled metropolitan growth has also been characterized by some distinct biases. It is biased in favor of those who profit from sprawl—particularly land speculators, real estate developers, and large retailing enterprises. It is biased against the conservationist and environmentalist vision of the public good. It is biased against effective citizen input. And, as will be examined in Chapter 10, it may be biased against the interests of poor people and racial minorities.

Chapter 10
Suburbia and
the Challenge of Exclusion

In discussing the myths about suburbanites' ideologies, Chapter 9 pointed out that suburban attitudes varied sharply from person to person and from suburb to suburb on most issues. On one issue, however, the study of Philadelphia suburbs showed remarkable agreement. An overwhelming percentage of white suburbanites of all social classes agreed that suburban communities have a right to exclude people they think are undesirable.[1] Although the survey data reviewed in Chapter 9 did not show that white suburban attitudes are substantially more segregationist than the attitudes of central-city whites, it is apparent that suburban whites in fact live in communities that are more segregated than the communities of central cities. Despite the dramatic gains in black suburbanization in recent years, most suburbs are overwhelmingly white. Does suburban segregation arise by design? Or is it simply the result of free choices that minorities make about where they want to live?

To answer this question, we must start with the issues that dominate local suburban politics, and these tend to be issues that affect exclusion and access. Almost universally in suburbs these issues are taxes, schools, and zoning. The issue of taxes inevitably arises, particularly when the suburb undergoes rapid development. Numerous expensive services must be provided, ranging from schools to police protection to sewers and water. Much of the revenue to provide these services comes from the local property tax. By 1980 property taxes accounted for about 40 percent of all locally raised revenue.[2] Unlike the central cities, in which the property tax burden is spread across the entire city, the property tax burden of suburbia varies from one suburb to another. Each suburban jurisdiction gets property tax revenue only from property within its boundaries. Consequently, suburbs are very sensitive to the politics of attracting industry that pays more than its share of property taxes and of keeping out people (especially low-income families with school-age children) who will add more costs of providing services than they will add revenue to the property tax base. Furthermore, there is growing evidence that the greater the reliance on property taxes in a metropolitan area, the greater are the disparities in income between suburbanites and central-city residents. The implication of this research is that suburbanites in these property-tax-reliant metropolises deliberately seek to keep low-income people out of their suburbs.[3]

Public education is a controversial issue for several reasons. As the central-city school systems were increasingly criticized for delinquency, segregation, racial unrest, and poor education over the past generation,[4] suburban schools were seen as places to escape these problems. Indeed, one oft-cited reason that is believed to motivate upper-middle-class professionals to live in suburbia is the belief that there will be decent schools where their children can be well educated and safe.* Suburbanites, like central-city dwellers, feel that public education is much too important to become bound up with party politics.† Yet several mutually contradictory themes flourish in suburban school politics. On the one hand, a complex of factors impel the suburbs to provide expensive school facilities. Not only do parents want the best for their children, but businesspeople and real estate brokers think that a reputation for good schools will attract upper-income residents with high-status professional occupations. On the other hand, good schools are expensive, and in most suburbs bitter battles recur periodically over school expenditures. Tax-conscious citizens charge that their money is being wasted on superfluous frills. Much of the tax-conscious animosity is directed at teachers who unionized during the 1970s and received substantial improvements in their salaries.

Finally, for the same reasons underlying the tax and school issues, zoning disputes always have the potential to disrupt the peace in the suburbs. Suburbs inevitably go through a phase of rapid growth. During this phase, subdividers and real estate developers construct and sell large numbers of houses. To service the new population, as discussed in the previous chapter, shopping centers and other facilities are built. This situation is always conducive to charges of conflict of interest, graft, sellouts to big developers, absence of planning, and absence of public concern. The conditions under which developers are allowed to operate and the zoning restrictions that are put on the kinds of housing they can build are significant battles at this stage in the suburb's growth.

All three of these issues—taxes, schools, and zoning—deeply affect who gets to live where in suburbia and the metropolis. Do the poor and racial minorities concentrate in the cities by their own free choice? Or are they kept out of the suburbs through the politics of exclusion? Are the upper-middle-income suburbs just naturally populated by people of a very narrow income range? Or do they deliberately exclude people of lower income? Finally, the rise of the women's movement in the past two decades has led to a line of research asking if suburban exclusionary politics has also affected women. How taxes and municipal finance affect these ques-

---

*There is some doubt, however, whether this belief is accurate. In Levittown, hardly anybody cited this as their reason for moving to the suburbs. The most common reason was the need for a bigger house and more space. See Herbert J. Gans, *The Levittowners: Ways of Life and Politics in a New Suburban Community* (New York: Vintage Books, 1967),pp. 32–33. In a study of six eastern and midwestern metropolises, housing and neighborhood conditions were the reasons most often given for moving to the suburbs. See Basil G. Zimmer, *The Metropolitan Community: Its People and Government* (Beverly Hills, Calif.: SAGE Publications, 1970), p.32.

†Roscoe Martin stressed: "Any contact between urban politics and the schools is held to be destructive of sound educational practice." See his *Government and the Suburban School* (Syracuse, N.Y.: Syracuse University Press, 1962), p. 58.

tions has already been discussed in Chapter 6. This chapter examines the question of exclusion as it relates to the three other policy areas—housing, education, and gender.

Exclusion and the Politics of Housing

Michael Danielson argues that racial and class segregation in the contemporary metropolis did not occur by accident. Rather, he sees them as resulting from a deliberate policy of exclusion.[5] The primary aim of the politics of exclusion is class homogeneity, not racial homogeneity. People in affluent neighborhoods do not want property values to drop by allowing cheaper homes to be built nearby or by allowing nonaffluent neighbors to move in. Parents of children in affluent schools do not want their schools flooded with nonaffluent children. Nor do they want their children forcibly transported to less affluent schools. To achieve these exclusionary goals, suburbs can rely on several legal tools. The main ones, as discussed below, are exclusionary zoning, limited-growth zoning, strict subdivision requirements, strict building codes, nonimplementation of fair housing legislation, and prohibitions against subsidized housing. Although the primary aim of these exclusionary devices may be class-based, they put a heavy burden on racial minorities because disproportionate numbers of them have low or moderate incomes.

The Strategies for Exclusion

Exclusionary Zoning

Zoning is the act of specifying what a piece of land may be used for. A zoning ordinance divides the city into different zones for different uses such as reserving some zones for heavy industry, some for commerce, some for light industry, some for single-family homes, some for apartments, and so on. Almost all suburbs of more than 5000 people exercise zoning powers, and about half of the smaller ones also do so.[6]

There are two main ways in which zoning can be used to exclude low-income people. The first is to establish minimum lot sizes and building floor-space requirements. For example, during the 1960s, two-thirds of the developable residential land in Cleveland's suburban Cuyahoga County was zoned for half-acre or larger lots.[7] In addition to specifying large lots, zoning ordinances may also specify minimum lot width and a minimum number of square feet for any home built on the lot. By requiring that big houses be built on wide, large lots, zoning ordinances effectively inflate the cost of housing. This is because it costs more to buy a half-acre lot than a quarter-acre lot, to build a house with 1200 square feet of floor space than one with 900 square feet, and to install sewers, curbs, and water lines in front of a 150-foot-wide lot than in front of a 60-foot-wide lot.

Because large-lot zoning inflates the cost of new housing, its net effect is to exclude people who cannot afford expensive houses. Since racial minorities have disproportionately low and moderate incomes, large-lot zoning imposes a special burden on them. The defenders of large-lot zoning argue, however, that it is needed to protect the value of other homes in the suburb. People who purchase $200,000 homes do not want someone building a $75,000 home next door to them.

A second exclusionary zoning tactic is to prohibit apartments with more than two bedrooms. The moxt exclusive suburbs prohibit apartments entirely. Relatively affluent suburbs permit apartments but prohibit three-bedroom apartments and require a high percentage of one-bedroom apartments in each complex. Michael Danielson reports that in 1976 "over 99 percent of all undeveloped land zoned for residential uses [in the New York metropolitan area] is restricted to single-family housing,"[8] thus excluding apartments.

Not only do these prohibitions discriminate against lower-income people unable to purchase a single-family home, they also discriminate against several categories of people who for one reason or another may not want to live in an entire house during certain periods of their lives—recently divorced people, young single adults, elderly people whose children have left home, and recently married couples. The rising numbers of people in these categories during the 1970s and 1980s created an economic demand for multiple-family buildings that has virtually forced the less exclusionary suburbs to permit apartment construction, townhouse construction, and condominium construction and conversion. Construction of multiple-family units in suburbs during the 1960s and 1970s increased almost five times as fast as did the increase in single-family homes.[9] Today, suburban multi-family complexes have become commonplace.

Limited-Growth Zoning

Limited-growth zoning refers to plans such as those of Ramapo and Petaluma (see Chapter 9) that limit the number of building permits issued each year. Although these are justified on aesthetic grounds of keeping the local community physically attractive or on fiscal grounds of keeping down the costs of adding expensive public services, growth limits inherently are biased against low- and moderate-income people.[10] By limiting the supply of houses while the demand for them is increasing, limited-growth zoning has the net impact of inflating the price of existing housing. This fact has led some observers to speculate that limited-growth zoningis a tool used by the well-to-do to keep out lower- and lower-middle income people.[11] However, a study of 97 northern California communities found that upper-income communities were no more likely to impose growth controls than were other communities,[12] and a study of voter reactions to a growth limitation initiative in Riverside, California, found that upper-status voters were no more likely to support the growth control initiative than were lower-status voters.[13] The most noticeable difference between the advocates and opponents of growth control was their attitude toward government's role in the economy generally. People with the liberal view that government should provide social services and protect the environment tended to support the growth control movement in Riverside regardless of their socioeconomic status. On the other hand, people with a conservative view emphasizing individual property rights and a minimal government role tended to oppose growth control. If these California findings apply to the rest of the nation, they point to an interesting conclusion. Growth control has an exclusionary impact even if the intent of its supporters is not necessarily to practice exclusion. Ironically, lower-income, non-homeowning, environmentally concerned liberals may be supporting policies that work to their economic disadvantage.

Strict Subdivision Requirements

Along with zoning ordinances, municipalities also pass subdivision requirements that oblige developers to put in improvements such as streets, sewers, water lines, and other services whenever they build a new subdivision of homes. By putting the burden for this on the developer, the city is saved the cost of paying for these improvements, and the purchasers of the homes are assured that they will not have to be added later at a much greater cost. In addition to necessary improvements such as streets, water lines, and sanitary sewers, subdivision ordinances may also require curbs, sidewalks, driveways, park space, storm sewers, and minimum setbacks of buildings from property lines. The more improvements that are required, the more expensive the subdivision becomes. Low-income and working-class suburbs often forgo many subdivision requirements.

Strict Building Codes

A city's building code specifies the quality of construction and the types of materials that must be put into a new house. There is clearly a tradeoff between holding down the cost of a new home and using expensive, high-quality construction materials and methods. People in wealthy suburbs often want very strict building codes to ensure that any new neighboring homes will not be cheap. People in low-income suburbs who envision that they might need to add an extension to their house such as a room or a garage will often be very content with lax building codes that will be cheaper to comply with. Strict building codes also tend to be favored by construction contractors and construction unions for the obvious reason that they generate larger sales and higher incomes.

Nonimplementation of Fair Housing Legislation

The federal Fair Housing Act of 1968 prohibits discrimination in the sale or rental of housing. Most states and many municipalities passed comparable laws and have established human rights commissions to investigate complaints of discrimination. Despite this extensive legislation, few human rights commissions have actively pursued their task. Few realtors or homeowners have been sued for refusing to show their homes to minorities. A realtor can easily meet the formal requirements of the law and still discourage minority applicants from buying homes in white neighborhoods. If a realtor simply does not exert as much sales effort while showing a suburban house to racial minorities as he or she exerts in showing the same house to prospective white buyers, the realtor probably will not make as high a percentage of sales to minorities as he or she does to whites. Realtors also "qualify" prospective buyers as to the types of neighborhoods they can afford and be comfortable in before they begin showing houses. Although this undoubt-edly save the realtors from wasting time showing people homes they would not be likely to purchase, it also tends to perpetuate the segregation of neighborhoods along income lines. Although none of these practices are illegal or unethical, they all discourage most racial-minority buyers from using the services of white realtors to find a home in a white suburb.

Prohibiting Subsidized Housing

One clear way to keep out many low-income people is to refuse all attempts to build subsidized housing in the community. All that is needed to accomplish this is for the city council to fail to take the positive steps needed to add subsidized housing. Few suburbs have public housing authorities that would be responsible for subsidized housing. And private organizations seeking to use federal housing programs must get building permits before they can undertake their projects. Many suburbs look favorably on granting such permits if the subsidized housing units will be used mainly for the elderly, but widespread opposition often occurs if the units will be used for low- and moderate-income families. In the upper-income suburb of Birmingham, Michigan, for example, three city council members were voted out of office in April 1978 after they had voted for a plan that would make housing available to low- and moderate-income families. Also on the ballot was a referendum on the housing plan itself. It was resoundingly defeated.[14]

Exclusion in Practice: The Case of Black Jack

How some of these exclusionary devices operate in practice can be seen in the case of a Missouri community with the fascinating name of Black Jack. In 1970 Black Jack was an unincorporated area of 2900 people in Saint Louis County. Although a number of apartment buildings existed in Black Jack, most residents lived in recently built single-family houses in the upper-middle price range. This prevailing upper-middle-income, single-family-home character of the community was threatened in 1969 when the Park View Heights Corporation (a church-sponsored nonprofit group) announced plans to construct 210 rental apartments under a federal program for moderate-income housing.[15]

When the plan was approved by HUD in 1970, the single-family homeowners formed the Black Jack Improvement Association and swiftly organized a drive to incorporate as a municipality in order to transfer zoning control from the county to the local suburb. The county would be less inclined to use its zoning powers to keep subsidized housing out of Black Jack than would a locally elected city council. This blatantly discriminatory motivation for incorporation did not on the surface appear to be a sufficient reason for creating a new municipality in Saint Louis County. Many local leaders felt that the county already suffered from an excess of suburban municipalities and governmental fragmentation. (There were 98 municipalities.) And even though leaders had been unsuccessful in their efforts to unify these fragmented governments, the county had since 1959 refused to grant any new incorporations. Consistent with this precedent, the Saint Louis County planning department recommended against Black Jack's incorporation.

Despite this unfavorable setting for incorporation, political support came from neighboring suburbs that sympathized with the desire of Black Jack residents to preserve the upper-middle-class, single-family-home character of their community. The county approved the incorporation in August 1970, and within three months Black Jack residents drafted a charter, elected a city council, and passed a zoning ordinance disallowing any new multiple-family residential buildings.

As these political events unfolded, Black Jack residents followed a tactic that is very common in exclusionary zoning disputes. Residents never directly mentioned racial integration as their reason for opposing the project. Rather they argued on the economic grounds of preserving the value of their property. Nevertheless, as Michael Danielson points out, many of these economic arguments were euphemistic substitutes for direct arguments against racial integration.[16] Black Jack residents used *code words* that did not mention race but that invoked racial fears in the minds of neighboring suburban whites whose political support was needed for Black Jack's petition for incorporation. The most effective word was Pruitt-Igoe, an infamous housing project in Saint Louis (see pp. 361–362) that conjured up images of poor black welfare recipients living in high-rise slum apartments amid crime, vandalism, and filth. To the sponsors of the project, using code words such as Pruitt-Igoe was simply another form of racial prejudice.[17]

Faced with what it believed to be blatant racial discrimination, the Park View Heights Corporation filed a suit against Black Jack. The incorporation of Black Jack and its new zoning ordinances were attacked as deliberate moves to prevent the housing project. Consequently they were charged with violating the Civil Rights Act of 1964 and the Fair Housing Act of 1968.

At this point, Black Jack became an issue in the national urban politics of the Nixon administration, whose stand on racial integration had not yet solidified. Civil rights groups, including the National Committee Against Discrimination in Housing, were pressuring the administration to take a strong stand on integrating both housing and schools. This was favored by HUD Secretary George Romney, who wanted the administration to swing its prestige against such blatant discrimination practices as those used in Black Jack. Attorney General John Mitchell, on the other hand, wanted the administration to stay aloof from such local matters. The Justice Department finally joined the suit against Black Jack, but did so in a way that made it clear that it would support such suits only when there was blatant discrimination.

While this split was developing within the administration, the federal courts were striking down actions similar to those of Black Jack. Lackawanna, New York, for example, was not allowed to prohibit a black subdivision in one of its white neighborhoods,[18] and Lawton, Oklahoma, was not allowed to zone out minorities or poor people.[19] Against this background, the federal district court ruled against the Park View Heights Corporation, but in 1974 the federal circuit court reversed this and struck down Black Jack's ordinances against the apartments.[20] This ruling was sustained by the United States Supreme Court.

As part of the court settlement, Black Jack was ordered to pay the Park View Heights Corporation $450,000 in damages. Black Jack residents apparently felt that this was a small price to pay to stop the project and buy out the Corporation's option on the land. Although this ended the city's fight with the developers, another suit was filed by black citizens of the St. Louis area. This suit ended by a consent decree in 1982 in which Black Jack agreed to adopt a fair housing ordinance and complete construction on a 135-unit project very similar to the one it had opposed a decade earlier.[21]

Although the Black Jack cases ended happily for St. Louis minorities, they did not set a very useful legal precedent against exclusionary zoning generally. In Black Jack the racial discrimination had been so blatant that it was possible to prove to the court's satisfaction that the intent of city officials had been to discriminate on the grounds of race. But in cases where discrimination was less obvious, federal courts refused to strike down exclusionary zoning. In Arlington Heights, Illinois, for example, the United States Supreme Court refused to strike down an exclusionary zoning ordinance that barred an integrated, subsidized townhouse project because no one could prove that the city officials had shown an intent to discriminate racially.[22]

Development in a Nonexclusionary Setting

What would happen if suburbs dropped their exclusionary tools and simply let developers construct homes in response to people's demands? To investigate this, Michael Danielson and Jamison Doig compared development patterns in two New York metropolitan communities.[23] The northern suburbs of Westchester County began adopting large-lot zoning and other exclusionary land use tactics as early as 1912. The result has been to preserve most of the county's semirural atmosphere for a fairly affluent citizenry, the most successful of whom live in communities such as the very wealthy Scarsdale. To the extent that Westchester County has working-class or lower-middle-class people, they tend to concentrate in the very old cities such as Yonkers. Most of Westchester County, however, stands as a model of how upper- and upper-middle-income elites can segregate themselves in communities that isolate them from the nastiest of today's urban problems.

In contrast to Westchester County's policy of exclusion, Danielson and Doig compared the development of Staten Island (the New York City borough of Richmond) during the 1960s. Until the 1960s, Staten Island remained about half undeveloped. Then the linking of Staten Island to Manhattan by bridge in 1964 spurred a construction boom, and about 72,000 new residents were added by 1970. Land use in Staten Island was unfettered by any of the usual legal devices discussed earlier. New York City had no comprehensive land use plan for the island. Minimum lot sizes put no constraints on builders. And no subdivision regulations were used.

As a result of this situation, building contractors were not obliged to build big, expensive homes that would exclude moderate- and low-income people. They were free to respond to the demands of the market and build whatever types of houses would bring them the greatest profit. What they built in fact were small, inexpensive homes packed together at a fairly high density of eight per acre. Although this practice was condemned by architectural critics for its lack of aesthetic concern, the houses were a big hit with working-class and lower-middle-class families that were excluded from Westchester and other suburbs but desperately wanted houses they could afford to buy.

Because there are so few studies of places like Staten Island that suburbanized without exclusionary controls, it is impossible to know for certain whether Staten Island is the model of what would happen if all exclusionary controls were removed. Rather, Staten Island and Westchester County exemplify the opposite extremes of a tradeoff between having no land use controls and having highly exclusionary controls. The less exclusionary a community makes its zoning laws, the more able builders are to respond to the demands of the market.

Exclusionary Politics: Suburbia and Beyond

Costs of Home Building

Compounding the problem of suburban exclusionary tactics is the general fact that the economies of home building throughout the nation have made it increasingly expensive to provide low-cost housing for low-income people regardless of where they live. One of the most telling statistics here is the percent of housing units that are owner-occupied. It jumped from 43 percent in 1940 to 61.9 percent in 1960, but in the next twenty-year period it edged upward much more slowly and reached only 64.7 percent in 1983.[24] The dramatic expansion of home ownership came to a halt in the 1970s because the costs of housing construction and purchasing began to escalate. Two of the most important factors driving up housing costs in the 1970s and 1980s were high interest rates and high land costs. In 1970, land comprised about 12 percent of the selling price of the average home. By the end of the decade this had risen to nearly 25 percent.[25]

If the suburbs had begun to open up to minorities in the 1950s instead of the 1970s (when costs began to soar), it would have been much easier for upwardly mobile racial minorities to suburbanize than it is today. Again, land was cheaper then in relation to the price of a house. There were fewer subdivision requirements such as sewers, sidewalks, and curbs, each of which drives up the initial cost of a home. And interest rates were lower. As we noted in Chapter 2, the great post-World War II suburban boom was funded in great measure by the long-term, low-interest, fixed-rate, low-down-payment mortgage. As these loans have become rarer in the 1980s, it has become harder for everybody to upgrade their housing. This has put a double burden on the racial minorities, whose average annual income is lower than that of most whites.

The above considerations most directly affect middle-income people who seek to purchase their homes, but indirectly they also affect lower-income people who seek to rent homes. By and large, racial minorities pay higher rents than whites for similar housing.[26] We will examine in Chapter 13 a wide variety of federal housing

policies that have sought to ease the rental costs of low-income people and to eliminate racial discrimination. In reference to the politics of exclusion it must be noted
that there is more publicly supported rental housing in suburbia today than at any
previous time. Some of this has gone to racial minorities, but the lion's share has
probably gone to low-income white families and to senior citizens.

Inclusionary Zoning

As an antidote to the exclusionary impact of all the above tactics, a number of
states have begun forcing suburbs to adopt *inclusionary zoning* plans that will
increase the size of their low-income populations.[27] The leader of inclusionary zoning was New Jersey whose supreme court obligated all municipalities to provide
housing opportunities for low-income and moderate-income people. The court
first imposed this burden on Mount Laurel, New Jersey, but in 1983,[28] after successful foot-dragging on Mount Laurel's part, the court in a decision popularly called
Mount Laurel II ordered all municipalities to discard zoning and subdivision
restrictions that are not necessary to protect health and safety and to take affirmative steps to increase their number of low-income housing units.[29]

A common tactic of inclusionary zoning is to oblige each subdivision developer
to set aside a minimum percent of housing units below a certain price level that
would be affordable by low-income people. Oak Park, Illinois, a Chicago suburb,
adopted a novel plan of subsidizing the integration of the city's apartment buildings. Under the plan, residents could obtain up to $300 in rent subsidies in 1985 if
they moved into an integrated apartment building, and owners of integrated
buildings could receive grants up to $1,000 for building improvements.[30]

Exclusion and the Politics of Schools

As discussed earlier, much of suburban school politics revolves around issues of
quality, cost, facilities, and teacher negotiations. Because such issues dominate
newspaper accounts of suburban school politics, it is easy to forget that all of this
occurs within a framework of racial and class exclusion. Although this exclusion is
not directly mentioned in law, its net effect in the typical metropolis is to concentrate racial-minority children in the central-city school district and to stratify a
large number of medium-sized suburban school districts into varying levels of
affluence.

Again, we must ask whether this stratification has come about by accident or by
design. Just as the Black Jack case illustrated that economic reasons given for exclusion in housing are often a subterfuge for underlying racial motivations, we also
must ask whether the exclusion of minorities from suburban schools is a natural
consequence of residential patterns or whether it results from deliberate attempts
to segregate. The terms given to these two possible explanations are *de jure* and *de
facto* segregation.

De Jure and De Facto Segregation

De jure segregation refers to segregated school systems that were required by law. Historically, an area with segregated schools had two separate school systems— one for white children and one for nonwhite children. Each system had its own separate school board, its own separate staff, and its own separate school build- ings. This practice was sanctioned by the United States Supreme Court. In 1896 the Court ruled that separate public facilities for blacks and whites met the Four- teenth Amendment's equal protection requirement as long as the separate facili- ties were equal.[31] This was the famous separate-but-equal doctrine, and several states used this ruling to justify the establishment of separate school systems for whites and nonwhites. In 1927 the Supreme Court specifically approved the separate-but-equal principal for public schools.[32] By the mid-twentieth century, seventeen states plus the District of Columbia legally required segregated schools, and another four states permitted segregation at the local level. However, the non- white systems were never given as many resources as the white systems, thus mak- ing a mockery of the provision that the separate systems be equal.

Black civil rights leaders, working through the National Association for the Advancement of Colored People (NAACP), spent the first half of the twentieth century attempting to get these dual systems declared unconstitutional. In a series of decisions from 1938 to 1950, the United States Supreme Court chipped away at the separate-but-equal doctrine by forcing state law schools in Missouri, Okla- homa, and Texas to admit black students.[33]

All of these developments came to a climax in the famous 1954 *Brown v. Board of Education* decision in which the Supreme Court unanimously struck down the dual school systems as violating the equal protection clause of the United States Constitution.[34] The schools were ordered to desegregate with all deliberate speed. However, the desegregation that followed was much more deliberate than speedy. The United States Army was required to protect students during the forced deseg- regation of the Little Rock, Arkansas, high school in 1957, and federal marshals were required to desegregate the University of Alabama and the University of Mis- sissippi in the early 1960s. Despite the slow progress of desegregation in its first dozen years, by 1980 southern public schools had achieved substantial integration and were in fact less segregated than the rest of the nation. About 57 percent of black children in the South still attended shcools that were over 50 percent minor- ity. By contrast, the figure nationwide for blacks attending such schools was approximately 63 percent.[35]

The reason why the South achieved greater desegregation by 1980 can be traced in part to differences in the patterns of segregation in the South and the rest of the nation. Outside the South, there were usualy no laws requiring racial segregation in schools. Rather, the schools were segregated in fact because minorities lived in one part of the city while whites lived in another. This has been called *de facto* segregation.

Coping with de facto segregation is much harder than coping with de jure segre- gation. Although a variety of techniques have been attempted in de facto segregated cities to get black and white children into the same classrooms (magnet schools, voluntary transfers, open enrollment plans, paired schools), the most direct tactic was the involuntary busing of both black and white school children to integrated schools. In 1971 the United States Supreme Court ruled that federal district courts may impose forced busing to desegregate if there is evidence that the segregation results from legal measures to alter school boundaries or to impose residential segregation.[36]

Busing and White Flight

The Court's busing decisions were extremely unpopular. As Table 10-1 shows, an overwhelming majority of whites opposed busing to achieve a better racial balance. From the perspective of metropolitan exclusionary politics, the most significant fact about the Court's busing decisions was that they placed the burden of desegregation squarely on the shoulders of working- and lower-middle-income central-city residents. The most controversial busing decisions of the 1970s involved central-city school systems such as Boston, Atlanta, Memphis, New York, Milwaukee, and Cleveland. Since the school-age populations of many of these cities were becoming overwhelmingly minority, however, there were limits as to how much desegregation could be achieved by busing within the central cities. In New York City, for example, the white population of public schools dropped from 68 percent in 1957 to 29 percent in 1977.[37] New York City's schools had not simply desegregated; they had resegregated. Nor is New York an extreme example. By 1980, only three of the nation's twenty-five largest school districts had more white students than minority students.[38]

According to critics of busing, the movement from segregation to desegregation to resegregation stems in large part from *white flight*. White parents with enough money could flee the whole problem of desegregation. If they did not want to flee by actually moving to the suburbs, they could send their children to private academies or parochial schools. Throughout the South and much of the North, private academies and parochial schools began to flourish in the 1970s, whereas only a decade earlier many of them had such deep financial difficulties that they were on the verge of extinction.[39]

Table 10-1. Opinion on Busing to Achieve a Better Racial Balance in Public Schools

	Favor	Oppose	Don't know
Whites	18.6%	79.1%	2.3%
Blacks	52.3%	39.6%	8.1%

Source: Davis, James Allan and Smith, Tom W.: *General Social Surveys, 1972–1985* [machine-readable data file]. Principal Investigator, James A. Davis; Senior Study Director, Tom W. Smith. NORC ed. Chicago: National Opinion Research Center, producer, 1985; Storrs, CT: Roper Public Opinion Research Center, University of Connecticut, distributor.

One of the most articulate spokespersons for the argument that busing precipi-tated white flight was Diane Ravitch, whose studies found that between 1973, when forced busing started in Boston, and 1975, the city lost more than a third of its white pupils, while its minority population increased.[40] In Atlanta busing went into effect in 1972. Between then and 1975 the black share of school enrollment increased from 56 to 87 percent. In Memphis busing started in 1973, and by 1976 the black share of enrollment increased from 50 to 70 percent.[41]

Although these percentages are important, they cannot be attributed solely to busing. Even where busing did not occur, white enrollment declined during the 1970s. Christine Rossell studied the enrollment records of eighty-six central-city school systems between 1963 and 1973. Only four of these cities had a statistically significant decline in white enrollment after busing began.[42] The biggest enroll-ment declines appeared to occur immediately before and after the busing deci-sion. In subsequent years, enrollment trends returned to their prebusing patterns. Even where busing was met with violence, a similar pattern emerged. During the three years after Boston started busing in 1973, the reaction was so violent that police had to be stationed all year in some of the schools. Descriptions of South Boston High School made it sound more like a battlefield than a school. But by the fall of 1977 most of the antibusing fervor had dissipated, and the children were bused to school without incident.

The policy implications of these facts are very difficult to sort out. But it is apparent that white flight was not anticipated very well by the advocates of deseg-regation, and it has led to problems we as a nation have failed to cope with success-fully.[43] It has left most large central cities such as Washington, Chicago, New York, and Atlanta with white school populations so small as to make meaningful central-city desegregation impossible. It has also led to demands that suburbs should share in the desegregation along with central cities.

Busing and the Suburbs

Is it possible to enlist the suburbs in the quest to desegregate the schools? The record to date is not very encouraging. The only places where desegregation could easily include the suburbs were those in which the school districts followed county lines. This happened primarily in southern and border states, where the county has traditionally been the strongest basic unit of government.

In most instances, however, suburbs were exempted from forced busing. A 1974 court ruling refused to extend busing to the Detroit suburbs because it could not be shown that the suburban school districts had drawn their boundaries delib-erately to exclude blacks.[44] And in 1977 the Supreme Court relied on the same principle (inability to show offical intent to segregate) to overrule a lower court order that would have forced desegregation of the suburbs and central city in the consolidated city-county of Indianapolis-Marion County, Indiana.[45]

Critics of the courts object to this principle that intent to desegregate must be shown before desegregation can be ordered between cities and suburbs. In Los Angeles, for example, supporters of desegregation attempted to get the California courts to merge City of Los Angeles schools with those of more than 100 school districts in three separate suburban counties.[46] Supporters of this plan argued that the concentration of racial minorities in the City of Los Angeles was in reality de jure segregation because governments at all levels had consistently sanctioned exclusionary practices such as the ones described earlier in this chapter. Federal loan programs had guaranteed many of the suburban mortgages. Federal and state highway programs had built the transportation network enabling suburbia to be built. And the state had sanctioned all the exclusionary zoning and planning devices that preserved suburbia from massive racial integration. These critics charged that application of the intent-to-segregate principle must be broadened to include the whole range of government actions whose effect is to concentrate minorities in the central-city schools. From this viewpoint, there is no distinction between de jure and de facto segregation. All segregation is de jure. Before the California Supreme Court could rule on this, however, California voters amended the state constitution to prohibit the state courts from imposing any busing in excess of principles established by the federal courts.[47] The net effect of this seemed to be to exempt Los Angeles suburbs from that city's school desegregation plans.

However much critics might argue that all segregation is de jure and that there is no valid distinction between de jure and de facto segregation, the federal courts appear to take that distinction very seriously. Even in central-city desegregation cases the Supreme Court relied on the principle of official intent to desegregate to uphold busing plans in Columbus[48] and Dayton, Ohio.[49] In desegregation cases involving busing across city boundaries into the suburbs, the courts have been very reluctant to call such segregation de jure.

The three major examples of involving the suburbs in school desegregation have been Louisville, Kentucky; Wilmington, Delaware; and St. Louis, Missouri. In Louisville, the central city and Jefferson County merged their two separate school systems in 1975 and initiated a countywide desegregation program. A federal court ordered that all schools in the county contain between 14 and 18 percent minority enrollment. Although greeted by considerable white protest, this project was carried out successfully.[50]

In Wilmington, the city school system was excluded from a 1968 statewide school district consolidation plan that changed the boundaries of all other local school districts in the State of Delaware. Ruling that this exclusion had the effect of legally concentrating the black students in the Wilmington school district, thus constituting de jure segregation, the federal courts ordered busing between the suburban and central-city schools.[51]

But the most imaginative central-city/suburban approach to desegregation was that in St. Louis. In 1980 the St. Louis city school system began a court-ordered desegregation plan only to find that a mere 22 percent of the children in the schools were white—too small a percentage to produce meaningful integration. Citing this statistic, the city schools asked the federal courts to extend the desegregation order to include 23 suburban school districts on the grounds that segregation was a metropolitan problem, not just a central-city problem.[52] Faced with the possibility that federal courts would force a prescribed desegregation plan on them, the suburban districts in 1983 voluntarily negotiated with the St. Louis schools and reached an agreement to gradually increase each suburban district's minority enrollment to between 15 and 25 percent over the next five years. According to their plan, this would be accomplished by busing an eventual total of 15,000 minority children from St. Louis to the suburbs and 15,000 white children from the suburbs into St. Louis. Because the busing of whites would be voluntary, it was necessary to make the city schools attractive to the suburban children. To accomplish this, several magnet schools were established to provide superior instruction in subjects like mathematics, arts, communications, and sciences.[53] Participating school districts were exempted from further litigation until 1988. By the time the first interdistrict busing began in the fall of 1983, the agreement was under fire from the City of St. Louis and the State of Missouri (both concerned about the cost of the plan), a small group of black parents (concerned that more black children than white children would be bused), and the federal government (which earlier had supported desegregating St. Louis schools).[54] Despite these objections, the federal courts upheld the agreement and ordered the State of Missouri to pay most of the plan's costs (estimated at $30–100 million per year).[55]

While these developments took place in St. Louis, political pressures were growing to restrict the role of federal courts in handling busing cases. Congress in 1980 passed bills that would prevent the Justice Department from suing to obtain school desegregation through forced busing, but that bill was vetoed by President Carter.[56] The need for such a bill became moot in 1981, however, when the Reagan administration declared its opposition to starting any new busing suits.[57] As if to emphasize its intent, the Justice Department asked the Supreme Court to uphold antibusing initiatives that had passed in California and Washington.[58] (The Supreme Court eventually upheld the California initiative but struck down the one in the State of Washington.[59]) And in 1984 the Reagan Justice Department entered into a consent decree with the Bakersfield, California, school district that would rely on magnet schools to attract white students voluntarily rather than forcing them into minority schools through involuntary busing.[60]

Where do these conflicting developments leave us as we enter the last decade of the twentieth century? Four generalizations seem reasonable. First, there no longer appears to be a great deal of political support in Congress, the public opinion polls, the federal courts, or the White House for achieving desegregation through involuntary busing, although Democratic administrations tend to be more receptive than do Republican ones. In 1987, the Supreme Court refused to review a lower court ruling that permitted Norfolk, Virginia, to end its desegregation plan even though that action would increase the number of black children attending all-black schools.[61] Although it is too early to say that the Supreme Court has thrown in the towel on desegregation, this ruling probably means that there will be less mandatory busing in the 1990s than there was in the 1970s and 1980s.

Second, despite the interdistrict desegregation plans in Wilmington, Louisville, and St. Louis, it seems very unlikely that the next few years will see an explosion of metroplitan-wide desegregation. Public school desegregation is likely to remain primarily a central-city responsibility. Third, despite the unpopularity of busing, several commentators have noted that no one has yet found any other effective way to desegregate.[62] A study of 879 Louisville-area whites in 1976 concluded that it was not primarily the busing that whites resent; it was the fact of having their children forced into schools with large numbers of blacks.[63] When the St. Louis plan reached the end of its first five-year phase in 1988, only 650 suburban white children were voluntarily riding into the city schools, barely one-fourth of the number hoped for.[64] This resistance to busing nonminority children into the city schools occurred even though these children were offered the chance to attend special magnet schools with superior educational offerings.

Finally, it must be asked what consequences busing has had for the educational achievement of the children involved. Although most scholarly research on this question appears optimistic, researchers are by no means united. On the pessimistic side, David Armor argues that busing has not made significant improvement in the educational achievement of minority children.[65] On the optimistic side of the argument, the most prominent spokesman is probably Willis Hawley, who conducted an elaborate study of ten court cases, desegregation activities in seventeen cities, and a review of over 1,200 other studies of desegregation. Hawley found that achievement scores of white children did not go down. He maintains that desegregation also reduced racial isolation of minorities.[66]

Disparities in School Financing

The division of public education in metropolitan areas into one large central-city school district surrounded by several medium-sized suburban districts has not only exaggerated racial separation, it has also generated severe disparities in the financing of public education. This is because nearly half the money for public schools comes from locally levied property taxes. Because of this, a small school district with an electric power plant, a large shopping center, or an industrial park will have abundant tax resources for public schools, whereas a neighboring district without these developments will be short on tax resources. The term for this uneven distribution of property tax resources is *fiscal disparities*.

The problem of fiscal disparities came to a head in 1971 in the California court case of *Serrano v. Priest*.[67] Serrano lived in a school district that lacked substantial property tax resources and that consequently found it hard to spend as much on schools as nearby districts that had a better property tax base. Serrano sued the State of California for not providing equal educational opportunity for all children and all school districts in the state. The California Supreme Court agreed that the fiscal disparities inherent in the property tax financing of public education violated the state constitution and ordered California to find an alternative financing method.

No sooner had the California Supreme Court made this decision than parents in other states sought to get the principle applied nationwide under the equal protection clause of the United States Constitution. A San Antonio, Texas, case came before the Supreme Court for decision in 1973. San Antonio was divided into several school districts, and the district for the Mexican-American community had very few property tax resources to support its schools. However, in *Rodriguez v. San Antonio School District*, the United States Supreme Court refused to apply the Serrano principle under federal law. The Court agreed that the states relied too heavily on the property tax. However, unless the state's constitution had a provision covering the allocation of school resources, the Court would not hear the case. The "ultimate solution must come from the lawmakers and from the democratic pressures of those who elect them."[68]

Although the Rodriguez case foreclosed the federal courts as an avenue for equalizing school finance, it did not foreclose the use of state courts, and several state courts ruled in favor of ending the fiscal disparities inherent in relying on the property tax to fund schools. The most volatile case occurred in New Jersey, where that state's supreme court in 1973 ordered the legislature to come up with a state income tax to equalize school finances.[69] In New Jersey the biggest fiscal disparities were between declining old central cities, such as Newark, and the growing, affluent suburbs. When the legislature repeatedly failed to follow these directions, the supreme court closed down all New Jersey schools in the summer of 1976 on the grounds that they were operating in violation of the state constitution. Faced with this pressure, the legislature relented and passed a state income tax that enabled the state to absorb a major share of school funding in New Jersey.

The policy of equalizing school finance has been plagued with political difficulties. First, if school district revenues must be equalized to a common level throughout the state, bitter political battles will occur over whether revenues of most districts will be brought up to that of the highest-spending districts or whether they will be brought down to that of the lowest-spending districts. Second, although the *Serrano* decision is based on the assumption that poor people live primarily in the property tax-poor districts, the truth of this assumption has not yet been demonstrated. In its *Rodriguez* decision, the Supreme Court specifically cited studies that this was not the normal pattern.

Some of these political difficulties materialized in the attempts to implement the court-ordered equalization of educational resources in New Jersey and California, although they did not prevent some progress from being made. A 1981 study of implementation in New Jersey found that the state portion of school finances rose from 23.6 percent in 1975 to 33.8 percent in 1980. This helped to equalize tax rates between school districts, but it still left the poorest districts unable to match the richest districts in per-pupil expenditure.[70] Likewise, in California the state's share of educational expenditures increased from 31.0 percent in 1971 to 59.4 percent in 1979. However, this still left room for the wealthier districts to spend more than the poorer districts, and the Proposition 13 tax-reduction movement in 1978 dissipated the attempts of reformers to make further equalization of school expenditures in that state.[71] In Texas, by contrast, continuing fiscal disparities brought the Texas school finance system back into the courts more than a decade after the *Rodriguez* decision. A Texas district court in 1987 ruled that the state's school finance system was unconstitutional. The 100 poorest districts in the state spent only $2,987 per pupil in 1985–1986, while the 100 wealthiest districts spent $7,233 per pupil.[72] The case will next go to the Texas Supreme Court for final ruling.

Exclusion, Housing, and Schools: Some Caveats

The previous discussion reviewed considerable research, court cases, and political events that all point toward the conclusion that the suburbs do indeed follow the politics of excluding racial minorities and low-income whites. Although it would be impossible to deny that the multicentered nature of the contemporary metropolis does indeed foster exclusion, we should be very careful not to overgeneralize about what this means. In fact we should specifically note some of the things that this does not mean.

First, the politics of exclusion does not mean that white suburbanites are racists or that they are unconcerned with the plight of the poor. Research reviewed in Chapter 9 showed that there is considerable heterogeneity in the beliefs and political attitudes of suburbanites.

Second, the politics of exclusion does not mean that all suburbs are exclusive. By definition, only a minority of suburbs can be exclusive. One might paraphrase Ortega y Gassett's famous quip and observe that when all the suburbs become exclusive, then none of them will any longer be exclusive. As noted in Chapter 9, suburbs fall into all income and class categories. Only about 15 to 20 percent are "homogeneous high-income enclaves."[73] The vast majority of suburbs contain a wide range of people as measured by their incomes and occupations.

Third, the politics of exclusion does not always mean that affluent suburbia is a noose around the neck of the impoverished central cities. Although this may indeed be the case in some of the big, old metropolises of the Northeast and Midwest, it is not universally true. As shown in Chapter 6, in the newer, smaller metropolises the central cities are usually more affluent than the suburbs. And some of the sharpest fiscal disparities occur between rich and poor suburbs rather than between suburbia as a whole and the central cities.[74]

Finally, even if all the exclusionary devices were removed and we lived in a world of perfect free choice, it seems likely that people would still cluster together in neighborhoods that had similar income, ethnic, and racial compositions.

Having expressed these caveats, however, we are still left with a multicentered metropolis that is not a perfect model of free choice. It is characterized by some distinctive consequences and biases.

Suburbs and Women

Do women in suburbs experience a lifestyle that is significantly better or worse than the lifestyles of central-city women? This is a very difficult question to answer, because there are so many different kinds of suburbs and such a great variety of women. Nevertheless, this question has been drawing increasing attention in feminist literature, and at least four generalizations seem plausible.

First, the myth of homogeneous, white, upper-middle-income suburbia (see pp. 249–253) with its ideal suburban family in which the husband brings home the paycheck and the wife devotes herself exclusively to the home is no longer accurate—if indeed it ever was. Some suburban women fit this image, but many suburban women work outside the home, are divorced parents, are widows, are single, or fall into any number of different life situations.

Second, some researchers argue that the suburbs were designed around this mythical image. With their low population density, their larger houses and yards, and their segregation of residential areas from commercial activities and busy streets, the suburbs encourage only one female role—wife and mother.[75] Single parents, for example, are likely to find these same design features hindrances to their attempts to find such things as day-care facilities, convenience stores within walking distance, and other needed services.

Third, for women without automobiles, or for women in one-automobile families, suburbia presents a major problem of access to stores, community facilities, and social services. Most suburbs are poorly served by public transportation. Even when bus service exists from the suburb to the central city, people are usually left to their own resources to travel around within the suburb itself. Without a car, a woman is at the disadvantage of having to walk down a major highway with no sidewalks just to visit a supermarket, a drugstore, or a doctor's office.[76] This disadvantage is especially severe for older women and for women with young children. Not surprisingly, a number of researchers report a greater physical and social isolation among suburban women than among central-city women.[77]

Finally, there is some evidence that married suburban women are less satisfied with where they live than are central-city women, suburban men, or central-city men.[78] It is difficult to evaluate this evidence, however, because the people interviewed did not constitute representative samples of any large population groups, and the samples tended to be disproportionately upper-middle-income people. Nevertheless, the aspect of suburban living most appealing to the men was that they viewed it as a retreat, a means to get away from the tensions of their jobs. Women tended to like the informal socializing they found in suburbs, but they complained about isolation and a lack of stimulation in their suburban settings.

The Consequences and Biases of the Politics of Exclusion

Because of the long-term housing boom from the end of World War II until the 1960s, the almost universal adaptation of the automobile as the basic means of mass transportation, the proliferating incorporation of suburban governments, and the decentralization not only of retail shopping but of many kinds of employment opportunities, the central business district lost its dominance over the metropolis. More and more the metropolitan areas became multicentered rather than centered on a single central business district. Los Angeles rather than New York became the model for the city of the future.

Politically, the multicentered metropolis is characterized by a series of geographic fiefdoms that feud with one another over commercial facilities and tax bases and that exercise almost unfettered control over zoning decisions. Individually, if a suburb is well located it can maximize both high services and low taxes for its residents by behaving as a geographic fiefdom and yielding few concessions to its less fortunate neighbors. As Robert Wood points out, all suburbs have hoped to emulate this model.[79] From the vantage point of the metropolis as a whole, however, this geographic fiefdomization has several negative political consequences. Since these consequences are described in considerable detail in the following chapters, they will simply be outlined here.

Separation of Public Needs from Available Resources

Because local governments rely excessively on locally imposed property taxes for their local revenue, the division of the metropolis into hundreds of relatively small taxing units tends to separate the public needs from the available resources. The property tax revenue generated by an electric power plant or a factory or a shopping center goes only to the local governments that operate in that locality. This has especially caused problems in financing small suburban school districts as well as school districts of central cities with a declining property tax base. If the school district area is very large—covering an entire central city or an entire county—it has schools located in affluent neighborhoods as well as in poor neighborhoods. It also has several large payers of property taxes within its boundaries. The residential areas of the city, including the poor neighborhoods, share in the property tax revenue generated by the factories, the central business district, and the commercial establishments. School districts are thus able to pool all of the available tax resources and redistribute them according to their priorities and their estimations of the public needs. If poor neighborhoods fail to get their fair share of these resources, the fault lies not in the lack of local resources but in the inequities of the established priorities.[80]

In most suburbs, however, the opposite situation prevails. There is no mechanism for sharing property tax resources. This fiscal imbalance has led to what the Advisory Commission on Intergovernmental Relations calls "the rise of lopsided communities."[81] The suburban school district with expensive homes, light industry, and elegant shopping centers will of necessity enjoy tremendous advantages over a neighboring school district that has lower-status homes, no industry, and no shopping centers.

These disparities in tax resources, it must be pointed out, do not derive from the fact of the multicentered metropolis itself as much as from the fact that the multicentered metropolis relies so heavily for its tax revenue on locally imposed property taxes. In order to alleviate these disparities, most states have taken steps to provide state aid to local school districts. The state aid normally derives from state sales taxes or income taxes and is normally distributed among the state's school districts according to complex formulas based on the number of pupils and the fiscal needs of the school districts. And, as shown earlier in the cases of California and New Jersey, the states moved decisively during the 1970s to reduce reliance on the property tax.

Despite attempts to iron out the differences in property tax inequities, most suburban municipalities and school districts in the United States still rely heavily on local property taxes for their revenue. As long as this remains the case, the multicentered metropolis will continue to separate public needs from available public resources. This separation will obviously continue to favor the residents of areas with the public resources (i.e., suburbs with a substantial tax base) and disfavor the residents of both central cities and suburbs with a scanty tax base.

Biases

The poor and the racial minorities are most directly disfavored by the multicentered metropolis. Because the multicentered metropolis separates public needs from available resources, local governments in the metropolis are not able to apply all of their potential resources to programs that deal with the special problems of the poor and the racial minorities. Because local municipalities can use their zoning powers to exclude low-income residents, low-income families (both white and black) are prevented from living near the places where the most dynamic growth is occurring both in jobs and other economic opportunities—around the suburban shopping centers.

The suburbs are not promoting extensive integration either racially or socioeconomically.[82] This bias of the multicentered metropolis has had several results, particularly in public education. The poorest school districts are often peopled with lower-income residents and the most affluent school districts with upper-middle-income residents. In metropolises with large minority populations, central-city schools have higher percentages of minority pupils. Furthermore, the greater the proliferation of governments in a metropolis, the more likely that metropolis is to have large disparities in average income among its municipalities.[83]

Theoretically, this bias against the racial minorities and the poor does not necessarily have to result from the multicentered metropolis. It is conceivable that within the existing pattern of suburban development, property taxes could be equalized, minorities could be given access to the better school districts, transit systems could be built to give inner-city residents easy access to suburban job locations, low-income public housing could be relocated into the suburbs, and exclusionary zoning could be minimized. But the controversy that has erupted over attempts to put these measures into practice in places such as Black Jack or South Boston indicates that significantly reducing the bias will be terribly difficult. Considerable progress has been made over the past decade, and progress will probably continue to be made in coming years. On balance, however, the contemporary state of governmental dispersion in the suburbs remains biased against the poor and racial minorities. Additionally, a certain segment of feminist thought also sees suburbia as having distinct biases against women.

Summary

1. Although there may not be significant differences in the political attitudes of suburbanites and central-city whites, there are clear differences in their living patterns. Central-city whites are much more likely to live in integrated com-

munities than are suburban whites. This chapter examines whether this results from free choice or whether the minorities are largely excluded from the suburbs.

2. The issues in suburban politics that focus on the politics of exclusion are taxes, schools, and zoning.

3. There are several legal tools in the politics of exclusion. These range from large-lot zoning to prohibitions against subsidized housing. Normally these tactics are justified on economic or aesthetic grounds. Their practical effect is to exclude low- and moderate-income people. Since racial minorities have disproportionate numbers of low- and middle-income people, exclusionary politics place a heavy burden on the minorities.

4. Black Jack, Missouri, presents the example of a community that incorporated and drafted an exclusionary zoning ordinance specifically aimed at keeping out a subsidized housing project that was expected to be heavily black.

5. The settlement of Staten Island in the 1960s presents an example of development in a nonexclusionary setting. Not faced with the rigid requirements of exclusionary zoning, building contractors constructed thousands of homes that could be afforded by working-class and lower-middle-income people.

6. The main issue of exclusionary politics in public education is whether the separation of white from minority schoolchildren has resulted from deliberate actions by officials (de jure segregation) or whether it is simply the natural result of residential patterns (de facto segregation).

7. Since the majority of federal court busing decisions have been restricted to single school districts and have not imposed busing between central cities and suburbs, lower- and lower-middle-income central-city residents have borne most of the burden of desegregation. As white parents have either taken their children out of the public schools or moved out of the city, some observers have called this "white flight" and charged that it is a natural reaction to the policy of busing. Other observers maintain that white flight has occurred even where busing was not implemented and thus is not evidence that the policy of busing is a failure.

8. Because school districts rely heavily on property taxes for their funding, they are particularly affected by the problem of fiscal disparities discussed in Chapter 6. Although the federal courts have not intervened in this issue, state courts in New Jersey, California, and elsewhere have actively sought to minimize fiscal disparities by reducing the heavy reliance of schools on the property tax.

9. A certain body of feminist literature perceives the design of suburbia as having certain exclusionary effects on some women. Particularly, the lack of public transit, the low-density housing, and the less extensive provision of social services than in the central cities make it hard for many suburban women to have access to commercial conveniences and to community facilities.

10. The existence of exclusionary politics does not mean that white suburbanites are racists, that all suburbs follow exclusionary policies, that the suburbs universally impose an economic burden on the central cities, or even that the metropolis would suddenly become integrated in terms of race and income if all the exclusionary devices were removed.

11. The existence of exclusionary politics in the multicentered metropolis does, however, have some definite consequences and biases. Its major economic consequence is that it separates public needs from available resources. Its major bias is against the low- and moderate-income elements of the population and against the racial minorities that have high percentages of low- and moderate-income people.

Chapter 11
The Politics of Metropolitan Reform

A major task of governments in metropolitan areas has been to cope with the consequences of the multicentered metropolis, outlined in the previous two chapters. *At a minimum*, pressures have increased rather than decreased on urban governments to provide services for growing populations in the suburbs. But the pressures on urban governments are rarely put in minimal terms. Urban governments are usually pressured by a variety of groups not only to provide at least minimum levels of service for all residents, but also, as shown in Chapter 9 and 10, to equalize tax inequities, to find the resources to satisfy public needs, to control suburban sprawl, and to simplify the overlapping and complex structure of governments in metropolitan areas.

The Rationale for Metropolitan Reform

How urban governments should cope with the problems associated with the multicentered metropolis has been the subject of considerable dispute involving a wide spectrum of opinions and value judgments. At one end of the spectrum are those who believe that the problems cannot be dealt with unless the whole system of government is scrapped and a new, general-purpose government established at the metropolitan level. At the other end of the spectrum are those who believe that adequate methods of governing the metropolis can be found without resorting to a metropolitan government as such.

The Scrap-the-System-and-Start-Over School of Thought

According to those who would scrap the whole contemporary system of metropolitan governments and start over, the flaws of the multicentered metropolis are so deeply rooted in its chaotic governmental structure that the structure itself must be rebuilt. The efficacy of the present governmental apparatus is brought into question. And the apparatus itself is seen as antidemocratic, not accountable to the electorate, inefficient, and not conducive to meaningful citizen participation. This is a devastating indictment of the present system, and it is presented by some distinguished scholars and prestigious organizations.

The argument that the present system is antidemocratic is made most forcefully, perhaps, by political scientist Robert Wood.[1] Participation in suburban political affairs is very limited. Election turnouts in suburban municipal elections are much lower than are turnouts for corresponding elections in the central cities or even for county offices. And the attempt of the suburbs to recapture the Jeffersonian ideal of small-town democracy very close to the people is misleading, for such small-town governments are seldom truly democratic. Even the famed town meetings of colonial New England inevitably fell under the dominance of a few local elites. For Wood, the "gargantuan" city provides a much better forum for the exercise of democratic values than does the proliferation of hundreds of small municipalities in suburbia.

The notion that small suburban governments are somehow closer to the people than large city governments is also challenged. Sociologist Scott Greer claimed that because the large city governments deal with more important issues than do small suburban governments, they dominate the media and capture people's attention. Suburban governments, in contrast, deal with such small issues that they "trivialize" local politics. Consequently, in the sense of getting people's attention and dealing with issues that are important to them, "the government of the greater urban polity is 'closer to the people'—they see its symbols with their morning coffee."[2]

Perhaps the most common complaint against the multicentered metropolis is its seeming inability to equalize the costs and benefits of government.[3] The Advisory Commission on Intergovernmental Relations (ACIR) has focused considerable attention on this issue, has attributed many of the inequities to the fragmentation of governmental authority, and has made several recommendations to improve the structure of local government.[4] The commission especially recommended a reduction in the number of special districts and local governments and encouraged steps that would lead to metropolitan and regional-level governments.

Finally, and perhaps most forcefully, a general-purpose government at the metropolitan level is felt to be needed for reasons of efficiency, administrative competence, and matching the level of government with the level of problems.[5] Political scientist Luther Gulick argues that many metropolitan problems—such as water supply, sewage disposal, and air pollution—are areawide problems that can only be handled on an areawide basis. To handle them on any other basis is to take indivisible problems and try to divide them up among many governments.[6] The problem of matching service needs with government size becomes even more complicated along the Mexican border where metropolitan problems become matters of international relations. San Diego's neighboring city, Tijuana, Mexico, lacks adequate sewage treatment facilities, which results in untreated sewage floating down the Tijuana River to San Diego beaches and agricultural land. Crop acreage has been reduced by one-third because of this pollution. But resolving the problem involves not only San Diego and Tijuana but also the governments of California, Mexico, and the United States, all of which have not yet agreed on the appropriate solution.[7]

San Diego's problem with Tijuana's sewage is distinct, of course, because of its international dimension, but the basic problem of service needs (in this case sewage) crossing over municipal boundaries exists in every MSA in the country. And these MSAs, according to Amos Hawley and Basil G. Zimmer, are characterized by the traits of "governmental chaos, of producing and service inefficiency and of administrative impotence."[8] In their minds, the only reasonable solution to this chaos is to "consolidate the many political units under a single, overarching municipal government."[9]

Institutionally, the most prestigious advocate of metropolitan government in recent years has probably been the Committee for Economic Development (CED), an organization of civic-minded businesspeople. CED was concerned about the two interrelated problems of efficiency at the metropolitan level and responsiveness to citizens at the local level. To meet these two needs, CED recommended that governments in metropolitan areas be entirely reshaped into a two-tier, federative-type system. As an excellent example of how this should be done, the CED cited the reorganization of government in metropolitan Toronto.[10]

The Metropolitan-Governance-Without-a-Metropolitan-Government School of Thought

Despite these arguments for performing major surgery on the structure of governments in the metropolis, very few major surgeries have taken place.[11] Seldom has it been concluded that the Jeffersonian ideal of small-town democracy ought to be scrapped in suburbia and replaced with a general-purpose metropolitan government. Suburban residents are generally unconcerned about the proliferation of governments in the metropolis.[12] And rather than make sweeping changes in governmental structures, local officials generally prefer to make incremental changes when they become necessary in order to deal with specific problems that arise. These incremental changes tend to protect and preserve the status quo and avoid any fundamental alterations in the governmental apparatus.

Criticisms of Metropolitan Government

It would be a mistake, however, to think that metropolitan reform is opposed only by self-seeking, petty, small-time politicians. Some prominent scholars have raised several disturbing questions about the logic of those who would make basic alterations in the government of the metropolis.

Political scientist Charles Adrian charges that reformers are unrealistic when they argue that metropolitan governments should be created so that needed services can be provided much more efficiently and economically.[13] The suburban "merchant or homeowner may value other things higher—in particular, access to decision-making centers and representatives of local government."[14] A study of suburbanites' attitudes in six different metropolitan areas also found that suburbanites were not greatly perturbed over the inadequacy of their public services. Even where they were concerned about the inadequacy of services, they seldom believed that a metropolitan government would improve the services.[15]

Furthermore, the reformers' belief that metropolitan government would save money through its professional administration and its practice of economies of scale is not very convincing to many opponents of metropolitan government. Political scientists Vincent and Elinor Ostrom have argued that recent public administration studies of selected public services tend to refute the notion that highly bureaucratized and centralized administration is more efficient than a proliferation of autonomous, smaller administrations that can compete with one another.[16] Political scientists Edward C. Banfield and Morton Grodzins discuss a point of diminishing returns beyond which economies of scale do not save money. They assert that costs per unit of services decrease up to about 50,000 people, but they do not decrease after that.[17] Some other studies put the point of diminishing returns much higher, in one case as high as 250,000 people.[18] Even at this level, however, the economies-of-scale argument works against the argument for creating a metropolitan-wide government, since the majority of the metropolitan population lives in MSAs larger than 250,000 people.

Additionally, since the levels of public services in suburbia are likely to vary greatly, any attempts to equalize these services could only mean bringing the service levels of the poorer suburbs up to the levels of the richer suburbs. And this undoubtedly would mean more expenditures. Although nobody has conducted an extensive empirical analysis of this question, an appraisal of metropolitan government reforms in Toronto, Nashville, and Dade County, Florida, concluded that expenditures in fact had increased since the adoption of metropolitan government.[19] Even though expenditures increased, the services could still have been operating at greater efficiency than previously. But average voters are more likely to be concerned with the net impact of the services on their property tax bill than with internal administrative efficiencies or with the costs per capita of the services. And empirical evidence does indicate that average suburbanites think that the creation of a metropolitan government would indeed raise their taxes.[20]

Also, according to Adrian, the reformers' belief that professional administration is preferable to part-time amateur administration may be at odds with the preferences of the majority of suburbanites. To the homeowner, "amateur firefighters provide enough services to meet his demands."[21] Many of the volunteer services such as fire fighting perform an important symbolic function in suburbia. Countless suburbs in the United States view the volunteer fire department as a source of local civic pride.

In addition to Adrian's questions of whether the demand to create general-purpose metropolitan governments is based on realistic assumptions, a second question is whether one can even talk realistically of such an entity as a metropolitan community. Political scientist Norton Long has argued persuasively that such a thing as a metropolitan community exists only in the minds of planners and metropolitan reformers.[22] For most people, the sense of community in public policy rarely encompasses the entire metropolis.

A third question that has been raised is whether creation of a metropolitan government is necessary in order to correct the flaws of the multicentered metropolis. Opponents of metropolitan reform contend that many of the flaws can be corrected simply by continuing to tinker with the existing system. Banfield and

Grodzins assert that many of the problems currently referred to as metropolitan problems involve only a portion of the metropolitan area. Thus they question why all the public water supply districts, for example, should be brought under one government. The same question may apply to other services such as solid waste disposal, sewerage, public health, recreation, and police and fire protection.[23]

Finally, several important value questions are involved in restructuring metropolitan government, especially the argument that the costs and benefits of the government in any given metropolitan area ought to be equalized among areas. Should all services be equal throughout the metropolitan area? Or should all areas simply be required to provide minimal standards of services? Once the minimal standards are achieved, should wealthier areas be allowed to maintain levels of services that are above the minimum? Banfield and Grodzins answer the last two questions affirmatively.[24] But among the vital services involved are education, public health facilities, and libraries. And it is difficult for this writer to admit that some residents of the metropolis should have inferior schools, hospitals, and libraries simply because they live in a portion of the metropolis that has no shopping center or commercial real estate, whereas other residents should have superior schools, hospitals, and libraries simply because their area of the metropolis is benefited by such tax-generating establishments.

The Public Choice Model

The most influential argument against metropolitan government was presented by Vincent Ostrom, Charles M. Tiebout, and Robert Warren, who articulate what is called the free market or the public choice model of metropolitan governance. Just as business firms compete with one another by producing or marketing goods, so do metropolitan municipalities compete with one another by producing or marketing public services. And this creates a "quasi-market choice for local residents in permitting them to select the particular community in the metropolitan area that most closely approximates the public service levels they desire." The net result is a "very rich and intricate 'framework' for negotiations, adjudicating, and deciding questions that affect their diverse public interests."[25]

Three problems arise with this free market economy as the model for producing and distributing public services in the metropolis. First, the availability of certain public services becomes dependent on whether the citizen can afford to live in a given municipality. The school district with the highest per-pupil expenditures is likely to be found in the suburban areas with the most expensive homes. Citizens who cannot afford such homes have no free market choice for their decision not to take advantage of these superior expenditures on public education. Although some private goods may legitimately be distributed on the basis of higher-quality goods to different classes of recipients, public services are normally intended to be distributed indivisibly on an equal basis to all classes of recipients.[26] In the realm of public education a persistent battle has been waged in state courts since 1971[27] over the question of whether school financing can follow the free market model.

Second, the free market model of metropolitan governance apparently assumes that the provision of public services needs no more governance than the provision of private goods and services. Even in the theoretical free market model of the economy, however, some overall regulation of the economy is necessary, either by the government or by a supposedly invisible hand that guides the marketplace. If the provision of public municipal services in the metropolis performs according to free market rules, then the regulation of public services of necessity becomes, as Matthew Holden has so aptly phrased it, a problem in diplomacy.[28] To state that there is a limited analogy between metropolitan governance and either a free market economy or international diplomacy is one thing; to posit it as a model for the way in which urban services ought to be provided in the metropolis is quite another. That transforms an empirical judgment into a normative judgment. Furthermore, it provides a theoretical justification for what is in most metropolises a very inequitable distribution of public services.

Finally, the free market model of metropolises is valid only to the extent that the free market model of the economy is valid. And if free market economies ever existed in the world, they certainly do not today. To posit the free market model as a norm to be adopted in the political sphere in urban America is to promote an economic model that does not exist even in the economic sphere.

Metropolitan Governance and Democracy

Still undiscussed is the proposal that the people obviously want a multicentered metropolis. Simply by moving to suburbia, post–World War II Americans have chosen small-town governance. They have also rejected an overwhelming majority of metropolitan government referendums put before them. For services that the small suburban municipalities could not handle, voters preferred that these services be removed from the arena of partisan politics by establishing a big-business type of special district organization to handle them on a supposedly nonpolitical basis. But establishing a metropolitan-level, general-purpose government would return politics to the administration of these services. And that was undesired. In the words of Robert Wood, the choices of residents of the metropolis were limited to two: "Grassroots democracy or big business—no other vehicle is trustworthy in the United States."[29] Confronted with such an apparent array of citizen preferences for the multicentered metropolis, any arguments against it were often dismissed as elitist, antidemocratic, or politically unrealistic.

There is a grain of truth in this assertion that a metropolitan-level government might be antidemocratic. But there is also an antidemocratic strain in the prevailing structures of governments in the multicentered metropolis. To the extent that the governing institutions in the multicentered metropolis are not accountable to the electorate and to the extent that they are more responsive to functional interest groups than they are to the citizenry at large, then to that extent the multicentered metropolis itself is also elitist and antidemocratic. Furthermore, to the extent that the very structure of the multicentered metropolis systematically excludes certain classes (such as racial minorities) or certain geographical areas (such as those suburbs that lack a high property tax base) from equal access to the major tax revenues of the metropolis, then to that extent it violates the spirit if not the letter of the constitutional provision that no state may deny any of its citizens the equal protection of the law.

These considerations show the sharp differences in value orientations between the approach that would scrap the whole system and the approach that seeks governance without a metropolitan government. It is not quite so apparent, however, that one approach is more democratic than the other. The notion that the multi-centered metropolis is nothing more than the democratic, free market choice for post-World War II Americans certainly has to be rejected, for the very choices that were available to the millions of migrants to suburbia were structured by decisions and nondecisions that had been made by both the federal government and the state governments.

Strategies to Attain Metropolitan Government

Whatever the intellectual merits of the metropolitan-governance-without-a-metropolitan-government theory, metropolitan reformers ideally preferred a more radical approach that would indeed scrap the whole system and start over. In practice, four types of metropolitan reorganization have occurred that meet some of the desires of the scrap-the-whole-system reformers. The first type has been central-city expansion through annexation or the use of extraterritorial powers. The second and third approaches, useful in metropolitan areas contained within one county, have been city-county consolidation and strengthening the urban county. The fourth type of reorganization involves the creation of a two-tier form of government, the first tier responsible for areawide functions and the second tier for local functions.

Annexation Strategies

Prior to World War I, metropolitan growth occurred largely through the expansion of the central-city boundaries by annexing the outlying territories. As the city's boundaries expanded outward, most of the growing metropolitan population was kept within the new boundaries, and few municipalities were incorporated as autonomous suburbs on the fringes of the cities. The consolidation of incorporated municipalities during this period was a frequent occurrence. Because of the frequent annexation to and consolidation with the central city, the growth of suburban fringe populations posed few problems until late in the nineteenth century. By 1900, however, successful annexation attempts became less popular and less frequent. Consequently, in most of the country, the growth of the central city through annexation peaked about the time of World War I.

This peaking resulted for two reasons. First, most state legislatures made incorporation easier for municipalities; and second, they made annexation more difficult. Particularly important were requirements that annexation be approved by dual referendums of the voters both within the city doing the annexation and within the area to be annexed. Because strong opposition to annexation existed among the new suburbanites, such annexation referendums were very difficult to pass in the suburban areas.* By the time the first phase of suburbanization ended during the Great Depression, the central cities of the Northeast and the Midwest were mostly encircled by a first tier of suburbs. Attempts by central cities to annex noncontiguous land beyond the first tier of suburbs were generally frowned upon by the courts. Following World War II, most states relaxed their annexation restrictions, and a new phase of annexation occurred. Except for the South and the Southwest, however, this second phase of annexation primarily consisted of unincorporated territories being annexed by suburbs and smaller cities, not by big central cities.† Central-city annexation since 1970 has largely been a southern and southwestern phenomenon.

The most imaginative use of annexation for central-city expansion took place in Texas. The Texas approach combined annexation with *extraterritorial jurisdiction*, which is a city's legal right to control subdivision practices in unincorporated territories on its borders. Extraterritorial jurisdiction was conferred on cities by the Texas Municipal Annexation Law of 1963, which let a city extend its control over subdivisions beyond the city boundaries and also let each city annex up to 10 percent of its territory each year without referendum.[30]

The most dramatic use of these powers has been through "spoke" or "finger" annexation by cities such as San Antonio or Houston.[31] By annexing highway rights of way, the central cities sent spokes or fingers out through the suburbs. This expanded the cities' zones of extraterritorial jurisdiction and prevented new suburban municipalities from incorporating. As parts of the extraterritorial zone urbanized, they were then annexed without referendum to the central city. These tactics enabled Texas central cities to keep growing and to capture the growing suburban tax base, while many northern and midwestern cities were increasingly surrounded by incorporated suburbs. If San Antonio, for example, were restricted to its 1950 boundaries, as were most northern big cities, it would have lost 55,000 people between 1960 and 1975. Instead it grew by 169,000 and kept 80 percent of Bexar County's population within the city boundaries. Equally important, the annexations enabled San Antonio to expand its tax base.[32] The growth of Houston through annexation has been even more dramatic. By 1980, Houston was the only one of the seven largest metropolitan areas to have more people living in the central city than in the suburbs.

---

*Historian Kenneth T. Jackson asserts that suburbanites' opposition to annexation was in great part a moral issue. They looked upon the central-city immigrants as the cause of much of the vice and corruption that characterized the politics of many central cities. See his "Metropolitan Government Versus Suburban Autonomy: Politics on the Crabgrass Frontier," in *Cities in American History*, ed. Kenneth T. Jackson and Stanley K. Schultz (New York: Knopf, 1972), pp. 442–446.

†The Advisory Commission on Intergovernmental Relations reports that post-World War II annexations have been most likely to occur in smaller cities with reform-style governments, cities whose residents are similar socioeconomically to the residents about to be annexed, and cities outside of the northeastern and mid-Atlantic regions. See the commission's *Report A-44, Substate Regionalism and the Federal System: The Challenge of Local Governmental Reorganization* (Washington, D.C.: U.S. Governnment Printing Office, 1974), vol. III, pp.82–84.

The annexation policies themselves came under considerable attack in the 1970s, however, and they are not likely to be used as much in the near future as they have been in the recent past. Substantial annexations in San Antonio in the early 1970s led to a resounding defeat of the dominant political coalition in the city, the Good Government League, in 1973 and sparked a civil rights suit that led to a city charter amendment that replaced the at-large council with a district-elected council in 1977. Houston faced a similar suit in 1978 when it attempted to annex 140,000 people. The United States Department of Justice has authority to review all boundary or electoral changes in local voting processes in counties that were covered under the 1965 Voting Rights Act (see Chapter 5, pp. 122–123). Arguing that Houston's annexations would dilute black and Hispanic representation on the at-large city council, Houston was literally forced to adopt a district-elected council. And this resulted in the election of a number of antigrowth advocates to the new city council in 1979.

City-County Consolidation

One metropolitan government approach that has been very appealing to reformers is to consolidate the central city and county into one government. Such a plan necessarily works best in the smaller MSAs where the entire metropolis is contained in a single county. In the multicounty MSAs, city-county consolidation would not create a metropolitan-wide government, but it would go a long way toward reducing the fragmentation of government services described in Chapters 9 and 10. For those reasons, considerable theoretical potential thus exists for using the county as a basis for metropolitan government, among both large and small counties.[33]

In the nineteenth century, consolidation of cities and counties occurred in New Orleans in 1805, in Boston in 1822, in Philadelphia in 1854, and in New York in 1898. After the consolidation in Honolulu in 1907, however, there were no more until after World War II. From then until 1976 only 17 consolidations have occurred out of 68 attempts in metropolitan areas.[34] Only three of these (Nashville–Davidson County, 1962; Jacksonville–Duval County, 1967; Indianapolis–Marion County, 1969) have involved more than 250,000 people.

Despite this pronounced lack of success, city-county consolidation was one of the most popular metropolitan reform proposals from the 1950s to the mid-1970s. Because of this, the most important features of consolidation merit investigation. Three basic questions arise: Why was consolidation proposed in these larger metropolitan areas? How did consolidation change the structure of government and representation in elected bodies? How did it change the handling of public services?

Why Consolidation Was Proposed

In the major consolidations of Nashville, Jacksonville, and Indianapolis, three background factors have usually been given. First, the provision of public services was usually broken down or at least was faced with serious complications. Although this is not always a precondition for consolidation, such problems often precede consolidation. Second, special political conditions have facilitated the movement toward consolidation. Third, most of the suburban areas and populations were not already contained in other incorporated municipalities.*

Service Deterioration   The most significant consolidation motivated by a deterioration in the provision of public services was that of Nashville–Davidson County, Tennessee. By the 1950s, most of Nashville's population growth was occurring in the suburban areas. An estimated 100,000 suburbanites were using septic tanks for disposing of human waste, and at least 25 percent of these septic tank systems were faulty. This posed a severe threat to the safety of the water supply, which was obtained primarily from private wells. Police and fire protection was very deficient.[35] Because of this, people turned more and more to private subscription for private police and fire services. Several firms competed to provide fire protection in the suburbs, and the inconsistent quality of this fire protection made the cost of fire insurance higher in the suburbs than in the city. Things came to such a pass that, in one instance, firefighters employed by a private fire company responded to the alarm of a burning house not to put out the fire—the burning house was not insured by their company—but to prevent the fire from spreading to a neighboring house, which was company-insured. They stood by and watched the one house burn to the ground.

In summary, Nashville's metropolitan area was characterized by sharp city/suburban political divisions, few areawide special districts, and deficiencies in the provision of public services in the suburbs. Taxable resources were distributed very unevenly throughout the metropolitan area. County expenditures, which benefited primarily the urbanized area, were often duplicated by the city's expenditures.

In the other areas where major consolidations occurred, similar situations existed. Baton Rouge had been plagued by a proliferation of special districts and a sprawling of the population beyond the city's boundaries.[36] Jacksonville was threatened by a loss of accreditation of its school system and a breakdown of its sewerage system, which was polluting the St. Johns River.[37] The main exception to this principle was Indianapolis, where the metropolitan problems had not reached a crisis stage. Through the creation of countywide service districts, Indianapolis had handled the problems of suburbanization with considerable success. The major complaint there seemed to be that the proliferation of these districts had gotten beyond the control of the elected county and city officials.[38]

Political Factors   A second feature common to these consolidations was the existence of special, favorable political conditions. In Jacksonville–Duval County, the

---

*These factors do not necessarily cause the movement toward consolidation, however, because the same factors were sometimes present in metropolises that did not experience a consolidation movement. But in the absence of some combination of these factors, consolidation is very unlikely to occur.

consolidation movement was accompanied by a long, drawn-out exposé of corruption in city government, which led to indictments of eight city government officials on counts ranging from grand larceny to bribery and perjury.[39]

In Nashville the passage of the consolidation charter in 1962 was linked not to public corruption but to extreme voter dissatisfaction with the city officials. A very similar consolidation proposal had been resoundingly defeated by the voters just four years earlier. What led to the final victory of the consolidation plan in 1962 was widespread discontent with two unpopular political moves during the intervening period: the annexation of considerable land and population without holding a referendum, and the passage of a so-called green sticker tax, which obliged suburbanites to purchase green stickers and display them on the windshields of their cars when they drove on the streets of Nashville. A vote for the charter was considered to be a vote against the mayor, who had imposed the unpopular green sticker tax.[40] One could vote for the consolidation in effect by casting a vote to throw out the unpopular rascals who inhabited city hall.[41]

In Indianapolis, the special favorable political circumstance was a change in control of state and local government offices. When the Republicans regained control in 1968, local leaders got the legislature to pass a consolidation proposal called Unigov.[42] Unigov was greatly aided by the fact that it needed no voter approval. The entire matter was handled in the state legislature.

If these consolidations were facilitated by peculiar political circumstances, they were also facilitated by the fact that not very many incorporated areas existed in the suburbs. Nashville–Davidson County had only six incorporated municipalities, and they were allowed to retain their separate existence. Baton Rouge had none. Jacksonville–Duval County had four small cities, which were allowed to retain their separate existence. Indianapolis–Marion County had sixteen small suburbs that were consolidated together with the City of Indianapolis; four larger suburbs were allowed to retain their separate existence. Thus in none of these four areas did consolidation pose a threat to any large suburban government.

Consolidation, the Structure of Government, and Representation

The most visible governmental change in consolidated governments is the creation of a new, countywide council to replace the previous city council and county board of commissioners. These new councils have usually been large (forty members in Nashville, twenty-nine in Indianapolis, and nineteen in Jacksonville), and have used a combination of at-large elections and single-member district elections. A result is that control over the new councils has gone, immediately or eventually, to the former suburbanites. In the case of Indianapolis, the Republicans got immediate dominance. The representation of blacks was critically affected by reorganization, as will be discussed later in the chapter.

Consolidation also brought substantial reorganization in some places. In Nashville, many public services that had previously been performed separately by the city and the county were merged. Instead of two school systems, there was now just one; instead of two public health departments, there was just one. In Jacksonville, the integration of public services under the control of the new council was less extensive than it was in Nashville. In fact, about two-thirds of the public spending in Jacksonville is conducted by independent agencies that are subject to very little control from the consolidated government.[43]

The least complete integration of the governmental structure came in the Indianapolis–Marion County consolidation. All of the existing governmental units were left intact. There are still over 200 governments,[44] eleven separate school districts, sixteen townships, some small cities, and some public authorities. The new government, entitled Unigov, consisted of the same elected county officers who were there prior to the consolidation, and there was no change in several key services.[45] What Unigov did accomplish was to subordinate old county and city administrative agencies to the mayor. In the opinion of one observer, this had led to "a much stronger degree of coordination than previously existed."[46]

Consolidation, Public Services, and Taxes

As pointed out in Chapters 9 and 10, one of the most persistent features of the metropolitan political economy is the wide disparity that exists in the quality of public services and the tax rates paid for these services. The four consolidated city-counties have dealt imaginatively with this problem by dividing the county into different service zones. Usually there is a rural zone that receives a minimum of public services and an urban zone that receives the maximum of public services. Since the rural zone residents receive fewer services, they pay a lower property tax rate. The residents of the urban zone, who receive more services, pay a higher property tax rate. Provision is made for the urban zone's boundaries to expand as population grows in the rural areas.

In Nashville, for example, all county residents pay a tax to the general-services district. This tax finances schools, public health facilities, police protection, courts, welfare, public housing, urban renewal, streets and roads, traffic, transit, library, refuse service, and building codes. In addition, the more densely populated urban areas, which need more extensive provision of government services, constitute an urban-services district. Residents of these areas pay a higher tax rate, and for this they receive fire protection, intensified police protection, sewage disposal, water supply, street lighting, and street cleaning. The charter provides for a gradual expansion of the boundaries of the urban-services district as the population continues to grow in the suburbs.

A very similar two-zone system of services is also utilized in Jacksonville–Duval County,[47] whereas Baton Rouge has a three-zone system. The third zone is an industrial district that enjoys a special taxing situation. The most complicated method of providing services and paying for them is found in Indianapolis–Marion County. Nine separate services each have their own taxing districts, which overlap with one another. Depending on where a person lives in the county, he or she pays a tax rate based on receiving from just one to all nine of these services. In fact, this structure of services and taxation changed very little with the consolidation.[48]

Traditional County Government

Despite being major service providers, most county governments have not been organized very effectively for the purpose of coping with urban ills. In particular, county government has lacked the capacity for decisive executive leadership. Almost 60 percent of all counties are governed by the traditional county governing body known as the board of commissioners.[49]* This board has responsibility for overseeing the operations of all the agencies and departments of the county. In practice, however, the boards of commissioners are usually ineffective in doing this. County agencies have tended to become very autonomous, and very little coordination has existed between them. Big county agencies, such as welfare departments, public hospitals, public health bureaus, and highway departments, have tended to create large bureaucracies and have gained the autonomy characteristic of the functional fiefdoms described in Chapter 7. The smaller agencies, such as tax assessors, license bureaus, registers of deeds, and bureaus of vital statistics, have in many instances become the patronage preserves of isolated political factions that strongly oppose centralized administrative control. Especially where the head of such a department is elected (as is often the case with registers of deeds and sheriffs), the boards of commissioners have little leverage to oblige these fiefdoms to implement general public policies.[50]

Reforming County Government

Most proposals for modernizing county government center on creating an executive office that would have the authority to subordinate these disparate agencies to some form of centralized control. Three particular proposals have received the most attention: the elected county executive, the county manager, and the county administrator. The elected county executive is analogous to the strong-mayor form of city government. As an elected official, the executive has a political base of support and is usually given considerable authority. The largest county with an elected executive is Wayne County, Michigan (Detroit), which created the position in 1981 in response to a severe fiscal and political crisis. Only about 6 percent of all counties have opted for an elected executive.

The county manager is analogous to the city manager. He is directly accountable to the board of commissioners. Although he lacks an electoral base of political support, he is given broad supervisory and budgetary control within the county government. County managers have been used with considerable success in Dade County, Florida, since 1957. But the county manager as a form of government has not been very popular; it has been adopted by only 6 percent of all counties.

Similar in concept to the county manager is the county administrator. The major difference between the two is that the county administrator is given much more limited supervisory control. He is less effective in coordinating various county

*Traditional county boards of supervisors are also included in this 60 percent.

agencies and thus is less threatening to them. This may be why the county administrator form of government has become fairly popular; it has been adopted in 29 percent of all counties.

Two-Tier Government

The third form of metropolitan government is the two-tier approach, which was promoted by the prestigious Committee for Economic Development (CED) in 1970. The CED was concerned primarily about two overriding needs of government in contemporary urban America, two needs that appear to be mutually exclusive. On the one hand is "the need for jurisdictions large enough to cope with problems that pervade entire areas," while on the other hand is the need for "jurisdictions small enough to allow citizens to take part—and take pride—in the process of government."[51] Table 11-1 shows how the CED proposal would divide powers between the local and metropolitan-level governments.

The two closest approximations to the CED two-tiered model are Miami, Florida, and Toronto, Canada. Miami's two-tier government utilizes the existing county as the basis for metropolitan government, whereas Toronto's two-tier system established a true federative form.

Miami: A Two-Tier Urban County

In 1957, Dade County, Florida, established a two-tier form of metropolitan government that seemed to promise a solution to the problem of metropolitan governance. The movement to establish this government was promoted by an increasingly widespread belief among business and good-government leaders that intergovernmental antagonisms and excessive parochialism on the part of the county's twenty-six municipalities were seriously impairing the efficient provision of public services in the region. Traffic conditions in particular had become intolerable. There were no expressways or overpasses. Because each town could set its own speed limits and other traffic regulations, some towns became renowned locally for the fines they collected through speed traps.[52] Civic leaders in Miami expressed open resentment at the parochialism practiced by some of the suburban communities, particularly Miami Beach. And the resentment was openly returned. When the mayor of Miami Beach denounced the plans for the new metropolitan government, a member of the Miami-Dade Chamber of Commerce retorted that Miami Beach was almost completely dependent on the city of Miami. "We Miamians furnish them with water, we burn their garbage, we house their servants, we furnish them with roads leading to Miami Beach . . . we even carry it to the ultimate extreme, we bury their dead."[53] The City of Miami's government was plagued with charges of corruption. Police were accused of not enforcing the city's ordinances on gambling and vice. In contrast, the county government was relatively well regarded. Over the years several public services had been transferred from municipal control to control by the county government.

Since the end of World War II, business and civic leaders in Miami had put forward various plans for consolidating city and county services. These civic leaders

Table 11-1. Division of Powers in Two-Tier Government

Primarily metropolitan	Shared	Primarily local
Transit *(with community participation)*	Planning	Solid waste collection *(with no recommendation on disposal)*
Water supply	Housing	Welfare *(with financing at the national level)*
Sewage disposal	Police	

Source: Adapted from *Reshaping Government in Metropolitan Areas* (New York: Committee for Economic Development, 1970), pp. 45, 51, 56. Reprinted by permission of the publisher.

forged a working alliance with the Dade County delegation in the state legislature, which guided through the legislature a constitutional amendment that granted a home rule charter to Dade County in 1955. The amendment was approved by the voters, a new charter was drafted, and in 1957 the new charter was narrowly approved by a countrywide majority of 44,404 to 42,620.

The new charter established a two-tier government. A restructured and modernized county government was given responsibility for what were deemed the areawide functions. These included mass transit, public health, planning, and some central police and fire services. Other functions have effectively been left to local municipalities, special districts, or school districts. These include police patrolling, public education, and control over local zoning and land use. For some of these functions, the county was authorized to establish minimum service standards. If a local government failed to meet these standards, the county was empowered to take over the service. The charter also allowed the local governments to maintain higher zoning and service standards if they so chose.[54]

This division of functions coincides very neatly with Oliver Williams's distinction between systems-maintenance functions and life-style functions.[55] All the functions turned over to the county involve maintaining the physical operation of the metropolis—keeping the traffic flowing, the water unpolluted, and the public services in operation. The functions that had the most sensitive relationship to controlling people's access to the most highly prized social amenities of the region—public education and residential location—remained in the control of the local governments.

This two-tier system of governance applies only in the municipalities. The unincorporated areas of the county have a one-tier system. In these areas, the county government handles both local and areawide functions.

The new county charter also replaced the traditional commission style of government with a county manager form of government. The county manager was given substantial executive responsibilities, and the county commissioners were removed from any direct control over the departments of government. The county board of commissioners became, in effect, a legislative body. Eight commissioners represent geographical districts, but they are elected at large. A ninth commissioner representing the whole county is also elected at large, and is given the title of mayor. The mayoral position is very weak, however, since the executive authority resides in the county manager.

The early years of the two-tier government were characterized by bitter conflicts between the county and the municipalities, as the county sought to take over functions that had traditionally been performed by the municipalities.[56] The board itself was deeply divided over many of these issues, and as a consequence, it was not until 1965 that the Metro government entered a period of political stability. A proposal to replace the county manager with a strong mayor was resoundingly defeated in a 1972 referendum.[57] But in 1975 and 1976 the charter was amended to expand the county government's responsibilities, strengthen the manager, and provide for a charter review commission every five years.[58]

The biggest problem facing the county today is an inadequate revenue base. Although Metro was given greatly expanded urban functions in 1957, it was not given the tax base needed to perform these functions adequately. Because of a peculiarity of Florida law, Metro was denied such traditional urban fundraising sources as excise taxes, franchise fees, a share of the state cigarette taxes, and the authority to impose taxes on utility bills.[59] Consequently, it was forced to rely almost exclusively on property taxes to finance the new services. This problem was eased considerably in recent years by broadening the county's revenue sources. By 1970–1971, the county's reliance on property taxes had diminished to the point that they provided only about a third of the total county revenue.[60] Even with this broadening of the fiscal base, considerable revenue problems remained.[61]

Toronto: A Federative Government

In contrast to Miami, Toronto represents a true federative government.[62] Whereas Dade County has unincorporated areas in which the two-tier system does not operate, Toronto's two levels of government operate throughout the entire metropolitan area. A second difference lies in the nature of representation: In Miami the city governments are not represented in the county government, while in Toronto the city governments themselves have been represented on the Metropolitan Council from the very beginning.

By the 1950s Toronto was plagued with the same metropolitan growth problems that plagued United States metropolises. Because of governmental fragmentation, there was an inability to plan regionally. The metropolis was without adequate water and sewerage facilities and a modern, coordinated public transit system, and individual jurisdictions were unable to finance major projects and programs.

In 1953 the Ontario Province Municipal Board studied various plans for coping with these metropolitan problems and came up with the Cumming Report, which recommended a federal system that would guarantee the continued existence of the existing thirteen municipalities in the Toronto area. Based on these recommendations, the Ontario Province legislature created a 24-member Metropolitan Council for the Toronto area. Half of the members were municipal officials from the City of Toronto, and the other twelve were municipal officials from each of the twelve suburbs. The Metropolitan Council selected its own chairperson, who was not obliged to be one of the 24 members.

The Metropolitan Council was made responsible for providing services that transcended local boundaries. These primarily included property assessment, construction and maintenance of freeways, and development of regional parks. Other functions such as streetlights, provision of public health services, fire protection, and marriage licenses were left to the individual municipalities.

The early years of metropolitan government in Toronto were a time of unmitigated success in providing services that had been neglected. The water and sewer systems were greatly expanded. More schools were built. An extensive program of expressway construction was undertaken. Subway and bus lines were extended, and a regional park system was created.

Despite these successes, a split occurred in the Metropolitan Council in the early 1960s that nearly destroyed it. In 1963 the Toronto representatives on the council proposed a subsidy for the Toronto Transit Commission, which had suffered a severe drop in passengers since Metro's inception in 1954. The subsidy was bitterly opposed by the suburbanites, who were not served by any of the subway lines. The net result of the conflict over transit was a 1966 reorganization of the Metropolitan Council, in which Toronto and the thirteen old suburbs were replaced with six new boroughs of a new municipality. Rather than each suburb having a seat on the Metropolitan Council, as had been the practice previously, seats were now allotted among the boroughs on the basis of one person, one vote.

A general assessment of Metropolitan Toronto after almost two decades of operation indicates that two-level federation in the metropolitan area is a viable form of government. Toronto does possess one advantage that does not exist in any state in the United States, however. Both at the creation of Metro in Toronto and at the time of the divisive split over transit in 1963, a provincial government existed that was capable of taking decisive action. The closest approximation to this in the United States occurred in Indianapolis and the Twin Cities, where the state legislature created the new metropolitan units without recourse to referendums.

Is Metropolitan Government an Improvement over the Multicentered Metropolis?

To justify the time and energy spent trying to achieve consolidation, urban counties, or two-tier governments, reformers at some point must ask whether these innovations are really an improvement over the multicentered metropolis in terms of better service delivery and better responsiveness to citizen demands. We can deal with this question by assessing the achievements of metropolitan government, its consequences and biases, and its impact on racial minorities.

Assessing the Achievements

One general assessment of metropolitan reorganization seems to be that it has led to improved public services, but this in turn has meant increased expenditures and taxes.[63] It must be recognized that inflation would have made property taxes rise anyway. A comparison of Jacksonville with nearby Tampa, Florida, however, concluded that city-county consolidation "produced no measurable impact on taxing and spending."[64] In Nashville and Jacksonville, the consolidated governments made significant headway in installing sewer lines and central water supplies. In Indianapolis, Unigov brought significant improvements in sewer and transportation services and provided a broader tax base for financing sewer construction costs.[65] In Nashville, a voter opinion survey conducted two years after the new charter was accepted found that 71 percent of the voters were satisfied with Metro's operation. The survey also discovered that citizens felt that the new government made it easier for them to know whom to call or see when they had a problem.[66]

Miami's Metro also has many significant accomplishments to its credit. First among these, undoubtedly, is the fact that it is the only successful two-tier experiment in the United States. Since its inception it has successfully integrated a haphazard county government. It has drawn up the area's first general land use plan, established uniform, countywide traffic laws and uniform subdivision ordinances, and taken steps toward the establishment of an areawide bus system. In the 1980s Miami opened a rapid-rail public transit system. Master plans for sewers and water have been prepared, and other public services have been improved considerably. Expensive duplication of many services by the county and the municipal governments has been reduced, and the provision of services to the minority populations has been significantly upgraded.[67]

The biggest failings of the metropolitan governments have been in coping with suburban sprawl and in dealing with social issues. In both Indianapolis and Nashville, the MSA now extends beyond the boundaries of the consolidated citycounties. However, in Miami–Dade and Jacksonville–Duval, most of the foreseeable future growth should occur within the central counties. On the critical social issues, metropolitan governments have probably fared no better than the multicentered metropolises.

The Consequences and Biases of Metropolitan Government

Consolidation, strengthening the urban county, and two-tier government: What conclusions can be drawn about these devices for restructuring metropolitan government? Are they really effective mechanisms for coping with the consequences of the multicentered metropolis? Do they provide effective means for responding to the needs of unorganized citizens as well as the demands of organized groups? And, whatever the merits of these reorganizations, are they really indicative of change when so few consolidations have occurred, only 6 percent of metropolitan counties are using the most advanced form of county government, and no United States metropolis has adopted a federative scheme of government? Have the reorganization movements really brought substantial change? Or have they simply been sound and fury, signifying nothing?

A response to these questions must first address the distinction made below between systems-maintenance issues and the issues of social access. Metropolitan governments are uniformly much more successful in dealing with the physical questions such as sewers, water supply, or parks and recreation than they are in dealing with social issues such as fiscal disparities, race relations, open housing, and the location of public, low-income housing in the suburbs. In terms of controlling metropolitan development and suburban sprawl, the metros do not seem to be much more effective than are the governments in metropolitan areas where metros have not been created. The proliferation of suburban incorporations has been greatly slowed down, but only recently has suburban development been tied to any metropolitan development plans.

Metropolitan government as it exists in Nashville, Jacksonville, Indianapolis, and Miami also has some inherent biases. First, these governments have not eliminated the biases of the multicentered metropolis on social access issues of zoning, schools, and housing. Oliver Williams has drawn a distinction between these social access issues and systems-maintenance functions, such as water supply or sewage disposal, which are essential for the sheer physical maintenance of the metropolis.[68] Although there has been little hesitation to give the metropolitan governments authority to perform the systems-maintenance functions, there has been considerable reluctance to allow land use controls or residential zoning practices to be turned over to metropolitan-level agencies. This can be seen in the fact that in all four of these major metropolitan reformed governments, existing suburban municipalities were allowed to continue existing with their authority over zoning and land use decisions unimpaired. In fairness to these governments, however, it must be noted that the formation of metropolitan governments reduced the likelihood of future suburban incorporations and, in the unincorporated areas of the counties, did indeed create a metropolitan-level land use authority.

Second, metropolitan governments appear biased against citizen participation in their affairs. Voting turnouts for the election of metropolitan councils have usually been low. And not one of the metropolitan governments created to date has moved very effectively to involve citizens in its activities.

Third, because the leaders of many urban groups take metropolitan government seriously enough to oppose its formation, these leaders probably think that metropolitan government will be biased against their interests. The opposition by suburban municipal officials, special district officials, and the administrative officers of city and county governments leads one to suspect that metropolitan government has the capacity to counter some of the existing biases toward the functional fiefdoms that now exist in the metropolis. Considerations of the impact of metropolitan government on black communities indicate that the inevitable dilution of black voting strength can be mitigated by certain structural arrangements to guarantee blacks a voice in the resulting metropolitan government. Consequently, the evidence suggests that metropolitan government, if it is designed appropriately, does have the potential to make some noticeable alterations in the structure of bias toward the existing functional fiefdoms.

The Impact of Metropolitan Government on Racial Minorities

Creation of metropolitan governments has had an immediate and apparently negative impact on the voting *potential* of central-city blacks. Especially in Jacksonville and Nashville, blacks had constituted a large and growing portion of the central-city populations prior to the consolidations and could reasonably have looked forward to wielding increasing influence over the city government. After consolidation, however, their percentage of the population was considerably reduced. Similar situations have led black leaders to oppose metropolitan reforms proposed in several metropolises. In Jacksonville, most black leaders supported consolidation, but opposition came from two black leaders who feared dilution of black voting strength and from one black who had been previously aligned with the old city government.[69] Black voters approved the plan by a margin of 59 to 41 percent.[70] In Nashville, the black leadership was also divided, while the black electorate voted against the plan by a margin of about 56 to 44 percent.[71]

Whether the *potential* decline in black voting strength actually occurred is dubious. Nashville blacks had been guaranteed a district system of representation in the new council, and this was a marked improvement over the complete lack of representation they had suffered under the old at-large system of electing councilmen in Nashville.[72] Furthermore, an analysis of all postconsolidation elections in Nashville found no evidence that any black candidates were defeated because of the dilution of black voting strength.[73] In Indianapolis, Unigov's district system of electing council members not only ensured blacks of representation on the new council, but it also gave the black militants and activists a stronger voice in both city and political party affairs.[74] In Jacksonville, the district system of election also guaranteed some black representation on the new council,[75] although some observers commented that the number of black seats ended up being fewer than the number tacitly agreed upon prior to the consolidation.[76] In summary, then, the numerical representation of blacks seems to have met or exceeded expectations in Nashville, Indianapolis, and Jacksonville. The establishment of metropolitan governments has not necessarily reduced black representation in terms of numbers.

Numerical representation is not the same thing as effective representation, however, and how the creation of metropolitan government affected the political efficacy of blacks seems to vary from city to city. In Indianapolis, Unigov has been much more successful than previous Democratic city administrations at getting federal grants for programs that operated primarily in black neighborhoods.[77] This no doubt is due to the fact that the Republican-dominated Unigov was able to maintain good relations with the Republican administrations in Washington. In Jacksonville, observers report that both black and white leaders view the postconsolidation system "as a vast improvement over pre-consolidation days."[78] Black employment increased under the new consolidated government, and black representatives have been appointed to every advisory board. Systematic efforts have been made to hire more black police officers and firefighters. In contrast to an underrepresentation in the preconsolidation council, black representation on the consolidated government council reflects the black percentage of the area's population. Apparently as a move designed to show good faith to the black population, the first sewers installed under the consolidated government's sewer construction program were in black neighborhoods.[79]

The examples of metropolitan reorganization in these three cities do not provide a definitive answer to the question of what minority populations can expect from metropolitan government. But they do indicate that the question is a good deal more complicated than simply asking whether metropolitan government will dilute the voting potential of blacks.* Some important tradeoffs are involved. In Jacksonville, for example, blacks, who already comprised 40 percent of the old city's population before consolidation, had looked forward to the day when they could have a majority and win the mayor's office. But it would have been the mayoralty of a city definitely on the decline. This tradeoff was expressed succinctly by one local black leader who was subsequently elected to one of the consolidated government's at-large council seats. "I might have been the black mayor, but I would have been only a referee in bankruptcy."[80] Immediate influence in a viable government was preferable to dominance over a nonviable one. Some scholars think that metropolitan reorganizations can be structured in ways that will protect the black population.[81] Finally, one scholar has pointed out that the special district forms of government that have proliferated in metropolitan areas have been "so rarely open to black influence . . . [that black leaders] . . . may become strong advocates for metropolitan forms that are answerable to the voters and that are not obstructed in decision making by ad hoc boards, and single function oriented agencies and districts."[82]

On balance, then, metropolitan government has not diminished black representation in Nashville, Jacksonville, or Indianapolis. It may even have made that representation slightly more effective. But the emphasis would have to be on the word *slightly*. The available evidence seems to suggest that metropolitan government has had very little impact, positive or negative, on black power. Black influence has remained relatively unchanged.[83]

Public Choice and Metropolitan Inequalities

Finally, we must return to the question that has concerned us for several chapters and with which this chapter began. Does the multicentered metropolis, as the metropolitan reformers charge, exacerbate the geographical separation of rich from poor and deprive the poor of access to the most lucrative tax resources of the

---

*This seems to have been the primary concern of much literature on the impact of metropolitan reorganization on the black population [See Frances Fox Piven and Richard A. Cloward, "What Chance for Black Power?" *The New Republic* 185, no. 13 (March 30, 1968): 23; and Lee Sloan and Robert French, "Race and Governmental Consolidation in Jacksonville," *Negro Educational Review* 2, no. 1 (April–July 1970): 72–78].

metropolis? Or, as the public-choice theorists contend, is the multicentered metropolis simply a benign way of sorting people into municipalities according to the level of services, taxes, and amenities that the people want?

These are very difficult questions to answer. John Logan and Mark Schneider attempted to answer them when they studied central-city suburban disparities in 55 metropolitan areas in 1960 and 1970.[84] They found that two key facets of the multicentered metropolis did indeed exacerbate income inequalities between central cities and suburbs. In particular, cities that had grown the least through annexation were plagued with greater inequalities than other areas, and areas that relied the heaviest on local property taxes to fund public services had the greatest inequalities. These findings were confirmed in a study of the 100 largest metropolitan areas in 1980.[85] However, the 1980 study also found that there were no important inequalities due either to the extent of fragmentation of government in metropolitan areas or to the extent to which suburbs were able to incorporate themselves. These two findings would seem to cast doubt on the proposition that income inequalities are caused by metropolitan fragmentation.

The strongest attack on the idea that the multicentered metropolis provokes social inequalities was probably that of public-choice theorist Elinor Ostrom. Reexamining the data of Schneider and Logan, she noted that of the 1139 suburbs they studied only 17.6 percent had an overconcentration of wealthy people and another 16.9 percent had an overconcentration of poor people. This left the overwhelming majority of suburbs (65.5 percent) having a mixture of poor people, rich people, and middle-class people.[86] Within the suburbs, at least, most people live in economically mixed rather than economically segregated communities.

Ostrom's critique hardly resolves the question of social inequalities in the multicentered metropolis. But it certainly makes clear that, however desirable metropolitan reform might be, it will take more than metropolitan reform to make a serious dent in the existing social inequalities in metropolitan America.

Why is Metropolitan Government So Hard to Get?

Whatever the accomplishments of existing metropolitan governments in Miami or Nashville, the fact remains that very few consolidations or two-tier governments have been established. To discover the reasons for this, scholars have spent considerable effort analyzing the campaigns for metropolitan reform, and these analyses point to several recurring factors that make the difference between victory and defeat. Five factors will be discussed here: (1) regional patterns and the suburban vote, (2) levels of public dissatisfaction, (3) the purification ritual, (4) the role of racial minority leaders, and (5) the role of other elites.

Regional Patterns and the Suburban Vote

Most metropolitan governments have been established in the South. Part of this must be attributed to the traditional reliance in the South on counties as the basic political and administrative units. Southern metropolises have typically been surrounded by fewer incorporated suburbs than have northern metropolises, so fewer local municipal officials have a vested interest that would be harmed by a metropolitan government. In both Saint Louis and Cleveland, two of the largest areas to suffer defeat in attempting metropolitan reform, the officials of many suburbs could and did oppose the new charter.[87] In Miami, by contrast, the suburbanites are generally emigrés from other areas of the country rather than ex-Miami residents. They therefore have fewer attachments to traditional political structures in Miami and fewer emotional ties to the Miami area.[88]

In the typical referendum on city-county consolidation, the suburban vote is usually against consolidation. Since passage normally requires separate majorities within the central city and suburbs (that is, concurrent majorities), suburban opposition is enough to kill the reform. This happened several times during the 1970s. In a 1973 consolidation referendum in Savannah, Georgia, for example, the total overall vote was in favor of consolidation by a three-to-two margin, but the consolidation failed because it did not get a majority of the suburban vote. The same thing happened to consolidation votes in Albuquerque, New Mexico (1973) and Knoxville, Tennessee (1978).[89] In many instances suburban voters interpret metropolitan reform as an attempt by central-city officials to "grab" their tax base and deprive them of their autonomy. One study indicates that the single most important factor in the defeat of metropolitan reforms was the fear of increased taxes.[90]

Levels of Public Discontent

In St. Louis, Cleveland, and some other cities where voter surveys were conducted,[91] voters were not markedly dissatisfied with the provisions of government services. In Nashville, as we saw, voters were dissatisfied. And for several years prior to the charter reform, voters in Miami were not only concerned over tax inequities but also upset about charges of corruption in police services in the city of Miami. It would seem, then, that substantial public discontent with public services creates a climate favorable to metropolitan reform if the proposed new governmental structure can offer some hope of satisfying that discontent.

The Purification Ritual

A third major difference between the successful and the unsuccessful reform attempts is closely associated with the level of discontent. The reform proposal has a much better chance for success if there is widespread public dissatisfaction with government officials, government agencies, government practices, or particular politicians. The new government can then be sold as a device for purging the government of its unpopular elements; and the campaign can be run as what Scott Greer terms a purification ritual.[92] In Nashville, the extremely unpopular green sticker tax and the city's annexation moves were successfully blamed on Nashville mayor Ben West. Thus a vote for the charter in 1962 could be sold as a vote against the mayor and his unpopular practices. In Miami, the charter proponents pointed out that the new charter government would be able to confront tax inequities and other aspects of government that drew strong feelings in much of the county. In Cleveland and St Louis, the charter proponents were unable to do either of these things. Thus charter campaigns appear to have a better chance to succeed if their organizers can make a credible attack on some aspect or feature of the incumbents that is unpopular with a substantial part of the electorate.

The Role of Racial Minority Leaders

In the creation of metropolitan governments, the role played by the minority communities has often been very important. It was least important in the creation of the Miami–Dade County Metro and the Indianapolis Unigov. In Jacksonville, Nashville, St. Louis, and Cleveland, however, the role of the blacks in particular was very important. In St. Louis, blacks were important primarily by their absence. No effort was made to enlist their support for the district plan, and no support was forthcoming. In Cleveland, where the homerule charter for the county was defeated by a very small margin, black interests had been needlessly ignored. Black leaders campaigned against the charter, and black wards voted resoundingly against it. The most success in getting black support came in Jacksonville and Nashville. In both places, blacks were given important positions on the commissions that drafted the consolidation charters, and a large council elected from districts was created in order to maximize black representation. The result of these concessions was that prominent blacks supported the consolidation in both places. Black wards strongly supported consolidation in Jacksonville but rejected it narrowly in Nashville.

From the foregoing, several propositions can be advanced. In some metropolises, such as Miami, the racial minority electorate may be so small that it will have a negligible role in the attempt to establish the new reform. Second, the approach of creating metropolitan governments by state legislative action minimizes minority influence. In most state legislatures, minority communities are severely underrepresented. Even the one-person, one-vote principle does not preclude a gerrymandering of legislative districts to divide minority populations among several districts. And this has happened to those populations in several cities. In contrast, a referendum at least gives minority voters a chance to exert as much influence as their numbers warrant.

The metropolitan governments can also be structured in ways that will minimize the dilution of the minority voting potential. In particular, large councils in which the members are elected from districts rather than at large will ensure some minority representation on the council. This assurance can be enhanced by promises to draw the council district lines so that the minority communities will have the maximum number of representatives warranted by their numbers. In addition, the charter can include guarantees for civil rights and equal opportunities in public employment. Such guarantees will be very important to those minority leaders who fear that the whole purpose of the metropolitan government is to keep them from appointive positions and jobs in the city government.

Finally, the metropolitan government promoters can include minority leaders in the planning, drafting, and promotion of the new charter. Certainly, the act of having minorities on the charter commission can be billed as an act of good faith that the new government will deal fairly with the minority communities.

The Role of Other Local Elites

Local political elites play a critical role in the passage or defeat of metropolitan reorganization proposals.[93] Where reorganization was successful, the reformers succeeded in gaining support from key political leaders and in neutralizing potential opposition. In Nashville, the effectiveness of Mayor Ben West's political opposition to consolidation in 1962 was neutralized by his own unpopularity. In Miami, the political party leaders and labor organizers were never very important in city politics. The metropolitan dailies, which had limited influence in St. Louis, were among the major molders of opinion in Miami. Thus one of the keys to victory was to turn the balance of politically important forces in favor of the charter, as in Miami and Nashville, rather than against it, as in St. Louis. Even this tactic is not a guarantee of success, however. In Cleveland, substantial political party support existed for the plan, but enough opposition still existed to kill it.

A reorganization plan would not seem to have much chance for passage unless there were a broad coalition of support from local government, business, civic, and media leaders. Division or opposition among these leaders is a signal to the voters that something is seriously wrong with the proposal.

Most of the factors that led metropolitan reorganizations to be defeated in the 1950s and 1960s still prevail today. This was reflected in a commentary in the *National Civic Review* on the defeat of a proposed city-county consolidation in Salt Lake City, Utah, in November 1978:

> An analysis of the situation suggests the existence of some fundamental factors which laid the ground work for the defeat: (1) unification lacked grassroots support, (2) abstract issues were rarely perceived, (3) justifications for unification were not inherently evident, and (4) political organizations required for success were missing.[94]

Although this explanation refers to Salt Lake City in 1978, one could easily apply it without changing a word to the defeats of reorganization in Cleveland and St. Louis two decades earlier. It probably would not be an overstatement to say either that the metropolitan reformers have not learned the lessons of history about how a campaign needs to be conducted or that the obstacles to reorganization are too overwhelming in most places.

Metropolitan Reform and Political Bias: Some Conclusions

The attempts to achieve metropolitan reform demonstrate certain political biases. The first of these involves the question of either stasis or change in metropolitan governance. The attitudes of the general metropolitan population and the leadership of many powerful interest groups seem biased toward stasis rather than change; many more reform campaigns have been lost than won.

Second, the perceptible changes that have taken place suggest that the attitudinal biases are more inclined toward incremental and limited changes than they are toward drastic and far-reaching changes. Although (as will be shown in Chapter 12) the reforms in the Twin Cities metropolitan area were far less extensive than complete consolidation of governments, they did nevertheless increase the capacity to deal with the metropolitan problems in their respective areas. And even though very few metropolitan counties have adopted the most advanced forms of urban county government (the county manager and the elected county executive), increasing numbers of metropolitan counties are adopting *some* reorganization proposals and assuming more responsibility for urban functions of government. Accomplishing limited reforms in metropolitan governance in an incremental fashion is apparently much easier than accomplishing sweeping reforms in one dramatic action.[95]* This is the major lesson of the Twin Cities and Indianapolis—especially the Twin Cities, where the creation of the Metropolitan Council culminated years of incremental changes, and the council itself has been subject to incremental growth since its creation.

To the extent that the public mistrusts metropolitan government, the examples of Indianapolis and the Twin Cities also indicate that substantial changes can best be obtained by limiting the metropolitan reform proposals to those that can be accomplished by legislatures without requiring voter approval in referendums. Although this may seem to be an undemocratic attempt to skirt the will of the electorate, the legislature is actually a much more appropriate forum for conducting metropolitan changes, as was shown above. In a referendum, the electorate is given a simple yes or no choice over a charter that, more likely than not, has been drafted by a blue ribbon committee of civic-minded reformers who lack electoral experience. Legislative committees, in contrast, are not limited to a take-it-or-leave-it option. They can debate any conceivable aspect of the proposal that any interest group or politician cares to raise. Whether this method of dealing with metropolitan reform is less democratic than the referendum approach depends primarily on how democratic the legislative committees are in their procedures. If one accepts the Madisonian preference for representative government over direct democracy,[96] then seeking metropolitan reform through the legislative approach is not so much an attempt to skirt the will of the people as it is an attempt to provide a forum where the people's representatives can work effectively.

All this considered, it must be admitted that very few metropolitan governments have been created. What has been the aftermath of the defeats of consolida-

---

*Thomas M. Scott demonstrates how changes in suburban governance occur in an incremental fashion as governments learn from one another. He concludes that innovations in government are viewed with less hostility in communities that can see the effects of such innovations in the neighboring communities [see his "The Diffusion of Urban Governmental Forms as a Case of Social Learning," *Journal of Politics* 30, no. 4 (November 1968): 1091–1108].

tion? If metropolitan government is rejected, what can be done? In fact, several options exist. And a considerable amount of incremental change has occurred. This will be examined in Chapter 12.

Summary

1. The two main schools of thought about metropolitan reform are (a) scrap-the-system-and-start-over, and (b) metropolitan-governance-without-a-metropolitan-government.

2. The strategies to attain metropolitan government have included central-city annexation, city-county consolidation, strengthening the urban county, and two-tier government.

3. Metropolitan governments have been more successful in addressing the systems-maintenance issues than they have been in addressing the social access issues. Central-city blacks have often opposed metropolitan reform on the grounds that it would dilute their voting strength. In Jacksonville and Nashville, however, some measures were taken to make the new metropolitan governments more responsive to black interests than the previous governments had been.

4. Whatever the accomplishments of metropolitan governments, few attempts to get them have succeeded. Most successes have been scored in the South and West. Other factors associated with success have been a high level of public dissatisfaction with the previous government, a charter campaign conducted on the model of the purification ritual, and tactics that gather the support of racial-minority leaders and other political elites.

5. The biases associated with metropolitan reform have included a bias in favor of the status quo in governmental organization and a bias of citizens toward incremental and limited change rather than drastic and far-reaching change. These biases have compounded the problems of getting metropolitan government.

Chapter 12
The Politics of Incremental Change in the Postreform Metropolis

The great hopes for achieving metropolitan government were, as Chapter 11 demonstrated, pretty well dashed by the mid-1970s. And in a sense, the period since then has become a postreform period. The problems of the multicentered metropolis did not disappear. Nor have the demands let up to increase the capabilities of urban governments to deal with these problems. In contrast to the 1950s and 1960s, however, the thrust of these demands is seldom any longer to create metropolitan governments. Rather, the focus today is much more likely to be on limited reforms and limited attempts at cooperation.

Four developments stand out. First, a distinction has been made between systems-maintenance issues of metropolitan politics and life-style issues. Second, under federal incentives a proliferation of metropolitan planning has occurred. Third, a new metropolitan institution, the council of governments (COG), has emerged. And fourth, through a process of incremental change, new models of metropolitan government took shape in Minnesota and Oregon.

A Matter of Life Styles

One feature of change that this chapter will discuss is the increased willingness to turn control of certain kinds of governmental functions over to centralized metropolitan agencies. But not all governmental functions are being turned over. Oliver Williams has posited what is called the "life-style model" of metropolitan politics, which seems to fit contemporary trends in metropolitan governance. Where there is no outside intervention by the federal government, Williams states that "policy areas which are perceived as neutral with respect to controlling social access may be centralized; policies which are perceived as controlling social access will remain decentralized."[1] The objectives of social access as discussed earlier in Chapter 10 are the life styles of upper-middle-class suburban areas, particularly the life styles of the expensive suburban school districts and the exclusive residential areas. The devices that control access to these life styles thus become the issues over which suburbanites fight most vehemently to retain local control. And the public issues that challenge most directly the exclusivity of these life styles are busing of pupils for the purpose of achieving racial balance, low- and moderate-income public housing, zoning, and possibly the equalizing of fiscal disparities in the metropolis. Suburban officials show great reluctance to allow these issues to be controlled by a centralized metropolitan government.

In contrast to these life-style issues, many of the problems of the multicentered metropolis—such as sewerage, water supply, health facilities, or solid waste disposal—represent what Williams labels systems-maintenance functions of government. Equal access to sewers does not threaten anybody's life style in the suburbs, but it is essential to maintain the health and safety of the majority of the population. As the seriousness of these systems-maintenance problems began to be recognized and as they began to be perceived as nonthreatening to the suburban life style, municipal officials became less and less opposed to centralizing and coordinating their operations in agencies that were large enough to practice economies of scale. Even in metropolises such as Toronto, Miami, and the Twin Cities, where major metropolitan reorganizations have been achieved, the new governments have been much more effective in the physical-development issues than they have in the social issues where questions of life style are at stake.[2]

The major battles of metropolitan politics today are less over the forms of metropolitan governance than over the substance of issues that threaten suburban life styles. The outlines for this may have been set in court battles over busing, the fiscal disparities inherent in relying on property taxes to finance public schools, and the extension of low- and moderate-income public housing into the suburbs.[3] As discussed in Chapters 9 and 10, these issues were just as volatile at the end of the 1980s as they had been earlier at the start of the 1970s.

In stressing the much more difficult problem of coming to terms with the life-style issues of the contemporary metropolis, however, it would be a serious mistake to underestimate the importance of the increased willingness of local officials to seek regional cooperation on the systems-maintenance issues. These issues are far from settled. What has changed has been the willingness of local officials to cooperate on centralizing control over the resolution of these issues. Much of this centralization, as Williams suggested, has resulted from the desire to provide the services as cheaply as possible. But much of it also has come from federal incentives to form metropolitan planning agencies and councils of government.

The Origin and Impact of Metropolitan Planning

City Planning: Background, Structures, and Implementation

Metropolitan planning is a historical outgrowth of urban planning. Urban planning is the attempt to make future urban development conform to pre-stated priorities and guidelines. Such attempts in the United States have a long history dating back to colonial plans for cities such as Boston, Philadelphia, Savannah, and New Orleans. L'Enfant's plan for Washington is the most famous of several such city plans. These plans, however, did little more than map out the central core of the city, and they were never able to keep pace with rapid city growth during the nineteenth century. In New York City, for example, the early-nineteenth-century planners expressed pride that they had planned for a city large beyond their wildest expectations. Within a generation the city had outgrown their plans. West of the Appalachians, cities were designed in grid patterns in the attempt to impose order on future growth.

Background

Contemporary urban planning dates not so much from these early endeavors as it does from the "city beautiful" movement at the turn of the century.[4] In 1893, the city of Chicago commissioned the design of an elaborate lakeshore development of lagoons, parks, boulevards, and classical architecture to house the Columbian Exposition. From then until about 1915, many progressive urban reformers sought to alleviate the social problems of the cities by beautifying them, by planning large, physical construction projects that were aesthetically pleasing. The most elaborate of these plans was undoubtedly the plan of development for Chicago, which provided for reversing the flow of the Chicago River to preserve the purity of Lake Michigan, landfills and park construction along the lakefront, forest preserves on the western edge of the city, and broad avenues that reached far into the hinterland. This "city beautiful" stage was succeeded by the "city functional" or the "city efficient" stage. This stage began with the drafting of a plan in 1909 for the development of Boston. Just as the Chicago plan had focused on physically beautifying the city, the Boston plan added the dimension of anticipating economic as well as physical needs. It focused on making the city more efficient. Public finances were to be made more open and honest. Public health facilities were to be provided, and the regional economy was to be strengthened.[5]

The "city efficient" stage of planning dominated until after World War II, when the concept of the comprehensive development plan came into general acceptance. Such plans attempt to present precise blueprints for the development of cities as they will look 20 or 30 years in the future.

Underlying all three of these stages was the assumption that city planning should be conducted for the general public interest of the city as a whole rather than for the private interest of particular clients. This assumption came under attack in the 1960s when the concepts of "pluralism in planning" and "advocacy planning"[6] were put forward to justify the use of professional planners by groups of citizens (especially the poor and the racial minorities) whose private interests were not being well served by the supposedly public interests advocated by the city planners.

Structures for Planning

All of these stages of planning have left their imprint on contemporary planning attitudes and institutions. One of the most important influences on planning was the progressive reform movement discussed in Chapter 4. In the words of political scientist Francine Rabinovitz, city planning was "conceived as a set of rules and structures designed to keep politics out of urban development."[7] By setting down in advance the rules of land use control and by dividing the city into a series of zones for different kinds of activities, it was hoped that the meddling of politicians in locational decisions could be minimized. Professional planners generally developed a scorn for politics and politicians that even today has not been entirely eradicated.[8] Partly as a result of this attitude, the earliest municipal planning commissions were isolated as much as possible from the political process. The planning commission was usually composed of prominent businesspeople and civic leaders who were independent of the local poltical machines, and the commissions themselves were independent of the mayor's office. But as time passed, the independence of the planning commission from the city's political leaders was found to be a liability in getting the plans accepted by the political officers. And recent decades have seen a move to incorporate planning into the administrative offices of the city government.[9] Presently, about two-thirds of all city planning agencies are directly subordinated to the chief executive of the city.[10]

In addition to the planning commission, other key actors in city planning are the city council, the city planner, the chief executive officers of the city, federal officials, and the business enterprises that wish to construct residential or commercial developments in the city. The city planner, who is the central person among these actors, is responsible for working with the planning commission to develop a comprehensive development plan for the city and for carrying out the plan once it is approved. City planners have historically tended to come out of the engineering and architecture professions and have concentrated on physical concerns such as building size, lot size, and zoning regulations. Since World War II, however, the educational background of planners has included more social science instruction, and many of these planners focus on social services such as health facilities, community development, poverty assistance, and other social resources.[11] The physical planners tend to predominate in the city planning departments,[12] whereas the social planners are found in other public and private agencies such as neighborhood councils, community action agencies, and health and welfare planning councils.[13]

These structures for urban planning exist not only in central cities but in suburbs and small towns as well. Over 90 percent of all cities under 10,000 people have developed city plans.[14] The physical layouts of many suburbs are originally designed by real estate developers, who plan curving streets, shopping centers, and other amenities that will give the suburban development an aesthetic appearance that is appealing to the residents and will put them within acceptable commuting distance of shopping and other service facilities. When the development incorporates, its residents may wish to retain the residential character of single-family homes, but the local officials responsible for planning very often find that these aesthetic concerns conflict with the need to approve developments such as industry, fast-food franchises, or apartment buildings that make a positive contribution to the suburb's property tax base. Even though they may have approved a comprehensive plan for the suburb's development, they often look favorably on deviations from the master plan if these deviations will contribute to the tax base of the suburb.

In the smaller suburbs, planning is often contracted out to a professional architect or planning consultant to provide a package deal consisting of a land use survey, population projections, a general plan, and recommendations on zonings. The planning consultants often have little long-range involvement with the communities, and the local planning officials lack the training and expertise to transform the planning document into an ongoing process of guiding municipal growth.[15]

Implementing Devices

The devices used by the city planner to implement the objectives of the comprehensive master plan are basically two—*zoning* and *subdivision control*. Through zoning, the planning commissioners can set aside certain blocks of the city for single-family homes, other blocks for multi-unit dwellings, other blocks for light industry, other blocks for heavy industry, other blocks for commercial retail facilities, and so forth. Under subdivision control, the planner can oblige subdivision developers to install streets, sidewalks, sewers, water facilities, lighting, and perhaps recreational facilities. The cost for these improvements are then passed on to the home buyers and need not be paid from general taxes.

When real estate developers present a proposal that is contrary to the city zoning code or to the general master plan, they have to apply for a *variance*, which is an official exemption from the code. If the developer is large enough to make a significant impact on the community, he or she can normally get projects approved by offering some minor concessions to the planning commissioners. In this way a convenient relationship is worked out between developers and the suburban officials. Developers get essentially what they want, and the suburban officials are able to extract enough compromises from the developers to prove to the suburban residents that they, the officials, are doing their jobs.

An excellent, if perhaps extreme, example of this is described by Herbert Gans in his account of planning in Levittown.[16] The local township planning officials "knew little about city planning," so they contracted with a consultant to serve as their city planner.

> The planner's sympathies were more with Levitt than with the residents. . . .
> His planner's philosophy and his judgment of where the power lay dictated that he work closely with the builder in planning for the township, and that he adapt his recommendations to the builder's proposals. As a result, the preliminary plan, completed in 1959, coincided closely with Levitt's own scheme.
> Yet even when [the public officials] had effective veto power over Levitt's operations, they did not often think to exercise it, because they felt Levitt was trying to do a good job and would make the township the best in the country.
> When the Township officials did question the Levitt proposals, it was almost always on matters of detail. On the larger issues they agreed. . . .[17]

The general trend in suburbia has been to use zoning powers to provide for very clearly and carefully segregated uses of land. Single-family homeowners tend to resent the construction of apartments or townhouses close to them. Consequently, buildings such as townhouses and apartments have commonly been constructed along the freeways, where the land is less desirable for single-family residences and where these larger buildings can serve as noise buffers for the single-family homes. Commercial activity is also quite clearly segregated, usually with the most extensive commercial retail activity being located in large shopping centers designed to be reached by automobile rather than by foot. A number of architectural critics have lamented the tendency toward segregated land use patterns in central cities as well as in suburbs.[18] The major exceptions to segregated land use are found in *planned unit developments* and in suburban new towns, such as Reston, Virginia, or Columbia, Maryland. Planned unit developments (PUDs) are relatively large neighborhoods of a city or suburb that have been zoned for development with a mixture of housing styles, commercial activity, and land uses.

In addition to zoning and subdivision controls as tools to implement the master plan, the city fathers also rely on a *capital improvements budget* to finance a long-range, planned schedule of public projects. The capital improvements budget will normally be drawn up and implemented by a separate capital improvements commission, but three-fourths of the city planners interviewed in one study indicated that they were involved with the capital improvement programs.[19] Since the capital improvements budget has a source of funds to locate public projects throughout the city, it is very important for implementing the master plan.

In the central cities and the larger suburbs, the planning process is much more professional than the process described above for the small suburbs. These larger municipalities hire their own planning staffs, which are usually subordinated to the mayor or the city manager. The focus of planning attention is also likely to differ from the focus in the suburbs. In the fast-growing suburbs, planning attention focuses on controlling future population growth and geographic expansion of the developed areas. By the time a suburb reaches a population large enough to afford the expense of a full-time planning staff and by the time it has transformed its government structure from that of a rural village or township to a municipal corporation, its physical growth pattern has normally been set and quite often its geographic area is practically filled with residential and commercial development. To impose strict development controls at this stage in suburban growth is really to gain control over very little. Nevertheless, if it wishes to get urban renewal funds or housing funds or some other funds from the federal government, the suburb may have to produce a comprehensive master plan for the function involved. Consequently, much of the planning activity in urban areas is defined in terms of urban renewal, urban redevelopment, highway construction, and other large-scale activities that depend on federal funding.

Metropolitan Planning

Because city planning is normally confined to the geographic areas within its municipal boundaries, there is difficulty in coping with problems that transcend municipal boundaries and in coordinating plans with those of neighboring communities. The realization of this in the post-World War II era sparked an interest in planning at the regional or metropolitan level.

The first metropolitan plan was probably the regional plan for New York and its environs, sponsored by a private foundation in 1929. Key provisions of the plan were not implemented, however.[20] And, left on their own, few other metropolises attempted to formulate their own metropolitan plans. Even as late as 1962 there were only 63 metropolitan planning commissions. These agencies were generally understaffed, underfinanced, and without authority to influence regional development. Less than half of the 38 largest planning agencies, in fact, had even developed comprehensive plans. Consequently, they concentrated on population studies, economic analyses, and traditional land use planning.[21]

Federal Funding

Whereas only 63 metropolitan planning commissions existed in 1960, by the end of that decade, their number had tripled to almost 200, and today they exist in almost all MSAs. What sparked this proliferation of planning agencies was federal funding. The 1965 Housing and Urban Development Act authorized funds for research and planning by regional planning agencies. This was a marked departure from the planning incentives written into earlier housing legislation in 1949 and 1954. Although the 1954 act provided incentives for metropolitan plans, most of the planning grants went to local housing and redevelopment authorities to plan for public housing and urban renewal. By contrast, the 1965 incentives were made available to metropolitan agencies, which could use the funds for a broader range of planning activities. This availability of funds was a significant spur to the officials in many metropolises to create metropolitan planning agencies in order to obtain these funds.

The A–95 Review Power

A second explanation for the expansion of metropolitan planning commissions in the 1960s is found in the evolution of the so-called A–95 review power. The Demonstration Cities and Metropolitan Development Act (Model Cities Act) of 1966 demanded that about 30 federal grant programs be approved by metropolitan review agencies before the grants could be awarded. Two years later Congress passed the Intergovernmental Cooperation Act of 1968, which strengthened the ability of each metropolitan review agency to subordinate federal grants to the priorities of its metropolitan development plan. This act stated, "To the maximum extent possible, . . . all federal aid for development purposes shall be consistent with and further the objectives of state, regional and local comprehensive planning."[22] The act gave the President the authority to establish rules and regulations for implementing the metropolitan review power. These rules were spelled out in 1969 by the Office of Management and Budget (OMB) A–95 Circular. For this reason the metropolitan review power was commonly referred to as the A–95 power. Under the terms of A–95, over 100 federal programs were eventually brought under the metropolitan review authority, which was vested in regional planning commissions directed by councils of local elected officials.[23]

This A–95 metropolitan review process was in effect from 1969 to 1983, when an executive order by President Ronald Reagan reduced the number of federal programs subject to review and turned the review authority over to the states. The intent of the executive order was to rectify some rigidities that had crept into the A–95 process over the years and to strengthen the authority of state governments.[24] The main bodies that had served as metropolitan review agencies under A-95 were the councils of government (COGs) set up in most metropolitan areas. Most of these COGs continued to perform the metropolitan review process under state authority after A–95 was terminated.[25]

Federal Impact on Metropolitan Planning

Despite the eventual demise of the A–95 process, the federal government made a significant impact on metropolitan planning. The availability of federal funds to underwrite planning, the emphasis on research, and the review power made it possible for metropolitan planning to be taken seriously for the first time in America. The metropolitan planning agencies now had the funds to hire professional staffs and to contract out particular jobs to consultants who could specialize in given areas. This gave the metropolitan plans a quality that could not be duplicated in most of the smaller municipalities. The metropolitan planning agencies also now have a larger focus that enables them to tackle certain planning issues the local municipalities are incapable of dealing with effectively. Some of these are land use, transportation, water supply, community facilities, air pollution, open space preservation, and recreation.

On these issues, planning has performed a very valuable service to the local suburban planners who have neither the staff nor the viewpoint to undertake the studies conducted by the metropolitan planning agency. This was particularly evident in Detroit, where carefully exercised leadership by the director of the Detroit Metropolitan Area Regional Planning Agency led to the formation of an extraordinarily cooperative Inter-County Committee of County Supervisors,[26] the forerunner of the councils of governments (COGs). Some planning commission studies found most valuable by the suburban officials were population research, industrial trends, land use, zoning regulations, and local public improvement plans.[27]

The Impact and Politics of Metropolitan Planning

Despite the tremendous proliferation of metropolitan agencies since 1965, it is doubtful whether the results of the planning have been very far-reaching. David Ranney writes that these agencies "have not been able to bring about a metropolitan planning policy which is followed by the governments comprising the metropolitan areas."[28] Geographer John Friedmann asserts that "the manifest purpose of this style of planning [i.e., comprehensive development planning]—to shape the development of cities and nations in accord with a preconceived design, and to do so on the basis of functionally rational criteria—was not being accomplished. Where it was tried, and judged by its own claims, comprehensive planning turned out to be a colossal failure."[29]

One reason for the limited effectiveness of metropolitan planning can be traced to the estrangement between politicians and the professional planners. Although planners are political actors in reality, they have traditionally viewed themselves as the self-styled guardians of the public good and as the promoters of long-range policies. But the planners inevitably confront politicians who are supposedly concerned with short-range private benefits for their constituents. This confrontation was described succinctly by Edward C. Banfield, who wrote: "No competent politician will sacrifice votes that may be needed in the next election for gains, however large, that may accrue to the public 10, 20, or 30 years hence."[30] Another reason for the limited effectiveness of metropolitan planning has been the absence of agreed-upon metropolitan goals that can be implemented through a metropolitan development plan. Planners may promote such goals, but they can implement them only if they are accepted by other political actors and if they also control budgets, investment decisions, locational decisions, and zoning practices.

Some evidence indicates that the spate of metropolitan planning since 1965 has apparently been little more than an exercise in drawing up plans merely to get federal money.[31] How useful such plans then become is questionable. One study by the Urban Land Institute found that of 102 cities surveyed that have a planning commission, only ten made specific use of the plans produced by these commissions.[32]

Other inhibiting factors stem from the high value placed on local autonomy. Local officials fear that strong metropolitan plans will force upon them development that they do not want and will deny them development that they may want. In particular, they are reluctant to allow control over zoning, public schools, and other life-style issues to be taken from local hands. Finally, the overwhelming majority of metropolitan planning agencies are not tied to a strong political base.[33] In contrast with a central-city planning agency, which can be tied directly to the mayor and benefit from his or her base of support, the metropolitan planning agency has no electoral constituency of its own nor any major elected political figure who can lend support to it. For all these reasons, the planner tends to view politics as an inhibiting factor that places an upper limit on what can be accomplished through planning.[34]

Advocacy Planning

Because of these obstacles to effective planning, successful planners adopt tactics and objectives that are commensurate with the prevailing organization and dispersion of power in their respective metropolises.[35] Quite often this causes the planners, like other political actors, to be much more responsive to the demands of the functional fiefdoms than to the needs of isolated citizens. Indeed, the uninformed, nontechnical, and often emotional input of the isolated citizen may well be disparaged by the persons planning the development projects in the metropolis. Very few private real estate developers seem inclined to invite citizen participation in the planning of their projects. From the developer's viewpoint, citizen input is negative since citizens usually object to some feature of any project. And since most citizens do not even hear about projects until considerable money has

Source: From *The Herblock Gallery* (New York: Simon & Shuster, 1968). Reprinted by permission.

The difficulties of coordinating federal, state, and local planning are aptly portrayed in this 1965 cartoon by Herblock. Note the monkey wrench which somebody has thrown into the works. Also note the 1754 cartoon. The 1754 unification proposal was the Albany Plan authored by Benjamin Franklin. After the eventual fruition of his unification efforts at the Philadelphia Constitutional Convention, Franklin is supposed to have glanced over his shoulder at a painting of the sun and declared that he believed the sun was rising over the dawn of a new union. It is not clear from Herblock's cartoon whether the sun is rising or setting.

been spent on them and they are presented to a planning commission or zoning board for approval, there is no mechanism for citizen input to be anything but negative. Nor is this inhibition of citizen participation limited to private developers. Big-city planning staffs, highway planners, urban renewal planners, or metropolitan planning agencies tend to be just as unreceptive to citizen groups as are the private developers. Many federal programs require citizen participation in the planning process. But such participation has usually occurred after the plan was drafted, so participation means it is presented at a public meeting for the purpose of enlightening the public. Rarely have citizens played a significant role in drafting city plans or urban renewal plans.[36]* Quite often the result has been a widespread feeling of alienation and helplessness in the face of drastic neighborhood changes caused by construction of locally unwanted freeways,[37] motels, commercial establishments, urban renewal projects,[38] university expansions, or any number of big projects. There is a basic tension between the traditional wish of the early-twentieth-century reformers to depoliticize politics and the Jeffersonian ideal of citizen participation. Thomas Scott has traced much of contemporary urban alienation to this tension. "In many ways, the present level of alienation toward political institutions is the result of the fact that we have moved very swiftly, especially in suburbs, to government by technocrat without raising and resolving the fundamental issues of the relationships between the governmental professionals and the part-time semi-interested citizen."[39]

One proposal to remedy this citizen malaise has been advocacy planning. The major spokesman for advocacy planning was city planner Paul Davidoff, who argued that the planning bureaucracies have aligned themselves with the prevailing local establishments and have neglected the legitimate needs of the poor and the racial minorities. To remedy this, Davidoff proposed that citizens' groups hire professional planners to prepare their own plans and propose them to the appropriate public agencies. In this way citizens can initiate positive proposals to the city government; and since they are represented by a professional planner, they are not overwhelmed by technical jargon.[40]

The concept of advocacy planning provoked a serious split within the planning profession. Traditional planning ideology demands that planning promote the public good rather than advocate the private good of specific clients. Traditionalists believe that city planners should restrict their official acts to land use planning and abstain from political or social issues. The smaller, proadvocacy planning faction rejected both of those beliefs.[41] Today a majority of planners lean more in the direction of pluralism in planning than they do in the traditionalist direction of believing that planners can determine the overall public good.[42] As a consequence of these rifts, however, and of the greater diversity that began to characterize planners when planning proliferated during the 1970s, the community of planners no longer shares a consensus on what the purposes of public planning are or on what role planners ought to play in the political process.[43]

---

*In the Model Cities and Community Action programs, to be sure, there was extensive citizen participation in the planning process.

If the advocacy planners are correct in their charges, urban planning as such has an inherent conservative bias. This statement is supported by empirical evidence at least in the areas of highway planning, urban renewal planning,[44] and comprehensive development planning in which the planners have been responsive primarily to their respective bureaucracies and functional fiefdoms. Such planning is conservative because the plans reflect the biases of past decisions and seek to protect the agency and the program from future encroachment.[45] Herbert Gans argues that the dominant faction of the American Institute of Planners is conservative.[46] Finally, some observers argue that all planning, even advocacy planning, is inherently conservative because it seeks merely to reform existing institutional practices rather than overthrow them.[47]

Most of the arguments for the conservatism of urban planning focus on city-level planning for highways or urban renewal. Metropolitan planning may be a more liberalizing force than these other kinds of planning, for it does represent a challenge to the status quo of municipal autonomy. And *if* the comprehensive metropolitan land use plans were implemented, they would have a sharp effect on the future of suburban sprawl. They would also, *if implemented*, broaden the social access to residences, schools, and jobs in the metropolis. The fact that they have not achieved these things is more a testimony to the strength of the status quo than it is to the conservatism of the metropolitan planners. In this sense the planners are exerting a liberalizing and not a conservative influence on metropolitan politics. The plans would provoke a change in the power relations—a slow, incremental change to be sure, but change nevertheless.[48] Finally, more recent surveys of planners suggest that planners are much more liberal than the general population and much more inclined to be Democrats than Republicans.[49]

Councils of Governments

For performing the metropolitan planning function and the former A–95 clearinghouse function of reviewing federal grant applications, the most popular form of metropolitan agency has been the *council of governments* (COG). A council of governments is a voluntary association of local municipalities and counties that join forces for the purpose of coordinating their activities concerning regional problems. COGs as a governmental device date back to 1954 and the establishment of the Supervisors Inter-County Committee in the Detroit, Michigan, area. Other COGs were created in Washington, D.C. (1957), San Francisco (1961), Salem, Oregon (1958), Seattle, Los Angeles, Atlanta, Philadelphia, and New York.

The Washington Metropolitan Council of Governments

A good example of the reasons for founding a COG and the possibilities and limitations it offers is presented by the Washington, D.C., Metropolitan Council of Governments.[50] This COG (WMCOG) grew out of a cooperative effort in Washington governance, which by the late 1950s was beginning to reach the limits of attacking areawide problems on a function-by-function basis.

There had been a long history of cooperation on functional activities in the Washington region. Eleven special authorities had been set up to regulate particular services in and around Washington. Considerable interstate and interjurisdictional agreement had been worked out on such matters as water supply, sewerage, roads, and recreational space. Nevertheless, most of these jurisdictional agreements had been adopted piecemeal for specific needs, and there was little coordination between them. Each organization was designed in functional terms, and within each functional sector there were often subregional jurisdictions. Maryland, Virginia, and the District of Columbia, for example, all had special agencies dealing with recreational open space. Most of these agencies were underfinanced, and no general body had planning or coordinating responsibility for the whole area.

In 1957 the Washington Metropolitan Regional Conference was organized, and five years later, in 1962, it changed its name to the Washington Metropolitan Council of Governments. Designed to stimulate cooperation between the federal government, the two states, and the various counties and municipalities involved, the WMCOG concentrated on noncontroversial issues such as demonstrating the need for mass transit, water supply, and pollution abatement.

The WMCOG developed an elaborate organization that has become typical of most COGs. Its ultimate governing body is the Conference, which meets semiannually and has representation from each of the constituent unit governments. In between the semiannual meetings, policy is established by an executive board, and day-to-day operations are carried out by an executive secretary and staff. The WMCOG was originally financed by voluntary assessments from each of the constituent units of government, but with the enactment of the 1965 Housing Act these voluntary assessments have been supplemented with federal planning grants.

During its early years, the WMCOG carried out a relatively successful program in the functions that have been referred to here as systems maintenance. Through its studies on transit, it recommended and saw created a National Capital Transportation Agency and subsequently a Washington Metropolitan Area Transit Commission that has successfully undertaken the construction of Washington's subway. WMCOG also drew up a Year 2000 Regional Development Plan in an attempt to focus public attention on several land use problems created by extremely rapid population growth. On the life-style issues, WMCOG has been less successful, but it did create the United Planning Organization, which became the local community action agency once the federal antipoverty program was started in 1965.

The Growth of COGs

COGs experienced their most rapid period of growth during the 1960s. As late as 1960 only seven COGs existed in the country. By 1972 there were more than 300[51] and by 1980, 660.[52] This rapid increase is due primarily to the availability of federal government planning grants and to federal demands for a metropolitan review process. Many metropolitan planning agencies became councils of governments when the 1965 Housing and Urban Development Act made COGs eligible to receive grants for planning and research in a broad range of activities,[53] and by the 1970s federal grants accounted for an estimated two-thirds of all COG expenditures.[54] A further federal stimulus was the designation of COGs as the A–95 review agencies.

In addition to the federal incentives, a second stimulus for the proliferation of COGs was simply that they are so easy to create. All that is required is a joint statement of principles by the affected local governments and the incorporation of an organization to implement those principles. Another important stimulus to the creation of COGs was the establishment in 1967 of a staff and program by the National Service to Regional Councils. The National Service now serves as a clearinghouse for information important to COGs. It consults with local councils and assists them with specific problems, providing information on federal programs.

An Assessment of COGs

COGs possess some very important advantages for intergovernmental cooperation. Not only are they relatively easy to create, but once created they become a mechanism for studying metropolitan problems and for formulating solutions to the problems. Most metropolitan areas never had such a mechanism prior to the formation of the COG. The COG also may have more influence on local governments than some other agencies by virtue of the fact that it is composed of elected officials. Although its proposals may not be as far-reaching as those of institutions further removed from locally elected officials, the very fact that locally elected representatives on the COG have backed the proposals may increase the possibilities of their acceptance.

Nevertheless, COGs also possess extreme limitations as a tool for metropolitan governance. Three limitations in particular stand out: the constituent-unit form of representation, the limitations on COGs' authority, and their lack of success in dealing with the social-access or life-style issues.

The fact that COG members are also officials of local governments means that COGs have a constituent-unit form of representation. This has caused disruptive bickering between the units of government in many COGs, but especially in San Francisco[55] and Cleveland.[56] In both places the problem was eventually resolved by moving toward granting each city representation that was roughly proportional to its population. In Cleveland this was attained only after a bitter conflict in which the Department of Housing and Urban Development threatened to remove from the COG its status as the A–95 review agency.

If the representational problems of COGs can be solved by applying the one-person, one-vote principle to its constituents, the second major problem, that of sufficient authority, is not so easily resolved. The coercive authority of most COGs lies exclusively in their status as the review agency for federal grants, but there is no guarantee that the federal granting agency will uphold a COG's review decision. In fact, in the Washington, D.C. COG, one of the constituent counties from the

State of Maryland temporarily withdrew from WMCOG in disagreement over the general direction of the organization. Cleveland temporarily withdrew from its COG. Because of this possibility of withdrawal, COGs cannot take decisive and effective action unless an overwhelming majority of members support any given proposal. And, of course, overwhelming majority support does not normally occur on the controversial life-style issues. Even in exercising the A-95 federal grant review power, COGs have been reluctant to exercise their authority to the fullest. A study of eleven COGs in Texas found that the review process was perfunctory. Only two COGs in Texas had ever made a negative review.[57] Melvin Mogulof, a knowledgeable student of COGs, has commented that "the COG finds it extremely difficult to do things such as make critical comments about applications of member governments for federal funds, establish priorities which affect member governments, or influence local governmental actions in an attempt to make them consistent with regional planning."[58] And political scientist Joseph F. Zimmerman asserts flatly that "No COG has solved a major problem."[59]

Finally, COGs have been very ineffective in dealing with the social-access and life-style issues discussed at the beginning of this chapter. There are two reasons for this. First, the 1966 Model Cities Act, which created the review power, specifically limited it to "federal loans or grants to assist in carrying out open-space projects or for the planning or construction of hospitals, airports, libraries, water supply and distribution facilities, sewerage facilities and waste treatment works, highways, transportation facilities, and water development and land conservation projects within any metropolitan area."[60] This language clearly ignores the social-access issues of tax disparities, low-income public housing in the suburbs, and busing of pupils to achieve racial balance in the schools. The second reason for the weakness of COGs in dealing with the life-style issues stems from the constituent-unit structure of COGs. This structure effectively grants a veto to the very suburban governments that do not want to lose control over the life-style issues. Consequently, the number of COG successes on social-access or life-style issues such as housing are very few.* A study of ninety-eight COGs, in fact, found that they rejected the idea that central-city problems should be one of their focal points.[61]

This ability of COGs to define metropolitan problems in a way that excludes central-city problems has provoked some sharp conflicts between the COGs and the central city. The sharpest conflict of this sort was probably that between Cleveland and the Northeast Ohio Areawide Coordinating Agency (NOACA). Formed primarily to meet federal A-95 review demands and to obtain federal grants, NOACA was heavily dominated by the suburban governments. NOACA rejected a Cleveland proposal that the COG take action to ensure the existence of middle- and low-income housing in the suburbs.[62] NOACA then refused to deal with the

---

*In Washington, the WMCOG prepared a model fair-housing ordinance that its constituent governments were urged to adopt. In Dayton, a procedure was established for allocating responsibility among the governments for low- and moderate-income housing [See Domestic Council Committee on National Growth, *Report on National Growth, 1972* (Washington, D.C.: U.S. Government Printing Office, 1972), p. 29].

question of rapid transit and instead favored a state-highway-department-proposed freeway that was opposed by both Cleveland and several eastern suburbs. Cleveland then withdrew its financial support from NOACA and sued for representation on the one-person, one-vote principle. NOACA retaliated by barring Cleveland from voting at board meetings. The immediate issue of representation was resolved when HUD threatened to strip NOACA of its A–95 review power if NOACA did not adopt the one-person, one-vote principle. But even with the proportional representation on the council, Cleveland is still entitled to only one-fourth of the NOACA board members, and the deep-rooted suspicions of the central city have not disappeared among the other 75 percent of the board.

Because of all these weaknesses, it was widely assumed that COGs would suffer heavily when the Reagan administration abolished the A–95 review process and sharply reduced the federal planning grants that the COGs relied on so greatly. And indeed, 125 of the 660 COGs closed down under these pressures.[63] But the remainder have adapted fairly well to the less favorable political environment of the 1980s. Although they relied on federal funds for 76 percent of their budgets on the average in 1977, this fell to 48 percent by 1983. They made up most of that shortfall by getting more funds from state and local governments, grants from foundations, and service contracts from other agencies and institutions that were willing to pay for planning studies as well as technical and advisory services.[64] As a consequence, COGs have become much more resilient than was expected, and they seem to be filling a need for a centralized metropolitan agency to provide planning, studies, and technical services to other governments.

Metropolitan Policymaking with Teeth

Although metropolitan planning, councils of government, and the metropolitan review process have not been very effective in coping with the problems of the multicentered metropolis, they could evolve into effective instruments for policymaking at the metropolitan level. To go from a council of government with metropolitan planning and metropolitan review authority to a metropolitan agency with real teeth to make and enforce metropolitan policies would be only a series of small steps. During the 1970s, an evolutionary, incremental process took place in two areas that led precisely in that direction. In the Minneapolis–Saint Paul, Minnesota metropolitan area, one model of metropolitan policymaking evolved, whereas a quite different model emerged in Portland, Oregon.

Minneapolis–Saint Paul: Separating Policymaking from Service Administration

Powers of the Metropolitan Council

In essence the Twin Cities Metropolitan Council is a metropolitan planning and policymaking agency. It has four major powers.[65] First, as the metropolitan planning agency, it is responsible for preparing the metropolitan development guide. The development guide is a statement of policies on topics that range from the location of airports to solid waste disposal to the distribution of low-income housing throughout the suburbs to the channeling of future growth into predetermined locations in the region (see Chapter 9).

The Council's second responsibility is reviewing the comprehensive development plans of the local governments in the region (see Chapter 8). Third, the Council oversees and coordinates the metropolitan commissions and special districts. As discussed in Chapter 9 (pp. 268–269), the Council appoints the members of the three metropolitan commissions responsible for transit, waste control (sewers), and regional parks and open space. Although the Council cannot appoint the members of the other two metropolitan commissions responsible for airports or sports facilities, it is empowered to review the budgets of these agencies and to veto capital expenditure projects. As discussed in Chapter 9, the Metropolitan Council has used this authority to bring the metropolitan districts in line with metropolitan policies for transit and airports.

A fourth power of the Metropolitan Council is to review applications from local governments and private organizations for many federal or state grant and loan guarantee programs. Although the A–95 process was used very timidly in most metropolitan areas, it was used with some forcefulness in the Twin Cities to encourage local governments to cooperate with the metropolitan policies. For example, in 1973 the Metropolitan Council refused to review one suburb's application for park funds until that suburb came up with a plan for low- and moderate-income housing.[66] When the A–95 power was replaced by a state-level review power in 1983, the Metropolitan Council was not greatly affected, because the state of Minnesota simply designated the Metropolitan Council as the agency to review grant proposals in that metropolitan area.

Creation and Incremental Growth of the Metropolitan Council

The Metropolitan Council was established by legislative act in 1967. Prior to 1967 the Twin Cities region was plagued for many years by governmental fragmentation, tax inequities and disparities, and inconsistent provision of services throughout the region. The two central cities were ringed by more than 130 incorporated suburban municipalities. This made central-city annexation and city-county consolidation strategies useless for coping with metropolitan problems. And the need to provide services in the suburbs led to a proliferation of municipalities, metropolitan agencies, special districts, and joint-powers agreements. By the mid-1960s, the region had more than 300 governments with very little coordination between them. The lack of coordination was beginning to produce a crisis in sewage disposal and water supply. A state Health Department investigation in 1959 discovered that 250,000 people in 39 suburbs were getting their drinking water from contaminated wells. More than 400,000 people used septic tanks rather than sewers.[67] When the Federal Housing Administration announced that it would no longer insure mortgages for homes that were not tied into central sewer and water systems, it became clear that some kind of metropolitan-wide coordinating action was necessary.

Concerning the kind of action that was needed, at least eleven major groups put forward ideas to establish some form of metropolitan coordinating agency. Much interest was expressed in the Toronto federative experience, and several reformers traveled to Toronto to gain firsthand impressions of its operations, but federation was rejected as unsuitable and politically unfeasible. More conservative reformers were interested in establishing a council of governments for the Twin Cities.

Perhaps the crucial event was the court-ordered reapportionment of the state legislature in 1965, which gave the metropolitan area its fair share of legislators for the first time. With the newly apportioned legislature, the breakdown in providing sewer services, the threat to the safety of the water supply, the non-coordination of metropolitan agencies, and the variety of civic groups pressing for action, by the time the legislative session opened in 1967 it was no longer a question of *whether* the legislature would establish some new metropolitan agency. The question had become: What powers would be given to the new agency and how would it be constituted?

Because of this evolution of consensus, metropolitan reform in the Twin Cities never went through a voting campaign. And the kinds of groups that surfaced in St. Louis, Cleveland, and other cities to defeat metropolitan reform schemes never argued against the creation of the Metropolitan Council. Suburban officials, who may have viewed the new Metropolitan Council suspiciously, never organized themselves against its creation. In fact, their lobbying agency, the League of Minnesota Municipalities, put forward a proposal for the Metropolitan Council that was more far-reaching than the bill that eventually passed the legislature. County officials in the metropolitan area formed an Inter-County Council in 1966 to offer an alternative to the Metropolitan Council. And a chain of suburban newspapers opposed the idea of a Metropolitan Council with teeth and proposed in its stead that the legislature create a Council of Governments for the Twin Cities. But the very fact that these interests spoke of an alternative rather than speaking in opposition indicates how much consensus existed about changing the status quo.

This lack of any significant opposition to the Metropolitan Council was explained by one observer as the result of a consensus of opinion that "something needed to be done, and [that] there was no push for a comprehensive home rule metropolitan government consolidation."[68] This lack of substantial opposition among the suburban officials might also have been a reflection of the particular nature of the political culture in Minnesota. This political culture has been described by Daniel J. Elazar as more moralistic than the political cultures of Cleveland or St. Louis. According to Elazar, a moralistic political culture is more receptive to governance for the common good than is either the individualistic or the traditional political culture.*

*In Elazar's terminology, the individualistic culture has a utilitarian concept of government that prefers a minimal amount of governmental intervention in what are considered private, individual matters. The traditional political culture is ambivalent toward governmental intervention in the private sphere and looks upon public officeholding as the perquisite of the social and economic elites. The moralistic political culture has no ambivalence about governmental intervention in the private sphere and believes that governments have a responsibility to act for the public rather than the private good [See Elazar's *American Federalism: A View from the States* (New York: Thomas Y. Crowell, 1966), pp. 89–97]. The importance of Minnesota's political culture to the establishment of the Metropolitan Council and the appropriateness of Elazar's concept of a moralistic political culture was suggested in a private communication by Frederick M. Wirt.

Another very important factor was the fact that the debate occurred in the forum of the legislature rather than in the forum of a voter referendum. When an issue comes to a referendum, one has only two choices: One can vote for the issue or against it. Given this choice, suburban newspapers, county officials, and municipal officials in the Twin Cities might have opposed such a referendum just as similar officials had done elsewhere. But in the forum of the legislature, the normal process is one of negotiation, bargaining, and compromise rather than adamant opposition, especially when strong interest groups are pushing for action on an issue that clearly needs legislation.

A final important feature about metropolitan reform in the Twin Cities is the incremental nature of the way in which the reforms have occurred. As indicated above, the creation of the Metropolitan Council was the culminating event in a long history of developing a consensus that some areawide approach to metropolitan problems was needed. Nor did the metropolitan reform cease with the creation of the Metropolitan Council in 1967. In every legislative session since then, the council's powers have been expanded, refined, and clarified. If the only forum for debating the Council's powers had been a referendum, it is highly unlikely that the Council's powers would have continued evolving after its creation.

Reflection on the Twin Cities' approach to metropolitan governance shows some advantages and some disadvantages. The major disadvantage is that a metropolitan reform enacted by a state legislature is not likely to be as far-reaching as one drafted by a charter commission and submitted to the electorate in a referendum. The interest groups that oppose metropolitan government are able to bargain with the legislators to dilute the scope of the reform. The Metropolitan Council created by the Minnesota legislature, for example, is not nearly as far-reaching a metropolitan government as are the governments created by referendum in Miami, Jacksonville, and Nashville.

The major advantages are two. First, as indicated above, the legislative approach to metropolitan reform increased the likelihood of some kind of reform governance being established, since most city-county consolidation proposals and other metropolitan government proposals are defeated at the ballot box. A weak, legislatively created government may be better than no reform at all. Second, the legislative approach is more conducive to an incremental evolution of the powers of the metropolitan government once it is created. In contrast to the gradual refinement of powers of the Twin Cities Metropolitan Council, the Miami–Dade County Metro can change its charter only through a referendum. And Miami voters have not usually been receptive to changes, such as switching to an elected county executive, that would broadly strengthen the Metro.

Distinctive Features of the Twin Cities Model

From the foregoing, several distinctive features of the Twin Cities model of metropolitan government are apparent. First, in the words of one of the Council's architects, the Council's role is one of policy leadership, not the swamp of administrative detail.[69] The Council does not operate anything. The bus system, for example, is run by the Transit Commission. The sewers are maintained by the Waste Control Commission and the airports by the Airports Commission. Exempt from operational and administrative responsibilities, the Council can devote its attention to the overall policies that guide the operation of these various services.

A second distinctive feature of the Twin Cities model is that it avoided the most debilitating aspects of a Council of Government. As noted earlier, many COGs were emasculated when member governments threatened either to withdraw or not make their financial contributions. This would not be possible in the Twin Cities, since the local governments are not members of the Metropolitan Council in the first place. Most Council districts overlap municipal boundaries, so Council members do not represent specific municipalities. Also, the Council has its own property tax authority, so it is not dependent on local governments for financial contributions.

Finally, the Twin Cities model is distinctive for the incremental, legislative approach that was taken to reform.[70] This provides a corrective feedback process. Each time the state legislature increased the Council's powers, those powers were tested in practice. In instances where the new authority was not working out well or it created conflicts with other governmental units, the problem could be brought back to the next legislative session for fine tuning. For example, in 1973 the Metropolitan Council and the Metropolitan Transit Commission were deadlocked over the question of who had the authority to plan for future transit development and whether that future development should rely on rapid rail or expanded bus service. The legislature responded to this conflict with the Metropolitan Reorganization Act of 1974, which clarified the Council's authority over the Transit Commission for policymaking purposes.

The Twin Cities: Some Caveats

Although the Twin Cities have created a truly distinctive model of metropolitan governance, it is important to remember that it still is not a true *metropolitan government*, and consequently it has important weaknesses in dealing with that area's metropolitan problems. For one thing, despite the Metropolitan Council's vaunted powers to control development, the Council was for all practical purposes bypassed in making some of the most important development decisions of the past decade, including a domed stadium, a racetrack, and a World Trade Center skyscraper. It also came under severe criticism in the mid-1980s for its shortcomings in transit planning and in overseeing a scandal-ridden Metropolitan Waste Control Commission. Because of this, the Metropolitan Council's extensive powers over the metropolitan districts began to look less impressive than they did a decade earlier when the Council had forced both the Transit Commission to back down on plans for a rapid-rail system and the Airports Commission to back down on its plans for a second airport. As the Metropolitan Council celebrated its 20th birthday in 1987, it was looking more and more like a stodgy, mature bureaucratic agency than the dynamic policymaking body it had been for its first decade of existence.[71]

Portland: Uniting Metropolitan Planning with Service Delivery

In 1978, voters in the three-county Portland, Oregon, metropolitan area approved a metropolitan governing structure that has most of the powers of the Twin Cities Metropolitan Council and some others as well.[72] The Columbia Region Association of Governments (Portland's COG) and the Metropolitan Service District (a special district responsible for the zoo and some other areawide functions, including solid waste) were combined into a single agency to be known as the Metropolitan Service District. The new Metropolitan Service District was given responsibility for areawide land planning, federal A–95 review powers, and direct provision of a limited number of services—sewage treatment, liquid and solid waste disposal, public transit, the zoo, and drainage and flood control. The Metropolitan Service District also was empowered to assume authority at some future date over a number of other functions if that seemed feasible. These were sports facilities, criminal justice, open-space preservation, parks, water supply, and libraries. The Service District is governed by a board elected for four-year terms from twelve single-member districts. Elections were held in November 1978, and in January 1979 the new metropolitan government began operation.

Like the Twin Cities model, the Portland model did not spring unexpectedly out of nowhere. The Council of Governments had existed for many years. In the early 1970s, a number of metropolitan services had been brought together under the Metropolitan Service District, making it one of the nation's few multifunctional metropolitan districts. In 1975 the National Academy of Public Administration began to study the possibility of forming a two-tier government in the region. Cooperating in the study was a sixty-five-member Tri-County Local Government Commission of local officials and private citizens who sent a two-tiered proposal to the Oregon legislature in 1978. The legislature limited the new government's authority to the urbanized and urbanizing area of the three-county region and then submitted the proposal directly to voters in the three counties. They approved it by a margin of 55 to 45 percent. Ironically, the wording of the issue on the ballot ("Reorganize Metropolitan Service District, Abolish CRAG") led many voters to think that they were voting to abolish a metropolitan planning agency, not to create a more powerful one.[73]

As the new government started business in 1979, it faced two major problems. First, it did not have a secure tax base, and Oregon at that moment was in the midst of a taxpayers' revolt. To get a property tax levy, the Metropolitan Service District would need approval from the voters. Voters defeated such a proposal in 1980.[74] Its second problem concerned the thorny question of solid waste disposal. The region did not have much suitable landfill space left for disposing of solid waste, and most communities did not want any more landfills in their own backyards. Metro, as the Metropolitan Service District is called in Portland, set the landfill problem as its highest priority and came up with a workable solution. It also attained control over the geographic sprawl of the urban population. Metro still faces a serious funding problem, however. If it can resolve that problem, it is likely to expand into other governmental operations as metropolitan needs arise.[75]

Although it is too early to assess the effectiveness of the Portland experiment, it does have some notable distinguishing features. First, unlike the Twin Cities model, the Portland model gives both operating responsibilities as well as policy-making responsibilities to its metropolitan government. It also makes the new government elective, which should give it a source of legitimacy that the Twin Cities Metropolitan Council lacks. Second, the Portland model, like the Twin Cities model, has used an incremental approach to reform. As pointed out above, considerable background work had been laid for the new government throughout the 1970s. Although the 1978 creation was much more than a simple incremental step, the full achievement of the Metropolitan Service District's potential seems destined to follow an incremental pattern.

Finally, it must be noted that the mere establishment of the Metropolitan Service District is an extraordinary achievement. Although it is not actually a general-purpose government such as Dade County, Florida, it goes far beyond the Twin Cities Metropolitan Council, which has no operating responsibilities. In sum, it is the first two-tier government since Miami–Dade County was established more than two decades earlier.

Conclusions: Change and Bias in the Planning and Review Functions

Metropolitan planning and the metropolitan review process since the mid-1960s represent a small but significant change in the politics of metropolitan governance. They illustrate well the incremental nature of urban political change. They represent change because they are a marked departure from the devices to preserve the status quo. However, they represent *incremental* change because they are not as drastic or as far-reaching as the city-county consolidations, the urban county governments, and the two-tiered metropolitan governments discussed in Chapter 11. Since few such metropolitan governments were actually created, and since those that were created were the result of extraordinary conditions, the drastic, far-reaching changes are not very attainable.

With drastic change unlikely and with the consequences of the multicentered metropolis still unsolved, the most successful innovations for governing the metropolis have been the combination of metropolitan planning and policymaking. In some metropolises, such as Minneapolis–Saint Paul, the federal review process has been augmented by state-granted review powers. In most metropolises, these functions have been given to the COGs. This change is incremental because it does not go very far, but it leaves open the possibility for further evolution of the COG toward becoming a stronger institution, as happened in Portland.

The incremental nature of the review process can best be seen in the distinction between the systems-maintenance and life-style issues. As indicated above, the metropolitan review power worked best on the systems-maintenance issues and in most metropolises was not applied very well to the life-style or social-access issues. This is incremental change because it touches only one small increment of the sum total of issues of metropolitan politics. As Oliver Williams suggested, the major cleavage in metropolitan politics today seems to be occurring over the question of equal access to upper-middle-class life styles as exemplified in the few exclusive suburbs. The cleavages are basically related to race and class. The issues that provoke these cleavages are zoning, the expansion of low- and moderate-income public housing into certain suburbs, busing to achieve racial balance in the public schools, and the elimination of fiscal disparities in the metropolis.

Because of this, the A-95 review process and metropolitan planning were not very effective in removing the class and racial biases of the multicentered metropolis that were discussed at the end of Chapter 10. Theoretically they could be effective for this. Given the stipulation of the Intergovernmental Cooperation Act of 1968 that federal grants be consistent with the objectives of metropolitan planning, there is no theoretical reason why the A-95 review agencies could not have used their planning and review power to remove the biases of the multicentered metropolis. They could have written into their metropolitan plans provisions for low- and moderate-income housing in the suburbs, for example, or provisions for coordinated land use zoning, and then used their review power to deny unrelated federal grants to those municipalities that refused to follow the plan's provisions. The agencies could also lobby before the state legislatures to make significant modifications in tax disparities in the metropolis and to equalize the financing of public education.

Metropolitan planning agencies *could* do these things. But it is obvious that most metropolitan planning agencies, especially the COGS, did not and are not doing them. Because of the limitations on COGs discussed earlier, COGs are very unlikely to reverse the biases of the multicentered metropolis, although they have demonstrated that they can deal effectively with some of the systems-maintenance problems. What authority they might have exercised seems to have been diminished even further by the elimination of the A-95 power.

Metropolitan planning agencies and COGs may also have a greater bias toward professional values in determining metropolitan priorities and in settling metropolitan problems than do the traditional general-purpose local governments.[76] The professionalism of the city planner and the public administration specialist becomes much more institutionalized in metropolitan government than it does in suburban or old central-city government. The party politician and the ward alderman do not necessarily disappear under metropolitan government, but they necessarily have to conduct themselves in the language of the professionals and on the terms of the professionals when they deal with certain items. A comprehensive development plan, for example, may be necessary to get some kinds of federal grants. And it must be drafted in language that is at least understandable if not acceptable to the federal planning officials involved in making the grants. Not only do the planning professionals determine the language to be used, they also play a significant role in setting the agenda for issues the metropolitan governments will confront.[77]

Some observers have suggested that this bias toward professionalism in metropolitan government also involves a bias toward public regardingness.[78] The professional planners will supposedly have in mind the overall interest of the public in the entire metropolitan area. However, such an assertion is based on the assumption that planners are public regarding. As shown earlier, such an assumption is difficult to verify.

Finally, the most striking aspect of contemporary metropolitan politics has been the role of the federal government. The 1960s and 1970s saw the emergence of the federal government as a force behind change. Legislation in those years transformed the federal government from a stimulator of both the multicentered metropolis and the expansion of functional fiefdoms to a promoter of metropolitan planning and coordination. It is primarily from actions by the federal courts and some agencies of the executive branch that substantial inroads have been made on the capacity to deal with the systems-maintenance issues.

This trend toward increasing involvement of the federal government in metropolitan affairs came under intense criticism in the 1980s. The Reagan administration sharply reduced federal funding for metropolitan problems and sought to reduce the federal government's domestic role. These issues will be discussed in Chapter 13.

Summary

1. Oliver Williams has posited a "life-style model" of metropolitan reform. In this theory, the systems-maintenance functions of government may get turned over to metropolitan authorities, but in the absence of outside intervention, the life-style functions that control social access to upper-middle-class life styles are performed by local-level governments.

2. Metropolitan planning emerged after city planning. Although there was some city planning in colonial times, most city planning dates from the early 1900s. Metropolitan planning did not begin to spread until the mid-1960s, when the federal government began to make planning grants available and also began to require a metropolitan plan in order for a region to be eligible for certain types of federal aid.

3. To date, metropolitan planning has had limited effectiveness.

4. Because of the availability of federal funding and because of federal review requirements to get federal grants (A–95), councils of government began to spread rapidly during the 1970s. Although COGs do perform planning and review functions, they have several inherent weaknesses, especially for dealing with the life-style issues. Since local governments are represented in a COG, those local governments can paralyze the COG by threatening to withdraw or to withhold their voluntary financial assessments.

5. During the 1970s, two innovations for metropolitan policymaking with some potential for strength emerged in Minnesota and Oregon. The Minnesota model stressed the separation of policymaking authority from the actual administration of service delivery. The Oregon model combined the planning

and policymaking functions of COGs with the actual administration of public service delivery.

6. The instruments of incremental change (metropolitan planning, COGs, and A–95 review) have a number of biases. They have not dealt with the life-style issues of metropolitan politics nearly as well as they have with the systems-maintenance issues. They have not reversed the exclusionary politics discussed in Chapter 10. They also may be biased in favor of the value systems of professional administrators rather than the value systems of traditional local government politicians.

Part V
Toward a National Approach to Metropolitan Policymaking

The involvement of the federal government in the political affairs of the metropolis has had a marked effect on both the tone of metropolitan politics and the structures of metropolitan governance. Primarily because of pressures from the federal government, the life-style issues are kept alive. And primarily because of pressures from the federal government, metropolitan planning, metropolitan planning agencies, and councils of governments have markedly increased. Whereas federal involvement prior to 1965 on balance supported the multicentered metropolis and the functional fiefdoms, federal involvement since then has been characterized by an ambivalence toward these structures. On the one hand it supports them. On the other hand, it seeks greater centralization of authority at the metropolitan level.

Because of this ambivalence, and because of the impact that federal programs have on cities, it is often argued that a national urban policy is needed to tie the hundreds of separate urban programs into coherent operations that strive to attain compatible objectives. Recent presidential administrations have come to grips with these developments in different ways, with each administration leaving its particular impact on the urban landscape. These developments and their relationship to the changing federal role in urban affairs are examined in Chapter 13. Finally, Chapter 14 speculates on the likely political changes in the American metropolis by the year 2010.

Chapter 13
The Changing Federal Role in Metropolitan Affairs

The developments discussed in Chapter 12 (metropolitan planning and councils of governments) share one feature: They were originally started because of the intervention of the federal government in urban affairs. Federal involvement in urban affairs extends to many other areas as well. Urban renewal and urban freeway systems resulted directly from federal activity. Urban welfare programs, criminal justice programs, and health care programs are heavily financed by the federal government. So extensive has the federal involvement become and so far-reaching have been the changes in the nature of its involvement that the changing federal role in urban affairs requires some detailed explanation.

Five broad changes can be seen in the evolution of the federal role. First was the invention of the grant-in-aid as a device for urban problem solving. This device saw its greatest expansion in the 1930s and the 1960s. Second were the grand designs of the Lyndon Johnson presidency: the waging of a War on Poverty and the creation of a Great Society. Third were the Nixon administration proposals of revenue sharing and grant consolidation, as well as the attempts to reorient federal domestic programs away from the big-city Democratic officials favored under Johnson's Great Society and toward more Republican-oriented officials in suburbs, small towns, and state governments. Fourth was the attempt of the Carter administration to articulate a coherent national urban policy that could guide the hundreds of specific programs the federal government promotes in urban areas. Fifth was the Reagan administration's efforts to reduce the federal urban role through initiatives such as New Federalism, budget reductions, and regulatory cutbacks. Presumably, Reagan's successor will put still another stamp on urban policy.

Although each presidency has contributed something new to the evolution of the federal urban role, it must be noted that these contributions did not always disappear as their sponsors left the White House. On the contrary, each change has been accompanied by the development of permanent constituencies that benefit from the new agencies and programs. These institutions, programs, and constituencies thus become a permanent feature of the urban political landscape.

358

Grants-in-Aid and the Federal Approach to Urban Problem Solving

Grants-in-Aid

A grant-in-aid is simply a federal payment to a state or local government to perform some specified activity. The state or local government usually must match a certain percentage of the federal funds and must adhere to program guidelines established by the federal government. Until 1930 there were only about ten such programs.[1]

Beginning with the Great Depression of the 1930s, the number of grants-in-aid grew steadily until 1960, when there were 132 such programs.[2] They were used to finance highway construction, public works, public assistance, public housing, airport construction, hospital construction, vocational education, and many other goals. During the 1960s and 1970s there was a greater emphasis than earlier to design grant-in-aid programs to accomplish nationally defined objectives rather than to help state governments accomplish state objectives. Federal grants increased for social programs and environmental protection. Consequently, the number of grants-in-aid proliferated to 539 in 1981 and amounted to $94.8 billion. President Ronald Reagan's New Federalism (to be discussed later) reduced the funding to $88.8 billion in 1982, and the number of grants was eventually reduced to 409. Despite these reductions, the funding for grants-in-aid began to grow again in subsequent years and by 1988 totaled nearly $110 billion.

As shown in Figure 13-1, grants-in-aid can be distinguished by narrowness or broadness of the purpose for which funds are granted. Categorical grants are specified for very narrowly defined purposes, and they give recipient governments very little discretion in spending the funds they receive. Interstate highway grants, for example, can be used only to build or maintain the Interstate Highway System.

When several categorical grants are consolidated under a single, broad grant in which greater discretion is given to the recipient agency, the result is a *block grant*. A prime example of a block grant is the 1981 Social Services Block Grant, which consolidated three separate social services grants into one program. While the federal funds for this block grant were sharply reduced from the level of funding for the previous social services grants, the SSBG sought to give states much greater flexibility in how they administer social service programs and to allow them much greater discretion in how they apply the federal funds. Some states took advantage of this flexibility to eliminate programs that had been previously required by federal law but were not serving many people, and also to establish fees for some social services.[3] Under the previous categorical grants, this flexibility would not have been possible.

The third type of grant, General Revenue Sharing (GRS), was initiated in 1972 and gave local governments broad discretion to use their GRS funds any way they wished, so long as it did not violate the law. GRS originally went to both state and local governments, but the program was amended in 1980 to provide funding for local governments only. In 1987 the program was essentially abolished.

Figure 13-1. Types of Grants-in-Aid

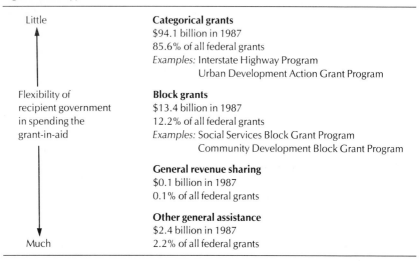

Little	**Categorical grants**
	$94.1 billion in 1987
	85.6% of all federal grants
	Examples: Interstate Highway Program
	Urban Development Action Grant Program
Flexibility of	**Block grants**
recipient government	$13.4 billion in 1987
in spending the	12.2% of all federal grants
grant-in-aid	*Examples:* Social Services Block Grant Program
	Community Development Block Grant Program
	General revenue sharing
	$0.1 billion in 1987
	0.1% of all federal grants
	Other general assistance
	$2.4 billion in 1987
Much	2.2% of all federal grants

In addition to being classified according to the flexibility they give to local governments, grants-in-aid are also distinguished by the degree of discretion permitted the federal granting agency to deny grants to applicants that fail to meet the agency's specifications. If the federal agency has no discretion but must allot its funds to states or communities by the terms of a rigid formula established by Congress, that grant is a *formula grant*. If the federal agency has lots of discretion to deny or award the grant, then that grant is called a *project grant*. Of the grants shown in Figure 13-1, the Community Development Block Grant is a formula grant because each city's share is automatically determined by a congressionally devised formula. A good example of a project grant would be the Urban Development Action Grant (UDAG) in Figure 13-1. To get a UDAG grant, a city must apply to the Department of Housing and Urban Development (HUD) and specify what projects will be built with the funds. HUD then has discretion to fund these project requests as it sees fit.

The grants-in-aid have been a very controversial tool for involving the federal government in domestic problems, and federal grants have attracted as much criticism as they have praise. Before analyzing their pros and cons, it will be useful to look at some specific grant-in-aid programs in operation. This will be done by examining the early urban grant programs for housing and urban renewal. We will then turn to the evolution of federal urban programs in the 1960s and 1970s and examine the relative merits of the narrow-based categorical grants as compared to the broader-based block grants and general revenue sharing.

Early Urban Programs: Housing and Urban Renewal

The first grants-in-aid that aimed most deliberately and directly at urban problems were the public housing and urban renewal programs. The legislation setting up these programs set the agenda for debating federal urban involvement throughout the 1950s and early 1960s.[4]

Housing

Federal housing programs date back to the 1930s, when federal action was required to limit the foreclosing of mortgages and to keep the mortgage-lending institutions from going bankrupt.[5] These actions were followed by the long-term, low-interest, low-down-payment, guaranteed mortgages of the Federal Housing Administration (FHA) and the Veterans' Administration (VA). As noted in Chapter 10, these FHA and VA programs served the suburban white working-class and lower-middle-class housing markets rather than the central-city poor and the racial minorities.

To provide housing assistance for the poor, the Housing Act of 1937 was passed. This act provided federal funds for local housing authorities to purchase land in blighted urban areas, tear down old buildings, construct apartments, and rent them out at subsidized rates to low-income persons.[6] For a variety of reasons, most of these housing projects failed to solve the housing problems of the poor. As of the mid-1960s the programs had actually torn down more housing than they had constructed.[7] They led to increasing concentrations of blacks in the big-city ghettos, and in some cities they were even used deliberately to relocate blacks from scattered locations to a few large ghettos.[8] Many housing projects themselves have degenerated into dangerous, high-rise slums.[9] So dangerous and unpleasant was the Pruitt-Igoe public housing project in St. Louis, for example, that people refused to live in it. Its 2700 apartments never maintained high occupancy rates. And in 1972 the failure of this project was publicly admitted when some of the buildings were torn down.[10] Public housing projects seldom related housing to the broader social and cultural environment.[11] Rather, they tended to concentrate large numbers of people with severe social problems in environments that lacked supporting social services or even more stable neighborhood structures. High-rise housing projects were especially vulnerable to crime.[12] To some critics public housing was virtually meant to fail.[13]

Since the early 1960s federal housing efforts have gone through several significant experiments with leased public housing, attempts to scatter public housing sites into middle-class and white neighborhoods, subsidized interest rates for low- and moderate-income home buyers, subsidized interest rates for developers to build low-cost rental housing, and experiments with housing vouchers. Many of these programs ran into severe difficulty. For example, the plan for subsidizing the interest rates of low-income home buyers got caught in a scandal that saw unscrupulous speculators making cosmetic repairs to basically unsound structures and then selling them to unsophisticated purchasers under the federal plan. When the new purchasers discovered that the basic defects would be extremely costly to repair, they often abandoned the houses and let their mortgages be foreclosed. Since the FHA guaranteed the mortgages, the FHA and its parent department HUD got stuck with billions of dollars of unpaid mortgages and hundreds of thousands of slum properties.[14] HUD became the nation's biggest slumlord. Another scandal involved a leased public housing program in Chicago that was found to be so flagrantly biased against integrated housing that the federal courts ordered the dispersal of subsidized housing into Chicago's suburbs and white neighborhoods.[15] In New York City, attempts by Mayor John Lindsay to scatter public housing projects in white neighborhoods ran into so much opposition that it had to be dropped.[16]

Because of these various federal experiments over the years, a wide variety of housing programs currently exist in cities, most of which are now run honestly and with reasonable effectiveness. These range from operating the old but still existing public housing projects to recent attempts at urban homesteading (the sale of government-owned dilapidated houses at very low prices to middle-income people who promise to rehabilitate them and live in them).

The single most important housing program today, the one that currently gets the greatest share of funds, is Section 8 of the 1974 Housing and Community Development Act. This program stimulates the rehabilitation of existing housing units for leased public housing. Until 1984, Section 8 was also used to get builders to include low- and moderate-income units in their new construction projects. With the ending of the new-construction component of the program in 1984, Section 8 has become primarily a rent supplement program. Typically a low-income family will pay 30 percent of its net income in rent to the apartment owners, and the local housing authority will pay the difference between that and a fair rental price, which it sets. To qualify for the program, apartment owners must maintain their apartments up to the city's housing codes. For this reason Section 8 provides an incentive to rehabilitate older buildings. Although Section 8 has been criticized for being very expensive,[17] it has turned out to be one of the most popular and least scandal-tainted housing programs for low- and moderate-income people. The number of Section 8 applicants in each city far exceeds the funds available, and a person often has to spend a long time on a waiting list before getting assistance. The Reagan administration proposed replacing Section 8 with a system of housing vouchers that recipients could use to help pay rent in any dwelling of their own choice without approval from the local housing authority. An experimental housing program passed Congress in 1983, but Congress has resisted turning it into a permanent program.

A major problem with both Section 8 and housing vouchers is that they provide large amounts of money for rent subsidies without adding to the permanent supply of public housing units. Under Section 8, developers received federal subsidies to construct apartment buildings. But after 5 to 20 years (depending on the contract) they have the right to pay off their long-term mortgage and give up any further subsidies. If they do this, they are permitted to drop out of the Section 8 program. By the late 1980s a number of Section 8 owners were beginning to find that the inflation of housing costs, urban gentrification, and central-city redevelopment processes had made their buildings much more valuable on the open market than they were within the Section 8 program. As a consequence they began withdrawing from the program, raising their rents and evicting the Section 8 tenants who could not afford the new rates.[18] Since the Reagan administration has stopped new housing construction under Section 8, there has been little new public housing construction to replace the Section 8 units that will disappear in the 1990s, causing a gap between the number of Section 8 eligible people and the number of available units. The Neighborhood Reinvestment Corporation projects that this gap will reach 3.7 million units in 1993 and grow to 7.8 million units by 2003.[19] In response to this threat, Congress passed a housing bill in 1987 that renewed the housing construction component of Section 8 and authorized $30 billion for housing programs.[20]

Urban Renewal

Urban renewal was started by the Housing Act of 1949 and its subsequent amendments, particularly those of 1954. Like the earlier public housing program, urban renewal provided federal funds to local public agencies (LPAs) to condemn land, clear it, and provide for its redevelopment. Urban renewal differed from public housing in two key respects. First, unlike public housing, urban renewal allowed up to 30 percent of the cleared land to be used for commercial purposes rather than for residential redevelopment. This made urban renewal popular with city officials, because the new commercial buildings added to the city's property tax base. Twenty-seven renewal projects in Chicago more than doubled the property tax values of the land that was redeveloped.[21]

A second difference between urban renewal and public housing was the involvement of the private sector in urban renewal. Public housing was both constructed and operated by public agencies, the local housing authorities. Under urban renewal, however, after the land was cleared by the LPA it was sold to private redevelopers who developed it at a profit in accord with agreements reached with the LPA. In some respects, this put the urban renewal plan at the mercy of the real estate market. Private redevelopers naturally were reluctant to purchase sites in undesirable neighborhoods. In Newark, for example, the LPA (the Newark Housing Authority) found that its first urban renewal project was stalled for several years because it could not find a private developer willing to build on the site the Housing Authority had cleared. In subsequent projects the Housing Authority did not clear any sites until it found developers willing to build on them. This made the developer's profit one of the criteria to be used in deciding where to place urban renewal projects.[22] Studies of urban renewal in New York indicate that similar criteria were applied there as well.*

Both public housing and urban renewal drew heavy criticism for their destruc-

---

*Urban renewal director Robert Moses would turn the title over to the redeveloper before the site had been cleared, thus allowing the developer to make a profit by renting slum housing even though he had paid the price for the cleared land, not for the buildings [Jeanne Lowe, *Cities in a Race with Time: Progress and Poverty in America's Renewing Cities* (New York: Random House, 1968), pp. 68–72].

tive effects on cities. As indicated above, more housing units have been destroyed through these programs than have been constructed.[23] They have increased rather than decreased racial segregation[24] and have destroyed viable, functioning, urban neighborhood communities.[25] The relocation of families from slum areas being demolished has been accompanied by extreme financial and personal hardships for those families.[26]

From the viewpoint of those who want effective government, the most damning criticism of urban renewal was its tendency to create a redevelopment functional fiefdom (see Chapter 7) that was much more responsive to bankers, real estate developers, construction contractors, construction unions, and federal officials in the Urban Renewal Administration than it was to city residents or city councils. This was particularly the case in Newark, New Jersey in the 1950s and early 1960s, where the Newark Housing Authority (NHA) produced some of the most extensive urban renewal projects in the nation. Harold Kaplan has documented how the NHA's executive director and administrative staff were able to both neutralize political opposition from residents who faced relocation and easily gain the cooperation of the city council.[27]

In the political turmoil of the late 1960s, however, urban renewal agencies began to lose their autonomy. Citing the NHA as a pertinent example of this, Michael Danielson and Jamison Doig attribute the decline of the NHA to two new political factors in the 1970s.[28] First was the emergence of black electoral power in the city and the election of a black mayor, Kenneth Gibson, who shared blacks' resentment of NHA. Second was NHA's loss of support from federal Urban Renewal Administration officials who were forced by events to become more attentive to Newark's angry black residents. The critical test came when Newark's city government and the NHA agreed to offer a substantial block of land in the black ghetto for the construction of an inner-city campus of the New Jersey Medical College. This construction would have forced many local residents to relocate to other housing that would certainly be more expensive but not necessarily be of better quality. Local residents protested the amount of land that was to be taken and the inadequate assistance offered to the residents who would be forced to relocate. Coming shortly after the extensive rioting in Newark's ghetto in 1967, these protests drew much more concern from federal Urban Renewal Administration planners than similar protests had drawn in the quieter days of the 1950s. When Gibson was elected mayor, he allied himself with the local residents and put pressure on the city council and other political officials to come out against the plan. The immediate result was a substantial cutback in the amount of land to be taken and guarantees of assistance in helping the residents relocate. Gibson succeeded in subordinating the NHA to the city government, and its long reign of autonomy in redeveloping the city was over.

While political changes in Newark dramatically affected urban renewal in that city, the 1974 Housing and Community Development Act eliminated urban renewal as a separate grant-in-aid program. Urban renewal was consolidated with six other urban grant programs into the community development block grant program mentioned above.

The Evolution of Federal Urban Policy from 1960–1990

The Great Society Approach

Of all the presidential administrations, Lyndon Johnson's "Great Society" produced the largest number of urban programs.[29] Johnson's most significant urban successes were as follows:

1. The creation of two cabinet-level departments to deal with urban problems. A number of transportation programs were brought together under the Department of Transportation (DOT). The Department of Housing and Urban Development (HUD) was created in 1965 and was made the central agency for coordinating most federal urban programs.

2. The Elementary and Secondary Education Act of 1965. Not only did this act provide extensive funding for elementary and secondary education, but its Title I provision established the principle of compensatory education by earmarking funds for schools with large numbers of economically disadvantaged children.[30]

3. The Economic Opportunity Act of 1964. This act established the War on Poverty and the Office of Economic Opportunity (OEO). The OEO saw its purpose as creating experimental innovations that the established bureaucracies were too timid or too conservative to initiate. Its most controversial creation was the community action program (CAP), which sought to involve local citizens in the planning and implementation of programs designed to end their poverty.

4. Fair Housing Act of 1968. This act outlawed discrimination in the sale or rental of housing.

5. Public Housing Legislation of 1968. This act called for 6 million publicly subsidized housing units by 1978. Unlike the 1949 housing act, the 1968 act was supported by appropriations.

6. Model Cities Act of 1966. This program sought to target diverse federal programs into specific blighted neighborhoods and use them as models of what could be accomplished through careful planning and coordination of federal programs. This approach was highly imaginative, but it had some inherent defects that will be discussed later (pp. 379–380).

Through these massive programs, the Great Society significantly changed the relationship between the federal government and the urban centers. The Great Society broadened the federal urban involvement beyond the housing and urban renewal concerns that had dominated up to the 1960s.[31] The Great Society programs raised a whole series of issues such as the participation of the poor in the planning and operation of programs, compensatory education, advocacy action in legal services and planning, equal opportunity in housing and employment, the role to be played by militant movements,[32] and a host of other social or human-related issues. This broadening of issues and programs for the first time forced the federal government to look seriously at coordinating all the programs it had unleashed. Under the Great Society, the grant-in-aid programs were designed for the first time to attain nationally defined objectives rather than state or locally defined objectives.[33]

Richard Nixon and the First New Federalism

As a result of Lyndon Johnson's Great Society programs there was a dramatic expansion in the number of grants-in-aid from about 100 in 1960 to nearly 500 when he left the White House in 1969. They had contributed 12 percent of all state and local government revenue in 1960; by the end of Johnson's presidency that had grown to 23 percent.[34]

Despite this tremendous growth in federal programs during the 1960s and despite the magnitude of the expenditures involved, there was no consensus that these programs were improving the quality of life. And for the federal programs that operated in metropolitan areas, hardly a major program existed that was not under attack from one group or another. The federal grant programs themselves were accused of distorting the ability of states and localities to establish their own priorities.[35] The welfare programs were accused of breaking up families, destroying people's initiative, and condemning people to live their entire lives on permanent public welfare.[36] The urban renewal programs were accused of engaging in "Negro removal" and destroying more housing than they replaced.[37] The Office of Economic Opportunity was accused by Nixon's urban adviser, Daniel Patrick Moynihan, of decimating the antipoverty program efforts through unthinking acceptance of the dogma of maximum feasible citizen participation.[38] The Model Cities programs were supposed to bring about a concerted interagency effort in target neighborhoods, but the funds were too few and were scattered over too many sites to have such an impact.[39] Even within the federal government, attempts to utilize federally owned land in key cities for the purpose of creating demonstration "new towns in town" were dismal failures.[40]

Not all of the federal programs were failures, of course, and many of the accusations were unfounded. There were also some startling success stories.[41] Legal aid programs initiated procedures for using the courts to force changes in living conditions in urban slums. Community action programs trained a generation of black youths in organizing techniques and pressure tactics. Head Start programs provided stimulating learning experiences for small children. Day care centers were established for mothers who wished to work or who needed to work.

But all these efforts did not eradicate poverty, rejuvenate the cities, or even provide a single city as a stunning success story that other cities could emulate. And when the moderately conservative Nixon came to the White House in 1969, he was influenced by his urban affairs adviser, Daniel Patrick Moynihan, who asserted that "Too many programs have produced too few results."[42]

Reaction to the Federal Urban Role

To appreciate Nixon's approach to a national urban role, we must first review how critics and supporters at the time viewed federal domestic programs. We can do this by comparing the positive impacts of federal programs with their negative impacts and then analyzing Nixon's reaction to the Great Society when he became president in 1969.

The Positive Impact of Federal Programs   The federal grant-in-aid programs have had at least five positive features. First, these programs have stimulated the states and municipalities to act on and spend considerable money on urban problems. Second, the federal programs have provided some very badly needed services. As Michael Reagan has pointed out, "To say that grant-in-aid funds account for over 20 percent of state-local revenues is to say that those governments would do one-fifth less for their citizens without federal aid."[43] Third, the multitude of federal programs have created a multitude of ways in which local governments could tie into federal funding, which is very consistent with the fragmented nature of metropolitan governance. Michael Danielson has characterized this as a "system in which the many pathways to the national capital attract numerous metropolitan actors, each motivated by a different perspective of the urban landscape and none representing the metropolis as a whole."[44] It could be argued that the fragmented nature of the grants-in-aid program made federal aid more accessible than it would have been if it had all been centralized and coordinated. Fourth, the federal urban programs have served as a stimulus to the local economy.[45] Urban renewal, highway construction, and housing programs have provided a great many jobs and have invested billions of dollars in the local economies. Finally, and most important, grants-in-aid programs have enabled the federal government to deal with national problems. Problems of urban poverty, public welfare, urban transportation, and public housing are widely recognized as national problems, not local problems. Without the grants-in-aid programs, these problems would not be dealt with nationally. Each state or locality would have to cope with its portion of the problem on its own, isolated from other states and localities that are also trying to deal with their portions of the problem.

The Negative Impact of Federal Programs   Despite these positive contributions, the grants-in-aid approach to urban problem solving has been severely criticized. First, some federal programs have seriously aggravated the decline in central cities. The federally sponsored freeway systems and interstate highways led to the physical dispersion of shopping areas, which siphoned retail shoppers away from the central cities. Federal housing programs were supposed to eliminate slums, yet after a decade of New York's housing program just as many people lived in slum housing as had lived there at the start. FHA/VA-insured home mortgages did provide a significant prop for the home mortgage system, but they also completely ignored community development. They stimulated growth in suburban areas that were already undergoing more growth than they could control. No attempt was made to set up a preferential condition for guaranteeing loans that would rank applicants according to community criteria rather than individual criteria. Such an action would have forced local communities to establish criteria for land development and would have given local communities a strong incentive to support metropolitan planning.[46] Urban renewal programs were similarly implemented without any relation to metropolitan development planning.

Second, as shown in the housing and urban renewal efforts, federal programs have led to extreme functional specialization. Third, and as a consequence of the first two negative impacts, federal programs have compounded the problems of accountability and control. By creating agencies that were semiautonomous and quasi-independent of mayors and elected local officials, the most important agencies for the physical development of a city were put beyond the reach of the local electorate. Finally, the grants-in-aid have skewed state and local budgets into the areas determined by federal programs, and this has made it more difficult for state and local governments to meet problems in areas not supported by grants-in-aid.[47]

Nixon's Perspective

Many of these criticisms of the federal grants-in-aid programs fell on receptive ears when Richard Nixon moved into the White House in 1969. As a conservative, Nixon had no philosophical attachment to the many programs that proliferated during the Great Society years. Nor did he have any political motivation to support programs that primarily benefited big-city, lower-income, and racial-minority constituencies. None of these constituencies had given Nixon a majority of their vote in 1968. Perhaps even more important was his philosophical commitment as a conservative to reverse the growth of federal power relative to that of the states. Nixon said in 1972:

> Do we want to turn more power over to bureaucrats in Washington in the hope that they will do what is best for all the people? Or do we want to return more power to the people and to the state and local governments so that people can decide what is best for themselves? It is time that good, decent people stopped letting themselves be bulldozed by anybody who presumes to be the self-righteous moral judge of our society. In the next four years, as in the past four, I will continue to direct the flow of power away from Washington and back to the people.[48]

Nixon sought to put this philosophy into practice with a two-pronged approach. First, as we will see here, he directly assaulted some of the central programs of the Great Society and the Democratic-controlled Congress. Second, as we will examine afterwards, he called for a New Federalism that would return power and authority to the state governments.

Assault on the Great Society

One of the first casualties of Nixon's assault on the Great Society was the Office of Economic Opportunity (OEO), the agency set up to head the War on Poverty. Popular OEO programs such as Head Start were spun off to regular departments. Many controversial ones, such as the Community Action Program, were simply starved of funds and left to die or to be picked up by local governments. The Legal Services Program was taken out of OEO and turned into a Legal Services Corporation, where its budget was trimmed and its mandate was sharply reduced to prevent controversial activities such as defending draft resisters, assisting voter registration, or defending abortion cases.

The most dramatic Nixon assaults on Democratic programs were his attempts in 1973 to impound (that is, refuse to spend) funds that Congress had appropriated for sewer construction, public housing, urban renewal, and model cities. Ultimately, the courts forced Nixon to spend the money, and Congress reacted with the

1973 Budget and Impoundment Control Act, which made future impoundments illegal. But the immediate effects of impoundment were to delay sewer plant construction for several years and to reduce federally subsidized housing starts in 1974–1976 to about 90 percent of their 1971 level.[49]

The New Federalism

Nixon responded to criticisms of the grants-in-aid system outlined earlier by proposing a New Federalism that would (1) consolidate about a fifth of the categorical grant programs into six (later reduced to four) huge block grants (or "special revenue sharing," as Nixon termed it) and (2) establish a general revenue sharing plan. Modified versions of these were passed into law during 1972–1974. The major thrust of these New Federalism proposals was to give greater authority to elected officials at the state and local levels.

Under Lyndon Johnson, federal grants particularly benefited traditionally Democratic constituencies such as racial minorities, big-city officials, and public employees hired to carry out the programs. In reaction, President Nixon called for a program that would give state and local governments more flexibility in using federal funds, that would distribute federal funds to a broader range of recipients so that more Republicans would benefit, and that would reduce the discretionary power of the federal bureaucracies (which Nixon suspected of having liberal, Democratic sympathies). To accomplish these goals, Nixon relied principally on general revenue sharing, grant consolidation, and switching emphasis from project grants to formula grants.

General Revenue Sharing   Revenue sharing was enacted in 1972 to turn $5 billion in federal revenues over to state and local governments to use as they saw fit, with none of the strings that were attached to categorical grants or block grants. The state share was eliminated in 1980, and the entire program was abolished in 1987 as part of the Reagan administration's efforts to cut domestic spending. The revenue-sharing idea had first surfaced during the Kennedy administration but died for lack of political support. There were many arguments both for and against revenue sharing.* What appealed to Nixon was the hope that general revenue

*Some arguments made in favor of revenue sharing were the unreliability of some categorical grants, the tendency of categorical grants to become hard and narrow, and the hope that revenue sharing would make the states more viable fiscally. There were several major arguments against revenue sharing. The unit that spends the tax money should also raise the tax money. The availability of many categorical grant programs gives the local government many options from which it can choose. State governments are too inadequate and in many instances too corrupt to be trusted with the funds and discretion they would receive through revenue sharing. The notion that the states are laboratories for governmental innovation has been overworked. The states in actuality are no closer to the people than is the federal government. Particularly for the racial minorities, the federal government has been more responsive than have the state governments. Revenue sharing might mean less funds going to urban and metropolitan problems. Finally, in Michael Reagan's words, revenue sharing "moves us back to the level of separate state political cultures (and to the extent that the pass through is required, even to the level of separate local political cultures) as the context-setting environment in which public expenditure decisions will be made." Reagan, in *The New Federalism* (New York: Oxford University Press, 1972), summarizes the case for revenue sharing (pp. 92–101) and the case against revenue sharing (pp. 102–132); the quotation is from pp. 126–127.

sharing would strengthen state and local governments and make it easier for them to perform needed urban services without having to rely on the initiative of federal grants-in-aid. For this reason, general revenue sharing fit neatly into Nixon's New Federalism plans to increase the authority of state governments while decreasing that of the federal government.

The Nixon Block Grants   A second key element of the New Federalism was the consolidation of several categorical grant programs into a few huge block grants. Nixon originally proposed in 1971 that Congress consolidate 129 categorical grant programs into six large block grants, which he called special revenue sharing. When Congress failed to do that, Nixon in 1973 reduced the proposal from six special revenue sharing packages to four (education, community development, law enforcement, and employment) that would consolidate only 70 categorical grants. As long as a state or locality spent its funds in the appropriate area, few restrictions were placed on how it was spent. From the conservative point of view, this had the advantage of allowing each state and locality to decide its own priorities for itself. Before Congress could act on these proposals, Nixon in 1973 began unilaterally dismantling some of the programs that were subject to being phased out, and he impounded funds for some of the others. Because of these premature acts, Nixon ran into enormous congressional opposition. Instead of passing the special revenue-sharing programs, Congress passed two significant block grant consolidations in the fields of employment and community development.

The Community Development Block Grant (CDBG) program was established by the 1974 Housing and Community Development Act. This act consolidated seven urban categorical grants, including urban renewal and model cities, into a single block grant of $8.4 billion for the three years from 1975 to 1977. It was renewed in 1977, 1980, and 1983, although the funding levels were reduced. Under this program, cities had discretion to use their CDBG funds for a wide variety of purposes ranging from code enforcement to economic development projects. To get its funds, a community had to submit a community development plan that identified its development needs and outlined a three-year program to meet those needs. Eighty percent of the CD funds were reserved for metropolitan areas. Under a complicated formula, each community of over 50,000 was automatically entitled to a specific sum. A "hold harmless" provision was inserted to protect big cities from receiving less than the annual average they had received under the consolidated programs over the preceding five years. Careful analysis of the first round of community development expenditures, however, showed that they redistributed federal money away from heavily Democratic big cities to more Republican-oriented suburbs and small cities. Of the 487 metropolitan communities entitled to receive CD funds, 204 got less money from CD funds than they had received under their old consolidated categorical grants. Of these 204 communities, 181 were central cities. Most of the communities that gained under the CD program were suburbs. Skokie, Illinois, for example, an affluent suburb of Chicago with virtually no racial minorities or people below the poverty line, had received nothing under the old categorical grants but received nearly half a million dollars during the first year of CD block grants.[50]

Although the community development program did create a cash loss to big cities, it had the positive feature of enabling them to recapture control over city redevelopment from the local public agencies (LPAs) that had dominated urban renewal. CD funds went directly to the city governments rather than to the LPAs and LHAs, as had occurred under the urban renewal and public housing programs. These agencies thus became more closely controlled by the mayors and city councils than they had been. They also were made more responsive to city residents. In order to get its CD funds, each city had to provide for citizen participation in planning CD expenditures.

Although some studies cast doubt on the effectiveness of citizen participation and the redevelopment use made of CD funds, it seems apparent that this type of block grant has indeed decentralized power in urban redevelopment away from Washington, away from the old urban renewal and public housing functional fiefdoms, and toward locally elected executives and councils.[51]

Assessing the Nixon Approach to Urban Policy

Even granting President Nixon the best of intentions, many of his proposals seemed biased toward Republican-oriented constituencies, perhaps in reaction to the Great Society's bias toward Democratic constituencies. His revenue sharing and grant consolidation proposals in particular could be viewed as a step backwards, away from formulating a national urban policy or coordinating programs in metropolitan areas. Michael Reagan called the grant consolidations, as originally proposed, a federal "cop-out." By eliminating the categorical grant programs and turning the money for those programs over to the states and localities, the federal government in effect was backing away from the attempt to establish national priorities in dealing with national domestic problems. Furthermore, because the federal programs to be phased out dealt with problems around which a new set of interest groups had emerged and because these interest groups found the national government more receptive to their problems than state or central-city governments, the special revenue-sharing proposals may have diminished the effectiveness of those interest groups.

> Having succeeded at the federal level, usually after years of protracted bargaining and political coalition building (i.e., log-rolling), the leaders of major interest groups representing the needs and demands of the schools, the children, the poor, the ethnic minorities, and the cities are not going to accept without a real fight the message that they should now begin over again in all the state capitals. After all, they have focused on Washington in the first place largely because of the proven unresponsiveness of those capitals. Again, it is a question of which priorities shall prevail, those of the national community or those of the lesser, narrower communities; those of the most inclusive majority, or those of the most exclusive status quo dominated pressure system?[52]

The Carter Urban Policy: 1977–1981

As the Nixon-Ford years drew to a close and Jimmy Carter entered the White House in 1977, two major new changes in urban America began to draw increasing national attention. First, as discussed earlier in Chapter 6, was the dramatic deterioration of many older cities in the Northeast and Midwest. Second was a growing conflict over the regional distribution of federal grants-in-aid. Northern governors and members of Congress teamed up to press for formula grants that would increase aid to their cities. Southern political leaders reacted by demanding that the formulas be written so as to benefit their cities.

Many of these political groups and interests looked to the new Democratic president in 1977 with the hope that he would respond to their pleas to provide more aid to deteriorating cities, stem the flow of federal funds from the Northeast to the Sunbelt, and channel more money into the surviving social programs of the Great Society. Referring to America's contribution to rebuilding Europe's devastated economies after World War II, National Urban League president Whitney Young demanded a Marshall Plan for the cities that would rebuild their devastated economies.[53] Analogies were drawn to the Apollo space program, which had put a man on the moon in the previous decade. Surely, if an all-out, concentrated program could perform such a feat as putting a man on the moon, an all-out Apollo-type program for the cities could revitalize them.

To deal with these demands, Carter appointed a cabinet-level Urban and Regional Policy Group, which spent a year studying federal urban programs. In March 1978, it gave him a list of 70 options on action to take on existing federal urban programs.

After making some modifications, Carter ended up approving a document that called for a "New Partnership" of the federal government, state governments, city governments, and private industry to cope with city problems. This New Partnership suggested the following remedies:

1. A national urban development bank that would channel investment funds into urban development projects.
2. Increased fiscal relief to help fiscally distressed cities.
3. An urban impact analysis that would force all federal agencies to delay domestic spending projects until it could be determined that they would not have an adverse impact on cities.
4. A renewed emphasis on economic revitalization of cities.[54]

If Lyndon Johnson's urban approach was characterized by providing social services directly to the poor, Carter's was characterized by stimulating corporations to invest in central cities, thus increasing job opportunities there and improving their economies. This economic revitalization would be achieved largely through tax credits, interest rate subsidies, and other incentives to get businesses to create jobs in cities and high-unemployment areas. Many of these incentives were to be administered by the National Development Bank, which would have the authority to provide more than $8 billion in loan guarantees to businesses and another $3.8 billion in interest-rate subsidies.

In practice, Carter achieved very little of this modest program. Urban impact analysis was initiated by his presidential order, but observers cast doubt on whether it accomplished anything,[55] and it was rescinded by his successor, Ronald Reagan. The most significant, lasting achievement was the UDAG program, which permitted HUD to make project grants for economic development programs. Many cities used UDAG grants as seed money to clear blighted areas and entice corporations to locate factories, office buildings, and other developments on the sites. Through 1985, UDAG had dispersed $4 billion to nearly 2,700 projects in 2,200 cities.[56]

Ronald Reagan and the Return of New Federalism

President Ronald Reagan's approach to urban policy was essentially embodied in the New Federalism he proposed. Unlike Carter, Reagan did not articulate a specific urban policy.[57] Indeed, some critics charged that he did not even have an urban policy.[58] Reagan strongly believed that the best antidote to urban problems lay in a healthy national economy and that urban development projects were best left to market forces and the private sector rather than be directed by government programs such as UDAG, which had been so popular under the Carter administration. In this president's view, government development programs do not encourage the expansion of business; they merely shift it from one location to another.[59] Rather than relocate the jobs to depressed areas where huge numbers of unemployed people live, Reagan preferred to let the people relocate to the places where jobs exist. Reagan's first budget director, David Stockman, was especially critical of urban development programs such as UDAG because "they encouraged companies to invest in high-cost and economically inefficient areas."[60] Although these ideas have considerable intuitive appeal, they rest on the dubious assumption that governments can do nothing to reverse the economic decline of faltering regions. But the experience of the Tennessee Valley Authority in the 1930s and 1940s as a major stimulant to economic growth in the Tennessee River region is evidence that governments can indeed stimulate declining regions if they have the will to do so.[61]

Urban Changes Under Reagan

The Reagan Administration's views on urban policy were best synthesized, perhaps, by the 1982 *National Urban Policy Report*. This report argued for the need to "restore balance in our federal system of government"[62] by reducing federal authority over the states. It expressed doubt about the effectiveness of many previous urban programs, urged a reduction in federal urban funding, and called for increased reliance on the private sector to improve urban conditions.[63]

Consistent with his faith in the private-market economy as the solution to urban problems, Reagan's only urban program initiative focused on helping the private sector. This was his proposal for *urban enterprise zones*. As this plan was originally conceived, the Department of Housing and Urban Development would be allowed to designate up to 25 urban neighborhhoods a year to qualify as enterprise zones. Any business firm that opened up in the qualifying zone would be eligible for special tax concessions from the local, state, and federal governments.

Reagan also proposed reducing the minimum wage for the enterprise zones and relaxing federal regulations on the environment and on occupational safety and health.[64] With these concessions, businesses could be expected to move into the affected neighborhoods and create jobs for the residents.

Although more than half of the states passed enterprise zone legislation, the national version never made it through Congress. Some critics noted that Puerto Rico has "a 35-year history as an 'enterprise zone.' Low wages and low taxation led to an economic boom in the 1950s and 1960s. But since 1970, disinvestment and stagnation have become the rule. Today, 30 percent of the Puerto Rican population is unemployed."[65] There is no evidence that any of the state-level enterprise zones are doing badly. But as the centerpiece for national urban policy, enterprise zones have a fundamental conceptual flaw. If they do succeed in raising living standards within the enterprise zone, this will be accompanied by higher wages and eventually higher taxes. At that point, the corporations involved will most likely pack up their investments and move to some other low-wage, low-tax area.[66] In this respect, a national policy of enterprise zones would reinforce the disinvestment practices of corporations that seek to move to low-cost areas and in the long run would make it harder to raise living standards overall.

In addition to the urban enterprise zones, Reagan's urban approach also consisted of the various elements of his New Federalism. Like his Republican predecessor Richard Nixon, Reagan sought to reduce federal authority over state and local governments. He said:

> My administration is committed heart and soul to returning authority, responsibility and flexibility to state and local governments. . . . The next years promise to be among the most exciting in the history of our intergovernmental system, as state and local governments assume responsibilities that have been preempted by the Federal Government over the past several decades.[67]

Key to the New Federalism were Reagan's budget cuts for domestic social programs and his efforts to devolve federal responsibilities to the states. Combined, these initiatives reduced the amount of federal money available for urban-related programs. By pushing nine new block grants through Congress, the president shifted much responsibility and administrative control for 54 previously categorical grant programs from the federal government to the state capitals. At the same time that he cut the budgets of federal urban programs, Reagan also sought to reduce the federal strings attached to them. In the Community Development Block Grant program, for example, he reduced the number of pages of federal regulations on how CDBG funds could be spent from 52 to two.[68] In the UDAG program, Reagan not only reduced the budget by a third but also gave communities greater discretionary power to use the funds for economic development rather than for a balance between that and neighborhood preservation projects, as the rules had previously required.

Finally, in addition to urban enterprise zones and New Federalism, the third part of Reagan's federal urban policy consisted of sharp budget cutbacks in direct urban programs (such as UDAG) and social welfare services (such as AFDC) that go disproportionately to central-city residents. Harold Wolman identified 24 specific federal aid programs for cities (ranging from CETA to the urban parks program); twenty of the twenty-four programs received budget cutbacks under Reagan.[69] The impact of these cuts on cities was severe. A survey of all cities with populations over 25,000 in four midwestern states (Illinois, Indiana, Michigan, and Wisconsin) in 1982 found that the federal budget reductions under Reagan had a significant negative impact on these cities' ability to provide all the services they had previously offered. Nineteen percent of the cities reported elimination of city services because of the federal cutbacks. One-third of the cities reduced the level of city services. Twenty-three percent reported laying off employees. And twenty-nine percent reported having to increase taxes in order to make up for the federal cutbacks.[70]

Reagan's Urban Legacy

What has Reagan's urban approach meant for American cities? What legacy has he left?

Judged on its own terms, the Reagan urban legacy is a failure. The Reagan theory had been to solve urban problems primarily through national economic growth. The economy did indeed grow steadily for six consecutive years (1983–1988) without a recession. And during those six years, economic conditions within central cities did indeed improve. Inflation rates dropped markedly, poverty rates marginally, and unemployment rates significantly. But barely a dent was made in underlying urban problems such as poverty, social disorganization, crime, poor schools, and economic disinvestment. By the end of the Reagan administration, the basic underlying conditions affecting these problem areas in most cities were as bad if not worse than they had been at the start of his administration.

In the eyes of Reagan's stronger critics, the judgment is even harsher. New public housing construction was brought to a virtual standstill by his administration's unwillingness to compromise with Congress on housing policy. Federal cutbacks in social services and welfare programs placed a bigger burden on city and county governments to care for impoverished people. The huge income tax cuts of 1982–1984 went primarily to upper- and upper-middle-income-people, with a mere pittance to urban lower-middle income people and the working poor. These tax and spending policies, as we saw earlier in Chapter 6, helped contribute to a long-term trend in which the national income is being redistributed away from the poor and toward the upper- and upper-middle-income groups. In the early years of his administration, city efforts to promote economic development were hampered by budget cuts in programs such as UDAG, CDBG, and the Economic Development Administration grant programs. Cities compensated for these cuts by increasing their reliance on tax incentives, especially IDRBs, to finance development projects and infrastructure rebuilding. But the Tax Reform Act of 1986 sharply limited the future use of IDRBs for development purposes.

In sum, Reagan's approach to urban policy was heavily marked by his own philosophical belief in laissez-faire: The best antidote to urban problems is economic growth. In all fairness to Reagan's approach, it would have to be admitted that economic growth is indeed a precondition to solving urban problems. Without economic growth, there probably is no way to reduce urban poverty rates and unemployment rates. But the Reagan years show conclusively, in this writer's mind, that economic growth by itself is not enough, for the eight years of Reagan's laissez-faire urban approach did nothing to tackle the underlying social problems that confront cities. Worse, the administration significantly reduced federal efforts to address those problems.

Can There Be a National Urban Policy?

Given the dramatic shifts in urban emphasis from one presidential administration to the next, it seems reasonable to ask what kind of urban policy role the federal government can in fact play. Are there any patterns to the successes and failures in the urban initiatives of Johnson, Nixon, Carter, and Reagan that future presidents can learn from to improve their own prospects for success in the balance of the twentieth century? Or would future presidents be better advised to concentrate on fields such as foreign policy, where their authority is less challenged, and stay out of the urban quagmire?

The Argument for a National Urban Policy

Although it might not be in the president's interest to get bogged down in the national in-fighting over urban policies, the same cannot be said for cities and metropolitan areas. In sending more than $100 billion in grants-in-aid to communities of all sizes, the federal departments and agencies have become significant urban actors. Many observers feel that the federal government needs to strongly articulate a set of national urban policy goals and objectives to coordinate the formulation and implementation of all federal urban programs.*[71] Programs deal with only specific aspects of the metropolis; without national goals, objectives, and priorities to tie the programs together, nothing provides overall guidance for all the federal urban programs. Consequently, the sheer magnitude of existing programs demands the articulation of national policy goals and objectives.

In addition to the need for guiding federal programs, there is controversy over the question of whether a national urban policy should seek to direct and channel the interregional population migrations discussed in Chapter 2. James L. Sundquist contends that the United States is the only large industrial democracy that has failed to establish such a policy.[72] He points out that the national population will grow substantially by the year 2000,† and these people will settle mainly in the

---

*A goal is a broad statement of something to be accomplished. An objective is a more specific statement of something to be accomplished. An objective operationalizes the goal. Whereas a goal need not always be measurable, an objective's attainment is always measurable.

†The Census Bureau projects a population increase of about 59 million people between 1980 and 2000 if immigration stays at current estimates and if there are 2.7 births per woman. If births fall to the replacement level of 2.1 per woman, the projected population increase is about 38 million people. See *Current Population Reports*, Series P-25, no. 704, "Projections of the Population of the United States: 1977 to 2050" (Washington, D.C.: U.S. Government Printing Office, July 1977).

four emerging megalopolises. Without effective growth policies, metropolitan sprawl will continue. Old metropolitan areas as well as central cities will continue to deteriorate as the population continues to shift to the newer growing metropolises of the Sunbelt. New metropolises will emerge and will be tempted to repeat the development mistakes of the older ones. This is both wasteful and inflationary, since it costs much more to provide new public services, infrastructure, private housing, and other amenities for a factory that locates on the metropolitan fringe than it does for one constructed within an area that is already urbanized. For all of these reasons, Sundquist believes we need national policies that will encourage private businesses to create jobs where unemployment is high rather thn following a market-dictated practice of letting workers migrate to where jobs are being created.

A third reason often given for a national urban policy is that urban problems are national problems. The fundamental causes of urban problems are found in such unexciting statistics as the national ratio of births to deaths and national migration figures. No given metropolis or state can hope to cope with these factors on its own. The number of people receiving aid for dependent children (AFDC) at any given time is very closely related to changes in the gross national product, and state or local governments acting individually can do very little to affect it. Nevertheless, they are left to cope with the brunt of the problems that face most AFDC recipients—the need for adequate housing, competent and often compensatory education, a variety of social services, and, in many instances, jobs. Very few of the causal factors of the urban problems can be dealt with by individual states and municipalities acting in isolation. Only the national government can coordinate the efforts of states and municipalities so that they act in concert rather than in opposition to one another.

Why We Do Not Have an Urban Policy

Demonstrating the need for a national urban policy is much easier than creating one. Even formulating such a policy at the highest levels of government would not guarantee that it meant anything in practice, as the Carter administration experience clearly shows.[73] Just as Chapter 12 demonstrated a distinction between planning as a document and planning as a process, so there is a distinction between policy as a document and the process of implementing it. The material covered so far in this chapter presents ample evidence for this distinction. For example, President Johnson articulated a policy that ordered the creation of "new towns in town," but this policy was never translated into action.

The reason it is so difficult to achieve a national urban policy is twofold, according to Peter Eisinger. First, political pluralism in the United States resulted in urban policy proposals under Nixon and Carter that were "great laundry lists of goals and programs that lacked internal coherence."[74] Each relevant interest group had its list of proposals, and many of these made it into the policy proposals of Nixon and Carter because of political pressures, regardless of whether the proposals interacted well together. Second, the commitment of the United States to the sanctity of the private sector has made it impossible to develop urban policy based on principles of nationalized central planning, such as is common in France, Great Britain, and much of western Europe.

The Elements of a National Urban Policy

While realizing these difficulties in creating a meaningful and effective national urban policy, it would be helpful to examine some of the key elements that would make up a national urban policy. These elements include some understanding of the urban and metropolitan role of state governments, the issues that should form the content of a national urban policy, and the process of carrying out a national urban policy once it is articulated.

The Role of States in National Urban Policy

No national urban policy can be effective if it ignores a role for state governments. State governments "occupy the strategic middle between the federal and local governments."[75] They determine the legal authority and fiscal power that local governments will have in coping with urban problems. In Indiana and Minnesota, as shown in Chapter 10, the state legislature enacted far-reaching metropolitan reform. State governments also take direct actions in urban areas. The New York Urban Development Corporation, for example, is able to override local zoning ordinances in building its various renewal and housing projects. And the California Coastal Zone Commissions can veto building permits issued by local governments on the Pacific Coast.

Particularly after legislative reapportionment increased suburban representation in the 1960s, state governments began to play a more active role in metropolitan problems. The most dramatic state action has probably been in the creation of state agencies to promote urban housing and redevelopment plans. One of the first examples of this was the New York Urban Development Corporation (UDC), created in 1968 to identify and redevelop target urban areas. It was given $1 billion in bonding authority, complete authority to develop a project from beginning planning stages to completion, eminent domain powers to enhance its ability to acquire land, and authority to override local zoning and building controls when necessary. The UDC is a state enterprise that is beyond the control of either local voters or local officials. It appeared to be making considerable strides in central-city redevelopment and housing until it defaulted on a bond issue in 1975.[76] Dealing with this fiscal problem kept the UDC fairly inactive for the next few years, but by 1980 it was recovering its initiative and sponsoring new projects aimed especially at office buildings and other commercial projects.

Despite the importance of states to urban problems, states for the most part have been bypassed in federal attempts at national urban policymaking. The Johnson urban programs operated directly with city governments and subcity units such as Model Cities and Community Action agencies. Nixon and Reagan, through their New Federalism approaches, did indeed decentralize considerable power to state governments, but they made little effort to relate the greater authority to urban revitalization. Carter's New Partnership called for a state role, but it seemed to have been added as an afterthought when the rest of the package was completed, and his proposal for state incentive grants was deleted by Congress.

The Targeting Problem

No discussion of national urban policy can fail to note the problem of targeting federal aid to the regions and people that are supposed to benefit from the aid. No federal program illustrates the targeting problem better than does the Model Cities program of 1966. For this reason it is worth discussing in some detail.

The Model Cities Program

Shortly after assuming the presidency, Lyndon Johnson was advised by the Council of Economic Advisors chairman, Walter Heller, of a Kennedy administration proposal to completely rebuild blighted neighborhoods of a few cities on an experimental, demonstration basis.[77] All existing federal programs would be concentrated on these areas. They could be used as models of what concerted and coordinated federal action might accomplish by working in partnership with local government. Other cities would then institute similar programs to emulate the model. Johnson liked the idea but informed Heller that such a program would have to include more than just a few cities if it were ever to pass through Congress. Johnson preferred instead something "big and bold."[78] A presidential Metropolitan and Urban Affairs Task Force was formed and given responsibility for designing a Model Cities proposal. The task force criticized existing federal programs, including the OEO, for fragmenting logically related services. Included in the task force's final proposal was a suggestion that the federal government "adopt two or three large cities and in addition build a brand-new one in order to show what could be accomplished by well-conceived, large-scale, concerted effort."[79]

Although Johnson thought that this recommendation was too theoretical to send to Congress, he did approve the creation of a second task force in 1965 and charged it with making a practical proposal that could be implemented and show results while he was still in office. The task force briefly considered the idea of concentrating all federal spending on just one demonstration city, but this was rejected because it would force his administration to choose between two of the most powerful Democratic supporters in the country: Mayor Richard Daley, who would propose Chicago, and labor leader Walter Reuther, who would propose Detroit. The task force also rejected a suggestion of five cities, because five cities would not attract enough members of Congress to vote for the bill. The task force report finally recommended that 66 demonstration cities be approved.

Cities would be invited to make an application that would identify a neighborhood to be redeveloped by the demonstration cities treatment. The applicants would be judged on the quality of their plans for redeveloping the Model City area. Once selected, two kinds of federal assistance would be available. First, the demonstration city neighborhoods would be eligible to receive all existing federal grants on a priority basis. Second, to make up any difference between what was available under existing programs and the costs of their demonstration cities experiment, they would receive supplemental grants on an 80:20 matching basis; for every $80 of federal supplemental grants, the city government would have to provide $20. These supplemental grants would ensure cooperation of all the federal agencies. Since the locally approved demonstration cities program could get whatever supplemental grants it needed (at a cost of 20 percent), it would thus be in a good bargaining position to get other federal agencies to join in what promised to be a very glamorous program.

In 1966, 63 cities were chosen to participate in the first round of Model Cities grants. Although most grants went to big urban centers, a few were passed out to small towns in the home districts of key members of Congress. Smithfield, Tennessee, was an appropriate winning city, since it was the home town of the chairman of the House Appropriations Subcommittee that dealt with HUD's budget. Another appropriate winner was Pikesville, Kentucky, which was the home town of another key subcommittee chairman. Montana, the home state of Senate Majority Leader Mike Mansfield, had two cities among the winners. And Maine, the home state of Senator Edmund Muskie, who had been the bill's floor leader, got three winners. To ensure that the program would not be blamed for political favoritism, Banfield writes that "at least one large city represented in Congress by a Republican had to be on the list. Happily, one—Columbus, Ohio—was found."[80] The next year, another round of winners was chosen, more than doubling the total number of Model Cities to 150.

Early evaluations of the Model Cities programs suggested that they had enormous potential for accomplishing their goals for long-range planning, citizen participation, and coordination of federal programs.[81] However, Congress never appropriated the full amount of money authorized for Model Cities, and the amount of money actually spent never added up to the amount appropriated. Furthermore, the White House never lent its full prestige to the implementation of Model Cities. And the federal agencies in charge of the categorical grant programs were never as cooperative with the Model Cities planners as had been anticipated.[82]

In 1973, the Nixon administration impounded money that was appropriated for Model Cities, thus bringing the program to a standstill, and the Housing and Community Development Act of 1974 consolidated Model Cities with six other urban grant programs into a large block grant for community development. This ended the Model Cities role as a coordinator of federal programs.

Other Targeting Problems

If a critical defect of Model Cities was the inability of Congress to target federal funds where they could have a significant impact, that defect has also permeated several other federal domestic policy efforts. For example, Alan Saltzstein studied the dispensing of HUD and LEAA grants to 20 medium-sized cities and found that instead of need, the most important factors were political and organizational. That is, the cities most adept at grantsmanship were likely to get the most grants.[83] As Congress and the Nixon administration moved toward formula grants, revenue sharing, and block grants during the 1970s, federal urban aid was spread among so many different small communities that, as Paul Dommel criticized, "increasing amounts of this aid are coming under the influence of a new 'something for every-one' distribution politics."[84] The problem persists today. An analysis of the Community Development Block Grant program since 1974 discovered that despite Congressional intent to target the money on communities suffering economic hardship, the number of communities eligible for the program grew from 590 in 1975 to 657 in 1980 and 814 in 1985. Between 1980 and 1985, the share of CDBG funds going to hardship communities declined, while the share going to well-off places increased. Detroit, one of the worst-off communities, saw its share of CDBG funds drop by 22.5 percent between 1980 and 1985, while well-off Hialeah, Florida saw a 101 percent increase over the same period.[85] Federalism specialist David B. Walker commented wryly that Washington "couldn't target if it tried. It spreads the money around."[86]

The Content of a National Urban Policy

If a national urban policy is to be developed out of the current melange of urban programs, of what would it consist? Four particular issues are of the utmost importance.

Perhaps most important, a policy should be established on the distribution of future population growth and on interregional migrations. Although nobody really knows how many people can fit comfortably into the southern California megalopolis and the other rapidly growing and water-short areas of the Southwest, southern California's shortfalls in water supply suggest that we may be approaching the limit under present technology. The federal government should discuss where the increased population should be housed and what kinds of realistic incentives can channel the interregional migrations into areas where they can be best accommodated.

Second, a national urban policy must confront the deterioration of the older central cities. Although hundreds of programs exist for these cities, many of them work at cross purposes and many still disrupt the governing capabilities of city governments. The federal government needs to decide what it wants for these urban centers, and the city governments need to define what they want for themselves. Unless broad policy goals and objectives can be formulated and unless the means can be found to tie specific programs into these policy goals, federal involvement is likely to remain piecemeal and ad hoc.

Third, a national urban policy must demand that the federal government consistently confront the life-style issues of social access that were discussed in Chapter 10. Unless the gross inequities in the distribution of public goods and services in housing, jobs, and schools that characterize most metropolitan areas can be reduced, the nation probably cannot avoid the two-societies fate predicted by the Kerner Commission: "Our Nation is moving toward two societies, one black, one white—separate and unequal."[87] Why should any parents who can really afford the choice live in a neighborhood where their children must attend inferior schools and confront what they think is a relatively high probability of physical assault?

And the answer, of course, is that very few people will live there if they can afford not to. For entirely rational reasons, they migrate into better neighborhoods where their children can have what they think are better and safer schools. And they strongly resist any efforts of local governments to make them share their advantages with the residents of less-advantaged neighborhoods. Continued federal pressure is thus an absolute must if the life-style issues are to be faced.

Fourth, a national urban policy must address the problems of suburban sprawl. Federally stimulated metropolitan planning has not done this. New town proposals have not done it. Incalculably valuable natural resources of farmland, recreational space, open space, water supply, and natural beauty have been plowed under and paved over in the past 30 years. And over the next 20 years they will continue to be wasted unless federal incentives and priorities are established.

The four aspects of urban policy indicated here refer to *national* problems, not local problems. And the existence of national problems involving federal expenditures of more than $110 billion demands that national policies be articulated to guide the ways in which that money is spent.

The Process of National Urban Policy

From these discussions on the difficulty of getting a national urban policy, it is apparent that the process of implementing national policies is just as important as the formulation of those policies in the first place. It is also apparent from earlier discussions that federal government programs have a mixed record of success in reaching their goals. Urban history in the 1960s and 1970s provides abundant examples of federal policies that were unimplemented or poorly implemented because the federal government did not possess the means or the unity to carry them out. On the other hand, these same years also present abundant examples of federal initiatives that worked very well and accomplished their policy objectives. In order to assess whether the White House can fulfill its stated intentions of implementing a national urban policy, it would seem useful to try and distinguish between the kinds of policies that the federal government is currently capable of implementing and those that it is not. Some things it does very well; other things it does very poorly.

What the Feds Do Poorly   First is the targeting problem. The federal government poorly implements policies that are adversely affected by traditional congressional logrolling. For example, the Model Cities program's prospects for success were seriously hampered from the beginning because its funds were spread among cities in so many congressional districts that no single model city got enough funds to carry out its objectives. If the goal behind Model Cities was in fact the creation of a demonstration project that all cities could emulate, then congressional logrolling hampered the attainment of that objective. Carter's proposals for supplementary fiscal assistance also failed in part because of the inability to reach agreement between some congressional members' desires to target benefits and other members' desires to spread benefits.

Second, coordination of federal policies during the 1960s was a dismal failure. The Office of Economic Opportunity was so unable to fulfill its legislative mandate to coordinate urban programs that it simply ignored the mandate and devoted itself to stimulating innovation and experimentation.[88] Model Cities was specifically created to coordinate federal programs at the neighborhood level, but its success at this was extremely limited.[89] The A–95 review process was devised to enable all federal grants to be coordinated at the metropolitan level, but the results were largely unencouraging and A–95 was discontinued under the Reagan administration.[90] Federal regional councils were created as a coordinating device, but these too were largely ineffective,[91] and Reagan abolished them in 1983. The federal government has stimulated the creation of a plethora of metropolitan, substate, regional agencies whose goal is to plan and coordinate federal grant programs in water quality, criminal justice, health services, transportation, and land use. It is not clear how much effect all these coordinating agencies actually have on the delivery of services.

Third, the federal government has a spotty record of ensuring that federal funds are spent in compliance with federal guidelines. HUD in particular has not effectively overseen the use of credit provisions for new towns programs, the prohibition of discrimination in public housing,[92] or the programs to stimulate home ownership among low-income families.

What the Feds Do Well　In contrast to the above activities, in which federal performance has been unsuccessful, there are many other federal activities in which the implementation process has worked very effectively—for example, transfer payments. Transfer payments are simply payments of cash from the federal treasury to individuals. They are called transfer payments because they in effect collect income taxes from some people and distribute (or transfer) those revenues to other people. The prime examples of transfer payments are Social Security and veterans' benefits. There may be disagreement about the adequacy of benefits or whether Congress has put too many obligations onto the Social Security tax or onto the general regressive nature of the Social Security tax, but once people qualify and register for Social Security benefits, the Social Security Administration accomplishes its objective of mailing checks to them with a minimum of disruption. A contrast of the Social Security Administration with the Office of Economic Opportunity suggests that it is much easier to do an effective job of mailing checks to people badly in need of cash than it is to create programs that will help those same people have an effective voice in how their neighborhoods are run.

Second, the federal government operates some kinds of programs much better than others. Its most successful programs are characterized by (1) well-defined agency responsibilities, (2) tangible, measurable objectives, (3) adequate resources, and (4) the absence of strong opposition among interest groups or government agencies that could divert the program from its original intentions. The Apollo mission to land a man on the moon in the early, successful days of NASA clearly had these characteristics, but the antipoverty programs lacked them. In the Apollo program, NASA's responsibilities were clearly defined, the objective of placing a man on the moon was tangible and measurable, adequate resources were provided, and some of the most powerful interest groups in the country strongly supported the economic boost the program would give to the economy. In the federal antipoverty programs, a multitude of agencies had overlapping missions. The objectives were not tangible, and appropriations to meet them were inadequate. In comparing the space program with the antipoverty programs, NASA was clearly given much better control to accomplish its program objectives than OEO or the other related agencies were given to eliminate poverty.

Third, the executive branch has been fairly successful at carrying out orders of the federal courts. Although desegregation of public schools and compliance with affirmative action orders have been slow, considerable progress has been made. Pursuant to court orders, children are now attending racially desegregated schools in places and numbers that only a few years ago would have seemed impossible.

Implications for Effective Policy

These statements comparing the things the federal government does well with those it does poorly are highly tentative. More systematic research is needed on the dynamics of implementing federal policies. If the above analysis is valid, however, important implications follow for the success of national urban policies.

First, the coordination problem is horrendous. Nothing that has yet been tried has worked well. Under the Johnson administration, first the Office of Economic Opportunity and then the Department of Housing and Urban Development was named as the agency to coordinate all federal urban programs. The Nixon administration probably devoted more effort toward coordinating and controlling urban policies than any other administration. Under Nixon, a Domestic Council was created to enable the White House to coordinate the formulation of domestic policies. The Domestic Council was to be chaired by the president, and membership consisted of the vice-president and the heads of the major departments and agencies concerned with domestic affairs. To ensure that the policies formulated by the Domestic Council were actually carried out, the Office of Management and Budget was given responsibility for evaluating the various domestic agencies in relation to the policies established by the Domestic Council. President Nixon, however, never exhibited the concern for urban problems that was needed to make this apparatus function effectively. His major policy considerations apparently centered on eliminating as many urban programs as possible and turning the funds for their operation over to the state governments. Under Carter the federal emphasis switched from stimulator of new services to facilitator of private investment in the economic revitalization of cities.

A second implication for successful urban policy is posed by the traditional congressional logrolling process. How can programs such as Model Cities, Community Action, or mass transit have a measurable effect anywhere if the appropriations are never adequate and if the funds are parceled out to the districts of every rural or small-town congressional representative who happens to head a subcommittee? In Carter's administration this same problem reemerged in the defeat of Supplementary Fiscal Assistance because of the incompatibility between those who wanted to target benefits and those who wanted to spread benefits.

The Bias of the Federal Involvement

Because the federal involvement in urban affairs is so massive and so heterogeneous, it is difficult to categorize its overall biases. If some federal programs (such as public housing) seem biased toward the status quo, others (such as the community action programs) seem equally biased toward rapid social change. Furthermore, the multitude of federal programs makes it difficult to categorize an overall bias of the federal involvement in terms of individual group benefits. Each program generates its own constituency. And if the residents of low-income residential neighborhoods are often disproportionately injured by some federal programs (such as those supporting urban renewal and freeway construction), other federal involvements (such as transfer payments, Aid For Dependent Children, and day care centers) disproportionately benefit these low-income people.

In order to assess the overall bias of the federal involvement, a concept is needed to calculate *net bias* or *net impact* of federal programs on identifiable constituencies and on major urban and metropolitan problems. If the total of federal programs biased against some identifiable urban constituency (for example, poor blacks) is outweighed by the total of federal programs biased in favor of that constituency, then the net bias or net impact of federal programs would be biased in favor of that constituency. If the total of federal programs promoting social change is outweighed by the total of federal programs protecting the status quo, then the net bias or net impact of federal involvement would be biased against social change.

To translate the concept of net bias into operational terms is very difficult, however. The constituencies of urban programs are not easy to identify precisely, and the criteria for deciding whether a program works for social change or for the status quo are not clear. Consequently, the task of operationalizing the concept of net bias lies beyond the scope of this book. What follows, instead, is an attempt to delineate six general patterns of federal involvement that strongly suggest a definite net bias. These patterns involve: (1) the creation of interest groups for the urban poor and minorities, (2) the attempts to equalize social access to middle-class life styles, (3) the attempts to control suburban sprawl, (4) the attempts to improve governmental accountability to the electorate, (5) the attempts to subordinate urban programs to comprehensive national urban policies, and (6) the attempts to use urban policies and programs as a device for redistributing income and resources.

Bias and the Creation of Interest Groups for the Urban Poor

Certain programs of Lyndon Johnson's Great Society were biased toward the creation of interest groups to represent the interests of the urban poor and the racial minorities. The Community Action programs and the Model Cities experiment greatly broadened the scope of community leadership in inner-city communities, particularly in the black communities. This leadership has been far from unified, but it did not disappear with the demise of the War on Poverty. Consequently, the black community in the 1980s is much stronger than it was a decade earlier in confronting urban governments about their operation in black neighborhoods. Particularly in relation to black communities, the federal programs created in the 1960s have solidified a number of urban interest groups that cannot be ignored: the Urban League, the Urban Coalition, the Conference of Mayors, and most of the racial improvement groups such as the NAACP. The importance of this was seen earlier in the example of Newark blacks effectively challenging the authority of the Newark Housing Authority.

The reverse of this bias of the Great Society, however, is that neither the national nor the state capitals are very responsive to the unorganized urban needy. Up to this point, the most disorganized urban communities have probably been American Indians and the Appalachian white, working poor. Neither group has benefited significantly from federal urban programs, which are biased toward more organized groups.

The revolutionary aspect of the New Deal in the 1930s was its institutionalization of organized labor as a mechanism for representing the interests of the working poor who were organized in unions. The major shortcoming of the Great Society during the 1960s was its inability to create a similar mechanism to represent the interests of those poor who were unorganized or not part of the unionizable labor force.

Bias and Social Access to Middle-Class Life Styles

A second net bias of the federal involvement has been against measures that would equalize social access to middle-class life styles. Federal housing programs illustrate this most clearly. Although some federal housing programs have indeed made it easier for moderate-income people to live in middle-class neighborhoods and although public housing has provided living space for millions of low-income people, no housing program has had a very far-reaching impact on integrating communities along either class or racial lines. Furthermore, as indicated by the estimates given in Table 13-1, the housing programs that facilitate social access are heavily outweighed by the housing programs that diminish social access. Federal Housing Administration (FHA) mortgage guarantees have been used overwhelmingly in the suburbs and have promoted little housing for the poor or for racial minorities. Public housing has been confined largely to the poor neighborhoods of central cities and has had the impact of increasing racial segregation.* Section 8

---

*Even though public housing does not improve social access for the poor, it must be noted that it *does* lower the cost of housing for those who live in the public projects and in that respect *does* constitute a redistribution of income. Because public housing is used by people poorer than those who use the HUD 235 and 236 programs, it can be considered more redistributive than those programs even though it does not do as much as they do to improve social access to middle-class life styles. For an analysis of the redistributive aspects of federal housing programs, see Henry J. Aaron, *Shelter and Subsidies: Who Benefits from Federal Housing Policies?* (Washington, D.C.: The Brookings Institution, 1972), pp. 121–126, 136–140.

leased public housing since 1974 has contributed to spreading low-income housing throughout cities and may indicate that current federal housing policies are less biased against social access than they were during the 1950s and 1960s.

Bias and the Containment of Suburban Sprawl

Federal programs have a net bias against attempts to contain suburban sprawl. The major federal programs to contain it, as indicated in this and the previous chapter, have been the stimulation of metropolitan planning and councils of governments. However, these have been extremely weak control mechanisms. Furthermore, the federal funds invested in them are small compared to the amount of federal funds invested in programs that stimulate suburban sprawl—especially guaranteed mortgages in the suburbs and the urban portion of the Interstate Highway System. It is difficult to conclude that the net bias of the federal involve-

Table 13-1. Selected Federal Programs and the Equalization of Social Access to Middle-Class Life Styles

Some federal programs that *diminish* lower-class access to middle-class life styles[a]		Some federal programs that *increase* lower-class access to middle-class life styles[b]	
Program	Dollars (millions)	Program	Dollars (millions)
Urban renewal: 1953–1974[1]	9,468	Rent supplements: 1966–1973[3]	403
Low-rent public housing: 1953–1974[1]	6,644	HUD 235: 1968–1973[4] *Home ownership assistance*	766
VA mortgage guarantees: 1945–1970[2]	4,005	HUD 236: 1968–1973[4] *Rental housing assistance*	407

[a]Urban renewal and public housing diminish social access because they have destroyed more slum housing than they have replaced. They have contributed to the residential concentration of low-income families and racial minorities, and they have seldom provided low-income housing in the suburbs. VA mortgage guarantees diminish social access because they seldom are made to low-income people. In 1970, the average VA home loan purchaser owned liquid assets of $2454, paid $21,264 for the home, and had an after-tax monthly income of $720 (an estimated before-tax annual income of $9600). This was slightly higher than the 1969 median family income ($9433) and more than twice as high as the poverty-level income for a family of five. (For source of data, see text note 4.)

[b]These programs increase social access because they provide assistance to low- and moderate-income households and they allow for these households to be dispersed among middle-income residential neighborhoods.

Sources:

[1]These data are extracted from U.S. Department of Commerce, Bureau of the Census, *Statistical Abstract of the United States* for the years 1974 (p. 249), 1968 (p. 383), 1965 (p. 398), 1962 (p. 385), and 1958 (p. 406).

[2]U.S. Department of Commerce, Bureau of the Census, *Statistical Abstract of the United States: 1971*, p. 262.

[3]Harold Wolman, *Politics of Federal Housing* (New York: Dodd, Mead, 1971), p. 146 for years 1966–1969. Reprinted by permission of the publisher. For 1970–1973, the sources are the same as the ones listed for note 4, below.

[4]Budget of the United States Government (Washington, D.C.: U.S. Government Printing Office). Fiscal year 1970, Appendix, pp. 520–521; fiscal year 1971, Appendix, pp. 500–501; fiscal year 1972, Appendix, pp. 496–497; fiscal year 1973, Appendix, pp. 509–510; fiscal year 1974, Appendix, pp. 497–498; fiscal year 1975, Appendix, pp. 492–493.

ment in urban affairs has been anything other than against containing suburban sprawl.

Having noted the net bias against containing suburban sprawl and the net bias against equalizing access to middle-class life styles, however, it must also be recognized that a number of federal initiatives over the past two decades do indeed seek to equalize access to middle-class life styles. The consistent commitments to affirmative action programs and to leased public housing should help equalize social access.

Bias and Governmental Accountability

Until at least the end of the 1960s the net impact of government programs was clearly to diminish the accountability of urban governments to the electorate. Many grants-in-aid programs stimulated the proliferation of special districts. Many other programs stimulated the creation of semiautonomous housing and redevelopment authorities. Welfare programs have been administered under a Byzantine system of administrative rulings that practically eliminated the accountability of the program to local elected officials.

The late 1960s and early 1970s, however, saw several coordinating devices aimed at making federal programs more accountable to identifiable officials. These devices include the A–95 review process, the stimulation of councils of governments, the federal regional councils, and the community development block grant program of the 1970s. This last item in particular has strengthened local elected officials' control over federally financed urban redevelopment. And the citizen participation provisions of the 1974 CD block grant program have also helped make the program more accountable to citizens' groups and neighborhood groups. In the 1980s, the Reagan administration downplayed the coordination devices such as A–95 and COGs. But its New Federalism efforts supported the trend toward increasing the authority of state governors and legislators.

Bias and Policymaking

The net bias of the federal urban involvement works to protect urban programs and highly particularistic interests from subordination to systematic policies. This has been shown repeatedly during the 1960s and 1970s. For example, the community development grant consolidation of 1974, as originally proposed by President Nixon, would have shifted influence away from those groups that are powerful at the national capital and toward those that are powerful at the state capitals. This would have been extremely detrimental to local big-city groups that had emerged around the Model Cities programs, the Community Action programs, and several others of the more than 100 grants-in-aid programs that Nixon was going to consolidate into special revenue sharing. The results were predictable. These groups and their allies in Congress and the federal bureaucracies fought bitterly against the proposals. The net result was a substantial amount of consolidation but within the framework of a compromise that effectively diluted the concept of special revenue sharing and ensured the major urban bureaucracies in HUD, DOT, and HEW that they would not suffer any setbacks. To give other examples, Carter's proposals for welfare reform, energy policy, and urban policy all were stymied by particular private interests unwilling to give in to Carter's perception of the public good. These examples suggest that very little incentive exists for any president to try to subordinate urban programs to national policy.

Bias and the Redistribution of Income

The preambles of federal urban legislation usually suggest that their objectives are to improve the lot of the disadvantaged. This was true of the Economic Opportunity Act, the Model Cities Act, the Elementary and Secondary Education Act, and may other acts that establish the urban-oriented grants-in-aid programs. One might therefore conclude that the objective of urban programs has been to redistribute income. By establishing programs to provide services for people who lack the resources to provide the services for themselves, the urban programs raise revenue from some people and turn it over to other people in the form of new services. This theoretically constitutes a redistribution of income.

Such a conclusion would be difficult to sustain, however. The effect of urban programs is not so much to redistribute income as it is to create wealth and to give a portion of that wealth to the constituencies of the programs, to the recipients of the new services. The major portion of such new wealth, however, goes not to the poor but to middle-class people connected to the organized groups that belong to the constituency of the program. By infusing new federal money into the economy, federal programs create jobs, purchasing power, and business activities. And the fact that the federal budget has operated at a deficit rather than being balanced since the inception of urban programs in the 1930s suggests that the money being poured into these programs was newly created money, money borrowed against the future rather than money taken out of the pockets of the middle and upper classes through the income tax.

This may all seem rather obvious and unimportant, but it has two significant ramifications. First, the pattern for federal involvement has been to justify urban programs in rhetoric that implies a redistribution of wealth. This is of symbolic importance, for it suggests that something is really being done to alter the living conditions of the urban poor. Second, the programs themselves infuse newly created wealth into the economy rather than redistribute old wealth. This new wealth is distributed through the prevailing economic institutions. Thus the major share of the new wealth will go to the middle and upper classes, and only a minor share will go to the poor. The bias implication of this is that under present conditions any urban program, no matter how radical its rhetoric, preserves the prevailing class structure. It does not stimulate radical social change nor does it redistribute the wealth.

The one possible exception to this may be the significant increase in transfer payments since 1965. In transfer payments, the money is paid out directly to the needy. Bureaucracies are kept to a minimum. And functional tie-ins between federal and local bureaucracies do not constitute functional fiefdoms that destroy the governing capabilities of local governments.

Conclusions

The federal involvement in urban affairs has evolved to the point where increasing pressures demand the coordination of urban programs under some form of executive-directed national urban policy. Ironically, the administration (Carter's) that sought the hardest to articulate such a policy enjoyed only modest success with it, while the administration (Reagan's) most vehemently opposed to articulating a national urban policy was one of the most successful in terms of reorienting the goals and purposes of federal involvement in urban affairs. The dynamics of the federal involvement thus suggest that several things will continue to happen throughout the 1990s. First, attempts to make the melange of federal programs accountable to the White House and to local elected officials will probably continue. Second, these federal actions probably will not significantly improve the access of the poor to middle-class life styles or significantly alter suburban sprawl. Finally, the biases of the federal involvement that were outlined above will change very little.

Summary

1. The main federal tool for coping with urban problems has been grants-in-aid. Two early grants-in-aid programs were public housing and urban renewal.

2. The most extensive outpouring of urban programs occurred during the administration of President Lyndon B. Johnson. Called the Great Society, his administration created two urban-related cabinet departments and sponsored the Elementary and Secondary Education Act, the Economic Opportunity Act, the Fair Housing Act, and the Model Cities Act.

3. During the presidential administrations of Richard M. Nixon and Gerald R. Ford, national urban policymaking focused on (a) reversing some key programs of the Great Society and (b) promoting a New Federalism based on general revenue sharing and grant consolidation.

4. President Jimmy Carter was the first president to articulate a specific urban policy. He did so in 1978, and his policies were characterized by the themes of economic revitalization, fiscal relief for distressed city governments, targeting of scarce federal resources to the most appropriate urban places, and improvement of existing urban programs.

5. President Ronald Reagan sought only one new urban initiative—Urban Enterprise Zones. However, his New Federalism, block grants, budget reduction, and regulatory changes had a marked impact on the federal urban role.

6. There are several factors that make it difficult to achieve a coherent and effective national urban policy. Some programs (such as the Apollo program) are implemented successfully by the federal government, but others (such as Model Cities) have been marked by much less success. It is important to distinguish between the things the federal government does well and the things it does poorly.

7. Because any particular group both pays costs under some federal programs and benefits from other federal programs, the concept of net bias was introduced to sort out the patterns of bias. During the Great Society period, one bias of federal programs was to facilitate the creation of interest groups for the urban poor. On balance, however, federal housing, renewal, and transportation programs have not facilitated lower-class access to middle-class life styles. Federal policies on balance have been biased in favor of suburban sprawl, although a number of policies in recent years have been trying to contain that sprawl. Because of the proliferation of programs and special districts, federal policies were biased against accountability of urban governments to the electorate. A number of developments since the mid-1960s, however, have attempted to promote greater accountability among urban governments.

Chapter 14
Political Change in the Metropolis of the Future

If present-day urban trends in the United States continue for another decade, what are the likely consequences? In order to answer this question, this chapter will make conservative projections of the developmental and political consequences of certain existing trends. First, reasons will be given why the 1990s probably will not witness the adoption of drastic national urban policies. Second, recent demographic and technological trends will be projected into the near future to show what changes can be expected by the year 2010. That is, how will the metropolis of 2010 differ from that of 1989? Third, speculations will be offered about likely political consequences of these changes. How will we be governed in the year 2010? And what will be the major changes in political processes?

The Difficulty of Establishing a National Urban Policy

Barring some unforeseen nuclear or ecological catastrophe, the migration and urban development patterns traced in Chapter 2 seem likely to continue through the 1990s. Coherent and enduring urban growth policies are no more likely to be achieved in the next decade than they were in previous decades. The reasons for this are deeply rooted in the structure of the American political system and in the nature of the American political culture.

The structure of the American political system has several features that impede the articulation and implementation of long-range policy goals for the kind of urban society we want to become. Foremost among these features are federalism and the separation of powers. Although the national government is still the dominant policymaker in the American federal partnership, national policies are carried out 50 different ways in 50 different states, and the New Federalism developments of the 1980s enhance state independence even further. The separation of powers makes different branches of the government responsive to so many different constituencies that achieving a consensus on controversial matters becomes almost impossible among all the branches and agencies of government. Furthermore, Congress and the executive agencies in particular are organized around the performance of specific service and regulatory functions that all have their own interest group clientele. This organization of government and private structures around specific service and regulatory functions gives the government a preference for making specific decisions that relate to specific projects. Even within given sectors of public life (veterans' benefits, for example), once a service is established it is very difficult to get either Congress or the appropriate executive agencies to make policy evaluations of the program in relation to its objectives and its performance.

In some functional sectors of public life, a long-range policy goal can be articulated and all efforts and programs subordinated to the achievement of that goal. The Apollo program and the specific decision to place an astronaut on the moon are prime examples of this.[1] In the operation of urban programs, however, there is no consensus on long-range policy goals to which separate programs can be subordinated. As a result, several hundred federal programs have proliferated in the metropolises in an uncoordinated, unplanned way. In more than one instance, the objectives of one program have been undone by the objectives of other programs. The New Federalism proposals of the Nixon and Reagan administrations were offered to give state and local governments more policy control over their usage of federal aid. However, studies found a tendency to recategorize the block grants,[2] and poor coordination seemed just as much a problem in the mid-1980s as it had a decade earlier.

Finally, the tradition of logrolling in Congress has been detrimental to urban programs such as Model Cities, in which program success depended on large appropriations being made for a few, carefully selected sites. In order to ensure the votes needed for passage, the number of Model Cities had to be expanded to so many locations that few cities received a sufficient concentration of resources to carry out a successful program. Although these geographical considerations have not necessarily proven detrimental to programs that are not essentially organized on a geographical basis (such as the Apollo program), they do work to the disadvantage of programs designed to operate for the select benefit of certain geographical locations.

These structural impediments to the creation of a long-range national urban policy are reinforced by certain prominent values of the American political culture. *American political culture* is taken to mean the sum total of beliefs, attitudes, opinions, and expectations about the way the American political system does function and should function.[3] Foremost among the aspects of the American political culture that impede the establishment of a national urban policy is a deep-rooted distrust of centralized control over domestic problems. Much of this stems from the colonial heritage and the Jeffersonian ideal of small-town democracy. It also stems from the reaction against the excessive corruption of the urban political machines. As a result, governmental authority in urban areas has been deliberately fragmented. One semiautonomous agency is given operating responsibility for one functional service sector, another semiautonomous agency is given operating responsibility in another functional service sector, and so on. The ideal of small-town democracy is resurrected in urban America by the proliferation of relatively small municipalities in the suburbs. General-purpose governments at the metropolitan level are so few and so difficult to establish that they can be considered a virtual impossibility as a way of ending the fragmentation of government authority in most metropolises.

Considerable centralization of authority has been achieved on a function-by-function basis in the area of key services needed to maintain the physical existence of the metropolis. However, on issues concerning access to middle-class life styles, such as zoning, school integration, and the construction of low-income public housing in the suburbs, there has been a strong reluctance to centralize control at the metropolitan level. Federal programs have supported the functional organization of authority and the creation of suburbia itself.

This inability to formulate a national urban policy and to form a national consensus about national objectives for our urban areas is perhaps the most apparent conclusion to be drawn about the governance of metropolitan America. Closely related to this lack of consensus is the lack of political power to confront directly some of the most obvious urban and metropolitan problems, particularly the lifestyle problems. We do not lack imaginative proposals; if anything, we are embarrassed by a wealth of creatively imaginative proposals that we have not been able to implement effectively. What has been sorely lacking is the organization of political power to make the programs work over the long run.

Technological and Demographic Effects on the Metropolis of the Future

A key question about the future of the metropolis concerns its technological viability beyond the next generation. The contemporary metropolis is contingent upon the availability of highly developed technologies for transit, transport, supply, employment, and provision of public services. The vulnerability of the contemporary metropolis is demonstrated at least once a year when some major central city undergoes a strike by transit workers, garbage collectors, teachers, police officers, or other public employees. The famous northeastern blackout of 1965 demonstrated how easily a whole network of metropolises can be paralyzed simply by an electrical failure. Periodic lines at the gasoline pumps during the 1970s, combined with escalating costs of gasoline, fuel oil, and other petroleum-based products, demonstrated just how dependent the whole system of metropolises is on the continual supply of gasoline, fuel oil, and natural gas. In trying to speculate on the viability of the contemporary metropolis as we move into the 21st century, certain assumptions have to be made about the state of the economy and the availability of energy sources.

First, it seems likely that there will be sufficient petroleum, natural gas, and electrical energy to maintain the physical existence and continued expansion of the contemporary metropolises for the next few decades. Second, although continued expansion of the metropolis is physically possible, it is becoming increasingly expensive. The economy grew more slowly in the 1970s than it did in the 1960s, and so far it has grown more slowly in the 1980s than it did in the 1970s.[4] The sources of petroleum, natural gas, and electrical energy are becoming much more costly to exploit than they were in the past. Ecological concerns will continue to require investments to reduce air pollution, to restore polluted waterways, and to reclaim land that will be strip-mined for coal. All of these factors will reduce the amount of money available for discretionary income and for improving individual standards of living. This, in turn, will limit the number of people who can afford to buy houses in and commute by auto from a new tier of suburbs created by developers who will want to leapfrog beyond the existing suburbs. Thus leapfrog development will probably slow down within the next decade. The 1980s have already begun to see a slowdown in the movement to small cities just beyond the metropolis. This may be a signal that leapfrog development itself is beginning to reach a limit. Ultimately, leapfrog development will stop—but probably not within the next decade.

Third, the expansion of the job market will probably continue in the pattern of the past quarter century. That is, the private job market will expand most rapidly in the suburbs, while the public-service job market will expand most rapidly in the central cities.

Predicting what effects these assumed conditions will have on metropolitan development is, of course, impossible. But one or some combination of three scenarios seems most likely.

One possibility that has been predicted in the media is that of an implosion in which the suburban populations begin migrating back into the central cities. In fact, recent years have seen a significant gentrification process as upper-middle-income professionals bought up old homes in run-down city neighborhoods and began restoring them. For a variety of reasons, however, only a small percentage of the suburban population is likely to do this. Despite the increased costs of leapfrog development because of the economic and energy factors cited above, leapfrogging is still likely to be cheaper for big developers than will be the costs of buying previously developed central-city land, destroying the buildings there, and clearing the sites for new construction. Furthermore, millions of workers now have jobs in the suburbs, and moving back into the central city will not necessarily put them closer to their places of employment. For all of these reasons, the preconditions that would sustain a massive in-migration into the central cities do not exist.

A second possible scenario, also suggested by the media, might be a genuine migration back to the country where families can live much more independently of natural resource shortages than they can in the large metropolises. The *Whole Earth Catalog*[5] implies tht such a movement is possible. And the Sunday supplements of the big-city newspapers periodically carry feature articles about young families that give up the comforts of the metropolitan rat race for idyllic, primitive homesteads in the wilderness. These publications suggest that it might be possible to create another golden age of thriving, small family farms. Small may be beautiful,[6] but it does not seem likely to be the destiny of the present generation of Americans. A massive movement back to the farm is no longer possible. In the nineteenth-century age of small and thriving family farms, most of the arable land was originally not owned by private individuals. It was given by the federal government under the terms of the Homestead Act. Today the most arable portions of rural land are privately owned, and they are increasingly owned by corporations that want either to cultivate them or to exploit their mineral wealth. Furthermore, as agricultural exporting becomes increasingly important to the national economy, arable farmland will become much too valuable an asset to be used merely for subsistence farming. For all these reasons, not much land will be available for the increasing millions of metropolitan people wishing to abandon the metropolis.

The back-to-the-county movement is likely to be limited in the future as it is now to three groups of people. One very small group consists of dropouts from the metropolitan rat race. The second, not much larger, consists of a new generation of nonfarmers and part-time farmers. These are professionals—doctors, lawyers, writers, artists, teachers, and others—who can afford the time and the money to absent themselves from the metropolis for days or weeks at a time. They often live in expensively refurbished farmhouses in places such as northern New England or the Blue Ridge Mountains, from where they can drive back to the metropolis on a few hours' notice. The third group consists of those people moving to growing small towns that have once again become economically viable due to the decentralizing impact of new communications technology.

The third possible scenario, and the one most likely for most of the population over the next decade, consists of continued metropolitan sprawl. Since 1970 there has been a net out-migration of MSA residents to small towns and new-tier suburbs just beyond the current MSA boundaries. As metropolitan sprawl has been continuing, the number of MSAs has increased.

The sprawl of the next decade is likely to proceed much more slowly than it has in the past because of more rigorous land use controls that were imposed in the 1970s and because of no-growth and slow-growth movements that appeared in the 1980s. But the metropolis of 2010 is not likely to be very much different from the metropolis of 1990—except that it will be larger and more spread out.

Beyond the year 2010, some basic alterations will have to be made in the patterns of metropolitan growth. Economically exploitable energy resources, on which the current technology of metropolitan growth depends, are not inexhaustible and probably do not extend more than a generation or two into the future. Major changes in the technology of transit and home heating may have to be made. Whenever such changes have occurred in the past, they have always made a stupendous impact on the patterns of urbanization. The railroads made the coal and canal towns of early nineteenth-century Pennsylvania obsolete. The automobile, the interstate highway, and the airplane made most of the late nineteenth-century railroad towns obsolete. And when newly emerging technology is applied to transit and home heating, it is likely to make a major impact on many contemporary suburbs and certain metropolises. Even now, if it were economically feasible, considerable electrical energy could be generated from solar cells and the burning of processed solid waste. The application of solar heating and energy-conscious building construction methods could reduce home heating dependence on natural gas. Natural gas itself could be supplemented by methane gas generated from human and animal waste. Personalized rapid transit could reach all but the neighborhoods of the lowest densities. High-speed, short-distance train travel between cities could diminish contemporary reliance on energy-intensive air travel.

As some of these methods are applied, the face and structure of the metropolis is certain to begin changing in ways that are not apparent now. By the year 2010 these physical changes will just be emerging and they may not be very perceptible. Beyond that date it is not possible to project very well.

Political Projections

What implications do the above projections have for political change in the metropolis over the next decade? Two areas seem to be of the most importance in answering these questions: (1) expected changes in the governing processes and structures, and (2) expected changes in the attempts of the racial minorities to gain equal access to middle-class life styles.

Projected Changes in Urban Governance

The first likely change is federal involvement in metropolitan affairs. Environmentalists will demand federal involvement to minimize the ecological impact of future metropolitan growth. Adherents of land use controls will demand more federal involvement when they lose battles at the state levels. Racial minorities will demand federal involvement to help them attain access to middle-class life styles and to break down segregation patterns in housing, education, and employment. Representatives of the housing and construction industries will demand more federal financial support for the construction of housing units. And the elements of the well-known highway lobbies will demand federal funds for more highways and for maintenance of existing highways. During the 1980s, many of these demands were on a direct collison course with the Reagan administration, which sought to reduce federal influence in most of those areas. Despite demands from fiscal conservatives that the federal government's influence be curbed, the mere existence of these powerful forces kept the federal government from withdrawing to a minimal role. The many urban interests that depend on federal funds will lobby strenuously for them. Some urban interests, particularly the racial minorities, rely heavily on the political intervention of the federal government to protect their welfare, and such groups will lobby energetically for a strong federal role, not a minimal one. Even under the conservative New Federalism of President Reagan, the federal role in metropolitan affairs was still substantial.

Another change to come will be more demands to be satisfied. The urban interest groups created during the turbulent 1960s and 1970s have not all disappeared. If anything, other potential groups are learning from the experience of blacks that gains can be won if people band together. The best example during the 1970s was probably the women's movement. Today, urban governments deal routinely with groups that did not exist only 20 years ago—groups for the retarded, alcoholics, ex-prisoners, welfare recipients, tenants, senior citizens, homosexuals, Hispanics, American Indians, and many others. None of these groups is likely to change the class structure of society, redistribute income, or terminate the functional organization of power. But they are likely to continue making demands that will challenge the prevailing distributions of wealth and power in the metropolis.

Finally, there will probably be an increasing atrophy of general-purpose municipal governments. As noted repeatedly in earlier chapters, consistently over the past 40 years general-purpose municipal governments have been bypassed in the creation of new governmental functions. And these newly created governmental functions have usually been made fairly independent of municipalities. That these patterns continue to the present day can be seen in the fact that the Census of Governments found that the number of special districts continued to grow. On many issues, such as transit, air pollution control, criminal justice planning, and health planning, control over these functions is localized in agencies other than municipal governments for many good reasons. For one thing, there may be a hundred or more municipalities in the metropolis, and to localize control over these functions in each municipality would compound the problems of coordination. Another reason is that the technical expertise and the bureaucratic structure needed to handle the new functions are much more likely to be found in functionally specialized agencies than they are in any of the existing municipalities, including the central-city government. Consequently, municipalities, including central-city governments, are in danger of either being bypassed entirely in the performance of governmental functions or being subordinated to policies predetermined at higher levels.

The major exceptions in the last ten years to this atrophy of local general-purpose governments have been general revenue sharing (until it was abolished in 1987), the block grant consolidations, and a movement in many states to grant more authority to cities. Many central cities have used the community development block grants to regain control over redevelopment and spur neighborhood citizens' groups. They have also exercised imaginative decisiveness in using industrial revenue bonds and other financial measures as seed money to set up public-private partnerships that would bring new industry into the city.

Implicit in all of the above is the possibility that the total urban governmental apparatus in 2010 could be less responsive to individual citizen demands and inputs than it is today. With the importance of federally supported regional planning agencies for growth, criminal justice, health care, air quality control, and water quality control, we are moving toward a de facto, two-tier arrangement of government without any prior agreement on the relative roles of each tier. As these changes occur, the emerging institutions are dominated by existing interest groups and public bureaucracies.

This change will be felt most dramatically in the suburbs, where the municipal governments are already very weak, except for their zoning powers. If the suburban municipal governments lose their control over zoning, their major *raison d'être* will disappear. Suburban governments will still be close to the people, but they will have so little authority and jurisdiction that the people will not be close to anything of any consequence. The major decisions will be made elsewhere—by school districts, special districts, counties, metropolitan districts, and federally financed planning agencies.

The projection for citizen input in central cities may be less bleak than it is in suburbia. Many cities have adopted some form of decentralized control sharing designed to give neighborhood residents more input into the political decisions of central-city governments. Central-city governments perform more functions and operate more services than do suburban governments. Because they are larger and because they are still the symbolic focal point for politics in the metropolis, they have more influence on state leaders, metropolitan leaders, and federal officials than do the officials of any given suburban municipality. And because the central-city governments still retain some importance, the neighborhood community councils may end up having considerable influence on the course of local governance. They even may become a more effective vehicle for citizen input than they would in suburban municipal governments.

Political Projections for Questions of Race

In the functional organization of power in the contemporary metropolis, one of the most urgent demands has been to give the powerless a stronger voice in the political system so that the metropolis can better meet their needs. This demand has been most publicized among the racial minorities, but it is important among other powerless citizens as well. Some observers show an almost nostalgic longing for old-style political machines that could advance the interests of the racial minorities today as they once enabled certain ethnic groups to gain effective political power. But a return to the past is impossible. Probably more and more attempts will be made to esablish shared control over the city government through decentralized administration or neighborhood governments. But since a high level of technical sophistication is needed to manage many of the services of the metropolis, reversing the functional organization of power would be difficult. Functionally organized power is necessarily power held by elites who are not accountable to a broad cross section of the population. Attempts throughout the 1960s and 1970s to organize the masses who did not belong to already existing, functionally organized interest groups generally failed. But these organization-building efforts did start a number of interest groups that still actively attempt to speak for the disadvantaged or for the public interest as they define it. Consequently, one of the key unresolved questions about the future of metropolitan America lies in working out the fundamental tension between demands of the racial minorities for improvement in their access to middle-class life styles and the functionally organized power structures in the sectors of welfare, education, renewal, public housing, and suburban development that have been so instrumental in building the segregated metropolis as it exists.

If one extends current trends in these matters into the next 10 years, four projections seem most likely.

First, de facto segregation will continue in housing. Increasing numbers of blacks are moving into predominantly white suburbs and neighborhoods, but the basic segregation of residential neighborhoods seems unlikely to be reversed. No programs now in existence or even in the planning stages could make a serious dent in the de facto segregation of housing patterns in the American metropolis. Continued pressure for affirmative action programs in the private employment sector and for low- and moderate-income public housing in the suburbs will make small dents in the patterns of segregation, but they are not capable of reversing the basic pattern.

Second, not only will de facto segregation continue, but the lessened growth of the economic pie will decrease the ability of the poor, especially the poor who are the racial minorities, to have access to middle-class life styles. During the 1960s, the percentage of blacks living below the federally defined poverty level declined.[7] Thus it looked as though increasing the size of the economic pie would do for the blacks what it did for the European ethnic minorities—that is, give them a larger piece. As the economy grew, succeeding generations of the European ethnic minorities lived more comfortably than did their parents' generations. However, the economy has not grown as fast since 1970 as it did during the 1960s.[8] The percentage of families living in poverty rose dramatically during the early 1980s. And if present trends continue, the poor and the racial minorities are likely to get a smaller share of a more slowly growing pie than they got during the 1960s, when the racial minorities achieved their most dramatic increase in living standards.

The European ethnic minorities created ethnic networks by moving into sectors of private or public life that were just being created. The big-city police departments and fire departments were disproportionately populated for so long by the Irish because the Irish were the dominant minority at the time that police and fire departments were created. The public school teacher professions and social worker professions in New York City were disproportionately populated by Jews for so long because the Jews were among those minorities strategically placed to move into those professions precisely at the time that they were created. It is difficult to foresee what new public-sector employment opportunities can arise by the year 2000 that can serve as a growth sector for black and minority employment. The antipoverty programs in the 1960s had aspects of performing this service for blacks, but it is hardly a growth sector any more. Health care and criminal justice planning are two obvious candidates. But the best positions in both of these sectors require highly sophisticated training beyond the bachelor's degree level. In the lower echelons, criminal justice administration and health care delivery have been substantially large employers of the minorities. And, as Peter Eisinger has shown, black control of city governments has produced some expansion of black employment.[9]

Third, a great question exists as to whether the poor and the racial minorities will continue to rely increasingly on the intervention of the federal government to help them increase their access to middle-class life styles. Their biggest ally has been the federal government. The interest-group structure of the black communities is much more effective at the federal level than it is at the state levels. With the black caucus in Congress and a sizable bloc of votes among urban, nonblack members of Congress, the ability of blacks to use leverage within the federal government to place demands on local governments is not likely to disappear. Certain federal agencies, particularly HUD, Education, and Justice, have direct mandates to carry out and implement congressionally approved programs to equalize access in certain key areas. Despite all these factors suggesting a continued reliance on the federal government to promote racial advancement, there are also some signs pointing in the opposite direction. Popular support for affirmative action and busing programs has declined, and at this time it seems unlikely that there will be any significant new busing programs put into effect. Indeed, in 1987 the federal courts approved the termination of a busing program in Norfolk, Virginia.

Fourth, there seems to be very little potential for a class-based political alliance between the racial minorities and the lower- and moderate-income whites. It is with these whites rather than with the upper middle classes that blacks have competed and will compete. Their children, more than the upper-middle-class children, are bused into black-dominated schools. These whites are more vulnerable than the upper middle class to periodic unemployment and hence are more resentful of affirmative action programs for hiring. And, more so than the upper middle class, they feel the squeeze on housing that is likely to persist in a more slowly growing economy and metropolis. Consequently, more individual contact will take place between working-class whites and working-class blacks by the year 2000, and much of this contact will be forced on them by federal action. Deeply felt resentments among lower- and moderate-income whites and blacks led to sporadic and disruptive violence during the 1970s. As an example, news stories about South Boston High School sounded more like battlefield reports than stories about an institution of learning. Some other desegregation efforts were achieved more peacefully. But every city will always have leaders who will try to postpone the inevitable (in this case, compliance with court orders on desegregation) as long as possible. And other leaders will always seek political gain by appealing to racial prejudice. The political manifestations of these tensions have been seen most clearly in the mayoral campaigns of black candidates. Few of them, as we noted in Chapter 7, drew much voting support from low-income white neighborhoods, although Jesse Jackson's 1988 presidential campaign drew a fairly large number of white votes.

To achieve desegregation peaceably and to promote the equalization of access of the minorities to middle-class life styles will certainly continue to be a most difficult task over the next decade—as it has over the previous decades.

Conclusions

Metropolitan politics over the next two decades will begin to reflect political adjustments that must be made to a basic change in the preconditions for continued growth in the post-World War II metropolis. In the past twenty years, two basic changes occurred in these preconditions. First, post-World War II metropolitan growth was contingent on the availability of cheap energy and the ability of the economy to sustain both the mass production of single-family homes in a suburban leapfrog development pattern and a mass consumption economy of continuously improving standards of living for most urban and suburban residents. The oil crises of 1973–1974 and 1978–1979 cast doubt on the precondition that the energy resources will be available to sustain metropolitan energy usage over the long run under current technology. And the economic pressures since then cast doubt on the ability of the economy to sustain continued post-World War II patterns of metropolitan growth over the long term. At the very least, the increased costs of energy and the prospect of a more slowly growing economy suggest that less money will be available for increases in most people's standard of living.

A second basic change in the preconditions relates to the role of the racial minorities. In post-World War II metropolitan growth, the vast majority of racial minorities were systematically excluded from access to middle-class life styles. The urban upheavals of the 1960s reflected the demand of the leaders of these minorities that this systematic exclusion be ended. In the opinion of this writer, this exclusion cannot be ended by the traditional method of relying on continued growth in the size of the economic pie. It cannot be ended without some redistribution of income and without major alterations in the distribution of political power in the metropolis. Hence urban political issues in the future will be much more intricately involved with national political issues and with economic issues than they ever have been before.

What the political complexion of the metropolis will look like beyond the year 2010 is highly conjectural, but certain trends seem likely to persist. One of the constants will be the long-range dwindling of supplies of certain natural resources that have been essential for the development of the modern industrial economy. If these long-range shortages mean, as many people are predicting, that we will move from an economy of abundance to an economy of scarcity, then the life-style issues of urban politics will undoubtedly assume increasing importance. If the benefits of the metropolis have proven impossible to equalize during the greatest growth boom that the country has ever seen, how can they be equalized when the amount of benefits grows relatively smaller rather than larger each year?

If the long-range shortages of natural resources do in fact lead to a long-range leveling off of the national economy while the metropolitan population continues to increase, then demands will most likely increase for both greater federal intervention and the centralization of political authority in general-purpose, metropolitan governments that can exert some control over the functional fiefdoms. Although it is difficult to imagine urban politics becoming any more explosive in the future than they were during the middle and late 1960s, the seeds for explosive politics are certainly present in the trends discussed above. Leaders of the new urban minorities will understandably fear the freezing of their racial and ethnic groups into a permanent urban underclass. White lower-middle-class and working-class people will fear an end to their social mobility. Upper-middle-class and professional-class people will fear the loss of their affluent life styles. The leaders of functional fiefdoms will rigidly oppose control-sharing schemes that will diminish their own influence over urban governments, and they will support citizen-representation schemes that give the appearance of shared control so long as the substance of their control is unaffected.

Of course, none of this is inevitable. The entire scenario is predicated on the twin assumptions that natural resource shortages will cause a permanent contraction in the growth of the American economy before the life-style issues of urban politics can be settled. Maybe the technological and economic adjustments to the scarcity of natural resources will be made before they reach the crisis stage. Maybe American business will become more competitive in the world arena, and the decline of America's industrial sector will reverse itself. Maybe the current glut of petroleum and natural gas will become permanent and the nation's energy problems will wither away. Maybe the life-style issues will be settled. Maybe the population growth will cease. Maybe the traditional American practice of muddling through with piecemeal, ad hoc remedies for specific problems will continue to suffice for the future as it has for the past. Maybe a national urban policy will be formed to deal with these matters. Maybe the present generation of economic and political leaders will act with more foresight and selflessness over the next decade than they have in the previous decades.

Then again, maybe they will not.

Notes

Chapter 1

1. *Plunkitt of Tammany Hall*, recorded by William L. Riordan (New York: E. P. Dutton, 1963), pp. 11–13.

2. See Chapter 11, pp. 328–329. On Cleveland, see Richard A. Watson and John H. Romani, "Metropolitan Government for Metropolitan Cleveland: An Analysis of the Voting Record," *Midwest Journal of Political Science* 5, no. 4 (November 1961): 376. On St. Louis, see Henry J. Schmandt, P. G. Steinbicker, and G. D. Wendel, *Metropolitan Reform in St. Louis* (New York: Holt, Rinehart and Winston, 1961), pp. 59ff. On Miami, see Edward Sofen, *The Miami Metropolitan Experiment* (Bloomington: Indiana University Press, 1963). On Indianapolis, see York Wilbern, "Unigov: Local Governmental Reorganization in Indianapolis," in Advisory Commission on Intergovernmental Relations, *Report A-41. Regional Governance: Promise and Performance: Substate Regionalism and the Federal System* (Washington, D.C.: U.S. Government Printing Office, May 1973), vol. II—Case Studies, pp. 71–72. On Jacksonville and Nashville, see Vincent L. Marando and Carl Reggie Whitley, "City-County Consolidation: An Overview of Voter Response," *Urban Affairs Quarterly* 8, no. 2 (December 1972): 181–204.

3. Harold Lasswell, *Politics: Who Gets What, When, How* (New York: McGraw-Hill, 1936).

4. Students not familiar with the input-output model of political analysis might find it useful to examine one of the many systems analysis models of politics. Much of the systems analysis terminology stems from the writings of David Easton and Gabriel Almond. See David Easton, *A Systems Analysis of Political Life* (New York: Wiley, 1965), and Gabriel Almond and G. Bingham Powell, *Comparative Politics: A Developmental Approach* (Boston: Little, Brown, 1966). Some interesting attempts to concentrate on the output side of this model in order to analyze the costs and benefits of policy outputs are

Thomas R. Dye, *Politics, Economics, and the Public: Policy Outcomes in the American States* (Chicago: Rand McNally, 1966), and Brett W. Hawkins, *Politics and Urban Policies* (Indianapolis, Ind.: Bobbs-Merrill, 1971).

5. A discussion of urban renewal is found in Chapter 13, pp. 363–364. For a documenteation of urban renewal's reducing the housing supply for the poor and the racial minorities, see John A. Weicher, *Urban Renewal: National Program for Local Problems* (Washington, D.C.: American Enterprise Institute, 1972), p. 6. For documentation of urban renewal's driving small business out of business, see Advisory Commission on Intergovernmental Relations, *Metropolitan America* (Washington, D.C.: U.S. Government Printing Office, 1966), p. 69.

6. Political change has proven to be an elusive term for political scientists to define precisely. Political-change literature has focused primarily on non-western countries that are perceived as undergoing a modernizing or a developmental process. Another focus has been the revolutionary aspects of some change. Some prominent examples of these focal points can be found in John H. Kautsky, *Political Change in Underdeveloped Countries: Nationalism and Communism* (New York: Wiley, 1962); David E. Apter, *The Politics of Modernization* (Chicago: University of Chicago Press, 1965); Leonard Binder, *Iran: Political Development in a Changing Society* (Berkeley and Los Angeles: University of California Press, 1962); Peter H. Merkl, *Political Continuity and Change* (New York: Harper & Row, 1967); and Chalmers A. Johnson, *Revolutionary Change* (Boston: Little, Brown, 1966).

7. Kenneth M. Dolbeare, *Political Change in the United States: A. Framework for Analysis* (New York: McGraw-Hill, 1974), p. 7.

8. This point is made particularly by Anthony Downs, *Urban Problems and Prospects* (Chicago: Markham, 1970), p. 1; and by Daniel N. Gordon,

"The Bases of Urban Political Change: A Brief History of Developments and Trends," in *Social Change and Urban Politics: Readings*, ed. Daniel N. Gordon (Englewood Cliffs, N.J.: Prentice-Hall, 1973), pp. 2–21. Dolbeare, however, argues that political change is an independent process because the political system has often failed to change along with changes in the economic system. See his *Political Change in the United States*, p. 3.

9. Murray Edelman, *The Symbolic Uses of Politics* (Urbana: University of Illinois Press, 1964).

10. This point is made by Yasumasa Kuroda in a study of a Japanese community. See his *Reed Town, Japan: A Study in Community Power Structure and Political Change* (Honolulu: University of Hawaii Press, 1974), pp. 7–8.

11. See Theodore Lowi, *At the Pleasure of the Mayor* (New York: The Free Press, 1964). Also see Edward C. Banfield and James Q. Wilson, *City Politics* (Cambridge, Mass.: Harvard University Press, 1963), pp. 107–110.

12. Political scientist Marilyn Gittell has described the difficulty of exercising electoral control over the New York City public school system. See her "Professionalization and Public Participation in Educational Policy Making: New York City, a Case Study," *Public Administration Review* 27, no. 3 (September 1967): 237–251. A similar point is developed by Norman I. Fainstein and Susan S. Fainstein in "The Political Evaluation of Educational Policies," in *Neighborhood Control in the 1970's*, ed. George Frederickson (New York: Chandler, 1973), pp. 195–216. See Harmon L. Zeigler et al., *Governing American Education* (Belmont, Calif.: Duxbury Press, 1974). Also, see Chapter 7, pp. 197–198.

13. See note 5.

14. See Chapter 13 for a fuller discussion of the attempts during the 1970s to articulate a national urban policy.

15. See *Urban America: Policies and Problems* (Washington, D.C.: Congressional Quarterly, 1978), pp. 1–2.

16. See Rochell L. Stanfield, "At Long Last an Urban Policy with the Carter Stamp," *National Journal* 10, no. 13 (April 1, 1978): 526–527; *Urban America: Policies and Problems*, pp. 5–22.

17. See Michael Parenti, "Ethnic Politics and the Persistence of Ethnic Identification," *American Political Science Review* 61 (September 1967): 717–726; and Raymond E. Wolfinger, "The Development and Persistence of Ethnic Voting," *American Political Science Review* 59 (December 1965): 896–908.

18. The definition of politics as the allocation of values, goods, and services is adapted from David Easton, *The Political System* (New York: Knopf, 1953). The definition of politics in terms of decision making is adapted from Robert A. Dahl, *Who Governs? Democracy and Power in an American City* (New Haven, Conn.: Yale University Press, 1961), and Nelson Polsby, *Community Power and Political Theory* (New Haven, Conn.: Yale University Press, 1963).

19. This approach to defining power is analyzed extensively by Robert A. Dahl in *Modern Political Analysis*, 2nd ed. (Englewood Cliffs, N.J.: Prentice-Hall, 1970), pp. 19–25 and 32–34. Dahl asserts that power is merely an extreme form of influence in which coercion is involved. "Severe losses for non-compliance can be invoked by the power holder" (p. 32).

20. Raymond E. Wolfinger, *The Politics of Progress* (Englewood Cliffs, N.J.: Prentice-Hall, 1974), pp. 7–9.

21. See J.E. Teele and C. Mayo, "School Racial Integration: Tumult and Shame," *Journal of Social Issues* 25 (January 1969): 137–156. For editorial accounts, see "Queen of the Backlash," *Economist*, June 25, 1966, p. 1417, and "Hicksville?" *Economist*, September 30, 1967, p. 1196.

22. This viewpoint is discussed in Chapter 7, pp. 206–207. For an article on the political efficacy of the poor and the unorganized see Michael Parenti, "Power and Pluralism: A View from the Bottom," *Journal of Politics* 32, no. 3 (August 1970): 501–532.

23. On central-city business interests, see especially Edward C. Banfield and James Q. Wilson, *City Politics* (Cambridge, Mass.: Harvard University Press, 1963), pp. 261–276. On suburban business interests, see especially Charles Gilbert, *Governing the Suburbs* (Bloomington: University of Indiana Press, 1967), pp. 145ff.

24. On Detroit, See Edward C. Banfield, *Big City Politics* (New York: Random House, 1965). On Chicago, see Banfield and Wilson, *City Politics*, pp. 277–278.

25. For a background article on this practice, see the *Wall Street Journal*, April 5, 1974, p. 1,

26. Historian Sam Bass Warner, Jr. has asserted the importance of privatism in American urban history. See his *The Private City: Philadelphia in Three Periods of Its Growth* (Philadelphia: University of Pennsylvania Press, 1968); Warner asserts that "The tradition of privatism is . . . the most important element of our culture for understanding the development of cities" (pp. 38–39).

27. See Juergen Habermas, *Legitimation Crisis* (Boston: Beacon Press, 1973), pp. 37, 75, and Robert D. Holloway and J. Harry Wray, *American Politics and Everyday Life* (New York: Wiley, 1982), p. 60.

28. Although he did not use the term privatism,

the argument against city governments financing substantial welfare or social services is made quite persuasively by Paul E. Peterson in his *City Limits* (Chicago: The University of Chicago Press, 1981).

29. Steven A. Peterson, "Privatism and Politics: A Research Note," *Western Political Quarterly* 37, no. 3 (September 1984): 483–489.

Chapter 2

1. The definition of urban in terms of volume, density, and heterogeneity was formulated by sociologist Louis Wirth in his article "Urbanism as a Way of Life," *American Journal of Sociology* 44 (July 1938): 1–24. The distinction between the sociological and demographic concepts of urbanization has been made by several scholars in addition to Wirth. See especially John Friedmann, "Two Concepts of Urbanization: A Comment," *Urban Affairs Quarterly* 1, no. 4 (June 1966): 78–79.

2. Federal Committee on Standard Metropolitan Statistical Areas, "The Metropolitan Statistical Area Classification," *Statistical Reporter*, no. 80-3 (December 1979): 35.

3. See Ira Rosenwaike, "A Critical Examination of the Designation of Standard Metropolitan Statistical Areas," *Social Forces* 48, no. 3 (March 1970): 322–333.

4. *The New York Times*, July 8, 1983, p. 7.

5. Peter Hall, *The World Cities* (New York: World University Library, 1971), p. 19.

6. John Friedmann and John Miller, "The Urban Field," *Journal of the American Institute of Planners* 21 (November 1965): 314.

7. Jean Gottman, *Megalopolis: The Urbanized Seaboard of the United States* (New York: Twentieth Century Fund, 1961).

8. Federal Committee on Standard Metropolitan Statistical Areas, "The Metropolitan Statistical Area Classification," pp. 33–34.

9. Population calculated from United States Bureau of the Census, *County and City Data Book: 1972* (Washington, D.C.: U.S. Government Printing Office, 1972), pp. 29–58.

10. Gottman, *Megalopolis*, chap. 1.

11. C. A. Doxiadis, *Urban Renewal and the Future of the American City* (Chicago: Public Administration Service, 1966), p. 75

12. Kingsley Davis, "The Origin and Growth of Urbanization in the World," *American Journal of Sociology* 60 (March 1955): 430–432.

13. The importance of transportation technology is cited by many urbanists. See especially Friedmann and Miller, "The Urban Field," and Gino Germani, "Urbanization, Social Change, and the Great Trans-

formation," in *Modernization, Urbanization, and the Urban Crisis*, ed. Gino Germani (Boston: Little, Brown, 1973), pp. 29–30.

14. Gerald M. Capers, Jr., "Yellow Fever in Memphis in the 1870's," *Mississippi Valley Historical Review* 24, no. 4 (March 1938): 483–502.

15. United States Bureau of the Census, *A Century of Population Growth: 1790–1900* (Washington, D.C.: U.S. Government Printing Office, 1909), p. 15.

16. United States Bureau of the Census, *Historical Statistics of the United States: Colonial Times to 1957* (Washington, D.C.: U.S. Government Printing Office, 1957), p. 14. Philadelphia's 1790 population found in United States Department of Commerce and Labor, Bureau of the Census, *A Century of Population Growth: 1790–1900*, p. 11.

17. United States Bureau of the Census, *Current Population Reports*, ser. P-20, no. 249, "Characteristics of the Population by Ethnic Origin: March 1972 and 1971" ((Washington, D.C.: U.S. Government Printing Office, 1973).

18. For an excellent interpretation of some of the political consequences of the third and fourth urban migration waves, see Steven P. Erie's "Rainbow's End: From the Old to the New Urban Ethnic Politics," in *Urban Ethnicity in the United States: New Immigrants and Old Minorities*, vol. 29, *Urban Affairs Annual Reviews*, eds. Lionel Maldonado and Joan Moore (Beverly Hills: SAGE Publications, 1985), pp. 249–275.

19. The classic interpretation of the importance of the western frontier to American history was made by Frederick Jackson Turner in his famous essay, *The Frontier in American History* (New York: Henry Holt and Company, 1920). His argument was rejected by historian Arthur M. Schlesinger, Sr., in "City in American History," *Mississippi Valley Historical Review* 27 (June 1940): 43–66, who argued that urbanization was the motive force behind the frontier movement and most of the important historical political movements. For a reformulation of the importance of the frontier in the urbanization process, see Daniel J. Elazar, *Cities of the Prairie: The Metropolitan Frontier and American Politics* (New York: Basic Books, 1970).

20. Roderick D. McKenzie, *The Metropolitan Community* (New York: McGraw-Hill, 1933), pp. 4–5.

21. See Charles N. Glaab and A. Theodore Brown, *A History of Urban America* (New York: Macmillan, 1967), pp. 113–144. For a fascinating, in-depth account of the creation of one city by the Northern Pacific Railroad, see Waldo O. Kliewer, "A Railroad City: The Foundations of Billings, Montana," *Pacific*

Northwest Quarterly (July 1940).

22. Sam Bass Warner, Jr., *Streetcar Suburbs: The Process of Growth in Boston, 1870-1890* (Cambridge, Mass.: Harvard University Press, 1962).

23. For a study of the impact of a subway on big-city growth, see James Leslie David, *The Elevated System and the Growth of Northern Chicago* (Evanston, Ill.: Northwestern University, Department of Geography, 1965).

24. See Kenneth Boulding, "The Death of the City: A Frightened Look at Post-Civilization," in *The Historian and the City*, ed. Oscar Handlin and John Burchard (Cambridge, Mass.: M.I.T. Press and Harvard University Press, 1963), pp. 133–145.

25. Sam Bass Warner, Jr. documents the small-scale nature of business in Philadelphia in the late eighteenth century, in *The Private City: Philadelphia in Three Periods of Its Growth* (Philadelphia: University of Pennsylvania Press, 1968), chap. 1. Oscar Handlin documents the late-nineteenth-century transition of Boston's economy from small-scale to large-scale enterprise in *Boston's Immigrants* (Cambridge, Mass.: Belknap Press of Harvard University Press, 1941), chap. 3.

26. Chapter 1, "The Metropolitan Explosion," in Hall, *The World Cities*, contains a more complete explanation of this idea.

27. Schlesinger, "City in American History."

28. Glaab and Brown, *A History of Urban America*, pp. 293–294.

29. For a summary of this anti-urban tradition, see Morton White and Lucia White, *The Intellectual Versus the City: From Thomas Jefferson to Frank Lloyd Wright* (Cambridge, Mass.: Harvard University Press, 1962).

30. Mark L. Gelfand, *A Nation of Cities: The Federal Government and Urban America 1933-1965* (New York: Oxford University Press, 1975), p. 220.

31. *Shelley v. Kraemer*, 334 U.S. 1 (1948).

32. Gelfand, *A Nation of Cities*, p. 220.

33. On the charge of economic discrimination, see Eugene Lewis, *The Urban Political System* (Hinsdale, Ill.: Dryden Press, 1973), pp. 221–223.

34. *Report of the National Advisory Commission on Civil Disorders* (Washington, D.C.: U.S. Government Printing Office, 1968), pp. 116–118.

35. Data on Spanish-speaking persons are taken from Bureau of the Census, *Current Popualtion Reports*, ser. P-20, no. 361, "Persons of Spanish Origin in the United States: March 1980" (Washington, D.C.: U.S. Government Printing Office, 1981), p. 5; and *Statistical Abstract of the United States: 1987* (Washington, D.C.: U.S. Government Printing Office, 1986), p. 11.

36. See Joan Didion, "Miami: 'La Lucha'," *New York Review of Books* 34, no. 10 (June 11, 1987): 15–18.

37. Calculated from *Statistical Abstract of the United States: 1987* (Washington, D.C.: U.S. Government Printing Office, 1986), p. 11.

38. United States census data cited in George Sternlieb and James W. Hughes, "The Uncertain Future of the Central City," *Urban Affairs Quarterly* 18, no. 4 (June 1983): 455–472.

39. Winston Moore, Charles P. Livermore, and George F. Galland, Jr., "Woodlawn: The Zone of Destruction," *Public Interest* (Winter 1973): 42. On this phenomenon, also see Ben Wattenberg, *The Real America* (Garden City, N.Y.: Doubleday, 1974), pp. 142–143.

40. *Wall Street Journal*, March 14, 1980, p. 1.

41. See Bureau of the Census, *Patterns of Metropolitan Growth* and *County Population Growth*, cited in *Minneapolis Star and Tribune*, November 21, 1985, p. 22a.

42. See *The New York Times*, March 3, 1987, p. 8.

43. On this point, see especially Brian J.L. Berry, "Islands of Renewal in Seas of Decay," in *The New Urban Reality*, ed. Paul E. Peterson (Washington, D.C.: The Brookings Institution, 1985), pp. 72–74.

44. See, for example, George Sternlieb and James W. Hughes, eds., *Revitalizing the Northeast* (New Brunswick, N.J.: Center for Urban Policy Research, 1978). Also see Donald B. Rosenthal, ed., *Urban Revitalization*, vol. 18, Urban Affairs Annual Reviews (Beverly Hills, Calif.: SAGE Publications, 1980).

45. John H. Mollenkopf, *The Contested City* (Princeton, N.J.: Princeton University Press, 1983), pp. 31–36.

46. For some examples of this viewpoint, see the following articles in *The New York Times*: Robert Lindsey, "Big Cities' Building Boom Belies Theory of Decline," July 23, 1979, p. A-12; Michael Knight, "Once-Blighted Cities of New England Are Booming," January 22, 1980, p. 1; "Dallas Helps Bring Expensive Houses into Inner City," January 2, 1980, p. A-18.

47. For example, see Paul Levy and Dennis McGrath, "Saving Cities for Whom?" *Social Policy* 10, no. 3 (November–December 1979): 20–28.

48. Neal Peirce, "Industrial Blackmail in the Cities?" *Public Administration Times*, December 1, 1980.

49. Alfred A. Watkins, "Intermetropolitan Migrations and the Rise of the Sunbelt," *Social Science Quarterly* 59, no. 3 (December 1978): 553–561.

50. Warner, *The Private City*, pp. 38–39.

51. Bayrd Still, "Patterns of Mid-nineteenth Century Urbanization," *Mississippi Valley Historical Review* 28 (September 1941): 187–206.

52. See David C. Ranney, *Planning and Politics in the Metropolis* (Columbus, Ohio: Charles E. Merrill, 1969), especially chap. 7, "Conflict and the Planning Process: The Politics of Planning," pp. 109–138.

53. See Richard Hamilton, *Class and Politics in the United States* (New York: Wiley, 1972), pp. 155–180.

54. See Chapter 9, pp. 249–253.

55. Karl Taeuber, "Racial Residential Segregation, 28 Cities, 1970–1980," Center for Demography and Ecology, University of Wisconsin, Madison, Working Paper 83-12. Joint Center for Political Studies, *Blacks on the Move: A Decade of Demographic Change* (Washington, D.C.: Joint Center for Political Studies, 1982).

56. See Katharine L. Bradbury, Anthony Downs, and Kenneth A. Small, *Urban Decline and the Future of American Cities* (Washington, D.C.: The Brookings Institution, 1982), pp. 187, 214–215.

Chapter 3

1. Ira Katznelson, *City Trenches: Urban Politics and the Patterning of Class in the United States* (New York: Pantheon Books, 1981), pp. 54–56.

2. U.S. Bureau of the Census, *Twelfth Census of the United States: 1900; Volume 1: Population; Part I*, p. cxxii.

3. William V. Shannon, *The American Irish* (New York: Macmillan, 1963), p. 28.

4. For a history of nativist movements and their effects on the immigrants, see John H. Higham, *Strangers in the Land* (New Brunswick, N.J.: Rutgers University Press, 1955).

5. Shannon, *The American Irish*, p. 46.

6. For a colorful history of the Know Nothing party, see Carleton Beals, *The Brass Knuckled Crusade: The Great Know Nothing Conspiracy 1820–1860* (New York: Hastings House, 1960). The decline of the party is described on pp. 252–279. The Massachusetts incident is described on pp. 227–233.

7. On lynching of Italians, see p. 58 in Chap. 3 of this book.

8. Robert Dahl, *Who Governs? Democracy and Power in an American City* (New Haven, Conn.: Yale University Press, 1966), p. 38.

9. John Tracy Ellis, *American Catholicism* (Chicago: University of Chicago Press, 1963), p. 102.

10. John Tracy Ellis, *Perspectives in American Catholicism* (Baltimore: Helicon, 1963), p. 61.

11. See Edwin Scott Gaustad, *Historical Atlas of Religions in America* (New York: Harper & Row,

1962), p. 169; and John F. Maguire, *The Irish in America* (London: Longmans, Green, 1968).

12. George Potter, *To the Golden Door: The Story of the Irish in Ireland and America* (Boston: Little, Brown, 1960), p. 359.

13. Shannon, *The American Irish*, pp. 36–37.

14. Ibid., p. 122.

15. Edward M. Levine, *The Irish and Irish Politicians: A Study of Cultural and Social Alienation* (Notre Dame, Ind.: University of Notre Dame Press, 1966), p. 119.

16. Ibid.

17. Shannon, *The American Irish*, p. 116.

18. Richard J. Whalen, *The Founding Father: The Story of Joseph P. Kennedy* (New York: E. P. Dutton, 1964), chap. 1.

19. Dahl, *Who Governs?*, pp. 41–52.

20. Herbert Gans, *The Urban Villagers: Group and Class in the Life of Italian-Americans* (New York: The Free Press, 1962), p. 167.

21. Levine, *The Irish and Irish Politicians*, p. 120.

22. The identification of Irish business interests as construction, food wholesaling, real estate, and transportation comes from Shannon, *The American Irish*, p. 122.

23. See Steven P. Erie, "Politics, The Public Sector and Irish Social Mobility: San Francisco, 1870–1900," *The Western Political Quarterly* 31, no. 2 (June 1978): 274–289.

24. Steven P. Erie, "The Organization of Irish-Americans into Urban Institutions: Building the Political Machine, 1840–1896," a paper presented at the Annual Meeting of the American Political Science Association, Chicago, Illinois, September 1–4, 1983.

25. Andrew M. Greeley, *Why Can't They Be Like Us?, America's White Ethnic Groups* (New York: E. P. Dutton, 1971), pp. 50–51.

26. Steven P. Erie, "Two Faces of Ethnic Power: Comparing the Irish and Black Experiences," *Polity* 13, no. 2 (Winter 1980): 268–269. Also see his "Rainbow's End: From the Old to the New Urban Ethnic Politics," in *Urban Ethnicity in the United States*, vol. 2, Urban Affairs Annual Reviews, eds. Lionel Maldonado and Joan Moore (Beverly Hills, Calif.: SAGE Publications, 1985), pp. 254–256.

27. See Nathan Glazer and Daniel Patrick Moynihan, *Beyond the Melting Pot; The Negroes, Puerto Ricans, Jews, Italians, and Irish of New York* (Cambridge, Mass.: M.I.T. Press, 1963), pp. 243–250. Also see Shannon, *The American Irish*, p. 67, and Andrew Greeley, *The Catholic Experience: An Interpretation of the History of American Catholicism* (New York: Doubleday, 1967), pp. 270–271. In Andrew M. Greeley, "American Catholics—Making It or Losing

It?" *The Public Interest* 28 (Summer 1972): 26–37, Greeley asserts that about a fifth of the faculty under age 30 at elite universities and colleges are Catholic (p. 28). The assumption of this author is that many of these are partially of Irish origin.

28. See Katznelson, *City Trenches*; and Erie, "Two Faces of Ethnic Power," pp. 270–271, who argues that the Irish machines served to control rather than reward the working class.

29. David Ward, "The Emergence of Central Immigrant Ghettoes in American Cities, 1840–1920," *The Annals of the American Association of Geographers* 58 (June 1968): 343–351.

30. Rudolf Glanz, *Jews and Italians: Historic Group Relations and the New Immigration 1881–1924* (New York: Shulsinger Brothers, 1970), p. 10.

31. Rudolph J. Vecoli, "Contadini in Chicago: A Critique of the Uprooted," *Journal of American History* 64 (1964): 404–417.

32. John S. MacDonald and D. Leatrice, "Urbanization, Ethnic Groups and Social Segmentation," *Social Research* 29 (Winter 1962): 435.

33. Carl Wittke, *The Irish in America* (Baton Rouge: Louisiana State University Press, 1956), p. 92.

34. Humbert S. Nelli, *Italians in Chicago, 1880–1930; A Study of Ethnic Mobility* (New York: Oxford University Press, 1970), pp. 189, 67.

35. Lawrence Frank Pisani, *The Italian in America: A Social Study and History* (New York: Exposition Press, 1957), p. 166.

36. Dahl, *Who Governs?*, p. 38. Also, see Raymond E. Wolfinger, *The Politics of Progress* (Englewood Cliffs, N.J.: Prentice-Hall, 1974), p. 30.

37. On the struggle between the Irish and Italians to control Italian wards in Boston, see William F. Whyte, *Street Corner Society: The Social Structure of an Italian Slum* (Chicago: University of Chicago Press, 1943), p. 195.

38. This is described by Samuel Lubell in *The Future of American Politics*, 3rd ed. (New York: Harper & Row, 1965), pp. 77–83.

39. Elmer E. Cornwell, Jr., In "Party Absorption of Ethnic Groups: The Case of Providence, Rhode Island," *Social Forces* 38 (March 1960): 205–211, documents a steady rise in the number of Italian ward committeemen in both the Republican and Democratic parties in Providence.

40. Lubell, *The Future of American Politics*, pp. 203, 216.

41. Ibid., pp. 79–80.

42. Theodore J. Lowi, *At the Pleasure of the Mayor* (New York: The Free Press, 1964), pp. 92, 117.

43. See Daniel P. Moynihan, "'Bosses' and 'Reformers': A Profile of the New York Democrats,"

Commentary 31 (June 1961): 461–470.

44. See Lowi, *At the Pleasure of the Mayor*, p. 40, on New York. On Chicago, see p. 68 in Humbert S. Nelli, "John Powers and the Italians: Politics in a Chicago Ward, 1896–1921," *Journal of American History* 57 (June 1970): 67–84.

45. Nelli, "John Powers and the Italians," p. 68.

46. Greeley, *Why Can't They Be Like Us?*, pp. 87, 92.

47. Nelli, *Italians in Chicago*, p. 196.

48. Andrew M. Greeley, *That Most Distressful Nation: The Taming of the American Irish* (Chicago: Quadrangle Books, 1972), pp. 147, 152.

49. Vecoli, "Contadini in Chicago," p. 268.

50. Edward C. Banfield, *The Moral Basis of a Backward Society* (New York: The Free Press, 1958).

51. Whyte, *Street Corner Society*, pp. 208–209.

52. Glanz, *Jews and Italians*, pp. 27–28.

53. Francis A.J. Ianni, "The Mafia and the Web of Kinship," *The Public Interest* (Winter 1971), p. 88.

54. On the New Orleans incident, see Richard Gambino, *Vendetta: A True Story of the Worst Lynching in America* (Garden City, N.Y.: Doubleday, 1977). On the Boston execution of Sacco and Vanzetti, see Leonard Dinnerstein and Frederic Cople Jaher, *The Aliens: A History of Ethnic Minorities in America* (New York: Appleton-Century-Crofts, 1970), p. 216; *The New York Times*, August 23, 1977, p. 47, and February 1, 1978, p. 10. For a fictional account of contemporary Italian reactions to the Sacco and Vanzetti trial, see Rick Boyer, *The Penny Ferry* (New York: Warner Books, 1984).

55. Pisani, *The Italians in America*, p. 62.

56. Andrew F. Rolle, *The Immigrant Upraised* (Norman: University of Oklahoma Press, 1968), p. 305.

57. Pisani, *The Italians in America*, p. 65.

58. Ibid., p. 269.

59. Rolle, *The Immigrant Upraised*, p. 379.

60. Ibid., p. 269.

61. Andrew M. Greeley, "American Catholics—Making It or Losing It?" *The Public Interest* 28 (Summer 1972): 32.

62. See Russell M. Posner's two-part article, "The Bank of Italy and the 1926 Campaign in California," *California Historical Society Quarterly* 37 (September 1958): 267–275, and (December 1958): 347–358; and also Russell M. Posner, "A.P. Giannini and the 1935 Campaign in California," *Historical Society of Southern California Quarterly* 39 (June 1957): 190–201 (cited in Rolle, *The Immigrant Upraised*, p. 281).

63. Lubell, *The Future of American Politics*, p. 83.

64. The governmental viewpoint is fairly well

summarized in two documents published by the President's Commission on Law Enforcement and Administration of Justice: *The Challenge of Crime in a Free Society* (Washington, D.C.: U.S. Government Printing Office, 1967), chap. 7; and the Commission's Task Force on Organized Crime, *Task Force Report: Organized Crime* (Washington, D.C.: U.S. Government Printing Office, 1967). The testimony of former Federal Bureau of Investigation director J. Edgar Hoover has been widely used in promoting the notion of the dominance of the Mafia over all organized crime in this country. See Hoover's testimony in U.S. Congress, Senate, Permanent Subcommittee on Investigations of the Senate Committee on Governmental Operations, *Organized Crime and Illicit Traffic in Narcotics*, 89th Cong. 1st sess. 1965, Senate Report 72. See also U.S. Congress House, Appropriations Subcommittee of the House Committee on Appropriations, testimony of J. Edgar Hoover, *Hearings Before the Subcommittee of Departments of State, Justice, and Commerce, the Judiciary and Related Agencies*, 89th Cong., 2nd sess., 1966, House Report 273.

65. Among popular exposé writings, several have dwelt heavily on the mystique of the Mafia and its supposed Sicilian origins. See Norman Lewis, *The Honored Society* (New York: Putnam, 1964); G. Schiavo, *The Truth About the Mafia* (El Paso, Texas: The Vigo Press, 1962); and Edward J. Allen, *Merchants of Menace: The Mafia* (Springfield, Ill.: Charles C. Thomas, 1962). A most spectacular book is Peter Maas, *The Valachi Papers* (New York: Putnam, 1968); the text is drawn from Maas's extended interviews with Valachi, who coined the phrase La Cosa Nostra and who supposedly was a member of that organization. A biographical account of one family in organized crime is Gay Talese, *Honor Thy Father* (New York: World Publishing, 1971). A journalistic account of selected criminal leaders is given by Ed Reid, *The Grim Reapers* (Chicago: Henry Regnery, 1969). A fascinating collection of anecdotes by an excellent investigative reporter is found in Nicholas Gage, *The Mafia Is Not an Equal Opportunity Employer* (New York: McGraw-Hill, 1971). The thoughts of a former police officer whose responsibilities dealt primarily with organized crime are found in Ralph Salerno and John S. M. Tompkins, *The Civic Confederation: Cosa Nostra and Allied Operations in Organized Crime* (Garden City, N.Y.: Doubleday, 1969).

66. Salerno and Tompkins, *The Civic Confederation*, p. 89.

67. Ibid., p. 277.

68. Richard D. Knudten, *Crime in a Complex Society* (Homewood, Ill.: Dorsey Press, 1970), p. 197.

69. Donald R. Cressey, *Theft of the Nation: The Structure and Operations of Organized Crime in America* (New York: Harper & Row, 1969), p. 21.

70. The President's Commission on Law Enforcement and Administration of Justice, *The Challenge of Crime*, p. 441.

71. Salerno and Tompkins, *The Civic Confederation*, pp. 232–235.

72. Ramsey Clark, *Crime in America* (New York: Simon & Schuster, 1970), p. 73.

73. Rolle, *The Immigrant Upraised*, p. 106.

74. Joseph S. Clark and others, *Crime in Urban Society* (New York: Dunnellen, 1970), p. 62. For an attempt to define organized crime and the difficulties in making such a definition, see Knudten, *Crime in a Complex Society*, p. 187.

75. Gordon Hawkins, "God and the Mafia," *The Public Interest* 14 (Winter 1969): 51.

76. Ianni, "The Mafia and the Web of Kinship," p. 86.

77. Ibid., p. 90.

78. See Herbert Asbury, *The Gangs of New York: An Informal History of the Underworld* (New York: Capricorn Books, 1970; originally published 1927).

79. R. Carlson and L. Brisson, "The Web That Links San Francisco's Mayor Alioto and the Mafia," *Look* 33 (September 23, 1969): 17–21; also *The New York Times*, May 4, 1977, p. 16.

80. See *The New York Times*, November 7, 1983, p. 1; October 25, 1984, p. 1; April 2, 1986, p. 1; September 19, 1986, p. 1; November 15, 1986, p. 9; March 11, 1987, p. 1.

81. See, for example, Wolfinger's comments on the lack of influence of organized crime in New Haven politics: Wolfinger, *The Politics of Progress*, p. 75n.

82. Ianni, "The Mafia and the Web of Kinship," pp. 96–98.

83. Ibid., p. 93. Humbert Nelli makes a similar observation about Italian organization in Chicago: Nelli, *The Italians in Chicago*, p. 224.

84. Whyte, *Street Corner Society*, pp. 140–146.

85. Bell, *The End of Ideology*, p. 130.

86. Ibid., pp. 128–136.

87. Humbert S. Nelli, "Italians and Crime in Chicago: The Formative Years 1890–1920," *American Journal of Sociology* 74 (January 1969): 389.

88. Rolle, *The Immigrant Upraised*, p. 163.

89. Ianni, "The Mafia and the Web of Kinship," p. 97; Daniel Bell, *The End of Ideology: On the Exhaustion of Political Ideas in the Fifties* (Glencoe, Ill.: The Free Press, 1960), pp. 128–136.

90. This is noted by several writers. See Gage, *The Mafia Is Not an Equal Opportunity Employer*, p. 135; Ianni, "The Mafia and the Web of Kinship," p. 97; and Salerno and Tompkins, *The Civic Confederation*,

p. 376.

91. Didion, "Miami: 'La Lucha,'" pp. 15–18.

92. See "The Mafia of the 1980's: Divided and Under Siege," *The New York Times*, March 11, 1987, p. 1.

93. *Minneapolis Star and Tribune*, January 14, 1987, p. 3A.

94. See *The New York Times*, November 7, 1983, p. 1; October 25, 1984, p. 1; September 19, 1986, p. 1; November 15, 1986, p. 9; March 11, 1987, p. 1.

95. Raymond E. Wolfinger, "The Development and Persistence of Ethnic Voting," *American Political Science Review* 59 (December 1965): 896–908.

96. Several surveys of the National Opinion Research Center (NORC) conducted at various times in the 1960s demonstrate this. Relevant examples can be found in Greeley, *Why Can't They Be Like Us?*, pp. 74, 75, 204, 207, and 208.

97. Lawrence Fuchs, *The Political Behavior of American Jews* (Glencoe, Ill.: The Free Press, 1956), p. 51.

98. Ibid., pp. 121–130.

99. On La Guardia, see Fuchs, *The Political Behavior of American Jews*, p. 158.

100. Glanz, *Jews and Italians*, pp. 31–32.

101. Ibid., p. 28.

102. Charles S. Liebmann, *The Ambivalent American Jew: Politics, Religion and Family* (Philadelphia: Jewish Publication Society of America, 1973), p. 136.

103. Glanz, *Jews and Italians*, p. 21.

104. For an interpretation of Jewish unity as motivated primarily as a reaction to anti-Semitism, see George Friedmann, *The End of the Jewish People?*, trans. Eric Mosbacher (Garden City, N.Y.: Doubleday, 1967).

105. Katznelson, *City Trenches*, pp. 84, 101–102.

106. Fred Massarik and Alvin Chenkin, "United States National Jewish Population Study: A First Report," *American Jewish Yearbook: 1973–74* (American Jewish Committee, New York, and Jewish Publication Society of America, Philadelphia, 1973), p. 295.

107. Herbert J. Gans, "Negro-Jewish Conflict in New York City: A Sociological Evaluation," *Midstream: A Monthly Jewish Review* 15, no. 3 (March 1969). Reprinted in *Ethnic Conflicts and Power: A Cross-National Perspective*, eds. Donald E. Gelfand and Russell D. Lee, (New York: Wiley, 1973), pp. 218–230.

108. Jonathan Rieder, *The Jews and Italians of Canarsie* (Cambridge, Mass.: Harvard University Press, 1985).

109. Liebmann, *The Ambivalent American Jew*, p. 35.

110. Ibid.

111. Despite the large size of America's Polish population, there is still a shortage of serious scholarship published on Polish politics. Except where otherwise noted, most of the interpretations in this book are taken from Joseph A. Wytrwal, *America's Polish Heritage: A Social History of the Poles in America* (Detroit: Endurance Press, 1961). Two more recent studies are Neil C. Sandberg, *Ethnic Identity and Assimilation: The Polish-American Community—Case Study of Metropolitan Los Angeles* (New York: Praeger, 1974); and Edward R. Kantowicz, *Polish-American Politics in Chicago* (Chicago: University of Chicago Press, 1975). The classic scholarly treatment of Poles in English is W.I. Thomas and Florian Znaniecki, *The Polish Peasant in Europe and America* (Boston: Richard C. Badger, 1918).

112. Oscar Handlin, *The American People in the Twentieth Century* (Cambridge, Mass.: Harvard University Press, 1954), p. 68.

113. Wytrwal, *America's Polish Heritage*, p. 256. The difficulty this creates for the aspiring Polish professional is described by Robert T. Golembiewski in the foreword to Brett W. Hawkins and Robert A. Lorinskas, eds., *The Ethnic Factor in American Politics* (Columbus, Ohio: Merrill, 1970), pp. v–x.

114. Robert A. Lorinskas, Brett W. Hawkins, and Stephen Edwards, "The Persistence of Ethnic Voting in Urban and Rural Areas: Results from the Controlled Election Method," *Social Science Quarterly* 49 (March 1969): 891–899.

115. Edward C. Banfield and James Q. Wilson, *City Politics* (New York: Vintage Books, 1963), p. 115.

116. Tammany Hall has been the subject of many fascinating studies. Among them see Seymour Mandelbaum, *Boss Tweed's New York* (New York: Wiley, 1955); Harold Zink, *City Bosses in the United States* (Durham, N.C.: Duke University Press, 1930); and Gustavus Meyers, *The History of Tammany Hall* (New York: Boni and Liveright, 1917).

117. See Duane Lockard, *New England State Politics* (Princeton, N.J.: Princeton University Press, 1959).

118. V.O. Key, *Southern Politics in State and Nation* (New York: Random House, 1949).

119. John Fenton, *Midwest Politics* (New York: Holt, Rinehart and Winston, 1966).

120. On California see Bernard L. Hyink, Seyom Brown, and Ernest W. Thacker, *Politics and Government in California*, 8th ed. (New York: Thomas Y. Crowell, 1973); and Clyde E. Jacobs and Alvin D. Sokolow, *California Government: One Among Fifty* (New York: Macmillan, 1970).

121. Frederick M. Wirt, *Power in the City* (Berkeley, Calif.: Institute of Governmental Studies, 1974).

122. In particular, see Wolfinger, "The Development and Persistence of Ethnic Voting"; Lorinskas, Hawkins, and Edwards, "The Persistence of Ethnic Voting in Urban and Rural Areas"; Gerald Pomper, "Ethnic and Group Voting in Non-partisan Municipal Elections," *Public Opinion Quarterly* 30 (Spring 1969): 79–97; and Richard A. Gabriel, "A New Theory of Ethnic Voting," *Polity* 4, no. 4 (Summer 1972): 405–428. Michael Parenti traces ethnic voting to a lack of ethnic assimilation. He argues that whereas ethnic acculturation took place, ethnic assimilation was much less extensive ["Ethnic Politics and the Persistence of Ethnic Identification," *The American Political Science Review* 61, no. 3 (September 1967): 717–726]. For a small collection of analytic articles on ethnic politics, see Hawkins and Lorinskas, eds., *The Ethnic Factor in American Politics*. For much less rigorous reportage on ethnic voting, see Mark R. Levy and Michael S. Kramer, *The Ethnic Factor: How America's Minorities Decide Elections* (New York: Simon & Schuster, 1972).

123. In 1974 the Center for the Study of Democratic Institutions devoted an entire issue of its journal to this ethnic self-consciousness. See *Center Magazine* 7, no. 4 (July–August 1974).

124. See Wolfinger, "The Development and Persistence of Ethnic Voting," pp. 896–908.

125. Martin Plax, "Uncovering Ambiguities in Some Uses of the Concept of Ethnic Voting," *Midwest Journal of Political Science* 15, no. 3 (August 1971): 571–582.

126. Robert Huckfeldt, "The Social Contexts of Ethnic Loyalties, Political Loyalties and Social Support," *American Politics Quarterly* 11, no. 1 (January 1983): 91–124.

127. Marcus Lee Hansen, *The Immigrant in American History*, ed. Arthur M. Schlesinger (New York: Harper & Row, 1964), chap. 4.

128. See Glazer and Moynihan, *Beyond the Melting Pot*, p. 128.

129. Wolfinger, *The Politics of Progress*, p. 69.

130. A more elaborate argument for social conflict as a conservative force can be found in Lewis Coser, *Functions of Social Conflict* (Glencoe, Ill.: The Free Press, 1964).

131. This conclusion is certainly borne out by a detailed study of ethnicity and social mobility in Detroit. See Olivier Zunz, *The Changing Face of Inequality: Urbanization, Industrial Development, and Immigrants in Detroit, 1880–1920* (Chicago: University of Chicago Press, 1982).

132. Zane L. Miller, "Boss Cox's Cincinnati: A Study in Urbanization and Politics, 1880–1914," *Journal of American History* 54 (March 1968): 823–838.

133. Melvin G. Holli, *Reform in Detroit: Hazen S. Pingree and Urban Politics* (New York: Oxford University Press, 1969), pp. 393–403.

134. For an excellent survey of black relationships with political machines in various cities, see Hanes Walton, Jr., *Black Politics: A Theoretical and Structural Analysis* (New York: J. B. Lippincott, 1972), pp. 56–69.

135. James Q. Wilson, *Negro Politics: The Search for Political Leadership* (Glencoe, Ill.: The Free Press, 1960).

136. Martin Meyerson and Edward C. Banfield, *Politics, Planning and the Public Interest* (Glencoe, Ill.: The Free Press, 1955).

137. The focus of this book on ethnic institutional development differs from most interpretations of American ethnicity, which focus more on individuals' voting or their adaptation to the larger society than on institution building. For a summary of sociological theories of ethnic adaptation to the larger society, see Greeley, *Why Can't They Be Like Us?*, pp. 23–25. For a summary of theories of ethnic voting, see Abraham H. Miller, "Ethnicity and Political Behavior: A Review of Theories and an Attempt at Reformulation," *Western Political Quarterly* 24, no. 3 (September 1971): 483–500.

Chapter 4

1. Edwin O'Connor, *The Last Hurrah* (Boston: Little, Brown, 1956). Examples of favorable treatments of machine politics are Frank R. Kent, *The Great Game of Politics* (Garden City, N.Y.: Doubleday, 1923; rev. ed. 1930); Sonya Forthal, *Cogwheels of Democracy: A Study of the Precinct Captain* (New York: The William Frederick Press, 1946); and Harold F. Gosnell, *Machine Politics: Chicago Model* (Chicago: University of Chicago Press, 1937, 2nd ed. 1967).

2. Raymond E. Wolfinger applied the term "conventional wisdom" to the notion that political machines have disappeared. See his "Why Political Machines Have Not Withered Away and Other Revisionist Thoughts," *Journal of Politics* 34 (May 1972): 365–398.

3. On Chicago, Philadelphia, New Haven, and Tammany, see Wolfinger, "Why Political Machines Have Not Withered Away." On upstate New York, see James A. Riedel, "Boss and Faction," *The Annals of the American Academy of Political and Social Science* 353 (May 1964): 14–26.

4. These scandals occupied much newspaper space during 1986 and 1987. For a succinct interpretation of their relation to machine politics, see Jack Newfield,

"Mayor Daley is Alive and Well in N.Y.C.," *The Nation* (April 4, 1987): 429–434. Also see Michael Tager, "Municipal Corruption in New York City," *Urban Politics and Urban Policy Section Newsletter* 1, no. 2 (Spring 1987): 14. On Boston, see Fox Butterfield, "Troubles of Boston's Mayor Are Tied to Political Machine," *The New York Times,* December 20, 1987.

5. Fred I. Greenstein, "The Changing Pattern of Urban Party Politics," *The Annals of the American Academy of Political and Social Science* 353 (May 1964): 3.

6. See Paul M. Green, "Making the City Work: Machine Politics and Mayoral Reform," a paper presented at the annual meeting of the American Political Science Association, Chicago, Illinois, September 3–6, 1987.

7. Bernard Hennessey refers to the decline of patronage as a "received wisdom." See his "On the Study of Party Organization," in *Approaches to the Study of Party Organization*, ed. William J. Crotty, Jr. (Boston: Allyn and Bacon, 1968), p. 32.

8. Frank J. Sorauf, "Patronage and Party," *Midwest Journal of Political Science* 3 (May 1959): 115–126. Although much of the belief in the decline in patronage is apparently traced to Sorauf's article, this article itself dealt with only one rural county in Pennsylvania. The belief also appeared in many government texts that antedated Sorauf's article.

9. Greenstein, "The Changing Pattern of Urban Party Politics," pp. 7–8.

10. On state-level patronage, see Daniel P. Moynihan and James Q. Wilson, "Patronage in New York State, 1955–1959," *American Political Science Review* 58 (June 1964): 286–301. On patronage at the state level in Illinois, Indiana, and Ohio, see John H. Fenton, *Midwest Politics* (New York: Holt, Rinehart and Winston, 1966). On patronage in New England, see Duane Lockard, *New England State Politics* (Princeton, N.J.: Princeton University Press, 1959). On county-level patronage, see W. Robert Gump, "The Functions of Patronage in American Party Politics: An Empirical Reappraisal," *Midwest Journal of Political Science* 15, no. 1 (February 1971): 87–107. On urban-level patronage, see Martin Tolchin and Susan Tolchin, *To The Victor: Political Patronage from the Clubhouse to the White House* (New York: Vintage Books, 1972), chaps. 2 and 4.

11. *Elrod v. Burns*, 427 U.S. 347 (1976); *Branti v. Finkel*, 445 U.S. 507 (1980).

12. This point is made by Wolfinger in his article, "Why Political Machines Have Not Withered Away."

13. A study of the strong machine in New Haven, for example, found that CETA jobs were tightly controlled by party boss Arthur T. Barbieri, but the jobs were apparently dispensed much more for reasons of ethnic favoritism than to maximize votes for the party. See Michael Johnston, "Patrons and Clients, Jobs and Machines: A Case Study of the Uses of Patronage," *The American Political Science Review* 73, no. 2 (June 1979): 385–398.

14. See Newfield, "Mayor Daley is Alive and Well in N.Y.C."

15. Elmer E. Cornwell, Jr., "Bosses, Machines, and Ethnic Groups," *The Annals of the American Academy of Political and Social Science* 353 (May 1964): 27–39. For a contrary argument that there was no necessary relationship between immigrant populations and the existence of machines, see Wolfinger, *The Politics of Progress* (Englewood Cliffs, N.J.: Prentice-Hall, 1974), pp. 122–130.

16. Theodore J. Lowi, *At the Pleasure of the Mayor* (New York: The Free Press, 1964), p. 112.

17. Joyce Gelb, "Blacks, Blocs and Ballots: The Relevance of Party Politics to the Negro," *Polity* 3, no. 1 (Fall 1970): 44–69.

18. Greenstein, "The Changing Pattern of Urban Party Politics."

19. James L. Gibson, Cornelius P. Cotter, John F. Bibby, and Robert J. Huckshorn, "Whither the Local Parties? A Cross-sectional and Longitudinal Analysis of the Strength of Party Organizations," *American Journal of Political Science* 29, no. 1 (February 1985): 139–160.

20. *Plunkitt of Tammany Hall*, recorded by William L. Riordan (New York: E. P. Dutton, 1963), pp. 17–20.

21. Although machine leaders usually arose from the immigrant lower classes, this was not always the case. Ed Crump put together a machine in Memphis, Tennessee, based on electoral support from that city's lower-income blacks and relatively affluent white ethnic Catholics. Crump was consistently opposed by low-income whites. The strange black-white ethnic alliance occurred because both groups were *socially marginalized* rather than economically marginalized in the context of Memphis society. See Kenneth D. Wald, "The Electoral Base of Political Machines: A Deviant Case Analysis," *Urban Affairs Quarterly* 16, no. 1 (September 1980): 3–30.

22. Howard Penniman, *Sait's American Parties and Elections*, 5th ed. (New York: Appleton-Century-Crofts, 1952), p. 283.

23. Richard Hofstadter, *The Age of Reform: From Bryan to F.D.R.* (New York: Knopf, 1955), p. 181.

24. Edward C. Banfield and James Q. Wilson, *City Politics* (New York: Vintage Books, 1963), p. 117, argue that friendship was perhaps the most important thing that the political leaders gave to the masses.

25. Hofstadter, *The Age of Reform*, p. 181.

26. Banfield and Wilson, *City Politics*, pp. 95–96, 101–107, 110–111. Also see James Q. Wilson and Edward C. Banfield, "Public Regardingness as a Value Premise in Voting Behavior," *The American Political Science Review* 58 (December 1964): 876–887.

27. Murray S. Stedman, Jr., *Urban Politics* (Cambridge, Mass.: Winthrop Publishers, 1972), p. 123. Another textbook accepts the ethos thesis and also states that it is "far from being simply of historical interest. If 'student radical' or 'black militant' was substituted for immigrant, a statement approximating some modern views of the 'power structure' might be created. . . . The feeling that government is 'the man' or 'the system' did not pass away with the immigrant" [Eugene Lewis, *The Urban Political System* (Hinsdale, Ill.: The Dryden Press, 1973), pp. 77–78]. In addition to influencing the textbook writers, this concept of public and private regardingness also heavily influenced much empirical urban research that was conducted during the balance of the 1960s. For a review of this literature, see Timothy M. Hennessey, "Problems in Concept Formation: The Ethos Theory and the Comparative Study of Urban Politics," *Midwest Journal of Political Science* 14, no. 4 (November 1970): 537–564.

28. Roger Durand, "Ethnicity, 'Public-Regardingness,' and Referenda Voting," *Midwest Journal of Political Science* 16, no. 2 (May 1972): 259–268.

29. James Q. Wilson and Edward C. Banfield, "Political Ethos Revisited," *American Political Science Review* 65 (December 1971): 1048–1062.

30. Abraham H. Miller and Stephen E. Bennett, "Political Ethos: Some Imperative Empirical and Conceptual Reconsiderations," a paper presented at the Annual Meeting of the Midwest Political Science Association, Chicago, April 24–27, 1974. The essence of their argument can be found in their "Communication" to *The American Political Science Review* 68, no. 3 (September 1974): 1265–1271.

31. Melvin G. Holli, *Reform in Detroit: Hazen S. Pingree and Urban Politics* (New York: Oxford University Press, 1969), pp. 393–403.

32. Joseph Lincoln Steffens, *Shame of the Cities* (New York: McClure, Phillips and Co., 1904).

33. See Jane Addams, *Twenty Years at Hull House* (New York: Macmillan, 1911).

34. Samuel P. Hays, "The Politics of Reform in Municipal Government in the Progressive Era," *Pacific Northwest Quarterly* 55 (October 1964): 157–166.

35. Lloyd Wendt and Herman Kogan, *Bosses in Lusty Chicago* (Bloomington: Indiana University Press, 1967), p. 169.

36. John M. Allswang, *Bosses, Machines, and Urban Voters*, rev. ed. (Baltimore: The Johns Hopkins University Press, 1986), p. 6.

37. William F. Whyte, *Street Corner Society* (Chicago: University of Chicago Press, 1970), pp. 313–315.

38. Riordan, *Plunkitt of Tammany Hall*, p. 46.

39. Bruce L. Felknor, *Dirty Politics* (New York: W. W. Norton, 1966), p. 160. On the effectiveness of various kinds of fraudulent electioneering practices, see Gosnell, *Machine Politics: Chicago Model*, pp. 85–90. A detailed account of early attempts to regulate corrupt campaign practices can be found in Earl R. Sikes, *State and Federal Corrupt-Practices Legislation* (Durham, N.C.: Duke University Press, 1928).

40. See John R. Owens, Edmond Costanti, and Louis F. Weschler, *California Politics and Parties* (London: Macmillan, 1970), p. 4.

41. Banfield and Wilson make the initial distinction between centralized power in Chicago's machine-style government and fragmented power in Los Angeles' reform-style government. See their *City Politics*, pp. 101–111. This distinction has been reinforced by later commentaries. On Los Angeles see Clyde E. Jacobs and Alvin D. Sokolow, *California's Government: One Among Fifty*, 2nd ed. (New York: Macmillan, 1970), pp. 147–148; and Francis M. Carney, "The Decentralized Politics of Los Angeles," *The Annals of the American Academy of Political and Social Science* 353 (May 1964): 107–122. The most extreme assessment of the centralization of power in Chicago is Mike Royko's polemical *Boss: Richard J. Daley of Chicago* (New York: E. P. Dutton, 1971).

42. Herbert Kaufman, "Emerging Conflicts in the Doctrines of Public Administration," *American Political Science Review* 50 (1956): 1057–1060.

43. Riordan, *Plunkitt of Tammany Hall*, pp. 11, 13.

44. Martin Meyerson and Edward C. Banfield, *Politics, Planning and the Public Interest: The Case of Public Housing in Chicago* (Glencoe, Ill.: The Free Press, 1955), p. 288.

45. Stedman, *Urban Politics*, p. 115.

46. Riordan, *Plunkitt of Tammany Hall*, pp. 11–16.

47. Royko, *Boss*, p. 84.

48. Hays, "The Politics of Reform in Municipal Government in the Progressive Era."

49. For a sympathetic history of the National Municipal League, see Frank M. Stewart, *A Half Century of Municipal Reform* (Berkeley: University of California Press, 1950). For a shorter and more recent history, see Alfred Willoughby, "The Involved Citizen, A Short History of the National Municipal

League: 1894–1969," a 75th Anniversary Edition of the *National Civic Review* 58 (December 1969): 519–564.

50. Robert L. Morlan, "Local Government—The Cities," in *The Fifty States and Their Local Government*, ed. James W. Fesler (New York: Knopf, 1967), pp. 469–471.

51. Ibid., p. 479. Also, for a general assessment of the city manager plan, see "Symposium on the American City Manager: An Urban Administrator in a Complex and Evolving Situation," *Public Administration Review* 31, no. 1 (January–February 1971): 6–42.

52. A study of district versus at-large elections in five cities found that a change to the district system is likely to provoke more controversy in council meetings. See Robert J. Mundt and Peggy Heilig, "Impacts of the Change to District Representation in Urban Government," a paper presented at the annual meeting of the Midwest Political Science Association, Chicago, April 25, 1980.

53. See *The New York Times*, December 21, 1982, p. 11.

54. See Banfield and Wilson, *City Politics*, chap. 13; Robert R. Alford and Harry M. Scoble, "Political and Socioeconomic Characteristics of American Cities," in *The Municipal Yearbook: 1965* (Chicago: International City Managers Association, 1965), pp. 82–97; and John H. Kessel, "Governmental Structure and Political Environment," *American Political Science Review* 56 (1962): 615–640.

55. Gladys Kammerer, "Is the Manager a Political Leader?—Yes," *Public Management* 34 (February 1962): 26–59.

56. Ronald O. Loveridge, *City Managers in Legislative Politics* (Indianapolis, Ind.: Bobbs-Merrill, 1971), p. 49.

57. George K. Floro, "Continuity in City-Manager Careers," *American Journal of Sociology* 61 (November 1955): 241.

58. George S. Blair, *American Local Government* (New York: Harper & Row, 1964), p. 213.

59. Morton Grodzins, *The American System*, ed. Daniel J. Elazar (Chicago: Rand McNally, 1966), pp. 190–194.

60. See William G. Colman, "The Role of the Federal Government in the Design and Administration of Intergovernmental Programs," *The Annals of the American Academy of Political and Social Science* 359 (1965): 28–29. Also see Roscoe Martin, *The Cities and the Federal System* (New York: Atherton Press, 1965), pp. 176–181.

61. *Elrod v. Burns; Branti v. Finkel.* For an assessment of these rulings, see Neil D. McFeeley, "The Supreme Court and Patronage: Implications for Local

Government," *National Civic Review* 71, no. 5 (May 1982): 257–258.

62. *Community Communications Co., Inc. v. City of Boulder*, 102 S. Ct. 835 (1982).

63. Banfield and Wilson, *City Politics*, pp. 123–127.

64. Michael Parenti, "Ethnic Politics and the Persistence of Ethnic Identification," *American Political Science Review* 61 (September 1967): 717–726.

65. Wirt, "Alioto and the Politics of Hyperpluralism," *Trans-action* 7, no. 6 (April 1970): 46–55; *Power in the City* (Berkeley, Calif.: Institute of Governmental Studies, 1974).

66. See Scott Greer, *Governing the Metropolis* (New York: Wiley, 1962), p. 70.

67. Gerald Pomper, "Ethnic and Group Voting in Non-Partisan Municipal Elections," *Public Opinion Quarterly* 30 (Spring 1969): 79–97.

68. Kessel, "Governmental Structure and Political Environment," pp. 615–620.

69. Raymond Wolfinger and John Osgood Field, "Political Ethos and the Structure of City Government," *The American Political Science Review* 60 (June 1966): 306–326. On the impact of education and Catholicism, see Terry N. Clark, "Community Structure, Decision-Making, Budget Expenditures, and Urban Renewal in 51 American Communities," *American Sociological Review* 33, no. 4 (August 1968): 576–593.

70. For an analysis of the impact of these variables on government forms, see Thomas R. Dye and Susan A. MacManus, "Predicting City Government Structure," *American Journal of Political Science* 20, no. 2 (May 1976): 257–271.

71. Robert Lane, *Political Life* (Glencoe, Ill.: The Free Press, 1959), pp. 269–271; and Albert K. Karnig, "Private-Regarding Policy, Civil Rights Groups, and the Mediating Impact of Municipal Reforms," *American Journal of Political Science* 19, no. 1 (February 1975): 91–106.

72. Robert H. Salisbury and Gordon Black, "Class and Party in Partisan and Nonpartisan Elections," *The American Political Science Review* 67, no. 3 (September 1963): 590.

73. Albert K. Karnig and B. Oliver Walters, "Decline in Municipal Turnout: A Function of Changing Structure," *American Politics Quarterly* 11, no. 4 (October 1983): 491–505.

74. Charles E. Gilbert and Christopher Clague, "Electoral Competition and Electoral Systems in Large Cities," *Journal of Politics* 24 (1962): 338–347.

75. In 88 San Francisco area cities, Willis Hawley found that nonpartisanship favored Republicans twice as often as it favored Democrats. See his *Non-Partisan*

Elections and the Case for Party Politics (New York: Wiley, 1973), pp. 31–33.

Also see Oliver P. Williams and Charles R. Adrian, "The Insulation of Local Politics Under the Nonpartisan Ballot," *The American Political Science Review* 53 (1959): 1052–1063; and Heinz Eulau, Betty H. Zisk, and Kenneth Prewitt, "Latent Partisanship in Nonpartisan Elections: Effects of Political Milieu and Mobilization," in *The Electoral Process*, eds. M. Kent Jennings and L. Harmon Ziegler (Englewood Cliffs, N.J.: Prentice-Hall, 1966), p. 215.

76. Karnig and Walter, "Decline in Municipal Turnout," pp. 491–505.

77. Howard Hamilton, "The Municipal Voter: Voting and Nonvoting in City Elections," *The American Political Science Review* 65, no. 4 (December 1971): 1135–1140.

78. Timothy Bledsoe and Susan Welch, "The effect of Political Structure on the Socioeconomic Characteristics of Urban City Council Members," *American Politics Quarterly* 13, no. 4 (October 1985): 467–484.

79. Carol A. Cassell, "Social Background Characteristics of Nonpartisan City Council Members," *Western Political Quarterly* 38, no. 3 (September 1985): 495–501.

80. Peggy Heilig and Robert J. Mundt, *Your Voice at City Hall: The Politics, Procedures and Policies of District Representation* (Albany, N.Y.: State University of New York Press, 1984), pp. 64–70.

81. Susan Welch and Albert K. Karnig, "Correlates to Female Office Holding in City Politics," *Western Political Quarterly* 31, no. 3 (September 1979): 478–491.

82. Janet A. Flammang, "Female Officials in the Feminist Capital: The Case of Santa Clara County," *Western Political Quarterly* 38, no. 1 (March 1985): 94–118.

83. Robert L. Lineberry and Edmund P. Fowler, "Reformism and Public Policies in American Cities," *The American Political Science Review* 61, no. 3 (September 1967): 701–716.

84. Clark, "Community Structure, Decision-Making, Budget Expenditures, and Urban Renewal," pp. 587–591. Clark found high correlations between reform-style government and decentralized decision-making structures. Decentralization was measured by the number of actors involved in making key decisions and by extent of overlap between the makers of decisions in the issue areas of urban renewal, the election of the mayor, air pollution, and the antipoverty program. For the controversiality of decisions and their vulnerability to disruption by community pressures, Clark used the term *fragile*. He wrote that, "for less fragile decisions, the more centralized the decision-making structure, the lower the level of outputs" (p. 588).

85. Ibid.

86. David R. Morgan and John P. Pelissero, "Urban Policy: Does Political Structure Matter?" *The American Political Science Review* 74, no. 4 (December 1980): 1005.

87. Peggy Heilig, "District Representation and Satisfaction With City Government," paper presented to the Annual Convention of the American Political Science Association, Chicago, September 14, 1983.

88. Timothy Bledsoe and Susan Welch, "Some Predictors of Service Representation in Urban Politics," paper presented to the Annual Convention of the American Political Science Association, Chicago, September 14, 1983.

89. Heilig and Mundt, *Your Voice at City Hall*, p. 96.

90. Scott Greer, *Governing the Metropolis* (New York: Wiley, 1962), p. 70.

91. For a discussion of special districts and a listing of sources, see Chapter 9 of this book.

92. Charles R. Adrian, "Some General Characteristics of Non-partisan Elections," *The American Political Science Review* 46 (1952): 775.

93. Robert Wood, *Suburbia, Its People and Their Politics* (Boston: Houghton Mifflin, 1958), p. 157.

Chapter 5

1. Andrew M. Greeley, "American Catholics—Making It or Losing It?" *The Public Interest* 28 (Summer 1972): 26–37; "The Ethnic Miracle," *The Public Interest* 45 (Fall 1976): 20–36.

2. These were the results of a Census Bureau study; see the *Wall Street Journal*, March 24, 1987, p. 35. Also see a similar study by the Urban Institute, reported in the *Minneapolis Star and Tribune*, February 8, 1987, p. 21A.

3. Thomas L. Van Valey, Wade Clark Roof, and Jerome E. Wilcox, "Trends in Residential Segregation, 1960–1970," *American Journal of Sociology* 82, no. 4 (January 1977): 836.

4. Based on 1980 census data, 5,815,000 blacks were suburbanites in 1980, compared to 4,039,000 in 1970. In percentages this accounted for 6.1 percent of all suburbanites in 1980, compared to 4.8 percent in 1970. See *Blacks on the Move: A Decade of Demographic Change* (Washington, D.C.: Joint Center for Political Studies, 1982), pp. 49–55.

5. Census Bureau data as reported in the *Wall Street Journal*, February 24, 1987, p. 35.

6. Morton D. Winsberg, "Changing Distribution of the Black Population: Florida Cities 1970–80,"

Urban Affairs Quarterly 18, no. 3 (March 1983): 361–370; quotes on pp. 364, 367.

7. Robert C. Smith, "The Changing Shape of Urban Black Politics: 1960–1970," *The Annals of the American Academy of Political and Social Science* 439 (September 1978): 24.

8. Howard Brotz, ed., *Negro Social and Political Thought, 1850–1900* (New York: Basic Books, 1966), p. 359.

9. Milton D. Morris, *The Politics of Black America* (New York: Harper & Row, 1975), pp. 215–220.

10. *Brown v. Board of Education of Topeka, Kansas*, 347 U.S. 483 (1954).

11. For a summary and critique of the internal colonialism argument, see Robert Blauner, "Internal Colonialism and Ghetto Revolt," *Social Problems* 16, no. 4 (Spring 1969): 393–408.

12. Allan Spear, *Black Chicago* (Chicago: University of Chicago Press, 1967), pp. 223–229.

13. Morris, *The Politics of Black America*, pp. 97, 104. Also see *The Autobiography of Malcolm X* (New York: Grove Press, 1965).

14. Carmichael's ideas are discussed in Stokely Carmichael and Charles V. Hamilton, *Black Power* (New York: Random House, 1967).

15. Bryan T. Downes, "A Critical Reexamination of the Social and Political Characteristics of Riot Cities," *Social Science Quarterly* 51, no. 2 (September 1970): 349–360.

16. Joe R. Feagin and Harlan Hahn, *Ghetto Revolts: The Politics of Violence in American Cities* (New York: Macmillan, 1965), p. 105.

17. See Morris, *The Politics of Black America*, p. 229.

18. This was essentially the conclusion of the National Advisory Commission on Civil Disorders, *Report of the National Advisory Commission on Civil Disorders* (Washington, D.C.: U.S. Government Printing Office, 1968).

19. Blauner, "Internal Colonialism and Ghetto Revolt."

20. Feagin and Hahn, *Ghetto Revolts*, pp. 122, 127, 132.

21. Ibid., p. 146.

22. James David Greenstone and Paul E. Peterson, "Reformers, Machines, and the War on Poverty," in *City Politics and Public Policy*, ed. James Q. Wilson (New York: Wiley, 1968), pp. 286–289.

23. *The New York Times*, August 12, 1985, p. 1.

24. Susan Welch, "The Impact of Urban Riots on Urban Expenditures," *American Journal of Political Science* 19, no. 4 (November 1975): 741–760.

25. See *The New York Times*, February 18, 1983, p. 8; and *Newsweek*, January 10, 1983, p. 23.

26. See Kenneth Clark, "The N.A.A.C.P.: Verging on Irrelevance," *The New York Times*, July 14, 1983, p. 23.

27. United States Bureau of the Census, *Statistical Abstract of the United States, 1986* (Washington, D.C.: United States Government Printing Office, 1985), p. 252; Also see *The New York Times*, July 9, 1984, p. 11.

28. *Gomillion v. Lightfoot*, 81 S. Ct. 125 (1960).

29. Lee Sloan, "Good Government and the Politics of Race," *Social Problems* 17 (Fall 1969): 161–175.

30. Leonard A. Cole, "Electing Blacks to Municipal Office: Structural and Social Determinants," *Urban Affairs Quarterly* 10, no. 1 (September 1974): 17–39.

31. See especially Susan MacManus, "City Council Procedures and Minority Representation: Are They Related?" *Social Science Quarterly* 59, no. 1 (June 1978): 153–161.

32. Ibid.

33. Albert Karnig, "Black Representation on City Councils: The Impact of District Elections and Socioeconomic Factors," *Urban Affairs Quarterly* 12, no. 2 (December 1976): 223–242.

34. Chandler Davidson and George Korbel, "At-Large Elections and Minority Group Representation: A Re-examination of Historical and Contemporary Evidence," *Journal of Politics* 43, no. 4 (November 1981): 982–1005. Also in support of the thesis that at-large elections diluted the black vote were Clinton B. Jones, "The Impact of Local Election Systems on Black Political Representation," *Urban Affairs Quarterly* 11, no. 2 (March 1976): 345–356; Margaret K. Latimer, "Black Political Representation in Southern Cities: Election Systems and Their Causal Variables," *Urban Affairs Quarterly* 15, no. 1 (September 1979): 65–86; Theodore P. Robinson and Thomas R. Dye, "Reformism and Black Representation on City Councils," *Social Science Quarterly* 59, no. 1 (June 1978): 133–141; and Delbert Taebel, "Minority Representation on City Councils: The Impact of Structure on Blacks and Hispanics," *Social Science Quarterly* 59, no. 1 (June 1978): 142–152.

35. Richard L. Engstrom and Michael D. McDonald, "The Election of Blacks to City Councils: Clarifying the Impact of Electoral Arrangements on the Seats/Population Relationship," *The American Political Science Review* 75, no. 2 (June 1981): 344–354.

36. *City of Richmond v. U.S.*, 442 U.S. 358 (1975). See Thomas P. Murphy, "Race Based Accounting: Assigning the Costs and Benefits of a Racially Motivated Annexation," *Urban Affairs Quarterly* 14, no. 2 (December 1978): 169–194.

37. *The New York Times*, March 28, 1979, p. 1.

38. *City of Mobile v. Bolden*, 446 U.S. 55 (1980). Although Mobile has not yet been forced to abandon its at-large system, the Supreme Court in 1982 did establish a precedent that may lead to Mobile's undoing. An at-large county commission in Burke County, Georgia was forced to establish wards when the Supreme Court ruled that its at-large system was being *maintained* for the purpose of preventing representation of the county's blacks (about half the county population). Since this situation is so similar to Mobile's, it suggests that Mobile's at-large council may eventually be struck down. *Rogers v. Lodge*, 102 S. Ct. 3272 (1982). See *The New York Times*, July 2, 1982. p. 9.

39. *City of Port Arthur v. United States*, 103 S. Ct. 530 (1982).

40. See *The New York Times*, January 9, 1980, p. A14; January 21, 1980, p. A12.

41. Hanes Walton, Jr., *Black Politics: A Theoretical and Structural Analysis* (New York: Lippincott, 1972), p. 59.

42. Martin Kilson, "Political Change in the Negro Ghetto, 1900–1940s," in *Key Issues in the Afro-American Experience*, eds. Nathan Huggins, Martin Kilson, and Daniel Fox (New York: Harcourt Brace Jovanovich, 1971), p. 182.

43. See Edward C. Banfield and James Q. Wilson, *City Politics* (New York: Random House, 1965), pp. 124–125.

44. See especially Michael B. Preston, "Black Politics and Public Policy in Chicago: Self-Interest Versus Constituent Representation," in *The New Black Politics: The Search for Political Power*, eds. Michael B. Preston, Lenneal J. Henderson, Jr., and Paul Puryear (New York: Longman, 1982), pp. 159–186; and Twiley W. Barker, "Political Mobilization of Black Chicago: Drafting a Candidate," *PS* 16, no. 3 (Summer 1983): 482–485.

45. A *New York Times* exit poll showed Washington winning 97 percent of the black vote, 57 percent of the Hispanic vote, 15 percent of the white vote, and 42 percent of the vote of all other races. *The New York Times*, April 9, 1987, p. 11.

46. Steven P. Erie, "Rainbow's End: From the Old to the New Urban Ethnic Politics," in *Urban Ethnicity In The United States*, vol. 29, Urban Affairs Annual Reviews, eds. Lionel Maldonado and Joan Moore (Beverly Hills, Calif.: SAGE Publications, 1985), pp. 253–255, 270.

47. Peter K. Eisinger, "Black Mayors and the Politics of Racial Economic Advancement," in *Culture, Ethnicity, and Identity*, ed. William C. McReady (New York: Academic Press, 1983), pp. 95–109.

48. Albert K. Karnig and Susan Welch, *Black Representation and Urban Policy* (Chicago: University of Chicago Press, 1980), pp. 122–128, 141.

49. Edmond J. Keller, "The Impact of Black Mayors on Urban Policy," *The Annals of the American Academy of Political and Social Science* 439 (November 1978): p. 51.

50. Ibid., p. 49.

51. Ibid., p. 51.

52. William E. Nelson, Jr., "Cleveland: The Rise and Fall of the New Black Politics," in *The New Black Politics: The Search for Political Power*, pp. 187–208.

53. Herrington J. Bryce, Gloria J. Cousar, and William McCoy, "Housing Problems of Black Mayor Cities," *The Annals of the American Academy of Political and Social Science* 439 (November 1978): 83.

54. See Chapter 7. Also see Bryce et al., "Housing Problems of Black Mayor Cities," p. 83.

55. Eisinger, "Black Mayors and the Politics of Racial Economic Advancement," p. 106.

56. Ibid., pp. 105–106.

57. V. O. Key, *Southern Politics* (New York: Vintage Books, 1949).

58. Eisinger, "Black Mayors and the Politics of Racial Economic Advancement," p. 106.

59. Peter K. Eisinger, "Black Employment in Municipal Jobs: The Impact of Black Political Power," *The American Political Science Review* 76, no. 2 (June 1982): 380–392.

60. Peter K. Eisinger, "The Economic Conditions of Black Employment in Municipal Bureaucracies," *American Journal of Political Science* 26, no. 4 (November 1982): 754–771.

61. Rufus P. Browning, Dale Rogers Marshall, and David H. Tabb, "Local Control Over Local Policies: Can City Politics Make a Difference for Minorities?" a paper presented to the Annual Meeting of the American Political Science Association, Chicago, September 1–4, 1983.

62. Daniel P. Moynihan, *The Negro Family: The Case for National Action* (Washington, D.C.: Office of Policy Planning and Research, U.S. Department of Labor, 1965).

63. See Nathan Glazer, *Ethnic Dilemmas: 1964–1982* (Cambridge, Mass.: Harvard University Press, 1983), pp. 7, 61; and Lee Rainwater and Martin Yancey, *The Moynihan Report and the Politics of Controversy* (Cambridge, Mass.: M.I.T. Press, 1967).

64. William Julius Wilson, "The Urban Underclass in Advanced Industrial Society," in *The New Urban Reality*, ed. Paul E. Peterson (Washington, D.C.: The Brookings Institution, 1985), pp. 132–133.

65. Paul Galloway, "Nine Weeks, Ten Murders,"

Chicago Sun-Times, March 22, 1981. Cited in Wilson, "The Urban Underclass," p. 137.

66. National Advisory Commission on Civil Disorders, *Report* (Washington, D.C.: U.S. Government Printing Office, March 1968), pp. 215–226.

67. Joseph P. Fitzpatrick and Lourdes Travieso Parker, "Hispanic Americans in the Eastern United States," *The Annals of the American Academy of Political and Social Science*, 454 (March 1981): 99.

68. Ibid., p. 103. For a graphic discussion of the question of color for one Puerto Rican, see Piri Thomas, *Down These Mean Streets* (New York: Knopf, 1967).

69. Harry P. Pachan and Joan W. Moore, "Mexican Americans," *The Annals of the American Academy of Political and Social Science*, 454 (March 1981): 114.

70. Ibid., p. 119.

71. Leo Grebler, Joan W. Moore, and Ralph C. Guzman, *The Mexican-American People: The Nation's Second Largest Minority* (New York: The Free Press, 1970), pp. 521–522.

72. Ibid., pp. 524–525.

73. Walter Prescott Webb, *The Texas Rangers: A Century of Frontier Defense* (Boston: Houghton Mifflin, 1935), pp. 479, 486.

74. Grebler et al., *The Mexican-American People*, p. 528.

75. *The New York Times*, July 17, 1978, p. A-8.

76. Clifton McCleskey and Bruce Merrill, "Mexican American Political Behavior in Texas," *Social Science Quarterly* 53 (March 1973): 785–798; and Susan Welch, John Comer, and Michael Steinman, "Political Participation Among Mexican Americans: An Exploratory Examination," *Social Science Quarterly* 53 (March 1973): 799–813.

77. F. Chris Garcia and Rudolph O. de la Garza, *The Chicano Political Experience: Three Perspectives* (N. Scituate, Mass.: Duxbury Press, 1977), pp. 36–37.

78. Susan A. MacManus and Carol A. Cassel, "Mexican-Americans in City Politics: Participation, Representation and Policy Preferences," *Urban Interest* 4, no. 1 (Spring 1982): 62.

79. *The New York Times*, September 15, 1985, p. 43.

80. Garcia and de la Garza, *The Chicano Political Experience*, p. 15.

81. Ibid., pp. 43–63.

82. John A. Garcia, "Y Soy Mexicano . . . : Self-Identity and Sociodemographic Correlates," *Social Science Quarterly* 62, no. 1 (March 1981): 90.

83. Garcia and de la Garza, *The Chicano Political Experience*, p. 38.

84. *The New York Times*, September 15, 1985, p. 43.

85. Garcia and de la Garza, *The Chicano Political Experience*, p. 82.

86. MacManus and Cassel, "Mexican-Americans in City Politics," pp. 60–62.

87. *Statistical Abstract of the United States, 1982-83*, pp. 22–24.

88. Tucker Gibson, "Mayoralty Politics in San Antonio, 1955–1979," in *The Politics of San Antonio: Community Progress and Power*, eds. David R. Johnson, John A. Booth, and Richard J. Harris (Lincoln, Neb.: University of Nebraska Press, 1983), p. 116.

89. Charles L. Cotrell and R. Michael Stevens, "The 1975 Voting Rights Act and San Antonio, Texas: Toward Federal Guarantee of a Republican Form of Government," *Publius* 8, no. 1 (Winter 1978): 79–100.

90. Neal R. Peirce and Jerry Hagstrom, "San Antonio's Mexican-American Mayor Seeks New Agenda for Minorities, Poor," *National Journal* 14, no. 42 (October 16, 1982): 1758–1759.

91. John A. Booth, "Political Change in San Antonio, 1970–82: Toward Decay or Democracy," in *The Politics of San Antonio*, eds. Johnson, Booth and Harris, pp. 209–211.

92. See Stuart Taylor, Jr., "Rising Voice of Cuban-Americans," *The New York Times*, March 7, 1984, p. 20; Bernard Weinraub, "Wooing Cuban-Americans in G.O.P.," *The New York Times*, May 22, 1987, p. 8; Joan Didion, "Miami: La Lucha," *New York Review of Books* 34, no. 10 (June 11, 1987): 15; and *New Yorker* article, May 1987.

93. See Didion, "Miami: La Lucha."

94. See *New Yorker* article, May 1987.

95. *Wall Street Journal*, October 15, 1985, p. 64; *The New York Times*, November 7, 1985, p. 1. On the 1987 runoff see *The New York Times*, November 12, 1987, p. 11.

96. Morrison G. Wong, "Post-1965 Immigrants: Demographic and Socioeconomic Profile," in *Urban Ethnicity In The United States: New Immigrants and Old Minorities*, vol. 29, Urban Affairs Annual Reviews, eds. Lionel Maldonado and Joan Moore (Beverly Hills, Calif.: SAGE Publications, 1985), p.69.

97. Philip Garcia, "Immigration Issues in Urban Ecology: The Case of Los Angeles," in *Urban Ethnicity In The United States: New Immigrants and Old Minorities*, vol. 29, pp. 84–86.

98. *Minneapolis Star and Tribune*, February 8, 1987.

99. Leon F. Bouvier and Robert W. Gardner, "Immigration to the U.S.: The Unfinished Story," *The Population Bulletin* 41, no. 4 (November 1986): 13–18.

100. *Statistical Abstract of the United States, 1987*, p. 86.

101. One Texas study found that illegal aliens received $132 million worth of services from the State of Texas and paid the state $162 million in taxes. *The New York Times*, November 15, 1983, p. 9.

102. MacManus and Cassel, "Mexican-Americans in City Politics," p. 66.

103. *Newsweek*, June 25, 1984, p. 21.

104. *Christian Science Monitor*, January 28, 1982, p. 1.

105. Bouvier and Gardner, "Immigration to the U.S.," p. 37.

106. Ibid.

107. *The New York Times*, July 10, 1987, p. 14; and *Wall Street Journal*, November 6, 1987, p. 1.

108. August 20, 1981, p. 11.

109. See Ricardo R. Fernandez and William Velez, "Race, Color, and Language in the Changing Public Schools," in *Urban Ethnicity In The United States: New Immigrants and Old Minorities*, vol. 29, p. 132.

110. This argument is stated by former Colorado governor Richard D. Lamm, who wrote: "I do not believe that massive immigration is the only cause of unemployment or poverty, but I know it is a significant cause of them. I do not think we can cure the ills of unemployment by eliminating illegal immigration, but I know that allowing it to continue certainly makes unemployment worse." See Richard D. Lamm and Gary Imhoff, *The Immigration Time Bomb* (New York: Dutton, 1985), p. 155.

111. This charge is exemplified by a *Wall Street Journal* editorial of June 12, 1987, which claimed that restrictions on immigration begun in 1987 would cause one-third of Oregon's strawberry crop to rot because there would not be enough pickers.

112. These generalizations are taken from Bouvier and Gardner, "Immigration to the U.S.," pp. 28–32.

113. Richard Murray and Arnold Vedlitz, "Racial Voting Patterns in the South: An Analysis of Major Elections from 1960 to 1977 in Five Cities," *The Annals of the American Academy of Political and Social Science* 439 (September 1978): 29–39.

114. Rufus P. Browning, Dale Rogers Marshall, and David H. Tabb, *Protest Is Not Enough: The Struggle of Blacks and Hispanics for Equality in Urban Politics* (Berkeley, Calif.: University of California Press, 1984), pp. 46–53.

115. Alvin J. Schexnider, "Political Mobilization in the South: The Election of a Black Mayor in New Orleans," *The New Black Politics*, pp. 221–237.

116. *Focus* 7, no. 11 (November 1979).

117. *The New York Times*, January 5, 1984, p. 9; November 10, 1983, p. 17.

118. Michael B. Preston, "The Election of Harold Washington: Black Voting Patterns in the 1983 Chicago Mayoral Race," *PS* 16, no. 3 (Summer 1983):

486–488.

119. *The New York Times*, April 9, 1987, p. 11.

120. Paul Green, "The Message From the 26th Ward," *Comparative State Politics Newsletter* VII, no. 4 (August 1986): 16.

121. Browning, Marshall, and Tabb, *Protest Is Not Enough*, pp. 121–124.

122. Joan Didion, "Miami: 'La Lucha'", 15–18.

123. Garcia and de la Garza, *The Chicano Political Experience*, p. 130.

124. *The New York Times*, July 18, 1986, p. 6. The percentage of Mexican-Americans and Puerto Ricans identifying themselves as Democrats is probably much higher, however, since this poll included Cubans, who overwhelmingly tend to be Republicans.

125. *The New York Times*, June 29, 1987, p. 13.

126. See Mark R. Levy and Michael S. Kramer, *The Ethnic Factor: How America's Minorities Decide Elections* (New York: Simon and Schuster, 1973), p. 83.

127. See Harold V. Savitch, "Powerlessness in an Urban Ghetto: The Case of Political Biases and Differential Access in New York City," *Polity* 5, no. 1 (Fall 1972): 19–56.

Chapter 6

1. See John Kenneth Galbraith, *The New Industrial State* (Boston: Houghton Mifflin, 1967); and Daniel Bell, *The Coming of Post-industrial Society: A Venture in Social Forecasting* (New York: Basic Books, 1973).

2. Lester C. Thurow, *The Zero-Sum Society: Distribution and the Possibilities for Change* (New York: Basic Books, 1980), pp. 7, 192.

3. Michael Harrington and Mark Levenson, "The Perils of a Dual Economy," *Dissent* 32, no. 4 (Fall 1985): 417–426.

4. *Minneapolis Star and Tribune*, December 9, 1986, p. 3M.

5. See especially Richard I. Kirkland, Jr., "Are Service Jobs Good Jobs?" *Fortune* 111, no. 12 (June 10, 1985): 38–47; and Warren T. Brookes, "Low-Pay Jobs: The Big Lie," *Wall Street Journal*, March 25, 1987.

6. Harrington and Levenson, "The Perils of a Dual Economy," p. 420. Kirkland, "Are Service Jobs Good Jobs?" showed the same relationship but cited different figures that showed a somewhat less severe discrepancy: $377 per week for nonsupervisory manufacturing workers versus $250 per week for nonsupervisory service workers in 1984.

7. Harrington and Levenson, "The Perils of a Dual Economy," pp. 421–422.

8. *Minneapolis Star and Tribune*, December 9, 1986, p. 3M.

9. Harrington and Levenson, "The Perils of a Dual Economy," p. 422.

10. Louis Uchitelle, "Narrowing a Wage Gap," *The New York Times*, June 26, 1987, p. 30.

11. Lester C. Thurow, "The Disappearance of the Middle Class," *The New York Times*, February 5, 1984, p. F-3.

12. The 1960s figure is for 1960–1969; the 1970s figure is for 1970–1979. U.S. Bureau of the Census, *Statistical Abstract of the United States, 1982–83* (Washington, D.C.: U.S. Government Printing Office, 1982), p. 421. The 1980s figure is for 1980–1984. *Statistical Abstract of the United States, 1986*, p. 434.

13. These data were calculated from U.S. Bureau of the Census, *County Business Patterns 1973* (Washington, D.C.: U.S. Government Printing Office, 1974), and *County Business Patterns 1981* (Washington, D.C.: U.S. Government Printing Office, 1982).

14. George Sternlieb and James W. Hughes, "The Uncertain Future of the Central City," *Urban Affairs Quarterly* 18, no. 4 (June 1983): 455–572.

15. Ibid., p. 463.

16. Ibid., p. 456.

17. Norton Long, "The City as Reservation," *The Public Interest* 25 (Fall 1971): 35. Long also developed the same idea in his "The City as Political Economy," *National Civic Review* 63, no. 4 (April 1974): 189–191.

18. George Sternlieb, "The City as Sandbox," *The Public Interest* 25 (Fall 1971): 14–21.

19. Alfred J. Watkins, "Intermetropolitan Migrations and the Rise of the Sunbelt," *Social Science Quarterly* 59, no. 3 (December 1978): 560.

20. Leon F. Bouvier and Robert W. Gardner, "Immigration to the U.S.: The Unfinished Story," *The Population Bulletin* 41, no. 4 (November 1986): 28–32.

21. See especially Alexander Ganz and Thomas O'Brien, "The City: Sandbox, Reservation, or Dynamo?" *Public Policy* 21, no. 1 (Winter 1973): 107–124.

22. Chester Hartman, Dennis Keating, and Richard L. Gates, with Steve Turner, *Displacement: How to Fight It* (Berkeley, CA: National Housing Project, 1982).

23. Roy Bahl, Bernard Jump, Jr., and Larry Schroeder, "The Outlook for City Fiscal Performance," in *The Fiscal Outlook for Cities: Implications of a National Urban Policy*, ed. Roy Bahl (Syracuse, N.Y.: Syracuse University Press, 1978), p. 14.

24. D. Stanley, "The Ambiguous Role of the Urban Public Employee," in *Managing Human Resources*, ed. C. Levine (Beverly Hills, Calif.: SAGE Publications, 1977), pp. 23–35.

25. James L. Greer, "The Structure of Economic Decline in Older Industrial Cities," a paper presented at the 1980 Conference of the Midwest Political Science Association, April 24, 1980.

26. Richard P. Nathan, "The Outlook for Federal Grants to Cities," in *The Fiscal Outlook for Cities*, p. 77.

27. James W. Fossett, *Federal Aid to Big Cities: The Politics of Dependence* (Washington, D.C.: The Brookings Institution, 1983), Tables 1 and 6. Data were from 1978.

28. Data from Figure 6-1 and United States Bureau of the Census, *City Government Finances in 1981–82* (Washington, D.C.: U.S. Government Printing Office, 1983), p. 7.

29. Paul E. Peterson, *City Limits* (Chicago: University of Chicago Press, 1981).

30. *The New York Times*, June 30, 1983, p. 8; August 30, 1983, p. 11.

31. *The New York Times*, November 28, 1983, p. 13.

32. Roger E. Alcaly and Helen Bodian, "New York's Fiscal Crisis and the Economy," in *The Fiscal Crisis of American Cities*, eds. Roger E. Alcaly and David Mermelstein (New York: Vintage Books, 1977), p. 33.

33. See Sidney Lens, "The City That Doesn't Work Anymore: Chicago in the Crunch," *Progressive* (April 1980): 34–38.

34. Todd Swanstrom, "Urban Populism, Fiscal Crisis, and the New Political Economy," in *Cities in Stress: A New Look at the Urban Crisis*, vol. 30, Urban Affairs Annual Reviews, ed. M. Gottdiener (Beverly Hills, Calif.: SAGE Publications, 1986), p. 90.

35. Alberta M. Sbragia, "The 1970s: A Decade of Change in Local Government Finance," in *The Municipal Money Chase: The Politics of Local Government Finance*, ed. Alberta M. Sbragia (Boulder, Colo.: Westview Press, 1983), p. 83.

36. On Cleveland's fiscal crisis, see John H. Beck, "Is Cleveland Another New York?" *Urban Affairs Quarterly* 18, no. 2 (December 1982): 187–206; Rochelle L. Stanfield, "Reagan Urban Policy—Count Us Out of Public-Private Partnerships," *National Journal* 14, no. 27 (July 3, 1982): 1173; and *The New York Times*, October 9, 1980, p. A-22.

37. This idea is contained in Sternleib, "The City as Sandbox."

38. See E.S. Savas, *Privatizing the Public Sector: How to Shrink Government* (Chatham, N.J.: Chatham House, 1982), pp. 10–26.

39. Pietro S. Nivola, "Apocalypse Now? Whither the Urban Fiscal Crisis," *Polity* 14, no. 3 (Spring 1982): 376.

40. Ibid. Also see Theodore J. Lowi, "Machine Politics—Old and New," *The Public Interest* 9 (Fall 1967): 86.

41. Ken Auletta, *The Streets Were Paved With Gold: The Decline of New York, An American Tragedy* (New York: Random House, 1979), p. 224.

42. Robert D. Reischauer, Peter K. Clark, and Peggy L. Cuciti, "New York City's Fiscal Problem," a Congressional Budget Office background paper, October 10, 1975. Reprinted in *The Fiscal Crisis of American Cities*, eds. Alcaly and Mermelstein, pp. 285–295.

43. Nivola, "Apocalypse Now?" p. 383.

44. Terry Nichols Clark and Lorna Crowley Ferguson, *City Money: Political Processes, Fiscal Strain, and Retrenchment* (New York: Columbia University Press, 1983), chap. 3.

45. Robert M. Stein, Elizabeth G. Sinclair, and Max Neiman, "Local Government and Fiscal Stress: An Exploration into Spending and Public Employment Decisions," in *Cities In Stress: A New Look at the Urban Crisis*, vol. 30, pp. 112–113.

46. Clark and Ferguson, *City Money*, p. 82.

47. Irene S. Rubin, *Running in the Red: The Political Dynamics of Urban Fiscal Stress* (Albany: State University of New York Press, 1982).

48. Ibid.

49. David R. Morgan and William Lyons, "The Impact of Intergovernmental Revenue on City Expenditures: An Analysis Over Time," *The Journal of Politics* 39, no. 4 (November 1977): 1088–1097.

50. Clark and Ferguson, *City Money*, pp. 245–261.

51. Dan Pilcher, "Assessing State Business Climates," *State Legislatures* 9, no. 8 (August/September 1983): 9–12.

52. *St. Paul Pioneer Press and Dispatch*, October 23, 1983, p. D-1.

53. David L. Birch, *The Job Generation Process* (Cambridge, Mass.: M.I.T. Program on Neighborhoods and Regional Change, 1979), p. 21.

54. Roy Bahl, *The Impact of Local Tax Policy on Urban Economic Development* (Washington, D.C.: U.S. Department of Commerce; Economic Development Administration; Urban Consortium Information Bulletin, September 1980), p. 15.

55. Roger W. Schmenner, *Making Business Location Decisions* (Englewood Cliffs, N.J.: Prentice-Hall, 1982), pp. 50–51.

56. Data for jobs gained in 1985 from the Bureau of Labor Statistics. Data for business climates taken from Grant Thornton Company, *Survey of Manufac-*turing Climates, 1985 (Chicago: Grant Thornton Company, 1986).

57. Data reported in the *St. Paul Pioneer Press and Dispatch*, June 4, 1986, p. B-10.

58. Committee on Economic Development, *Leadership for Dynamic State Economies* (New York: Committee on Economic Development, 1986).

59. Robert Mier and Scott E. Gelzer, "State Enterprise Zones: The New Frontier?" *Urban Affairs Quarterly* 18, no. 1 (September 1982): 39–52. For specific details on the Connecticut urban enterprise zones, see *The New York Times*, July 7, 1981, p. 1.

60. Jane F. Roberts, "State Actions Affecting Local Governments: Upheaval for Fiscal Relations," *The Municipal Year Book: 1987* (Washington, D.C.: International City Management Association, 1987), pp. 56–57.

61. Stein, Sinclair, and Neiman review the relevant research on this question in their "Local Government and Fiscal Stress," p. 102.

62. Jane Carroll, "Economic Development Through Venture Capital," *State Legislatures* 11, no. 3 (March 1985): 24–25.

63. *The New York Times*, June 23, 1986, pp. 1, 9.

64. *St. Paul Pioneer Press and Dispatch*, March 13, 1983, p. A-11.

65. *Minneapolis Tribune*, June 5, 1983, p. 6-D.

66. *The New York Times*, March 15, 1981, p. 12; April 30, 1981, p. 23; *Minneapolis Tribune*, June 5, 1983, p. 6-D.

67. George Sternlieb and James Hughes, *Atlantic City Gamble* (Cambridge, Mass.: Harvard University Press, 1984).

68. *The New York Times*, July 11, 1986, p. 11.

69. Committee on Economic Development, *Leadership for Dynamic State Economies*, p. 6.

70. Ibid.

71. Lester C. Thurow, *The Zero-Sum Society: Distribution and the Possibilities for Change* (New York: Basic Books, 1980), p. 192.

72. See especially Barry Bluestone and Bennett Harrison, *The Deindustrialization of America* (New York: Basic Books, 1982), pp. 8, 35, 63–66, 86–92.

73. Thomas J. Leary, "Deindustrialization, Plant Closing Laws, and the States," *State Government* 58, no. 3 (Fall 1985): 113–118; and *The New York Times*, July 12, 1984, p. 7.

74. David Corn, "Dreams Gone to Rust: The Monongahela Valley Mourns for Steel," *Harper's* 273, no. 1636 (September 1986): 56–65.

75. Terry F. Buss and F. Stevens Redburn, "Religious Leaders as Policy Advocates: The Youngstown Steel Mill Closing," *Policy Studies Journal* 11, no. 4 (June 1983): 640–647.

76. Thomas A. Pascarella and Richard D. Raymond, "Buying Bonds for Business: An Evaluation of the Industrial Revenue Bond Program," *Urban Affairs Quarterly* 18, no. 1 (September 1982): 73–89.

77. John E. Peterson, "The Municipal Bond Market: Recent Changes and Future Prospects," in *Financing State and Local Government in the 1980s: Issues and Trends*, eds. Norman Walzer and David L. Chicoine (Cambridge, Mass.: Oelgeschlager, Gunn and Hain, Publishers, 1981), pp. 129–142.

78. Peterson, *City Limits*.

Chapter 7

1. See especially Robert S. Lynd and Helen M. Lynd, *Middletown in Transition* (New York: Harcourt, Brace and Company, 1937); W. Lloyd Warner et al., *Democracy in Jonesville* (New York: Harper & Row, 1949); and August B. Hollingshead, *Elmtown's Youth* (New York: Wiley, 1949). A short summary and methodological critique of these early major works can be found in Nelson Polsby, *Community Power and Political Theory* (New Haven, Conn.: Yale University Press, 1963).

2. Floyd Hunter, *Community Power Structure* (Chapel Hill, N.C.: University of North Carolina Press, 1953).

3. Lawrence J.R. Herson, "The Lost World of Municipal Government," *The American Political Science Review* 51 (1957): 330–345.

4. T. J. Anton, "Power, Pluralism, and Local Politics," *Administrative Science Quarterly* 7 (March 1963): 425–454; Polsby, *Community Power and Political Theory;* Herbert Kaufmann and Victor Jones, "The Mystery of Power," *Public Administration Quarterly* 14 (Summer 1954): 2–5; Raymond Wolfinger, "Reputation and Reality in the Study of Community Power," *American Sociological Review* 25 (October 1960): 636–644: and Robert A. Dahl, "A Critique of the Ruling Elite Model," *The American Political Science Review* 52 (June 1958): 463–469.

5. In particular, this is Polsby's critique. See *Community Power and Political Theory*.

6. Robert Dahl, *Who Governs? Democracy and Power in an American City* (New Haven, Conn.: Yale University Press, 1966).

7. See, for example, Delbert C. Miller, "Decision-Making Cliques in Community Power Structures: A Comparative Study of an American and an English City," *American Journal of Sociology* 64 (November 1958): 299–310; William H. Form and William V. D'Antonio, "Integration and Cleavage Among Community Influentials in Two Border Cities," *American Sociological Review* 24 (December 1959): 804–814; Robert Presthus, *Men at the Top: A Study in Community Power* (New York: Oxford University Press, 1964); and Robert E. Agger, Daniel Goldrich, and Bert Swanson, *The Rulers and the Ruled: Political Power and Impotence in American Communities* (New York: Wiley, 1964).

8. See, for example, Presthus, *Men at the Top;* Agger et al., *The Rulers and the Ruled;* Linton C. Freeman et al., *Local Community Leadership* (Syracuse, N.Y.: University College, 1960).

9. John Walton, "Discipline, Method, and Community Power: A Note on the Sociology of Knowledge," *American Sociological Review* 31, no. 5 (October 1966): 684–689.

10. Floyd Hunter, *Community Power Succession: Atlanta's Policy-Makers Revisited* (Chapel Hill, N.C.: University of North Carolina Press, 1980).

11. William G. Domhoff, *Who Really Rules? New Haven and Community Power Re-examined* (New Brunswick, N.J.: Transaction Books, 1978).

12. Clarence N. Stone, "Community Power Structure—A Further Look," *Urban Affairs Quarterly* 16, no. 4 (June 1981): 506.

13. Robert S. Lynd and Helen M. Lynd, *Middletown* (New York: Harcourt, Brace and Company, 1929), and *Middletown in Transition*.

14. Lynd and Lynd, *Middletown in Transition*, p. 74.

15. Robert D. Schulze, "The Bifurcation of Power in a Satellite City," in *Community Political Systems*, ed. Morris Janowitz (New York: The Free Press, 1961).

16. Ronald J. Pellegrin and Charles H. Coates, "Absentee-Owned Corporations and Community Power Structure," *American Journal of Sociology* 61 (March 1956): 413–419.

17. Banfield and Wilson, *City Politics*, pp. 261–276.

18. Peter Clark, "Civic Leadership: The Symbols of Legitimacy," a paper presented at the 1960 Annual Meeting of the American Political Science Association. Edited and reprinted in *Democracy in Urban America*, 2nd ed., eds. Oliver P. Williams and Charles Press (Chicago: Rand McNally, 1969), pp. 350–366.

19. Peter Bachrach and Morton S. Baratz, "The Two Faces of Power," *The American Political Science Review* 56, no. 4 (December 1962): 948.

20. Clarence N. Stone, "Social Stratification, Non-Decision-Making, and the Study of Community Power," *American Politics Quarterly* 10, no. 3 (July 1982): 293.

21. On the methods of researching nondecisions see Matthew Crenson, *The Unpolitics of Air Pollution: A Study of Non-Decision-Making in the Cities* (Baltimore: Johns Hopkins Press, 1971). Raymond Wolfinger finds the concept of nondecisions so fraught

with methodological problems that it is virtually unresearchable. See his "Non-decisions and the Study of Local Politics," *The American Political Science Review* 65, no. 4 (December 1971): 1063–1080. Frederick W. Frey takes a more optimistic viewpoint. See his "Comment: On Issues and Non-issues in the Study of Community Power," *The American Political Science Review* 65, no. 4 (December 1971): 1081–1101. Other criticisms of nondecisions can be found in Geoffrey Debnam, "Nondecisions and Power: The Two Faces of Bachrach and Baratz," *The American Political Science Review* 69, no. 3 (September 1975): 889–899; and Richard Merelman, "On the Neo-Elitist Critique of Community Power," *The American Political Science Review* 62, no. 2 (June 1968): 451–460.

22. For example, see Bernard Asbell, "Dick Lee Discovers How Much Is Not Enough," *The New York Times Magazine*, September 3, 1967, p. 6.

23. See Delbert C. Miller, *Leadership and Power in the BosWash Megalopolis* (New York: Wiley, 1975).

24. Peter J. Steinberger, *Ideology and the Urban Crisis* (Albany, N.Y.: State University of New York Press, 1985), p. 138.

25. Richard Child Hill, "Fiscal Collapse and Political Struggle in Decaying Central Cities in the United States," in *Marxism and the Metropolis*, eds. William K. Tabb and Larry Sawyers (New York: Oxford University Press, 1978), pp. 213–240.

26. See Richard Child Hill, "Crisis in the Motor City: The Politics of Economic Development in Detroit," in *Restructuring the City: The Political Economy of Urban Redevelopment*, by Susan Fainstein et al. (New York: Longman, 1983), pp. 98–102.

27. Several projections are analyzed in David Fasenfest, "Community Politics and Urban Redevelopment: Poletown, Detroit, and General Motors," *Urban Affairs Quarterly* 22, no. 1 (September 1986): 114.

28. See, for example, Susan S. Fainstein et al., *Restructuring the City.*

29. See Michael Peter Smith, "Urban Structure, Social Theory, and Political Power," in *Cities in Transformation: Class, Capital, and the State*, vol. 26, Urban Affairs Annual Review, ed. Michael Peter Smith, (Beverly Hills, Calif.: SAGE Publications, 1984), pp. 9–11.

30. David C. Perry, "Structuralism, Class Conflict, and Urban Reality," in *Cities in Transformation: Class, Capital, and the State*, vol. 26, pp. 219–234.

31. Michael N. Danielson and Jamison Doig, *New York* (Berkeley: University of California Press, 1982).

32. Harvey Molotch, "The City as a Growth Machine: Toward a Political Economy of Place," *American Journal of Sociology* 82 (September 1976): 309–332.

33. G. William Domhoff, "The Growth Machine and the Power Elite: A Challenge to Pluralists and Marxists Alike," in *Community Power: Directions for Future Research*, ed. Robert J. Waste (Beverly Hills, Calif.: SAGE Publications, 1986), p. 57.

34. Paul E. Peterson, *City Limits* (Chicago: University of Chicago Press, 1981).

35. See, for example, Domhoff, "The Growth Machine and the Power Elite," p. 70.

36. Clarence N. Stone, "Toward An Urban-Regimes Paradigm," *Urban Politics and Urban Policy Section Newsletter* 1, no. 2 (Spring 1987): 7.

37. Clarence N. Stone, "Systemic Power in Community Decision Making: A Restatement of Stratification Theory," *The American Political Science Review* 74, no. 4 (December 1980): 978–990.

38. Ibid., p. 164.

39. Bryan D. Jones and Lynn W. Bachelor with Carter Wilson, *The Sustaining Hand: Community Leadership and Corporate Power* (Lawrence, Kan.: University Press of Kansas, 1986).

40. Ibid., pp. 206, 212.

41. Ibid., p. 8.

42. Pietro S. Nivola, "Apocalypse Now? Whither the Urban Fiscal Crisis," *Polity* 14, no. 3 (Spring 1982): 376.

43. Terry Nichols Clark and Lorna Crowley Ferguson, *City Money: Political Processes, Fiscal Strain, and Retrenchment* (New York: Columbia University Press, 1983).

44. Theodore J. Lowi, *At the Pleasure of the Mayor* (New York: The Free Press, 1964). See especially chap. 7.

45. Theodore J. Lowi, "Machine Politics—Old and New," *The Public Interest* 9 (Fall 1967): 86.

46. See Roger Starr, "Power and Powerlessness in a Regional City," *The Public Interest* 16 (Summer 1969): 10.

47. Lowi, "Machine Politics—Old and New," p. 89.

48. David Rogers, *The Management of Big Cities: Interest Groups and Social Change Strategies* (Beverly Hills, Calif.: SAGE Publications, 1971), p. 117.

49. Jeffrey L. Pressman, "The Preconditions for Mayoral Leadership," *The American Political Science Review* 66, no. 2 (June 1972): 514.

50. Arnold W. Reitze, Jr., and Glenn L. Reitze, "Law: Deus Ex Machina," *Environment* 16 (June 1974): 3–5, 42. The charge was originally made by Bradford C. Snell in *American Ground Transport, A Proposal for Restructuring the Automobile, Truck, Bus, and Rail Industries*, a report to the Subcommittee on Antitrust and Monopoly of the Committee on the Judiciary, U.S. Senate, February 26, 1974.

51. See the *Transit Fact Book: 1975-1976* (Washington, D.C.: The American Public Transit Association, 1976), p. 32.

52. For an in-depth study of this in Boston and other cities, see Alan Lupo, Frank Colcord, and Edmund P. Fowler, *Rites of Way: The Politics of Transportation in Boston and the U.S. City* (Boston: Little, Brown, 1971).

53. Rogers, *The Management of Big Cities*, pp. 36-37.

54. Frances Frisken, "The Metropolis and the Central City: Can One Government Unite Them?" *Urban Affairs Quarterly* 8, no. 3 (June 1973): 403.

55. Jeffrey Pressman, "Foreign Aid and Urban Aid," in *Neighborhood Control in the 1970's*, ed. George Frederickson (New York: Chandler, 1973), p. 152.

56. Douglas Yates, *The Ungovernable City* (Cambridge, Mass.: The M.I.T. Press, 1977), p. 7.

57. John F. Dillon, *Commentaries on the Law of Municipal Corporations*, 5th ed. (Boston: Little, Brown, 1911), vol. I, sec. 237.

58. Roland J. Liebert, *Disintegration and Political Action: The Changing Functions of City Governments in America* (New York: Academic Press, 1976), p. 53. Also see Thomas R. Dye and John A. Garcia, "Structure, Function, and Policy in American Cities," *Urban Affairs Quarterly* 14, no. 1 (September 1978): 103-126.

59. Supreme Court treatment of the impact of federal laws on state and local authority has spawned considerable research and writing. For some current reactions, see Stephanie Beckes, "Boulder and NLC Revisited: An Introduction," *Intergovernmental Perspective* 9, no. 4 (Fall 1983): 5-6.

60. Doyle W. Buckwalter, "Dillon's Rule in the 1980s: Who's in Charge of Local Affairs?" *National Civic Review* 71, no. 8 (September 1982): 399-406.

61. Lowi, *At the Pleasure of the Mayor*, p. 225.

62. See James David Greenstone and Paul E. Peterson, "Reformers, Machines, and the War on Poverty," in *City Politics and Public Policy*, ed. James Q. Wilson (New York: Wiley, 1968), pp. 286-289.

63. J. David Greenstone, "Party Pressure on Organized Labor in Three Cities," in *The Electoral Process*, eds. M. Kent Jennings and L. Harmon Ziegler (Englewood Cliffs, N.J.: Prentice-Hall, 1966), pp. 55-80.

64. Martin E. Meyerson and Edward C. Banfield, *Politics, Planning, and the Public Interest* (Glencoe, Ill.: The Free Press, 1955), pp. 285-300.

65. Ibid.

66. James L. Gibson, Cornelius P. Cotter, John F. Bibby, and Robert J. Huckshorn, "Whither the Local Parties? A Cross-Sectional and Longitudinal Analysis

of the Strength of Party Organizations," *American Journal of Political Science* 29, no. 1 (February 1985): 139-161.

67. See James M. Perry, *The New Politics: The Expanding Technology of Political Manipulation* (New York: Clarkson N. Potter, 1968).

68. See Alexander L. George, "Political Leadership and Social Change in American Cities," *Daedalus* 97, no. 4 (Fall 1968): 1194-1217; and Robert H. Salisbury, "Urban Politics: The New Convergence of Power," *The Journal of Politics* 26, no. 4 (November 1964): 775-797.

69. Pressman, "The Preconditions for Mayoral Leadership," pp. 512-513, 522.

70. John P. Kotter and Paul R. Lawrence, *Mayors in Action: Five Approaches to Urban Governance* (New York: Wiley, 1974), chap. 7.

71. Ibid., p. 107.

72. Ibid., p. 111.

73. Norton Long, "The City as Reservation," *The Public Interest* 25 (Fall 1971): 35.

74. Allan R. Talbot, *The Mayor's Game: Richard Lee of New Haven and the Politics of Change* (New York: Harper & Row, 1967), p. 29.

75. Jewell Bellush and Murray Hausknecht, "Entrepreneurs and Urban Renewal: The New Men of Power," *Journal of the American Institute of Planners* 32, no. 5 (September 1966): 289-297.

76. See Dahl, *Who Governs?*, pp. 200-214; and Raymond Wolfinger, *The Politics of Progress* (Englewood Cliffs, N.J.: Prentice-Hall, 1974), pp. 157-202.

77. Yates, *The Ungovernable City*, p. 165.

78. Peter K. Eisinger, "Black Mayors and the Politics of Racial Advancement," in *Culture, Ethnicity, and Identity*, ed. William C. McReady (New York: Academic Press, 1983), p. 106.

79. See pp. 144-145. In Ernest N. Morial's first election as mayor of New Orleans in 1977, he received only 19 percent of the white vote but 95 percent of the black vote. In Richard Arrington's first election as mayor of Birmingham in 1979, he won less than 15 percent of the white vote. Philadelphia's Wilson Goode won about 20 percent of the white vote in his 1983 victory. Chicago's Harold Washington won few white votes but an estimated 95 percent of the black vote in his 1983 election. In his 1987 reelection, Washington expanded his vote in white neighborhoods but still received a small minority of white votes.

80. Eisinger, "Black Mayors and the Politics of Racial Advancement," pp. 95-109.

81. Grace Hall Saltzstein, "Female Mayors and Women in Municipal Jobs," *American Journal of Political Science* 30, no. 1 (February 1986): 128-139.

82. John F. Sacco and William M. Parle, "Policy

Preferences Among Urban Mayors: A Comparative Analysis," *Urban Affairs Quarterly* 13, no. 1 (September 1977): 49–72.

83. Arnold M. Howitt, "The Expanding Role of Mayoral Staff," *Policy Studies Journal* 3, no. 4 (June 1975): 363–369.

84. Peter Trapp, "Governors' and Mayors' Offices: The Role of the Staff," *National Civic Review* 63, no. 5 (May 1964): 242–249.

85. Wen H. Kuo, "Mayoral Influence on Urban Policy Making," *American Journal of Sociology* 79, no. 3 (November 1973): 637.

86. Glen Sparrow, "The Emerging Chief Executive: The San Diego Experience," *National Civic Review* 74, no. 11 (December 1985): 538–547.

87. Russell D. Murphy, "Whither the Mayors? A Note on Mayoral Careers," *Journal of Politics* 42, no. 1 (February 1980): 277–290.

88. Michael Parenti, "Power and Pluralism: A View from the Bottom," *Journal of Politics* 32, no. 3 (August 1970): 501–532.

89. Ibid. Quotations are found on pp. 519, 521, 526, 528.

90. Ibid., p. 529.

91. Michael Lipsky, *Protest in City Politics: Rent Strikes, Housing and the Power of the Poor* (Chicago: Rand McNally, 1970). See especially pp. 163–185.

92. Michael Lipsky, "Rent Strikes: Poor Man's Weapon," *TRANS-action* (February 1969): 10–15.

93. Peter K. Eisinger, "The Conditions of Protest Behavior in American Cities," *The American Political Science Review* 67, no. 1 (March 1973): 11–28.

94. In Toledo, young black leaders criticized the city's urban renewal programs for not consulting black leadership. See Jean Stinchcombe, *Reform and Reaction: City Politics in Toledo* (Belmont, Calif.: Wadsworth, 1968), pp. 147–148.

95. One Chicago study seeking to identify blacks holding key decision-making positions in the city government and in private business concluded that blacks were systematically underrepresented in every area of public and economic life. Harold Baron, with Harriet Stulman, Richard Rothstein, and Rennard Davis, "Black Powerlessness in Chicago," *TRANS-action* 6, no. 1 (November 1968): 27–33.

96. A study of Oakland found blacks exercising considerable influence in no area of public life except for the anti-poverty programs. See Edward C. Hayes, *Power Structure and Urban Policy: Who Rules in Oakland?* (New York: McGraw-Hill, 1972), especially pp. 156–160, 185–200.

97. A school decentralization experiment in Brooklyn was ended after a local governing board of blacks and Puerto Ricans attempted to transfer teachers out of the ghetto schools and usurp authority held by the New York City Board of Education. See Maurice R. Berube and Marilyn Gittell, *Confrontation at Ocean Hill-Brownsville: The New York School Strike of 1968* (New York: Praeger, 1969).

98. John A. Perrotta, "machine Influence on a Community Action Program: The Case of Providence, Rhode Island," *Polity* 9, no. 4 (Summer 1977): 481–502.

99. Rufus P. Browning, Dale Rogers Marshall, and David H. Tabb, *Protest is not Enough: The Struggle of Blacks and Hispanics for Equality in Urban Politics* (Berkeley: University of California Press, 1984).

100. This is suggested by several commentaries on Chicago. Michael Novak charges that Poles and Italians are grossly underrepresented in executive positions in Chicago. He also charges that there are fewer Polish and Italian college students than there are black college students. See Michael Novak, "The New Ethnicity," *The Center Magazine* 7, no. 4 (July–August 1974): 18–25. Studs Terkel's interview with Florence Scala, a leader of the unsuccessful movement to save the Hull House neighborhood from demolition, is a graphic example of the sense of powerlessness among whites. Studs Terkel, *Division Street: America* (New York: Avon Books, 1967), pp. 29–38. On Appalachian in-migrants into the city, see Todd Gitlin and Nanci Hollander, *Uptown: Poor Whites in Chicago* (New York: Harper & Row, 1970).

101. See Jonathan Rieder, *Canarsie: The Jews and Italians of Brooklyn against Liberalism* (Cambridge, Mass.: Harvard University Press, 1985).

102. See Eric Nordlinger, *Decentralizing the City: A Study of Boston's Little City Halls* (Cambridge, Mass.: M.I.T. Press, 1972), p. 9.

103. For some samples of this criticism, see Jonathan Kozol, *Death at an Early Age: The Destruction of the Hearts and Minds of Negro Children in the Boston Public Schools* (Boston: Houghton Mifflin, 1967); Bel Kaufman, *Up the Down Staircase* (Englewood Cliffs, N.J.: Prentice-Hall, 1964); Robert Coles, *Teachers and the Children of Poverty* (Washington, D.C.: Potomac Institute, 1970); Herbert Kohl, *36 Children* (New York: New American Library, 1967).

104. Mario Fantini and Marilyn Gittell, *Decentralization: Achieving Reform* (New York: Praeger, 1973), pp. 53–55.

105. Ibid., p. 48.

106. Most of this account of decentralization in Detroit is taken from William R. Grant, "Community Control v. School Integration in Detroit," *The Public Interest* 24 (Summer 1971): 62–79.

107. Fantini and Gittell, *Decentralization: Achieving Reform*, pp. 53–55.

108. National Advisory Commission on Civil Disorders, *Commission Report*, pp. 32–33.

109. George J. Washnis, *Municipal Decentralization and Neighborhood Resources: Case Studies of Twelve Cities* (New York: Praeger, 1973). The twelve cities studied were Los Angeles, San Antonio, Kansas City (Missouri), Chicago, Norfolk, New York, Atlanta, Houston, Boston, Baltimore, Columbus, and San Francisco.

110. John Mudd, "Beyond Community Control: A Neighborhood Strategy for City Government," *Publius* 6, no. 4 (Fall 1976): 113–136.

111. Jeffrey R. Henig, "The Political Consequences of Neighborhood Change," a paper presented at the 1983 meeting of the American Political Science Association, Chicago, Illinois, September 1–4, 1983.

112. Joseph Zimmerman, *Participatory Democracy: Populism Revived* (New York: Praeger, 1986), pp. 150–151.

113. Ibid., pp. 152–153.

114. Milton Kotler, *Neighborhood Government* (Indianapolis, Ind.: Bobbs-Merrill, 1969).

115. Richard L. Cole, "Citizen Participation in Municipal Politics," *American Journal of Political Science* 19, no. 4 (November 1975): 761–782.

116. John Hamer, "Neighborhood Control," *Editorial Research Reports*, October 31, 1975, pp. 787–804.

117. Mudd, "Beyond Community Control," pp. 113–136.

118. John M. Orball and Toru Uno, "A Theory of Neighborhood Problem Solving: Political Action vs. Residential Mobility," *The American Political Science Review* 66, no. 2 (June 1972): 471–489.

119. Cole, "Citizen Participation in Municipal Politics," pp. 761–782.

120. Matthew A. Crenson, *Neighborhood Politics* (Cambridge, Mass.: Harvard University Press, 1983), p. 299.

121. See Lewis Lipsitz, "A Better System of Prisons? Thoughts on Decentralization and Participation in America," in *Neighborhood Control in the 1970's*, ed. George Frederickson (New York: Chandler, 1973), pp. 46–47.

122. Crenson, *Neighborhood Politics*, p. 300.

Chapter 8

1. John P. Blair and David Nachmias, "Urban Policy in the Lean Society," in *Fiscal Retrenchment and Urban Policy*, vol. 17, Urban Affairs Annual Reviews, eds. John P. Blair and David Nachmias (Beverly Hills, Calif.: SAGE Publications, 1979), p. 16.

2. P. Clark, "What's Happening Outside of California?" *Nation's Cities* 15 (August 1978): 26–27.

3. U.S. Bureau of the Census, *Statistical Abstract of the United States, 1987* (Washington, D.C.: U.S. Government Printing Office, 1986), pp. 249, 417. The 1980s period covered 1980 to 1985. Also, *Statistical Abstract of the United States, 1979*, p. 283.

4. Quoted in Blair and Nachmias, "Urban Policy in the Lean Society," p. 38.

5. Albert O. Hirschman, *Exit, Voice, and Loyalty: Response to Decline in Firms, Organizations, and States* (Cambridge, Mass.: Harvard University Press, 1970), p. 57.

6. E. S. Savas, "Municipal Monopolies versus Competition," in *Improving the Quality of Urban Management*, vol. 8, Urban Affairs Annual Reviews, eds. Willis D. Hawley and David Rogers (Beverly Hills, Calif.: SAGE Publications, 1974), p. 483.

7. Robert L. Lineberry, *Equality and Urban Policy: The Distribution of Urban Services*, vol. 39, SAGE Library of Social Research (Beverly Hills, Calif.: SAGE Publications, 1977), p. 167.

8. Roger Allbrandt, "Efficiency in the Provision of Fire Services," *Public Choice* 16 (Fall 1973): 1–15.

9. *The New York Times*, February 20, 1984.

10. Committee for Economic Development, *Improving Productivity in State and Local Government* (New York: Committee for Economic Development, 1976).

11. See Dennis Smith, *Report from Engine Co. 82* (New York: McCall Books, 1972), p. 27.

12. Arnold Meltsner and Aaron Wildavsky, "Leave City Budgeting Alone!: A Survey, Case Study, and Recommendations for Reform," in *Financing the Metropolis*, volume 4, Urban Affairs Annual Review, ed. John P. Crecine (Beverly Hills, Calif.: SAGE Publications, 1970), p. 344.

13. Lewis Friedman, *Budgeting Municipal Expenditures* (New York: Praeger, 1975), p. 79.

14. On decision rules, see Lineberry, *Equality and Urban Policy*, pp. 153–160.

15. On the distinction between line and staff personnel in public administration, see George E. Berkley, *The Craft of Public Administration* (Boston: Allyn and Bacon, 1975), pp. 58–62.

16. See William C. Baer, "Just What Is Urban Service Anyway?" *Journal of Politics* 47, no. 3 (August 1985): 881–898.

17. See Michael Lipsky, *Street-Level Bureaucracy* (New York: Russell Sage Foundation, 1980).

18. James Q. Wilson, *Varieties of Police Behavior* (Cambridge, Mass.: Harvard University Press, 1968), chap. 4.

19. *Miranda v. Arizona*, 384 U.S. 436 (1966).

20. Jonathan Kozol, *Death at an Early Age* (Bos-

ton: Houghton Mifflin, 1967).

21. See especially Lipsky, *Stree-Level Bureaucracy.*

22. Daniel Katz et al., *Bureaucratic Encounters: A Pilot Study in the Evaluation of Government Services* (Ann Arbor, Mich.: Institute for Social Research, 1975), pp. 120, 182.

23. John Clayton Thomas, "The Personal Side of Street-Level Bureaucracy," *Urban Affairs Quarterly* 22, no. 1 (September 1986): 89–100.

24. Elaine B. Sharp, *Citizen Demand-Making in the Urban Context* (University, Ala.: The University of Alabama Press, 1986).

25. Morton Grodzins, "The Federal System," in *Goals for Americans: The Report of the President's Commission on National Goals* (Englewood Cliffs, N.J.: Prentice-Hall, 1960), pp. 365–366.

26. There are two different versions of incrementalism. The *rational incremental* model argues that the largest increments go to the agencies that run programs consistent with the short-term political interests of the legislators who approve the budget. See Charles E. Lindblom, "Decision Making in Taxation Expenditures," in National Bureau of Economic Research, *Public Finances: Needs, Sources and Utilization* (Princeton, N.J.: Princeton University Press, 1961), pp. 295–329. In contrast, the *role-constrained* model of incrementalism argues that budget increments get determined by individual actors playing out predetermined roles. It is essentially this model that is described in the text. See Thomas J. Anton, "Roles and Symbols in the Determination of State Expenditures," *Midwest Journal of Political Science* 11, no. 1 (February 1967): 27–43.

27. This argument was made by Ira Sharkansky in reference to state legislators and state agencies. See his "State Administrators in the Policy Process," in *Politics in the American States: A Comparative Analysis*, 2nd ed., eds. Herbert Jacob and Kenneth N. Vines (Boston: Little, Brown, 1971), p. 259.

28. Lineberry, *Equality and Urban Policy*, p. 152.

29. Sharkansky, "State Administrators in the Policy Process," p. 259.

30. Examples of a school district budget organized in both a line-item format and a program budget format can be seen in Frederick S. Lane, ed., *Managing State and Local Government: Cases and Readings* (New York: St. Martin's Press, 1980); Richard L. Montesi, "Sunset Hills," pp. 213–223.

31. See Allen Schick, "PPB: The View from the States," *State Government* 45, no. 1 (Winter 1972): 13.

32. Aaron Wildavsky says of PPB, "I have not been able to find a single example of successful implementation of PPB," and he makes specific reference

to attempts at zero-based budgeting in the U.S. Department of Agriculture. See his *The Politics of the Budgetary Process*, 2nd ed. (Boston: Little, Brown, 1974), pp. 195, 200. Also see John A. Worthley, "PPB: Dead or Alive?" *Public Administration Review* 34, no. 4 (July–August 1974): 393.

33. Donald J. Borut, "Implementing PPBs: A Practitioner's Viewpoint," in *Financing the Metropolis*, pp. 285–310.

34. See Herbert P. Dooskin, "Zero-base Budgeting: A Plus for Government," *National Civic Review* 66 (March 1977): 119–121.

35. John D. La Faver, "Zero-base Budgeting in New Mexico," *State Government* 47, no. 2 (Spring 1974): 112.

36. Michael J. Scheiring, "Zero-base Budgeting in New Jersey," *State Government* 49, no. 3 (Summer 1976): 174–179.

37. David R. Morgan, *Managing Urban America* (North Scituate, Mass.: Duxbury Press, 1979), p. 230.

38. David W. Singleton, Bruce A. Smith, and James R. Cleaveland, "Zero-Base Budgeting in Wilmington," in Lane, *Managing State and Local Government*, pp. 223–240.

39. On MBO, see Jong Jun, "Introduction: Management by Objectives in the Public Sector," *Public Administration Review* 36, no. 1 (January–February 1976): 1–4; and Frank Sherwood and William Page, "MBO and Public Management," *Public Administration Review* 36, no. 1 (January–February 1976): 5–11. For general overviews, see Robert D. Miewald, *Public Administration: A Critical Perspective* (New York: McGraw-Hill, 1978), pp. 153–155.

40. Peter F. Drucker, "What Results Should You Expect? A User's Guide to MBO," *Public Administration Review* 36, no. 1 (January–February 1976): 12–19.

41. Morgan, *Managing Urban America*, p. 194.

42. See Harry Hatry et al., *Program Analysis for State and Local Governments* (Washington, D.C.: The Urban Institute, 1976), p. 1.

43. Orville F. Poland, "Program Evaluation and Administrative Theory," *Public Administration Review* 34, no. 4 (July–August 1974): 334.

44. Ibid., p. 335.

45. Ibid., pp. 333–338.

46. For an assessment of program evaluation generally, see Carol H. Weiss, *Evaluation Research: Methods of Assessing Program Effectiveness* (Englewood Cliffs, N.J.: Prentice-Hall, 1972).

47. On Scottsdale, see Edward C. Hayes, "In Pursuit of Productivity: Management Innovation in Scottsdale," *National Civic Review* 73, no. 6 (June 1984): 273–277.

48. Data from a 1985 survey by the International City Management Association. Reported in *The New York Times*, May 28, 1985, p. 9.

49. E. S. Savas, *Privatization: The Key to Better Government* (Chatham, N.J.: Chatham House Publishing Company, 1987), pp. 58–92.

50. See Julia Marlowe, "Private Versus Public Provision of Refuse Removal Service: Measures of Citizen Satisfaction," *Urban Affairs Quarterly* 20, no. 3 (March 1985): 355–363. In the Tucson area, she found that public provision of garbage removal was cheaper than private subscription. However, private monopoly contract in an area was cheaper than either public removal or private subscription.

51. Peter Hames, "When Public Services Go Private: There's More Than One Option," *National Civic Review* 73, no. 6 (June 1984): 282.

52. *The Book of the States: 1974–75* (Lexington, Ky.: Council of State Governments, 1974), pp. 184–187. In six states (Montana, Nebraska, North Dakota, Tennessee, Texas, and West Virginia) merit systems cover only employees in federal grant programs. An official of the Bureau of Intergovernmental Personnel Programs of the U.S. Civil Service Commission cites a survey indicating that 95 percent of all local employees are covered by some form of merit system. Whether all of these systems are free of political influence, however, seems debatable. See Andrew W. Boesel, "Local Personnel Management: Organizational Problems and Operating Practices," *Municipal Yearbook: 1974* (Washington, D.C.: International City Management Association, 1974), pp. 92–93.

53. York Wilbern, "Administrative Organization," in *The 50 States and Their Local Governments*, ed. James W. Fesler (New York: Knopf, 1967), pp. 341–342.

54. Frank J. Thompson, "Bureaucratic Responsiveness in the Cities: The Problem of Minority Hiring," *Urban Affairs Quarterly* 10, no. 1 (September 1974): 40–68.

55. *Carter v. Gallagher*, 452 F.2d 315 (8th Cir. 1972).

56. Peter K. Eisinger, *Black Employment in City Government, 1973–1980* (Washington, D.C.: Joint Center for Political Studies, 1983), pp. 34–41.

57. *Boston Firefighters Union v. Boston Chapter NAACP*, 103 S. Ct. 2076 (1983).

58. Marion Reber, "Comparable Worth: Closing a Wage Gap," *State Legislatures* 10, no. 4 (April 1984): 26–31.

59. Keon S. Chi, "Developments in State Personnel Systems," in *Book of the States: 1984–85* (Lexington, Ky.: Council of State Governments, 1984), p. 289–291; Debra A. Stewart, "State and Local Initiatives in the Federal System: The Politics and Policy of Comparable Worth in 1984," *Publius* 15, no. 3 (Summer 1985): 81–96.

60. Morgan, *Managing Urban America*, p. 194.

61. *The New York Times*, April 24, 1977, p. 5.

62. See Boesel, "Local Personnel Management," pp. 87–90.

63. Ibid., pp. 87, 90.

64. "Unions Go Public," *State Government News* 15 (October 1977): 5.

65. Morgan, *Managing Urban America*, p. 255.

66. As of this writing, Chicago's 1980 financial problems were too new for competent scholarly research to have been conducted and published about them. One critical background article is Sidney Lens, "The City That Doesn't Work Anymore: Chicago in the Crunch," *The Progressive* (April 1980): 34–38.

67. Bureau of the Census, *Statistical Abstract of the United States: 1986* (Washington, D.C.: U.S. Government Printing Office, 1985), p. 423.

68. Ibid., p. 412.

69. The following analysis of equality and bias in urban service delivery relies heavily on Lineberry, *Equality and Urban Policy*.

70. See John Rawls, *A Theory of Justice* (Cambridge, Mass.: Harvard University Press, 1971); and Michael Nozick, *Anarchy, States and Utopia* (New York: Basic Books, 1974).

71. See Lineberry, *Equality and Urban Policy*, chap. 1.

72. *Hawkins v. Shaw*, 437 F.2d 1286 (5th Cir. 1971).

73. *Hobson v. Hansen*, 269 F. Supp. 401, 517 (1969).

74. *Rodriguez v. San Antonio Independent School District*, 411 U.S. 1 (1973).

75. Lineberry, *Equality and Urban Policy*, p. 48.

76. Ibid., pp. 74–76.

77. James S. Coleman, "The Concept of Equality of Educational Opportunity," *Harvard Educational Review* 38 (1968): 16–17; "Equal Schools or Equal Students?" *The Public Interest* 4 (Summer 1966), p. 72.

78. On ESEA Title I, see Jerome T. Murphy, "The Education Bureaucracies Implement Novel Policy: The Politics of Title I of ESEA, 1965–1972," in *Policy and Politics in America: Six Case Studies*, ed. Allan P. Sindler (Boston: Little, Brown, 1973), pp. 160–198.

79. Lee Rainwater, *What Money Buys: Inequality and the Social Meanings of Income* (New York: Basic Books, 1974), p. 168.

80. See Lineberry, *Equality and Urban Policy*.

81. American Library Association, *Access to Public Libraries* (Chicago: American Library Association, 1963), p. 57.

82. See Lineberry, *Equality and Urban Policy*, pp. 108–109.

83. Ibid.

84. Ibid.; and Steven D. Gold, "The Distribution of Urban Government Services in Theory and Practice: The Case of Recreation in Detroit," *Public Finance Quarterly* 2 (January 1974): 107–130.

85. Frank S. Levy, Arnold J. Meltsner, and Aaron Wildavsky, *Urban Outcomes: Schools, Streets, and Libraries* (Berkeley: University of California Press, 1974), p. 219.

86. Lineberry, *Equality and Urban Policy*.

87. Glenn Abney and Thomas P. Lauth, "A Comparative Analysis of Distributional and Enforcement Decisions in Cities," *Journal of Politics* 44, no. 1 (February 1982): 193–200.

88. Kenneth R. Mladenka, "Citizen Demands and Urban Services: The Distribution of Bureaucratic Response in Chicago and Houston," *American Journal of Political Science* 25, no. 4 (November 1981): 693–714.

89. Arnold Vedlitz and James A. Dyer, "Bureaucratic Responses to Citizen Contacts: Neighborhood Administrative Reaction in Dallas," *Journal of Politics* 46, no. 4 (November 1984): 1207–1216.

90. Thomas, "The Personal Side of Street-Level Bureaucracy," pp. 89–100.

91. John Boyle and David Jacobs, "The Intra-City Distribution of Services: A Multivariate Analysis," *The American Political Science Review* 76, no. 2 (June 1982): 371–379.

92. Albert O. Hirschman, *Exit, Voice, and Loyalty: Responses to Decline in Firms, Organizations, and States* (Cambridge, Mass.: Harvard University Press, 1970).

93. See especially Paul Schumaker and Russell W. Getter, "Structural Sources of Unequal Responsiveness to Group Demands in American Cities," *Western Political Quarterly* 36, no. 1 (March 1983): 26–27; Matthew Crenson, *Neighborhood Politics* (Cambridge, Mass.: Harvard University Press, 1983) and Browning, Marshall, and Tabb, *Protest is not Enough*.

Chapter 9

1. See, for example, Louis H. Masotti, ed., "The Suburban Seventies," *Annals of the American Academy of Political and Social Science*, no. 422 (November 1975); William G. Colman, *Cities, Suburbs and States* (New York: The Free Press, 1975); John Kramer, ed., *North American Suburbs: Politics, Diversity, Change* (Berkeley, CA: Glendessary, 1972); Louis H. Masotti and Jeffrey K. Hadden, eds., *Suburbia in Transition* (New York: Watts, 1974); Barry Schwartz, ed., *The Changing Face of the Suburbs* (Chicago:

University of Chicago Press, 1976); Robert C. Wood, *Suburbia: Its People and Their Politics* (Boston: Houghton Mifflin, 1958); Frederick M. Wirt et al., *On the City's Rim: Politics and Policy in Suburbia* (Lexington, Mass.: D.C. Heath, 1972); Karl A. Lamb, *As Orange Goes: Twelve California Families and the Future of American Politics* (New York: W.W. Norton, 1974).

2. See, for example, William H. Whyte, *The Organization Man* (Garden City, N.Y.: Doubleday, 1957); David Riesman, *The Lonely Crowd* (Garden City, N.Y.: Doubleday, 1956); John Keats, *The Crack in the Picture Window* (Boston: Houghton Mifflin, 1957). For an interesting and readable critique of the antisuburban literature, see Scott Donaldson, *The Suburban Myth* (New York: Columbia University Press, 1969).

3. Leo F. Schnore, "The Social and Economic Characteristics of American Suburbs," *The Sociological Quarterly* 4, no. 2 (Spring 1963): 122–134.

4. Charles R. Adrian and Charles Press, *Governing Urban America,* 4th ed. (New York: McGraw-Hill, 1972), p. 42.

5. Wood, *Suburbia*, p. 9.

6. For one example, see James A. Maxwell, "Kentucky's Open City," *The Saturday Evening Post*, March 26, 1960, p. 22.

7. *The New York Times*, November 15, 1978, p. B-4.

8. Adrian and Press, *Governing Urban America*, p. 47.

9. Wood, *Suburbia*, p. 153.

10. Murray S. Stedman, Jr., *Urban Politics* (Cambridge, Mass.: Winthrop Publishers, 1972), p. 33.

11. Reported in Bennett M. Berger, *Working Class Suburbs* (Berkeley and Los Angeles: University of California Press, 1960), p. 23. Also see William Dobriner, *Class in Suburbia* (Englewood Cliffs, N.J.: Prentice-Hall, 1963).

12. Adrian and Press, *Governing Urban America*, p. 46.

13. *Blacks on the Move: A Decade of Demographic Change* (Washington, D.C.: Joint Center for Political Studies, 1982), pp. 49–55.

14. Thomas A. Clark, *Blacks in Suburbs: A National Perspective* (New Brunswick, N.J.: Rutgers University Center for Urban Policy Research, 1979), p. 32.

15. Ibid., pp. 58, 61; Reynolds Farley, "The Changing Distribution of Negroes Within Metropolitan Areas: The Emergence of Black Suburbs," *American Journal of Sociology* 75, no. 4 (January 1970): 524–525; and Clifford E. Reid, "Are Blacks Making It in the Suburbs? A Correction," *Journal of Urban*

Economics 16, no. 3 (November 1984): 357–359.

16. Harold X.Connally, "Black Movement into the Suburbs: Suburbs Doubling Their Black Population During the 1960s," *Urban Affairs Quarterly* 9, no. 1 (September 1973): 100.

17. Norman M. Bradburn, Seymour Sudman, and Gulen G. Gockel, *Racial Integration in American Neighborhoods: A Comparative Survey* (Chicago: National Opinion Research Center, 1970), p. 76.

18. Leo F. Schnore, Carolyn D. Andre, and Harry Sharp, "Black Suburbanization: 1930–1970," in *The Changing Face of the Suburbs*, ed. Barry Schwartz (Chicago: University of Chicago Press, 1976), p. 69. Also, a study of 1363 suburbs based on 1970 census data found very high levels of racial segregation in both southern and northern suburbs. See Avery M. Guest, "The Changing Racial Composition of Suburbs 1950–1970," *Urban Affairs Quarterly*, 14, no. 2 (December 1978): 195–206.

19. John E. Farley, "Metropolitan Housing Segregation in 1980: The St. Louis Case," *Urban Affairs Quarterly* 18, no. 3 (March 1983): 355.

20. Michael Gutkowski and Tracey Feild, *The Graying of Suburbia* (Washington, D.C.: Urban Institute, 1979).

21. See Herbert J. Gans, *The Levittowners: Ways of Life and Politics in a New Suburban Community* (New York: Vintage Books, 1967). Levittown was named after its master builder William J. Levitt. Levitt made a fortune off his tract developments, becoming the proud owner of a 68-acre estate, a yacht, and a multimillion-dollar stock portfolio. But his methods, which worked well in the 1950s, did not fare well in the 1980s. In 1987, the then 80-year-old Levitt declared bankruptcy and was evicted from his New York offices. *Forbes*, May 4, 1987, p. 40.

22. *The New York Times*, November 4, 1980, p. 15.

23. Louis H. Masotti, "Prologue: Suburbia Reconsidered—Myth and Counter-Myth," *The Urbanization of the Suburbs*, vol. 7, Urban Affairs Annual Reviews, eds. Louis H. Masotti and Jeffrey K. Hadden (Beverly Hills, Calif.: SAGE Publications, 1973), pp. 18–21.

24. David Listokin and W. Patrick Beaton, *Revitalizing the Older Suburb* (New Brunswick, N.J.: Rutgers University Center for Urban Policy Research, 1983), pp. 4–8.

25. See Ernest W. Burgess, "Urban Areas," in *Chicago: An Experiment in Special Research*, eds. T.V. Smith and Leonard D. White (Chicago: University of Chicago Press, 1929), pp. 113–138. Also see John C. Bollens and Henry J. Schmandt, *The Metropolis: Its People, Politics, and Economic Life*, 2nd ed.

(New York: Harper & Row, 1970), pp. 48–51.

26. See Homer Hoyt, "The Structure of American Cities in the Post-War Era," *American Journal of Sociology* 48 (January 1943): 476–477.

27. See Amos Hawley, *Human Ecology* (New York: Ronald Press, 1950), pp. 268–275.

28. See John Fine, Norval Glenn, and J. Kenneth Monts, "The Residential Segregation of Occupational Groups in Central Cities and Suburbs," *Demography* 8 (February 1971): 91–101. Using census tracts as their unit of analysis and using diversity in occupation as their measures of heterogeneity, Fine and his coworkers discovered that suburban neighborhoods were very heterogeneous occupationally. In seven of the eight SMSAs studied, they found that the suburban census tracts were more heterogeneous than the central cities. Those data refer only to occupational heterogeneity, and different results might be obtained if heterogeneity were measured in median educational levels or median income.

29. Wirt et al., *On the City's Rim*, pp. 32–33.

30. Fred I. Greenstein and Raymond E. Wolfinger, "The Suburbs and Shifting Party Loyalties," *Public Opinion Quarterly* 22 (Winter 1958–1959): 80–82.

31. Wood, *Suburbia*, pp. 141–149.

32. Wirt, *On the City's Rim*, p. 85.

33. Herbert Hirsch, "Suburban Voting and National Trends: A Research Note," *Western Political Quarterly* 21 (September 1968): 508–514.

34. Angus Campbell, Philip E. Converse, Warren E. Miller, and Donald E. Stokes, *The American Voter* (New York: Wiley, 1960), p. 459.

35. Benjamin Walter and Frederick M. Wirt, "The Political Consequences of Suburban Variety," *Social Science Quarterly* 52, no. 3 (December 1971): 746.

36. John C. Bollens et al., *Metropolitan Challenge* (Dayton, Ohio: Metropolitan Studies, 1959).

37. John M. Orbell and Toru Uno, "A Theory of Neighborhood Problem Solving: Political Action vs. Residential Mobility," *The American Political Science Review* 66, no. 2 (June 1972): 471–489.

38. Thomas R. Dye, "City–Suburban Social Distance and Public Policy," *Social Forces* 44, no. 1 (September 1965): 100–106.

39. Joseph Zikmund II, "A Comparison of Political Attitude and Activity Patterns in Central Cities and Suburbs," *Public Opinion Quarterly* 31, no. 1 (Spring 1967): 74.

40. Wirt et al., *On the City's Rim*, p. 194.

41. Oliver P. Williams, Harold Herman, Charles S. Liebman, and Thomas R. Dye, *Suburban Differences and Metropolitan Politics: A Philadelphia Story* (Philadelphia: University of Pennsylvania Press, 1965), pp. 211–220.

42. Wood, *Suburbia*, p. 14.

43. Kenneth T. Jackson, "Metropolitan Government Versus Suburban Autonomy: Politics on the Crabgrass Frontier," in *Cities in American History*, eds. Kenneth T. Jackson and Stanley K. Schultz (New York: Knopf, 1972), pp. 442–462.

44. Daniel J. Elazar, "Suburbanization: Reviving the Town on the Metropolitan Frontier," *Publius* 5, no. 1 (Winter 1975): 33–80.

45. Joseph F. Zimmerman, *The Federated City: Community Control in Large Cities* (New York: St. Martin's Press, 1972), pp. 12–13. Also see David C. Perry, "The Suburb as a Model for Neighborhood Control," in *Neighborhood Control in the 1970s*, ed. George Frederickson (New York: Chandler, 1973), pp. 85–99.

46. The classic account of developing a subdivision is Gans, *The Levittowners*.

47. Michael N. Danielson, *The Politics of Exclusion* (New York: Columbia University Press, 1976).

48. Advisory Commission on Intergovernmental Relations, *Urban America and the Federal System* (Washington, D.C.: U.S. Government Printing Office, 1969), pp. 12–13.

49. Wood, *Suburbia*, pp. 198–258.

50. Robert O. Wood describes Los Angeles County as a producer of services in his *Government in Metropolitan Regions: A Reappraisal of Fractionated Political Organizations* (Davis, Calif.: Institute of Governmental Affairs, University of California, 1966), pp. 92–117.

51. Richard M. Cion, "Accommodation Par Excellence: The Lakewood Plan," in *Metropolitan Politics: A Reader*, 2nd ed., ed. Michael N. Danielson (Boston: Little, Brown, 1971), pp. 224–226.

52. Ibid., p. 230.

53. Charles Hoch, "Municipal Contracting in California: Privatization with Class," *Urban Affairs Quarterly* 20, no. 3 (March 1985): 303–324. Hoch studied incorporation attempts in the San Gabriel section of Los Angeles County for the period 1955 to 1970.

54. Cion, "Accommodation Par Excellence," pp. 230–231.

55. Advisory Commission on Intergovernmental Relations, *Report A-44: Substate Regionalism and the Federal System: The Challenge of Local Governmental Reorganization* (Washington, D.C.: U.S. Government Printing Office, 1974), vol. III, pp. 67–68.

56. Virginia Marion Perrenod, *Special Districts, Special Purposes: Fringe Governments and Urban Problems in the Houston Area* (College Station, Tex.: Texas A & M University Press, 1984).

57. Stanley Scott and John Corzine, *Special Districts in the San Francisco Bay Area: Some Problems and Issues* (Berkeley, Calif.: The Institute of Governmental Studies, 1962).

58. Perrenod, *Special Districts, Special Purposes*, pp. 22, 34–44.

59. Ibid., pp. 39–42.

60. *The New York Times*, August 2, 1987, p. F-28.

61. See Michael N. Danielson and Jamison W. Doig, *New York: The Politics of Urban Regional Development* (Berkeley: University of California Press, 1982), pp. 245, 318.

62. *The New York Times*, April 28, 1977, pp. 1, 48.

63. See *The New York Times*, October 13, 1977, p. 1; and November 8, 1977, p. 1.

64. For a concise summary of these developments, see Danielson and Doig, *New York*, pp. 244–250.

65. *The New York Times*, August 2, 1987, p. F-28.

66. For a discussion of the constituent unit idea of representation on metropolitan districts, see Arthur W. Bromage, *Political Representation in Metropolitan Agencies* (Ann Arbor: University of Michigan Institute of Public Administration, 1962).

67. See John J. Harrigan and William C. Johnson, *Governing the Twin Cities Region: The Metropolitan Council in Comparative Perspective* (Minneapolis: The University of Minnesota Press, 1978).

68. Not all researchers agree with this assessment. One attempt to measure the effects of freeways on urban neighborhoods found that the freeways had only a marginal effect on population and housing characteristics. Michael Chernoff, "The Effects of Superhighways in Urban Areas," *Urban Affairs Quarterly* 16, no. 3 (March 1981): 317–336.

69. See Alan Lupo, Frank Colcord, and Edmund P. Fowler, *Rites of Way: The Politics of Transportation in Boston and the U.S. City* (Boston: Little, Brown, 1971).

70. *Citizens to Preserve Overton Park, Inc. v. Volpe*, 401 U.S. 402 (1971).

71. *Statistical Abstract of the United States, 1986* (Washington, D.C.: U.S. Government Printing Office, 1985), p. 608. The period is for 1970 through 1983.

72. See *Transit Fact Book: 1985* Washington, D.C.: American Public Transit Association, 1985), p. 32. Ridership bottomed out at 6,567 million riders in 1972, climbed to 8,235 million in 1980, and then dropped off again.

73. Sheldon M. Edner and Edward Weiner, "Urban Transportation: A Time for a Change," *Public Administration Review* 42, no. 1 (January/February

1982): 84–89.

74. Peter Hall, *Great Planning Disasters* (Berkeley: University of California Press, 1982), pp. 109–137.

75. *The New York Times*, August 1, 1987, p. 10.

76. Some of these criticisms can be found in William H. Whyte, *The Last Landscape* (Garden City, N.Y.: Anchor Books, 1970).

77. For a more extended treatment of these four models, see John J. Harrigan and William C. Johnson, "Can Metropolitan Sprawl Be Controlled? The Twin Cities Experiment in Comparative Perspective," a paper presented to the annual meeting of the Midwest Political Science Association, April 28, 1978. Also see William C. Johnson and John J. Harrigan, "Planning for Growth: The Twin Cities Approach," *National Civic Review* 69, no. 4 (April 1969): 189–194.

78. On Ramapo, see *Golden v. Planning Board of Town of Ramapo*, 39 N.Y.2d 359, 334 N.Y.S.2d 138, 285 N.E.2d 359 (1972).

79. *City of Petaluma v. Construction Industry Association of Sonoma County*, 522 F.2d 897 (1975).

80. *The New York Times*, September 11, 1977, p. 47.

81. *The New York Times*, March 19, 1978, p. 26; December 30, 1978, p. 7.

82. Michelle J. White, "Self Interest in the Suburbs: The Trend Toward No-Growth Zoning," *Policy Analysis* 4, no. 2 (Spring 1978): 185–204.

83. Elizabeth H. Haskell and Victoria S. Price, *State Environmental Management* (New York: Praeger, 1973), pp. 173–194.

84. See Carl E. Lutrin and Allen K. Settle, "The Public and Ecology: The Role of Initiatives in California's Environmental Politics," *Western Political Quarterly* 28, no. 2 (June 1975): 352–371.

85. See Melvin B. Mogulof, *Saving the Coast: California's Experiment in Inter-Government Land Use Regulation* (Lexington, Mass.: Lexington Books, 1975).

86. See Harrigan and Johnson, *Governing the Twin Cities Region*, pp. 68–74.

87. For example, see David R. Goldfield, "The Limits of Suburban Growth: The Washington, D.C. SMSA," *Urban Affairs Quarterly* 12, no. 1 (September 1976): 83–102.

88. *First English Evangelical Lutheran Church of Glendale v. County of Los Angeles*, 107 S. Ct. 2378 (1987).

89. *The New York Times*, June 10, 1987, p. 1.

90. Raymond and May Associates, *Zoning Controversies in the Suburbs: Three Case Studies* (Washington, D.C.: U.S. Government Printing Office, 1963), p. 75 (Research Report no. 11, prepared for the consideration of the National Commission on Urban Problems).

91. Williams et al., *Suburban Differences and Metropolitan Policies*, p. 294.

92. *Wall Street Journal*, March 26, 1987, p. 22; and Mary H. Cooper, "Downtown Suburbia," *Editorial Research Reports* (November 14, 1986): 841–844.

93. See Robert Cervero, *Suburban Gridlock* (New Brunswick, N.J.: Rutgers University Center for Urban Policy Research, 1986).

94. *The New York Times*, July 15, 1987, p. 13. Data taken from a U.S. Department of Agriculture study.

95. Scott and Corzine, *Special Districts in the San Francisco Bay Area*.

96. Perrenod, *Special Districts, Special Purposes*, pp. 86–87.

97. Ibid., pp. 89–93.

Chapter 10

1. Oliver P. Williams, Harold Herman, Charles S. Liebmann, and Thomas R. Dye, *Suburban Differences and Metropolitan Politics: A Philadelphia Story* (Philadelphia: University of Pennsylvania Press, 1965), pp. 211–220.

2. U.S. Bureau of the Census, *Governmental Finances in 1981–82*, GF Series, no. 5 (Washington, D.C.: U.S. Government Printing Office, 1983), p. 1.

3. See John R. Logan and Mark Schneider, "Governmental Organization and City/Suburb Income Inequality, 1960–1970," *Urban Affairs Quarterly* 17, no. 3 (March 1982): 303–318; Scott A. Bollens, "A Political-Ecological Analysis of Income Inequality in the Metropolitan Areas," *Urban Affairs Quarterly* 22, no. 22 (December 1986): 221. The Logan-Schneider analysis was based on 1960 and 1970 census data; the Bollens analysis was based on 1980 census data.

4. For two examples of this criticism, see Jonathan Kozol, *Death at an Early Age: The Destruction of the Hearts and Minds of Negro Children in the Boston Public Schools* (Boston: Houghton Mifflin, 1967); or Bel Kaufman, *Up the Down Staircase* (Englewood Cliffs, N.J.: Prentice-Hall, 1964). For an analysis of suburban school system politics, see David W. Minar, "Community Basis of Conflict in School System Politics," *American Sociological Review* 31 (December 1966): 822–835.

5. See Michael N. Danielson, *The Politics of Exclusion* (new York: Columbia University Press, 1976).

6. Ibid., p. 61.

7. Ibid.

8. Ibid., p. 53.

9. U.S. Bureau of the Census, *Census of Population and Housing 1970: General Demographic Trends for Metropolitan Areas, 1960 to 1970,* Final Report PHC(2)-1 (Washington, D.C.: U.S. Government Printing Office, 1971), p. 82.

10. Michelle J. White, "Self Interest in the Suburbs: The Trend Toward No-Growth Zoning," *Policy Analysis* 4, no. 2 (Spring 1978): 185–204.

11. John R. Logan, "Growth, Politics and the Stratification of Place," *American Journal of Sociology* 84, no. 2 (Summer 1978): 404–416.

12. William Protash and Mark Baldassare, "Growth Policies and Community Status: A Test and Modification of Logan's Theory," *Urban Affairs Quarterly* 18, no. 3 (March 1983): 397–412.

13. M. Gottdeiner and Max Neiman, "Characteristics of Support for Local Growth Control," *Urban Affairs Quarterly* 17, no. 1 (September 1981): 55–74.

14. See *The New York Times*, April 12, 1978.

15. On Black Jack, see Danielson, *The Politics of Exclusion*, pp. 31–33, 84–85, 166–167, 184–186, 231–233.

16. Ibid., p. 90.

17. *The New York Times*, June 20, 1971.

18. *Kennedy Park Homes v. City of Lackawanna*, 436 F.2d 108 (1971).

19. *Dailey v. Lawton*, 425 F.2d 1037 (1970).

20. *United States v. City of Black Jack, Missouri*, 508 F.2d 1179 (1974).

21. *The New York Times*, February 25, 1982, p. 12.

22. *Arlington Heights v. Metropolitan Housing Development Corporation*, 429 U.S. 252 (1977).

23. Michael N. Danielson and Jameson W. Doig, *New York: The Politics of Urban Regional Development* (Berkeley, CA: University of California Press, 1982), pp. 79–81, 105–108.

24. U.S. Bureau of the Census, *Statistical Abstract of the United States: 1987* (Washington, D.C.: U.S. Government Printing Office, 1986), p. 712.

25. George Sternlieb and James W. Hughes, "The Post-Shelter Society," in *America's Housing: Prospects and Problems*, eds. George Sternleib and James W. Hughes (New Brunswick: Rutgers University Center for Urban Policy Research, 1980), pp. 95–96.

26. An analysis of the Census Bureau's 1975 and 1976 Annual Housing Surveys in nineteen SMSAs with both large Hispanic and black populations found that blacks, Mexican-Americans and Puerto Ricans tended to pay higher rents than Anglos or Cubans. However, they did not pay higher prices to purchase homes. See Lauren J. Kriva, "Housing Price Inequalities: A Comparison of Anglos, Blacks, and Spanish-Origin Populations," *Urban Affairs Quarterly* 17, no. 4 (June 1982): 445–462.

27. Barbara Taylor, "Inclusionary Zoning: A Working Option for Affordable Housing?" *Urban Land* 40, no. 3 (March 1981): 6–12.

28. Mount Laurel II. For analysis, see *The New York Times*, June 21, 1983, p. 1; June 22, 1983, p. 9.

29. Ibid.

30. *Minneapolis Star and Tribune*, November 7, 1984, p. 21A.

31. *Plessy v. Ferguson*, 163 U.S. 537 (1896).

32. *Gong Lum v. Rice*, 275 U.S. 78 (1927).

33. *Missouri ex rel. Gaines v. Canada*, 305 U.S. 337 (1938); *Sipuel v. Oklahoma*, 332 U.S. 631 (1948); *McLaurin v. Oklahoma State Regents*, 339 U.S. 637 (1950); *Sweatt v. Painter*, 339 U.S. 629 (1950).

34. *Brown v. Board of Education*, 347 U.S. 483 (1954).

35. Gary Orfield, *Public School Desegregation in the United States 1968-1980* (Washington, D.C.: Joint Center for Political Studies, 1983), p. 4.

36. *Swann v. Charlotte-Mecklenburg Board of Education*, 402 U.S. 1 (1971).

37. *The New York Times*, November 21, 1977, p. 57.

38. Orfield, *Public School Desegregation*, p. 26.

39. See *The New York Times*, October 9, 1977, p. 1.

40. Diane Ravitch, "The 'White Flight' Controversy," *The Public Interest*, no. 51 (Spring 1978): 142.

41. Mary Costello, "Busing Reappraisal," *Editorial Research Reports*, December 26, 1975, pp. 945–964.

42. Christine H. Rossell, "School Desegregation and White Flight," *Political Science Quarterly* 90, no. 4 (Winter 1975–1976): 692. This has been a very controversial article. It has been criticized for its methods and policy suggestions by Diane Ravitch in her article, "The 'White Flight' Controversy," pp. 135–150. Also see the exchange of views by Christine H. Rossell, Diane Ravitch, and David J. Armor, "Busing and 'White Flight'," *The Public Interest*, no. 53 (Fall 1978): 109–115.

43. Charles S. Bullock III, "School Desegregation After a Quarter Century," *Urban Affairs Quarterly* 18, no. 2 (December 1982): 295–296.

44. *Millikin v. Bradley*, 418 U.S. 717 (1974).

45. *The New York Times*, Jan. 30, 1977, p. 2; July 21, 1977, p. E-6.

46. *The New York Times*, November 20, 1978, p. 18; January 4, 1979, p. 19.

47. *The New York Times*, November 8, 1979, p. A-21.

48. *Columbus Board of Education v. Penick*, 443 U.S. 449 (1979).

49. *Dayton Board of Education v. Brinkman*, 443 U.S. 526 (1979).

50. John B. McConahay, "Self-Interest Versus Racial Attitudes as Correlates of Anti-Busing Attitudes in Louisville: Is It the Buses or the Blacks?" *Journal of Politics* 44, no. 3 (August 1982): 692–720.

51. *The New York Times*, July 20, 1977, p. 10.

52. *The New York Times*, January 10, 1981, p. 12.

53. *The New York Times*, March 10, 1983, p. 10.

54. *The New York Times*, December 8, 1983.

55. *The New York Times*, February 9, 1984, p. 4.

56. *The New York Times*, March 22, 1981, p. 14.

57. *The New York Times*, March 16, 1981, p. 11.

58. *The New York Times*, September 11, 1981, p. 1.

59. *The New York Times*, July 1, 1982, p. 13.

60. *The New York Times*, January 26, 1984, p. 1.

61. *The New York Times*, November 4, 1986, p. 1. Also see *Newsweek*, November 17, 1986, pp. 60–61.

62. Frederick M. Wirt, "Institutionalization: Prison and School Policies," in *Politics in the American States: A Comparative Analysis*, 4th ed., eds. Virginia Gray, Herbert Jacob, and Kenneth N. Vines (Boston: Little, Brown, 1983), p. 310.

63. McConahy, "Self-Interest Versus Racial Attitudes," pp. 692–720.

64. *The New York Times,* June 8, 1988, p. 23.

65. David J. Armor, statement submitted to the Committee on the Judiciary, United States Senate, *Hearings on the Fourteenth Amendment and School Busing*, 97th Congress, 1st sess., May 14, 1981.

66. Willis O. Hawley, ed., *Effective School Desegregation* (Beverly Hills, Calif.: SAGE Publications, 1981).

67. *Serrano v. Priest*, 5 Cal. 3d 584 (1971).

68. *Rodriguez v. San Antonio School District*, 411 U.S. 59 (1973).

69. *Robinson v. Cahill*, 355 A.2d 129, 69 N.J. 1449 (1975). For an excellent background on the history of this case, see Richard Lehne, *The Quest for Justice: The Politics of School Finance Reform* (New York: Longman, 1978).

70. Margaret E. Goertz, *Money and Education in New Jersey: The Hard Choices Ahead* (Princeton, N.J.: Education Policy Research Institute, Educational Testing Service, 1981), pp. 3, 31.

71. Richard F. Elmore and Milbrey Wallin McLaughlin, *Reform and Retrenchment: The Politics of California School Finance Reform* (Cambridge, Mass.: Ballinger, 1982), pp. 5, 214–215.

72. *The New York Times*, April 30, 1987, p. 11.

73. Mark Schneider and John Logan, "Fiscal Implications of Class Segregation," *Urban Affairs Quarterly* 16, no. 1 (September 1981): 29.

74. See Richard Child Hill, "Separate and Unequal: Governmental Inequality in the Metropolis," *The American Political Science Review* 68, no. 4 (December 1974): 1560–1561.

75. Janet K. Boles, "Making Cities Work for Women," *Urban Affairs Quarterly* 18, no. 4 (June

1983): 573–580.

76. Rosalie G. Genovese, "A Women's Self-Help Network as a Response to Service Needs in the Suburbs," in *Women and the American City*, eds. Catharine R. Stimpson, Elsa Dixler, Martha J. Nelson, and Kathryn B. Yatrakis (Chicago: University of Chicago Press, 1981), p. 248.

77. See Sylvia Fava, "Women's Place in the New Suburbia," in *New Space for Women*, eds. Gerda R. Wekerle, Rebecca Peterson, and David Morley (Boulder, Colo.: Westview, 1980); and Boles, "Making Cities Work for Women."

78. Boles, "Making Cities Work for Women," p. 574; and Susan Saegert, "Masculine Cities and Feminine Suburbs: Polarized Ideas, Contradictory Realities," in *Women and the American City*, pp. 100–104.

79. Robert C. Wood, *Suburbia: Its People and Their Politics* (Boston: Houghton Mifflin, 1958), p. 9.

80. See Wilbur R. Thompson, *A Preface to Urban Economics* (Baltimore: The Johns Hopkins Press, 1965), pp. 115–120.

81. Advisory Commission on Intergovernmental Relations, *Urban America and the Federal System* (Washington, D.C.: U.S. Government Printing Office, 1969), pp. 9–10.

82. A study of suburbs of Buffalo, New York, and Milwaukee, Wisconsin, found very little class integration. Richard F. Hamilton, *Class and Politics in the United States* (New York: Wiley, 1972), pp. 155–180.

83. Hill, "Separate and Unequal."

Chapter 11

1. Robert C. Wood, *Suburbia: Its People and Their Politics* (Boston: Houghton Mifflin, 1958), chap. 7 and pp. 232–241. On the concept of "Gargantua," see Robert C. Wood, "The New Metropolis: Green Belts, Grass Roots or Gargantua," *The American Political Science Review* 52, no. 1 (March 1958): 108–122. Also see his *1400 Governments: The Political Economy of the New York Metropolitan Region* (Cambridge, Mass.: Harvard University Press, 1961).

2. Scott Greer, *The Emerging City* (New York: The Free Press, 1962), pp. 141, 149.

3. Wood, *Suburbia*, pp. 282–285.

4. Advisory Commission on Intergovernmental Relations, *Urban America and the Federal System* (Washington, D.C.: U.S. Government Printing Office, 1969), pp. 82–83.

5. See Joseph F. Zimmerman, "Substate Regional Government: Designing a New Procedure," *National Civic Review* 61, no. 6 (June 1972): 286. Zimmerman writes that "Govermental irresponsibility exists in the typical substate region encompassing two or more counties. . . . A regional government is needed now

in most metropolitan areas."

6. Luther Gulick, *The Metropolitan Problem and American Ideas* (New York: Knopf, 1962), p. 24.

7. Glen Sparrow and Dana Brown, "Black Water, Red Tape; Anatomy of a Border Problem," *National Civic Review* 75, no. 4 (July–August 1986): 214–218.

8. Amos H. Hawley and Basil G. Zimmer, *The Metropolitan Community: Its People and Government* (Beverly Hills, Calif.: SAGE Publications, 1970), pp. 2–3.

9. Ibid., p. 3.

10. *Reshaping Government in Metropolitan Areas* (New York: Committee for Economic Development, 1970).

11. John C. Bollens et al., *Exploring the Metropolitan Community* (Berkeley: University of California Press, 1961), pp. 70–71. The surgical metaphor is Bollens's and Schmandt's.

12. Hawley and Zimmer, *The Metropolitan Community*, pp. 91–92.

13. Charles R. Adrian, "Metropology: Folklore and Field Research," *Public Administration Review* 21, no. 3 (Summer 1961): 148–157.

14. Ibid., p. 150.

15. Hawley and Zimmer, *The Metropolitan Community*, pp. 91–92.

16. Vincent Ostrom and Elinor Ostrom, "Public Choice: A Different Approach to the Study of Public Administration," *Public Administration Review* 31 (March 1971): 203–216.

17. Edward C. Banfield and Morton Grodzins, *Government and Housing in Metropolitan Areas* (New York: McGraw-Hill, 1958), p. 34.

18. Joseph F. Zimmerman, "Can Government Functions Be 'Rationally Assigned'?" *National Civic Review* 73, no. 3 (March 1983): 125–131.

19. Daniel R. Grant, "Metro's Three Faces," *National Civic Review* 55, no. 6 (June 1966): 317–324.

20. Hawley and Zimmer, *The Metropolitan Community*, pp. 95–96.

21. Adrian, "Metropology," p. 151.

22. Norton E. Long, "The Local Community as an Ecology of Games," *American Journal of Sociology* 64 (November 1958): 251–261. Also see his *The Polity* (Chicago: Rand McNally, 1962), pp. 156–164.

23. Banfield and Grodzins, *Government and Housing*, p. 42.

24. Ibid., pp. 36–38.

25. Vincent Ostrom, Charles M. Tiebout, and Robert Warren, "Organizing Government in Metropolitan Areas: A Theoretical Inquiry," *The American Political Science Review* 55, no. 4 (December 1961): 838, 842.

26. On the distinction between public and private goods, see Ostrom and Ostrom, "Public Choice: A Different Approach," pp. 206–207.

27. *Serrano v. Priest*, 5 Cal.3d 584, 487 P.2d 1241 (1971).

28. Matthew Holden, Jr., "The Governance of the Metropolis as a Problem in Diplomacy," *Journal of Politics* 26 (August 1964): 627–647. Also see Thomas R. Dye, "Metropolitan Integration by Bargaining Among Sub-Areas," *American Behavioral Scientist* 5 (May 1962): 11.

29. Wood, *Suburbia*, p. 84.

30. Stuart A. MacCorkle, *Municipal Annexation in Texas* (Austin: Institute of Public Affairs, University of Texas, 1965), pp. 28–36.

31. Arnold Fleischman, "Sunbelt Boosterism: The Politics of Postwar Growth and Annexation in San Antonio," in *The Rise of the Sunbelt Cities*, vol. 14, Urban Affairs Annual Reviews, eds. David C. Perry and Alfred J. Watkins (Beverly Hills, Calif.: SAGE Publications, 1977), pp. 151–168.

32. Arnold Fleischman, "The Politics of Annexation: A Preliminary Assessment of Competing Paradigms," *Social Science Quarterly* 67, no. 1 (March 1987): 128–142.

33. Advisory Commission on Intergovernmental Relations, *Report A-44: Substate Regionalism and the Federal System, Volume III. The Challenge of Local Government* (Washington, D.C.: U.S. Government Printing Office, 1974), p. 77.

34. Vincent L. Marando, "City–County Consolidation: Reform, Regionalism, Referenda, and Requiem," *Western Political Quarterly* 32, no. 4 (December 1979): 409–422.

35. Daniel R. Grant, "Urban and Suburban Nashville: A Case Study in Metropolitanism," *The Journal of Politics* 17 (February 1965): 85. Also on the background to Nashville, see Brett W. Hawkins, *Nashville Metro: The Politics of City-County Consolidation* (Nashville, Tenn.: Vanderbilt University Press, 1966); and David A. Booth, *Metropolitics: The Nashville Consolidation* (East Lansing, Mich.: Institute for Community Development and Services, Michigan State University, 1963).

36. William C. Havard, Jr., and Floyd C. Corty, *Rural-Urban Consolidation: The Merger of Governments in the Baton Rouge Area* (Baton Rouge, La.: Louisiana State University Press, 1964), pp. 146–147.

37. Melvin B. Mogulof, *Five Metropolitan Governments* (Washington, D.C.: The Urban Institute, 1973), p. 22.

38. This point is made by R. Steven Hill and William P. Maxam in their article, "Unigov: The First Year," *National Civic Review*, June 1971, pp. 310–

314, especially p. 310. Also see York Wilbern, "Unigov: Local Government Reorganization in Indianapolis," in Advisory Commission on Intergovernmental Relations, *Report A–41: Substate Regionalism and the Federal System, Volume II, Regional Governance: Promise and Performance—Case Studies* (Washington, D.C.: U.S. Government Printing Office, 1973), pp. 49–51.

39. John M. De Grove, "The City of Jacksonville: Consolidation in Action," in Advisory Commission on Intergovernmental Relations, *Report A–41: Volume II*, pp. 19–20.

40. Daniel R. Grant, "Metropolitics and Professional Political Leadership: The Case of Nashville," *Annals of the American Academy of Political and Social Sciences* 353 (May 1964): 78.

41. Scott Greer, *Metropolitics: A Study of Political Culture* (New York: Wiley, 1963), pp. 7–18.

42. Howard W. Hallman, *Small and Large Together: Governing the Metropolis*, vol. 56, Sage Library of Social Research (Beverly Hills, Calif.: SAGE Publications, 1977), p. 85.

43. De Grove, "The City of Jacksonville," p. 20.

44. Patricia S. Florestano and Vincent L. Marando, *The States and the Metropolis* (New York: Marcel Dekker, 1981), p. 200.

45. Zimmerman, "Metropolitan Reform," p. 533.

46. Willbern, "Unigov," p. 63.

47. Mogulof, *Five Metropolitan Governments*, p. 46; and De Grove, "The City of Jacksonville," p. 20.

48. Willbern, "Unigov," pp. 61–62.

49. Advisory Commission on Intergovernmental Relations, *Report M–72: Profile of County Government: An Information Report* (Washington, D.C.: U.S. Government Printing Office, 1972), p. 13. Later references to the percentage of counties using the county manager, county administrator, and county executive forms of government are also taken from this source.

50. On the weaknesses of traditional county government and proposals for reform, see Advisory Commission on Intergovernmental Relations, *Report M–61: For a More Perfect Union: County Reform* (Washington, D.C.: U.S. Government Printing Office, 1971). The discussion that follows in the text is taken principally from this source.

51. *Reshaping Government in Metropolitan Areas*, pp. 16–18.

52. See Hallman, *Small and Large Together*, p. 96. Also see League of Women Voters of the United States Education Fund, *Supercity/Hometown, U.S.A.: Prospects for Two-Tier Government* (New York: Praeger, 1974).

53. D.B.S. Paul, "Metropolitan Dade County Government: A Review of Accomplishments," from an address presented to the Local Government Law Section, American Bar Association, Miami Beach, Florida, August 8, 1965. The printed text can be found in Joseph F. Zimmerman, *Government of the Metropolis: Selected Readings* (New York: Holt, Rinehart and Winston, 1968), pp. 202–203.

54. Quoted in Edward Sofen, *The Miami Metropolitan Experiment* (Bloomington, Ind.: Indiana University Press, 1963), p. 72.

55. Aileen Lotz, "Metropolitan Dade County," in Advisory Commission on Intergovernmental Relations, *Report A–41: Volume II*, p. 7.

56. Oliver P. Williams, *Metropolitan Political Analysis: A Social Access Approach* (New York: The Free Press, 1971), pp. 86–93.

57. Grant, "Metro's Three Faces," p. 407.

58. See Thomas J. Wood, "Dade County Voters Reject Amendment," *National Civic Review* 61, no. 5 (May 1972): 254–255.

59. "Dade County Reviews Charter," *National Civic Review* 71, no. 5 (May 1982): 265–266. The first charter review in 1981 called for extending the two-tier system to the unincorporated areas of the county by creating limited-purpose municipalities there to handle zoning and purchase of services. This has not been done, however.

60. Irving G. McNayr, "A Report to the Chairman and the Members of the Board of County Commissioners," September 25, 1962. The printed text of this report can be found in Joseph F. Zimmerman, *Government of the Metropolis*, p. 199.

61. Lotz, "Metropolitan Dade County," p. 10.

62. Mogulof, *Five Metropolitan Governments*, pp. 48–49.

63. The following account relies heavily on *Reshaping Government in Metropolitan Areas*, pp. 7–83, and Frank Smallwood, *Metro Toronto a Decade Later* (Toronto: Bureau of Municipal Research, 1963). For another analysis of the Toronto experiment, see Harold Kaplan, *Urban Political Systems: A Functional Analysis of Metro Toronto* (New York: Columbia University Press, 1967).

64. See Grant's "Metro's Three Faces."

65. J. Edwin Benton and Darwin Gamble, "City/County Consolidation and Economies of Scale: Evidence from a Time Series in Jacksonville, Florida," *Social Science Quarterly* 65, no. 1 (March 1984): 190–198.

66. C. James Owen and York Willbern, *Governing Metropolitan Indianapolis: The Politics of Unigov* (Berkeley, Calif.: University of California Press, 1985), chapter 7.

67. Grant, "Metro's Three Faces," p. 322. Also see McArthur, "The Metropolitan Government of Nashville," pp. 31–32.

68. For a positive assessment of Miami's Metro, see Lotz, "Metropolitan Dade County," p. 10. A less complimentary assessment is given in Mogulof, *Five Metropolitan Governments*, pp. 27–48, 59.

69. Williams, *Metropolitan Political Analysis*, pp. 86–93.

70. Lee Sloan and Robert M. French, "Black Rule in the Urban South?" *TRANS-action* (November/December 1971): 29–34.

71. Advisory Commission on Intergovernmental Relations, *Report A-44; Volume III, The Challenge of Local Governmental Reorganization*, p. 102.

72. Hawkins, "Nashville Metro: The Politics of City–County Consolidation," pp. 132–133.

73. Grant, "Metro's Three Faces," p. 403.

74. Daniel R. Grant, "A Comparison of Predictions and Experiences with Nashville 'Metro'," *Urban Affairs Quarterly* 1, no. 1 (September 1964): 34–54, especially 51–53.

75. Willbern, "Unigov," pp. 71–72.

76. Vincent L. Marando and Carl Reggie Whitley, "City–County Consolidation: An Overview of Voter Response," *Urban Affairs Quarterly* 8, no. 2 (December 1972): 181–204, especially 190.

77. Joan Carver, "Responsiveness and Consolidation: A Case Study," *Urban Affairs Quarterly* 9, no. 2 (December 1973): 246.

78. Willbern, "Unigov," p. 63.

79. De Grove, "The City of Jacksonville," p. 24.

80. Mogulof, *Five Metropolitan Governments*, p. 117.

81. De Grove, "The City of Jacksonville," p. 24.

82. See Willis Hawley, *Blacks and Metropolitan Governance: The Stakes of Reform* (Berkeley, Calif.: Institute of Governmental Studies, University of California, 1972).

83. Mogulof, *Five Metropolitan Governments*, p. 119.

84. Steven P. Erie, John J. Kirlin, and Francine F. Rabinovitz, "Can Something Be Done? Propositions on the Performance of Metropolitan Institutions," in *Reform of Metropolitan Governments*, ed. Lowdon Wingo (Washington, D.C.: Resources for the Future, 1972), p. 24.

85. John R. Logan and Mark Schneider, "Governmental Organization and City/Suburb Income Inequality, 1960–1970," *Urban Affairs Quarterly* 17, no. 3 (March 1972): 303–318.

86. Scott A. Bollens, "A Political-Ecological Analysis of Income in the Metropolitan Areas," *Urban Affairs Quarterly* 22, no. 2 (December 1986): 221–224.

87. Elinor Ostrom, "The Social Stratification–Government Inequality Thesis Explored," *Urban Affairs Quarterly* 19, no. 1 (September 1983): 91–112.

88. On St. Louis's failure to achieve its metropolitan reform, see Robert H. Salisbury, "Interests, Parties, and Governmental Structures in St. Louis," *Western Political Quarterly* 13, no. 2 (June 1960): 500–501; Edward C. Banfield, *Big City Politics* (New York: Random House, 1965), pp. 121–124; Henry J. Schmandt, P.G. Steinbicker, and G.D. Wendel, *Metropolitan Reform in St. Louis* (New York: Holt, Rinehart and Winston, 1961); and Scott Greer, *Metropolitics: A Study of Political Culture* (New York: Wiley, 1963). On Cleveland's failure, see James A. Norton, *The Metro Experience* (Cleveland, Ohio: The Press of Western Reserve University, 1963); Estal E. Sparlin, "Cleveland Seeks New Metro Solution," *National Civic Review* 69, no. 3 (March 1960): 143; and Richard A. Watson and John H. Romani, "Metropolitan Government for Metropolitan Cleveland: An Analysis of the Voting Record," *Midwest Journal of Political Science* 5, no. 4 (November 1961): 365–390.

89. Edward Sofen, *The Miami Metropolitan Experiment* (Bloomington, Ind.: Indiana University Press, 1963), pp. 74–75.

90. *National Civic Review* 62, no. 8 (September 1973): 449; 63, no. 1 (January 1974): 32–33; 68, no. 1 (January 1979): 43.

91. Sharon P. Krefetz and Alan B. Sharof, "City–County Merger Attempts: The Role of Political Factors," *National Civic Review* 66, no. 4 (April 1977): 178.

92. For sources on these surveys, see note 90. For surveys in addition to St. Louis and Cleveland, see Amos H. Hawley and Basil G. Zimmer, "Resistance to Unification in a Metropolitan Community," in *Community Political Systems*, ed. Morris Janowitz (Glencoe, Ill.: The Free Press, 1961), pp. 164–167. A similar result was discovered from a survey in Dayton, Ohio; see John C. Bollens et al., *Metropolitan Challenge* (Dayton, Ohio: Metropolitan Community Studies, 1959), p. 241.

93. Greer, *Metropolitics: A Study of Political Culture*, pp. 7–18.

94. Thomas A. Henderson and Walter A. Rosenbaum, "Prospects for Consolidation of Local Governments: The Role of Local Elites in Electoral Outcomes," *American Journal of Political Science* 17, no. 4 (November 1973): 695–720.

95. Doyle W. Buckwalter, "No on Merger for Salt Lake," *National Civic Review* 68, no. 3 (March 1979): 150–151.

96. This question is examined extensively by

Thomas M. Scott in his article, "Metropolitan Government Reorganization Proposals," *Western Political Quarterly*, 21, no. 2 (June 1968): 489, 498–507.

97. See *The Federalist Papers*, ed. Clinton Rossiter (New York: New American Library, 1961), No. 10, by James Madison, pp. 77–84.

Chapter 12

1. Oliver P. Williams, *Metropolitan Political Analysis* (New York: The Free Press, 1971), p. 93.

2. This has been noted above. For Miami, see Edward Sofen, *The Miami Metropolitan Experiment* (Bloomington, Ind.: Indiana University Press, 1963). For Toronto, see Frank Smallwood, *Toronto: The Problems of Metropolitan Unity* (Toronto: Bureau of Municipal Research, 1963).

3. H. Paul Friesema, "Cities, Suburbs, and Short-lived Models of Metropolitan Politics," in *The Urbanization of the Suburbs*, vol. 7, *Urban Affairs Annual Reviews*, eds. Louis H. Masotti and Jeffrey K. Hadden (Beverly Hills, Calif.: SAGE Publications, 1973), p. 242.

4. For a summary of the stages of planning discussed here, see Thad L. Beyle and George T. Lathrop, "Planning and Politics: On Grounds of Incompatibility?" in *Planning and Politics: Uneasy Partnership*, eds. Thad L. Beyle and George T. Lathrop (New York: Odyssey Press, 1970), pp. 3–5.

5. For a detailed discussion of the Chicago and Boston Plans and their relation to the City Beautiful and the City Functional movements, see Mel Scott, *American City Planning Since 1890* (Berkeley, Calif.: University of California Press, 1971), chaps. 2 and 3.

6. See Alan Altshuler, "Decision-making and the Trend Toward Pluralistic Planning," in *Urban Planning in Transition*, ed. Ernest Erber (New York: Grossman, 1970), pp. 183–186, 327–331.

7. Francine Rabinovitz, *City Politics and Planning* (New York: Atherton Press, 1969), pp. 8–9.

8. Deil S. Wright, "Governmental Forms and Planning Functions: The Relation of Organizational Structures to Planning Practice," in Beyle and Lathrop, eds., *Planning and Politics: Uneasy Partnership*, pp. 68–105, especially p. 69.

9. Rabinovitz, *City Politics and Planning*, pp. 9–11.

10. Wright, "Governmental Forms and Planning Functions," p. 73.

11. Scott, *American City Planning Since 1890*, pp. 541–547.

12. Wright, "Governmental Forms and Planning Functions," p. 87. Wright's study of 300 city planners found that two-thirds of them defined planning in physical or economic terms. Only a third defined

planning in terms of what the author called people's human needs.

13. John C. Bollens and Henry J. Schmandt, *The Metropolis: Its People, Politics, and Economic Life*, 2nd ed. (New York: Harper & Row, 1970), p. 274.

14. Rabinovitz, *City Politics and Planning*, pp. 3, 132–133.

15. Scott, *American City Planning Since 1890*, pp. 507–508.

16. See Herbert Gans, *The Levittowners: Ways of Life and Politics in a New Suburban Community* (New York: Random House, 1967), especially chap. 1, "The Planners of Levittown," and chap. 14, "Politics and Planning."

17. Ibid., pp. 386, 17, and 18.

18. See Jane Jacobs, *The Death and Life of Great American Cities* (New York: Vintage Books, 1961).

19. Wright, "Governmental Forms and Planning Functions," p. 79.

20. The New York Regional Plan of 1929 is discussed by Scott, *American City Planning Since 1890*, pp. 260–265, 447–448.

21. William H. Nash, Jr., "The Effectiveness of Metropolitan Planning," a paper presented to the Metropolitan Area Planning Council of the Commonwealth of Massachusetts, June 18, 1965. The text of a revised edition can be found in H. Wentworth Eldredge, ed., *Taming Megalopolis: Vol. II, How to Manage an Urbanized World* (Garden City, N.Y.: Doubleday, 1967), pp. 699–700.

22. Quoted in Terrance Sandalow, "Federal Grants and the Reform of State and Local Governments," in *Financing the Metropolis: Public Policy in Urban Economics*, vol. 4, *Urban Affairs Annual Reviews*, ed. John P. Crecine (Beverly Hills, Calif.: SAGE Publications, 1970), p. 182.

23. For background on the evolution of the A–95 process, see Advisory Commission on Intergovernmental Relations, *Report A-43: Substate Regionalism and the Federal System, Vol. I, Regional Decision Making: New Strategies for Substate Districts*, (Washington, D.C.: U.S. Government Printing Office, 1973), pp. 140–166.

24. Cole Blease Graham, Jr., "State-Local Responses to Federal Overhaul of The A–95 Review Process," a paper presented at the Annual Meeting of The American Political Science Association, Chicago, Illinois, September 1–4, 1983.

25. David B. Walker, "Snow White and the 17 Dwarfs: From Metro Cooperation to Governance," *National Civic Review* 76, no. 1 (January–February 1987): 14–27.

26. Scott, *American City Planning Since 1890*, pp. 513–518.

27. Ibid.

28. David C. Ranney, *Planning and Politics in the Metropolis* (Columbus, Ohio: Merrill, 1969), p. 104.

29. John Friedmann, "The Future of Comprehensive Urban Planning: A Critique," *Public Administration Review* 31, no. 3 (May/June 1971): 317.

30. Edward C. Banfield, "The Uses and Limitations of Metropolitan Planning in Massachusetts," a paper presented to the Metropolitan Area Planning Council of the Commonwealth of Massachusetts, June 18, 1965. The text can be found in Eldredge, ed., *Taming Megalopolis: Vol. II*, pp. 712–714.

31. This charge is made of the Cleveland COG by Frances Frisken, "The Metropolis and the Central City: Can One Government Unite Them?" *Urban Affairs Quarterly* 8, no. 3 (June 1973): 395–422.

32. Rabinovitz, *City Politics and Planning*, p. 7.

33. Ranney, *Planning and Politics in the Metropolis*, pp. 104–107.

34. F. Stuart Chapin, Jr., *Urban Land Use Planning*, 2nd ed. (Urbana, Ill.: University of Illinois Press, 1965), pp. 60–62.

35. Rabinovitz, *City Politics and Planning*, pp. 154–157.

36. Ranney, *Planning and Politics in the Metropolis*, p. 155.

37. For an excellent discussion of citizen involvement in freeway controversies, see Alan Lupo, Frank Colcord, and Edmund P. Fowler, *Rites of Way: The Politics of Transportation in Boston and the U.S. City* (Boston: Little, Brown, 1971).

38. There are many excellent descriptions of the battles over urban renewal and urban renovation. One of the most highly readable, interesting descriptions of a resident's frustrations in fighting the destruction of the old Hull House neighborhood in Chicago is contained in Studs Terkel's interview with Florence Scala in Studs Terkel, *Division Street: America* (New York: Avon Books, 1967), pp. 29–38. The battle over the expansion of the University of Chicago into the Hyde Park–Kenwood section is analyzed by Peter H. Rossi and Robert A. Dentler, *The Politics of Urban Renewal: The Chicago Findings* (New York: The Free Press, 1961).

39. Thomas M. Scott, "Suburban Governmental Structures," in *The Urbanization of the Suburbs*, vol. 7, *Urban Affairs Annual Reviews*, eds. Louis H. Masotti and Jeffrey K. Hadden (Beverly Hills, Calif.: SAGE Publications, 1973), p. 236.

40. See Paul Davidoff, "Advocacy and Pluralism in Planning," *Journal of the American Institute of Planners* 31, no. 4 (November 1965): 331–338.

41. Herbert Gans, *People and Plans: Essays on Urban Problems and Solutions* (New York: Basic Books, 1968), pp. 72–74.

42. Michael L. Vasu, *Politics and Planning* (Chapel Hill, N.C.: University of North Carolina Press, 1979), p. 175.

43. Michael L. Vasu, "Planning Theory and Practice in the 1980s," *Urban Affairs Quarterly* 17, no. 1 (September 1981): 114.

44. On highways, see Lupo, Colcord, and Fowler, *Rites of Way;* on urban renewal see Jewell Bellush and Murray Hausknecht, eds., *Urban Renewal: People, Politics and Planning* (Garden City, N.Y.: Doubleday, 1969).

45. Thad L. Beyle and George T. Lathrop, "Planning and Politics: On Grounds of Incompatibility?", p. 9.

46. Gans, *People and Plans*, pp. 72–74.

47. See Alan S. Kravitz, "Mandarinism: Planning as Handmaiden to Conservative Politics," in Beyle and Lathrop, eds., *Planning and Politics: Uneasy Partnership*, pp. 240–267. Also see Robert Goodman, *After the Planners* (New York: Simon & Schuster, 1971), pp. 171–175.

48. John W. Dyckman, "Social Planning in the American Democracy," in *Urban Planning in Transition*, ed. Ernest Erber (New York: Grossman, 1970), pp. 27–44, especially p. 28.

49. Vasu, *Politics and Planning*, pp. 113, 127, 132.

50. This account of the Washington Metropolitan Council of Governments is taken principally from Roscoe C. Martin, *Metropolis in Transition* (Washington, D.C.: U.S. Housing and Home Finance Agency, 1964), pp. 39–50.

51. Melvin B. Mogulof, *Governing Metropolitan Areas* (Washington, D.C.: The Urban Institute, 1971), p. 1.

52. Walker, "Snow White and the 17 Dwarfs," pp. 14–27.

53. Royce Hanson, *Metropolitan Councils of Government*, a report for the Advisory Commission on Intergovernmental Relations (Washington, D.C.: U.S. Government Printing Office, 1966), p. 27.

54. Alan Edward Bent, *Escape from Anarchy: A Strategy for Urban Survival* (memphis, Tenn.: Memphis State University Press, 1972), p. 85.

55. Victor Jones, "Bay Area Regionalism: Institutions, Processes, and Programs," in Advisory Commission on Intergovernmental Relations, *Report A-41: Substate Regionalism and the Federal System, Regional Governance: Promise and Performance* (Washington, D.C.: U.S. Government Printing Office, 1973), pp. 75–110.

56. See Frisken, "The Metropolis and the Central City," 395–422.

57. Philip W. Barnes, *Metropolitan Coalitions: A Study of Councils of Government in Texas* (Austin, Tex.: Institute of Public Affairs, University of Texas, 1969), p. 67.

58. Mogulof, *Governing Metropolitan Areas*, p. 15.

59. Joseph F. Zimmerman, "Can Governmental Functions be 'Rationally Reassigned'?" *National Civic Review* 73, no. 3 (March 1983): 125–131.

60. Demonstration Cities and Metropolitan Development Act of 1966, section 204. Quoted in Barnes, *Metropolitan Coalitions*, p. 14. However, the I.C.A. of 1968 did grant review authority for social issues.

61. Frisken, "The Metropolis and the Central City," p. 399.

62. This account of NOACA is taken from Frisken, "The Metropolis and the Central City," pp. 395–422.

63. Walker, "Snow White and the 17 Dwarfs," pp. 14–27.

64. *Intergovernmental Perspectives* 10, no. 2 (Spring 1984): 4.

65. See John J. Harrigan and William C. Johnson, *Governing the Twin Cities Region: The Metropolitan Council in Comparative Perspective* (Minneapolis: The University of Minnesota Press, 1978), pp. 39–64.

66. Ibid., p. 61.

67. Mogulof, *Governing Metropolitan Areas*, p. 82.

68. Stanley Baldinger, *Planning and Governing the Metropolis: The Twin Cities Experience* (New York: Praeger, 1971), pp. 120–124.

69. Ted Kolderie, "Policy Leadership, Not Swamp of Detail is Council's Role," *Metro Monitor*, Metropolitan Council Publication 6, no. 1 (November 1979): 2.

70. See "Innovation by Increments: The Twin Cities as a Case Study in Metropolitan Reform," *Western Political Quarterly* 31, no. 2 (June 1978): 206–218.

71. See John J. Harrigan and William C. Johnson, "Trouble in River Cities: Metropolitan Governance Under Attack," a paper presented at the Midwest Political Science Association convention, Chicago, Illinois, April, 1986. Also see William C. Johnson and John J. Harrigan, "Political Stress and Metropolitan Governance: The Twin Cities Experience," *State and Local Government Review* 19, no. 3 (Fall 1987): 108–113.

72. This account relies heavily on Anthony G. White, "Portland Merges Regional Agencies," *National Civic Review* 67, no. 7 (July 1978): 329; *The New York Times*, March 22, 1979, p. A-16; Carl Abbott, *Portland: Planning, Politics, and Growth in a Twentieth-Century City* (Lincoln, Nebr.: University of Nebraska Press, 1983), pp. 254–263.

73. Abbott, *Portland*, p. 262.

74. Ibid., p. 263.

75. Interview with Portland Metropolitan Service District Executive Director Rick Gustafson at Portland, Ore., March 4, 1983.

76. Steven P. Erie, John J. Kirlin, and Francine F. Rabinovitz, "Can Something Be Done? Propositions on the Performance of Metropolitan Institutions," in *Reform of Metropolitan Governments*, ed. Lowdon Wingo (Washington, D.C.: Resources for the Future, 1972), p. 24.

77. Ibid.

78. Joan Carver, "Responsiveness and Consolidation: A Case Study," *Urban Affairs Quarterly* 9, no. 2 (December 1973): 243, 246.

Chapter 13

1. James L. Sundquist, *Making Federalism Work: A Study of Program Coordination at the Community Level* (Washington, D.C.: The Brookings Institution, 1969), p. 279.

2. Data on grants-in-aid taken from *Significant Features of Fiscal Federalism 1982/83* (Washington, D.C.: The Advisory Commission on Intergovernmental Relations, 1983), p. 66.

3. National Governors' Association, *1982 Governors' Guide to Block Grant Implementation* (Washington, D.C.: National Governors Association; Federalism Information Center, February, 1982), p. 29.

4. Suzanne Farkas, *Urban Lobbying* (New York: New York University Press, 1971), p. 60.

5. For a concise background on early public housing programs, see Jewell Bellush and Murray Hausknecht, "Urban Renewal: An Historical Overview," in *Urban Renewal: People, Politics and Planning*, eds. Jewell Bellush and Murray Hausknecht (Garden City, N.Y.: Doubleday, 1967), pp. 3–16.

6. A concise summary of the operating procedures of the public housing programs under the Public Housing Administration is provided by Roscoe C. Martin, *The Cities and the Federal System* (New York: Atherton Press, 1965), pp. 128–132.

7. Jeanne Lowe, *Cities in a Race with Time: Progress and Poverty in America's Renewing Cities* (New York: Random House, 1968), pp. 232–233.

8. Theodore Lowi, *The End of Liberalism: Ideology, Policy and the Crisis of Public Authority* (New York: Norton, 1969), pp. 251–266.

9. See, for example, Harrison Salisbury's description of the Fort Greene project in Brooklyn, *The Shook-Up Generation* (New York: Harper & Row, 1958), pp. 73–88.

10. For background on the Pruitt-Igoe housing project, see Nicholas J. Demerath, "St. Louis Public Housing Study Sets Off Community Development to Meet Social Needs," *Journal of Housing* 19 (October 15, 1962): 472–478. For information on the demise of Pruitt-Igoe, see Jane Holtz Kay, "Architecture," *Nation* 217 (September 24, 1973): 284–286; and G. McCue, "$57,000,000 Later: New Effort to Put Pruitt-Igoe Together Again," *Architectural Forum* 138 (May 1973): 42–45. Also see Lee Rainwater, "The Lessons of Pruitt-Igoe," *Public Interest*, no. 8 (Summer 1967): 116–126; and Eugene J. Meehan, *Public Housing Policy* (New Brunswick, N.J.: Rutgers University Press, 1975).

11. Jewell Bellush and Murray Hausknecht, "Public Housing: The Contexts of Failure," in Bellush and Hausknecht, eds., *Urban Renewal*, p. 456; and Bellush and Hausknecht, "Public Housing: It Was Meant to Fail," in Bellush and Hausknecht, eds., *Urban Renewal*, pp. 413–414.

12. See Oscar Newman, *Defensible Space: Crime Prevention Through Urban Design* (New York: Macmillan, 1972).

13. Bellush and Hausknecht, eds., *Urban Renewal*, pp. 413–414.

14. See Leonard Downie, Jr., *Mortgage on America: The Real Costs of Real Estate Speculation* (New York: Praeger, 1974), p. 115.

15. *Hill v. Gautreaux*, 96 S. Ct. 1538 (1976).

16. Mario Cuomo, *Forest Hills Diary: The Crisis of Low-Income Housing* (New York: Vintage Books, 1975).

17. For criticisms of Section 8, see Irving Welfeld, "American Housing Policy: Perverse Programs by Prudent People," *The Public Interest*, no. 48 (Summer 1977): 128–144.

18. *The New York Times*, April 14, 1987, p. 1.

19. *Wall Street Journal*, June 3, 1987, p. 15.

20. *Wall Street Journal*, December 23, 1987, p. 40.

21. Robert L. Lineberry and Ira Sharkansky, *Urban Politics and Public Policy* (New York: Harper & Row, 1971), p. 336.

22. Ibid., p. 337. On redevelopment in Newark, see Harold Kaplan, *Urban Renewal Politics* (New York: Columbia University Press, 1963).

23. Lowe, *Cities in a Race with Time*, pp. 68–72.

24. Lowi, *The End of Liberalism*, pp. 251–266.

25. See Jane Jacobs, *The Death and Life of Great American Cities* (New York: Vintage Books, 1961).

26. See Chester W. Hartman, "A Rejoinder: Omissions in Evaluating Relocation Effectiveness Cited," *Journal of Housing* 23, no. 2 (February 1966): 88–89. Also see Herbert Gans, "The Failure of Urban Renewal: A Critique and Some Proposals," *Commen-*

tary, April 1965, pp. 29–37.

27. See Kaplan, *Urban Renewal Politics*.

28. Michael Danielson and Jamison Doig, *New York* (Berkeley, Calif.: University of California Press, 1982), pp. 297–310.

29. Douglas M. Fox, "Federal Urban Policies Since 1945," in *The New Urban Politics: Cities and the Federal Government*, ed. Douglas M. Fox (Pacific Palisades, Calif.: Goodyear Publishing, 1972), pp. 96–97.

30. Implementing the principle of compensatory education, however, proved very difficult. See Jerome T. Murphy, "The Education Bureaucracies Implement Novel Policy: The Politics of Title I of ESEA, 1965–1972," in *Policy and Politics in America*, ed. Sindler (Boston: Little, Brown, 1973), pp. 160–198. Also see Stephen K. Bailey and Edith K. Mosher, *ESEA: The Office of Education Administers a Law* (Syracuse, N.Y.: Syracuse University Press, 1968).

31. Farkas, *Urban Lobbying*, p. 60.

32. For a discussion of urban movements see Norman I. Fainstein and Susan S. Fainstein, *Urban Political Movements: The Search for Power by Minority Groups in American Cities* (Englewood Cliffs, N.J.: Prentice-Hall, 1974).

33. Sundquist, *Making Federalism Work*, pp. 3–5.

34. U.S. Office of Management and Budget, *Special Analyses: Budget of the United States Government, Fiscal Year 1975* (Washington, D.C.: U.S. Government Printing Office, 1974), p. 210. FY 1973 grants-in-aid equaled 23.5 percent of state and local budgets. In FY 1961 they equaled 12.6 percent.

35. Criticisms of grants-in-aid as not enabling states to establish their own priorities can be found in many textbooks on state and local government. See Thomas R. Dye, *Politics in States and Communities* (Englewood Cliffs, N.J.: Prentice-Hall, 1969), pp. 471–472; Duane Lockard, *The Politics of State and Local Government*, 2nd ed. (New York: Macmillan, 1969), pp. 36–42.

36. For critiques of the welfare system see Gilbert Y. Steiner, *The State of Welfare* (Washington, D.C.: The Brookings Institution, 1971); Frances Fox Piven and Richard A. Cloward, *Regulating the Poor: The Functions of Public Welfare* (New York: Pantheon, 1971); and Daniel P. Moynihan, *The Politics of a Guaranteed Income: The Nixon Administration and the Family Assistance Plan* (New York: Random House, 1973), especially chap. 2.

37. Lowe, *Cities in a Race with Time*, pp. 232–233.

38. Daniel P. Moynihan, *Maximum Feasible Misunderstanding: Community Action in the War on*

Poverty (New York: The Free Press, 1969).

39. See Edward C. Banfield, "Making a New Federal Program: Model Cities, 1964–1968," in *Policy and Politics in America: Six Case Studies*, ed. Allan P. Sindler (Boston: Little, Brown, 1973), pp. 124–169.

40. Martha Derthick, *New Towns in Town: Why a Federal Program Failed* (Washington, D.C.: The Urban Institute, 1972).

41. For a more positive view of the Great Society, see Sar A. Levitan and Rupert Taggart, "Great Society Did Succeed," *Political Science Quarterly* 91 (Winter 1976–77): 601–618.

42. Daniel P. Moynihan, "Toward a National Urban Policy," *The Public Interest* 17 (Fall 1969): 7.

43. Michael Reagan, *The New Federalism* (New York: Oxford University Press, 1972), p. 84.

44. Michael N. Danielson, *Federal-Metropolitan Politics and the Commuter Crisis* (New York: Columbia University Press, 1965), p. 189.

45. Roscoe C. Martin, *The Cities and the Federal System* (New York: Atherton Press, 1965), p. 146.

46. Robert C. Wood, *The Federal Government and the Cities*, pp. 52–54.

47. Reagan, *The New Federalism*, pp. 87–88.

48. The Advisory Commission on Intergovernmental Relations, *The Future of Federalism in the 1980s*, Report M-126 (Washington, D.C.: Advisory Commission on Intergovernmental Relations, July, 1981), p. 49.

49. *The New York Times*, March 19, 1978, p. E-6.

50. Paul R. Dommel, "Distribution Politics and Urban Policy," *Policy Studies Journal* 3, no. 4 (June 1975): 370–374.

51. See Raymond A. Rosenfeld, "Implementation of the Community Development Block Grant Program: Decentralization of Decision-Making and Centralization of Responsibility," a paper presented to the Midwest Political Science Association, Chicago, Illinois, April 21–23, 1977. Also see Danielson and Doig, *New York*, (chap. 9, "The Politics of Urban Regional Development").

52. Reagan, *The New Federalism*, pp. 130–131.

53. Norton Long, "A Marshall Plan for Cities?" *The Public Interest*, no. 46 (Winter 1977): 48–58.

54. See Myron A. Levine, "The President and National Urban Policy," a paper presented to the 1979 Annual Meeting of the Northeastern Political Science Association, Newark, New Jersey, November 9, 1979.

55. Rochelle L. Stanfield, "Federal Policy Makers Now Must Ask: Will It Hurt Cities?" *National Journal* (July 21, 1979): 1203–1206.

56. Michael J. Rich, "Learning to Live with Less: Federal Aid for Housing and Community Development in the 1980s," *Urban Politics and Urban Policy*

Section Newsletter I, no. 1 (Summer 1986): 13.

57. Myron A. Levine, "The Reagan Urban Policy: Efficient National Economic Growth and Public Sector Minimization," *Journal of Urban Affairs* 5, no. 1 (Winter 1983): 17–28.

58. John R. Logan, "Symposium: Urban Theory and National Urban Policy," *Urban Affairs Quarterly* 19, no. 1 (September 1983): 3–4.

59. Rochelle L. Stanfield, "Economic Development Aid—Shell Game or Key to Urban Rejuvenation?" *National Journal* (March 21, 1981): 497.

60. Ibid., pp. 494–495.

61. Norman J. Glickman, "Emerging Urban Policies in a Slow-Growth Economy: Conservative Initiatives and Progressive Responses in the United States," *International Journal of Urban and Regional Research* 5, no. 4 (December 1981): 492–527.

62. United States Department of Housing and Urban Development, *The President's National Urban Policy Report* (Washington, D.C.: U.S. Government Printing Office, 1982), p. 46.

63. Ibid., p. 66.

64. These proposals were enunciated by Reagan in various speeches. For the core of his message on enterprise zones, see *The New York Times*, March 24, 1982, p. 14.

65. Richard Child Hill, "Market, State, and Community: National Urban Policy in the 1980s," *Urban Affairs Quarterly* 19, no. 1 (September 1983): 5–20.

66. Ibid., p. 12.

67. Ronald Reagan, *Federalism: The First Ten Months* (Washington: The White House, 1981), p. 1.

68. Levine, "The Reagan Urban Policy," p. 24.

69. Harold Wolman, "The Reagan Urban Policy and Its Impacts," *Urban Affairs Quarterly* 21, no. 3 (March 1986): 311–335.

70. David A. Caputo and Steven E. Johnson, "New Federalism and Midwestern Cities: 1981–1985," *Publius* 16, no. 1 (Winter 1986): 81–96.

71. Daniel P. Moynihan, "Toward a National Urban Policy," *The Public Interest* 17 (Fall 1969): 6; and Robert C. Wood, *The Federal Government and the Cities* (Washington, D.C.: George Washington University Press, 1964), pp. 52–54.

72. James L. Sundquist, "Needed: A National Growth Policy," *The Brookings Bulletin* 14, no. 4 (Winter–Spring 1978): 3.

73. Domestic Council Committee on National Growth, *Report on National Growth, 1972,* (Washington, D.C.: Government Printing Office, 1971), pp. ix–x.

74. Peter K. Eisinger, "The Search for a National Urban Policy, 1968–1980," *Journal of Urban History* 12, no. 1 (November 1985): 3–24.

75. Patricia S. Florestano and Vincent L. Marando, *The States and the Metropolis* (New York: Marcel Dekker, 1981), p. 12.

76. See *The New York Times*, March 16, 1975, sec. 8, p. 1.

77. This account of the creation of the Model Cities program relies heavily on Banfield, "Making a New Federal Program," pp. 124–169.

78. Ibid., p. 125.

79. Ibid., p. 129.

80. Ibid., p. 148.

81. Sundquist, *Making Federalism Work*, pp. 117–119.

82. Marshall Kaplan, *Urban Planning in the 1960's: A Design for Irrelevancy* (New York: Praeger, 1973), pp. 110–111.

83. Alan Saltzstein, "Federal Categorical Aid to Cities: Who Needs It Versus Who Wants It," *Western Political Quarterly* 30, no. 3 (September 1977): 377–383.

84. Paul R. Dommel, "Distribution Politics and Urban Policy," *Policy Studies Journal* 3, no. 4 (June 1975): 370–374.

85. Paul R. Dommel and Michael J. Rich, "The Rich Get Richer: The Attenuation of Targeting Effects of the Community Development Block Grant Program," *Urban Affairs Quarterly* 22, no. 4 (June 1987): 552–579.

86. Interview between David B. Walker and the author, Washington, D.C., December 29, 1983.

87. National Advisory Commission on Civil Disorders, *Report* (Washington, D.C.: U.S. Government Printing Office, 1968), p. 1.

88. Sundquist, *Making Federalism Work*, pp. 74, 78, 81.

89. Kaplan, *Urban Planning in the 1960's*, pp. 109, 118; and Banfield, "Making a New Federal Program," pp. 124–169.

90. See Chapter 10. Also see Melvin B. Mogulof, *Governing Metropolitan Areas* (Washington, D.C.: The Urban Institute, 1971).

91. Mogulof, *Federal Regional Councils*.

92. *Hills v. Gautraux*, 96 S. Ct. 1538 (1976).

Chapter 14

This distinction between the efficacy of the Apollo program and the inefficacy of urban programs is elaborated more fully by Anthony J. Catanese, *Planners and Local Politics: Impossible Dreams*, vol. 7, SAGE Library of Social Research (Beverly Hills, Calif.: SAGE Publications, 1974), pp. 55–60.

2. Advisory Commission on Intergovernmental Relations, *Report A-62, Summary and Concluding Observations: The Intergovernmental Grant System: An Assessment and Proposed Policies*, (Washington, D.C.: U.S. Government Printing Office, June 1978), p. 6.

3. A more elaborate discussion of the concept of political culture can be found in Gabriel A. Almond and Sidney Verba, *The Civic Culture: Political Attitudes and Democracy in Five Nations* (Boston: Little, Brown, 1965), chap. 1, "An Approach to Political Culture." A short compendium of survey research findings of American opinions on a variety of issues over the past generation is compiled by Rita James Simon, *Public Opinion in America: 1936–1970* (Chicago: Rand McNally, 1974). The acquisition of political attitudes and the transmission of the political culture to new generations is referred to as *political socialization*. For a discussion of these processes see Kenneth P. Langton, *Political Socialization* (New York: Oxford University Press, 1969).

4. See Herman E. Daley, ed., *Toward a Steady-State Economy* (San Francisco: W. H. Freeman, 1972).

5. The Portola Institute, *The Last Whole Earth Catalog* (New York: Random House, 1971). See the catalog's statement of purpose, p. 1.

6. Ernst F. Schumacher, *Small Is Beautiful: A Study of Economics as if People Mattered* (New York: Harper & Row, 1973).

7. Ben Wattenberg, *The Real America* (New York: Doubleday, 1974).

8. Daley, *Toward a Steady-State Economy*.

9. Peter K. Eisinger, *Black Employment in City Government, 1973–1980* (Washington, D.C.: Joint Center for Political Studies, 1983), pp. 34–41.

Index of Names

This index lists names of authors and other persons mentioned in the text. The letter n after a page number indicates either an end note or a footnote.

Index of Subjects